ANZACS

ON THE
WESTERN FRONT

ANZACS

ON THE
WESTERN FRONT

THE

AUSTRALIAN WAR MEMORIAL
BATTLEFIELD GUIDE

PETER PEDERSEN

WITH CHRIS ROBERTS

WILEY

John Wiley & Sons Australia, Ltd

coll AU

First published 2012 by John Wiley & Sons Australia, Ltd
42 McDougall Street, Milton Qld 4064
Office also in Melbourne

Typeset in Myriad Pro

National Library of Australia Cataloguing-in-Publication entry:

Author: Pedersen, P. A. (Peter Andreas), 1952-

Title: ANZACs on the Western Front: The Australian War Memorial Battlefield Guide /
             Peter Pedersen.

ISBN: 9781742169811 (pbk.)

Notes: Includes index.

Subjects: Battlefields — Europe — Guidebooks.
             World War, 1914–1918 — Battlefields — Europe — Guidebooks.

Other Authors/Contributors: Australian War Memorial.

Dewey Number: 940.4144

Cover design by saso content & design pty ltd

Cover images supplied by the Australian War Memorial: map — RC09857; Rising Sun — REL28780; back cover photograph — E03142. Poppy image © iStockphoto.com/dabjola.

Printed in China by Printplus Limited
10 9 8 7 6 5 4 3 2 1

Disclaimer

The publisher and the author make no representations or warranties with respect to the accuracy or completeness of the contents of this work and specifically disclaim all warranties, including without limitation warranties of fitness for a particular purpose. No warranty may be created or extended by sales or promotional materials. The advice and strategies contained herein may not be suitable for every situation. This work is sold with the understanding that the publisher is not engaged in rendering legal, accounting, or other professional services. If professional assistance is required, the services of a competent professional person should be sought. Neither the publisher nor the author shall be liable for damages arising herefrom. The fact that an organisation or website is referred to in this work as a citation and/or a potential source of further information does not mean that the author or the publisher endorses the information the organisation or website may provide or recommendations it may make. Further, readers should be aware that internet websites listed in this work may have changed or disappeared between when this work was written and when it is read. Please be advised that travel information is subject to change at any time. We therefore suggest that readers write or call ahead for confirmation when making travel plans. The author and the publisher cannot be held responsible for the experiences of readers while travelling.

CONTENTS

ABOUT THE AUTHOR

Dr Peter Pedersen has written seven books on the First World War and contributions to several others, as well as numerous articles on campaigns from the Second World War, the Vietnam War, and battlefields and military and aviation museums worldwide. He appears frequently on Australian television and radio and has spoken at military history conferences and seminars in Australia and abroad. He has also guided many tours to the Western Front and other battlefields in Europe and Asia, which included leading and organising the first British tour to Dien Bien Phu in Vietnam. A graduate of the Royal Military College, Duntroon, the Australian Command and Staff College, and the University of New South Wales, he commanded the 5th/7th Battalion, the Royal Australian Regiment, and was a political/strategic analyst in the Australian Office of National Assessments. Dr Pedersen is currently Head of the Research Centre at the Australian War Memorial.

Other books by Peter Pedersen
Monash as Military Commander
Images of Gallipoli
Hamel
Fromelles
Villers-Bretonneux
The Anzacs. Gallipoli to the Western Front
Anzacs at war

ACKNOWLEDGEMENTS

Many people contributed to this book in various ways.

Brigadier Chris Roberts AM, CSC (Retd) stood head and shoulders above all of them. Chris served with the SAS in Vietnam and has always been keenly interested in military history. He's done some excellent work on the Gallipoli campaign. I know Chris from our army days together and was delighted when he volunteered to help with the project as a researcher. From the outset he was infinitely more than that. He plotted the data gleaned for each battle on the relevant map and then drew up a detailed framework for the drive or walk that was invaluable for me. His comments, as a soldier who has led in battle and also held senior command, on tactics and terrain during our visits to the battlefields were immensely helpful. Never hesitating to go the extra mile, Chris also undertook the myriad ancillary tasks, some unforeseen, that arose during the project's course. Mate, without your enthusiastic help, I'd have laboured to get the book done. I dedicate it to you with 'the deepest of gratitude and respect'. It's also a pleasure to have you on the cover.

The wonderful staff of the Australian War Memorial took the project to their hearts. Major-General Steve Gower, the Memorial's Director, gave me every encouragement and support. So did Nola Anderson, Head of National Collections Branch, and Helen Withnell, Head of Public Programs Branch. Marylou Pooley, Head of Communications and Marketing, who had the idea for the project, was a tower of strength throughout. My colleagues in the Research Centre and the Military History Section shouldered extra duties so that I could concentrate on my writing. I must mention Craig Tibbits, Senior Curator of Official and Private Records, in this context. Craig did a superb job while filling in for me as Head of the Research Centre towards the end of the project, which gave me a clear run to the last full stop. Janda Gooding, Head of Photographs, Sound and Film, Hans Reppin, Manager, Multi-Media, and Bob McKendry, Image Interpreter in Multi-Media ensured that the illustrations were of the highest quality possible. They patiently taught me about the wizardry of modern digital processing along the way. Nothing was too much trouble for Anne Bennie, Head of Retail and Online Sales, who deftly handled the considerable administrative dimensions of the project.

The maps reflect Keith Mitchell's cartographic skill. Less obviously, they also reflect his forbearance and good humour in accommodating the frequent changes that were necessary to get them exactly right.

On the battlefields, Martial Delabarre in Fromelles, Jean Letaille in Bullecourt, Claude and Collette Durand in Hendecourt, Philippe Gorczynski in Cambrai, Charlotte Cardoen-Descamps in Poelcapelle, and Johan Vanderwalle at Polygon Wood were unstinting in their advice, assistance and hospitality. They are great friends of Australia. Closer to home, Dolores Ho, Archivist at the Kippenberger Military Archive in the New Zealand Army Museum at Waiouru, and, in Wellington, the staff of both the National Library of New Zealand/Alexander Turnbull Library and Archives New Zealand exemplified the ANZAC bond by handling every request for information promptly and efficiently.

To one and all, a heartfelt thanks.

Congratulations on buying this guide. You may have done so out of an interest in the Australian and New Zealand role on the Western Front. You may have wanted to follow in the footsteps of a forebear or to see where he fell and where he rests. Each of these reasons is an acknowledgement of what Australia and New Zealand did on the Western Front. It was the decisive theatre of the First World War and both nations made their greatest contribution to victory there. Gallipoli was a sideshow, though it helped to establish the Australian and New Zealand national identities and enriched the English language with the word ANZAC. But for Australians and New Zealanders a certain romance attaches to Gallipoli, with its idealised images of bronzed men storming ashore at ANZAC Cove and clinging to cliff-top positions. The Western Front, on the other hand, evokes only images of appalling slaughter for a few acres of mud. It cost Australia and New Zealand more casualties than all of the conflicts they have fought since put together. Not surprisingly, then, the Western Front has always stood in Gallipoli's shadow. You are helping to bring it out into the sunlight.

Walks and drives

Australians and New Zealanders often forget that the term 'ANZAC' refers to both of them and not to just one or the other. As the title of this guide contains the term, the pages that follow lay out detailed instructions on walking or driving the major battlefields on which the Australians AND the New Zealanders fought on the Western Front. The battles are covered more or less in the order in which they occurred from 1916 to 1918. This format allows them to be fitted clearly within the context of the war, which, in turn, makes for an easier understanding of how the war played out, the important tactical milestones passed along the way and how the Australian Imperial Force (AIF) and the New Zealand Expeditionary Force (NZEF) evolved to meet the war's changing demands.

Unfortunately, the chronological order doesn't match the geographical one. The AIF and NZEF areas of operation stretched 150 km from the Belgian coast at Nieuport to the Hindenburg Line near St Quentin in France. In 1916 the AIF and NZEF started off in French Flanders in the north before moving south to the Somme River. In 1917 most of their major battles were in the north again, around Ypres in Belgian Flanders. In 1918 they headed back to the Somme and then advanced eastwards. Following the battles in chronological order would necessitate duplication in the geographical order; following the geographical order would reduce the chronological one to incomprehensible nonsense.

By grouping the battlefields into four operational sectors, though, and travelling to and within these sectors in a prescribed sequence, the chronological order can be approximated. The Australian War Memorial has successfully used a similar structure in its battlefield tours for many years. Simply start from Ypres in Belgian Flanders in the north, continue south to the Somme and then travel east to the Hindenburg Line. To reach Ypres from Calais, head east from the ferry terminal on the A16-E40 autoroute and then swing onto the N8 as

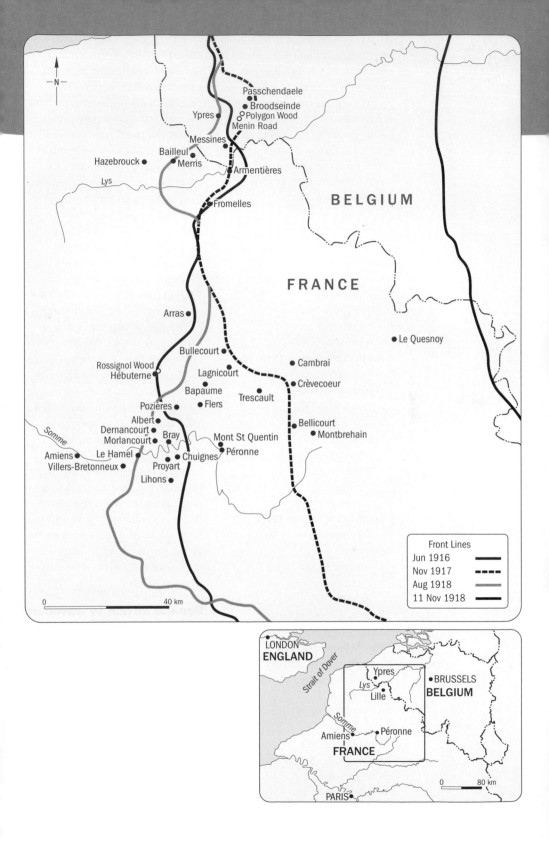

you approach the Belgian town of Veurne. From Paris, head north on the A1/E17 to Lille, pick up the A27/E42 (direction Tournai) and then the A17 and A19. On leaving Ypres, take the N366 and N365 to Armentières, followed by the A1 to Bapaume and then the D929 to Albert or Amiens. You are now on the Somme. The recommended sequence of battlefield walks and drives in each sector is:

- **Flanders 1916–18:**
  - Ypres
  - Messines
  - Menin Road
  - Polygon Wood
  - Broodseinde
  - Passchendaele
  - Bois-Grenier/Fleurbaix
  - Fromelles
  - Hazebrouck
- **North of the Somme 1916–18:**
  - Pozières/Mouquet Farm
  - Flers (NZ)
  - Flers/Gueudecourt
  - 1917 Hindenburg Line advance
  - Bullecourt
  - Hébuterne/Le Signy Farm/Rossignol Wood/Puisieux
  - Bapaume (NZ)
  - Dernancourt/Morlancourt
- **South of the Somme 1918:**
  - Villers-Bretonneux
  - Hamel
  - Amiens 8 August
  - Lihons, Proyart and Chuignes
  - Etinehem, Bray, Curlu
  - Mont St Quentin/Péronne/ Bouchavesnes
- **Hindenburg Line 1918:**
  - Hindenburg Outpost Line
  - Hindenburg/Beaurevoir Lines
  - Montbrehain
  - Trescault Ridge to Beaurevoir Line (NZ)
  - Le Quesnoy (NZ)

Of course you can be selective and only visit the battlefields that interest you. There are plenty to choose from!

Each battle has its own chapter. As well as the battlefield walk or drive, the chapter includes information on nearby places of interest, perhaps text boxes on relevant personalities and issues, and, where relevant, the locations of the bas-relief commemorative plaques hand sculpted by Melbourne periodontist Dr Ross J. Bastiaan. These can now be found on virtually every battlefield on which Australians have fought. Local cemeteries pertinent to Australians and New Zealanders are also covered. There is a tendency nowadays in both guidebooks and on battlefield tours to 'do' the battlefields by going from cemetery to cemetery. Make no mistake, this guide emphatically puts the fighting that took place then on the ground as it is now. Everything else is secondary.

The length of each walk or drive is given but the time you spend on it is up to you. To do them all thoroughly would take about three weeks. If you have the time and inclination, fine. Few people do. But you can whiz around most of them in half a day; less if you decide to go only to the locations of particular actions. The walks can be partly driven. Whether walking or driving, do not forget that the Australians and New Zealanders fought as part of a British Expeditionary Force (BEF) that also included Canadians and South Africans as well as, predominantly, soldiers from Britain. Large French and, towards the end, American armies fought alongside the BEF.

General advice to travellers

Your first decision is when to go. In making it, consider one factor above all else: the old Western Front is a long way from Australia and New Zealand, so you can't come back tomorrow to see what you missed out on today. That means doing as much as possible in whatever time you have, which suggests the European summer, June to August, as the optimal time. The weather is at its best, by European standards anyway, and the days are long, so you can pack a lot into them. The trouble is, everyone else thinks like that. The battlefields are crowded — half of Britain seems to be on the Somme in July — and accommodation is at a premium. If the crops haven't been harvested, forget extensive battlefield panoramas. You avoid most of these problems in spring and autumn, although the weather is sharper then. But winter is a rotten time to be outdoors, particularly for us antipodeans. The days are short and sometimes entirely fog-bound, and the battlefields are muddy and often snow-covered.

Whatever the season, you'll almost certainly experience the tendency of the weather, even in summer, to cram the four seasons into an hour. So pack a hat, sunglasses, sun cream and a waterproof smock. Most travellers bring a camera but overlook binoculars, without which you won't be able to appreciate the views from the various vantage points or pick out the more remote locations. A compass will help you orient the maps to the ground. You'll probably have some reference material like maps (and this guide!) as well. By wearing an angler's or hunter's vest, with its many pockets, or carrying a small haversack, you can have these things always on hand. It's very annoying to leave your car to walk to a particular location and find when you get there that you've left what you need in the car.

As the battlefield walks occasionally utilise farm tracks and the adhesive qualities of Western Front mud are legendary, good hiking shoes or boots are a must. While walking, carry plenty to drink, particularly in summer, and something to munch on. To make the best use of your time, get the necessary victuals in the nearest town and have a picnic lunch. In an ironic contrast to the war years, there are many idyllic spots on the battlefields today where you can do so — the banks of the Somme and the Ancre immediately spring to mind.

The battlefields are in rural areas and you really do need a car to get about on them, just as you would in rural Australia or New Zealand. Hiring a bike is an option in some places, particularly Ypres, where the battlefields are flat and compact, but you'll still require a car to get from one battlefield to another. A car is also the quickest way of seeing the battlefields. Whatever means of locomotion you use, remember that the locals generally make their living from the soil. They get understandably angry when unthinking visitors tramp across

Hat, sunglasses, multi-pocketed angler's jacket and camera and binoculars on belt: the author, properly kitted out, at Caterpillar Crater, Hill 60.

their fields and unthinking drivers block their tractors on the narrow roads. Stick to the farm tracks and the edges of the fields and, if in doubt, ask. The goodwill on which all battlefield tourists depend rests on these simple courtesies.

Two points relate specifically to cars: in the vast majority of stops on the drives there is plenty of room for parking, but on occasion you will have to pull over onto the verge. Be careful when you do so. Secondly, the huge growth in tourism to the Western Front has naturally resulted in a huge increase in the number of cars, hired or otherwise, driven by battlefield tourists. They represent rich pickings for those with a malevolent bent. The upshot is a surge in car break-ins. Do not have your trip ruined by leaving valuables on view and becoming a victim. Lock them out of sight in the boot. As you would anywhere else in the world, carry important items on you. That angler's vest really does come in useful.

One positive result of the rise in battlefield tourism has been the commensurate growth in battlefield accommodation. Quite a few bed and breakfasts have started up on the main battlefields, such as the Somme and Ypres. Some are run by British (and New Zealand) expatriates and English is spoken in most of them. They'll generally do a packed lunch but don't serve dinner. The towns relevant to the ANZAC battlefields — Albert, Ypres, Pèronne Armentières and Cambrai — offer a range of accommodation, as well as restaurants that will take care of your dinner needs. The main cities, Amiens and Lille, offer a broader range of both but are less conveniently located. Take the busy city traffic into account and you'll easily find yourself spending well over an hour a day getting to and from the battlefields, which amounts to the best part of a day out of a week's stay. Details of local tourist offices, from which advice on accommodation can be obtained, and some handy websites are at the end of the guide.

Anyone who has been a soldier will recall the warning given before entering a live fire training area about unexploded ammunition. 'Ammunition is designed to kill', it went. 'If you come across any, leave it alone.' The battlefields weren't training areas. Millions of shells, including gas shells, were fired on them, not counting those the Germans sent the other way. A good percentage were duds. Farmers turn up about 90 tonnes' worth every year while ploughing. As the ravages of time may well have rendered this ammunition extremely sensitive and, therefore, still extremely capable of fulfilling its original purpose of killing and maiming, the warning is very relevant today. If you see shells stacked by the road awaiting disposal by the military authorities, or the odd shell or grenade lying about in fields or woods, DO NOT TOUCH THEM. Otherwise you risk becoming the last ANZAC casualty of the Western Front.

At the time of writing, a number of interpretive centres were about to be set up by the Australian Department of Veterans' Affairs on key Australian battlefields as part of an Australian Remembrance Trail on the Western Front. Some may be in place at the time of your visit.

Maps

You can complete the battlefield walks and drives using the maps in the guide. The *Institut Geographique Nationale* Blue Series 1:25 000 maps listed at the start of each walk or drive will enable you to orient yourself in relation to locations outside the battlefield area and to navigate to cemeteries and places of interest that are also outside it. The IGN 1:250 000 Nord, Pas-de-Calais, Picardie R01 is useful for navigating from an arrival location, such as Calais or Paris, to the battlefields, and for navigating between battlefield areas that are some distance apart. These maps can be obtained from good bookshops in France, Belgium and the UK and in *Maison de la Press* shops or major supermarkets in France. You can also order them online from IGN at **www.ign.fr**

A few words of caution. French road numbers have a life of their own. Indeed, they seemed to mutate in between the research trips done for this guide. Numbered roads aren't necessarily continuous either. They can end at one place and start up somewhere else, yet still have the same number. A road might also have several names along its course. This guide reflects the state of play as regards roads at the time of writing. It may well have changed when you get to the Western Front. As you're now prepared for the eventuality, don't have a trip-destroying sense of humour failure if it turns out to be the case. Armed with the maps herein, the IGN maps and the initiative for which Australians and New Zealanders are famous — and which our soldiers here had in heaps — you'll still be able to get around comfortably.

How to use this book

Before starting a battlefield walk or drive, READ THE BATTLE NARRATIVE. It places the battle within the wider strategic and operational setting, outlines the planning factors and also helps you to overcome a very real practical limitation. The directions that the available roads and tracks take often preclude following the battle as it actually unfolded. You may be able to retrace an advance from start to finish on one flank, for example, but have to go from finish to start on the other flank.

On big battlefields, such as the Hindenburg Line advance in April 1917 or the Amiens offensive on 8 August 1918, many key locations cannot be seen from one another. The battle narrative brings coherence and order to the battle, enabling you to visualise where the principal locations were in relation to each other and to set the local actions described along the route within the context of what was happening elsewhere. As you read, try to see the battlefield in your mind's eye, which will

Leave well alone. A dud near the A29 autoroute at Villers-Bretonneux.

give you a head start when you set foot upon it.

The walks are more detailed than the drives. You can stop anywhere, and more frequently, on a walk than on a drive, which allows the action to be covered in greater depth. It is appropriate then, that Fromelles, Pozières, Mouquet Farm, Bullecourt and Passchendaele, perhaps the toughest battles fought by the Australians or New Zealanders on the Western Front, are covered in walks. But the itineraries for the drives and walks have one thing in common: they explain not only WHAT happened during the battle but also HOW it happened on the ground. This entails describing where the opposing lines ran and the successive objectives for an attack lay, the direction that the advance took and from whence the counterattack came, the location of German machine-guns, and what the ground itself offered to the Australians and New Zealanders on the one hand and to the Germans on the other. Considerations such as fields of fire, observation and keeping direction are constantly mentioned. Taken together, all of these things go a long way towards explaining why a fight turned out the way it did. Think about them and make up your own mind.

There is nothing arcane about any of this. On reaching a location, you will be asked to position yourself in relation to an obvious reference point, such as a road, railway or wood, which gets you facing a certain direction. To follow the action in that location, just look to your front, right or left, or your right front and left front, the directions in between, as directed. Throughout the guide you will see the names of places, features and landmarks in bold font. Some of these bold names appear on the maps; others are in the text and denote locations of interest. At the back of the guide you will find a glossary of the military terms used throughout.

In the end, it has been said, every battle comes down to the infantryman's willingness to go forward. The walks and drives will bring you closer to him, to his problems, to his fears. But you will be doing them in daylight, whereas much of the fighting took place in darkness made more impenetrable by smoke and mist. So pay particular attention to the soldiers' descriptions. The apprehension on moving up to the start line, the deafening noise and bone-jarring concussion of the barrage, the frenzy of infantry combat with bayonet and bomb, the gruesome spectacle of tanks crushing machine-gunners, the overwhelming sadness at the loss of a comrade held

dear and the juxtaposition of humanity with brutality — the soldiers spare nothing. But this guide cannot fully bring their words alive. You have to breathe life into them by putting your imagination to work. You will then gain some understanding of what it must have been like to be there and also appreciate the battlefields as places where ordinary men achieved great things. The guide will then have fulfilled its aim.

A note on place names

This guide uses wartime spellings for the towns and villages mentioned in it. In the case of Belgian Flanders, these were invariably French spellings. Since the war, though, the Flemish spellings have been adopted. Look out for the following changes:

Wartime (French)	Modern (Flemish)
Lille	Rijsel
Messines	Mesen
Nieuport	Nieuwpoort
Passchendaele	Passendale
Poperinghe	Poperinge
St Yves	St Yvon
Warneton	Waasten
Ypres	Ieper

Using ground. How a German machine-gun was sited to catch the 51st Battalion in enfilade as it advanced across the Cachy Switch at Villers-Bretonneux.

CACHY

51ST BATTALION ADVANCE

CACHY SWITCH

GERMAN MACHINE-GUN

THE ANZACS ON THE WESTERN FRONT

After their withdrawal to Egypt at the end of the Gallipoli campaign in December 1915, the AIF and NZEF were greatly expanded. Largely by splitting veteran battalions and using the huge pool of reinforcements in Egypt to bring the resulting half battalions up to strength, the number of Australian divisions went from two to four. Another division was raised in Australia and sailed directly to England. There were now five Australian infantry divisions. A brigade formed from reinforcements and another that had arrived from New Zealand joined the New Zealand Infantry Brigade in a separate New Zealand Division. The New Zealand and Australian Division, in which the New Zealanders had served with the 4th Australian Brigade on Gallipoli, was disbanded.

I and II ANZAC

The AIF and NZEF had made up a single corps on Gallipoli, the Australian and New Zealand Army Corps, known, like those who belonged to it, as the ANZAC. The extra formations necessitated the creation of another corps. I ANZAC, comprising the 1st and 2nd Australian Divisions, and the New Zealand Division, was commanded by Lieutenant-General Sir William Birdwood, who had led the original ANZAC. The 4th and 5th Australian Divisions made up II ANZAC, which Lieutenant-General Alexander Godley commanded. These arrangements were not ironclad. The 4th and 5th Divisions mostly served alongside the 1st and 2nd in I ANZAC, which left Egypt for France in March 1916. II ANZAC followed in June and the New Zealand Division transferred to it soon after. The 3rd Australian Division joined II ANZAC on reaching the Western Front from England in November.

Whereas the isolation of its enclave on Gallipoli had made the ANZAC essentially an independent force, on the Western

Brigadier-General Brudenell White.

Front I and II ANZAC constituted a fraction of a BEF that was already 50 divisions strong. The decisions of British commanders affected them much more directly. Those commanders faced the problem that the combination of trench, machine-gun and barbed wire had decisively tilted the balance in warfare in favour of the defence over the attack. Although the same problem had existed on Gallipoli, an open flank offered a way around the defence, but the ANZAC's attempt to take advantage of it in August 1915 failed. On the Western Front there was no way around. The trenches stretched from the North Sea to the Swiss border and the Germans defending them were highly skilled. They could only be attacked frontally, in other words, into the teeth of the defence.

Somme

Service in colonial wars, which all the British commanders and some Australian

Lieutenant-General Sir William Riddell Birdwood

Commander ANZAC 1915, I ANZAC 1916–November 1917, Australian Corps November 1917–May 1918 and the Fifth Army from then until war's end

1865–1951

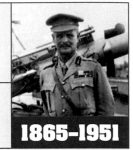

Birdwood had an imperial pedigree that matched his mandatory imperial moustache. The grandson of a general and the son of the under-secretary to the government of Bombay, he was born in India, educated in England and had served abroad since 1885, mainly in Indian frontier campaigns until going to South Africa as Kitchener's military secretary. A teetotaller with an occasional stammer, he had the ambitious man's flair for self-promotion. But Birdwood also took men for what they were rather than what their appearance suggested. He had commanded a brigade though not a division, and was secretary to the Government of India in the Army Department and on the Governor-General's Legislative Council before being appointed to command the ANZAC. He also commanded the AIF.

Birdwood's indifference to danger and informal manner won him many friends among the ANZACs, whose affection he reciprocated. But he was no tactician and often failed to grasp the big picture. On both Gallipoli and the Western Front, he depended heavily on his Australian chief-of-staff, Brigadier-General Brudenell White. Courteous, restrained, cerebral, White had planned the withdrawal from ANZAC, which went off without a hitch. Birdwood told him to make sure all the signal wire was reeled up. White was flabbergasted: 'Heavens! What does he think we are doing here — why I would gladly have left all the guns behind if we could only get the men off safely.' This episode highlighted Birdwood's limitations. Not for nothing did he take White with him on leaving the Australian Corps to command the Fifth Army in May 1918. Looking back, White could not recall Birdwood ever having drafted a plan, and as for his much-vaunted visits to the trenches, 'he never brought back with him a reliable memory of what he had seen'. Lieutenant-General Sir John Monash, who replaced Birdwood as commander of the Australian Corps, had the vision, intellect and tactical grasp that Birdwood lacked.

After the war, Birdwood returned to the Indian Army and became its commander-in-chief in 1925. He lobbied, unsuccessfully, to become Governor-General of Australia. Knighted in 1914 (KCMG) and 1917 (KCB), Birdwood was appointed GCMG, created a baronet and granted £10 000 in 1919. He became a field marshal in 1925.

Lieutenant-General Sir Alexander John Godley

Commander New Zealand and Australian Division 1915, II ANZAC 1916-November 1917, XXII Corps 1918

1867–1957

An ambitious but impecunious mounted infantry officer who preferred the Boer War to Staff College, the 191-centimetre-tall British-born Godley had been appointed by Kitchener to command the New Zealand Defence Forces before the war. He showed his considerable organizational skills by revamping the territorial forces and in the raising of the NZEF, which he commanded. But Godley was highly unpopular among the New Zealanders owing to his aloof manner, short temper, sharp tongue and forceful wife, Louisa. 'Make 'em run, Alex', which she allegedly said while Godley reviewed some New Zealanders on parade, became his nickname.

ANZAC, where Godley led the New Zealand and Australian Division, quickly showed his feebleness as a field commander. He lost control of the all-important offensive to outflank the Turks in August 1915. Commanding II ANZAC on the Western Front, he was carried by his two outstanding divisional commanders, General Monash of the 3rd Australian Division, and the New Zealand Division's General Russell. When II ANZAC was disbanded at the end of 1917, he took over XXII Corps.

Knighted (KCB and KCMG) during the war, Godley was promoted to general in 1923 while commanding the British Army of the Rhine. He served as governor and commander-in-chief of Gibraltar from 1928 to 1932.

ones had, was no help in these conditions. They had to be mastered virtually from scratch. The process was costly. When the 5th Australian Division attacked at Fromelles, in French Flanders, in July 1916, the British plan was poor and the Australian commander lost control of the battle. The 5th Division was destroyed in one night. Faulty planning, some of it Australian, cost the 1st, 2nd and 4th Divisions dearly in attacks on the Somme at Pozières and Mouquet Farm between July and September. Even when an attack succeeded, the crushing retaliatory German bombardments still caused grievous loss. Modern military technology had transformed warfare into 'mechanical slaughter', one Australian said. The 28 000 Australian casualties from the Somme and Fromelles amounted to the equivalent of over half of the

48 Australian battalions in France. But the possibility of obtaining the needed replacements through conscription disappeared when a proposal to bring it in was defeated in a divisive referendum in Australia in October 1916. Though the AIF would remain the war's only volunteer army, manpower shortages dogged it from now on.

Tanks made their debut when the New Zealand Division attacked on the Somme in September but they held more promise than substance at this early stage in their development. The New Zealanders also advanced behind a 'creeping' barrage, a curtain of shells that lifted steadily ahead of the infantry advance, suppressing the defences as it went. This really was an important tactical innovation and it remained standard for the rest of the war. Though the

The Australian Prime Minister, William Morris Hughes, urges a vote in favour of conscription while on the stump in Sydney's Martin Place during the 1916 referendum campaign. Voters weren't convinced. He failed to convince them in 1917, too.

New Zealanders did not experience fighting of the same intensity as the Australians, their losses were comparable because they stayed in the line for twice as long as any of the Australian divisions. But New Zealand had introduced conscription in August 1916, enabling the losses to be made up with reasonable certainty. Indeed for much of 1917, the New Zealand Division had a fourth brigade, making it the largest division in the BEF.

After several weeks' rest, the Australian divisions returned to the Somme towards the end of 1916. As the autumn rains had turned the battlefield into a swamp, their attacks got nowhere. It was also evident that their fighting efficiency had gone backwards as there had not been enough time to properly train the replacements for the losses from the first stint. Though its severity strained morale, winter brought a respite that allowed some of the deficiencies to be fixed.

Bullecourt

When the Germans withdrew to the Hindenburg Line in February 1917 to shorten their line overall and thereby save manpower, the Australians followed up skilfully. The switch from trench warfare to

open warfare was as welcomed as it was easily made but it did not last long. Trench warfare returned with I ANZAC's attacks on the Hindenburg Line at Bullecourt in April and May in support of a British offensive at Arras. Results were mixed.

The artillery had little chance to shred the wire before the 4th Australian Division's attack in April. At British insistence, a dozen tanks attempted to crush the wire instead even though the Australians had never worked with tanks, while Australian lapses precluded effective artillery support for the infantry. The 4th Division was shattered for no gain. Better preparation enabled the 2nd Australian Division to take its part of the Hindenburg Line in May but the fight was gruelling and also drew in the 1st and 5th Divisions. I ANZAC was then thoroughly rested. Recognising that the term 'Digger', by which British troops had praised the New Zealand pioneers and engineers for their entrenching exploits on the Somme, richly met their own conception of their job, the Australians now commandeered it.

Flanders

On 7 June II ANZAC participated in the British attack on the Messines Ridge. It was the first time that the Australians and New Zealanders had fought together in a big battle on the Western Front. Messines was a watershed for the BEF too. It now enjoyed artillery superiority over the Germans, which permitted a massive preliminary bombardment and a creeping barrage of great density and depth. The infantry's advance was to stop well before resistance hardened. In order to keep German counterattacks at bay, a heavy standing barrage would surround the objectives while they were being consolidated. The new scientific techniques of flash-spotting and sound-ranging located German guns so that they could be knocked out beforehand. No detail was overlooked in the preparation. Numerous rehearsals

Diggers. In what has become perhaps the iconic image of Australian soldiers in the First World War, Lieutenant Rupert Downes addresses his platoon during the great battle before Amiens on 8 August 1918. As a result of the AIF's chronic manpower shortage by then, the platoon consists of 17 men, about half its normal strength.

were carried out on ground almost identical to that in the attack sector. Preceded by 19 mines blown under the German line, the attack yielded a great British victory.

Using the same methods, except for the mines, during the subsequent Third Ypres offensive, I and II ANZAC spearheaded the assaults at Menin Road and Polygon Wood, and at Broodseinde, where they attacked alongside each other for the first time. Continuous heavy rain had earlier rendered the battlefield a muddy wilderness. But good weather blessed the ANZAC attacks and they succeeded. Only the final one, by II ANZAC against Passchendaele, failed. Though the rains had returned, again reducing the battlefield to an impassable quagmire, the British high command, and General Godley in II ANZAC, insisted on the attack going ahead. The Ypres campaign cost the Australians 38 000 men and led to a second conscription referendum in Australia. Even more bitter than the first, it was similarly defeated.

The Australian Corps

Yet this cloud did have a silver lining. Ever since the Australian divisions had arrived on the Western Front, the Australian government had wanted them to be together. But the British high command thought that a corps of five divisions would be too large for one man to handle and the system of reliefs within it too complex. A corps of four divisions avoided the problem because two could be in the line with the other two ready to relieve them. When the manpower crisis intervened, Birdwood suggested that the 4th Division, which was the most battle-worn, should temporarily become a depot division to supply reinforcements for the others. Besides averting the 4th's break-up, the proposal meant a corps of the magical four divisions.

The British agreed and the Australian Corps came into being under Birdwood on 1 November 1917. Following a brilliant German counterattack at Cambrai at the end of November, the 4th Division was best positioned to go into close reserve at Péronne in case the Germans went further. Its brief stint as a depot division was over.

The creation of the Australian Corps came as a total surprise and was greeted with joy. Grouping the Australian divisions in a single formation took full advantage of one of the AIF's major strengths, its homogeneity. When Australian divisions attacked alongside each other for the first time on the Menin Road, one commander estimated that the effectiveness of his formation had been increased by a third. As casualties and sickness in the Australian Corps were minimal during a mild winter, the steady flow of returning wounded briefly eased its manpower shortage. Having disbanded the 4th Brigade as a result of its losses at Ypres, the New Zealand Division now belonged to XXII Corps, as II ANZAC became.

Stemming the tide

Utilising divisions freed by Russia's collapse, the Germans unleashed a colossal offensive in March 1918 in a bid to win the war before America's involvement put victory beyond reach. The Australians and New Zealanders missed the start of the offensive and it was already faltering when the 4th Australian Brigade temporarily joined the New Zealand Division in the British IV

New Zealanders lunching in the front line at Le Signy Farm, near Hébuterne, where they were heavily engaged during the German offensive in March and April 1918.

Corps at Hébuterne, north of the Somme. Fighting astride the Somme on the BEF's right flank, the other Australian formations played the main role in shielding the vital communications centre of Amiens. Their crowning achievement was the recapture of the town of Villers-Bretonneux in a difficult night attack on 24 April. When the Germans attacked in Flanders in April, the 1st Australian Division was rushed north to defend Hazebrouck, another important communications hub. Its stubborn resistance ensured the town's retention.

Advancing to victory

At the end of May, the final 'Australianisation' of the Australian Corps occurred when Lieutenant-General Sir John Monash replaced Birdwood as its commander. Monash was Australian. His divisional commanders were now either Australian or had lived in Australia for many years. These changes coincided with the ebbing of the German tide. The British, French and American counteroffensives that ended in Germany's defeat could now begin. In July 1918 the Australian part got underway in an attack that effortlessly captured the village of Hamel. Combining infantry, artillery, tanks and aircraft, and utilising surprise, Monash's plan became the blueprint for the much bigger British thrust before Amiens on 8 August, in which the Australians and Canadians swept all before them. This was the first battle in which all five Australian divisions operated together. The Australian Corps broke through the German bastions at Mont St Quentin and Péronne on the Somme at the start of September in one of the Western Front's rare manoeuvre battles. It went into action for the last time at the end of the month in the successful assault on the Hindenburg Line.

Along with the Canadians, the Australian Corps had spearheaded the BEF's advance to victory in the war's final months. At a cost of 23 243 casualties,

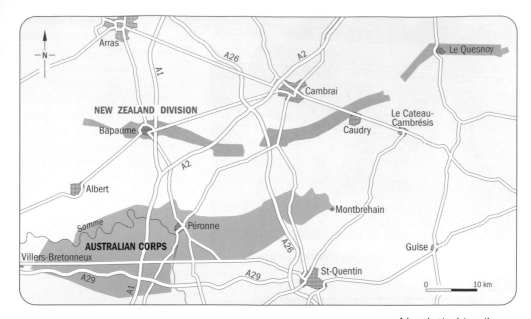

just over a quarter of whom were killed, it took 29 144 prisoners, 338 guns and countless machine-guns as well as liberating 116 towns and villages. These figures represented about 22 per cent of the captures of the entire BEF, of which the Australian Corps comprised just over 8 per cent, in this period. Through this achievement, Australia had influenced the destiny of the world for the first time in the nation's history and arguably more than at any time since. For its part, the New Zealand Division took Bapaume in August 1918, conducted a brilliant advance to the Hindenburg Line from the Trescault Spur and then stormed Le Quesnoy just before the Armistice. As the New Zealanders comprised just a single formation in one of many British corps, their feats were overshadowed by what the Australians did. But they lost nothing in comparison. They lost over 4000 men.

Reflections

Nowadays historians are fond of pointing out that technical and tactical innovation and material superiority, particularly with regard to artillery, and the German decline gave any British division a good chance of battlefield success as 1918 went on. This is quite true but it does not devalue the accomplishments of the Australians and New Zealanders a jot. Judgements on how good they were are perhaps best left to the soldiers who fought on the two-way rifle ranges with and against them, rather than to historians writing from the comfort of their studies almost a century afterwards.

Captain Hubert Essame, who had fought on the Somme in 1916, been wounded alongside the Australians at Villers-Bretonneux and who rose to become a general in the British Army, thought the Australian soldier in 1918 'the best infantryman of the war and perhaps of all time'. Some had reached that conclusion months beforehand. After Polygon Wood a British general told the 5th Division: 'You men have done very well here.' 'Only as well as ability and opportunity allow', a Digger shot back. 'Very well put young man', the general retorted, 'but you have undoubtedly the best troops in the world'. The normally reserved British Official Historian, Brigadier-General Sir James Edmonds, remarked: 'Nothing too good' could be said of the Australians of 1918. They were 'the finest'. In 1919 Marshal Foch, who had been Allied generalissimo the previous year, declared the Australian 'the greatest

Advancing to victory: the ground captured by the Australian Corps and the New Zealand Division.

Loss. Australian fallen, Lijssenthoek Military Cemetery, near Ypres.

Loss. New Zealand fallen, Caterpillar Valley Cemetery and New Zealand Memorial to the Missing, Somme

individual fighter in the war'. A German sergeant-major captured at Dernancourt maintained that the Germans 'generally considered that the Australian troops were about the finest in the world'. Generally, however, they thought the Australians and Canadians about equal. The New Zealanders were no less highly regarded but they always tended to be lumped in with the Australians.

There could be no argument, though, about the overall cost. Over the four years of war, Australia enlisted a total of 416 809 men, a mind-boggling effort for a country of about four million people. About 80 per cent, or 331 781, took the field, mostly on the Western Front. In all, 59 342, almost 20 per cent, were killed — over 46 000 on the Western Front — and 152 171, nearly 45 per cent, wounded. The overall casualty figure amounted to 215 585. Hence, only one out of every three Australians who enlisted got through unscathed, at least physically. Proportionate to forces fielded, the Australian casualty rate was the highest in the British Empire. New Zealand was not far behind. With a population of 1.3 million, it sent 100 444 men overseas, of whom 18 166 were killed and 41 317 wounded, again, mostly on the Western Front. These figures amounted to a 60 per cent casualty rate.

CHAPTER 1

1916

BOIS-GRENIER/ FLEURBAIX

'Splendid, fine physique, very hard and determined looking…The Australians are also mad keen to kill Germans and to start doing it at once', the BEF's commander-in-chief, General Sir Douglas Haig, wrote after reviewing the 7th Brigade on 27 March 1916. It had just arrived on the Western Front. Six weeks later, the New Zealand Division and the 2nd and 1st Australian Divisions of I ANZAC were side by side in that order on the right flank of the Second Army. They held the 15 kilometres of front in French Flanders that stretched from the River Lys and past the town of Armentières to a point opposite the Sugarloaf, a German salient near the village of Fromelles. Called the Bois-Grenier sector — although the Australians knew it as the Fleurbaix sector, after the half-ruined village two kilometres behind the line — the area had seen no serious fighting for almost a year. The BEF used it as a 'nursery' where new formations could be introduced to trench warfare. In June and July respectively, the 4th and 5th Australian Divisions also received their baptism of fire there, as did the 3rd, in November.

The line

In contrast to the precipitous terrain at ANZAC on the Gallipoli peninsula, the nursery was barely above sea level and ironing-board flat. Where ANZAC was parched, the nursery was covered by coarse, scrubby grass that had choked the crops in the abandoned fields. Where the opposing trenches at ANZAC were virtually on top of one another, the width of no-man's-land in the nursery varied from as little as 70 metres to as much as 450 metres. As the water table was 45 centimetres below the surface, diggings soon filled with slush. Both sides built upwards.

Though referred to as a trench, the front line was really a breastwork of earth-filled sandbags. The support line was 70 metres to 90 metres rearwards, supposedly far enough back to prevent both lines being bombarded simultaneously. If the Germans broke into the front line, reserves would concentrate for counterattacks in the appropriately named reserve line another 450 metres back. Communication trenches, spaced 230 metres apart and often dubbed 'avenues', led to the front-line system. Comprising posts and trenches that would only be garrisoned in an emergency, the second line was 1.5 kilometres further in rear. This was

General Sir Douglas Haig. He was promoted field marshal on 1 January 1917.

the standard arrangement for the trenches along the entire Western Front. In what was also standard, the Germans held the high ground, in this case the Aubers Ridge, along which their second line ran through the villages of Aubers, Fromelles and Le Maisnil. It was more like a flattened speed bump than a ridge but it still gave the Germans excellent views.

Heaven after hell?

Charles Bean, the Australian Official Correspondent and, later, Official Historian, wrote of the early days in the nursery that 'the sound of a rifle shot rarely broke the silence'. One ANZAC veteran likened it to 'heaven after hell'. At ANZAC everything had been scarce except for the unvarying ration of corned beef, apricot jam, cheese and biscuit, and there was no safe area where battalions could rest. In the nursery water was piped forward, and fresh meals were brought up from field kitchens. After leaving the line, battalions walked through green fields to billets in villages and farms for reasonably frequent breaks. Field baths gave temporary relief from lice, although the rats were worse than on Gallipoli. Each village had its own estaminet selling wine and beer.

The one similarity with ANZAC and, for that matter, the rest of the Western Front, was the routine in the line. Day began as it ended, with stand-to, when all men were on alert to repel any German attempt to take advantage of the change from night to day routine and vice versa. After an officer had checked the cleanliness of weapons, the men would be stood down, leaving sentries to keep watch. Some of the remainder did fatigues, perhaps thickening the traverses that gave breastwork and trench the zigzag shape necessary to prevent an attacker firing along them and to localise

Heaven after hell. Australians relax at Bois-Grenier, probably in the reserve-line breastwork. The front-line breastwork would have been higher. One man catches up on the news while two others hunt the lice in their shirts.

shell or bomb explosions. Others rested. But machine-guns were manned continually and trained on selected points in the German line opposite. Night was the most active period. Patrols went out into no-man's-land and increased fatigue parties did the repair and porterage tasks that were too hazardous by day.

Starting with steel helmets to protect heads against shrapnel and splinters, equipment and weapons that would have been godsends at ANZAC were issued. Each battalion received four Lewis light machine-guns. By the end of the war, the same battalion would have close to 50. In place of the crude bomb improvised from a jam tin filled with odd bits of metal came the Mills bomb, whose segmented ovoid body burst into numerous small fragments each capable of killing. The standard issue per division was 52 000. Two four-tube batteries of light Stokes mortars went to each brigade. Setting up in the support line, mortar teams could lob 22 bombs per minute onto targets pinpointed by observers in the front line. The three field artillery brigades in each division received additional guns and were augmented by a howitzer brigade, whose high-angle fire had greater reach than the flatter trajectory fire of the field-guns.

The enemy

Those who cared to think about the capabilities of these new weapons realised that the Western Front, appearances in the nursery notwithstanding, would be much tougher than ANZAC. The omnipresence of aircraft was new. Gas masks, which came in handy at ANZAC to ward off the stench, now had to be employed for their true purpose. The German medium trench mortar or *minenwerfer* seemed more plentiful than the Stokes and was

much more destructive. German snipers were deadly and could not be suppressed. German shells fell suddenly and accurately.

The Australians might have impressed Haig with their keenness to kill Germans immediately but the Germans got in first. On 5 May they raided the 20th Battalion in the Bridoux Salient, near Bois-Grenier, inflicting well over 100 casualties and taking 10 prisoners as well as two Stokes mortars. As the Stokes were still secret, both Haig and the commander of the Second Army, General Sir Herbert Plumer, were livid. The Australians were embarrassed for a long time. On 30 May the 9th and 11th Battalions lost 131 men when the Germans struck at Cordonnerie Farm, three kilometres from Bridoux. Six of the eight German casualties were due to a grenade that accidentally went off when they returned to their line. Major-General Gordon Legge, the commander of the 2nd Australian Division, admitted that the initiative lay with the enemy, who was 'somewhat superior in the offensive'. For that matter, the Germans were making the running along the Western Front.

Strategy

The Allied plan for 1916 had called for simultaneous summer offensives on the Eastern and Italian fronts, and on the

Steel-helmeted soldiers from the 2nd Australian Division at Bois-Grenier. The man on the left wields a newly issued Lewis-gun. Standing on the firestep, the next man peers over the parapet. As this would have been suicidal in the front line, the photo was probably taken in the support line. The order and cleanliness also suggest a staged shot.

Western Front, where the British and French would attack astride the Somme River. But in February 1916 the Germans launched a massive offensive against the French at Verdun, a historic fortress town on the Meuse River for which they hoped France would fight to the last man and, ultimately, 'bleed to death'. According to the German calculus, Britain would be unwilling to fight on alone in the west, while Russia was tottering in the east. The Allied plan began to unravel as the French appealed for help to relieve the pressure at Verdun, while the Italians were in trouble against the Austrians. Named after the Russian general who conceived it, the famous Brusilov offensive helped the Italians but ended up costing over a million men. It hastened Russia's collapse in 1917. Still, the Russians had done their bit. Ground down at Verdun, the French had to skimp on theirs. By mid-June they could only spare 16 divisions for the Somme offensive instead of the 39 originally offered. The BEF had to assume the main role. Haig gave the task to General Sir Henry Rawlinson's Fourth Army. Meanwhile the rest of the BEF was to carry out as many raids as possible in order to divert German attention from

Rawlinson's preparations and wear down divisions the Germans might use as reinforcements after the offensive began.

Raids

I ANZAC's first offensive action had been a raid. These 'minor trench operations' were originally intended to identify the Germans opposite, usually by taking a prisoner, in the belief that a new formation signified imminent activity. But they were also launched to maintain the offensive spirit and to keep the Germans off balance. Revolvers, bombs, knives and clubs were the instruments of mayhem. On the night of 5 June, a 66-strong raiding party drawn from the 26th and 28th Battalions attacked the German line near Bois-Grenier. Though the casualties caused by the German retaliatory bombardment meant that Australian losses exceeded German, the raid was considered a success. The New Zealanders carried out their first raid, with mixed results, on the night of 16 June.

Following Haig's demand for an increased raiding tempo, I ANZAC launched a dozen raids from the nursery between 25 June and 2 July. In the first, 18-year-old Private William Jackson of the 17th Battalion brought in wounded despite being severely wounded himself. He became the first Australian to be awarded the VC on the Western Front and remains its youngest Australian recipient. Striking near the Sugarloaf on 1 July, the 9th Battalion captured a troublesome machine-gun. In simultaneous raids two kilometres away the following night, the barrage supporting the 11th Battalion inflicted over 100 casualties on the Germans but the 89 men from the 14th Battalion were caught in uncut wire. Almost half were lost, and for nothing, as the German line was practically empty. On 13 July,

General Sir Henry Rawlinson.

175 raiders from the 1st Otago Battalion were all but wiped out before they reached the German line. The hit-and-miss nature of raids was becoming evident and I ANZAC, like the rest of the BEF, came to detest them.

7.30 am 1 July 1916. The Tyneside Irish Brigade advances over the Tara-Usna hills to be destroyed by German machine-guns around the village of La Boiselle. The 34th Division, to which the Tynesiders belonged, lost 6380 men, more than any other British division on the first day of the Somme. This photograph is one of the most recognised of the war.

Somme

At 7.30 am on 1 July 1916, 13 British divisions attacked on a 24-kilometre front astride the D929, the Albert–Bapaume road, on the rolling chalk uplands of the Somme. Five French divisions assaulted on a nine-kilometre front that was mainly south of the river on their right. During the week the bombardment lasted, the Fourth Army's 1537 guns and howitzers fired 1.5 million shells but the Germans sheltered in dugouts up to nine metres deep that were impervious to it. Dense wire entanglements girded their line. Emerging from their dugouts at the end of the bombardment, the Germans mowed down the rows of heavily laden infantrymen advancing towards them. The British Army suffered 57 470 casualties, the greatest loss in a single day in its history. The smaller follow-up attacks also failed.

On 7 July, I ANZAC was ordered to the Somme. In exchange for the New Zealand Division, which joined II ANZAC in order to remain under General Godley, the 4th Australian Division was to go with I ANZAC after being relieved by the newly arrived 5th Australian Division. Between April and June, the 1st, 2nd and 4th Australian Divisions had suffered 2384 casualties, while the New Zealand Division lost 2239 between May and July. By then the nursery was no longer heaven-like. 'Machine-gun fire went on almost continuously', the 30th Battalion's history records. 'Shrapnel had also to be contended with, and occasionally 5.9-inch shells played havoc with our parapets.'

DRIVING THE BATTLEFIELD

Those who have been to Gallipoli will appreciate how the nursery's flatness must have struck the Australian and New Zealand veterans of that campaign. Despite the lack of elevated vantage points, though, the views are often extensive. Hence most of the actions described during this drive can be followed in their entirety. But it only takes a tree line or a hamlet to block the view; when that happens relating one action to another is impossible. This does not really matter because the actions were not major attacks but small-scale raids, certainly in 1916. They were related to each other in that they were part of a raiding program rather than in a tactical sense on the ground. Don't forget that the lines on both sides comprised breastworks rather than trenches.

MAP IGN Blue Series, 1:25 000, 2404E Armentières

From Ypres take the N336 and swing right onto the N58 freeway just before Warneton. Continue over the Lys into France, where the N58 becomes the D7.

Once over the Lys, which the front lines crossed on your left, continue over the roundabout to the **red and white shed** ❶ between the agricultural machinery dealership and the power lines and look along the D7. Crossing the D7 at the roundabout behind you, the British front line, which the New Zealand Division entered on 13 May 1916, stretched to your right front. The power lines run above the centre of no-man's-land, which was generally about 400 metres wide. On the other side of it the German front line went through **Quatre Hallots Farm** on the D7 directly ahead of you. In the New Zealand

Division's first raid on the Western Front, an 87-man party drawn from the 2nd Brigade passed through your location on its way to the **Breakwater**, a trench to the right of the farm. Designed to seal off the trench from the Germans, the New Zealanders' box barrage wiped out the officers leading the raid. Two snipers were bayoneted but no prisoners were taken. The New Zealanders lost 10 men.

Return to the roundabout, head left on the D945 past **Houplines** and left again after 900 metres onto Rue Brune. Continue 500 metres to **Pont Ballot** ❷ at the T-junction by the electricity sub-station. Stand with Rue Brune at your back. The New Zealand line ran diagonally through the junction and on to your right front. The apex of a German salient directly opposite you reduced the width of no-man's-land to 125 metres, making this location an ideal starting point for raids. The New Zealanders launched several, with mixed results. On 25 June 1916 the 2nd Rifles took nine prisoners; on 11 July the 2nd Otago got a bloody nose when the supporting barrage left the German wire intact.

Now walk to the dumping area under the power lines to your left, look along them towards the red and white shed and leap ahead to 27 February 1917. That night the 3rd Division, which became the pre-eminent Australian division at raiding, carried out the 'big raid'. You are standing on the right flank, from where the 824-man raiding party, drawn from the 10th Brigade, spread across the divisional front line almost to the shed. General Monash, the 3rd Division's commander, used 'flavoured smoke', probably for the first time in the BEF. The preliminary bombardment included

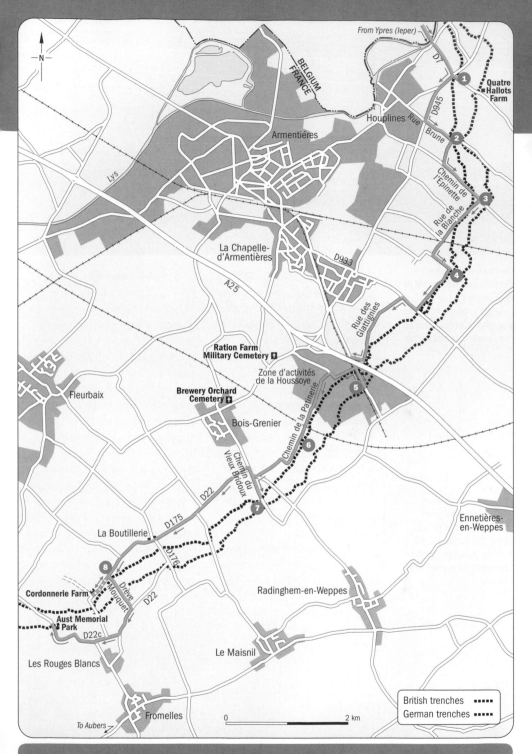

The drive starts at the northern end of the nursery sector in the vicinity of Houplines and follows the British front line to Fromelles at the southwestern end of the nursery. It includes the sites of the major raids carried out by the ANZACs in 1916 and early 1917, and the location of Private Jackson's VC action.

DISTANCE COVERED: 18 km

DURATION: 2.5 hours

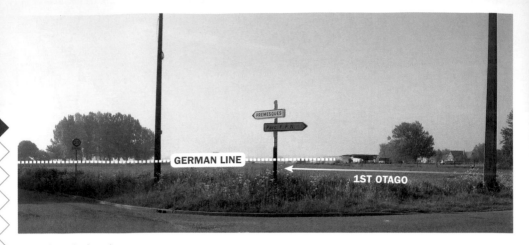

GERMAN LINE

1ST OTAGO

No-man's-land, where 1st Otago was wiped out trying to cross on 13 July 1916. To the right of where this picture was taken, 1st Auckland had lost heavily 10 days earlier.

The 'big raid', as seen from the 10th Brigade's right flank. At the far end of the German line is the Breakwater, where the New Zealanders carried out their first raid.

smoke and gas to inveigle the Germans into wearing their gas masks whenever they saw smoke. The final bombardment omitted the gas, enabling the raiders to attack without gas masks and catch the Germans in theirs. Attacking to your right front, the raiders reached the third German line and occupied an 800-metre stretch of it for 35 minutes while protected by a box barrage so straight, said Captain Charles Peters of the 38th Battalion, 'You could have toasted bread at it'. This was the most important raid launched by an Australian division. In the following days the Germans struck the 3rd Division seven times but only reached its line twice.

Head right on Chemin du Pont Ballot, then left at the T-junction onto Chemin de l'Epinette and stop 800 metres further

on at the **T-junction ③** with Rue de la Blanche on your right. Face the 50-kilometre speed sign on Chemin de l'Epinette. You are standing in no-man's-land. The German line was 180 metres ahead of you. Late on 3 July 1916, two intense bombardments, each an hour long and the second using *minenwerfers*, pummelled 1st Auckland's line, which ran behind the house on your right and met Rue de la Blanche 150 metres to your right. German raiders twice tried to enter but were beaten off. The Aucklanders lost 102 men. Next morning the area around you defied belief. The breastwork was flattened, men were buried alive and body parts lay everywhere. Torrential German shrapnel and machine-gun fire accounted for 163 of 1st Otago's 175-man raiding party to your right front 10 days later.

AUSTRALIAN LINE

> The whole system of enemy works was thoroughly demolished, a minimum of over 200 dead have been counted, 17 prisoners were brought back; as also a very large quantity of material, including several quite new types of Minenwerfer Fuzes, a complete portable electric searchlight plant, several medical panniers, a miscellaneous collection of rifles, helmets and equipment, and a large mass of papers, maps and documents.
>
> Monash on the 'big raid' (letter to Birdwood, 27 Feb 1917, MS1884, National Library of Australia)

Continue to the right along Rue de la Blanche, turn left beyond the railway at the T-junction and park 350 metres along at the **sharp right turn** 4. Stand with the railway on your left and the power lines ahead of you. The New Zealand line ran along the road to your right, through your location and then jutted to your front at the **Mushroom Salient**. It reached to within 50 metres of the German line, which would have passed under the power lines at that point. While standing sentry in the Mushroom late on 29 June, Private William Nimot became the only New Zealander to desert to the Germans. His parents were German, with the family name of Nimodt. The family needed police protection when news of the desertion reached New Zealand. It also brought trouble for those with Germanic names there. On 8 July the Germans raided the Mushroom twice within 45 minutes. 1st Canterbury repelled the first raid but the second got into the breastwork. The Germans were driven back yard by yard and finished off by a counterattack. All told, the Canterburys suffered 116 casualties.

Carry on for 850 metres and turn right onto the D933. Keep your eyes peeled and turn left opposite a grey concrete wall after 300 metres onto Rue des Glattignies. At the T-junction below the A25 autoroute, turn right onto Rue du Bois then immediately right again. The 2nd Rifles ejected German raiders who entered Rue de Bois redoubt here on 19 July. Head left at the T-junction onto Avenue Industrielle and pass under the A25. The British line crossed the Avenue Industrielle 100 metres beyond the underpass and ran along Rue François Arago, the first road on the right; the German line crossed 400 metres further on, at the slight leftwards bend in the road. As there is no parking there, continue another 400 metres to the old railway station, **Ennetières en Weppes**, and walk back to the **bend** 5. Face the A25.

You are standing where the Australians opened their raiding account on the

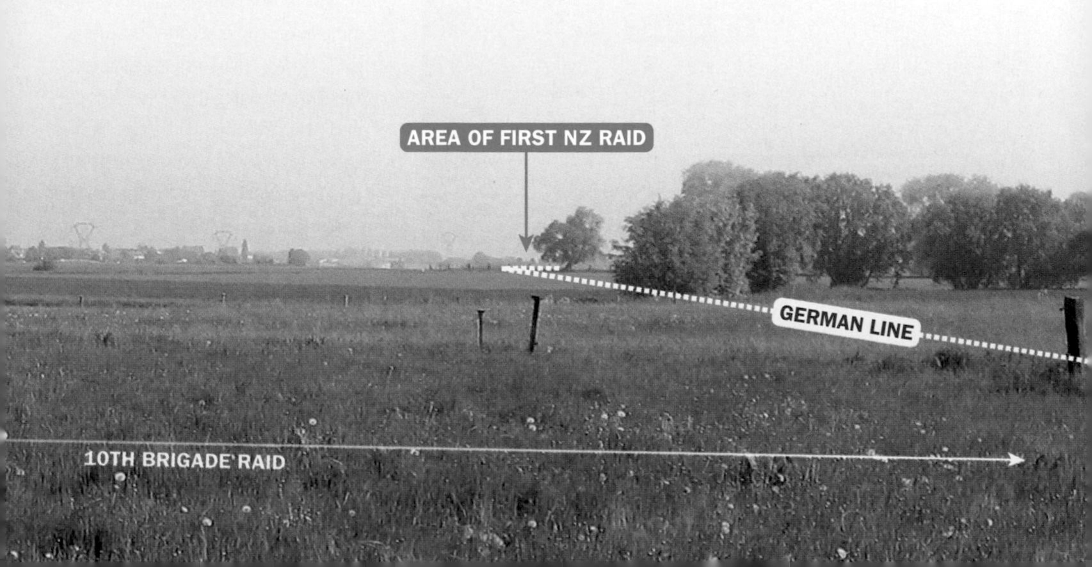
AREA OF FIRST NZ RAID
GERMAN LINE
10TH BRIGADE RAID

Western Front at 11.35 pm on 5 June 1916. Led by Gallipoli veteran Captain Maitland Foss, who was already known for his scouting of no-man's-land in the nursery, the 66 raiders advanced towards you wearing unmarked British clothing to confuse the Germans and with faces and bayonets blackened. A box barrage protected them during the seven minutes they spent in the German breastwork here. Six Germans were killed and three captured but six raiders, and 20 men in the Australian line, fell victim to the bombardment that the Germans called down as the raiders returned across no-man's-land. On 29 June, 312 men from the 6th Brigade struck the stretch of German line that extended from your location 500 metres leftwards. Entering it at three points under a heavy box barrage, they suffered 32 casualties but inflicted 111 in what the Germans admitted was very severe fighting. The 14th Battalion's costly raid against the deserted German line on 14 July also occurred in this area.

Head back along Avenue Industrielle and turn left just before the A25 onto Rue François Arago. Head right onto Rue Ambroise Paré at the roundabout then left after 100 metres onto Chemin de la Patinerie. Once over the railway bridge, pause by the **electricity sub-station** 6

to your left. The British and German lines paralleled the road on your side of the sub-station, which lies in the old no-man's land, and the far side respectively. During a raid on the German line to your left front by a 73-strong party drawn from the 5th Brigade on 25 June, Private Jackson carried wounded men back three times under heavy shellfire, and went out after a shell burst mangled his arm to recover two more wounded.

After another 1.1 kilometres turn right onto the D62 (Rue du Bas), then left straightaway onto Chemin du Vieux Bridoux, which you should follow around to the left, past the memorial to the 2/10 Scottish Battalion, The King's Liverpool Regiment. Park after 400 metres at the slight **leftwards bend** 7 and walk down the road until you can see the German **bunker** 500 metres to your right front and the spire of **Fromelles church** beyond it. You are now on the front line at the **Bridoux Salient**. The 20th Battalion held it when the Germans started out from their own line, which crossed the road on the near side of the houses to your front, at 7.40 pm on 5 May. This was one of the first occasions on which the Australians were able to glean the true texture of the Western Front. The heaviest bombardment they had yet known bashed them. 'Some fellows' nerves gave way & they became gibbering idiots, Sergeants and all sorts, god it was little wonder … fighting here is simply a massacre', wrote Corporal Arthur Thomas. The Germans inflicted on the 20th six times their own loss of 19 men. Their capture of the two Stokes mortars, which should have been withdrawn after firing to the support line behind you, resulted in the sacking of the 20th's commanding officer.

Head back along Chemin du Vieux Bridoux towards Bois-Grenier and take the first left, the D22, at **White City**, where the 20th Battalion's headquarters was located. The D22 soon becomes the

The view from the 20th Battalion's front line in the Bridoux Salient.

FROMELLES

GERMAN LINE

GERMAN RAID 5 MAY

20TH BATTALION LINE

D175. Continue for 2.5 kilometres along it to the **intersection** 8 with Drève Mouquet on the left and park. Look along Drève Mouquet. The Australian line ran to your front along the D22/D175 and the German line, based on the **Tadpole** strongpoint, paralleled it 250 metres ahead. Thanks to the supporting barrage, the 11th Battalion raided the Tadpole successfully on 2 July. As a 'No Entry' sign precluded further progress on the D175 at the time of writing, walk 400 metres along the D175, passing **Cordonnerie Farm** on the right, just beyond which the road bends sharply left.

Stand on the bend with the farm over your left shoulder and face the copse on the left of the road ahead of you. The Australian line stretched left to right along the front of the copse while the German line stretched along the rear of it. No-man's-land, which the copse straddles, was therefore quite narrow, which made this location attractive for raiders on both sides. When the Germans raided the 9th and 11th Battalions here

on 30 May, their barrage obliterated 60 metres of the Australian breastwork. The German raid report stated that: 'Bodies, buried and torn in shreds, were found in great number, and also very many dead, apparently unwounded, were seen in dugouts'. But the 9th got its own back in its raid on 1 July. For the loss of 33 men, its 148-man raiding party killed or wounded 58 Germans and captured 21.

Return to your car, head down Drève Mouquet and turn right at the T-junction onto the D22. At the three-way intersection by the crucifix, head right on the D22c and follow it to the **Australian Memorial Park** to begin the Fromelles battlefield walk. To return to Ypres, continue past the park on what is now Rue Delvas to Sailly-sur-Lys and turn right onto the D945. On reaching the big roundabout beyond the TGV railway, bear half left onto the D945n, cross the Lys and turn right onto the D933 in Nieppe. Turn left after 400 metres onto Rue de la Chapelle Rompue and follow it to the N365, which takes you to Ypres.

The crater made by a *minenwerfer* bomb during the bombardment that preceded the raid on the 11th Battalion on 30 May 1916.

LOCAL INFORMATION

Many of those who fell in the nursery lie in cemeteries on the Fromelles battlefield and are described in the chapter on that battle.

Brewery Orchard Cemetery, Bois-Grenier

Firmly linking this cemetery to the fighting in the nursery, 20 men from the 20th Battalion who fell in the German raid on the Bridoux Salient lie in one long grave at IV.C. Of the cemetery's 344 burials, all but two of them known, 125 are Australian and 13 New Zealand. Started in an orchard at the end of 1914 to serve the British advanced dressing station set up in the cellar of the adjacent brewery, the cemetery was sheltered by the surrounding ruins of Bois-Grenier and remained in use for the next three years. Located next to the modern brewery that dominates the site today, it can be reached on the tour route by heading back from the Bridoux Salient along Chemin du Vieux Bridoux and continuing into Bois-Grenier. Turn right onto the D222 near the end of the village and the cemetery is on your left.

Ration Farm Military Cemetery

The cemetery is on the left of the D222 one kilometre past Brewery Orchard. A communication trench ran from the farm opposite to the British front line one kilometre beyond. Ration parties returning from the line along the trench brought the dead back with them to cemeteries either side of the D122. Ration Farm Old Cemetery, behind the ruined original farm buildings, was begun in February 1915. After the war, its graves, along with those from other small cemeteries and from battlefield burials, were concentrated in Ration Farm New Cemetery, which had been started in October 1915. It eventually became Ration Farm Military Cemetery. Of its 1317 burials, 639 of them known, 259 are Australian and 32 New Zealand. Gallipoli veteran Private Robert Jack of the 24th Battalion at I.I.6 was killed in the 6th Brigade's raid on 29 June.

Armentières

Initially held by the Germans, Armentières was captured by the British in October 1914 and became the main behind-the-lines centre in French Flanders. It was also immortalised as the home of the Mademoiselle featured in a humorous, and, in some versions, ribald, wartime ditty. Australians and New Zealanders stationed in the nursery in 1916 frequented the estaminets and restaurants around the main square, while premises offering more worldly delights could be found on the streets behind it. Armentières was largely intact when abandoned at the start of the German offensive on the Lys in April 1918. When the Germans left on 2 October 1918 it was in ruins. You pass by the town while driving between Ypres and the nursery.

CHAPTER 2

1916

FROMELLES

Sitting atop Aubers Ridge, Fromelles has always been a sleepy French Flanders village. But in the fields below it on any Sunday after the harvest, clusters of men festooned with ammunition bandoliers check their weapons as if gearing up for the Gunfight at the OK Corral, move off in line and then stop as one to send a volley of shots rippling through the stillness. Weekend hunters blasting rabbits and anything else that moves to smithereens, they unknowingly create an atmospheric link to the past. Across these same fields on 19 July 1916, the 5th Australian and the 61st (South Midland) Divisions carried out an attack that constitutes a rare vintage for connoisseurs of military incompetence.

Planning

Arriving in France in June 1916, the 5th Division, commanded by Major-General James McCay, began entering the line in the nursery opposite Fromelles on 10 July. The raiding program carried out earlier by the other Australian divisions before they left to take part in the Somme offensive had not stopped the Germans sending troops from the nursery to the Somme too. As stronger action was required, General Haig's headquarters re-examined a proposal from Lieutenant-General Sir Richard Haking, the commander of XI Corps, for an attack on Aubers Ridge. It blocked the western approaches to Lille, the industrial centre of Flanders, 20 kilometres east. Haking wanted to take 'the two main tactical localities on the ridge', the high ground around Fromelles and Aubers.

Initially it was decided to rejig Haking's scheme as an artillery demonstration, using a long bombardment to suggest that a new offensive was starting. But the commander of the First Army and Haking's superior, General Sir Charles Monro, insisted on an infantry advance,

although only to the German support line, 140 metres to 180 metres behind the front line and 1.4 kilometres short of Aubers Ridge. Though the ridge is nowhere more than 25 metres above sea level, the Germans ensconced on it still looked down on the front lines. Given its modest objective, the attack was never going to deprive the Germans of their view. Monro got his way nonetheless.

Provisionally fixed for 17 July, the attack would be carried out by the 5th Australian Division, which was loaned to XI Corps, and the 61st Division, also recently arrived in France, from XI Corps. Haking would be in charge. On 14 July he directed that '[Each] Division will attack with 3 brigades in line, each brigade with 2 assaulting battalions, and each battalion on a front of assault of about [300 metres]'. The preliminary bombardment was to last seven hours. Half of the 5th Division's 12 battalions had been in the front line for two days and the other six had not seen it at all at this stage. The 4th Australian Division's artillery, which would support them, was deemed too raw to go to the Somme;

Lieutenant-General Sir Richard Haking. In 1918 he featured prominently in a War Cabinet discussion of officers judged to be incompetent.

The view that the Germans had across the plain from Fromelles church in 1916; the same view today as the morning mist starts to lift.

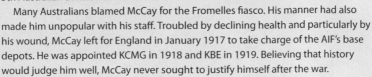

Major-General Sir James Whiteside McCay

Commander, 2nd Brigade 1914–15, 5th Australian Division 1916

1864–1930

Irish-born McCay was intelligent, energetic and brave but also conceited, pedantic and abrasive. A fine scholar, he became a successful teacher, solicitor and militia officer before entering state politics in Victoria in his early 30s. Shifting to federal politics, McCay became Minister for Defence in 1905. By 1914, he had left politics altogether but remained active in the law and was a colonel in the militia. He led the 2nd Brigade at the ANZAC landing and was seriously wounded a fortnight later. Invalided back to Australia, McCay received a hero's welcome. He took command of the new 5th Australian Division in March 1916.

Many Australians blamed McCay for the Fromelles fiasco. His manner had also made him unpopular with his staff. Troubled by declining health and particularly by his wound, McCay left for England in January 1917 to take charge of the AIF's base depots. He was appointed KCMG in 1918 and KBE in 1919. Believing that history would judge him well, McCay never sought to justify himself after the war.

the 5th's was rawer still. Nevertheless, McCay was gratified that his division, the last Australian division to reach France from Egypt, would be the first to see serious action on the Western Front. He placed the 14th Brigade between the 8th Brigade on the left and the 15th on the right.

Problems

The tactical difficulties were immense. Protected by wire entanglements five metres deep, the German front-line breastwork comprised a sandbag wall over two metres high and six metres across that was impervious to all but the heaviest shells. Machine-guns in the Sugarloaf Salient enfiladed the ground on either side. Owing to its flatness, they were also capable of grazing fire, in which the centre of every burst does not rise above the height of a standing man. The combination of enfilade and grazing fire maximises a machine-gun's lethality

by enabling it to catch an assault flank on with no dead ground for cover. Haking gave the Germans another ace by setting the interdivisional boundary for the attack virtually on the Sugarloaf. As this meant that the strongpoint could rake both the British and Australian assaults, the commanders either side of the boundary had to be able to act instantly without compromising each other, not easy when they were out of touch in the heat of battle. The boundary should have been drawn so that only one division was directly affected.

Moreover, the Germans knew the area intimately. The 6th Bavarian Division had held it for well over a year and many in its ranks, such as Lance-Corporal Adolf Hitler, had been fighting since the start of the war. In May 1915 they helped to shatter a British assault on Aubers Ridge in which Haking and Monro were senior commanders. What experienced divisions had been unable to do on much the

KASTENWEG

SITE OF AUSTRALIAN MEMORIAL PARK

DELANGRÉ FARM

FROMELLES

LAIES

RUE DELVAS

SUGARLOAF

A wartime oblique aerial photograph showing the ground over which the 5th Australian Division attacked. The Australians held the lower trench; the Germans the upper one.

same ground then, they were ordering two green divisions to do now with next to no notice against strong defences manned by veterans. Birdwood and White protested from the Somme that the Germans would have to be dopes to take such a limited attack seriously. It would hardly deter them from sending local units there. On the spot, Brigadier-General Harold 'Pompey' Elliott of the 15th Brigade showed a British liaison officer the 400 metres of no-man's-land in front of the Sugarloaf that the 15th had to cross. The officer predicted 'a bloody holocaust'. Despite their rawness, the soldiers were uneasy at the rushed

preparations. Many had not yet been issued steel helmets.

On 16 July Haig's headquarters suggested cancelling the attack because the transfer of German reserves to the Somme had slowed. Claiming that morale would suffer, Haking resisted and the attack stood. But with rain hampering observation on 17 July, Haking was forced to seek a postponement. This time Monro advocated cancellation. He was told that Haig now wanted it to proceed because a German counterattack on the Somme seemed imminent. The attack was rescheduled for 19 July. At dawn that morning the Australians saw a sign on Aubers Ridge asking: 'Why so long, you are twenty four hours late?' They had shot away the previous one, which read: 'ADVANCE AUSTRALIA — IF YOU CAN!'

The attack

As the clock wound down, some Australians relaxed with a pre-battle drink in the local estaminets. Used only to puny shelling, the Gallipoli veterans were awed by the intensity of the bombardment. But the gunners' inexperience told as many 'dropshorts' landed on the Australian line. The German artillery pummelled it too. At 6 pm, with over two hours of daylight left, the assault began. Shot down before the Sugarloaf, the 61st Division made only small gains elsewhere that it could not hold. The Germans in the Sugarloaf now dealt with Elliott's assault. Cheering as the 59th and 60th Battalions clambered over the parapet, they wiped them out.

Marked today by VC Corner Cemetery, no-man's-land was much narrower ahead of the 8th and 14th Brigades. They overran the German front line and the muddy ditches behind it, and then set up in them after going 600 metres further without finding the support line. The smoke and dust from the shelling reduced visibility. Taking over the 53rd Battalion on the right of Rue Delvas after its commanding officer was killed, 21-year-old Captain Charles Arblaster had intermittent contact across the road with the 54th Battalion and thought he was in touch with the 60th until bombing started on his right. Moving along their old front line, which was empty because McCay had directed each wave to keep going, the Germans struck the open right flank where the 60th should have been. Arblaster hurriedly organised its defence.

The 32nd Battalion anchored the left flank 1.1 kilometres away in the Kastenweg, a communication trench running past German-held Delangré Farm. A mine had been blown in no-man's-land there in the hope that the

The attack at the Sugarloaf

The 60th climbed on the parapet, heavily laden, dragging with them scaling ladders, light bridges, picks, shovels and bags of bombs. There was wire to go through, and stinking ground; a creek to cross, more marsh and wire; then the German lines. Stammering scores of German machine-guns spluttered violently, drowning the noise of the cannonade. The air was thick with bullets, swishing in a flat criss-cross lattice of death. There were gaps in the lines of men — wide ones, small ones. The survivors spread across the front, keeping the line straight. There was no hesitation, no recoil, no dropping of the unwounded into shell-holes. The bullets skimmed low, from knee to groin, riddling the tumbling bodies before they touched the ground. Still the line kept on. Hundreds were mown down in the flicker of an eyelid, like great rows of teeth knocked from a comb, but still the line went on, thinning and stretching. Men were cut in two by streams of bullets. And still the line went on.

Downing, WH, *To the Last Ridge,* Sydney, 1998, p. 8

Unlike at Gallipoli, cameras were strictly forbidden in the front line on the Western Front but Lance-Corporal Charles Lorking of the 53rd Battalion fortunately had one on him before the 53rd attacked. Of the eight men shown above having a tense last-minute smoke, only three, all wounded, would be alive the next day.

Another photograph taken by Lance-Corporal Lorking of the 53rd Battalion just before the attack.

abandoned them when they thinned out the forward defences months earlier. Aerial photographs revealed the change but Haking's headquarters missed it. Standing in knee-deep water, the Australians tried to fill the few sandbags they had with soil so clayey that it clung to their shovels and had to be put into the sandbags by hand. As shell-bursts choked the Laies, an irrigation ditch in no-man's-land into which other ditches drained, the water rose higher and mud had to be used. Any man hit while working drowned unless his mates were close enough to help him.

As ammunition and bombs were constantly needed, the carrying parties faced the daunting prospect of having to shuttle back and forth. Most did not. On reaching the old German line, they joined the fight instead of returning to their own line for another load. Fresh parties had to be formed. With reinforcements also being drip-fed into it, the battle became a black hole that sucked in most of the 5th Division. Meanwhile, Haking, upon hearing of the 61st Division's drubbing, had countermanded a previous order for it to attack again at 9 pm. McCay's headquarters was advised but failed to inform Elliott, who had readied the 58th Battalion to support the attack. Duly going over the top, the 58th crumpled in a torrent of fire from the Sugarloaf that sounded like a thousand sheets of calico being rent at once.

By then German reserves, newly arrived from Aubers Ridge, were counterattacking. The 8th Brigade on the left flank held on grimly. On the right flank, where the Germans had earlier been halted, the 53rd Battalion was all but cut off by 1 am. Arblaster led a charge to break out but it was doomed. Lieutenant-Colonel Walter Cass, the 54th Battalion's commander, signalled: 'Position almost desperate'. But McCay had

spoil might shield the 32nd from the strongpoints at Mouquet Farm and the Tadpole beyond. It did not, leaving this flank exposed as well. Barricading the Kastenweg, the 32nd Battalion extended rightwards to link up with the 31st's advanced line in the ditches but not with the bulk of the 31st, which was in the old German front line. The 54th Battalion's advanced line did not connect with the 31st's at all.

The bitter end

At 7.30 pm, the 8th and 14th Brigades held a disjointed position with both flanks open. The support line they sought once ran along the muddy ditches they were occupying but the Germans had

The Germans recapture part of the advanced line held by the 31st Battalion. This ditch, part of the old German support line, was typical of those held by the Australians during the battle. Note the dead in the mud and the sandbags that the Australians stacked on the left of the ditch in an effort to make a parapet.

virtually no men left to send him. At 2.30 am the Germans swamped what remained of the 8th Brigade. At 5 am news arrived that the 14th Brigade's situation was dire. Monro ordered a withdrawal.

Some in the 14th Brigade pulled out along a communication trench dug 150 metres across no-man's-land during the night, a Herculean feat. Many of those who could not reach it were shot down trying to cross no-man's-land, or were killed in the German line. The scene in the Australian trenches was likened to 'the stock of a thousand butcher-shops'. 'They'll get used to it', McCay remarked. The Germans offered a truce to gather the wounded but McCay, aware of the British policy on truces, rejected it. Men took matters into their own hands and slipped out to rescue their comrades.

Sustaining the highest loss rate in all of Australia's conflicts, 5533 casualties in a single night, the 5th Australian Division was destroyed as a fighting formation for

Seemingly asleep, a dead Australian in the German line. He may well have been one of those the Germans buried at Pheasant Wood.

several months. Of the 1917 Australians killed, 1299 had no known grave. Some 400 were taken prisoner. The 61st Division had 1547 casualties. The Germans lost 1582.

WALKING THE BATTLEFIELD

Several points need to be kept in mind on the Fromelles battlefield. Because it is so flat, good vantage points are nonexistent. The area around Fromelles church does offer useful views but is well outside the battle area. Be aware that Rue Delvas ran diagonally *across* the axis of the Australian assault until it passed VC Corner Cemetery, which is in no-man's-land and *not* the Australian front line. Of the 700 blockhouses the Germans built in the area, 90-odd survive but many postdate the battle.

On the plus side, landmarks that serve as markers to key sites abound. The hornbeams in VC Corner Cemetery are visible almost anywhere, making the cemetery an excellent orientation point and allowing the position of Rue Delvas and the two front lines to be estimated from a long way away. 'Cobbers', the statue dominating the Australian Memorial Park, is similarly prominent. The heaviest fighting took place around the park, which is situated where the German front line met Rue Delvas. As the battle in its entirety can be grasped from the park, a full description of it from there follows. The park is also the starting point for a walk around what is the smallest of the AIF's major battlefields.

MAP IGN Blue Series, 1:25 000, Sheet 2404E, Armentières, Edition 4, 1996

From Ypres, take the N365 and swing left onto Rue de la Chapelle Rompue at the Y-junction on the outskirts of Armentières. Turn right on reaching the D933 and left at the roundabout onto the D945n. Once over the A25 autoroute and the Lys, head right at the roundabout onto the D945 for Sailly-sur-Lys. Turn left there onto the D166/D175, signposted Fromelles.

'Cobbers'

You are now following the route that the 5th Australian Division took to the battle. Stop after seven kilometres at the **Australian Memorial Park** and stand in the park with 'Cobbers' on your right and Rue Delvas on your left. **VC Corner Cemetery** is to your front on the right of Rue Delvas 200 metres along. Broken by farm buildings, the tree line to its right follows Rue Petillon. The D171 (Rue du Bois) extends across the horizon to its left. Overlooked by the needle-like spire of **Laventie church**, the D171 goes through **Fauquissart**, whose squat church steeple rises to your left. The 61st Division's line began there and roughly paralleled the near side of the D171 before swinging towards VC Corner Cemetery below Laventie church, where the Australians took over. Crossing Rue Delvas 250 metres beyond the cemetery, their line passed well in front of **Cellar Farm**, which is the long house facing the

VC CORNER AUSTRALIAN CEMETERY MEMORIAL

LE TROU AID POST

AUSTRALIAN LINE

14TH BRIGADE   14TH BRIGADE

park 750 metres away, and brushed the left side of the prominent copse on your right.

The tree line to the left of the copse masks **Cordonnerie Farm**, while **Delangré Farm** and the **Kastenweg** are behind the tall, thickish growth to the right of the copse. Following the path of the telegraph poles between the two farms, the German front-line breastwork ran towards the park and passed just beyond the fence in front of you. A clump of bush in the field to your right hides two blockhouses that formed part of the front-line system. In the opposite direction, the German line headed to the **Sugarloaf**, whose apex was in the fields 720 metres away on your left. Unfortunately, no convenient reference point exists to indicate its position. But all is not lost!

Turn left and face the road. An old corner café 130 metres to your left front marks the junction of Rue Delvas with Rue Deleval. The first house on Rue Deleval after the café is **Delaporte Farm**, site of a major strongpoint, and the next, a long white building, is **La Ferme Equestre L'Hippocrate**, **Orchard House** to the British. Draw an imaginary line from it left to right across your front, and the intersection with another line running at right angles to Rue Delvas from the park is the approximate location of the Sugarloaf.

Now turn left again. On the sharp bend 220 metres away, where Rue Delvas swings eastwards past Rouge Bancs, stands a **crucifix memorial** erected by his family to Lieutenant Paul Kennedy of 2/Rifle Brigade, who fell in the British attack in May 1915. The pillbox, in which Hitler possibly sheltered during the Australian attack, can be discerned to the right of the crucifix one kilometre further on. The ground in rear rises to **Aubers Ridge**. Although the wooded slope conceals **Aubers**, **Fromelles church** is visible on the skyline to your left front.

No-man's-land was much narrower to your left than your right. It was 220 metres across at the park. Attacking on the far side of Rue Delvas behind you, the 53rd Battalion was badly enfiladed from the Sugarloaf, before which the 15th Brigade had been shot down. 'Parapet Joe', a notoriously accurate machine-gun firing down Rue Delvas from the entrance to the park, was also troublesome. Captain Arblaster took over the 53rd when its commanding officer, Lieutenant-Colonel Ignatius Norris, was killed on the breastwork.

The 54th Battalion on this side of Rue Delvas had an easier crossing and caught the Germans emerging from the breastwork and the deep dugouts behind it. The 54th's assault continued over the light tramway, which ran along the fence in front of you and on to

The attack of the 14th and 8th Brigades as seen from the Australian Memorial Park, along which the German front-line breastwork ran.

CELLAR FARM

8TH BRIGADE

8TH BRIGADE

GERMAN LINE

Pheasant Wood below Fromelles church, while the 53rd on your right now crossed Rue Deleval. Some men from both battalions went 400 metres further. Unable to find a clearly defined trench, they returned to some watery ditches in the fields ahead of you, which were the remains of the support line they had been seeking.

The 53rd Battalion held a line of posts that began 70 metres to your front on Rue Delvas, paralleled the near side of Rue Deleval for 180 metres, then curved towards the German breastwork. A shallow wall of sandbags across Rue Delvas connected to the 54th Battalion, whose posts were in a ditch that ran across your front towards the track opposite the **Pension pour les Chiens**, the dog kennels in the two buildings to the left of the Kennedy Crucifix. A gap existed between these posts and the 31st Battalion, most of which was on the far side of the track to your left front. Lieutenant-Colonel Cass set up the 54th's headquarters in a luxurious dugout 45 metres past the end of the park on your left. The 54th's communication trench struck the German line behind the headquarters after being extended across no-man's-land from the farm buildings on Rue Petillon during the battle.

Shortly after the 53rd Battalion arrived, Arblaster saw Germans streaming along the vacant front line behind him towards Rue Delvas. They struck the 53rd's open flank in the field to your right, which the 60th Battalion from the 15th Brigade

should have been occupying. With anyone who could be spared, Arblaster held them for an hour until a lack of bombs forced him back. By then the Germans were virtually at the entrance to the park and only some barricades hastily thrown up by the 55th Battalion stopped them going further.

Just after 1 am fresh German troops advanced from Delaporte Farm to your right front and struck along the breastwork and ditches. Some worked their way behind the 53rd Battalion's advanced line in the ditches and fired into them from the rear. Arblaster led a charge against these Germans but it was instantly destroyed. Badly wounded, he died in a German hospital. Sergeant Arthur Stringer rallied a dozen men and temporarily halted the Germans by hurling bombs from the parapet of the breastwork near the park entrance. Then Lieutenant Bill Denoon and 50 men regained 40 metres of the breastwork in an hour-long bomb fight that kept the Germans on the far side of the road.

At 2.30 am the Germans assaulted frontally astride the track to the left of the Kennedy Crucifix. They soon reached their old front line and rolled along it to the Kastenweg, forcing the remnants of the 8th Brigade to charge through them to the Australian line. A group from the 31st Battalion, led by its commanding officer, Lieutenant-Colonel Frederick Toll, held out in the breastwork near the track until 5.45 am, by which time they had run out of

The 14th Brigade's right flank on Rue Delvas, which was held by Captain Arblaster and the 53rd Battalion.

AUBERS RIDGE

DELAPORTE FARM

RUE DELEVAL

ADVANCED LINE 53RD BATTALION

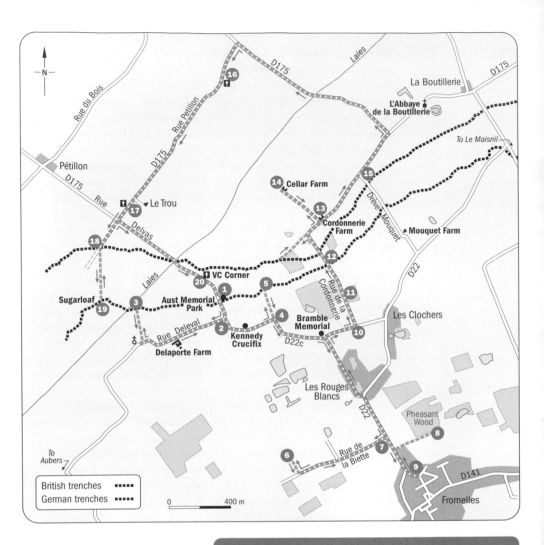

bombs and their single machine-gun was crippled.

Linking up with this assault, another frontal attack came in between Rouge Bancs and Delaporte Farm, directly towards you. With its entire perimeter now being pressed, the 14th Brigade withdrew. As the advanced line in the ditches to your front was cut off, many had to charge rearwards to the breastwork, which Captain Norman Gibbins' rearguard was holding at the head of the newly dug communications trench to your left. Safety lay at the other end but Gibbins did not reach it. After the battle, Australian wounded littered no-man's-land and their comrades went out nightly to bring them in.

This walk covers the assault of each of the Australian brigades. It passes through the furthest points reached by these assaults, the main positions eventually held in the German line, and the German counterattacks. The Australian line, from which the assault started, and the Sugarloaf, from where the right flank was carved up, are also included.

DISTANCE COVERED: 13 km
DURATION: 6 hours

The walk

Study the battle from the **Australian Memorial Park** ① using the previous narrative, then head left on Rue Delvas. After 130 metres, turn right at the old corner café onto **Rue Deleval** ②. The 1 am counterattack against the 53rd Battalion's right flank came through **Delaporte Farm**, which is on the left after 300 metres. Continuing almost to the chapel on the right a little further on, walk to the end of the **track 3** that is also on the right. You are now on the German front line between the Sugarloaf and the Australian Memorial Park, and also near the boundary between the 14th and 15th Brigades. The dead and wounded of the 59th and 60th Battalions covered the ground on the left, back to and beyond the **Laies**, which runs across your front.

Return to Rue Delvas and continue past the **Kennedy Crucifix**. Some men from the 14th Brigade crossed the road here and kept going in their search for the German support line. The road makes a right-angle turn at the **Pension pour les Chiens 4**, opposite which a track heads left. Walk 50 metres along it and look to your right front. Sections of derelict trench running in that direction were occupied by the 8th Brigade's advanced line, whose right flank, held by part of the 31st Battalion, was 160 metres away. Walk another 70 metres and look left towards the corner café. You are now level with the 54th Battalion's ditch, which did not meet the track but swung back to the breastwork, 90 metres further along near the bush-covered blockhouses.

Walk to the **telegraph poles 5**, which approximate the line of the breastwork, then turn about and look

towards **Fromelles**. Colonel Toll and the rest of the 31st Battalion were in the breastwork on your left and Captain Gibbins' men were in it on your right but the 270-metre gap between the advanced lines of the 8th and 14th Brigades to your front remained open. Having come down the road from Fromelles, the Germans attacked astride the track at 2.30 am and overran the 31st Battalion's advanced line. Reaching the breastwork on Toll's left, they raced along it to the Kastenweg, forcing the 8th Brigade's chaotic withdrawal. Toll's group exited around 5.45 am. The 14th Brigade withdrew a few hours later.

Return to Pension pour les Chiens and continue along Rue Delvas. Just past the next bend, the raised bank of a pond on the right marks the end of Toll's attempt to find the German support trench at the start of the attack; he had walked through the Australian barrage to it.

Continue to the **memorial** to Sergeant Kenneth Bramble of 609 Squadron RAF, whose Spitfire crashed here on 21 July 1941, and head right at the fork towards Fromelles on what is now the D22. After 460 metres, take the right branch of the next fork and stop 300 metres along at Rue de la Biette on the right. If you are feeling energetic *and* there is little or no crop growth, it is worthwhile walking along it for 800 metres to the football field on the right. Just beyond the far end of the field is a platoon-sized **pillbox 6** with machine-gun platforms at either end. Stills from the film footage of Hitler's

Looking towards Fromelles from where the German breastwork crossed the farm track in the area held by the 31st Battalion. The Germans counterattacked along the axis of the track at 2.30 am on 20 July.

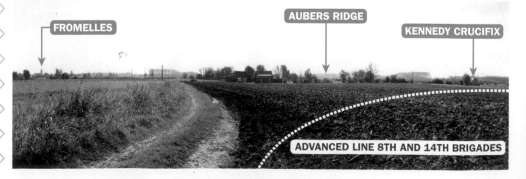

FROMELLES

AUBERS RIDGE

KENNEDY CRUCIFIX

ADVANCED LINE 8TH AND 14TH BRIGADES

return to his old Western Front haunts in June 1940 show him examining it minutely, which suggests he may have sheltered in it during the battle. Local tradition says, though, that he parked himself in another blockhouse on Aubers Ridge 500 metres west of Fromelles on the D141. Perhaps, but the Rue de la Biette blockhouse seems a likelier *Führerbunker*! The Australian Memorial Park can be seen from it one kilometre north. Parts of the 14th Brigade came almost this far in their search for the German support line.

Return to the D22 and turn right for **Fromelles (Pheasant Wood) Military Cemetery 7**, 100 metres along on the right. At the time of writing, a track on the other side of the D22 led to the field before **Pheasant Wood** in which the **burial pits 8** containing the remains of those re-interred in the cemetery were discovered. The Germans no doubt brought the corpses here on the trench

The blockhouse to which Hitler, a runner, may have come during the battle.

railway that ran to the site of the Australian Memorial Park. The work compound for the exhumation, identification and reburial of the remains was on the corner of the track and the D22. As you are now just 300 metres from **Fromelles church 9**, you might as well call in! The original church did not survive the war, but the concrete observation post that the Germans built

The area where the burial pits were located at Pheasant Wood.

Fromelles church after the war, when all that remained intact was the concrete observation post.

inside it did. Some stained glass and a table from the original church, and the first Kennedy Crucifix, are in the new church. Despite the trees and the urban sprawl, a brief walk around this area conveys some idea of the views it commanded over the plain. The site of the Pheasant Wood burial pits can also be reached by taking the track to the left of the church.

Now return to the Bramble memorial, head right at the fork and continue looking in the direction in which you have been walking when you reach **Rue de la Cordonnerie** ❿ on the left after 200 metres. A machine-gun at **Les Clochers**, the hamlet 220 metres straight ahead at the end the road, ended the 31st Battalion's advance. The **Türkenecke** strongpoint was to your right in the area of the blockhouses. Reserves from both locations reinforced **Delangré Farm** ⓫, which was in the copse on the right 200 metres down Rue de la Cordonnerie, to which you should now proceed. A path

at the near edge of the copse leads to the pit from which a *minenwerfer* heavy trench mortar most probably smashed the 58th Battalion's line before a raid on 15 July that inflicted 160 casualties. The Delangré Farm strongpoint stood on the mutilated ground further on in the copse and overlooked the 32nd Battalion's barricade in the **Kastenweg**, which crossed the road next to the gate and ran along the left side. Captain Frank Krinks and 11 men from the 32nd set up in shell holes on the right of the Kastenweg at the far edge of the torn ground, from where the Germans on the higher ground of the strongpoint were silhouetted against the night sky. Together with the 32nd's posts on the left of the Kastenweg, they blocked counterattacks from Delangré Farm along it.

Continue 250 metres past the *minenwerfer* pit to a large shed. The **German breastwork** ⓬ followed the path beside it. When the end was near, half of Krinks' XI withdrew to the breastwork near your location but the Germans seized two of them. The others turned back and freed their mates with a flurry of punches. Krinks and three men reached friendly territory. From here the breastwork can be tracked to the Australian Memorial Park by looking along the line of telegraph poles through the clearing on the left. In the opposite direction, it slanted past the three blockhouses in the field, which were probably infantry shelters. The buildings around the prominent barn to their right 500 metres away approximate the location of the **Mouquet Farm** strongpoint. Its enfilade advantage against the Australians' left flank, on Rue de la Cordonnerie 100 metres beyond the telegraph poles, is obvious. The Australian mine went off in no-man's-land to the right of the road but the spoil did not shield the 32nd Battalion from the flanking fire.

Now walk to the sharp bend, 100 metres short of the buildings of **Cordonnerie Farm** ⑬. Trying to dig a trench across no-man's-land from here during the

> *[We found] a solid cube of concrete, except for a stair so narrow that only with difficulty could a normally built man ascend… It terminated in a loophole for an observer, who with a telescope could, with perfect safety to himself, count every sentry in our lines. He also had an extensive view across our back areas, and could at once detect any preparation for attack.*

Brigadier-General Elliott on visiting Fromelles church in March 1919 (quoted in McMullin, R, *Pompey Elliott*, Melbourne, 2002, p. 508)

battle, the 30th Battalion was within 20 metres of the German line when the withdrawal occurred. The trench saved many lives. Take the track on the left and, after 250 metres, you will be on the Australian front line at the boundary between the 8th and 14th Brigades. The narrowness of no-man's-land, which greatly helped their attack, is evident from the Australian Memorial Park and the telegraph poles denoting the German line. But it also accounted for the pounding the Australians took from

No-man's-land where the Australian mine was blown.

AUSTRALIAN MINE CRATER

CORDONNERIE FARM

The entrance to the underground accommodation at Cellar Farm.

gasped. He was never seen again. From this area, too, Lieutenant Waldo Zander of the 30th Battalion witnessed the end of a Lewis gun crew cut off in the German line ahead of you as the battle wound down: 'After all the rest had fallen back they could still be heard firing. We could see the Bosche working in along the trench on both their flanks toward them, but they still stuck to their post and the gun kept firing. We saw some stick bombs thrown into their little stronghold—then silence!' The rumpled mounds on the left as you return to the road enclose the moat of a medieval farm.

Return to Cordonnerie Farm. **Cellar Farm** 14 is behind it and can be reached by taking the track on the left that runs beside both. In the field between them on the right, some deep dugouts, begun in September 1916 to accommodate a battalion, are being excavated. The pump piping and its wooden sheaths are in perfect condition and thousands of rat paw prints indent the concrete lining the four shaft heads. **Cellar Farm Avenue**, a communication trench on the 8th Brigade's left flank, passed through Cellar Farm en route to Rue Petillon, which it met to the left of Rue-Petillon Military Cemetery. The cemetery's Cross of Sacrifice is clearly visible.

Return to the road and turn left past Cordonnerie Farm. As you walk the

their own artillery, especially in the 31st Battalion before they went over here. Some remembered a legless Australian crawling back towards your location on his stumps later in the battle. 'Make way please', the mortally wounded man

LE TROU AID POST

15TH BRIGADE

400 metres to the **Drève Mouquet** 15, the British line ran to your right. Look down the Drève Mouquet on reaching it. The German line crossed 300 metres along, at which point the **Tadpole** stood on a slight rise on the left of the road. Mouquet Farm was 150 metres beyond the Tadpole. After another 300 metres, turn left onto the D175 and again onto Rue Petillon 1.1 kilometres later. **Rue-Petillon Military Cemetery** 16 is next to the site of **Eaton Hall dressing station**, which received Australian wounded. Cellar Farm Avenue began 230 metres further on. Starting after another 350 metres, **Brompton Road**, the 14th Brigade's communication trench, parallelled it and was used by Corporal Henry Williams to move forward with the 56th Battalion.

Continue 250 metres to beautiful **Le Trou Aid Post Cemetery** 17. Brigadier-General Elliott's headquarters and the aid post were in the hamlet on the left of the road. Looking like a man 'who had just lost his wife', Elliott wept openly as he shook hands in this vicinity with what was left of the 15th Brigade and assisted the wounded.

Proceed to the corner of Rue Petillon and Rue Delvas, face left along Rue Delvas and look towards Cellar Farm and Cordonnerie Farm to your left front. The Australian line ran from there to the near side of the farm buildings ahead of you, on the other side of which is VC Corner Cemetery, before crossing Rue Delvas. Having crossed Rue Delvas yourself, walk 200 metres down the **track** 18 on the far side to where the 15th Brigade's right flank met it. Turn left and face Aubers Ridge. If the field to your front has been harvested, you can reach the **Sugarloaf** 19 from this location by walking straight ahead across the field for 370 metres. Spent cartridge cases still come to the surface at the site. Striking the Laies means you have veered to the left.

As you walk, it is hard not to be numbed at the thought of the fate of those whose footsteps you are following. Reaching the Laies, the first wave of the 59th and 60th Battalions was hit by a devastating fusillade and 'went down like

The view from the Sugarloaf site of the ground over which the 15th Brigade attacked.

VC CORNER AUSTRALIAN CEMETERY MEMORIAL

AUSTRALIAN MEMORIAL PARK

GERMAN FRONT LINE

The Laies, as crossed by the 15th Brigade in 1916 (top), and today.

Rue Delvas to see the route that the German line took. Then look back to your starting point for the German perspective. As you retrace your steps, consider the folly of putting the interdivisional boundary so close to the Sugarloaf that it could despatch the British attacking it on your left and then catch the 15th Brigade in enfilade to your right.

Return to Rue Delvas and turn right. **VC Avenue**, the communication trench leading to the 15th Brigade's line, crossed the road 60 metres along. The line itself went over after another 300 metres, past which Rue Delvas bridges the **Laies** and passes **VC Corner Cemetery** 20. Both are in the old no-man's-land. On your way back to the Australian Memorial Park, you might care to pause at the cemetery. The fields around it were carpeted with dead, Charles Bean said, and also with wounded who 'could be seen everywhere raising their limbs in pain or turning hopelessly, hour after hour, from one side to the other'. They moaned for water or for an end to their agony. Their cobbers made nightly forays to fetch them.

Humanity, tragedy and cruelty intermingled. Krinks and the three men who escaped with him were returning with their wounded when a panicky Australian sentry killed two of them with a single shot. Two Germans carried a wounded Australian to his own parapet, saluted and walked away. Unaware of what had happened, other Australians shot them. Preventing all attempts to save a man who had been blinded, the Germans let him stumble around near the Sugarloaf for several days before shooting him. Many simply could not be recovered. Wracked by pain, driven mad by thirst and the attentions of ants and flies, they met a ghastly finish. Some of them lie in these grounds. All of them are named on the wall at the far end.

From the Australian Memorial Park, return to Ypres the way you have come.

wheat before the reaper', wrote Lieutenant Frank Knyvett. The second got to the middle of no-man's-land. Seeing no movement ahead, the third wave pressed on towards where it imagined the first two must have been lying ready for the final rush. It was also mown down, as a machine-gun firing down the Laies made the ditch a death-trap. Leaning over their parapet, the Germans looked 'as if they were wondering what was coming next', said Lieutenant Tom Kerr. The fourth wave gave them their answer. They obliterated it. But the tragedy was not over, for the 59th Battalion was scythed later in the evening while trying to get across this ground.

On reaching the Sugarloaf, look half left to the Australian Memorial Park on

LOCAL INFORMATION

CEMETERIES

Anzac Cemetery

On the D945 500 metres outside Sailly-sur-la-Lys, Anzac Cemetery was begun by the 2nd Australian Field Ambulance near an advanced dressing station just before the Fromelles attack and remained in use until the Germans overran the area in April 1918. Of the 300-plus burials, 111 are Australian and they include many Fromelles fallen, especially from the 31st Battalion. Captain Gibbins rests at I.A.5. There are eight New Zealand burials in the cemetery. Nineteen Australians lie in Sailly-sur-la-Lys Canadian Cemetery across the road.

Aubers Ridge British Cemetery

Established postwar to concentrate the burials from smaller wartime cemeteries nearby and from the battlefields around Aubers, this cemetery is on the D41 750 metres from the village. Of the 718 graves, 445 are unknowns. Most of the Fromelles dead were picked up from where they had fallen. Plot I consists almost entirely of 108 unidentified Australians. Of the 16 named Australians, 14 were from the 59th Battalion, which was on the 5th Division's right flank and closer to Aubers than the other Australian battalions.

Fromelles (Pheasant Wood) Military Cemetery

On the D22 300 metres short of Fromelles church, this was the first new war cemetery to be built by the Commonwealth War Graves Commission in 50 years. It contains the remains of 250 Australian and British soldiers who fell at Fromelles and were buried by the

Pheasant Wood Military Cemetery.

The grave of Private Billy Ellsdale, Rue-David Military Cemetery.

now contains 356 graves. Most of the 207 unknowns, 155 British and 52 Australian, were probably killed during the Fromelles battle.

Rue-David Military Cemetery

Located 900 metres along the D176, Rue des Davids, which heads left from the Boutillerie crossroads beyond the Drève Mouquet, the cemetery was begun in December 1914 and became a concentration cemetery after the armistice. Almost half of its 893 burials are unidentified. The proportion is even higher for the Australians, 256 of whose 353 dead are unknowns. Many of them are thought to have fallen at Fromelles. Resting at II.E.44, Private Billy Ellsdale was probably the first Aboriginal soldier killed in France. He died on 7 July 1916. Eighteen New Zealanders lie in this cemetery.

Rue-du-Bois Military Cemetery

Many Fromelles dead rest in this cemetery, which is on the D171 500 metres from the Petillon crossroads. It was started by the British in November 1914. As a result of graves brought in postwar from the battlefields and other cemeteries, the cemetery now contains 832 burials, of which 242 are Australian and five are New Zealanders. Major Geoff McCrae, who led the 60th Battalion at Fromelles, lies at I.F.33.

Germans in five pits just outside Pheasant Wood across the road. Following the discovery of the pits, exhumation and DNA tracing to identify the remains began in 2009. By the time the Prince of Wales dedicated the cemetery on 19 July 2010, the 70th anniversary of the battle, almost 100 of the Australians had been named. Their numbers are likely to increase as the identification process will continue for several more years.

Le Trou Aid Post Cemetery

Shaded by poplars and willows and surrounded by a natural moat, this cemetery is literally an island of tranquillity. Passed during the walk, it is on Rue Petillon near its junction with Rue Delvas. Begun in October 1914 to serve Le Trou Aid Post on the other side of the road, it was enlarged after the war and

Rue-Petillon Military Cemetery

Along with Le Trou, Rue-Petillon is one of the most beautiful of the local cemeteries, with entrance portals and grounds enhanced by weeping willows and other trees. Named after the road on which it is located at the opposite end to Le Trou and passed during the walk, it was begun

Rue-Petillon Military Cemetery.

in December 1914. Like some of the other local cemeteries, Rue-Petillon was used for concentration purposes postwar. Of its 1136 burials, about half of them known, 292 are Australian and 24 New Zealand. Chaplain Spencer Maxted of the 54th Battalion, killed while stretcher-bearing, is at I.K.2. Perhaps the last burial in Rue-Petillon was Major Roy Harrison, the 54th's second-in-command, whose remains were found in 1927 and identified by his silver cigarette case. He rests at I.D.20.

VC Corner Australian Cemetery Memorial

Established after the Armistice on Rue Delvas in the old no-man's-land crossed by the 14th Brigade, VC Corner is one of only two all-Australian cemeteries on the Western Front (Toronto Cemetery at Ploegsteert is the other) and, uniquely, contains no headstones. As none of the remains of the 410 Fromelles dead collected around it in 1918–19 could be identified, they were interred in two areas, each marked by a flat white cross, either side of a central grass avenue. The names of all 1299 Australian fallen with no known grave grace a screen wall memorial at the rear.

MEMORIALS

The Australian Memorial Park

The park was opened on 5 July 1998. Its centrepiece, a 2.1-metre bronze statue by Melbourne sculptor Peter Corlett, is based on Sergeant Simon Fraser's response to a wounded soldier's cry, 'Don't forget me, Cobber'. Fraser was one of those who had scoured the battlefield for wounded. Officially known as 'Cobbers', the statue depicts a soldier from the 57th Battalion, whom Corlett modelled on Fraser, carrying a wounded

VC Corner Australian Cemetery Memorial.

'Cobbers'.

mate from the 60th over his shoulder. Though it may be seen as unrealistic, the action of the cobber, Australian slang for mate, in clinging to his slouch hat unmistakeably identifies where the men are from and hence the memory sustaining them as they head towards their line.

According to the local battlefield preservation group, the blockhouses

The Australian Memorial Park and its blockhouses.

in the park were built in 1917 and their damaged state reflects the postwar efforts of farmers to remove them. Exploration has revealed that the one closest to the road was an infantry shelter and the one furthest from it a stores dump. The centre blockhouse was a miners' shelter covering the head of an unfinished mine gallery. Partially collapsed and full of water, it juts 38 metres towards the British line.

MUSEUMS

Fromelles Museum

Housed on the second floor of the town hall and school building, which is on the left of the D141 150 metres past the junction with the D22, the Fromelles museum contains many relics of all the battles fought in the area. At the time of writing, opening hours were 9 am to midday and 2 pm to 7 pm on every second Sunday between April and December, excluding August. Visits at other times can be arranged by calling the mairie (03 20 50 20 43) three weeks in advance.

The Fromelles museum. The ladder was recovered from a mine gallery in the Tadpole strongpoint in 1994.

CHAPTER 3

1916

SOMME: POZIÈRES/ MOUQUET FARM

Two things are visible from almost any part of the rolling chalk uplands on which the 1916 Somme campaign was fought. One is the Thiepval Memorial to the Missing. The other is a communication tower. Across the road from the tower is an excrescence once crowned by a windmill. Both the memorial and the tower stand on the same ridge. The road is the D929, which follows the course of the arrow-straight Roman road from Amiens, 21 kilometres south-west of the ridge. Straddling it like a barricade before dropping into the valley of the Ancre below Thiepval, three kilometres away, the ridge takes its name from Pozières, an agricultural village on the D929 between Albert and Bapaume.

Plumb on the ridge's summit, the windmill site, Hill 160 on German maps, occupies one of the highest points of the Somme battlefield. It was just behind the German second-line system, dubbed by the British the 'Old German' (OG) Lines, whose twin trenches, OG1 and OG2, followed the ridge. As Pozières squatted on a broad spur in front of the ridge, the Germans made it an outlying bastion of the OG Lines. Pozières Trench ran from them around the southern side of the village to Gibraltar, a multistorey blockhouse on the D929. From there K Trench went to the redoubt at Mouquet Farm, 1.5 kilometres north, and on to the fortress of Thiepval.

Enter the Australians

General Haig had wanted the Fourth Army to capture the German second line north of the D929 on the opening day of the Somme offensive. Its commander,

General Rawlinson, worried that the strength of the German first line would prevent all but a handful of troops getting that far. He advocated a 'bite and hold' policy, which meant taking a limited objective that could be easily defended. Rawlinson was right. Despite its enormous cost, the opening attack on 1 July 1916 left the first line largely intact. Only on the right flank, to the right of the D929, where the Fourth Army advanced alongside the French, had it been breached. Now adopting 'bite and hold' himself, Haig told Rawlinson to strike the German second line there. General Sir Hubert Gough's Reserve Army, originally formed to exploit a breakthrough by advancing on Bapaume, would tie down the Germans on the left of the D929.

The assault, on 14 July, seized three kilometres of the second line and briefly gained a foothold in Pozières Trench. On 16 July the OG Lines were taken almost

Pozières windmill: the Australian Memorial Park.

General Sir Hubert Gough.

as far as the junctions of OG1 with Pozières Trench and OG2 with Munster Alley, a switch that ran back opposite Pozières Trench to High Wood. By now Rawlinson considered Pozières 'the key of the area'. It hemmed in his army's left, prevented the forward move of British guns, and blocked views over the German rear area behind the ridge. Haig was less concerned. Encouraged by Rawlinson's recent success, he ordered a third major attack, in which the Fourth Army was to extend the breach in the second line on the right of the D929 on 23 July. Its advance would eventually turn both Pozières and Thiepval on the left, so all that was required on that flank 'was a methodical, step-by-step advance'. Haig gave the task to Gough and reinforced his army with I ANZAC.

On arrival from Flanders, I ANZAC concentrated around Vignacourt, 40 kilometres from the battlefield, to assimilate the lessons of the recent fighting. Successive objectives were now set so close that the infantry attacking one was still protected by the barrage when it lifted onto the next. As they had to follow on the heels of the lift, troops crept by night into no-man's-land as close to the German line as the fire allowed, so that when it moved on they could strike before the Germans set up their machine-guns. Instead of every wave going to the final objective as at Fromelles, the first wave took and consolidated the first objective, the second wave leapfrogging it to take the next one, the third wave leapfrogging the second and so on. Hearing, too, that the Germans tried to isolate every assault with a heavy barrage of their own, the 1st Australian Division left for the line on 19 July.

Preparations

While stipulating a 'methodical advance', Haig had also directed Gough to capture Pozières as soon as possible. That suited Gough's natural impetuosity. Preferring to control operations directly rather than through his corps commanders, he told the 1st Division's commander, Major-General Harold Walker, on 18 July: 'I want you to go into the line and attack Pozières tomorrow night'. With no time

for a reconnaissance and his division not yet in the area, Walker protested and secured a 24-hour delay. Birdwood and White weighed in and had the attack deferred another day. The attack was finally fixed for 12.30 am on 23 July, to coincide with the Fourth Army's advance.

Nor did Walker agree with Gough's idea of attacking from the south-west. He preferred to go in from the south-east, where his left would be more sheltered and his right protected by Rawlinson's attack. Gough relented. Gough also envisaged capturing Pozières over two nights, the attack on the first merely gaining Pozières Trench. Birdwood and White felt that the D929 was reachable on the first night. A new trench along the southern branch of the derelict light railway from Bapaume could form an intermediate objective halfway to it. Gough again concurred. Reflecting the recent training, the attack would comprise three waves, the first taking Pozières Trench, the second 'New Trench' and the third going to the D929. The postponements allowed the nightly digging of jump-off trenches in no-man's-land to reduce the distance

Major-General Sir Harold Bridgwood Walker

Commander, 1st Brigade/1st Australian Division 1915, 1st Australian Division 1916–May 1918

1862–1934

A British general, Walker was initially Birdwood's chief of staff on Gallipoli. But he was far more effective as a fighting leader and temporarily commanded Australian and New Zealand brigades before permanently replacing Major-General William Bridges as commander of the 1st Australian Division after Bridges was mortally wounded in May 1915. Badly wounded himself in October, Walker resumed command of the 1st Division in early 1916 and led it over the next two years through its toughest battles. Direct and decisive, he had a good tactical sense. With the appointment of Australians to command the Australian divisions in 1918, Walker went to the British 48th Division, which had attacked alongside the 1st Australian Division at Pozières. Knighted in 1918 (KCB) and 1919 (KCMG), he held a senior command in India before his retirement in 1928.

across it from 500 metres to as little as 180 metres.

Taking Pozières

At 10 pm on 22 July, the bombardment of Pozières intensified. The assault battalions were in the jump-off trenches by midnight and at 12.10 am on 23 July, the first wave edged towards the tapes that scouts had laid in no-man's-land. At 12.30 am the artillery lifted to New Trench and the first wave set off. Pozières Trench fell with little resistance. The second wave found that New Trench hardly existed. The third wave easily got to the D929. On the right flank, though, the Germans held out at the junctions of the OG Lines with Pozières Trench and Munster Alley despite the actions of Private John Leak and Lieutenant Arthur Blackburn, who were both awarded the VC. A 500-metre gap separated the Australians there from those on the D929. A German counterattack into it was swept away nonetheless.

On either side of the Australians, the British made little progress. Realising that a breakthrough was unlikely, Haig ordered local assaults to wear down the Germans until conditions favoured a resumption of the wider offensive. On the right flank, the Fourth Army would slog away at Delville and High Woods. I ANZAC was to be the leading agent on the left flank, where the loss of Pozières had set German alarm bells ringing. Such was its tactical importance that the Germans were determined to regain it. The preparatory bombardment for a counterattack by fresh troops on 25 July started early the day before and continued for hour after hour. I ANZAC got its own attack in despite it.

Gough wanted to secure the summit of Pozières Ridge and then swing along the crest past Mouquet Farm to cut off Thiepval. On 24 July he ordered Walker to gain a jump-off line beyond Pozières cemetery for a later attack on the OG Lines on the summit. Assaulting them south of the D929 at 3.30 am on 25 July, the 5th Battalion found that the Germans had mostly fled. But they soon recovered. Eventually drawing in the 7th as well as the 9th and 10th Battalions, a titanic bomb fight raged around the OG1/Pozières Trench junction, with little progress being made. But the 4th and 8th Battalions, attacking 90 minutes earlier, cleared most of Pozières on the other side of the D929. Private Thomas Cooke of the 8th was awarded a posthumous VC for firing his Lewis gun from an exposed position until he was killed. Caught in the open, the German counterattack next morning was massacred.

The Germans abandoned the idea of recapturing Pozières but continued the shelling to inflict damage and loss. The last traces of the village disappeared. Handing over to the 2nd Australian Division on 26 July after sustaining 5285 casualties, the 1st Division was benumbed.

To the windmill

The 2nd Australian Division was to gain the summit. Just as he had done Walker, Gough hustled its commander, Major-General Gordon Legge. Despite its Gallipoli service, Legge was aware that his division had yet to fight a major battle whereas the 5th Division, the most junior, had already done so at Fromelles. Even though the 2nd Division had only fully

> They looked like men who had been in hell. Almost without exception each man looked drawn and haggard, and so dazed that they appeared to be walking in a dream, and their eyes looked glassy and starey. Quite a few were silly, and these were the only noisy ones in the crowd. In all my experience I've never seen men so shaken up as these.
>
> Sergeant Edgar Rule, 14th Battalion, on seeing the 1st Australian Division leave the line (Rule, E, *Jacka's Mob*, Sydney, 1933, p. 61)

taken over the line on 27 July, he ordered the assault for 12.15 am on the 29th. The rush doomed it. Carrying out the main attack on the left of the D929, the 7th Brigade had to form up 550 metres from OG1 on the 'Tramway', the northern branch of the old Bapaume railway, because there was no time to link the posts that the 1st Division had established further forward. The 7th was flayed on the wire of OG1. A gas bombardment crippled the 20th Battalion south of the D929, where the Germans still held most of the OG Lines. Three days earlier, a good deal of the 5th Brigade had been sucked into another massive but inconclusive bomb fight in them near Munster Alley.

Legge was given another chance. He set the next attack for 9.15 pm on 2 August. Over 1.5 kilometres of approach and jump-off trenches were dug to reduce the distance across no-man's-land. 'Demolition' bombardments interspersed with sudden barrages confused the Germans as to when the real attack was coming. They replied in kind. The digging thus became one of the most dreadful tasks the AIF undertook. Two grudging postponements from Gough were necessary before it was completed on 4 August. But the work paid off for the OG Lines were easily taken. When the Germans counterattacked on 5 August, Lieutenant Percy Cherry mortally wounded one of the officers leading the assault. He went over to the dying German, who took some letters from his pocket and asked Cherry in English to post them. Cherry agreed and the German handed the letters over, saying 'And so it ends'. The windmill was occupied once the attack was seen off.

Jacka

In a ghastly state after 12 days in the line — twice as long as the 1st Division — and 6846 casualties, the 2nd Division was relieved by the 4th. No sooner had it taken over than the Germans, desperate after the loss of the Pozières crest, counterattacked again, on

Major-General James Gordon Legge

Commander, 2nd Australian Division, 1915–16

A scholar, teacher and barrister before becoming a professional soldier, Legge had great intellect and energy. But he was also arrogant and quarrelsome, which made him many enemies. Nonetheless, his career flourished after the South African War, during which he saw action and also served as a staff officer. He was the architect of Australia's prewar compulsory training scheme. When war

1863–1947

came again in 1914, Legge was returning from England, where he had been Australia's representative on the Imperial General Staff, to become Chief of the Australian General Staff. He quickly raised a force to capture German New Guinea. After Bridges' death, Legge temporarily replaced him before going to Egypt to form the 2nd Australian Division. He returned to Gallipoli with it in August. Haig blamed Legge, not unfairly, for the 2nd Division's initial failure at Pozières. Though its next attack was a success, he never recovered. Birdwood took the opportunity, when Legge became ill in January 1917, to have him removed. 1918 brought personal tragedy with the death of his son on the Western Front. After the war Legge became commandant of the Royal Military College, Duntroon. He retired from the army in 1922.

OG1 near the windmill at the end of the battle. The entrances to some of the deep dugouts that sheltered the Germans — and the Australians — are visible.

7 August. Preceded by an annihilating bombardment, they swept over lightly held OG2 and bombed several dugouts in OG1. The remnants of Lieutenant Albert Jacka's platoon occupied one. His ears ringing from the explosion, Jacka darted up the stairs and shot the German sentry at the top. Seeing 40 Australian prisoners being escorted back by a much stronger guard, he lined up the eight men nearest him and charged. Half of the guards fled; the rest fought. The prisoners and other Australians joined in, and the Germans were sent packing.

Mouquet Farm

The thrust along the crest towards Thiepval could now begin. I ANZAC would advance on the intermediate objective, Mouquet Farm (Moo Cow Farm to the Australians). Charles Bean derided Gough's plan as 'springing from an impossible tactical conception — that of forcing a salient gradually behind an enemy salient on a strongly fortified front … giving a bang with the hammer every day or two to drive the wedge in

another fraction of an inch'. The width of the crest meant that the new salient would be much narrower than the one just created at Pozières, making the German bombardments even more concentrated.

Realising its importance to the defence of Thiepval, the Germans held Mouquet Farm strongly. Several cellars sheltered its garrison, and two fortified communication trenches passed in front of it: Park Lane and Skyline Trench. Fabeck Graben trench added depth to it. British Official War Office photographer Geoffrey Malins called the farm 'the most wonderful defensive point that could possibly be conceived'.

Banging with the hammer

The farm was to be reached in stages, which the 4th Brigade started off. On 8 August the 15th Battalion took part of Park Lane but the British on their left were mown down on the D73, the Pozières–Thiepval road. Its flank exposed, the 15th withdrew. Gough extended I ANZAC's flank to the D73. Over the next

Captain Albert Jacka

Legendary Australian front-line soldier

1893–1932

A forestry worker when he enlisted in the AIF in 1914, Jacka was awarded the war's first Australian VC for single-handedly, and successfully, counterattacking some Turks who had penetrated the 14th Battalion's line on Gallipoli on 19–20 May 1915. Many felt that his bravery at Pozières in 1916 and again at Bullecourt in 1917 were just as outstanding but he received the MC for both actions instead. Not only was he renowned within the AIF, to the extent that the 14th Battalion was known unofficially as 'Jacka's Mob', but he also became a national hero. Although the war took its toll — he was a long time recovering from his wounds after Pozières and was badly gassed in 1918 — Jacka became active in business and public affairs afterwards. He served on the St Kilda Council, including as mayor. Jacka bore his fame and its obligations with dignity until his death in 1932. He had done the same in the AIF, remaining in the line instead of accepting offers from Prime Minister Hughes to help with recruiting campaigns in Australia.

two nights, the 15th and 16th Battalions reclaimed the ground given up and advanced 100 metres beyond Park Lane towards the quarry in front of Skyline west of the farm, while the 13th reached a sunken road 350 metres east of it. On 12 August the 50th Battalion, with the British attacking on the far side of the D73, took Skyline Trench apart from the quarry.

With just over 500 metres gained, the Fabeck Graben and the farm itself were to be attacked on 14 August. The British lost their section of Skyline Trench the night before. As the advance on the farm would be enfiladed from there, Gough dropped the farm from the plan. The British would retake Skyline while the 13th Brigade seized the Fabeck and the quarry. German shelling was so brutal shortly before the attack fell due that the Australian battalion commanders recommended abandoning their part of it. As the British assault would then be jeopardised, they were overruled. Ironically the British were successful but the 13th Brigade was not. Having lost 4649 men, the 4th Australian Division handed over to the 1st.

Over the next three weeks, the divisions of I ANZAC went in again. The farm was now a rubble heap, with few identifiable landmarks left on the slope below it. On 18 August uncertainty over locations resulted in the supporting bombardment crippling the 3rd Battalion's assault towards the Fabeck. The 3rd Brigade struck it on 21 August for a trifling gain. After sustaining 2650 casualties, the 1st Division was relieved by the 2nd. On 26 August the 21st Battalion veered off course on the D73 side of the farm. Only a single post near the ruins was captured. Having lost 1268 men, the 2nd Division made way for the 4th.

Mouquet Farm, on the far crest, under bombardment as seen from Pozières.

Mouquet Farm before ... and after.

THIEPVAL

D73

The attacks towards Mouquet Farm from Park Lane.

The 14th Battalion was unable to clear other posts near the ruins on 27 August, after which heavy rain transformed the battlefield into a quagmire. Slurping through it on 29 August, the 16th Battalion was seen off at the farm, which necessitated the withdrawal of the 13th from the Fabeck. On 3 September the 51st Battalion was overwhelmed at the farm but parts of the 49th and 52nd held on in the Fabeck until some Canadians showed up. The Canadian Corps had just entered the battle. After losing 1346 men, the 4th Division left on 5 September to join the remainder of I ANZAC in rest at Ypres.

Reckoning

In its 45 days on the Somme, I ANZAC had launched 19 attacks at a cost of 23 000 casualties. Virtually every survivor had shell shock to some degree. Lieutenant Alec Raws of the 23rd Battalion wrote shortly before his death, that many were 'murdered … through the incompetence, callousness, and personal vanity of those high in authority'. Gough was loathed. Birdwood, 'the soul of ANZAC', temporarily became 'the arsehole of France'. There was also a grim

Shelling

Charles Bean vividly expressed the feeling of helpless vulnerability the shelling engendered:

> Shell after shell descends with a shriek … each one an acute mental torture, each shrieking, tearing crash bringing a promise to each man … I will rend your flesh and pulp an arm and leg; fling you half a gaping, quivering man like these that you see smashed around you to lie there rotting and blackening like all the things you saw by the awful roadside. Ten or twenty times a minute, every man in the trench has that instant fear thrust upon his shoulders — I don't care how brave he is — and with a crash that is physical fear and a strain to understand.

Birdwood said much the same thing about the Pozières bombardments, though more prosaically. 'Until one has been personally subjected to such a thing, it really is impossible to conceive what it means', Birdwood remarked. A French officer judged the bombardments to be as severe as those around Verdun, considered the heaviest of the war. Eventually the strain caused by the shelling spilled over into shell shock, a neurosis causing psychological breakdown that was permanent in severe cases.

postscript. Thiepval fell during a wider attack by Gough's army on 26 September 1916. It was struck frontally, which made the salient that I ANZAC had tried to batter behind it via the farm irrelevant and justified the Australian charge of needless sacrifice. In a final irony, Mouquet Farm was taken *after* Thiepval.

MOUQUET FARM

SKYLINE TRENCH

DRIVING/WALKING THE BATTLEFIELD

Three tours follow. The first, which retraces I ANZAC's route to the battlefield, has been included because it confronted the Australians with the sights, sounds and stinks of a big Western Front offensive for the first time. Best done by car, it also passes some of the key areas of the tragic 1 July attack and hence sets the context for the Pozières attacks. The second, a visit to the Australian Memorial, allows the course of the battle to be grasped from a single location. It is intended for those lacking the time to walk the battlefield. The third is a walk for those who do have the time. It necessitates moving along, crossing and recrossing the D929, along which a stream of juggernauts and cars hurtle all year round. So be careful.

MAPS IGN Blue Series, 1:25 000: 2407E Bapaume; 2407W Acheux-en-Amiénois; 2408E Bray-sur-Somme; 2408W Albert

Pozières is 12 kilometres south-west of Bapaume. If driving from Paris use the A1/E15 autoroute and take exit 14, signposted Bapaume, onto the D917/N17. On reaching the roundabout on the Bapaume ring road, swing onto the D929, direction Albert. Stay on the D929 until you reach the village. If you want to follow I ANZAC's entry into the battle, continue to Albert.

I ANZAC's route to the battlefield

Start from the town square of **Albert**. At the start of the war, Albert had a population of 7343 and was briefly occupied by the Germans. On 1 July 1916 it was 2.5 kilometres behind the Fourth Army's line. The town became the main logistic and administrative centre for the British in the Somme offensive and it was also the location of the 1st Australian Division's headquarters. Damaged by a shell in 1915, the Golden Virgin atop the 70-metre spire of **Notre Dame de Brebières Basilica** hung horizontally over the square like a diver about to leap. 'You could readily imagine that she had purposely leaned down over the street to bless the thousands of soldiers who pass', said Captain Gordon Maxfield of the 21st Battalion as the Australians marched by. They nicknamed her Fanny after Fanny Durack, Australia's first female Olympic champion, who had won the 100-metre freestyle swimming in 1912.

The superstition arose that the war would end when the Madonna fell, with the side responsible as the loser. When the Germans took Albert in March 1918, British guns destroyed the spire. The war ground on for eight months, the British recaptured Albert in August, and were on the winning side when the war ended in

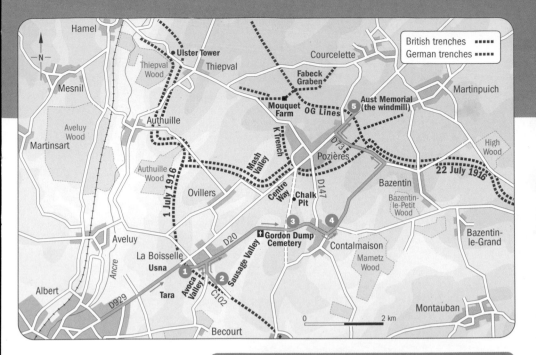

November! By then the town was a ruin and only 120 inhabitants remained. Even as Albert was being rebuilt, it became a centre for battlefield tourism, and so it remains today. The **Musée des Abris** under the Basilica is worth visiting.

Leave the square on Rue de Birmingham and turn left at the T-junction onto the D929, which soon starts to climb. After passing an industrial zone on the left on the outskirts of Albert, it crosses a saddle between two hills, **Tara** on the right and **Usna** on the left. From the saddle, **La Boiselle** is immediately right of the D929 on the far side of **Avoca Valley**, which is the lower end of **Mash Valley**. Running along the left of the road past **Ovillers**, to your left front 2.5 kilometres distant, Mash Valley stretches towards **Pozières**, which also

In following I ANZAC's march to the line at Pozières, this drive passes over the Tara and Usna Hills and through the village of La Boiselle. It includes a stop at the vast preserved mine crater just outside La Boiselle and provides good views of Avoca and Sausage Valleys before reaching the village of Contalmaison, one of the furthest points reached by the Fourth Army on 1 July. The drive then skirts Pozières en route to the Australian Memorial at the windmill.

DISTANCE COVERED: **12 km**
DURATION: **1 hour**

extends to the left of the D929 on the high ground on the horizon 3.5 kilometres off. The German second line was behind it on that high ground. The German front line on 1 July ran just in front of La Boiselle and Ovillers. The British front line paralleled it and, across Mash Valley, followed the line of the D20, which straddles the D929 at the foot of Tara and Usna.

Albert's Golden Virgin then... and now.

Advancing at a slow walk under drenching fire, some men from the 8th Division, which was supposed to take Pozières, miraculously got across the 750 metres of no-man's-land in front of Ovillers and penetrated the German front line. They were soon forced out. Next to them, the 34th Division advanced astride the D929 on La Boiselle. Its reserve, the Tyneside Irish Brigade, was destroyed as it advanced down the slope ahead of you. Only a small section of the front line to the right of La Boiselle was captured.

Continue on the D929. Just before the village, turn right onto the D20 at the **Poppy Restaurant**. The crater of **Y Sap**, the second largest of the four mines blown at La Boiselle on 1 July, was on the left of the D929 100 metres past the junction. It is now filled in. A **memorial seat** ❶ to the Tynesiders is at the top of the grassed area on the left of the D20, virtually on the German front line. On the right of the D20 100 metres further on is the **Glory Hole**, its rumpled ground evidence of the vicious mine warfare that went on here. The smallest of the 1 July mines went up just beyond it.

Now drive along the D20 for another 200 metres before turning right onto the C9, signposted **La Grande Mine**, and then left at the fork onto the C102. You are roughly following the course of the German front line. **Lochnagar Crater** ➋, 500 metres down the C102 at the upper end of **Chapes Spur**, is where the largest of the La Boiselle mines, with 30 tonnes of ammonal, obliterated the Schwaben Höhe strongpoint and left a void 90 metres across and 30 metres deep. The remains of the garrison, and of some British soldiers, still lie in and around it. Those of Private George Nugent of the Tyneside Scottish were uncovered after a storm in 1998 at the spot marked by a small cross. In order to preserve the crater, Englishman Richard Dunning purchased the site in 1978, and it now serves as memorial to those who fought on the Somme. The dangers caused by erosion preclude descending into it but you can walk around the rim.

The views make the walk worthwhile. To the north, four kilometres away across the D929, the **Thiepval Memorial** peeks around Pozières church. To the north-east, 4.2 kilometres distant, is the communication tower next to Pozières windmill. In the opposite direction, the Golden Virgin pokes above the Tara-Usna hills, denoting Albert, and Chapes Spur separates Avoca Valley from **Sausage Valley** (Sausage Gully to the Australians), which swings past the eastern side of the crater towards **Gordon Dump Cemetery**. From Albert, some of the Australian formations destined for Pozières took the D929 to La Boiselle, while others hived off it at Tara Hill, descended into Avoca Valley and crossed Chapes Spur near the crater before following the trench railway along Sausage Valley to Gordon Dump. 'Unexploded shells, debris, equipment were everywhere among the shell craters and in the mouths of the smashed dugouts were corpses', said Private Dick

Lochnagar Crater.

Roberts of the 3rd Battalion of the area around you. 'That which we took to be spongy ground that we were walking over was the bodies of dead soldiers.'

Returning the way you have come, turn right onto the D20, as the Australians who had gone through La Boiselle did. Drive 650 metres past the church to the sign for **Gordon Dump Cemetery**, on the right. It is at the head of Sausage Valley, whose slopes were crammed with the Australian reserve battalions. Around them the noise was deafening as field batteries, including Australian ones, fired from the crests, heavy batteries from lower down the valley, and troops and transport moved unceasingly back and forth.

Sausage Valley during the battle.

Gordon Dump Cemetery at the head of Sausage Valley. The D20, which the Australians used to enter the battle, runs along the crest behind it.

Continue on the D20 from this point, which is where the two approach routes to Pozières converged. The road is sunken, and hence concealed from the village, but was heavily shelled nonetheless. Climbing the bank to see Pozières would have been suicidal. The Australians dismissed as duds shells landing with a dull plop in this vicinity but then they noticed a smell like mouldy hay. It was their initiation into gas warfare. The Germans were using phosgene, which dissolves the membranes of the lungs. After another 900 metres, the D20 strikes a north–south track cut steeply into the banks on either side. The junction was called **Casualty Corner** ❸, after the advanced dressing station located at the first corner on the left.

Here the approach routes separated again. Those entering the line at the Albert end of Pozières took the left branch of the track, which reaches the village after 1.5 kilometres. If driving, do not turn onto it because your end of it is unsuitable for cars. Instead, walk a little way up the right branch and into the

field on the left, and look towards Pozières. The high banks on the downhill stretch of the track to the **Chalk Pit**, a disused quarry about halfway along on the right, gave some protection, but the relatively exposed uphill stretch beyond it to the village was called, for good reason, **Dead Man's Road**. Used to enter the line at the Bapaume end of Pozières, the other approach route followed the D20 for another 700 metres before turning left onto the D147, which runs roughly parallel to the track you have just passed.

Continue on the D20 into **Contalmaison**, which, incredibly, a few men reached on 1 July. At the end of the village, turn sharp left on the D20, which then heads sharp right after 300 metres. At this point take the sunken road on the left near the **water tower** ❹. Pozières eventually comes into view on the D929, 1.3 kilometres away on the left. The cramping that the village imposed on the Fourth Army's advance is clear. Looking in that direction, note how distinct the re-entrant below you becomes. On 23 July, the 1st Division attacked from it towards Pozières. To follow this assault, and those after it, continue to the D73, turn left and, on reaching the D929, right for the **Australian Memorial** ⑤.

The Australian Memorial, Pozières windmill

A windmill had stood on the crest of the Pozières Ridge since the start of the 17th century. When I ANZAC attacked in July 1916, it had been destroyed and the Germans used the ruins, enclosed by stone walls 1.5-metres high, as an observation post. Lumps of concrete, embedded in a grass-covered mound of rumpled earth, are all that is left of it. Passing some information panels and a Bastiaan plaque, the entrance path ends at a tablet at the base of the mound. Its inscription states that the windmill 'was the centre of the struggle in this part of the Somme Battlefields in July and August 1916. It was captured on 4 August by Australian troops who fell more thickly on this than on any other battlefield of the war'. The area where the vast majority were killed can be seen from here.

Stand with the D929 on your right. The rearward slope of the ridge bottoms out in the valley behind Courcelette, which can be seen two kilometres off and to the left of the D929. The German third line ran across the valley floor 2.5 kilometres beyond the village, where the ground gradually rises towards Bapaume. The Pozières Ridge was a naturally stronger position than the third line, and also sheltered the artillery batteries, reserves and logistics echelons arrayed on the valley floor to support the resistance to the British advance coming from the direction of Albert. The Germans were desperate to hold it.

Now turn about. The forward slope of the ridge is far gentler. Descending almost imperceptibly from the windmill towards Pozières village, the D929 heads south-west past the water tower, which is adorned with a mural of a Digger's head,

a rising sun badge, a poppy and a VC, with the names of the Australian, Canadian and British soldiers who won it in the Pozières area added. Heralded by a sign board bearing the figure of an ANZAC, the village is strung out for one kilometre along the D929 behind the water tower. In 1916 it also began from this point, and was surrounded by orchards. The four-day bombardment before the 1st Australian Division's attack on 23 July completed the work, started by the shelling that preceded the earlier British attacks, of reducing the orchards to shattered stumps and the village to rubble.

If the water tower is taken as 12 o'clock, Pozières cemetery is in the vicinity of the prominent white farm building at the right-hand end of the village at 1 o'clock. The northern branch of the derelict light railway from Bapaume crossed the D929 between the water tower and the 'Grainor' agricultural complex to the left of the road. With Tramway Trench alongside, the railway tracked to the cemetery and on to Ovillers. Further to the right, the British Memorial to the Missing of the Somme at Thiepval comes into view at 2 o'clock on the skyline. About halfway to the Memorial and 1.7 kilometres to your right front is Mouquet Farm.

Courcelette from the windmill.

Now look to the left of the D929. The D73 passes the 'Grainor' complex and skirts Bazentin-le-Petit Wood at 9 o'clock. By mid-July the British had taken the stretch of the OG Lines that cut across the left end of Bazentin-le-Petit Wood to the D73 roughly halfway between the windmill and the wood. But further progress was blocked by Munster Alley, the switch trench that arced back from this point to High Wood, visible to your left rear, and the 450 metres of the OG Lines that remained between Munster Alley and the D929. About 180 metres short of the D929, the OG Lines straddled the southern branch of the light railway. It went to the left of Pozières, parallel to the D929 and down to La Boiselle. From the railway, along which the Germans were believed to have constructed a 'new trench', OG1 and OG2 went over the D929 respectively 230 metres and 80 metres ahead of you. Bending at the Elbow, 300 metres to your right, they followed the ridgeline and passed to the right of Mouquet Farm.

Note how the ground not only slants down towards Pozières but also falls away into re-entrants on either side of it. The drop is more pronounced on the right side, where it forms the head of Mash Valley. Jutting from Pozières Ridge between the re-entrants, the spur on which Pozières stands blocked an attack on the ridge itself. Grazing fire from it could enfilade any advance up the re-entrants towards the crest. Quick to appreciate this advantage, the Germans turned Pozières into a forward extension of the OG Lines. Enclosing the lower half of the village, Pozières Trench left OG1 450 metres from the D929, directly opposite where Munster Alley sprang back from OG2, and paralleled the left edge of the village before curving towards the D929 at the far end. Starting there on the other side D929, K Trench headed across the head of Mash Valley and past the cemetery. Thick belts of wire screened all of these trenches.

Had the 1st Australian Division attacked Pozières from the south-west, as Gough wanted, it would have been strung out mainly to the right of the D929 and followed its general direction towards K Trench, with the British 48th Division on its flank extending well past the cemetery. Aware of the danger on that flank from Mouquet Farm and Thiepval, General Walker insisted on attacking from the south-east, on the left of the D929. The 1st and 3rd Brigades stretched from the OG Lines 700 metres to your left to the D929 at the far end of the village. Meeting feeble resistance, they swept over Pozières Trench and the railway to the D929. Still spoiling for a fight, some men pursued 30 Germans fleeing up the road towards you. Killing the lot near your location, they ran into the barrage protecting those entrenching in Pozières and headed back.

In the OG Lines on your left, the Germans resisted stubbornly. Supposed to reach the D929 where the OG Lines crossed it, the advance remained stuck at the junction of Pozières Trench and OG1. The new Australian line bent back from there across your left front to the forward edge of Pozières, near the water tower.

The battlefield on the right of the D929.

POZIÈRES

RAILWAY AND TRAMWAY TRENCH

> There were four Huns in a shell hole. All I could see were their heads, shoulders, and rifles. As I went towards them, they began firing point-blank at me. They hit me three times and each time the terrific impact of the bullets swung me off my feet. But each time I sprang up like a prize-fighter, and kept getting closer. When I got up to them, they flung down their rifles and put up their hands. I shot three through the head and put a bayonet through the fourth. I had to do it — they would have killed me the moment I turned my back.

Jacka on the counterattack near the Elbow (quoted in Rule, *Jacka's Mob*, p. 72)

Starting from near your location at the windmill, the Germans counterattacked across this area at 5.30 am on 23 July, and were shot down. The 5th and 7th Battalions from the 2nd Brigade made little progress when they renewed the advance along the OG Lines, now barely recognisable owing to constant shelling, on the left of the D929 early on 25 July. On the right, the 4th and 8th Battalions fought their way to the cemetery, clearing the rest of Pozières village. German reinforcements rushing up to the OG Lines were smashed in the area around you by Australian machine-guns and artillery.

By 27 July the 1st Division had been relieved by the 2nd. Attacking towards you from Pozières on 29 July, it was to seize the windmill and the OG Lines on the crest. Caught by gas and machine-guns, the 5th Brigade's assault to the left of the D929 never got going. The Germans in the OG Lines to the right of the road saw the 7th Brigade forming up along the line of the railway and responded with torrential fire. Only a few Australians reached OG1 ahead of you. Securing the flank, the 23rd Battalion dug in along the Ovillers–Courcelette road, soon to be named after Major Eric Brind of the 23rd, which can be seen running along the bottom of the re-entrant

halfway between the windmill and Mouquet Farm.

The jumping-off trenches that the 2nd Division dug for its attack on 4 August were, on average, 270 metres from the OG Lines. They ranged across virtually the entire 1450-metre assault frontage, which extended from Brind's Road and crossed the D929 in front of the water tower. Though the diggers were shelled remorselessly, their work enabled the attackers to assemble under cover and closer to the OG Lines than on 29 July. The Germans were swamped. Lieutenant Cherry's machine-guns at the Elbow scattered their counterattack, which struck between the windmill and Brind's Road at dawn on 5 August. From the ruins of the windmill, the Australians saw the Germans hurriedly pulling field-guns out of Courcelette.

The 4th Division relieved the 2nd. Finding the windmill deserted, as its occupants had withdrawn to escape the ongoing shell fire, Sergeant David Twining of the 48th Battalion set up a post 40 metres to your right. Twining and the remnants of his section held the post for three days, an action that is depicted in a diorama in the Australian War Memorial. The main weight of the German counterattack on 7 August fell

CEMETERY

THIEPVAL MEMORIAL

MOUQUET FARM

OG LINES

between your location and Brind's Road. It overran OG2 and parts of OG1. Lieutenant Jacka's counterattack started from a dugout in OG1 at the grassy bump 350 metres to your right, just past the Elbow. Look in that direction. A deadly brawl soon spread across the field as Australians and Germans took each other on in close quarter combat, resulting in one of the most bizarre scenes in the history of the AIF.

The drive along the crest towards Mouquet Farm now got underway. Look towards the farm to appreciate the validity of Bean's criticism of Gough's concept. The width of the crest, and the need to stick to the lee to avoid being skylined from Courcelette, limited attacks to narrow frontages that magnified the effectiveness of the German artillery. Starting from Brind's Road on 8 August, the 4th Division had almost reached Mouquet Farm by the time it was relieved a week later. Subsequent attacks by the 1st and 2nd Australian Divisions, and again by the 4th, failed to take it. Concurrently with the 18 August assault, the 2nd Brigade advanced either side of your location in an attempt to gain

ground beyond the windmill. The 6th Battalion, on the farm side of the D929, got 200 metres past you but the 7th and 8th Battalions, on the other side, were repulsed with heavy loss.

After Pozières the 2nd Division erected a cross on the windmill site. It remained the divisional memorial until the 2nd's veterans chose Mont St Quentin as the new location when permanent memorials to the Australian divisions were built in the 1930s. The site then took on the flavour of the national memorial that it has today. Now cross the D929 to the memorial to the fallen of the Tank Corps, which centres on finely crafted metal models of four tanks: a Mark IV, a Mark V, a Whippet and a carrier tank. The fence is made from tank driving chains suspended between tank gun barrels. The tanks formed up here and at several other points nearby before going into action for the first time in warfare on 15 September 1916.

Walking the Australian attacks

Begin at the **Australian Memorial, Pozières windmill**. Having used the previous narrative to orient yourself on

The battlefield on the left of the D929, showing the 1st Division's assault.

BAZENTIN-LE-PETIT WOOD

RAILWAY

THIEPVAL MEMORIAL

BRIND'S ROAD

MOUQUET FARM

ELBOW (CHERRY)

JACKA

TWINING

OG LINES

The area between the windmill and Mouquet Farm in which the actions of Jacka, Cherry and Twining occurred. Note that locations are approximate.

the battlefield and follow the course of the battle, walk down the right side of the D929 towards Pozières. After 250 metres, you will have crossed the OG Lines and reached **the line of the wire in front of OG1** ❶. Much of this wire was uncut when the 7th Brigade advanced from the village towards you on the right of the road in the 2nd Australian Division's failed attack on 29 July. By the light of flares, the Germans saw the few men who reached the wire frenziedly trying to get through, some trying to bash a path with their rifles, others using wire cutters and still others trying to wrench the stakes from the ground. They poured a hail of lead into them.

Lines of dead from the 28th Battalion stretched into the field from your location.

Once past the water tower, turn right onto the C6, the Courcelette road. The jumping-off trench dug for the 2nd Division's successful attack on 4 August extended from the junction across the fields to Brind's Road. Now head down the C6 and stop after 320 metres at the **track** ❷ on the left. From here, OG1 and OG2 crossed the C6 respectively 50 metres behind you and 100 metres ahead of you. During the German counterattack on 5 August, Captain Cherry accepted the letters from one of the leaders, whom he had mortally wounded, in the field to your left

DIRECTION OF 1ST DIVISION ATTACK

OG LINES

The Tank Corps Memorial.

Taking the D73, turn left after 80 metres onto a track and walk to where the **power lines** 5 cross. This track follows the line of the light railway, which forked where you are standing. The northern branch swung behind you to the D929/D73 junction from where you have just come. OG1 crossed the track at the fence corner on the left 150 metres ahead of you, and OG2 crossed another 150 metres beyond it to pass in front of the windmill. Your location approximates to the right flank of the 1st Division's line in Pozières after the 23 July attack. The OG Lines should have been taken as far as the D929 but the assault stalled 500 metres from it, leaving a gap on your right that remained until the 18th and 20th Battalions advanced between the road and railway to the OG Lines in the 2nd Division's attack on 4 August. In its earlier attack on 29 July, the 20th Battalion was seen crossing the northern branch of the railway to your rear and machine-gun fire from the OG Lines and a phosgene cloud ensured that it went no further. Sergeant Claude Castleton of the 5th Machine-Gun Company was awarded a posthumous VC for bringing in wounded during this attack from no-man's-land in the field to your left front.

front, in the angle between the track and the road. Follow the track for 200 metres, to where the **Elbow** 3 in OG1 grazed the left side of it at the dirt pile. Jacka's counterattack started near this point.

Return to the D929, turn right and continue for 150 metres to the **junction** 4 with the D73, signposted Bazentin, on the left. The northern branch of the light railway from Bapaume crossed the D929 just before the junction, and the southern end of **Tramway Trench**, which was the 7th Brigade's start line on 29 July, ran along the railway on the other side. A large dugout, virtually on the D929 where the Tramway began and full of surgical dressings, was promptly called the **Medical Dugout**. The 12th Battalion captured the improbably named Hauptmann (Captain) Ponsonby Lyons in it on 23 July. Ponsonby, who had an English grandfather, introduced himself as the commandant of Pozières.

Return to the D73 and turn left. The southern branch of the railway crossed it at the leftwards bend by the **'Grainor' building** 6. A trench thought to follow the railway down the near side of Pozières was the 1st Division's second objective on 23 July. It did not exist. During the crushing German bombardment on 5 August, Major Duncan Chapman of the 45th Battalion, reputedly the first man ashore at ANZAC Cove, was killed near where you are standing.

Now walk another 300 metres along the D73 to the **dumping area** 7 on the right and look towards the far end of Pozières. Starting there, **Pozières Trench** skirted the village and went under the

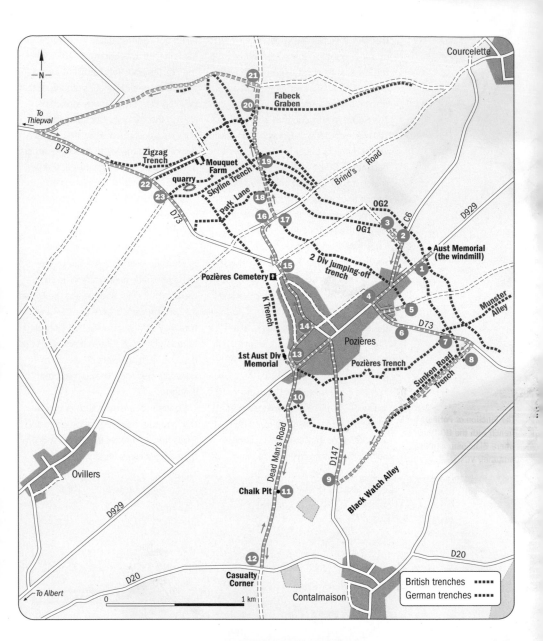

British trenches ••••••
German trenches ••••••

D73 via a tunnel at your location to join OG1 90 metres away on the other side. Face in that direction. **Munster Alley** ran back from OG2 150 metres in rear of OG1's junction with Pozières Trench, and was linked to the junction by a communication trench. Trying to advance along the OG Lines to the D929 on 23 July, the 9th and 10th Battalions found OG2, pounded beyond recognition and swept by fire from posts in and around Munster Alley, untenable. The action was

Examining in detail the capture of Pozières and the windmill, this walk encompasses the OG Lines, Dead Man's Road, Pozières village, trench and cemetery, Gibraltar, K Trench and Brind's Road. The advance on Mouquet Farm is followed from either flank, with the option of a walk around the farm itself. An optional extension visits the Chalk Pit and Casualty Corner.
DISTANCE COVERED: 16 km
DURATION: 7 hours

confined to the section of OG1 to your front. Private Leak of the 9th and Lieutenant Blackburn of the 10th won their VCs there. Leak charged a machine-gun post just to the left of the Pozières Trench junction, silenced it, and was found in it wiping the blood off his bayonet with his slouch hat. The Germans subsequently charged 100 metres beyond the junction. Blackburn led four attacks under murderous fire back along OG1 from your right front to snatch it back. Turning down Pozières Trench and through the tunnel, he and his small party then linked up with the right of the 9th Battalion.

Instead of reaching the D929, the advance along the OG Lines hardly got beyond the junction ahead of you. Look half left at your previous location, where the power lines crossed the track, to see the other end of the gap that resulted. The Germans counterattacked into it from the OG Lines to the right of the windmill at 5.30 am on 24 July. Attacking into the gap between your location and the railway early next morning, the 5th Battalion had trouble distinguishing OG1 and OG2 from the surrounding shell holes. OG2 was finally identified and

taken but counterattacks from both flanks forced a withdrawal to OG1, where the 7th, 9th and 10th Battalions joined the 5th in the three-hour bomb fight that developed in the 35-metre stretch of OG1 to the left of its junction with Pozières Trench. 'Bombs at the double — machine guns at the double—carriers at the double—more bombs at the double — strings of men going up', recalled one Australian of the scene around you.

The Germans conceded this part of OG1 and the communication trench to Munster Alley. Both sides left the OG Lines to the railway unoccupied thereafter. The 5th Brigade and the British 1st Division were unable to make any headway in Munster Alley in a 13-hour bomb fight on 26 July. As it enfiladed the gap, the Germans were desperate to keep Munster Alley. They did so until 6 August.

Continue 200 metres further on the D73 and turn right onto another track. Stop after 100 metres ⑧ and look down the track. Pozières Trench roughly

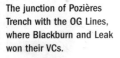

The junction of Pozières Trench with the OG Lines, where Blackburn and Leak won their VCs.

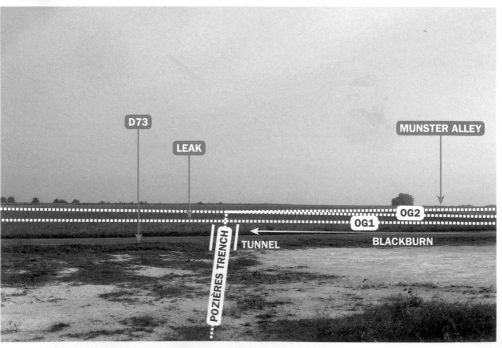

paralleled it on your right, about halfway to the village. **Black Watch Alley**, a squalid ooze full of British and German corpses when the 3rd Brigade occupied it on first entering the line, followed the track 250 metres on your left. Running down from the higher ground beyond it, OG1 crossed the track where you are standing and continued diagonally to the D73. Held by the 9th Battalion, the extreme right flank of the 1st Australian Division on 23 July was in OG1 50 metres to your left. By then, **Sunken Road Trench** had been dug along the right of the track as a jumping-off position so that the attack could start closer to Pozières Trench. As the 3rd Brigade filed into this trench just before the attack began, the supporting bombardment reached its height, shredding what was left of the orchards and hedges on the outskirts of Pozières. Private Jack Bourke of the 8th Battalion was awestruck. 'No description, however realistic, can give any idea of what it was like', he wrote. 'The ground shook with the thunder of guns, while the whole battle line was lit up as bright as day with the thousands of rockets, flares and flashlights of every colour.'

Continue along the track, which follows the re-entrant on the southern side of the village. Wanting to reach Pozières Trench as soon as the fire lifted at 12.30 am, the first wave crawled out into no-man's-land on your right. A few men were seen. Some machine-guns opened. The tension was agonising. Sergeant Ben Champion of the 1st Battalion could not stop urinating. At 12.28 am two minutes' hurricane fire

The enemy came towards us like swarms of ants rushing from shell hole to shell hole… In our trench each man full of fight and confidence lined the parapet and emptied magazine after magazine. Men pulled one another down from the parapet to get a shot at them. The machine-guns caused great losses and artillery, which had been brought up, tore great gaps in the oncoming lines. The attack just melted away.

Sergeant Harry Preston, 9th Battalion, on the German counterattack on 24 July (Preston's notebook, 2DRL/0811, AWM)

began, and bursting shrapnel illuminated Pozières Trench. 'The concussion made our ears ring', wrote Champion. 'It is strange how men creep together for protection', he noted. 'Soon, instead of four paces between the men, we came down to lying alongside each other, and no motioning could make them move apart.'

As you walk, the re-entrant deepens and Pozières disappears. The cover that the re-entrant offered made Sunken Road Trench an ideal forming-up place for the attack. After 800 metres, the track bends to the left. The Australian line left it here and cut diagonally across your right front to the D929. Called **Howitzer Avenue**, this was the stretch from which the 1st Brigade assaulted on the left of the 3rd. After passing between **Sunken Road Cemetery** on the left and **2nd Canadian Cemetery** on the right, the track peters out at the **D147** **9**, on which you should turn right. Howitzer Avenue crossed it towards the far end of the cutting 350 metres along, and

> [I saw] the bullets cutting their stems off right against my head … I lay as flat to the ground as possible, jammed the steel helmet onto my head and brought the body of my rifle across my face to stop anything that might happen to drop low … a man alongside of me was crying like a child and saying we will never get out of this. I kept replying yes we will!
>
> Sergeant Preston, on lying among the poppies in no-man's-land under machine-gun fire before the attack (Preston's notebook, 2DRL/0811, AWM)

The Chalk Pit.

The 1st Division's attack as seen from Sunken Road Trench. The ground rises slightly towards the village, which sheltered the first part of the attack.

used as a headquarters crumbles away on the left about halfway along.

Return to the D929, cross and walk past a Bastiaan plaque to the **1st Australian Division Memorial** 13, which the 1st's veterans wanted here because it lost more heavily at Pozières than anywhere else. The two German field-guns that originally flanked the memorial disappeared during the Second World War. **Gibraltar's** remains are in the copse opposite. Standing three metres high, this pillbox was clobbered by an Australian gun manoeuvred under cover of the bombardment onto the left of the D929 in the area of the traffic signs 200 metres from your location before the 1st Division's attack on 23 July. The 11 soldiers from the 2nd Battalion who captured it found range-finders, binoculars, four machine-guns and two kettle-drums inside. When the 21st Battalion's headquarters moved in several days later, the pillbox was being called Gibraltar, possibly because it stood out like Gibraltar; more probably because that name was inscribed on the cap badges of its Hanoverian defenders. It was mostly demolished after the war. Excavations in the mid-1980s uncovered the underground chambers. They are in a sorry state and have been fenced off. Entry is forbidden.

Pozières Trench went over it 350 metres further on.

On reaching the D929, head left for 300 metres to **Dead Man's Road,** the unsealed road on the left. The walk down Dead Man's Road is optional but it passes some interesting sites. The **cutting** 10, where various headquarters were, and which was lined with corpses, is 250 metres along. The unmistakeable **Chalk Pit** 11 then looms on the left. Site of lesser headquarters and a small supply dump, the old quarry is now a rubbish tip that is slowly being filled in. From here, the track climbs markedly to meet the D20 from La Boiselle at **Casualty Corner** 12. A large concrete **dugout** that some Australian battalions probably

POZIÈRES CHURCH

POZIÈRES BRITISH CEMETERY ON D929

1ST BRIGADE

3RD BRIGADE

The superb view that the Germans had from Gibraltar is evident from the nearby viewing platform, which is the same height as the pillbox was. Orientation markers relate the Pozières battlefield to other key locations of the Somme offensive. Almost straight ahead on the right of the D929 is **Pozières British Cemetery and Memorial** and, to its right, the spire of **Ovillers church** at the far end of **Mash Valley**. As you contemplate the bare slope in front of you, ask yourself if the aim of taking both Ovillers and Pozières on the first day of the offensive was realistic, envisage the difficulties confronting the 48th Division advancing towards you on 23 July, and appreciate General Walker's wisdom in insisting that the 1st Australian Division alongside it attack from the more favourable ground that you have just walked on the far side of the D929. Continue looking right, past the **Thiepval Memorial** on the skyline, to the white farm building 600 metres away, immediately to the right of which is **Pozières Cemetery**. From the D929, **K Trench** ran in front of the 1st Division Memorial and through the shed's location towards Mouquet Farm behind it.

Continue to the T-junction and turn left onto the D73. Only the chancel

Dugout on Dead Man's Road.

window of the **church** 14 on the left was still standing by 23 July. That night patrols from the 11th and 12th Battalions cleared the water-tower end of Pozières, while the 8th Battalion swept mainly to the right of the D73 and dug in 100 metres beyond the church. Shells

POZIÈRES TRENCH

The remains of Gibraltar in 1919, with the 1st Australian Division memorial in rear.

and coffee as they went, the 4th Battalion bombed along K Trench towards you early on 25 July. Simultaneously advancing on their right astride the D73, the 8th Battalion reached the cemetery area first, trapping the Germans withdrawing before the 4th Battalion. They screamed 'Mercy, Kamerad!' but the Australians were reluctant to take prisoners in this advanced position and kept on firing. The two battalions eventually met on the small knoll behind the cemetery and the white farm building.

Return to the D73 and stand with your back to the track, from which the railway line ran diagonally, with **Tramway Trench** alongside the last third of it, to meet the D929 to the right of the water tower. The 8th Battalion's advance on this side of the D73 met stiffer resistance. Private Cooke's posthumous VC action possibly occurred near the trees midway to the village outskirts. After the rest of the gun crew had been killed, Cooke fought on with his Lewis gun against German counterattacks. He was found dead beside it. At the end of the advance, the Australian line went well to the right of the railway line but converged on it at the Tramway.

Head left to the intersection and take the middle road, which ends at a **T-junction 16**. Look straight ahead. You are now on **Brind's Road**, from which the 4th Australian Division kicked off the attacks on **Mouquet Farm**, among the trees 650 metres directly in front of you,

and other relics are piled high in the front yard of a house that you will pass on the right as you walk to this location. On the left 300 metres further along, just before a four-way intersection, is the **cemetery 15**, with the white farm building behind it. The dip here is the head of the re-entrant on the northern side of Pozières, which broadens into Mash Valley. You have now crossed the spur on which Pozières sits. By fortifying the spur, the Germans buttressed the OG Lines, whose general location is indicated by the communications tower off to your right.

The northern branch of the light railway ran to Ovillers along the track on the left of the cemetery, down which you should walk until you can see the 1st Division Memorial on your left. This is the reverse of the view along K Trench that you had from the memorial. Swilling German rum

The 4th Battalion's advance down K Trench.

POZIÈRES

1ST AUSTRALIAN DIVISION MEMORIAL

K TRENCH

4TH BATTALION

on 8 August. The **quarry** was in the copse to the lower left of the buildings. **Skyline Trench** ran past the quarry from the D73, while **Park Lane**, 200 metres to your front, paralleled Brind's Road. During a German bombardment on 11 August, and over the next four days, Private Martin O'Meara of the 16th Battalion carried out 25 wounded from the area below the quarry and brought up ammunition, food and water on his return trips. He was awarded the VC.

Brind's Road was the objective for the 23rd Battalion, which attacked from the railway on the left flank of the 2nd Australian Division on 29 July. In the only success that night, it reached Brind's and extended as far as OG1, which crossed the road on the crest of the ridge 250 metres off. But the failure at the Tramway end of the attack left the 23rd hanging. It pulled back to the junction with the **track** ⑰ 100 metres rightwards from your location. Walk to

this junction, which marked the left end of the jumping-off trench that the 2nd Division dug for its assault on 4 August. The trench ran from here to the D929 just to the right of the water tower. Knowing what the work meant, the Germans pulverised the fields in between, making the digging a nightmare. Thanks to the jumping-off trench, though, the 6th (nearer to you) and 7th Brigades were over no-man's-land so quickly that the Germans could only get one machine-gun into action. It was in the field on the left of Brind's 60 metres further along. With the OG Lines taken, the advance headed for Mouquet Farm.

Take the track for 200 metres to the end of a slightly sunken section ⑱. Crossing here, Park Lane ran leftwards to K Trench and the D73, which follows the line of white posts on your left. The objective for the attack from Brind's on 8 August, it fell to the 15th and 16th Battalions but they had to withdraw

The 2nd Division's successful assault on 4 August. It had tried to cover the same ground in the disastrous one on 29 July.

when the British failed to take the K Trench/D73 stretch. After the Australian left was extended to the D73, the two battalions attacked on 9 August and Park Lane was theirs. Next evening, the 16th Battalion almost reached Skyline Trench, while the 13th Battalion established an advanced post where OG2 crossed the again slightly sunken track on the slope 300 metres ahead of you. The rest of the 13th's line ran along Park Lane to your location and then down the track for 90 metres, where OG1 crossed. From this point, to which you should now walk, the line extended 200 metres to OG2 on your right, which the 14th Battalion held back to Brind's Road to secure the right flank. On 11 August the 13th Battalion caught in enfilade a counterattack from the quarry on your left against the 16th and smashed it.

Continue for another 200 metres to the location of the **13th Battalion's**

advanced post **19**. The 13th drew up to it on 12 August. On the opposite flank to your left, most of Skyline Trench was also taken. Cresting the slope along the way, walk a further 300 metres and face left along the line of the **Fabeck Graben 20**. After running through your location from the site of **Courcelette British Cemetery** in the re-entrant behind you, the Fabeck crossed OG2 100 metres in front of you and OG1 150 metres beyond it before cutting behind the farm buildings to your left front. The original buildings were among the trees to the right of them but the risk of subsidence from the German underground workings precluded their rebuilding there. Some lumps of concrete are all that remain of the defences. On 14 August the farm was to be attacked but the loss of Skyline Trench on the far side of the D73 by the British the night before scuppered the plan. Skyline, the quarry and the Fabeck were to be taken instead.

The Fabeck, OG Lines and Mouquet Farm.

MOUQUET FARM (NEW)

OG1

OG2

On the left, the British regained Skyline but the 50th Battalion could not get beyond the quarry. Advancing on the Courcelette side of the track, the 51st Battalion on the right got to within 150 metres of your position but was sent reeling in disarray back to your previous location. The 13th Battalion in the centre, which had moved up OG1 and taken the Fabeck between it and OG2 directly in front of you, was left isolated. When the Germans counterattacked from your right, Captain Harry Murray ordered a fighting withdrawal through the posts he had set up in the advance along OG1. Carrying a wounded man on his back, Murray, a distinguished original ANZAC, was the last to leave each post as his men leapfrogged through. The 13th, too, ended up at your previous location.

For the German view from the Fabeck, look at the farm and the slope descending towards Park Lane below it. With the Australian attack preparations in plain sight, the Germans were easily able to register their artillery on them, turning the slope into a surreal wilderness of putrid pockmarked brown. Without identifiable landmarks to use as reference points, the supporting barrage scattered the 3rd Battalion's assault on the Fabeck

on 18 August. On 21 August the 10th Battalion reached the Courcelette side of the Fabeck and the 12th next to it got to the farm. Both were soon ejected. The weight of the attack on 26 August was on the far side of the farm. On this side, the 24th Battalion almost got beyond it before being forced back.

Heavy rains had turned the area around you into a sea of mud before the 29 August attack. The 16th Battalion's withdrawal from the farm in that attack caused the 13th under Murray, which had taken the same stretch of the Fabeck between the OG Lines in front of you as it had done a fortnight earlier, to retire as well. In the final attack on 3 September, the 51st Battalion took the farm and the Fabeck behind it before being overwhelmed. The 49th, which held a 180-metre section of the Courcelette side of the Fabeck behind you, and the 52nd, which set up a post on the track 90 metres to your left, managed to stay in place until relieved by the Canadians.

Continue for 350 metres to a **cross-track** 21 and turn left for the D73, where you should turn left again. Mouquet Farm is on the high ground to your left front. **Zigzag Trench** stretched from the track junction on the right

SITE OF ORIGINAL FARM

THIEPVAL MEMORIAL

FABECK GRABEN

500 metres along to **Point 77**, on the high ground midway between the farm and D73, and then broke left for the farm. The road to the farm crosses a pronounced re-entrant to meet the D73 at what was **Point 54**. Walk to this **junction** 22, which is marked by a Bastiaan plaque. Cutting from it to **Point 27** on the right-hand corner of the old farm buildings, which were on the left of those you see now, **Constance Trench** overlooked the quarry, which was in the copse 250 metres to your right front. The ground on which the farm stood herefore dominated the approaches across the lower ground to its front and from this flank.

The attacks on this side of the farm followed the same pattern as those on the other side. On 26 August the Germans in Constance Trench fled before the 21st Battalion but the 21st, unable to recognise its objective, Zigzag Trench, continued to the farm ruins. It was flayed as it went past your location at Point 54. Point 77 was the only gain. A platoon from the 14th Battalion briefly took Point 27 on the following night. On 27 August a

party under Sergeant Rule crept up the D73 from the quarry and entered Point 54 but withdrew almost immediately under a hail of bombs. Carved up from your location while crossing the D73 to your right rear and advancing diagonally up the muddy slope in front of you on 29 August, the 16th Battalion got into the farm ruins but was quickly forced out. Attacking over the same ground on 3 September, the 51st Battalion went further, seizing the Fabeck beyond the farm on the high ground to your left front. There they were cut off and either killed or taken prisoner.

Continue on the D73 for another 250 metres to the **track** 23 coming off the high ground on the right. After following this track, Skyline Trench ran in front of the quarry. On 12 August, when Skyline apart from the quarry was captured, a platoon from the 50th Battalion reached the farm before having to pull back to your location. The British lost Skyline on your right on the 13th and regained it next evening, when the 50th Battalion also managed to advance beyond the quarry. Heavily shelled, and

The attacks on the quarry side of the farm. Note the short distance between the quarry, which the Australians held, and the farm, which the Germans held.

SITE OF ORIGINAL FARM

POINT 27

CONSTANCE TRENCH

machine-gunned from Constance Trench, it was soon back behind the quarry. Not until 21 August was the quarry incorporated into the line.

Now follow the D73 all the way back to the D929. On reaching it, look right to see **Le Tommy Café**, where a restorative drink may be in order! A replica trench filled with battlefield relics is at the back. From the café, return along the D929 to the windmill. By dawn on 23 July, after the 1st Australian Division's attack, a trench 1.2 metres deep, its parapet built up with dead Germans and bristling with over 20 machine-guns, fringed the D929 through Pozières. In the growing light, German snipers fired from the ruins, so groups of Australians moved through the village throwing phosphorous bombs into the cellars and dugouts that hid them. Forced out by the choking smoke, the Germans were shot as they emerged, or chased and bayoneted. Having got their man, the Australians would sit down for a smoke while waiting for another German to bolt.

When the Germans began the bombardment of Pozières, the cellars

offered some protection from the shelling; the trenches that most of the Australians were holding offered none. Frantic digging went on to extricate those buried by the constant collapses. The wounded were laid in the bottom of the trenches, which filled with half a metre of soil in an hour. As you walk to the windmill, imagine an ash heap two metres deep, pitted by shell craters lying edge to edge like the scratchings of gigantic hens. This was all that remained of the village.

Shelling. The main street of Pozières, crossed by Centre Way Trench, at the end of August 1916.

QUARRY

LOCAL INFORMATION

CEMETERIES

Courcelette British Cemetery

Easily seen from the windmill, this cemetery can be reached by taking the C6 near the water tower in Pozières and turning left at the T-junction after 1.7 kilometres. Started under the name 'Mouquet Farm' in an area captured by the Canadians on 15 September 1916, it was used postwar as a concentration cemetery for burials from nearby smaller cemeteries and the surrounding battlefields. The track in front partly marks the course of the Fabeck Graben. The track that forked left at the bend in the road just before the cemetery is an extension of Brind's Road. Of the 1970 burials, 513 are Australian.

Gordon Dump Cemetery

At the head of Sausage Valley on the right of the D20 650 metres past La Boiselle, this cemetery was used until September 1916 and then became a postwar concentration cemetery. It includes 91 Australians among its 1676 burials. The gun line of 106 Howitzer Battery, 6th Australian Field Artillery Brigade, was nearby when the battery's ammunition dump was hit on 7 August 1916. The resulting explosion killed Bombardier Henry White, Gunners Frank Cromellin, Allan Mercer and Gladstone Page, and Drivers William Cracknell and George Denness, all of whom lie in I.A.

London Cemetery and Extension, Longueval

To reach this cemetery, head towards Bapaume on the D929 but turn right, 1.3 kilometres past the windmill, onto the D6 for Martinpuich. Continue two kilometres beyond the village to High Wood, where the fighting before its fall in September 1916 rivalled that at Pozières and Mouquet Farm as regards hideousness and cost. Started when 47 British dead were turfed into a shell hole soon after the wood's capture, the cemetery was selected for concentration purposes postwar, which took it from 101 graves to the third-largest cemetery on the Somme with 3873 graves. Of these, a staggering 3114 are unidentified. Most of the 299 Australians were killed at Pozières or Mouquet Farm. Only 102 are known.

Pozières British Cemetery and Memorial

On the D929 600 metres from the south-western end of Pozières, the cemetery was started as soon as the village had been secured. Used in 1917 and 1918, it was greatly enlarged after the war. More Australian dead from the 1916 Somme battles now rest in it than anywhere else, 714 out of 2756 burials. Among them are Sergeant Castleton VC at IV.L.43, and Major Chapman at III.M.22. Nineteen Australians believed to rest somewhere in the cemetery are remembered on a special memorial. Some 251 of the Australian burials are unidentified.

Serre Road Cemetery No 2

This cemetery is the largest of the Somme cemeteries and also one of the largest British cemeteries in France. To reach it, continue through Thiepval on the D73 to the T-junction with the D163 at Auchonvillers. Turn right and then left after 400 metres onto the D174, which you should follow for 1.2 kilometres before turning right onto the D919 for Serre. The cemetery is on the right 1.3 kilometres short of the village. One of the three Serre Road cemeteries begun in 1917, it became a postwar concentration cemetery with 7127 graves, of which almost 5000 are unidentified. Most of the 699 Australian burials, of whom over half are unknown, fell in July–August 1916. One Australian who died later was Sergeant William O'Brien of the 29th Battalion at XXIV.C.2, who leans on a stick in front of the platoon being briefed by Lieutenant Downes in an iconic photograph taken on 8 August 1918. O'Brien fell next day.

Sunken Road Cemetery

On the track between the D147 and the D73 followed by part of the Australian jumping-off line for the 23 July attack on Pozières, this small cemetery is passed on the walking tour. Started in July 1916 and used until October, it contains 200 burials, 61 of them Australian.

Grave of Sergeant Castleton VC, Pozières British Cemetery and Memorial.

MUSEUMS

The 230-metre tunnel system under the Notre Dame de Brebières Basilica houses the **Musée des Abris**, also called the **Somme '14–18' Trench Museum**. Using appropriate sound effects and lighting, it depicts typical trench scenes on the Somme and includes life-size re-creations of dugouts for headquarters, trench mortar positions, medical posts and accommodation, as well as raiding and tunnelling activities. A huge range of relics are incorporated in them. Opening hours are 9.30 am to midday and 2 pm to 6 pm 15 March to 15 December, and all day in July and August. An entry fee is charged. Contact details are: telephone 33 3 22 75 16 17; musee@somme-1916.org. See also www.somme-1916.org.

NEARBY PLACES OF INTEREST

Thiepval and Thiepval Memorial to the Missing

Signposted on the D73 from Pozières, Thiepval was one of the largest villages on the Somme before the war but is barely a hamlet now. The main British ceremony on 1 July is held at the 45-metre-high Memorial to the Missing, designed by the great imperial architect Sir Edward Lutyens, which commemorates

Thiepval Memorial to the Missing.

Thiepval, let alone Mouquet Farm, the Germans had a grandstand view of what was happening as it happened.

Ulster Tower

Emerging from their trenches in Thiepval Wood (now Authuille Wood on French maps), on the D73 1.5 kilometres past Thiepval, early on 1 July, the Ulstermen of the 36th Division crept out into no-man's-land to cut down the length of their assault, just as the Australians would do at Pozières. When the barrage lifted, they charged across five German trenches and took the Schwaben Redoubt near the crest above them, becoming the only formation north of the D929 to breach the German line. But the attacks on either side failed and the Ulstermen had to pull out, having sustained over 5000 casualties. To put these events into perspective, stand facing the tower. Thiepval Wood is behind you, the Thiepval memorial is on your right, and Mill Road Cemetery, slightly to your right front and the resting place of many of the Ulstermen, is close to where the Schwaben Redoubt was.

the 1916 Anglo-French offensive on the Somme and also the 73 000 British and South African soldiers who fell there between then and March 1918 (their ANZAC counterparts are commemorated on the memorials at Villers-Bretonneux and Longueval). Unveiled in 1932, it is the largest British war memorial in the world. Opened in 2004, the Visitor Centre boasts informative displays and databases, and a shop.

From the mound at the entrance to the memorial grounds, you can easily see the communication tower at Pozières and the traffic crawling along the D929. This is a good vantage point from which to grasp I ANZAC's task in its entirety. Having advanced astride the D929 to the tower, it turned left for Mouquet Farm along the ridge that you see running towards you. As is obvious from its location in relation to Thiepval, the farm had to be taken if a salient, to use Charles Bean's words, was to be pushed behind Thiepval in order to pinch it out. From

The tower, a replica of Helen's Tower at Clandeboye in Northern Ireland, where the Ulstermen trained, commemorates their achievement and loss. Unveiled in November 1921, it was the first official commemorative monument on the Western Front. The Visitor Centre includes a memorial chapel as well as a small café. Safety issues have precluded access to the top of the tower for some years. A German soldier carved a swastika on the wall there during the Second World War. The remains of trenches and shell holes are in the copse behind the tower. Thiepval Wood has been the scene of major archaeological excavations but the work can only be seen on guided tours from the tower, which is open daily except on Mondays and in December and January. Entry is free.

Newfoundland Memorial Park, Beaumont-Hamel

Field Marshal Haig opened the park on 7 June 1925, after its purchase by the government of the dominion of Newfoundland (now part of Canada) in memory of the Newfoundland Regiment, which was virtually destroyed in the grounds on 1 July 1916. When the 29th Division attacked here, the Newfoundlanders were in reserve in St John's Road, a support trench behind the Caribou monument. The attack foundered. The Newfoundlanders were urgently ordered forward to assist. Finding the communication trenches clogged with dead and wounded, they took to the open and walked downhill under heavy machine-gun fire towards the front line 275 metres off. Of the few who got as far as no-man's-land, none made it past the 'danger tree', a dead tree used a landmark. Only 68 of the 778 Newfoundlanders who went into action answered the roll call that night.

The park's 16 hectares comprise the largest part of the 1916 Somme battlefield that has been preserved. Screw pickets stand forlornly in no-man's-land and the trenches and craters, though grass-covered, are clearly defined. The Caribou was the Newfoundland Regiment's emblem, and the Caribou monument bears the names of those from the regiment who fell. Staffed by Canadian students, who give frequent tours of the battlefield, the Visitor Centre is housed in a replica of a typical Newfoundland log cabin. The copse one kilometre north of the park is the site of the Hawthorn Ridge Mine, whose explosion before the attack was filmed by Geoffrey Malins. It is probably the war's most famous footage. On the D73 five kilometres from Ulster Tower, the park is open daily except on Christmas Day and New Year's Day. Entry is free.

Trenches in the Newfoundland Memorial Park.

CHAPTER 4

1916

SOMME: NEW ZEALANDERS AT FLERS

When the Australians left the line at Mouquet Farm on 3 September 1916, the Somme offensive was just short of its halfway point. But the visitor experience on the 1916 Somme battlefields today is slanted towards what happened in the first half of the offensive and, in particular, on the first day, 1 July 1916. Nothing like the same level of attention is given to the battlefields of the second half of the offensive. The New Zealand Division, taking part in its first set-piece battle on the Western Front, distinguished itself in several attacks around Flers, at the heart of those battlefields, in September and October.

Planning

Believing that attritional assaults, such as the one at Mouquet Farm, were grinding the Germans down to breaking point, General Haig ordered a resumption of the wider offensive. Using tanks for the first time, it was slated for 15 September across an 11-kilometre front. The Fourth Army on the right of the D929 was to seize the German third line at Flers, in the valley before Bapaume, and push on to the fortified villages of Morval, Lesboeufs and Gueudecourt, whereupon the cavalry would gallop up the far slope to Bapaume. The Canadian Corps from the Reserve Army would protect the left flank by taking Courcelette, on the other side of the D929, while the French advanced on the Fourth Army's right. XV Corps in the centre of the Fourth Army was to capture Flers and Gueudecourt.

Forming the left-hand formation of XV Corps, the New Zealand Division, under Major-General Andrew Russell, would advance across the high ground between Delville and High Woods, and into the valley beyond. Its first objective, the Green Line, was a section of the Switch Trench that ended at Munster Alley, where the Australians had such trouble in July and August. After the 2nd Brigade had taken it, the 3rd (Rifle) Brigade was to capture the Brown Line 800 metres further on and continue another 900 metres, passing over Flers Trench and Flers Support in the German third line, to the Blue Line beyond Flers. It would then establish a protective flank on the Red Line, a triangular-shaped wedge on the spur immediately north-west of Flers.

The advance was three kilometres long, over twice as far as the Australians

Major-General Sir Andrew Hamilton Russell

Commander, New Zealand Mounted Rifles 1915, New Zealand Division 1916-18

1868-1960

After graduating from the Royal Military Sandhurst with the Sword of Honour in 1887 and serving briefly in the British Army, Napier-born Russell returned to New Zealand in 1892 and became a pastoralist. Having impressed as an officer in the prewar citizen forces, he gained command of the New Zealand Mounted Rifles when the NZEF was raised in August 1914. After leading the Rifles with aplomb at ANZAC, Russell took charge of the newly formed New Zealand Division in 1916. On the Western Front, he did well in the set-piece attacks of 1916–17 but exhaustion made for a patchy performance in the mobile warfare of 1918.

Anticipation, detailed planning and an insistence on thorough training underpinned Russell's command of the New Zealand Division. He always argued his corner, even disagreeing on occasion with Haig. Nonetheless Haig offered Russell command of a British corps in June 1918 but he chose to stay with his division. A very strict disciplinarian who expected the utmost of his officers, Russell refused to support any VC recommendation for an officer on the basis that, however brave the officer may have been, he was simply doing what was expected of him. Appointed CB in 1916, he was knighted (KCB) in 1917. After the war, Russell returned to farming but also devoted his time to the welfare and care of ex-servicemen. His last stint in uniform was in 1940–41 as inspector-general of the forces in New Zealand.

had gone in their opening attack at Pozières. But the frontage was narrow, 900 metres, allowing General Russell to concentrate a brigade against both Switch Trench and the third line, where the toughest resistance could be expected. Arriving on the Somme in mid-August 1916, the New Zealanders spent the next three weeks practising assaults in waves behind a creeping barrage and consolidating the objective. They also got four of the 54 tanks available to crush wire and knock out strongpoints.

To Flers

On 12 September the bombardment commenced. Having established its advanced headquarters near Meaulte, on the eastern outskirts of Albert, the New Zealand Division had begun moving through Fricourt to the front line north of Longueval two days earlier. Trenches were started in no-man's-land on arrival to reduce the distance to Crest Trench and Coffee Lane in the German front line to as little as 150 metres. On the night of 14 September, the tank and infantry commanders huddled by candlelight to discuss how they would cooperate. None of the battalions had any chance to practise with the tanks.

A slight mist wreathed the valley as dawn ushered in brilliant autumn weather. At 6.20 am the barrage began its creep. The lanes left in it for the tanks were clearly defined but of the tanks themselves, there was nothing to be seen. Old shell holes had delayed them at the exit from Delville Wood. But the

age was very effective, and 2nd
ckland and 2nd Otago between them
viftly took Coffee Lane and Crest Trench.
hen a hail of fire whipped in from High
Wood on the left. The tanks supporting
the 47th (London) Division from III Corps
could not negotiate its shattered remains,
leaving the Londoners stalled.

Though the Otagos were enfiladed
from the wood and lost heavily, the
advance was unchecked. Sergeant
Donald Brown helped it along by
knocking out two machine-guns. By
6.50 am, the Otagos and the Aucklanders
had captured the Switch Trench. As they
dug in, 4th Rifles from the Rifle Brigade
spread across the divisional frontage and
struck out for the Brown Line. There was
still no sign of the tanks but it did not
matter for the Brown Line fell without
incident at 7.50 am. Thirty minutes later,
the 2nd and 3rd Rifles started for the
Blue Line. The tanks finally appeared,
which was fortunate because stiff
resistance had temporarily brought the
advance to a standstill.

Running into the uncut wire of Flers
Trench, 3rd Rifles on the left could make
no progress until Tanks D11 ('Die Hard')
and D8 created breaches in it. Abbey
Road, which connects Flers with the
hamlet of L'Abbaye d'Eaucourt on the
D11 two kilometres north-west, was then
crossed and the link-up made on the
Blue Line with 2nd Rifles on the right.
Getting through the wire unaided at
great cost, the 2nd had flushed out Flers
Trench and continued to Flers Support
Trench, which was deserted. As Abbey
Road was approached, resistance
stiffened. The 1st Rifles lent support and
it was cleared by 9.30 am. Before the Blue
Line was occupied at 10 am, Lieutenant
CE Butcher from the 2nd Rifles had made
history by scribbling a note that Rifleman
JW Dobson took to Tank D12. It read:
'Enemy machine-guns appear to be
holding up infantry in valley on your
right. Can you assist in pushing forward?'

Though he did not know it, Butcher had
written the first communication to a tank
in action. His note is preserved at the
Tank Museum at Bovingdon in England.

Meanwhile, one of the most famous
incidents of the war had occurred in
Flers, which the 41st Division was to
capture. Many of its supporting tanks had
been lost, resulting in grievous casualties
by the time it neared Flers. But one of the
surviving tanks, D17 'Dinnaken', with
parties of infantry in tow, lurched over
the wire of Flers Trench and up the D197
to the far end of the village, blasting
German strongpoints as it went. After
witnessing the scene, the crew of a
British observation aircraft dropped a
message behind the British line that
made front pages worldwide: 'A tank is
walking up the High Street of Flers with
the British Army cheering behind.'

But the 41st Division's heavy losses
disrupted its advance through the village.
The New Zealanders extended into its
sector and also pushed up the D197
beyond Flers to the Red Line. They were
now in a pronounced salient, which had
been created by the inability of the
41st Division to go further and the
47th Division on the left to get past
High Wood. Raked by fire and heavily
counterattacked, they had to give the
Red Line up.

By nightfall four kilometres of the
German third line had been taken.
Besides the capture of Flers and High
Wood, Courcelette had fallen to the
Canadians and Martinpuich to the 15th
(Scottish) Division. Compared with 1 July,
twice as much ground had been gained
in what became known as the Battle
of Flers-Courcelette at half the cost. For
the New Zealand Division that meant
an advance of 2.3 kilometres, the
longest in the Fourth Army, for the loss
of 2000 men. But the failure to capture
Gueudecourt and Lesboeufs dashed
any prospect of the hoped-for
breakthrough by the cavalry. The French

New Zealanders after capturing and consolidating a trench at Flers.

achieved little. Nonetheless, Haig and Rawlinson felt that enough had been accomplished to warrant continuing the attack.

The days following

On 16 September the 1st Brigade took over the advance, with 1st Wellington trying for the Red Line. Packed between Abbey Road and the D197 at the far end of Flers, the Wellingtons had an enormous stroke of luck just as they were about to assault at 9.25 am. Attacking towards them from Grove Alley, just past which the Red Line lay, was a 500-strong German force trying to regain the ground lost the previous day. With 350 metres of open no-man's-land to cross, the Germans had no chance. They crumpled before a wall of fire from the Wellingtons, who now had a clear path to Grove Alley and the Red Line.

The 41st Division on the right of the New Zealanders still could not get past Flers. III and XIV Corps on the flanks of the Fourth Army also stalled. Rain set in, forcing a postponement of the next big attack from 18 to 25 September. In the interim, the 41st Division was relieved by the 21st but the New Zealand Division stayed put. It played a leading role in the minor operations to consolidate the new line, especially before High Wood, where, on 18 September, the 47th Division took its final first-day objective, the Flers System, apart from two 90-metre stretches of Flers Trench and Flers Support. The Germans could reinforce them using Goose Alley, which ran back atop a spur towards L'Abbaye d'Eaucourt. They resisted stubbornly. Starting on 19 September, it took the 2nd Brigade, along with the Londoners and the Black Watch from the 1st Division who relieved them, three nights to close the gaps.

> The New Zealand Division has fought with greatest gallantry in the Somme Battle for twenty-three consecutive days, carrying out with complete success every task set, and always doing even more than was asked of it. The Division has won universal confidence and admiration. No praise can be too high for such troops.
>
> Haig to the New Zealand Division and the
> New Zealand government, 4 October 1916

For the New Zealand Division, the assault on 25 September was the easiest so far, in part because the objective was not a defended trench line but 1.5 kilometres of high ground. The 1st Brigade was to extend the line from the Goose Alley/Flers Support junction over the Goose Alley Spur and on down to the D197's junction with the D74 at Factory Corner, so-called because of the ruined sugar factory there. After advancing behind a very precise creeping barrage, it was digging in across the spur by mid-afternoon. The way was now clear to strike the Gird Trenches on the far side of the D74. They would be attacked from Factory Corner on 27 September by the 1st Brigade on the left of the D197 and the 55th Division on the right. Gird and Gird Support from the D197 to Goose Alley fell easily but 1st Otago could not take Goose Alley's junction with Gird Trench on the left flank. It lay in a hollow and the Otagos, skylined as they approached, were lashed by artillery and machine-gun fire. A trench dug around the hollow on 28 September finally linked 1st Auckland in Gird with the Otagos in Goose Alley.

Pressing on regardless

Though the battle of Morval, as it became known, finally delivered Morval, Lesboeufs and Gueudecourt into British hands, and Gough's army had taken Thiepval on 26 September, there was no question of the cavalry pouring through. Aerial reconnaissance had picked up Reserve (R) 1, a fourth German defensive line anchored on Le Transloy, three kilometres from the positions reached. The Gird Trenches screened it. Behind R1, two more lines, R2 and R3, were under construction either side of Bapaume. Notwithstanding their existence and the failure to achieve a breakthrough, Haig was sufficiently encouraged by the results so far to continue the offensive. The Fourth Army would capture the Transloy Line as the next step. As part of the preliminaries, the 47th Division was to seize L'Abbaye d'Eaucourt on 1 October. On its right, the 2nd New Zealand Brigade would take the Goose Alley/Gird Trench junction as well as the Circus, a strongpoint near L'Abbaye d'Eaucourt, and Circus Trench, which ran from the Circus to the junction.

Within half an hour of the advance starting, 2nd Canterbury had captured the junction and the first half of Circus Trench. On its left, 2nd Otago advanced against the Circus and the other half of Circus Trench. One machine-gun wreaked havoc until Sergeant Brown charged it and shot the crew. A sniper's bullet subsequently killed him. For his actions in this attack and on 15 September, he was posthumously awarded the first VC won by the New Zealand Division. The Circus was taken but L'Abbaye d'Eaucourt did not fall to the 47th Division until 3 October. The New Zealand Division had left the line the previous day. At a cost of almost 7000 casualties, it had reached the end of the longest unbroken stint by any division on the Somme, and the longest sustained battle it would fight in the war.

DRIVING/WALKING THE BATTLEFIELD

Unlike the D929 at Pozières and Mouquet Farm, no arterial roads slice across the Flers battlefield, so the hazards caused by busy traffic do not arise. As two locations cannot be reached by car, some walking is necessary. This problem will not arise if you walk the battlefield.

MAPS IGN Blue Series, 1:25000, 2407E Bapaume; 2408E Bray-sur-Somme

> Passing between Delville and High Woods, this drive (or walk) follows the New Zealand advance to Flers in the attack on 15 September. It then covers the later fighting to secure the Goose Alley Spur and the assaults on the Gird Trenches and the Circus.
> DISTANCE COVERED: **10 km**
> DURATION: **2 hours (driving); 4 hours (walking)**

From both Bapaume and Albert, the New Zealand battlefield at Flers is easily reached by taking the D929 to Pozières and turning there onto the D73, signposted Bazentin. Once through Bazentin, head left on the D20 for Longueval.

From the crossroads in the centre of **Longueval**, turn left onto the D197, direction Flers, by the **Pipers' Memorial**. The four-metre-high statue of a piper climbing over a sandbagged trench parapet commemorates the pipers of the wartime regiments that had them, and is located in Longueval because the village was captured by the 9th (Scottish) Division. On 15 September 1916, the four tanks supporting the New Zealand Division's attack started from the Y-junction 250 metres along the D197 and moved up the minor road straight ahead. This is North Street,

which you should take for 350 metres before parking by the **calvary** ① on the right.

Face the **New Zealand Memorial** ②, 800 metres away at the far end of North Street. In 1916 both North Street and the D197 ran through the western side of **Delville Wood**, to your right, whereas they skirt that side of it now. Repeatedly attacked since 14 July 1916, **High Wood**, 1.4 kilometres to your left front, was still largely in German hands when the New Zealanders began entering the line on 10 September. Looping from the wood, the British line ran around the re-entrant on your left to your location and across the front of Delville Wood. The New Zealanders' first task was to get closer to the German line, which followed the high ground on which the memorial stands, by pinching out this re-entrant. They did so over the next few nights by digging three trenches either side of North Street, 330 metres ahead of you, which halved the width of no-man's-land. **Auckland Trench** ran 400 metres from the right of North Street, **Fern Trench** 600 metres from the left of it, and **Otago Trench** ran 50 metres in front of Fern.

Noting the location of these trenches, drive to the New Zealand Memorial. The first of the New Zealand obelisk memorials to be constructed after the war, it was designed by Samuel Hurst Seager, the official architect of New Zealand battlefield memorials, and unveiled in October 1922 by Sir Francis Bell, leader of New Zealand's Legislative Council. A sign subsequently affixed to the memorial, which claims that the New Zealanders launched the successful attack on Flers, ignores the fact that Flers

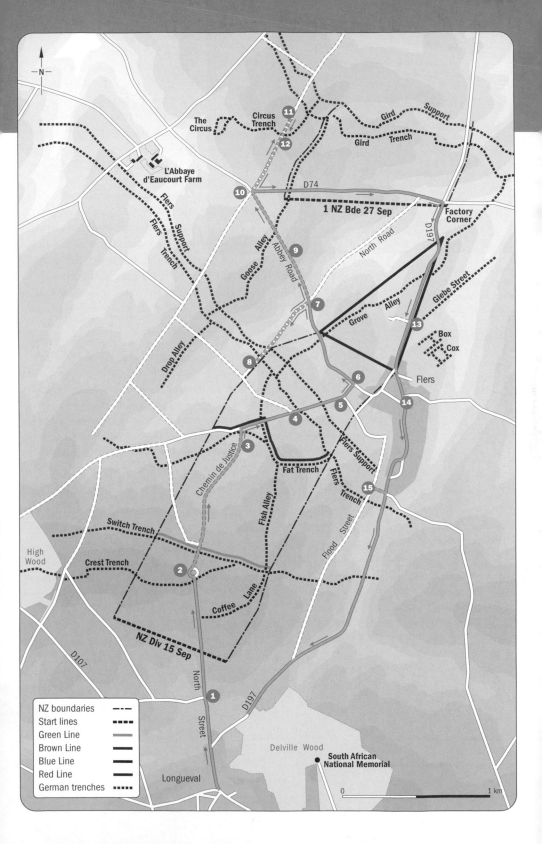

High Wood from Crest Trench, showing how the wood enfiladed the New Zealand advance.

Looking down North Street from Crest Trench at the start of the New Zealand Division's attack.

was outside the New Zealand boundary and the tanks and the 41st Division had the main role in capturing the village!

The ridge on which you are standing stretches from the Somme, through High Wood and the Pozières windmill, where it is called Pozières Ridge, to Thiepval. It was the most important terrain of the Somme campaign. To appreciate the edge it gave the Germans here, look at the view over the low ground, where the British line ran and from which you have come. The advanced trenches dug by the New Zealanders were still only halfway up the slope and 150 metres short of Coffee Lane, the German outpost trench, which ran around the slope from the left of North Street, 250 metres from your location. On the Crest itself, Crest Trench started near the right hand corner of

High Wood, crossed North Street just in front of you and curved back to the Switch Trench in your left rear.

North Street was NOT the centre line of the 2nd Brigade's attack on 15 September. Instead the axis ran diagonally across your front from Otago and Auckland Trenches. When the attack reached your location, 2nd Otago stretched 300 metres from your right and 100 metres over North Street, from where 2nd Auckland extended 500 metres to your left. The two battalions moved up the slope towards you, many of the Otagos singing, and twice betrayed their inexperience by stumbling into the creeping barrage. Thanks to the preliminary bombardment, which was more effective in the New Zealand Division's sector than anywhere else, the Aucklanders overran Coffee Lane and Crest Trench on your left. This trench had been heavily manned but the occupants were dispirited after their own guns had mistakenly shelled them earlier. Most of those in front of the Otagos fell victim to Lewis gunners or the barrage as they streamed back to the Switch Trench. A machine-gun crew 250 metres to your right did stay and fight, holding up the Otago's left flank until Sergeant Brown silenced it.

Look at High Wood on your right. After the 47th (London) Division's failure to take it, the German machine-guns there

swung onto the Otagos' left flank, which was in enfilade to them. Though casualties were again heavy, the Otagos struggled on to **Switch Trench**, as did the Aucklanders on their right. High Wood fell towards midday, the last of the major woods to be captured by the British on the Somme. To trace the line of the Switch, walk to the back of the memorial and look down the road. Emerging from High Wood midway along the right half of the wood as you look at it, the Switch crossed the road 150 metres ahead of you and ran on down to the D197 on your right. To the British on the other side of the crest, it was a classic reverse slope position. Unable to see the Switch from their line, they needed aerial observers to direct artillery fire onto it but bad weather often made for poor results. On the other hand, the Germans had excellent fields of fire from it up to the crest, against which any attack would be skylined. As it happened, the creeping barrage ahead of the New Zealanders softened the Switch up, ensuring its easy fall. Sergeant Brown again distinguished himself by knocking out a machine-gun in it 250 metres to your left front.

The Switch was the **Green Line**, the New Zealanders' first objective. They beheld from it a view as extensive as the one that unfolded before the Australians when they reached the Pozières windmill

six weeks earlier. Looking over it today, **Flers** is 1.8 kilometres to your right front, with **Gueudecourt** directly behind it. Flers was in the 41st Division's sector. Its boundary with the New Zealand Division paralleled the D197 to the left edge of Flers, where the water tower is a useful point of reference. Advancing on the left of the boundary, the New Zealanders were to cross the Brown Line, which stretched leftwards from the near side of Flers, and then the Blue and Red Lines, which did likewise on the far side. Flers and Flers Support Trenches, which comprised the German third line, ran into the village between the Brown and Blue Lines. Beyond Flers, the ground rises towards Bapaume. The New Zealand attack on 1 October and the Australian attacks in November were directed mainly at the Gird Trenches on the lower slope facing you, which screened other German lines further back.

Head down the road, known locally as Chemin de Justice, which follows its wartime course to meet the High Wood–Flers track at a **T-junction** ❸ in a shallow re-entrant one kilometre further on. Park and look back towards the New Zealand Memorial. Crossing the High Wood–Flers track 150 metres to your left, **Fish Alley** ran up the spur to the Switch, paralleling Chemin de Justice. The **Brown Line** began at the near divisional boundary 200 metres to your right and

NORTH STREET

FERN TRENCH

OTAGO TRENCH

ran through your location to Fish Alley, which it then followed for 350 metres before turning sharp left and extending 400 metres eastwards along **Fat Trench** to the far divisional boundary. Having taken over the advance at the Switch, 4th Rifles extended between the two boundaries and moved down the slope towards you, the creeping barrage hanging like a curtain before them. They had occupied the Brown Line by 7.50 am. The tanks were struggling to catch up, D8 on the track from the memorial and the others astride Fish Alley.

Now head right along the High Wood–Flers track and park after 300 metres at the **Quatre Voies junction** ④, where a track enters from the left. **Flers** and **Flers Support Trenches** paralleled it before crossing the road 100 metres and 270 metres ahead of you respectively to enter the southern end of Flers on your right. As these trenches comprised the German third line, General Russell knew they were well defended by barbed wire and machine-guns, whose long fields of fire become obvious once you look along the line the trenches followed. Had Russell drawn an objective line close to them, the attack would have struck the trenches at either the end of a long advance, when its momentum was flagging due to casualties and exhaustion, or soon after the assault began, when it lacked momentum. He wisely set the Brown Line sufficiently far forward of the trenches that the momentum of 2nd and 3rd Rifles, starting out for the **Blue Line** at 8.20 am, would be at its peak when they were reached. The Blue Line ran 350 metres behind Flers Support Trench from the far end of the village.

Stand with your back to the New Zealand Memorial. Encountering uncut wire before Flers Trench in the field to your left front, 3rd Rifles were unable to bomb their way forward even when reinforced by part of 1st Rifles. Fortunately the tanks had caught up. Tank D10 was knocked out while crossing Fat Trench behind you. Lumbering past it and through your location, 'Die Hard' flattened the wire and then machine-gunned Flers Trench before similarly dusting up Flers Support. Tank D8 did the same on your left, just beyond the junction of Chemin de Justice with the High Wood–Flers track, through which you have passed. Streaming through the breaches created, 3rd Rifles took 145 prisoners, and a small follow-up party from 4th Rifles another 100.

Head towards Flers for another 450 metres and park near the **track** ⑤ on the right where the road swings leftwards. Tank D12 was destroyed at the point where an imaginary line drawn along this track meets the village. Losing heavily in getting through the wire unaided, 2nd Rifles had found Flers Support, which crossed the road 80 metres behind you, empty, but took 80 prisoners in Flers Trench. Now walk to the junction with **Abbey Road**, today's **Chemin l'Abbaye** ⑥, at the water tower. Used sometimes now as a dumping ground for dud ordnance recovered from the fields,

The view from Switch Trench over the later stages of the New Zealand attack. The Red Line ran beyond the Blue Line.

BROWN LINE

GREEN LINE

the embankments along this stretch of Abbey Road were riddled with German dugouts. Again keep your back to the New Zealand Memorial. Seeing 2nd Rifles advancing on your left towards them, the dugout occupants fought doggedly and had to be prised out. Nonetheless the Blue Line, which extended from the end of the village and ran 200 metres to your front parallel to Abbey Road, was reached at 10 am. Left hanging when the remnants of the neighbouring 41st Division were shelled out of Flers, 2nd Rifles stretched over the other side of the village and into its sector.

Turn left onto Abbey Road, which eventually becomes unsealed, and park after 630 metres by the **pumping shed** ⑦ on the left, where North Road crosses over. Look back towards Flers. Tank D8 covered the Rifles from here as they dug in on the Blue Line, which ran from the village to the bend in Abbey Road 150 metres to your front. The Red Line met the Blue Line there and continued over the tip of the spur to your left front to the D197, with which it formed the apex of the triangular-shaped final objective, one kilometre away. Weathering heavy fire, 1st Rifles had by midday captured **Grove Alley**, which tracked 100 metres behind the Red Line to the D197, along with two field-guns. As the 47th Division was stuck in High Wood, to your right, and the 41st Division had not progressed beyond Flers, it is easy to appreciate how vulnerable 1st Rifles were. Harried from both sides and with a counterattack

looming across the D197, they withdrew to the Blue Line — under fire from the field-guns, which the Germans, bombing along Grove Alley, had recaptured. The 1st Wellingtons snatched Grove Alley back next day.

Leaving your car, head right on North Road, which cannot be driven. The high ground on your right is **Goose Alley Spur**, named after the communication trench that ran along its crest. Flers Support crossed the road 400 metres along, where the track cuts through a low spur, **Flers Trench** ⑧, after another 150 metres. Stop here and face right, looking along the line of the trench to Goose Alley Spur. The Flers Trenches there were in the 47th (London) Division's sector. By 18 September it had taken all but the 90-metre sections at the junction of Flers Support with Goose Alley and, in front of it, Flers Trench with Drop Alley. As long as the Germans held these junctions, they could enfilade the New Zealanders' flank and direct artillery onto their communications rearward. Bombing

FLERS

BLUE LINE

Captions for image 1:
DELVILLE WOOD
NEW ZEALAND MEMORIAL
HIGH WOOD

The Blue Line on Abbey Road looking back towards Switch Trench on the crest. This view vividly conveys the length of the New Zealanders' advance and how open it was.

up from the base of Goose Alley Spur ahead of you, 2nd Auckland, in conjunction with the Londoners attacking along the crest from your left front, took all but 30 metres of the junctions on 19 September. 2nd Canterbury rushed the Goose Alley junction next evening but the Black Watch could not hold the Drop Alley one. With the Germans now behind them and attacking down Goose Alley to their front, Captain Fred Starnes led repeated bombing attacks to keep the Cantabrians from being cut off. A Starnes-inspired bayonet charge on 21 September finally saw the Germans off. Recommended for a VC, Starnes received a DSO.

Return to your car and continue on Abbey Road up the side of the Goose Alley spur. Once through the cutting, park and walk back to the **crest ⑨**. Stand facing Flers across the re-entrant below you. L'Abbaye d'Eaucourt, to which the Germans back-pedalled after Starnes's

counterattack, is in the low ground to your left rear. The New Zealand Division's peripheral role in the Battle of Morval on 25 September involved the 1st Brigade advancing from Grove Alley, on the slope above the far side of the re-entrant, at 12.35 pm. The first objective ran along North Road below you to the D74 one kilometre to your left front, where a ruin can be discerned just to the left of **Factory Corner** at the D74/D197 intersection. Next, 1st Otago stormed through your location to take Goose Alley between its junction with Flers Support, 500 metres to your right, and Abbey Road, which it crossed on the slope to your left. Gueudecourt, in the trees on the skyline to the right of Factory Corner, also fell, securing the New Zealanders' right flank.

Now drive to the **five-way intersection ⑩**, where Abbey Road meets the D74, and park. **Gird Trench** ran along the spur ahead of you. From your

The attack on the Flers Trench/Drop Alley and Flers Support/Goose Alley junctions.

Captions for image 2:
GOOSE ALLEY SPUR
FLERS SUPPORT/GOOSE ALLEY
FLERS/DROP ALLEY

FLERS

The assault on Goose Alley
on 25 September.

previous location on Abbey Road, Goose Alley crossed the D74 and passed 250 metres to the right of the **track** that leaves the far side of the intersection. Walk up the track for 600 metres ⑪, where the hollow in which Goose Alley met Gird Trench is out of sight on the right. It came as a nasty surprise to 1st Otago, which had to take Goose Alley up to this junction to secure the left flank of the 1st Brigade's attack on the Gird Trenches between the hollow and the D197 above Factory Corner on 27 September.

Look towards the hollow. On reaching it after advancing from the D74 on your right, the Otagos' right flank made an easy target for the Germans at the junction in the hollow and in Gird Trench on either side, who were also protected by uncut wire. The Otagos took cover in the shell holes that pockmarked the slope on your right. The junction had held out. But the rest of Goose Alley had fallen to the Otagos, and 1st Auckland on their right had taken the Gird Trenches almost to the far side of the hollow. Next day the Otagos and some 1st Wellingtons entrenched across the slope to your right just below the hollow to link up with the Aucklanders.

On the way back to your car, stop after 150 metres ⑫. After leaving Gird Trench on the near side of the hollow on your left, **Circus Trench** crossed the track here and crabbed down the slope to the **Circus strongpoint** 350 metres to your

right front. In the lead-up to the attack on the Transloy Line, the 2nd Brigade advanced from the D74 diagonally over the slope to your left front at 3.15 pm on 1 October. The elusive Gird Trench/Goose Alley junction finally fell to 2nd Canterbury, which also captured Circus Trench up to your location and a German battalion commander to boot. On your right, 2nd Otago came under withering fire as it attacked the rest of Circus Trench and the Circus. Subsequently killed in this vicinity, the redoubtable Sergeant Brown silenced one of the deadliest machine-guns before both positions were captured. The 47th Division attacked L'Abbaye d'Eaucourt on the D74 to your right front but it held out for two more days. Before leaving, look back towards the New Zealand Memorial on the distant skyline. The New Zealanders' advance started there; it finished here.

Now head left on the D74 towards Factory Corner. The Gird Trenches, which were the 1st Brigade's main objective in the attack on 27 September, paralleled the road 400 metres to 600 metres to your left. The 1st Canterbury easily took them on the Factory Corner flank. In the attack two days earlier, it had captured a German artillery headquarters there. You should now turn right at Factory Corner onto the D197 for Flers.

The New Zealanders' Red Line for the opening attack on 15 September, whose other extremity you crossed on Abbey

L'ABBAYE D'EAUCOURT

CIRCUS

CIRCUS TRENCH

The attack on the Circus.

Road, met the D197 100 metres into the cutting that you almost immediately enter. This point was the apex of their triangular final objective, and the D197 from here to Flers was the boundary with the 41st Division. Grove Alley straddled the D197 near the other end of the cutting, 350 metres past which is a **track** ⓭ on the right. Park there, cross the road and walk back along it until the Cross of Sacrifice in **AIF Burial Ground, Grass Lane Cemetery** comes into view just to the right of the poplars. **Glebe Street** went diagonally from the track to the cemetery area. **Box** and **Cox Trenches** ran between Glebe Street and Flers, 300 metres away.

With 'Die Hard' standing sentinel on the D197 near your location, 2nd Rifles occupied Box and Cox to protect their right flank after the 41st Division pulled back through the village. The 1st Rifles reached your location but it was too exposed to hold. Advancing from the Blue Line at the edge of Flers through heavy fire on the other side of the D197, they subsequently took Grove Alley and two field-guns. But a counterattack along Glebe Street from the cemetery area threatened to cut them off and they had to withdraw. Attacking from Grove Alley towards you next day, the Germans were mown down by 1st Wellingtons and 'Die

Hard'. German dead littered the surrounding fields. The Wellingtons easily took Grove Alley between the D197 and Abbey Road.

Carry on to Flers. Just after the Wellingtons' attack started, 'Die Hard' was destroyed on the D197 100 metres short of the fork, where a chapel stands at the village entrance. The Blue Line ran at right angles to the fork for 1.2 kilometres to Abbey Road on your right. About 200 metres past the fork is the triangular **Place des Britanniques** ⓮, where the bronze figure of a fully equipped British soldier commemorates the 41st Division. It is one of the finest and best-known memorials on the Western Front. The soldier gazes intently north, the direction in which he and his comrades advanced behind 'Dinnaken' on the D197, 'the main street of Flers'.

On leaving Flers, you will reach a crossroads at a crucifix. Turn right and park after 100 metres at the **T-junction** ⓯. The road on your left, paralleling the D197, is Flood Street, along which Tanks D16 and D18 moved, while 'Dinnaken' forged along the D197 and another tank advanced on the far side of it. All four machines crashed through the wire of Flers Trench, which ran 50 metres in front of you. Now look across Flood Street into the New Zealand Division's sector.

The 'Tommy' in Flers.

Lieutenant Butcher was near the crest 400 metres ahead of you when he summoned Tank D12 to deal with a German outpost. Rifleman Dobson, who conveyed his message, later wrote: 'The Germans had a pop at me once, and I got into a shell hole, and waited and then got going again. I got inside the tank and guided it to where these machine guns were, in a farm building, and the tank just pushed it over. Germans scattered in all directions'. Now return to your car and follow the D197 to your start point at Longueval.

LOCAL INFORMATION

CEMETERIES

Caterpillar Valley Cemetery and New Zealand Memorial to the Missing

On the right of the D20, just before the intersection with the D107 at the entrance to Longueval, this cemetery overlooks Caterpillar Valley, captured in the major attack on 14 July 1916. It is the second largest of the Somme cemeteries with 5568 burials, of which 1773 are identified. In November 2004 the remains of an unknown New Zealander were exhumed from XIV.A.27 and re-interred in a stone-and-bronze tomb at the National War Memorial in Wellington in probably the largest commemorative event in New Zealand's history. One of the 9000 New Zealand fallen from all wars who have no known grave, the Unknown Warrior was selected from Caterpillar Valley as more New Zealand units fought in this area than anywhere else. The Caterpillar Valley (New Zealand) Memorial along the east (left) wall lists all 1205 New Zealand missing from the 1916 Somme battles. Some 214 New Zealanders rest in the cemetery, which also contains 98 Australians.

Bull's Road Cemetery

The 41st Division's Blue Line, which was the limit of its advance on 15 September, ran along the road that heads east from the Place des Britanniques. It was then called Bull's Road, and the eponymous cemetery is 500 metres along on the right. Of the 776 burials, 480 are unknown. Most of the 120 New Zealanders were brought in after the war from their division's sector on the other side of Flers. Many of the 148 Australians were wartime burials, reflecting their presence here over the winter of 1916–17.

Caterpillar Valley Cemetery and New Zealand Memorial to the Missing.

South African Memorial, Delville Wood.

Private Frank Thompson of the 9th Battalion in I.C.21 was killed on Christmas Day 1916. Sergeant Les Black of the 1st Battalion at I.B.30 was sniped on New Year's Day 1917.

NEARBY PLACES OF INTEREST

Delville Wood South African National Memorial

Attacking from Longueval as part of the 9th Scottish Division on 15 July 1916, the South African Brigade took most of the wood and held it for five days against attacks interspersed between bombardments that sometimes reached rates of over 400 shells per minute. Rain added to the ordeal. When the South Africans were relieved on 20 July, just 143 were left from the 3150 who had entered it. Delville Wood was not completely taken until 27 August. By then it was a surreal wilderness of charred stumps, waterlogged craters and pulped bodies.

Acorns from South Africa were used in the replanting, which more or less followed the wood's original outline. Grassy rides run the course of the prewar bridle paths; the names given to them on trench maps can be read on the stone markers at the intersections. As the ground was otherwise left as it was, innumerable trenches and shell holes can be seen in the undergrowth. Visibly peppered by shrapnel, a hornbeam near the Princes Street/Regent Street intersection is the only tree from the original wood to survive the war. Many of the dead from both sides still lie within the wood's 63 hectares, effectively making it a huge gravesite.

Unveiled in 1926, the South African National Memorial at the entrance to the wood now commemorates the 15 000 South Africans who fell in the Second World War and Korea as well as South Africa's 10 000 dead from the First World War. The museum behind it is open daily except on Mondays and French public holidays, and in December and January. Entry is free. The Visitor Centre includes a café, and a shop that sells artefacts. Just follow the signs on the D20 in Longueval.

CHAPTER 5

1916–17

SOMME: AUSTRALIANS AT FLERS AND GUEUDECOURT

Embittered by its first stint on the Somme, I ANZAC was dismayed at having to return there in November 1916. Having recuperated after Fromelles, the 5th Division went too. The line on their arrival was practically where it had been when the New Zealand Division left at the start of October, well beyond Flers but just past Gueudecourt. Charles Bean remarked that the fighting in which the Australians tried to advance further was 'undoubtedly the most difficult in which the AIF was ever engaged'; the conditions 'the worst ever known to the AIF'.

Back to the Somme

By the end of September 1916, the Fourth Army had gained a footing on the upward slope of the valley before Bapaume. On 2 October the autumn rains began in earnest, turning the valley into a swamp and blinding the artillery observers. The Germans had also strengthened their line. With the odds stacked so heavily against them, British assaults on 7, 12 and 18 October stalled. But General Haig had no intention of stopping, especially as the French did not halt their attacks. He insisted that their flank had to be protected and that a better winter line was needed. I ANZAC was among the formations Haig called upon to carry on the advance. But at least it would form part of

General Rawlinson's army rather than General Gough's.

Resting at Ypres, the Australians had been anticipating a quiet winter. When the orders for their return to the Somme arrived, Bean wrote, 'they all looked very serious — sturdy and solid, but not the least buoyancy about them'. I ANZAC began taking over the Flers–Gueudecourt area astride the D197/D10 to Ligny-Thilloy on 21 October. Marching towards it, the Australians beheld a sea of waterlogged shell holes that started well before the old Pozières battlefield. Passing by devastated Delville Wood, they followed the D197 through Gun Valley to the ruins of Flers and beyond. The mud was omnipresent and easily sucked the boots off those struggling through it. In the

Part of the Maze trenches in February 1917.

quagmires that passed for trenches, 'hands and faces protruded from the slimy, toppling walls. Knees, shoulders and buttocks poked from the foul morass', wrote Private Walter Downing of the 57th Battalion. 'There was no hot food, and no prospect of it… We did not sleep, but waited in a torpor as the minutes crawled past.'

Bayonet Trench and the Maze

After another attack on 23 October gained a few yards, the 5th Australian Division was earmarked for the next one on the 25th. Rain caused its post-ponement to 5 November, by which time the 1st and 2nd Divisions had the job. The 1st Battalion and bombers from the 3rd were to capture the salient formed by the junction of Bayonet and

Lard Trenches on the outskirts of Gueudecourt. From this point, Bayonet Trench ran west for 1.5 kilometres to a knot of trenches called the Maze. In the main attack, the 7th Brigade would strike the Maze on the right of the British 50th (Northumbrian) Division, which was to assault the Butte de Warlencourt on the D929.

Drenched by shrapnel, the 1st Battalion got to Bayonet Trench. The wire was uncut. Most men bolted, forcing the 3rd Battalion's bombers to withdraw from Lard Trench. The 7th Brigade's attack was a worse fiasco. Lieutenant-Colonel James Walker had held the 25th Battalion back to wait for rations. The one company to arrive in time joined the composite battalion formed to take the place of the 25th by robbing the other assault battalions of their reserve companies.

A timings mix-up caused the attack to start after the creeping barrage, enabling the Germans to fire with impunity. Part of the Maze, and Bayonet Trench alongside, were momentarily entered. The 50th Division's attack on the Butte also failed.

On 14 November the 5th Brigade attacked the Maze. After languishing in the ooze for nine days, it was in such a poor state that the 25th and 26th Battalions had to be borrowed from the 7th Brigade. Barely recovered from their assault on 5 November, they floundered in the mud of no-man's-land under withering fire. On the left of the Maze, the 19th Battalion and some Northumbrians took part of Gird Trench. Ordered to help the 19th by renewing their assaults, Walker and Lieutenant-Colonel George Ferguson of the 26th Battalion dithered for two days. The Germans counterattacked and regained their line. Walker and Ferguson were relieved.

Winter

On 18 November Haig closed the Somme offensive down. I ANZAC's assaults in this last phase, which were just as futile as those before Mouquet Farm and no different in outcome, cost it 2000 men. Though serious action had now ceased, the harshest French winter in 40 years saw temperatures plummet to minus 15 degrees Celsius, ensuring that conditions for the Australians in front of Flers and Gueudecourt remained awful.

Private Alfred Binskin of the 24th Battalion saw one man die at his post. Another man shot himself rather than return to the trenches. Still another deserted to the Germans. Malingering increased. The digging of dugouts had to

A working party from the 16th Battalion tries to make a section of Gird Trench habitable during the Somme winter.

Lieutenant-Colonel Henry ('Harry') William Murray

Stormy Trench was his battle

1880–1966

A prewar timber cutter, Tasmanian-born Murray enlisted in the AIF in October 1914 and became a machine-gunner in the 16th Battalion. During the Gallipoli campaign, Murray won the DCM, was twice wounded, and transferred to the 13th Battalion on being commissioned. Awarded the DSO for his audacious leadership at Mouquet Farm in August 1916, he followed up his VC at Stormy Trench with a second DSO for his actions in the 4th Brigade's attack at Bullecourt in April 1917. As a lieutenant-colonel in May 1918, Murray took over the 4th Machine-Gun Battalion. He received the French Croix de Guerre and was appointed CMG before the war's end.

Murray remains the most decorated of all Australian servicemen, and is usually considered to be the most highly decorated infantryman of the British and Empire armies in the First World War. A born leader, he was tactically astute and had a shrewd eye for ground. Like his great contemporary Albert Jacka, Murray could sum up a situation and come up with the appropriate action almost instinctively. Every risk he took was calculated, which belied his nickname 'Mad Harry'. Yet Murray did not possess Jacka's seeming indifference to fear. In his postwar writings, he claimed to be a nervy and highly strung man who owed his unshakeable resolve to the power of discipline. It is hard to disagree with Bean's assessment of him as 'the most distinguished fighting officer in the AIF'.

Murray became a Queensland grazier after the war and remained on the land, except during his service in the Second World War, when he commanded the 26th Battalion in North Queensland until April 1942, and then his local Volunteer Defence Corps battalion until August 1944. He died after a car accident in January 1966.

be forbidden after several men were smothered when the slimy trench walls collapsed. Trench foot, a form of frostbite that sometimes resulted in gangrene and amputation, became rampant. Covering the few kilometres to the line took all night, with numerous slides off the slippery tracks into the shell holes. Stuck in the mud, men drowned or died of exposure unless found by rescue teams, who often had to use mules and ropes to haul them out. Losing a pair of boots and trousers was the best result; a broken back the worst. Several relays of

stretcher-bearers were needed to evacuate the wounded. Brigadier-General Duncan Glasfurd of the 12th Brigade died in the 10 hours it took to get him back. Morale plunged.

Gradually conditions improved. With the offensive over, the priority for transport switched to engineering materials. Timber and iron for dry standing, revetting and dugouts reached the trenches in quantity. Thanks to Brigadier-General Brudenell White, I ANZAC's chief-of staff, battalions received hot food there and returned to

An Australian intelligence officer searches prisoners taken by the 13th Battalion during the capture of Stormy Trench.

warm hutments once relieved. The ground froze over with the New Year frosts, ending the misery caused by the mud. Morale rose.

Gueudecourt

A small success kicked off the fighting in 1917. Haig had agreed with the French to renew the Somme offensive when the weather improved in spring. Rawlinson called for a more aggressive policy on the Fourth Army's part beforehand. On 1 February the 15th Battalion took Stormy Trench just outside Gueudecourt. But weak artillery support, and a crushing German barrage that precluded a resupply of bombs, forced its withdrawal. Attacking three nights later, the 13th Battalion took no chances. Every man

carried six bombs, carriers with 480 more followed each company and another 20 000 bombs were stockpiled well forward.

This time the barrage was perfect. The Germans were ejected from 350 metres of Stormy Trench but shelled and counterattacked it repeatedly. The 13th's bomb supply never faltered. Captain Murray's company held the open right flank, where the struggle was the most intense he ever experienced. Stricken with influenza, he had told the doctor, 'I'm going to take Stormy Trench, and what's more, I'm going to keep it'. Murray kept his word but of the 140 who attacked with him, 48 remained. He was awarded the VC for his inspirational leadership.

DRIVING/WALKING THE BATTLEFIELD

Like the New Zealand battlefield at Flers, the Australian one can be walked or driven. Walking it or driving it, always remember the atrocious conditions that prevailed. Never mind the Germans, simply enduring on this battlefield took all of a man's reserves of willpower and grit. Flers reduced the infantryman's traditional role of dominating the enemy irrespective of weather or terrain to a counsel of perfection.

MAPS IGN Blue Series, 1:25 000, 2407E Bapaume; 2408E Bray-sur-Somme

From both Bapaume and Albert, take the D929 to Pozières and turn there onto the D73, signposted Bazentin. Once through Bazentin, head left on the D20 and, on reaching Longueval, turn left at the crossroads by the Pipers' Memorial onto the D197 for Flers.

Flers was in ruins and frequently shelled but the Australians used its cellars during the winter for headquarters and to accommodate reserve units. Knocked-out tanks littered the surrounding fields. Leave the village on the D197 and turn left after 1.2 kilometres onto the D74 at the crossroads. The sugar factory that once stood at this location gave the crossroads its nickname of **Factory**

The German view from Gird Trench of the slope up which the Australian attacks in November came. The crest on the far side of the valley had been captured on 15 September.

Corner. As you continue on the D74, the **Gird Trenches** paralleled it on the higher ground 400 metres to 600 metres to your right. At the L'Abbaye d'Eaucourt crossroads, turn right onto the partly sunken road, shown on trench maps as **Blue Cut**, and park after 850 metres beside the **steel post 1** on the right.

Look back the way you have come. **High Wood** is on the skyline to your front, with **Delville Wood** to its left. The spire of **Flers church** is visible to the left of Delville Wood; the spire of **Gueudecourt church** on the skyline to your left. Heavy rain from the start of October turned the valley to your front, which the Fourth Army crossed in the preceding fortnight, into a sea of mud. The Australian infantry, whose soaked equipment already felt 'like the load of Atlas' trudged forward through it in sodden greatcoats weighing 18 kilograms. In the trenches, both sides sometimes had no option but to climb onto the parapets and stand looking at each other. The Germans in the village of **Le Barque**, 1.2 kilometres along Blue Cut behind you, used the road to enter **Gird Trench**, which ran from your half left across the slightly higher ground. Crossing Blue Cut at your location, it tracked to your right to the **Butte de Warlencourt**, the treed hillock just this side of Le Sars on the ubiquitous

DELVILLE WOOD

NEW ZEALAND MEMORIA

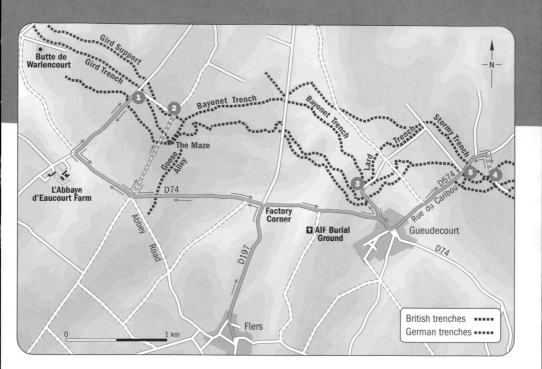

British trenches ·····
German trenches ·····

D929. As their line crossed Blue Cut 150 metres ahead of you, the Australians had to attack uphill through the bog.

Advancing towards you at 6.45 am on 14 November, the 19th Battalion stretched 200 metres into the field on your left. In order to avoid falling behind the barrage in the mud, it had left its trenches early and arrived at Gird Trench 'with the last shell'. Catching three Germans scurrying from a dugout close to where you are standing, Sergeant Perce Jones shot two and bayoneted the third. Many more bolted down Blue Cut towards Le Barque. Together with the Northumbrian Territorials of the 50th Division on your right, the 19th Battalion

Starting from Flers, this walk/drive goes to the sites of the Gird Trenches and the Maze at one end of the line held by the Australians in winter 1916 and passes through Gueudecourt to the Bayonet/Lard Trench junction at the other. It concludes in the area of Stormy Trench.
DISTANCE COVERED: **8 km**
DURATION: **2 hours driving; 3.5 hours walking**

seized 450 metres of Gird Trench and occupied **Gird Support**, 200 metres behind you. Of the 25th and 26th Battalions, which should have been alongside the 19th further to your left, nothing was seen. The next day, the 19th was using captured German rifles and ammunition to hold on. On 16 November a counterattack from your right rear drove

HIGH WOOD

GUEUDECOURT

AREA OF THE MAZE

BAYONET TRENCH

GIRD TRENCH

The area of the Maze, Bayonet and Gird Trenches.

in the British. The 19th responded with a bayonet charge to your right across the open, which failed. It had to withdraw.

Return to the D74 and head left towards Factory Corner, stopping after 700 metres at the five-way intersection. Leave your car on the farm track that you will be taking up the slope on your left as it is not driveable. Walk 700 metres to the end of the **track 2**, where you can clearly see Le Barque to your front, and turn about. The formidable **Gird Trench/ Goose Alley** junction captured by the New Zealanders on 1 October was in the hollow 250 metres to your left front. They had already taken the Gird Trenches between there and the D197 above Factory Corner, and the 55th Division had captured them on the other side of the D197. In the faint hollow 250 metres to your left front and at the apex of a sharp salient that projected towards the Australian line, but hidden by the curve

of the slope, was the **Maze**. It connected the uncaptured part of the Gird Trenches, which ran rightwards from here to your previous location, to **Bayonet Trench**. In turn, Bayonet Trench ran almost to Gueudecourt on your left.

On 14 November the 25th and 26th Battalions assaulted from your right and left front respectively. Caught by a German bombardment, they were also 'chopped about by our own artillery fire, which was falling fearfully short', wrote Corporal Peter Gaffney of the 26th, 'and the Hun fairly mowed them down with m. gun fire and shells'. Though they had no need to, the Germans charged. Both battalions were repulsed. The 20th Battalion, which had been loaned to the 26th, renewed the attack on the Maze and Bayonet Trench on your left during the afternoon but was cut down. Another attempt by the 25th Battalion against Gird Trench on your right never got going.

1ST BATTALION

BAYONET TRENCH

On 15 November Gird Trench was found to be empty but inept Australian command procedures and the deep mud delayed its occupation. The Germans got in first, quickly installing a post on your left.

The 7th Brigade had also attacked here in a raging gale at 9.30 am on 5 November. Owing to command lapses and poor communications, the 25th Battalion arrived late and the other battalions were not in position when the barrage lifted. As they arose 150 metres to 200 metres ahead of you, the barrage was already well behind you. The Maze was unscathed as it had been wrongly marked on the artillery maps. From Blue Cut through your location to the Maze and beyond, the Germans crowded their parapet, and many clambered onto it, to mow the advancing Australians down. The British attack beyond Blue Cut had failed, so the Germans there poured enfilade fire across your front too. 'We couldn't hear ourselves speak for the crackle of the machine-guns and the whistling of the bullets', said Private Bob Mann of the 25th Battalion. Mann 'looked around to see how the rest of them were getting on. There wasn't anybody on their feet'. Part of the 27th Battalion managed to enter Bayonet Trench 400 metres to your left but was soon driven out.

Now continue along the D74 beyond Factory Corner for 1.2 kilometres and turn hard left at the entrance to **Gueudecourt**. Follow this road, which soon becomes sunken, for 300 metres to a sharp rightwards bend, and park by the **track 3** that heads up the side of the bank on the left. Walk to the top of the bank, where Bayonet Trench joined **Lard Trench**. From there, Bayonet Trench followed the crest of the spur for 300 metres before swinging behind the captured part of the Gird Trenches to the Maze. Now face the sunken road. Running atop the bank on your left for 150 metres and then along the left of the road, Lard Trench crossed the re-entrant and ran to the top of the spur to your left front, where it cut right to the copse around the **Newfoundland Memorial Park** on the skyline directly ahead. You are therefore at the apex of the acute salient formed by the junction of Bayonet and Lard Trenches. The dead from three unsuccessful British attacks against it thickened the wire entanglements atop the bank.

The 1st Brigade delivered the fourth attack on the salient at 12.30 am on 5 November from trenches that arced around it at distances ranging from 100 metres to 250 metres. Advancing up the sunken road on your right in monsoonal rain, a bombing party from the 1st Battalion was annihilated by a machine-gun post that guarded the apex at your location. But three bombing parties from the 3rd Battalion scrambled up the bank and through the wire to seize about 100 metres of Lard Trench on your left. They were digging a trench

Bayonet and Lard Trenches.

back to the Australian line in the low ground to your front when a withdrawal order arrived, for the 1st Battalion's attack on Bayonet Trench behind you had failed. No live Germans were to be left behind in Lard Trench. 'We had just got away', Sergeant Arthur Matthews wrote, 'when we heard the awful screams of the men who were being slaughtered through military necessity'.

To follow the 1st Battalion's attack, turn about so that the sunken road is behind you. The 1st's line was over the rise ahead but it had scooped out a jump-off trench nearer the crest to reduce the width of no-man's-land before Bayonet Trench, over which you are now looking. Seeing the move into the jump-off trench, the Germans deluged no-man's-land with shrapnel, making it impossible to leave the trench to form up. Expecting the trench to be vacant, the supporting waves found the leading waves still in it. They bridged the top with their bodies to make room for the supports underneath. The need to stay in the jump-off trench allowed the creeping barrage to get away. Given plenty of time to get ready, the Germans cut down the 1st Battalion as it came over the rise towards you. The slope in front of you was covered with wounded and dead, who sank slowly into the mud. Only a few men cleared the wire.

Return to your car and enter Gueudecourt. During the winter, the Germans lobbed a 5.9-inch shell into its ruins every minute to prevent the Australians using the dugouts and cellars. At the crossroads in the village centre,

turn left onto the D574 and park by the farm track on the right 100 metres past the Newfoundland Memorial. Walk 200 metres along the **track 4** and look straight ahead. **Stormy Trench** ran diagonally through this location from your left front. It was taken by the 13th Battalion, which advanced behind an arrow-straight barrage across a snow-covered no-man's-land from **Shine Trench**, 250 metres to your front, on 4 February 1917. You are standing on the **open right flank**, where Captain Murray's company attacked.

Leading his men through the wire and finding Stormy Trench almost empty, Murray deployed them either side of you. Unwilling to get caught up in the tangle of old saps into which the trench ran, he established a barricade in it about 50 metres to your left. The first counterattack struck the barricade soon afterwards. It was repulsed. So were two more. Murray often took his men onto the parapet, from where they bombed the Germans or raced across the open to bayonet them. When they got into the trench on your side of the barricade, he shot three and captured three while leading the rush that forced them out. His uniform shot through, Murray then carried three wounded men to safety.

Return to your car and drive back to the **Newfoundland Memorial 5**. One of the five caribou memorials, it commemorates the capture of this area by the Newfoundlanders on 12 October 1916. From here, return to Longueval on the D574/D74 and thence to Albert or Bapaume.

Stormy Trench from the Newfoundland Memorial.

STORMY TRENCH

← 13TH BATTALION

LOCAL INFORMATION

CEMETERIES

AIF Burial Ground, Grass Lane, Flers

Signposted from the D74 roughly halfway between Gueudecourt and Factory Corner, this cemetery lies 100 metres down a track that was known in 1916 as Grass Lane. The only military cemetery to have the acronym AIF in its title, it was set up in November by Australian medical units working in the nearby chalk caves. Expanded by the concentration of burials from other cemeteries postwar, its 3475 graves include 417 Australians and 80 New Zealanders. Many of the Australians fell in the Flers fighting, 2nd Lieutenant Fred Matthews DCM of the 6th Machine-Gun Company at X.L.2 among them. Matthews died on 8 November 1916. Along with his brothers, Henry and Arthur, he was manning a machine-gun in the Armentières nursery on 4 July 1916 when the Germans launched a raid. His brothers were killed but Fred broke up the raiders by firing over 1000 rounds at them.

Thistle Dump Cemetery, High Wood, Longueval

Begun in August 1916 and used for the next six months, Thistle Dump Cemetery was expanded post-armistice by the addition of 56 graves. Of its 192 burials, 36 are Australian. Major Ivan Sherbon of the 19th Battalion, who had won the MC at Pozières, was killed while deploying his company for the 14 November attack at Flers. He rests at E.4. The cemetery is on the D20 halfway between Bazentin and Longueval.

AIF Burial Ground, Grass Lane.

Grave of 2nd Lieutenant Matthews DCM.

Grave of Sergeant Brown VC, Warlencourt British Cemetery.

Warlencourt British Cemetery

On the D929 seven kilometres from Pozières, this cemetery was made in late 1919 by concentrating burials from the small cemeteries and grave sites that dotted the battlefields of the closing stages of the Somme offensive. There are 3505 graves but the most graves moved from a single location was 17. Most of the 477 Australians, 138 of them unknown, were killed in the November 1916 fighting or during the winter. Resting at VI.A.25, 2nd Lieutenant William Healy MC had led the 25th Battalion in the 4 August attack at Pozières after all the other officers became casualties. He fell on 14 November. 2nd Lieutenant

> *That ghastly hill, never free from the smoke of bursting shells, became fabulous. It shone white in the night and seemed to leer at you like an ogre in a fairy tale. It loomed up unexpectedly, peering into trenches where you thought you were safe; it haunted your dreams. Twenty-four hours in the trenches before the Butte finished a man off.*
>
> Carrington, C, *A Subaltern's War*, London, 1929, p. 117

William McMullen at III.A.7 and Lance-Sergeant Abel Skinner at II.B.30, both of the 25th Battalion, and Corporal Leslie Sneyd of the 27th Battalion at II.E.32, had all won the DCM at Pozières. They died on 5 November. The 79 New Zealanders include Sergeant Donald Brown VC of the Otago Regiment, who fell in the New Zealand Division's final attack on the Somme, on 1 October 1916. He rests at III.F.11.

NEARBY PLACES OF INTEREST

Butte de Warlencourt

Charles Carrington was a subaltern in the Royal Warwickshires. His description of the Butte is as well known as the Butte itself was notorious. An ancient burial ground of excavated chalk that commanded the D929, it was riddled with dugouts and trenches, and girded by rows of wire, all of which enabled the Butte to exert the same demoralising grip on the minds of the British soldiers huddled in its shadow as Monte Cassino did in the next war. Repeatedly attacked, the closest it came to falling was during the 50th Division's assault on 5 November 1916. A strong counterattack drove the Northumbrians from the foothold they had gained and the Butte remained uncaptured until the Germans abandoned it on 24 February 1917.

Steps lead to the crest but dense vegetation obscures the views its German defenders beheld. The Butte now belongs to the Western Front Association, whose plaque and a French sign at the foot both state that the Butte marks the limit of the British advance on the Somme in 1916. It is located on the right of the D929 six kilometres from Pozières and 500 metres past Le Sars.

The Butte de Warlencourt in 1919.

CHAPTER 6

1917

AUSTRALIAN ADVANCE, GERMAN COUNTERATTACK

If 1917 had begun well for the Australians on the battlefield, there were plenty of surprises for them off it. The command of three of I ANZAC's four divisions changed hands, with Major-Generals Smythe VC, Holmes and Hobbs taking over the 2nd, 4th and 5th Divisions respectively from Legge, Cox and McCay. Then, to their dismay, the Australians returned to General Gough's army, now titled the Fifth Army. But it was not to be for a renewal of the Somme offensive as they had expected. The French had decided on a massive offensive in April on the Chemin des Dames instead and wanted Field Marshal Haig to carry out supporting attacks at Arras. In the biggest surprise of all, the Germans, seeking to conserve their overstretched resources, reduced their front by almost 50 kilometres by withdrawing up to 50 kilometres to the pre-prepared Hindenburg Line at the end of February.

Following up the Germans on I ANZAC's front, the Australians were able to engage for the first time in their experience in the open warfare for which they had trained in Egypt both before and after the Gallipoli campaign. The exhilaration that attended the advance in those few weeks went a long way towards purging the lingering ills of the Somme campaign and the winter months.

They've gone!

Before the First and Third Armies struck at Arras, the Fifth Army was to thrust north-eastwards to draw the Germans away from them. I ANZAC was gearing up to begin its part in the advance with renewed assaults on the Maze, and Gird and Bayonet Trenches, when the Germans retired on Bapaume on 23 February 1917. Suspecting that they might be luring him forward with a view to counterattacking, and not wanting to disrupt preparations for the Arras offensive, Haig ordered a cautious advance.

The 2nd Australian Division easily took Gird and Bayonet Trenches, and Warlencourt beyond them, on 25 February as the Germans had fallen back on R1 and R2, their first and second lines before Bapaume. On 26 February the outpost line in front of R1 was captured, apart from Malt Trench on the left. Running into the Loupart Bastion, a spur shielding the Loupart Wood sector of R1 on the heights west of Bapaume, it was strongly held. Assaults by the 5th and 6th Brigades failed. The gunners took over, creating enough gaps in the wire for the 5th and 7th Brigades on 2 March to swarm into Malt Trench and carry on to the Loupart Bastion.

Having advanced five kilometres, I ANZAC now closed up on R1. Gough intended to attack it on 13 March, allowing time for another thorough bombardment. The Germans left the day before. Thick smoke rising from Bapaume and a spike in train movements eastwards suggested that their withdrawal was continuing to the Hindenburg Line. On 17 March Australian patrols found R2 empty. Shortly afterwards the 30th Battalion was chasing the Germans though Bapaume. 'Fritz waits until we are ready to have a go and then clears out', wrote Captain William Braithwaite of the 22nd Battalion. Braithwaite was acknowledging the reality of the withdrawal. The Germans were pulling back in their own time and slowing down their pursuers by cratering roads and leaving a web of booby traps.

Chasing Fritz

Still fearing a counterattack, Haig wanted every chance of maintaining pressure on the Germans taken but only if minimum forces could be used. Subject to these constraints, the Fifth Army was to close on the Hindenburg Line. Gough saw that by breaching it in the Bullecourt-Quéant area, 13 kilometres off, he could swing northward against the German flank while the Germans were fending off the Third Army at Arras. He told each of his forward divisions to furnish all-arms columns as advance guards to clear the way.

Chosen because of their strong leadership, Brigadiers-General Charles Gellibrand and 'Pompey' Elliott led the columns from the 2nd and 5th Australian Divisions respectively. Each had his own brigade, the 6th under Gellibrand and the 15th under Elliott, augmented by an artillery battery and some light horse for scouting. The green Bapaume plateau stretched ahead, blighted only by R3, behind which the German rearguards tried to impose as much delay as possible from villages that were more strongly held as the Hindenburg Line was reached. Early on 18 March the two columns headed out from Bapaume on an eight-kilometre front, Elliott's astride the D930, the Bapaume–Cambrai road, Gellibrand's on his left.

Moving across open country after over two years in the trenches initially took

Privates Charles Marsh (left) and Leo Dixon (right) of the 30th Battalion move through the smoking ruins of Bapaume on the morning of 17 March. The Germans wrecked the town to prevent its use for billeting.

some getting used to. Elliott had inculcated in his brigade the tactics of envelopment but they were forgotten in the rather clumsy capture of Frémicourt, the first village in its path. Things got back on track a few hours later when the Germans at Delsaux Farm in front of R3 were properly enveloped and had to withdraw. Next day, the Germans were manoeuvred out of Beugny, Lebucquière, Vélu and Vélu Wood. On 20 March the 60th Battalion reached Beaumetz and the 59th took Morchies. Having raced five kilometres past the British on its right, Elliot's column now faced Doignies, Louverval and Hermies, 'outpost' villages of the Hindenburg Line. General Hobbs ordered it to halt.

Capitalising on the pause, the Germans nearly recaptured Beaumetz on 23 March. Hollering 'I'll teach the bastards to attack me', Elliott ordered an assault on Doignies and Louverval but without telling Hobbs as it would contravene his halt order. Hobbs found out anyway and cancelled the assault. Next morning the Germans had another go at Beaumetz and failed again. Elliott also took Bertincourt because it enfiladed his flank and the British, who should have taken it, had fallen behind. When a British cavalry patrol turned up, Elliott considered it too weak to hold the village and refused to go. General Birdwood reprimanded him.

Gellibrand also ran foul of Birdwood. Finding R3 abandoned, his column took Vaulx-Vraucourt. Learning that villages behind the Hindenburg Line were burning, which suggested that the Germans might even be withdrawing further, Gough wanted the columns to advance rapidly. But Brudenell White urged caution. Upset with the progress made on 19 March, Gough told Birdwood that he hoped the outpost villages of Noreuil and Lagnicourt would be occupied next day. Poor staff work saw this message passed on unchanged to Gellibrand, who thought it superseded White's instructions. At 12.50 am on 20 March, with snow falling, he ordered the 21st and 23rd Battalions to envelop Noreuil, 2.5 kilometres away, at 3 am. Neither battalion had a chance to reconnoitre, and both were dead beat after two days on the move. Birdwood blamed Gellibrand for the ensuing fiasco but was not blameless himself. Gellibrand estimated that 150 Germans with several machine-guns were in Noreuil rather than the few snipers originally thought.

Beaumetz from Vélu, showing how close some of the villages captured during the advance were to each other.

Brigadier-General Harold Edward Elliott

Commander, 15th Brigade, 1916–18

1878–1931

Nicknamed 'Pompey', Elliott had a huge frame and a matching personality. He was also an outstanding soldier and leader. No Australian general got more out of his men. But he was temperamentally flawed.

On Gallipoli, Elliott commanded the 7th Battalion, which won four of the seven VCs awarded for Lone Pine. On the Western Front, he led the 15th Brigade in most of the AIF's great battles. His finest hour was probably at Polygon Wood in September 1917, when he had to redeploy his brigade rapidly to secure its flank after the Germans struck the neighbouring British division just before a major attack. The 15th went on to take the British division's objective in the attack as well as its own. During the war, Elliott, who had won the DCM in the Boer War, was awarded the DSO and appointed CB and CMG.

Yet Elliott's lack of self-control undid much of his good work. Hobbs dismissed his proposed 'private' retaliatory attack at Doignies and Louverval as an instance of Elliott's impetuosity. After Polygon Wood, Elliott wrote an inflammatory report on the British, largely in ignorance of their situation. Birdwood had all copies destroyed. During the German offensive in March 1918, Elliott ordered the shooting of British stragglers who refused to stop. Hobbs quickly countermanded the order. No doubt Elliott's mercurial nature led to his being overlooked for divisional command in May 1918. It was a tremendous personal blow that developed into an obsession. As a senator in Canberra during the postwar decade, Elliott used his position to air his grievance and seek redress. He was unsuccessful and committed suicide in March 1931.

Taking the outpost villages

Gough now directed that the outpost villages would be attacked only after thorough preparation. Those in I ANZAC's path were ringed with trenches and wire, and linked by a series of strong posts, often dug into the banks of the sunken roads between the villages, rather than continuous trenches. Lacking the punch necessary for this second phase of the advance, the columns were dispensed with. The 7th Brigade attacked Lagnicourt behind a creeping barrage before dawn on 26 March. While the 27th Battalion secured the spur between Noreuil and Lagnicourt, part of the 26th Battalion struck Lagnicourt frontally and the rest enveloped it. Counterattacking mid-morning, the Germans seemed set to regain Lagnicourt but their morale suddenly slumped and they retired.

On 2 April the 13th Brigade from the 4th Division carried out a dawn envelopment of Noreuil. The 50th and 51st Battalions were to meet beyond the village, which lay in a valley. Advancing along the northern slopes, the 51st stumbled onto an unmarked trench, where it remained on being engaged from Noreuil in its rear. Striking the southern side of the village, the 50th ran into posts missed by the barrage. They slowed progress to a crawl until Private Joergen Jensen charged one and forced it to surrender. His action, which earned a VC, enabled the left of the 50th Battalion to move through Noreuil to meet the 51st in the unmarked trench. But the parties set aside to mop up Noreuil were too weak. The Germans left in the village took them prisoner. Counterattacks overran the right of the 50th and only the timely arrival of reserves saved the unmarked trench from the same fate.

Concurrently with the 13th Brigade's attack, the 14th Brigade took Louverval and Doignies, either side of the D930 several kilometres away, in another predawn envelopment. Both villages were heavily wired, though much of the 800-metre gap between them was not. Dispensing with a barrage to ensure surprise, the 56th Battalion was to swing around the northern side of Louverval and its adjacent wood, while the 55th following entered the gap and went around the northern side of Doignies. Each village could then be taken from the rear. The Germans in Doignies bolted. Those in Louverval blew two mines to create an obstacle; the felled trees of Louverval Wood were an even bigger one. Perhaps none of this would have mattered had the 56th Battalion gone around the village and the wood as intended but its commanding officer, Lieutenant-Colonel Humphrey Scott, apparently changed his mind and ordered an advance through them. Only when the original plan was reverted to did the village fall.

On 5 April the 49th Battalion reached the embankment west of Bullecourt, along which the Boisleux–Marquion railway ran parallel to the Hindenburg Line 900 metres away. The 1st Division took over the entire Australian front on 6 April, the 3rd Brigade deploying on the left of the D930 and the 1st Brigade on the right. Facing them were the last three villages before the Hindenburg Line: Boursies on the D930, Hermies three kilometres south of it and Demicourt in between. Their capture on 9 April was intended as a feint to divert German attention from the opening of the Arras offensive. A heavily flagged attack on Boursies the day before would, in turn, divert the German gaze from Hermies, so

that the attack on it came as a surprise. Once both villages had fallen, the Germans were expected to abandon Demicourt.

Early on 8 April, the 10th Battalion charged across the valley below Louverval Wood towards the Boursies Spur one kilometre away, on which lay Boursies. Though there was no barrage to alert the Germans, they saw the movement and quickly halted it. Next to the 10th, the left of the 12th Battalion stalled between the wood and the D930 but the right, under Captain James Newland, braved torrential fire to take a ruined mill on the outskirts of Boursies. Continuous counterattacks against the mill peaked at 10 pm and Newland's men wavered. He and Sergeant Percy Whittle rallied them.

The 2nd Battalion's assault on Hermies was to have gone in at 3.30 am on 9 April but started early when a haystack ignited by a German flare lit up the attackers. On reaching the village, the left company hooked around the eastern side to cut the village off. As the rest of the 2nd started through the village, the right company was pinned down on the western side. It was saved by the arrival of the centre companies and the advance of the 3rd Battalion. By 6 am German resistance had collapsed and both battalions had linked up. Watching Demicourt, the 1st Battalion reported at 6.10 am that the Germans appeared to be withdrawing. Those in the village were pulling out to escape some Australian shelling; those on the outskirts stood fast and they held up the 1st Battalion's advance. Patrols worked their way into the village. At noon the Germans were discovered to have left. Lasting three weeks and costing I ANZAC over 2500 casualties, the open warfare interlude had ended.

The German counterattack

Though the fighting now moved to Bullecourt, it did return briefly to the

The ruins of Hermies.

outpost villages when the Australians, who had attacked almost nonstop since their arrival on the Western Front a year earlier, were themselves heavily attacked. Heeding Haig's order to conserve forces during the advance to the Hindenburg Line, Gough had proceeded with three divisions spread over an 18-kilometre frontage. On reaching it, the 4th Australian and the 62nd Divisions were concentrated onto a six-kilometre stretch to attack Bullecourt on the Fifth Army's left, which required the 1st Australian Division to hold the 11 kilometres between Lagnicourt and Hermies on its right.

After the 4th Division was shattered at Bullecourt on 11 April, the 1st pushed to within one kilometre of the Hindenburg Line to mislead the Germans into thinking that Gough would next attack on its front rather than at Bullecourt again. This advance increased the 1st Division's frontage to 12 kilometres. Its front line was therefore eggshell thin, comprising a string of sentry posts ahead of half-platoon piquets over 300 metres

apart. These forward positions could rarely be seen by the support platoons up to 800 metres rearwards. Themselves one kilometre apart, the support platoons were invisible to each other. The supporting artillery was packed into the Noreuil and Lagnicourt Valleys behind these fragile defences.

The Germans knew the Australian line was lightly held. Wanting to capitalise on the Bullecourt success, they decided to strike on 15 April. Four divisions were to capture or destroy as many men and guns as possible in seizing the seven villages behind the 1st Division's line — Noreuil, Lagnicourt, Morchies, Doignies, Boursies, Demicourt and Hermies — holding them for the day and withdrawing that night. When the bombardment fell at 4 am, the sentries withdrew to the piquets, some of which were lost. Lieutenant Pope of the 11th Battalion was awarded a posthumous VC for holding his position to the very end. Resistance such as Pope's at the piquet line let reinforcements reach the supports, which then drove the Germans off. Only at the junction of the 1st and 2nd Divisions, where the 12th Battalion from the 3rd Brigade and the 17th Battalion from the 5th met between Lagnicourt and Noreuil, did a crisis arise.

Attacking here without a bombardment, the Germans surprised the inner flanks of the two battalions. In front of Noreuil, the right of the 17th Battalion gave way. Overrunning Lagnicourt, except for a small pocket held by Captain Newland and his piquets, the Germans poured into the valley behind the village, where the 2nd Australian Field Artillery (AFA) Brigade was located. The gunners could not engage them for fear of hitting their own infantry, some of whom were coming back with the Germans on their heels. Taking the breech-blocks and dial sights, they left shortly after 5 am, as did the 1st AFA Brigade behind the 2nd. A scratch force, hastily assembled at the 12th Battalion's headquarters 700 metres from Lagnicourt, held the Germans until the 9th Battalion's arrival from the rear at 6.30 am.

Brigadier-General Robert Smith, the commander of the 5th Brigade, directed the 19th Battalion, bivouacked in the valley behind Noreuil, and the 20th Battalion further back, to secure the Noreuil Valley and the spur between it and Lagnicourt, and to extend across the front of Noreuil to meet the rest of the 17th Battalion. They did so none too soon. The Germans were surging up the spur from the Lagnicourt Valley but the 19th reached the crest first and barred their way. The 17th and 19th between them stopped those attacking Noreuil. The 20th Battalion linked with the 9th in the Lagnicourt Valley and the two battalions cleared both the valley and the village. By 8.30 am it was all over. Four thousand Australians had held most of their largely unwired line against an attack by 16000 Germans. As opposed to 1010 Australian casualties, the Germans had lost 2313. Five of the 2nd's AFA's 21 guns were damaged; the 1st AFA's guns were unharmed.

The valley behind Lagnicourt where the Germans overran the Australian gun lines. Those of the 1st AFA were in the foreground; those of the 2nd AFA closer to the village.

DRIVING THE BATTLEFIELD

The Australian follow-up of the German withdrawal to the Hindenburg Line started near Bapaume and finished 13 kilometres beyond it on the general line Noreuil–Lagnicourt–Boursies–Demicourt–Hermies. Dead flat on the eastern outskirts of Bapaume, the terrain over which the Australians advanced soon becomes rolling like the Somme but, uncluttered by woods, it is more open and offers great fields of fire. As they had not been fought over, the fields were grassed rather than pockmarked by endless craters.

Try to visualise at all times the effects of the scorched-earth policy through which the Germans left nothing behind that might be useful. The extent of the destruction was astonishing. 'All the fruit trees in the orchards are cut down close to the ground', said Lieutenant Ronald McInnis of the 53rd Battalion, 'houses are burnt and destroyed by mines … telegraph poles are cut down and the insulators smashed'. Captain Louis Roth of the 22nd Battalion saw that every well was 'either poisoned or filled with rubbish and manure'.

As this tour covers the locations that figured prominently in the Australian advance and the mid-April German attack on the Australian line, the descriptions switch between both. Leave your car on reaching Lagnicourt, where a leisurely walk is the best way to study the action!

> **MAPS** IGN Blue Series, 1:25 000: 2407E Bapaume; 2408E Bray-sur-Somme

From Pozières, take the D929 towards Bapaume. A kilometre beyond Le Sars and 100 metres before Warlencourt British Cemetery, turn left onto Loupart Road, as it was known in 1917. Continue through two crossroads and past a communications pylon to the top of the hill, and park where a farm track runs off to the left. Face down the **track 1**. The high ground on which you are standing is the **Loupart Bastion**, across which the **R1 Line** ran well to your right rear after curving around **Loupart Wood** on your right. Snaking up to your left rear after passing over the D929 one kilometre past the Loupart Road, **Malt Trench**, part of the outpost line in front of R1, crossed the track 100 metres to your front and, contrary to expectation, was strongly held. Branching right off Malt Trench a few hundred metres further along it at a powerful redoubt, **Gamp Trench** went down to the valley floor ahead of you, where **Warlencourt-Eaucourt** nestles. Launched from this side of the village, the late-afternoon attacks on Malt Trench by the 5th and 6th Brigades on 25 February had to cover 500 metres and then overcome intact wire.

Starting from the flats near the D929, the 18th Battalion was halted short of Malt Trench at the D10E1, the Warlencourt–Le Barque road, which forms the first crossroad you drove over. The neighbouring 22nd Battalion attacked without artillery support up the bare slope to your left front. Lashed by fire from machine-guns in and around your location, the assault became entangled in the uncut wire. Also hammered by these guns, the 21st Battalion's attempt on Gamp Trench bogged down near the track. After a two-day bombardment to cut the wire, the 5th and 7th Brigades launched another attack at 3.10 am on 2 March.

The 26th Battalion followed in the tracks of the 22nd Battalion's earlier attack up the slope but got through the wire and into Malt Trench between the point where it crossed the track to your front and the Loupart Road on your left. Most of the Germans in this stretch broke. On the right of the 26th, the 27th Battalion bombed down Malt Trench towards the D929 but was driven back to the Loupart Road. There it rallied and linked up with the 17th Battalion from the 5th Brigade, which had bombed up Malt Trench from the D929. Unable to make much headway against Malt Trench down the slope to your right front, the 28th Battalion swung around to your left and into the part of Malt Trench captured by the 26th, along which it struck towards Gamp. When the redoubt at the junction of the two trenches, which had been the chief obstacle, was rushed, the Germans abandoned it. By mid-afternoon the 2nd Division was established on the Loupart Bastion.

Drive back down Loupart Road and turn left onto the D10E1, which was as far as the 18th Battalion got in the attack on 25 February. Turn left again onto the D929 towards **Bapaume**. Malt Trench, the 18th's objective, crossed it after 350 metres and ran diagonally up the rear slope of the Loupart Bastion on your left. In conjunction with the 12th Battalion's successful advance towards Le Barque 500 metres on the far side of the D929, the 18th exacted some revenge on 26 February, securing a lodgement in Malt Trench on the right of the D929. From here on 2 March the 17th Battalion

bombed up Malt on the left of the road to meet the 27th coming the other way. R1, which the Germans abandoned just before it was to be attacked, stretched along the high ground on your left for two kilometres before descending to cross the D929 just past the intersection with the Grévillers–Thilloy road.

The **R2 Line** straddled the D929 about 50 metres before the railway line that you will cross just before entering Bapaume. Its course paralleled the track and cut through the urban build-up on your right, an area of open fields in 1917. At this stage, the 2nd Division was advancing on the left of the D929 and the 5th Division on the right. The Germans vacated R2 half an hour before they reached it on 17 March. Follow the D929 to the T-junction in Bapaume, turn right onto the D917 and park in the **town square ➋**. Haig had hoped to take Bapaume at the start of the Somme offensive in July 1916 but it remained out of reach. Now, eight and a half months later, the 19 kilometres separating Bapaume from Albert, where the offensive began, had finally been covered. The streets along which you have just driven were cratered and criss-crossed by chains linked to explosives when the Australians moved through them. They beheld a town reduced to a smoking ruin by systematic German demolitions. The stench of destruction was all-pervading.

As the **town hall** on the square was one of the few intact buildings, the Australian Comforts Fund took it over to offer passing troops hot food and drinks and a temporary resting place. These comforts were not available for long. On 25 March a delayed-action mine

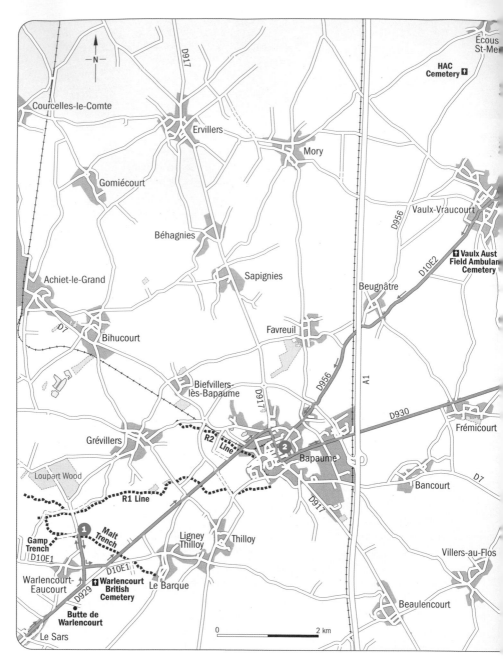

The following labels appear on the map:

N (compass)

Écous St-Me

HAC Cemetery ✝

Courcelles-le-Comte

Ervillers

Mory

Gomiécourt

D917

Vaulx-Vraucourt

D956

Béhagnies

Vaulx Aust Field Ambulan Cemetery ✝

D10E2

Achiet-le-Grand

Sapignies

Beugnâtre

D7

Favreuil

Bihucourt

D956

A1

Biefvillers-lès-Bapaume

D917

D930

Frémicourt

Grévillers

R2 Line

Bapaume

Loupart Wood

R1 Line

Bancourt

D7

Gamp Trench

Malt Trench

Ligney Thilloy

Thilloy

Villers-au-Flos

D10E1

Warlencourt-Eaucourt

D10E1

Le Barque

D929

Warlencourt British Cemetery ✝

Beaulencourt

Butte de Warlencourt

Le Sars

0   2 km

①   ②   (map markers)

obliterated the town hall, killing 24 Australians. 'Fritz is a dirty dog, the lowest of the low', Captain Braithwaite remarked, forgetting that the Australians, on leaving ANZAC, had left all sorts of creative booby traps for the Turks to discover. The town hall was rebuilt between 1931 and 1935. To the left of the entrance is a memorial to the two visiting French parliamentary deputies who also died in the blast but not the Australians. The square is named after General Louis Faidherbe, one of the better French commanders in the Franco-Prussian War of 1870–71. The statue of him in the centre is a replica,

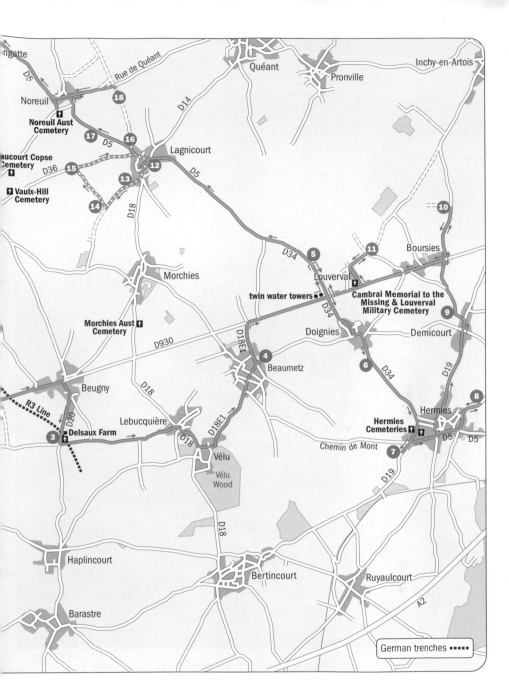

Rue de Quéant

Quéant

Inchy-en-Artois

Pronville

Noreuil

18

D14

Noreuil Aust
Cemetery

17 D5 16

Lagnicourt

uucourt Copse
Cemetery

D36 15

12

D5

Vaulx-Hill
Cemetery

13

D18

14

10

D34

5

11

Boursies

Louverval

twin water towers

Cambrai Memorial to the
Missing & Louverval
Military Cemetery

Morchies

9

D34

Morchies Aust
Cemetery

D930

D18E1

Doignies

Demicourt

4

Beaumetz

6

D34

D19

D18

Beugny

R3 Line

D20

Lebucquière

D18E1

D18

Hermies

8

Hermies
Cemeteries

3 Delsaux Farm

Vélu

Chemin de Mont

D5 D5

7

Vélu
Wood

D19

D18

Haplincourt

Bertincourt

Ruyaulcourt

A2

Barastre

German trenches •••••

as the Germans took the original for scrap.
They left the base, on which the damage
caused by shell fire remains a reminder of
what the war did to Bapaume. The names
that the Australians scratched into it are
now almost illegible.

Leave the square on the D917, which is
signposted Cambrai and becomes the

Starting at the Loupart Bastion and Malt Trench, the drive
passes through Bapume and then Frémicourt, Delsaux Farm,
Beugny, Lebucquière, Vélu, Beaumetz, Louverval, Doignies,
Hermies, Demicourt, Boursies, Lagnicourt and Noreuil. The
walk covers the loss of Lagnicourt and the valley behind it as
well as the counterattack to regain both.
DISTANCE COVERED: 55 km (Lagnicourt walk 4 km)
DURATION: 7 hours

Bapaume town hall, with General Faidherbe keeping an eye on things in front of it.

HIGH WOOD

WARLENCOURT-EAUCOURT

MALT TRENCH

D930 on crossing the A1 autoroute just outside Bapaume. You are now on the axis of the 15th Brigade's advance. On your right is **Frémicourt**, 1.4 kilometres beyond which the **R3 Line** went over the D930 just past a track that does likewise. Proceed into **Beugny**, turn right onto the D20 and stop after 1.3 kilometres at **Delsaux Farm Cemetery** ❸, behind which R3 ran. Look back towards Frémicourt, whose capture, though easy, was marred by a tendency to gravitate towards any point from which fire came. This mistake was not made at your location, where the 60th Battalion pinned down the German posts in R3 with heavy frontal fire while simultaneously creeping around the shallow re-entrant to your left front to get behind them. Beugny fell in the same way. The 15th Brigade was through R3.

Turn left at the cemetery and, after two kilometres, swing right in **Lebucquière** onto the D18 for **Vélu** and **Vélu Wood**, which loom ahead. All three were enveloped, the Germans offering little resistance before withdrawing. Just before entering Vélu, leave the D18, which heads 2.3 kilometres south to **Bertincourt**, the village that Elliott's light horse occupied, even though it lay in the British sector, to secure his right flank. Turn left instead onto the D18E1 (Rue de Beaumetz) and follow it through **Beaumetz** to the **cemetery** on the far side. The D18E1 breaks left at the cemetery but you should continue straight on and park after about 500 metres at an appropriate place on the verge ❹.

While the 59th Battalion spread over a wide frontage to capture **Morchies** on the other side of the D930, which you can see 700 metres to your left, on 20 March, the 60th Battalion had a harder time at Beaumetz. Before they left that night, the Germans in the village stubbornly resisted the centre of the attack and their reinforcements threatened the advances around either side. Look down the road towards Doignies, 1.4 kilometres ahead. The German counterattack on 23 March that made Elliott apoplectic barrelled across the low ground on your left to the cemetery behind you, and also struck the southern end of Beaumetz on your right, getting behind the 29th Battalion. The 29th, which had relieved the 60th, was almost driven from the village before counterattacking itself and restoring most of the line. Next morning the Germans attacked again through your location but failed to penetrate Beaumetz at all. 'We fired and fired until the iron-work of our rifles burnt our hands', recalled Sergeant Downing. 'At about eight the enemy retired, leaving very many dead, and all grew quiet again.' The dead lay thickest along the D18E1, on which you should turn right after returning to the cemetery. Many Germans had sought shelter at the roadside, only to be caught in enfilade by a machine-gun from the 57th Battalion firing from the cemetery down the D18E1 towards the D930.

On reaching the D930, turn right onto it. Just past the **twin water towers** 1.5 kilometres along, turn left onto the

The attacks on Malt Trench. Note the steepness of the slope up which the attacks came.

POZIÈRES

22ND/26TH BATTALION ATTACKS

FRÉMICOURT

COVERING FIRE FROM FRONT

OUTFLANKING ATTACK

The 60th Battalion's advance from Frémicourt to Delsaux Farm.

D34 and, where the power lines cross after 900 metres, park in the open area beside the pylon **5**. You are on the **Louverval Spur**, from which some of the outpost villages can be picked out and their positions relative to each other established. Look along the D34 in the direction in which you have been travelling. Lagnicourt is on the road to your front, while **Bullecourt**, in the Hindenburg Line, is 7.5 kilometres to your right front. Now turn about and look down the D34 towards the water towers. **Doignies** is 1.4 kilometres in front of you on the other side of the D930 with **Boursies** on the D930 one kilometre to its left, while **Louverval** is below the eastern side of the spur 800 metres to your left front on this side of the D930. In 1917 **Louverval Wood**, which had been cut down by the Germans, extended from Louverval onto the high ground to your left. Today almost nothing remains of the wood or of the château it enclosed.

For its attack on Louverval and Doignies on 2 April, the 14th Brigade

formed up beyond the crest to your right. The disappearance of Louverval Wood makes it difficult to envisage the 56th Battalion's assault on Louverval. Instead of swinging around the wood and the village to the D930 after passing through your location, most of the 56th headed directly into the wood, where the combination of felled trees and heavily laden infantry all but halted its advance. The left company regained the initiative by moving up onto the spur to your left to bypass the wood and then heading down the slope to the far side of Louverval. Gradually emerging from the wood, the rest of the battalion reinforced it. Louverval was cut off. Frustrated by what turned out to be a difficult attack, the Australians took few prisoners.

Supposed to be assaulting concurrently with the 56th, the 55th Battalion started prematurely when the right company under Captain Eric Stutchbury advanced across your front 200 metres in from the D930 15 minutes early and blundered into Louverval's

LOUVERVAL/D930

outskirts. Stutchbury promptly faced his men south towards Doignies, expecting the rest of the battalion to move around his left to the rear of the village. Instead, it wheeled diagonally across the D930 on his right — your right front — and directly into Doignies, whereupon he led his company behind the village. As the danger of encirclement was still very real, the Germans pulled out. The fall of Doignies had been rapid and almost bloodless.

Now follow the D34 over the D930 to Doignies. Stutchbury's company advanced on your left, the rest of the 55th Battalion on your right. Remaining on the D34, park 600 metres past Doignies at the **track** 6 that heads right along the crest of a spur. **Hermies** is 1.5 kilometres further along the D34 to your front, **Demicourt** two kilometres to your left. You are standing on the end of the start line for the 2nd Battalion's attack on Hermies on 9 April, which extended 800 metres into the field on your left and was lit up by the burning haystack. At

least with Doignies in Australian hands, the 2nd did not have to worry about crossing the trench linking the village to Hermies, which ran to the right of the road. The assault went down its inner side. The 3rd Battalion's subsidiary attack went in on the right of Hermies from beyond the far crest.

Continue on the D34 along the line of the 2nd Battalion's advance on the left of the road, in which all but the left company headed directly for Hermies. As you enter the village, turn right at each of the two forks onto the D5E1 (Rue Saint Michelle), which climbs past **Hermies British Cemetery** and **Hermies Hill British Cemetery**. The fire that flayed the right company came from the cemeteries area, which was a brick pit in 1917, and from the ruins that were on your left. 'Laying men low on all sides, and throwing showers of earth over those who lived through the deadly hell' was how Private Hartnett described the fusillade. 'Moans and groans could be heard on all sides from the wounded.'

The ground over which the German counterattack that maddened Brigadier-General Elliott came.

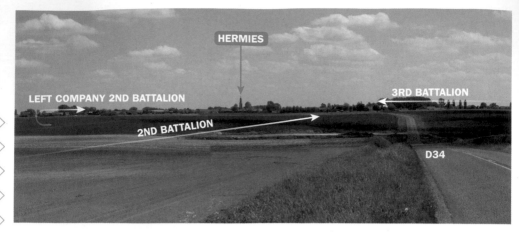

The assault on Hermies.

Hugging the lower slope around you for 90 minutes, the company fought back as best it could but the coming dawn threatened annihilation. Just as the order to charge was given, the fire died down. Scrambling through the ruins, the centre companies had overrun the Germans in the nick of time.

Carry on up the hill past the grain silo at Chemin de Mont crossroad, which was also the crossing point of the old railway, to the crest beyond the village and park on the left of what is now the **D19** ⑦. With Hermies to your right rear, look across the road. The 3rd Battalion assaulted on the left of Chemin de Mont towards you. That flank was temporarily held up behind the buildings to your right but the rest of the battalion kept going on your left. When it reached the railway, which skirted the near side of Hermies behind you, resistance in this vicinity crumpled, and the 3rd Battalion soon met the 2nd on the train line.

Return to the crossroad, turn right onto the D19 (Rue de la Gare here) and follow it into the village square, where it meets the D5. Continuing on the D5 (direction Havrincourt/Marcoing), turn left 350 metres from the square onto Rue Neuve and drive downhill to the end of the village. Park there, walk along the road to a cutting and take the overgrown **track** ⑧ up the left side. At the top, look towards Hermies. As the left company of the 2nd Battalion swung to your front

around the village, catching many Germans asleep in their cellars on the way, it was engaged by a machine-gun firing from the sandpit that marked your location in 1917. A VC resulted from what happened next. Hurling several bombs from the cutting, Lance Corporal Bede Kenny rushed the gun and killed a German who tried to stop him.

Return to the square in Hermies. Paying careful attention, as this part of the drive is too finicky to show in detail on the map, turn right onto the D5 (direction Doignies/Arras), and right again onto Rue de Lesboeufs, the D19 for Demicourt. Turn left onto Rue de Boursies 450 metres after entering Demicourt and stop at the **cemetery** ⑨. Face the village, which the Germans, on losing Hermies, did not immediately abandon as anticipated. Covered by a company of the 1st Battalion from the crest behind you, two other companies twice tried to envelop Demicourt by passing to your left and right before the Germans withdrew.

Continue along Rue de Boursies for 600 metres to a calvary in a stand of trees at a Y-junction and turn right towards Boursies. Crossing over the D930 at the far end of the village, descend into the broad valley on the far side and stop after one kilometre at the **track** ⑩ on the left on the valley floor. Look along it. The high ground to your left front is the **Boursies Spur**, on which Boursies itself can be

The site of Lance-Corporal Kenny's VC action.

seen; the high ground to your front across the valley is the continuation of the Louverval Spur. In the 3rd Brigade's feint on 8 April to distract the Germans from the attack on Hermies next day, the 12th Battalion advanced on Boursies Spur along the D930 almost to the far end of Boursies. It did not get much further in the next attack on 9 April but the 10th Battalion advanced the line on the Louverval Spur to a point on it directly ahead of you. Outflanked by the fall of Hermies and Demicourt, the Germans left Boursies that day.

A Company of the 11th Battalion subsequently held the area around you with three piquet posts. If you stay facing down the track, one was 100 metres to your left, another 700 metres distant near the crest to your right front and, in between, Lieutenant Pope and his 30 men 400 metres to your right front. When the German pre-dawn attack on 15 April swept through your location after coming up the valley behind you, the post on the left was surrounded but held out. So did Pope's until it ran out of ammunition, whereupon the survivors fixed bayonets for a suicidal charge. Ex-London bobby Pope was later found among the Australian and German dead. The Germans got through but could not penetrate the reinforced support positions on the Boursies and Louverval Spurs 800 metres to your front and withdrew. This story was repeated along most of the 1st Division's line.

Return to the D930, turn right and drive through Boursies, which straggled along both sides of the road in 1917 just

> The lance corporal on the left [was] ... charging a gun ... served and defended by eight men. From thirty yards he dropped a bomb amongst them and at twenty yards — just as the bomb burst — he was wounded in the left arm. Undaunted he continued his rush and leapt into the trench and bayoneted in quick succession the remaining three Germans ... he is L.Cpl Kenny.
>
> Sergeant Matthews on Lance Corporal Kenny's VC action at the sandpit
> (Matthews, A, 'Diary of Experiences', 2DRL/0219, AWM)

as it does now. Once through the village, the D930 crosses the crest of the Boursies Spur and passes a long concrete screening wall on your right. The area behind it was the location of the derelict mill that Captain Newland's men took on the 8 April feint and which the Germans, moving on the right of the road in the direction in which you are driving, counterattacked repeatedly. A machine-gun firing from this vicinity also caused no end of trouble for the 55th Battalion in its attack on Doignies, off to your left, on 2 April. Immediately before the D930 bottoms out at the **Cambrai Memorial to the Missing** and **Louverval Military Cemetery**, turn right onto the minor road to Louverval. Turning right again at the T-junction at the far end of the hamlet, drive 400 metres to another T-junction, where a **calvary** ⑪ is set in trees, and park. As this stand is in the low ground between the Louverval and Boursies Spurs, a bit of walking will be necessary to get full value from it!

First, though, look back along the road down which you have just driven. It skirted the southern face of Louverval Wood, whose felled trees held up the 56th Battalion's advance on 2 April. Bounded by the road on your right and broken by the grounds of the **château** halfway along, the wood's eastern face extended almost to the crest. The 56th's line at the end of the advance ran along both faces of the wood and across to the D930 at the Cambrai Memorial. After a hard assault through your location in the Boursies feint on 8 April, the 10th Battalion gained another 400 metres on the Louverval Spur and the re-entrant below it on your right.

Now walk towards the D930 until the spire of Boursies church appears to your left front. Concurrently with the 10th's attack, the left of the 12th Battalion advanced from Louverval but could not get beyond this track. Ploughing through heavy fire as it moved along the Boursies Spur on the D930, the right flank under Captain Newland bombed its way into

The area of Lieutenant Pope's post.

POPE'S POST

BOURSIES

GERMAN ATTACK

the ruined mill that stood near the clump of trees on the crest. This was the area shielded by the concrete wall you passed earlier, and where Newland and Sergeant Whittle between them stemmed the retirement before the German counterattack at 10 pm, which struck along the D930 from Boursies and, against Newland's flank, from the high ground on your left. Restoring its line on 9 April, the 12th Battalion got closer to Boursies, while the 10th grabbed more of the Louverval Spur after the Germans on it pulled back.

Return to the Cambrai Memorial, turn right onto the D930 and, after 750 metres, right again just before the twin water towers onto the D34, which you took earlier. This time remain on the D34, which becomes the D5 on entering, after almost four kilometres, a long, deep cutting as it climbs the spur to **Lagnicourt**. This cutting featured prominently in the Lagnicourt fighting but you will have to consider what happened before driving through as parking in it is impossible and walking down the busy D34 into it from Lagnicourt is dangerous. The description assumes that you are looking up the cutting towards the village.

Having taking Lagnicourt early on 26 March, the 26th Battalion established posts along the crest either side of the cutting, which Captain Cherry's company held. Counterattacks soon struck them. The one that swept in from the high ground to the right was held. Corporal Edgar Morrow fired at a German machine-gun crew setting up. 'My man dropped, and "Got him", I said delightedly.' Another machine-gunner ran forward. 'He was hardly fifty yards away when I shot him in the stomach. He crumpled forward and fell on his gun.

The site of the mill on the D930 held by a 12th Battalion party under Captain Newland and Sergeant Whittle.

GERMAN COUNTERATTACK

MILL SITE (NEWLAND AND WHITTLE)

BOURSIES

GERMAN COUNTERATTACKS

Captain Percy Herbert Cherry

Awarded the VC posthumously for his role in the capture of Lagnicourt.

1895–1917

Though already an officer in the militia, Cherry was considered too young to be one in the AIF when he enlisted in March 1915. Made a quartermaster-sergeant instead, he was finally commissioned at the end of the Gallipoli campaign in 1915. His promise to post the letters given to him by the German he had mortally wounded at Pozières showed that Cherry was capable of great compassion. Yet he was also a strict disciplinarian who could have been unpopular were it not for his aggression, almost fanatical bravery, and insistence on leading from the front. These qualities were amply demonstrated in his VC action at Lagnicourt. At Malt Trench three weeks before, he had rushed two machine-guns to win the MC. As the award was not announced until the day of his death, Cherry never knew of it. He had been wounded four times and was not yet 22 when killed.

I laughed.' Then Morrow was sent flying. 'Something had hit my right shoulder like a kick from a horse, and I found my right arm useless. Blood was running down my sleeve onto my hand.' But the thrust that crossed the D5 halfway along the sunken stretch and rocketed up the side of the spur on the left almost reached Lagnicourt before the Germans backed off. German shelling of the cutting area killed Cherry at 4 pm.

In their attack on 15 April, the Germans again advanced along the high ground on the right and overran Lagnicourt except for the cutting, which was held by Captain Newland's company from the 12th Battalion. Lining both banks, they kept the Germans from breaking out of the eastern side of the village, which faced Newland's men on the left. Newland's leadership was inspirational. In desperation, the Germans set up a machine-gun on the crest to fire down the D5 but Sergeant Whittle bombed it and brought it back before it got a shot away. Newland and Whittle received the VC for this action and their earlier one at Boursies.

On reaching the T-junction in Lagnicourt, turn left and then, bearing left onto the D18 (direction Bertincourt), park beside the **church** ⑫. Remembering that Cherry's name is inexorably linked to the capture of the village, look back the way you have come. Having fought its way along the D18 behind you to the church, Cherry's company was blocked by torrential fire that came from a giant crater blown in the road at the junction where you first turned left. Cherry called for trench mortars to pound the crater area but became frustrated at the time needed to organise the bombardment. Deciding not to wait, he led a rush under cover of Lewis-guns and rifle grenades that reached the crater, overwhelmed the Germans in it and found Lieutenant Harry Bieske at the bottom of it. Detached earlier by Cherry, Bieske and a few others had swung around the village to your right. As they moved down the D5, Bieske went on ahead and blundered from the rear into the Germans opposing Cherry. Leaping over their heads as they fired at him, he landed with a shattered ankle in the

The cutting on the D34 below Lagnicourt held by Captain Newland's men during the German counterattack. Captain Cherry's company had earlier captured the crest.

crater. The distraction gave Cherry's men the edge needed to take it. For his leadership and bravery, which included staying to help hold Lagnicourt against counterattacks, even though he had been wounded and his company ordered to withdraw, Cherry was awarded a posthumous VC.

You can now start the **Lagnicourt walk**. Continue along the D18, on which Cherry's Lewis-gunners had to aim at the Germans, who engaged them from the ruined houses either side, by gripping the slings as continuous firing was making the barrels too hot to hold. After 300 metres, turn right and walk another 300 metres to **Lagnicourt Hedge Cemetery** ⑬. Stand at the rear of it with your back to the entrance and look across the valley. On 15 April the gun lines of the 2nd AFA Brigade were spread over the valley floor: those of the 5th AFA Battery and the 102nd AFA Battery 300 metres to your left front and in front of you respectively, those of the 4th AFA Battery to your right in the low ground this side of the houses. Starting about 300 metres to your left, the line reached by the Germans when they

overran these batteries and most of Lagnicourt early that morning cut through the 5th Battery's position in the valley and passed this side of the line of trees spilling over the crest of the far spur.

Leaving the cemetery, turn right and, after 650 metres, right again at the junction in the large tree covered cutting. Stop at the **track** ⑭ on the left in the valley floor, 250 metres away, and face Lagnicourt. You are now looking along the axis of the 7th Brigade's attack on 26 March, which captured the village. The road on which you are standing was the start line for the attack. In light rain, the 27th Battalion stretched along it on the slope to your left. The 26th Battalion extended through your location and over the road you took from the cemetery to the cutting, which was the centre line and the route Cherry used to get to Lagnicourt. Passing right and left of the village and setting up posts on the far side, the rest of the battalion had a relatively easy advance, unlike Cherry's company.

The street along which Captain Cherry's company advanced into Lagnicourt then ... and now.

Continue up the slope on the other side of the valley to the crest, where the Australian Artillery Group Headquarters was located on the right of the road. The Germans got to within 250 metres of it before being driven back by the 20th Battalion's right flank, which sped along the crest to your left and crossed the road here, eventually meeting the left flank of the 9th Battalion. As you walk over the crest, look across the next valley. Moving left to right along the far slope in the 7th Brigade's advance on 26 March, the 27th Battalion linked up with the 26th on the high ground to the left of Lagnicourt.

Now walk down to the **crossroads** 15 with the D36 in the valley itself. This was the apex of the penetration by the Germans on 15 April. Coming from your right, they overran the gun lines of the 1st AFA Brigade, which comprised the 2nd AFA Battery's virtually on the crossroads and 1st AFA Battery's to its right, and those of the 3rd AFA Battery to your front on the slope ahead. The guns were retaken in the 20th Battalion's counterattack, the centre of which moved down the valley through your location, and the left along the slope.

Head right on the D36 for Lagnicourt. At the edge of the village, head left onto the D5 for 200 metres and face the two large white buildings just beyond the junction with the sunken track on the right, which is the start of the old **Lagnicourt–Bullecourt road** 16. Captain Vowles' post on the 12th Battalion's left flank was in this location during the German attack. Advancing towards you at right angles to the D5, the Germans struck it after swamping a machine-gun section 200 metres along the track. More Germans emerged from the village, having taken all but the D34 cutting area held by Captain Newland's men on the far side, and swung behind the post. Vowles, who had captured Hauptmann Ponsonby Lyons, the commander at Pozières, several months

On 15 April the Germans hurtled up the valley towards you and along the spur to your left front before being blocked 300 metres short of your location by a hotchpotch of cooks, batmen and anyone else who could fire a rifle, which had been thrown together by Lieutenant-Colonel Charles Elliott at the 12th Battalion's headquarters in the cutting. After forming up beyond the far right corner of the cutting, the 9th Battalion came across it and fanned out in front of your location. Hurtling in the opposite direction to the Germans, the 9th swept down the valley and, joined by the 20th Battalion along the slope to your left front, retook the gun lines and carried on into Lagnicourt.

GERMAN ATTACK 15 APRIL

LAGNICOURT

27TH BATTALION 26 MARCH
20TH BATTALION 15 APRIL

26TH BATTALION 26 MARCH

9TH BATTALION 15 APRIL

The capture, and recapture, of Lagnicourt.

before, gave the order to pull out along the valley down which you have just walked. The Germans could now take the 6th AFA Battery's gun line, which was on the slope 150 metres behind you. When the 26th Battalion had earlier captured Lagnicourt, its left flank passed through your location before swinging right beyond the village.

Following the D5 into Lagnicourt, return to your car at the church and drive back along the D5 towards **Noreuil**. About 600 metres past the site of Vowles' post, the D5 crosses the crest of the spur separating Noreuil from Lagnicourt. Pull off here and park on the **strip** 17 between the road and the edge of the fields. Pick your spot carefully as the D5 can be busy and the strip is narrow, in places *very* narrow! Look down the road towards Noreuil, which nestles on the bank of the tiny **l'Hirondelle** below you. Before the first battle of Bullecourt on 11 April, the artillery batteries arrayed along the valley to the left of Noreuil suffered some of the worst counter-battery fire that Australian gunners experienced in the war.

In the 6th Brigade's ill-fated attack in the snowstorm early on 20 March, the 23rd Battalion advanced from your left astride the spur on which you have

parked. Crossing the D5 below you, the left company pushed to the right of the village along the near bank of the l'Hirondelle but was recalled when the rest of the battalion could not get beyond the D5. Reforming on your left, the 23rd then tried to assault down the spur and parallel to the road. Skylined to the Noreuil garrison and in enfilade to the Germans on your right, who had prevented the advance across the road, it was met by blistering fire and forced to take cover among the dung heaps that littered the slope to your front. A German bombardment increased its misery. Moving along the spur on the other side of the valley, the 21st Battalion also ran into a wall of fire and was pinned down to the left of Noreuil. Both battalions withdrew.

In the 13th Brigade's successful envelopment of Noreuil on 2 April, the battalions advanced at right angles to each other. Attacking from the left on the far spur, the 51st Battalion passed behind the village and occupied an unmarked trench on the slope to its right. On this side of the valley, the 52nd Battalion on your right protected the flank of the 50th. Starting from the crest on your left, the 50th Battalion moved down the slope parallel to the D5 as the 23rd had done a fortnight earlier. Its right company crossed the road just in front of you but the rest of the battalion remained on the left-hand side. Behind a barricade in the cutting through which the D5 bends 400 metres further on was the post that Private Jensen knocked out. It had held up the centre company before Jensen rushed it, chucked in a bomb and brandished two others to bluff the 40-odd defenders into surrendering. An advanced company of the 19th Battalion lined the cutting and hurriedly established a few posts to the left of its near end when the Germans struck from Lagnicourt behind you on 15 April. Waiting until they had just passed your location, the 19th unleashed a massive volley. The Germans recoiled and went to ground around you.

Passing through the cutting, turn right once over the l'Hirondelle onto Rue de Quéant, which almost immediately becomes high-banked on the left. The

5th Brigade's headquarters, from which Brigadier-General Smith watched the Germans blocked at the cutting, was in a wrecked house on the corner. Their simultaneous advance along the valley and the spur on your left was the right flank of their penetration. The 17th Battalion and newly arrived companies of the 19th halted it 300 metres from the headquarters. After another 300 metres, you will drive through a Y-junction, which the Germans had cratered in 1917. Ignore the grass track, similarly banked, that branches off to the left and up the side of the spur, and remain on Rue de Quéant until it crosses a dirt track, all that remains of the Lagnicourt–Bullecourt road here, 300 metres further on. Turn right onto this track, which was the 13th Brigade's objective on 2 April, and park near the **pumping station** 18 just beyond the partly sunken bed of the old railway that ran alongside the l'Hirondelle.

Stand with Noreuil on your left. The unmarked trench, in which the 51st

The attacks on Noreuil on 20 March and 2 April, and the site of Private Jensen's VC action.

JENSEN'S VC

NOREUIL

21ST BATTALION 20 MARCH/
51ST BATTALION 2 APRIL

23RD BATTALION 20 MARCH

23RD BATTALION 20 MARCH/
50TH BATTALION 2 APRIL

Battalion sheltered at the end of its advance along the spur in front of you, ran up the facing slope 100 metres to 300 metres to the left of the Lagnicourt–Bullecourt road objective. After sweeping through Noreuil, all but the right company of the 50th Battalion joined it there. Having bypassed Noreuil, this company, commanded by Captain David Todd, advanced towards you along the valley floor. Halfway between your location and the village, it was seen by a German post in the road behind you, which was masked from the 52nd Battalion on the crest to your rear. Devastating fire from this post, and another one on the bank of the railway 200 metres to your right, pinned down Todd's men to your left front. Noreuil's garrison came up Rue de Quéant and took them in rear. As the Germans were using the Australian 'moppers-up' taken prisoner in the village as shields, Todd's men could not fire back. The remnants were captured and herded to **Quéant**, the village on your right. Only

a handful had reached the Lagnicourt–Bullecourt road.

Covered by the posts near you, the Germans now began bombing up the unmarked trench from the Rue de Quéant. After three attempts, they gained a foothold and the trench had to be barricaded. They also lined the embankment above the grass track, marked by the tree line to your left front, to fire into the flank of it. So absorbed were they that Major Noel Loutit was able to dribble a reserve platoon unobserved along the embankment above Rue de Quéant, up which he had crept from Noreuil. As a lieutenant at the Gallipoli Landing, Loutit had gone further inland than any other Australian. Now he told each of his men to aim at a man on the embankment above him, then gave the order to fire. Dead Germans slid down the slope. The Germans in the post on the railway turned their fire onto Loutit's men,

The view from the pumping station over the action around the unmarked trench, where the Germans missed Major Loutit's party.

50TH BATTALION

The enfilading of the 50th Battalion on the spur above Noreuil Australian Cemetery. All of the headstones mark Australian fallen.

forcing their retirement to the crater at the Y-junction. During the night, the Germans withdrew to Quéant.

Rejoin the D5 in Noreuil and follow it past the church to the five-way junction, where you may care to turn sharp left for **Noreuil Australian Cemetery**. A machine-gun dug into the bank there enfiladed the left of the 50th Battalion as it began the wheel through the village after coming down the spur behind the cemetery. Casualties were severe, even though the 50th's Lewis-gunners had blazed away from the hip in an effort to silence it. Now continue on the D5 as it climbs the spur along which the 21st Battalion tried to steal in the 6th Brigade's abortive attack on 20 March. Heavy fire from machine-guns dug into the sunken bank of the D5 stopped it 500 metres to your left. On 2 April the 51st Battalion stormed these guns before passing to your right and behind Noreuil to link up

with the 50th on the far side of the village.

Just before entering **Longatte**, turn left onto the D36E1 for **Vaulx-Vraucourt**, three kilometres away. It was the first village taken by the 6th Brigade, on the left flank of the advance from Bapaume. The 6th surprised some of the garrison shaving. Captain Vowles' men retired on the village when they were driven out of Lagnicourt, three kilometres northwest of it, and the 20th Battalion was quartered in it before being rushed forward to Noreuil. Having set up in Vaulx-Vraucourt at the start of April, the Australian 15th Field Ambulance handled the wounded from the fighting in these and the other outpost villages and the two battles at Bullecourt. From Vaulx-Vraucourt follow the signs to Bapaume, from which you can return to Pozières, otherwise return to Longatte and take the D956 to Bullecourt.

LOCAL INFORMATION

CEMETERIES

Many of the villages captured by I ANZAC contain a military cemetery that, in turn, contains the graves of Australians who fell in the advance to the Hindenburg Line and the German riposte from it. Only those with a substantial number of Australian burials are covered here.

Bapaume Australian Cemetery

Begun in March 1917 by the 3rd Australian Casualty Clearing Station, the cemetery was used until June. Of its 88 Commonwealth burials, 74 are Australian and all of them are identified. Resting next to each other, Private Albert Scott of the 5th Battalion at A.28, Private Alexander Gunn of the 6th Battalion at A.27, and Scotch College old boy Private Charles Neild of the 8th Battalion at A.29 were killed when the Bapaume Town Hall blew up. All over 40 years old, they had been seconded to the Australian Comforts Fund. Signposted from the D917 to Péronne 150 metres south of its junction with the D930 near the centre of Bapaume, the cemetery is tucked away on the Rue du Chemin Blanc behind a small park with a statue depicting the death of Abel Guidet, Bapaume's mayor in the Second World War. The Germans executed him for his Resistance ties.

HAC (Honourable Artillery Company) Cemetery, Écoust-St-Mein

On the D956 one kilometre south of Écoust-St-Mein, this cemetery opened soon after the British 7th Division

captured the village in early April 1917. The first Australian burials were 12 gunners added to what is now Plot I, Row A. They fell when the Germans overran the gun lines at Lagnicourt. But most of the 176 Australian graves, almost two-thirds of them unidentified, date from postwar when the cemetery was enlarged to almost 2000 graves by the concentration of burials from smaller nearby cemeteries.

Hermies British and Hermies Hill British Cemeteries

Straddling the D5E1 (Rue Saint Michelle) in Hermies, these cemeteries feature on the tour route because stubborn resistance came from the old brick pit area that they occupy when the 2nd Battalion attacked the village. Of the 109 burials in Hermies British Cemetery, 27 are Australian and they are mostly fallen from this attack. 2nd Lieutenant Malcolm Patterson at A.7 was shot through the head when he tried to get a better view of the German strongpoints at the brick pit. The Australians started the cemetery soon after capturing Hermies.

Hermies Hill British, on the other hand, was begun in November 1917 and became a postwar concentration cemetery with over 1000 graves. Among its 43 Australian burials are Lieutenant Vic Robins of the 2nd Battalion at III.D.11, who was killed while leading his company towards the eastern end of Hermies in the 2nd Battalion's assault, and 2nd Lieutenant Alf Cassidy, who fell when the 1st Battalion took nearby Demicourt.

Moeuvres Communal Cemetery Extension

Moeuvres did not figure in the Australian advance. On the contrary, it stayed in German hands until the British took it in September 1918. They immediately began using the cemetery extension, which the Germans had started in September 1917, and it was greatly expanded after the war. Only eight of its 565 Commonwealth burials are Australian but they include Lieutenant Pope VC at V.D.22. The cemetery is on the northern side of Moeuvres, which can be reached by turning left off the D930 onto the D34B one kilometre past Boursies.

Morchies Australian Cemetery

Australian units started this cemetery, which is on the D18 just south of Morchies, soon after the 59th Battalion took the village on 20 March and they used it until the end of April. The Germans took it back a year later and briefly used it themselves. Of the 61 Commonwealth burials, 20 are Australian.

Noreuil Australian Cemetery

Commenced soon after Noreuil's capture, this cemetery was used until the following December and, briefly, at the end of 1918. Justifying its name, 182 of its 244 burials are Australian, of whom 82 are commemorated by special memorials along the southern wall as their original marked graves were destroyed by shelling during the Bullecourt fighting. Most of the 82 were 50th Battalion men killed in the attack that came down the slope behind the cemetery. Particularly

The Clayton brothers, Noreuil Australian Cemetery.

poignant are the graves of the Clayton brothers from Tasmania, William, 42, and Edward, 29, both of the 52nd Battalion. Killed at Bullecourt on 12 April, they have been inseparable since, resting side by side in F.5 and 6. Visited on the tour route, the cemetery is signposted from the D5 in Noreuil.

The Vaulx-Vraucourt cemeteries

On the D36 one kilometre from Vaulx-Vraucourt, **Vaulx-Hill Cemetery** is the largest of the three cemeteries near the village. Look eastwards from the eastern end of it and you can just see Lagnicourt to the right of the road 2.5 kilometres off. Started in September 1918 with 17 graves, the cemetery was used for postwar concentration purposes that expanded it to 858 burials, of which 106 are Australian. Resting at II.B.3, Lieutenant-Colonel Bertram Watts DSO was killed by German counter-battery fire near Lagnicourt on 10 April while commanding the 4th AFA Brigade. The same shell accounted for three of his staff, who are appropriately buried next to him: the medical officer, Captain Brian Mack in II.B.4, and Lieutenants Herb Harding and Guy Davenport MC, who share II.B.6. Lieutenant Roy Fordham of the 10th Battalion, who had accompanied Loutit inland at the Gallipoli Landing, lies at III.B.4. His luck ran out in front of Louverval Wood in the Boursies feint on 8 April.

Vaulx Australian Field Ambulance Cemetery, 200 metres off the D10E2 to Beaugnâtre and a kilometre from Vaulx-Vraucourt, contains 52 Commonwealth graves, 32 of

Grave of Lieutenant-Colonel Watts DSO, Vaulx-Hill Cemetery.

them Australian, and, interestingly, 61 German graves. The Germans used the cemetery, which opened in April 1917, after they captured the village in March 1918. It was retaken in September. Reached along a track that is signposted from the D36E1 to Écoust-St-Mein a kilometre from Vraulx-Vraucourt, **Vraucourt Copse Cemetery** includes 38 Australians among its 104 Commonwealth burials.

CHAPTER 7

1917

BULLECOURT

On 11 April 1917 the Australians captured the Hindenburg Line at Bullecourt and became the first troops in the BEF to take any part of it, though their stay was brief. On 3 May they attacked at Bullecourt again and this time the Hindenburg Line was theirs. It had occasionally been glimpsed in the distance during the advance from Bapaume. On 5 April the 49th Battalion got a better look when it reached the embankment of the Boisleux–Marquion railway, which ran past Bullecourt towards Quéant 3.5 kilometres away. Peering out from it at the rust-brown ribbon 900 metres across no-man's-land, the 49th beheld three belts of barbed wire, each nine to 13 metres wide and four metres apart before the front trench, and arranged in a zigzag pattern to funnel attackers into the fire of appropriately sited machine-guns, and a single belt before the support trench. Reminded of the set-up at Pozières, the Australians dubbed the two trenches, which were 2.5 metres deep, 140 to 180 metres apart and linked by numerous cross-trenches, OG1 and OG2.

OG1 diverged from OG2, which ran behind Bullecourt, and swung around the front of the village. From Bullecourt, which was therefore incorporated within the OG Lines, the two trenches ran in parallel across a pronounced re-entrant before snaking past Riencourt-lès-Cagnicourt 1.8 kilometres away. It guarded their junction with the newly dug Wotan Line, known to the British as the Drocourt–Quéant Switch, which ran behind the Hindenburg Line as a reserve line in case of a breakthrough at Arras. To make the junction more secure, Balcony Trench jutted from it and ran in front of the Hindenburg Line to enclose Quéant. Balcony Trench and Bullecourt thus stood like jutting jaws either side of the re-entrant.

Gough again

Field Marshal Haig wanted General Gough to seize a stretch of the Hindenburg Line through which a cavalry division could pass in order to join the two cavalry divisions that were to go through the main breach created by the Third Army's attack from Arras. Lying on the flank of the Third Army's advance, Bullecourt seemed the logical place. Gough felt that greater prizes were on offer. The ultimate prize was the Drocourt–Quéant Switch as a German withdrawal before the Third Army would end up there. Seizing its junction with the Hindenburg Line would render the switch untenable. Gough therefore sought to break the Hindenburg Line in two places. The 62nd Division from V Corps would attack west of Bullecourt

The section of the Hindenburg Line assaulted by the 12th Brigade, eight days before the attack. Linked by cross-trenches, the OG Lines zigzag across the picture. The bands in front of them are wide entanglements. Another entanglement lies between them, as does the track of a trench railway. The prominent line running diagonally from the left bottom is the bed of a dismantled tramway. Bullecourt is just past the left edge of the photograph.

and take Hendecourt 1.5 kilometres beyond, from where the cavalry link-up was to be made. Starting from the railway embankment east of Bullecourt, the 4th Australian Division would go 1.3 kilometres across the bare re-entrant to capture Riencourt, turn right and go another kilometre to close up on the junction. The attack was set for 10 April.

As the 4th Division's task was exceedingly ambitious, the Australian commanders were anxious. Gough deleted the Hindenburg Line/Drocourt–Quéant Switch junction as an objective. But crossing the re-entrant to Riencourt still necessitated a deep penetration on a narrow frontage, 1.2 kilometres, that was overlooked from the jaws at either end. The lee of the high ground on which Balcony Trench ran gave some protection on the right flank but the danger from Bullecourt on the left could only be suppressed by the artillery. A more pressing problem was the undamaged wire across the entire frontage of the attack. General White told Gough on 8 April that at least another eight days' wire-cutting by the guns were necessary.

The Arras offensive opened spectacularly on 9 April, with the Canadian Corps taking Vimy Ridge and the Third Army alongside it advancing five kilometres. Gough seethed because the uncut wire precluded action on his front. Then a tank officer suggested that the 12 tanks available could crush the German entanglements, obviating the need for the artillery to do so. Once the tanks were through the wire, the guns could open up to cover the infantry's advance. Gough was jubilant. The attack could go ahead at dawn next day as originally intended.

With dawn only 12 hours off, the existing plan was simply adjusted to accommodate the tanks. At 4.30 am on 10 April the 4th and 12th Brigades, each led by four tanks, were to advance along the slopes above the re-entrant. Another four tanks would move next to Central Road in the 300-metre gap left between the two brigades at the bottom of the re-entrant. On breaching the wire, the tanks would wheel outwards and trample OG1 and OG2, with the two on the left going on to Bullecourt with the 46th Battalion. On the fall of the village, the tanks would lead the 62nd Division to Hendecourt and the Australians to Riencourt. The tanks were clapped-out Mark II's, under-armoured training machines unable to move even at walking pace. With snow falling, whether they could arrive in time from their 'tankodrome' 10 kilometres away was doubtful.

The 4th and 12th Brigades had never worked with tanks before. At 2.30 am they lay in their jump-off positions in front of the railway embankment. At 4.15 am word arrived that the tanks could not make it until well after dawn. General Holmes, the 4th Division's commander, recalled the two brigades. Gough rescheduled the attack for 4.30 am next day. The plan was slightly altered. As the Hindenburg Line wire was now reported partly cut, the infantry would advance automatically at 4.45 am, 15 minutes after the tanks started.

'The bloody fiasco'

At 1 am on 11 April a phosgene-laced bombardment drenched Bullecourt. At 3 am, when all of the tanks should have been ready, the first one arrived. Guiding it into position, Captain Jacka ascertained that the tanks could not reach the wire in the 15 minutes allowed, which meant that the infantry would get there first. It was too late to change the plan. When

The 16th Battalion has fought its way into OG1, with one tank reaching the wire, which was much denser than shown. The snow reflects the light of the flares, giving the battlefield a surrealistic look. This is a scene from the Australian War Memorial's diorama of the Bullecourt attack.

the infantry stepped off at 4.45 am, they soon overtook the few tanks ahead of them, whereupon the Hindenburg Line in front of Riencourt erupted in a cyclone of fire that whipped the 4th Brigade on the right of Central Road.

Urging the 16th Battalion through the fusillade to the wire, Major Percy Black hustled it over damaged stretches into OG1 but was killed while doing the same at OG2. Captain Murray rushed the 13th Battalion's first wave forward to assist. The

The Germans inspect a crippled tank after the attack.

13th mopped up OG1 and joined the 16th in the hand-to-hand fight for OG2. On their left, the 14th Battalion, badly mauled in taking OG1, was joined by the 15th in OG2. By 5.30 am the 4th Brigade held 800 metres of both. But there was no chance of reaching Riencourt in the growing light.

A slip-up cost the 12th Brigade on the left of Central Road dearly. An ambiguity in the brigade orders led the 46th Battalion to assume that it was to advance 15 minutes after its tanks, no matter when they arrived, instead of at 4.45 am regardless. The first tank did not appear until 4.45 am. Disoriented in the dark, it shot up the 46th and was knocked out. The next came at 5 am and broke down. When the assault finally began at 5.15 am, the shelling of Bullecourt had ceased as the attack should already have reached it, leaving the Germans free to rake the 46th's open flank. Pressing on, the 46th found much of the wire at OG1 untouched, as did the 48th Battalion following at OG2. Both were mauled in getting through but by 7 am they held 450 metres of each trench.

Only four tanks had got to the wire and one reached Bullecourt. With sunrise, all of them appeared to the German gunners like slugs against a white background.

Lieutenant Walter Shelley of the 22nd Australian Machine-Gun Company looks for movement in the gaps made in the wire by the Australian artillery during the bombardment of the Hindenburg Line before Second Bullecourt. The village, which lies between OG1 and OG2, is on the left skyline.

Major-General Sir John Gellibrand

Commander 6th Brigade 1916–17, 12th Brigade 1917–18, 3rd Australian Division 1918

1872–1945

Tasmanian-born Gellibrand had joined the British Army, graduating top of his class from Sandhurst in 1893, and serving in the Boer War and attending the Camberley Staff College before returning to Australia in 1912. After serving as a staff officer on Gallipoli, where he was awarded a DSO, Gellibrand took the 6th Brigade to the Western Front. He was an able commander.

A bohemian who usually wore a private's uniform, Gellibrand lived close to his men and won their loyalty through his bravery and sometimes quirky ways. But those ways and his independent outlook often put him offside with his superiors. He showed both sides of his nature at Bullecourt. The success in the second battle rested on Gellibrand's handling of the 6th Brigade when it stood alone in the Hindenburg Line. But Gellibrand considered that the way the 2nd Division handled things insulted his brigade's efforts and asked to be relieved of his command. He was duly sent to the AIF training depots in England. In November 1917 Gellibrand returned to France to command the 12th Brigade, and in May 1918 succeeded Monash in command of the 3rd Division. He was knighted (KCB) in 1919 and held the federal seat of Denison between 1925 and 1928. The Remembrance Club he founded in Hobart in 1923 ultimately grew into the Legacy Movement.

Burning tank carcasses soon dotted it. Nonetheless the 4th and 12th Brigades were firm in the Hindenburg Line. Murray reported at 7.15 am, 'With artillery support we can keep the position until the cows come home'. None came. Deceived by the snow, which hid the lie of the land, the Australian artillery observers thought that Riencourt had been reached. Gough ordered the cavalry forward. It was smashed.

The Germans struck the outer flanks of both brigades and from the gap between them. Running out of bombs and ammunition, the 4th Brigade was driven inwards around 11 am. Pointing to the torrential fire behind them, Murray yelled: 'There's only two things now — either capture, or go into that!' He was among the last to leave. The Germans could now concentrate on the 46th and the 48th Battalions. So did the Australian guns, which were pounding the Hindenburg Line in the belief that it had been lost. By 12.30 pm both battalions had pulled out. As Bullecourt had not fallen, the 62nd Division stayed put. Against the Germans' 749 casualties, the 4th Division lost almost 3500 men, of whom 1182 were prisoners, the highest number of Australians captured in one action during the war. The British Army later used Bullecourt as an example of how an attack should not be undertaken.

Another go

Believing that the Germans were about to withdraw, Gough geared up to try gain but the Germans got in first with their attack on the Australian line on 15 April. The French offensive on the Chemin des Dames began next day but soon stalled with the loss of over 100 000 men. Hearing rumours that the French now wanted to sit tight and wait for the Americans, who had just entered the war, Haig sought to bolster their flagging offensive spirit by continuing at Arras, where his own offensive had also bogged down. The First and Third Armies would assault on 3 May, with the Fifth Army advancing the right flank using the 62nd Division and the 2nd Australian. Gough's objectives were largely unchanged: OG1 and OG2, which included Bullecourt for the 62nd, in the first phase, and the Fontaine–Quéant road behind OG2, which partly survives as today's D38, in the second to gain a jump-off line for the capture of Riencourt and Hendecourt in the third.

In the 2nd Division, the 5th and 6th Brigades would assault on 600-metre frontages respectively right and left of Central Road behind a creeping barrage and with no gap between them. In contrast to the first attack, the preparations were thorough and included rehearsals on similar terrain. The Hindenburg Line had been bombarded from mid-April. By month's end Bullecourt, Riencourt and Hendecourt resembled rubbish heaps and great swathes of wire had been destroyed.

'Well done, Australia!'

At 3.45 am on 3 May, the 5th and 6th Brigades headed for the Hindenburg Line. On the 5th Brigade's right, the 19th Battalion veered towards Balcony Trench and was savaged by machine-guns. As the 17th Battalion alongside stayed on track, a gap yawned. The rear waves poured into it. Realising its error, the 19th changed direction leftwards and the line became densely packed, giving the machine-guns an even better target. When dawn broke, so did the line. By 4.45 am it was strewn along the sunken

Major-General Sir Nevill Maskelyne Smyth VC

Commander, 2nd Australian Division, 1917–18

1868–1941

A British regular officer, Smyth had won the VC at Khartoum in the Sudan in 1898. During the Gallipoli campaign, he commanded the 1st Australian Brigade in its epic attack on Lone Pine and was one of the last officers to leave ANZAC. In 1913 he had learned to fly and, as commander of the 2nd Division, occasionally flew his own aerial reconnaissances of the German line. When Australians took over the Australian divisions in 1918, Smyth went back to the British Army and led the 59th Division in the liberation of Lille. A man of few words, he was nicknamed 'the Sphinx' and was noted for his thoroughness and caution. Smyth was appointed CB in 1916 and knighted (KCB) in 1919. His affection for the men he had led for most of the war greatly influenced his decision to emigrate to Australia in 1925.

Australians relax by a dugout in the Hindenburg Line in front of Riencourt after the battle. The depth of the trench, which is probably OG2, and the protection provided by the dugout, give some idea of how formidable the Hindenburg Line was.

road in front of the railway embankment. But the 6th Brigade had taken its stretch of the OG Lines. Its commander, Brigadier-General Gellibrand, had established his headquarters in the railway embankment and saw everything.

Sheltered by the slope on the right of Central Road from the fire that shattered the 5th Brigade, the 23rd and 24th Battalions reached the OG Lines before the Germans emerged from their dugouts, and took them with little loss. On their left, half of the 21st and 22nd Battalions were raked from Bullecourt and pinned down at the wire. The other half, further away from the village, joined

the 23rd and 24th in the Hindenburg Line. Also seized was the start of the sunken Diagonal Road, which OG2 briefly followed as it ran 800 metres to Bullecourt from a six-way junction, called the Six Cross Roads, at the bottom of the re-entrant. Parties from the 23rd and 24th Battalions got to the Fontaine–Quéant road but were heavily engaged from Riencourt. As the village was clearly unattainable, Gellibrand ordered a protective barrage around the 500-metre stretch of the Hindenburg Line his brigade held.

Aware that the fate of the pocket depended on shoring up the right flank,

Gellibrand told Captain Walter Gilchrist to rally the 5th Brigade's scattered troops. Gilchrist was near the wire with about 300 men from the 5th at 5.30 am when the German machine-guns opened. He and a few survivors reached OG1 and began bombing along it. Twice they were driven back to Central Road, twice they went forward again. Gellibrand had seen the 62nd Division's attack on the left flank cut to pieces but the 2nd Division's commander, Major-General Smyth, swallowed the 62nd's assurance that it was 'bombing towards the Anzacs'. Overruling Gellibrand's protests, he directed the 25th Battalion to attack in support. Gellibrand tested the waters with two platoons. They were shredded.

The numerous cross-trenches linking OG1 and OG2 complicated the defence of both flanks. If the Germans recaptured part of one line, they could zip down the nearest cross-trench and get behind the Australians in the other. The first counterattack, at 8.45 am, fell heaviest on the right. It was thrown back, although the line on the Fontaine–Quéant road had to be given up. Counterattacks by both sides now went on in a continuous cycle. The 28th Battalion captured and lost 350 metres of OG1 on the right of Central Road three times until it withdrew at dusk on hearing a mistaken report the 6th Brigade was retiring. But the 6th remained in place until relieved by the 1st Brigade early on 4 May. 'Well done, Australia!' read the note dropped by a British airman at Gellibrand's headquarters.

As long as the Germans held Bullecourt, the Australian pocket was endangered. General Birdwood demanded its capture. The 7th Division,

which had relieved the 62nd, was to keep bashing away at the village, while the 1st Brigade extended the flanks of the pocket in order to get the extra space needed to absorb counterattacks. On 4 May the 1st and 3rd Battalions bombed 180 metres closer to Bullecourt and the 2nd and 4th Battalions recaptured the 350-metre stretch of OG1 held by the 28th Battalion on the opposite flank the previous day. Two German counterattacks, one using flamethrowers, were unsuccessful. On 5 May the 3rd Brigade took over on the right of Central Road. The 11th and 12th Battalions reeled back to it when the Germans struck again with flamethrowers. Inspired by the solo bombing attack of Corporal George Howell of the 1st Battalion, they rallied and hurled the Germans beyond their starting point. Howell was awarded the VC.

On 7 May the 9th Battalion bombed down OG1 to connect with the 7th Division, which had partly taken Bullecourt. As the 1st Australian Division, which had also worn the brunt of the Lagnicourt attack, was now exhausted, the 5th Australian relieved it. Spearheaded by Lieutenant Rupert Moon, the 58th Battalion advanced along OG2 to Bullecourt on 12 May. Moon won the VC. Finally deciding that the cost of trying to regain the Hindenburg Line was prohibitive, the Germans withdrew to a new position behind it. 'The Australian capture and defence of the double trench line', wrote Haig, 'exposed to counter-attack after counter-attack, through two weeks of almost constant fighting, deserves to be remembered as a most gallant feat of arms'. The cost to the 1st, 2nd and 5th Divisions was 7000 men.

WALKING THE BATTLEFIELD

The Bullecourt battlefield is unspoiled by urban sprawl or busy roads, so there is no traffic noise to intrude on the senses. Instead, Bullecourt has a timeless, even haunting quality because its silence and stillness, and the subtle reminders of 1917 that remain, let the past speak. Just listen as you walk.

You should also remember two things that will help set the stage for what you hear. At the time of the first battle, Bullecourt was freezing cold, snow-covered, bleak. For the second battle, the snow had vanished, such trees as were left were blossoming, and patchy growth was sprouting in the few mildly shelled places. The Germans fought like tigers in both battles. As Australians on Australian battlefields, we inevitably focus on our own side. On this Australian battlefield, think of the Germans as well.

You will see, too, that the locals have maintained a strong Australian connection. For many years, Jean Letaille, a long-time mayor of Bullecourt, his wife, Denise (before she passed away), and Claude and Collette Durand of Hendecourt have gone out of their way to welcome visitors. They have all been made honorary Members of the Order of Australia. A signposted walking trail around the Australian battlefield has been established by *Les amis de la nature*, a walking group. The walk that follows takes a different route and traces the fighting in much greater detail.

MAP IGN Blue Series, 1:25 000: 25070 Croisilles

From Albert/Pozières, take the D929 towards Bapaume. Turn left at the roundabout 4.5 kilometres past Le Sars, where the D929 becomes the ring road around Bapaume, and, following the signs to the A1 autoroute, go through two more roundabouts before taking the third exit at the next one onto the D956 (direction Vaulx-Vraucourt). Bullecourt is about 11 kilometres along.

Just before entering Bullecourt, note the water tower on the right. The Australian, British and French flags and AIF and British insignia were painted on it in 2007 to commemorate the 90th anniversary of the battle. Once in the centre of the village, park at the **church** ❶, in front of which is a memorial to the Australian and British divisions that fought in the battle. Built using funds raised locally by M Letaille, then mayor, and M Durand, it was dedicated on 24 May 1981. Facing the car park is a memorial to the Tank Corps, on which is set several track links from one of the tanks lost at Bullecourt. In the **town hall** across the road hangs a painting by Australian war artist James Scott that depicts the death of Percy Black. The Australian War Memorial

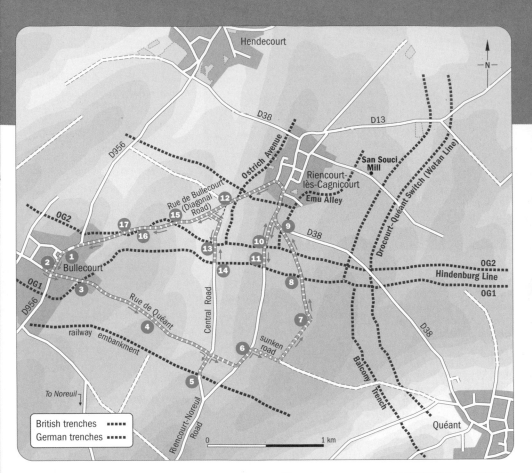

British trenches ·····
German trenches ·····

presented it to Bullecourt in 1988 in recognition of the way the villagers have commemorated the Australians who fought there.

Walk back along the D956 to the crossroads and look straight ahead. Parallelling Rue de Quéant and Rue d'Arras (D5e2) on your left and right,

This walk covers both Bullecourt battles. Starting in Bullecourt itself, it offers perspectives on the fighting from locations on the start line, the railway embankment and Central Road, and, in particular, the OG Lines. Riencourt and the sites of the two VC actions are also included.

DISTANCE COVERED: 9 km
DURATION: 5 hours

The memorial in front of Bullecourt church. As the Australian War Memorial commissioned Victorian sculptor Roy McPherson to make the bronze slouch hat, the belief that it is an original one from the First World War covered in bronze is baseless.

OG1 crossed the D956 150 metres in front of you and was here called **Tower Trench**. Coloured red on trench maps, the area between it and Rue d'Arras was bitterly contested and became infamous as the **Red Patch**. The 62nd and 7th Divisions attacked it frontally astride the D956 and the 7th Division also struck it from your left astride Rue de Quéant. Adding depth to OG1 was another trench that crossed the road 100 metres behind you. These defences ensured that this end of Bullecourt was the last part of the village to fall. Now head along Rue d'Arras to **M Letaille's house** (No 1, the first on the right) to visit, by prior arrangement, his **battlefield museum** ❷.

On returning to the crossroads, walk 450 metres along Rue de Quéant to the crest on the far side of a small **re-entrant** ❸ and stand with Bullecourt at your back. Having enclosed the right

side of the village, OG1/Tower Trench swung across Rue de Quéant and ran through your location before curving around in front of the **Australian Memorial Park**, shown by the flagpoles, 500 metres to your left. From in front of the two poplars to the right of the park, OG1 tracked diagonally across the re-entrant and then cut back in front of **Riencourt**, 1.7 kilometres to your left front on the higher ground. OG2, which ran behind Bullecourt and through the park site, was 150 metres in rear of OG1 and roughly paralleled it. After OG1 passed Riencourt, Balcony Trench diverged from it and followed the course of the power lines on the far crest before descending to enclose **Quéant**, which is over the crest. The **Drocourt–Quéant Switch** ran past the far side of Riencourt to meet OG2 directly behind the OG1/Balcony Trench junction. Following the tree line 300 metres on your right is the **railway embankment** from which the Australians and British attacked.

Note how the Germans here resisted the temptation to 'chase ground' and defended back instead of forward. By siting OG1 on this spur, they accepted that the dip before the next spur, and especially the main re-entrant beyond, would largely be hidden. This dead ground made an ideal forming-up place for an attack up Rue de Quéant towards you but the observation gained by moving OG1 forward to the next spur would have resulted in a longer line that required more men to hold. An attack

AUSTRALIAN MEMORIAL PARK

HINDENBURG LINE

12TH AND 6TH BRIGADES

from this direction was, in any case, far less likely than one from the embankment. In the one time it was tried, on 7 May, the British formed up in the dip 200 metres ahead. Advancing astride the road, they easily took OG1 but were pinned before the depth trench by counterattacks from the Red Patch. On 11 April the Australian 12th Brigade had also formed up in the dead ground but attacked towards the Australian Memorial Park. Its left flank came into view from OG1 to your left and was hammered.

Continue along Rue de Quéant for 550 metres to the crest of the spur on the other side of the dip ❹ and look towards the twin poplars. On your right is the start of the main re-entrant, into which the spur falls ahead of you. The dark line that passes two trees as it runs along the lower slope above the re-entrant is **Central Road**. The Hindenburg Line went between these trees after crossing the re-entrant from the poplars. Around you is the area in which the 12th Brigade formed up for the attack on 11 April. With its left flank 100 metres on your left, the 46th Battalion's start line crossed Rue de Quéant where you are standing and ended with its right flank 250 metres short of Central Road, on the other side of which was the 4th Brigade. The 48th Battalion lay behind the 46th, just this side of the railway embankment. Owing to the error over the start time, both battalions were caught in these positions by the German guns, which had begun

firing when the 4th Brigade attacked. In the gap to your right between the 4th and 12th Brigades, a breakdown before the tanks set off reduced the number of tanks advancing to three. Arriving after the 12th Brigade had left, one of them was abandoned 200 metres in front of you after a direct hit decapitated the driver.

For the attack on 3 May, the 6th Brigade formed up on a parallel start line that was 150 metres closer to the Hindenburg Line and extended to Central Road, thus avoiding any gap between it and the 5th Brigade on the other side of the road. With its right flank 250 metres ahead of you, the 22nd Battalion stretched 300 metres to your left front, while the right flank of the 21st behind it was near where you are standing. The 24th Battalion was to your right front with the 23rd behind it on the slopes to your right.

On reaching Central Road, turn right and walk to the embankment of the old **Boisleux–Marquion railway** ❺. The course of both battles can be more easily followed from this location than anywhere else. It is also where, in the first attack, the tanks were to cross the embankment and meet Captain Jacka, who would guide them to the start line. Look down Central Road towards the Hindenburg Line. Partly masked by the tree line on the horizon to the left of the road, **Hendecourt** was not an objective for the 11 April attack but the 62nd Division's objective in the 3 May one.

Central Road from the railway embankment, showing the two attacks carried out by I ANZAC. There was no gap between the brigades in the second one.

CENTRAL ROAD

RIENCOURT

4TH AND 5TH BRIGADES

Riencourt to your right front was the Australian objective in both attacks, and Central Road formed the boundary between the two assaulting brigades in each.

When the first attack started, only three tanks were in place ahead of the 4th Brigade, whose line ran past the prominent clump of bushes below the crest to your right front and down towards Central Road. None were ahead of the 12th, through whose forming-up area to your left front you have just walked, and one was on the left of Central Road just beyond Rue de Quéant in the 250-metre gap between the 4th and 12th. Three tanks had not yet reached the embankment, two more were moving from it to Rue de Quéant and another had temporarily broken down on Central Road 150 metres in front of you. Unsupported by tanks or a creeping barrage, as the tanks were supposed to obviate the need for one, the 46th Battalion got into OG1 from the left of the Australian Memorial Park to a point in line with the twin poplars, while the 48th reached OG2 at the poplars and bombed along it to Central Road at the two trees. The 4th Brigade took both trenches from just to the right of Central Road almost to the power lines beyond the crest. But the gap that the Germans still held between them in each trench could not be closed. Counterattacked outwards from it and inwards from the outer flanks, both brigades were eventually forced to return to the embankment either side of you.

In the second battle, the 6th Brigade on the left captured the OG Lines from the poplars to Central Road. The 5th Brigade's attack on the right failed, only small parties of the 18th Battalion gaining a footing in both trenches at Central Road. Ghastly trench fighting, which also involved the 1st and 5th Australian Divisions, went on over the next 12 days

as the advance ground remorselessly left and right along the OG Lines from the captured stretch towards Bullecourt and Riencourt.

Notice how the crest to your right front screens the area in front of Riencourt through which the Hindenburg Line ran. Some of it is in dead ground from your location, just as it was to the artillery observers here. The blanket of snow that rendered the ground almost featureless during the first attack further complicated their task, which helps explain their belief that Riencourt had been reached. They stuck to it despite the sheaves of SOS rockets from the Hindenburg Line that proved otherwise, fatally delaying the barrage needed to protect the captured stretch. Looking on from their headquarters among the dugouts that riddled the back of the embankment, the infantry commanders seethed. The 16th Battalion's head-quarters was 200 metres to your right, the 13th's 200 metres past it and the 14th's collocated with the 15th's another 200 metres along, the 48th's and 46th's respectively 700 metres and 900 metres away on your left. The tanks leaguered near **Noreuil**, whose church steeple pierces the skyline behind you, on 10 April after their late arrival led to the 24-hour postponement of the attack but they still could not reach the start line in front of your location on time next day.

On 3 May Brigadier-General Smith of the 5th Brigade had his headquarters in Noreuil, whereas Brigadier-General Gellibrand commanded the 6th Brigade from a dugout in the embankment 90 metres to your left. As a result, Gellibrand could follow the battle closely and exert some control over it. He became very frustrated when his reports were questioned and pointedly recommended that a sceptical Smith should come forward and see for himself after the 5th Brigade was shattered. When the 28th

Battalion mistakenly withdrew up Central Road that evening, raising the possibility that the Hindenburg Line would have to be given up, Gellibrand rallied it and strung it out with all other available men, including his own staff, along the embankment because it was the next line of defence.

Walk back to Rue de Quéant, which continues as a dirt track on the right. Take this track. It soon runs into a T-junction with the Riencourt–Noreuil road, on which you should head left for 150 metres to a **cutting** ⑥, where a second dirt track runs uphill to the right through another cutting. Known as the **sunken road** in 1917, this track was a continuation of Rue de Quéant but the stretch of it down to Central Road no longer exists. Already livid at the late arrival of the tanks and on learning that they were too slow to lead the infantry to the wire, Captain Jacka had to be restrained from shooting the crew of one when it got stuck in the non-existent part before the 11 April attack. During a night reconnaissance on 7 April, Jacka had found the track unoccupied and the 14th and 16th Battalions moved into it next evening in order to get closer to the Hindenburg Line. The 14th and 16th and, later, the 17th and 19th Battalions then advanced left and right respectively of the Riencourt–Noreuil road. Jacka laid a jump-off tape for the 14th and 16th that was 180 metres to the left of the sunken track here. A German officer, Lieutenant Reich, sprung him while he laid it. Pistol-whipped on trying to escape, Reich complained to Jacka's superior, who replied that as Jacka had captured him, he was lucky to be alive.

Now walk up the sunken track for 220 metres, take the metalled track on the left for another 220 metres and face Bullecourt. You are now on the right of the 4th Brigade's start line. Waiting for the tanks in the early morning of 10 and 11 April, men lay shivering in the snow along it from here almost to Central Road, which is hidden by the crest to your front. Carry on to the **pumping shed** on the left, at which point the track crosses Hill 98 and has become a bitumen road that bends leftward ⑦. The right of the 5th Brigade's start line was in this vicinity.

From the pumping shed, walk another 400 metres to where the road bends slightly left again ⑧, turn about and look back along it. OG1 crossed the road in this location and OG2 went over 200 metres behind you, whereupon both trenches headed directly to the junction with Balcony Trench on the far side of the power lines to your left. Two machine-gun posts formed outworks of Balcony Trench as it tracked along the power lines to the railway embankment and down to Quéant over the crest. One was 500 metres to your left front and just this side of the power lines, the other 200 metres to its left, near the pylon. Between them they enfiladed the wire in front of OG1 and Balcony Trench and also had superb fields of grazing fire across no-man's-land before you. As you can see by looking right though, Central Road and much of the main re-entrant were in defilade to them, which greatly helped the 12th and 6th Brigades attacking on that flank. From the strongpoint at **San Souci Mill**, which stood near the

> *Some dropped in the middle of the wire and hung there like scarecrows wounded and helpless only to be riddled. Others got entangled and escape was out of the question. They were like birds in a snare and just had to stand there until bullets had ended their suffering.*
>
> Private W Gallwey on the sights at the OG1 wire (Gallwey, W, 'Silver King', MS1335, AWM)

pylon taking the power lines over the D38 on your left, the Drocourt–Quéant Switch skirted the far side of Riencourt. A few stones are the only remaining trace of the mill.

The scene when the 4th Brigade attacked towards you in darkness on 11 April was surreal. Standing out starkly against the snow, its four waves stretched in perfect dressing 'illimitably to right and left … a glorious sight', wrote Sergeant William Groves of the 14th Battalion. They soon passed the few tanks. The Hindenburg Line and Balcony Trench seemed eerily quiet until the leading wave neared the wire of OG1 50 metres in front of you and, 'with a fury of hell, the enemy machine-guns spit out incessant fire'. Bullets glancing off the wire sparked like swarms of fireflies. Many men met their end in it.

One of the most dramatic moments of the battle now occurred. Moving forward to the wire on the right of the road, Major Black yelled to the 16th Battalion, 'Come on, boys, bugger the tanks!' Utilising torn stretches of wire as the illumination from a stream of German flares was reflected by the snow to shroud the battlefield in a ghostly light, Black got the 16th across and into OG1

but was killed soon after doing the same at the wire of OG2 150 metres behind you. He fell 100 to 200 metres from the right of the road. Meanwhile Murray was coolly 'strolling along as if death was something which only came with old age', recalled Lance-Corporal Bert Knowles in the 13th Battalion following. Seeing Black's men mown down, Murray shouted, 'Come on, 13th! The 16th are getting hell!' Reaching the wire 90 metres from the right of the road, he found Tank D28, outlined by sparks from bullet strikes, blocking his way. Pushing past it, he silenced a machine-gun 10 metres from the tank that had accounted for 30 of his own men.

The 4th Brigade captured OG1 100 metres short of Central Road to a point 200 metres on your left and, behind it, OG2 200 metres short of Central Road to a point 350 metres on your left. Launched at 10 am, the main German counterattack struck the 4th heaviest at the left extremities in both trenches while covered by fire from houses in Riencourt. When they were abandoned 90 minutes later, the two machine-guns in the outworks of Balcony Trench laid a solid wall of fire across no-man's-land in front of you. The chance

OG LINES

Major Percy Charles Herbert Black

His great front-line career ended in OG2 at Bullecourt.

A 36-year-old miner in Western Australia when he joined the 16th Battalion as a private in 1914, Black was a born leader. He was a machine-gunner with Harry Murray at Gallipoli, where both won the DCM, were commissioned, and became very close friends. Like Murray, who thought him 'the bravest of us all', Black led a company at Pozières and Mouquet Farm, and was awarded the DSO. Gripped by a premonition before the Bullecourt attack, he confided to Murray: 'Well, Harry, we have been in a few stunts together, but this is my last. But I'll have that Hun front line first'. Black was shot through the head while directing his men through the wire at OG2. Murray found time during the battle to search, unsuccessfully, for his body. Shattered by the loss, he was inconsolable for a long time afterwards.

1877–1917

of getting through it, Murray wrote later, was akin to running 'for hundreds of yards through a violent thunderstorm without being struck by any of the raindrops'. He was one of the nine officers and a handful of other ranks from all four battalions of the 4th Brigade to reach the safety of the sunken track.

When the 19th Battalion strayed to the left of the road in the 5th Brigade's attack on 3 May, the Balcony Trench machine-guns ripped into it, together with another gun at San Souci. The 19th veered back on track but the 20th Battalion following it was already in the gap that had opened with the 17th Battalion to your right front. When the line went to ground before the OG1 wire in front of you for two minutes to wait for the barrage to lift, it was packed. Ignoring

On the 5th Brigade's start line looking at the ground that both the 4th and 5th Brigades had to cover to reach Riencourt.

RIENCOURT

the barrage, the Germans climbed onto the parapet either side of you to add their fire to that of the machine-guns. Shrapnel shells from the German counter-barrage were bursting at head height and shredding whole groups. As dawn broke, a half-crazed officer shouted: 'Pull out — retire — get back for your lives'. The line either scarpered back to the sunken road or hunkered down in shell holes.

Continue to the junction with the D38 **9**, through which **Emu Alley** ran back from OG2 to Riencourt. During the 4th Brigade's attack, a 16th Battalion party cleared this communication trench to your location, where it threw up a barricade and held it until the 4th Brigade withdrew. Now head left to the **chapel** at the end of the Riencourt–Noreuil road, which you crossed after leaving the railway embankment. Walk towards the embankment for 150 metres to where OG2 straddled the road after running down from the twin poplars to your right **10**. The 4th Brigade held it either side of you but in the second attack, on 3 May, the 28th Battalion bombed along it to a cross-trench 200 metres on your right before being driven back to Central Road by a counterattack that started near your location. Next day, the 2nd and 4th Battalions between them bombed to a cross-trench 90 metres on your right, which marked the limit of the gain in OG2. Passing either side of your location,

the seventh, and last, German counter-attack on 15 May regained this corner as well as 60 metres of OG2 and most of the cross-trench. The 54th Battalion bombed back along both to trap the Germans in the corner, where another party from the 54th cleaned them up after storming across the open from OG1 to your right front.

Proceed another 170 metres to where OG1 crossed the road **11**. It was much the same story here. On 11 April the 4th Brigade took OG1 either side of you. On 3 May Captain Gilchrist charged 200 metres to the right of the road towards it with the survivors of the 5th Brigade that he had gathered at the railway embankment and other remnants picked up along the way. Plastered when they reached the wire that crossed the road 50 metres in front of you, very few got into OG1. Bombing along it towards you, they twice reached the cross-trench, 200 metres to your right, which the 28th Battalion later got to in OG2. Incongruously clad in a cardigan, as he had discarded his jacket and helmet in the stifling heat, Gilchrist often threw from the parapet in full view of the Germans before he was killed. Afterwards, the 28th Battalion thrice reached your location only to be driven back to Central Road by counterattacks from your left. On 4 May the 2nd and 4th Battalions bombed to the cross-trench, 90 metres to your right, that the 28th had also reached in OG2. On 6 May the day began

The death of Major Black.

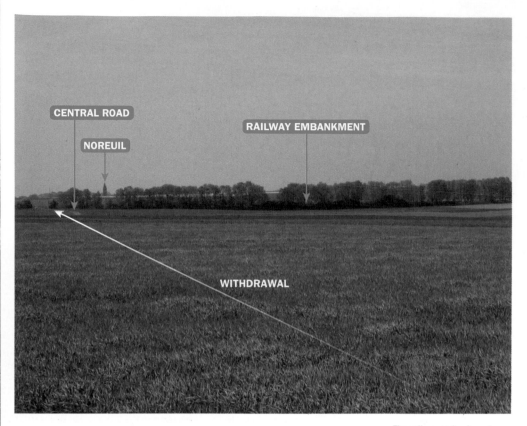

CENTRAL ROAD

NOREUIL

RAILWAY EMBANKMENT

WITHDRAWAL

with OG1 lost to Central Road in the flamethrower attack that came along the trench from your left, and ended with its recapture up to the cross-trench again. This was the limit of the gain in OG1 too.

Retracing your steps, enter Riencourt. Follow the first left, Rue de Bullecourt, downhill out of the village to a confluence of tracks at the bottom of the slope. You are now at what remains of the **Six Cross Roads 12**. Standing with

your back to Riencourt, look along Rue de Bullecourt, which now became Diagonal Road because it passed diagonally through OG2 on the slope ahead. The drainage ditch on your left is the modern continuation of Central Road, which carries on as the overgrown track to your right rear. To your right front, the track up the slope is the old Fontaine–Quéant road, which here was part of the 6th Brigade's objective in the second

The railway embankment seen from the area seized by the 4th Brigade. It later withdrew to the embankment.

RIENCOURT

OG2

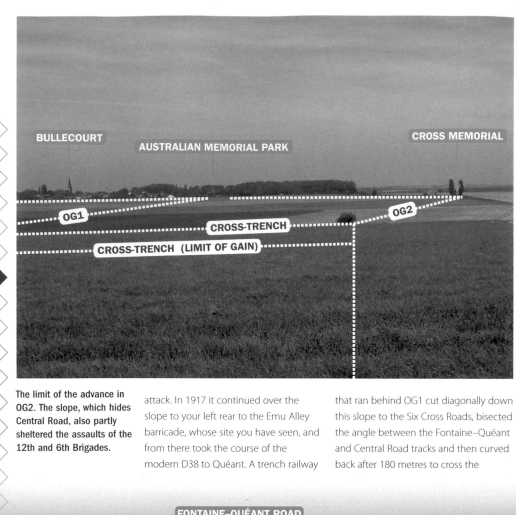

BULLECOURT

AUSTRALIAN MEMORIAL PARK

CROSS MEMORIAL

OG1

CROSS-TRENCH

CROSS-TRENCH (LIMIT OF GAIN)

OG2

The limit of the advance in OG2. The slope, which hides Central Road, also partly sheltered the assaults of the 12th and 6th Brigades.

attack. In 1917 it continued over the slope to your left rear to the Emu Alley barricade, whose site you have seen, and from there took the course of the modern D38 to Quéant. A trench railway

that ran behind OG1 cut diagonally down this slope to the Six Cross Roads, bisected the angle between the Fontaine–Quéant and Central Road tracks and then curved back after 180 metres to cross the

FONTAINE–QUÉANT ROAD

TRENCH RAILWAY

MAXFIELD

Fontaine–Quéant track just beyond the crest.

At the start of the second attack, Captain Maxfield's party from the 24th Battalion reached the curve of the railway on the crest to your right front; Captain John Pascoe's from the 23rd filled in between it and the Six Cross Roads. Both dug in along the low embankment that carried the track. Lining Central Road on your left, another party from the 23rd under Captain Percy Parkes faced Ostrich Avenue, a major communication trench that paralleled it after crossing Diagonal Road 60 metres behind you. Part of the first counterattack came down Ostrich Avenue from Riencourt but was repelled from the 23rd's barricade on it at the Fontaine–Quéant track to your rear. But the parties under Maxfield and Pascoe were exposed to fire from the Germans at the Bullecourt end of Diagonal Road, which struck them from behind, from Riencourt, and to German shelling. The survivors withdrew into OG2 on your left about 11.30 am when their own overstretched artillery could no longer support them. Maxfield did not make it; Pascoe did.

Continue along Diagonal Road and turn left after 250 metres onto a track. It soon meets Central Road, which is high-banked on the left. Head right on Central Road, stopping 200 metres along at the tree on the bank ⑬. Look across the re-entrant towards the twin poplars on the Diagonal Road. OG2 ran from there to a point 100 metres in front of you, where it turned sharply to cross Central Road at your location and go over the bank and crest. During the first battle the 48th Battalion reached OG2 at the poplars and bombed down it to where you are standing, while the 4th Brigade captured OG2 beyond its junction with Ostrich Avenue on the slope 90 metres to your rear. Using the cover that Ostrich Trench provided, the Germans channelled fresh troops into this gap from Riencourt to counterattack the inner flanks of the 4th and 12th Brigades. In the second battle, the 6th Brigade took essentially the same poplars–Central Road stretch of OG2 as the 48th Battalion had. Subsequent bitter bomb-fighting by other formations seesawed along OG2 behind you and eventually captured 300 metres of it.

The fight at the Six Cross Roads.

PASCOE

Walk another 200 metres **14** and look across the re-entrant again to follow what happened in OG1. Paralleling OG2 down the slope behind you, it went through your location, swung half right 80 metres in front of you and left 200 metres later to run up the far slope past the left of the Australian Memorial Park. On 11 April the 46th Battalion captured OG1 from its leftwards swing to just beyond the park, while the 4th Brigade's left flank was 200 metres to your rear. Practically cut off by the 48th Battalion once it reached Central Road in OG2 behind them, the Germans in your location not only fought off all attempts to close the gap but relentlessly bombed and fired at a tank that had become enmeshed in the wire 50 metres to your left until it caught fire. The failure to eliminate the gaps in OG1 and OG2

divided the effort of each brigade by requiring it to defend both of its flanks instead of just the outer one.

It is worth the effort if you can climb the bank here. Once on top, look directly ahead to the power lines, which is the track that OG1 followed. Advancing from your right on 3 May, the 5th Brigade was shot down in front of it. With OG1, and OG2 on your left, still in German hands, the threat to the 6th Brigade in OG1 and OG2 behind you was dire. The junctions of the two trenches with Central Road became the starting points for the many bombing attacks along them towards the Noreuil–Riencourt road that sought to gain elbow room. Counterattacks came the other way, so the action in the OG Lines went back and forth. The 6 May flamethrower one rattled the group from the 11th and 12th Battalions holding OG1 for 400 metres to your front. They bolted back to Central Road below you,

The business end of Central Road, showing the protection that the bank afforded. Corporal Howell won his VC near this location.

OG2

where an officer with revolver drawn halted them. Taking matters into his own hands, Corporal Howell leapt onto the parapet where you are standing and bombed away from you along OG1. He soon fell wounded; the Germans fled up OG1. The lost stretch was promptly retaken. The battle ended with 400 metres of both trenches in Australian hands on this side of Central Road.

Descend to Central Road and look along it towards the railway embankment to see the field of fire in that direction that the Germans in the gap astride the road here had during the first attack. As there was no gap in the second attack, this difficulty did not recur. The bank sheltered Central Road from the fire from your left that had smashed the 5th Brigade, and the 6th Brigade's capture of the OG Lines behind you and to your right rear reduced the fire that would otherwise have whipped in from there. So Central Road became the artery that sustained the battle. The traffic in both directions was nonstop. By the evening of 3 May the 2nd Division's pioneers had dug a roadside trench that linked the embankment to the Hindenburg Line. Running on your left, it was lined with the corpses of many of the pioneers who made it. Central Road was known as **Pioneer Trench** from then on.

Return to Diagonal Road and walk towards Bullecourt. Stopping after 300 metres in the cutting, climb the stairs to the **Cross Memorial** ⓯ at the twin poplars atop the embankment on your right. Look across the road, which OG2 met to your front but did not cut through. Instead, Diagonal Road blocked the trench, which began again on this side of it just to the right of the memorial. From here it ran along the embankment for 150 metres before going over the road once more near the head of the cutting to pass through the right side of

The 'step' where OG2 met Diagonal Road.

the Australian Memorial Park. Having to step up to Diagonal Road rather than rushing across it exposed the 48th Battalion in the 11 April attack to deadly enfilade fire from where OG2 recrossed the road on your right. The 48th stalled at OG2 in front of you but bombed down it on your left front to Central Road. Meanwhile the 46th Battalion held OG1 150 metres in rear from roughly in front of you to just beyond the Australian Memorial Park.

The two battalions were therefore skew-whiff, preventing the mutual support that would have stopped the Germans picking them off piecemeal. They struck along OG1 first, simultaneously with their counterattack against the 4th Brigade on the other side of Central Road. The 46th's exposed left flank near the park was always vulnerable but the attack also came from the gap in OG1 astride Central Road to pummel its right flank to your front.

The 46th was squeezed out of OG1, isolating the 48th in OG2. It counterattacked away from you along two cross-trenches, one directly in front of you, the other 200 metres to its left, to gain OG1. The Germans followed along both trenches to attack the 48th frontally, and also began pressing against its flanks as they had done to the 46th. With the

When the Germans were about forty yards away I saw a fellow shoot a jet of flame into the bank. It was the first flammenwerfer I had seen. I fired and shot the carrier through the belly; my bullet went through the flammenwerfer can, and it caught fire at the back. You could hardly see for smoke. There was a hole in the road; the man fell into it, and about a dozen men on top of him — they all appeared to catch fire.

Sergeant Pat Kinchington of the 3rd Battalion on the German counterattack on OG2 (quoted in Bean, CEW, *The AIF in France. IV. 1917*, Sydney, 1938, p. 493)

Australian artillery now shelling the area around you, the 48th withdrew as well.

In the 6th Brigade's attack on 3 May the outer flank of the 21st and 22nd Battalions to your right front had no protection from enfilade fire, unlike the 23rd and 24th on the Central Road flank, and was badly mauled from Bullecourt. German shelling also severely disrupted their advance. Though those closest to the outer flank were temporarily pinned down at the wire before OG1, the 6th Brigade took OG1 from Central Road to about 200 metres this side of the Australian Memorial Park, and OG2 from Central Road to Diagonal Road in front of you. Just as it had done to the 48th Battalion, which had captured the same stretch of OG2 in the earlier attack, the

The 46th and 48th Battalions in the OG Lines, from the Cross Memorial. After the attack, Germans shot the dying and left the wounded in front of OG1 for the Australians to collect in an informal truce.

problem caused by the need to step up to the road prevented any exploitation along OG2 to your right. During the 1st Brigade's relief of the 6th early next morning, 150 Germans came down the road to your right to counterattack OG2. They were unsuccessful. The concurrent flamethrower attack along OG1 from your right front was also beaten off and the 3rd Battalion got across Diagonal Road at the step. Now began the same cycle of attack and counterattack along both trenches, only towards Bullecourt, that was underway on the far side of Central Road.

Continue towards the **Australian Memorial Park 16**. OG2 recrossed the road 250 metres along to run on its left. OG1 was 150 metres further in. When the

CENTRAL ROAD

OG2

48TH BATTALION

58th Battalion attacked along both trenches from here at 3.40 am on 12 May, Lieutenant Rupert Moon's platoon between them had to take a pillbox on the park site. Charging across the open, the platoon faltered as fire from the pillbox lashed it. Hit in the face, Moon yelled 'Come on, boys, don't turn me down'. Following him, they cleared the pillbox in 20 minutes' hard fighting. Walk to the Digger statue at the far end of the park to see the area in which it stood. OG2 cut through the park 20 metres in from Diagonal Road and was barricaded as it crossed the road a third time just past the park boundary.

Proceed along Diagonal Road. Moon's men now joined the attack on OG2, which had been held up at the barricade. When the Germans broke back from it into the road ahead of you, he leapt onto the road alone, emptied his rifle into them, was hit again and bombed back into OG2. Inundating the road with bombs themselves, he and a few others ran along it, shooting into the dugouts on either side of the cutting to trap the Germans, who had sheltered in them,

until reinforcements arrived. Moon almost reached the track on the right 100 metres past the park. He had been hit a third time but 186 Germans surrendered. As he joked 'I've got three cracks and not one of them good enough for Blighty', a fourth crack broke his jaw and smashed 12 teeth.

Now look along Diagonal Road from the junction with the track ⑰. OG2 crossed the track 50 metres to your right and passed to the right of Bullecourt, while OG1 curved away 150 metres to your left to run along the facing side of the village. In the last Australian attack at Bullecourt, the 58th Battalion advanced after dark on 12 May down the slope to your left from OG1, and reached Diagonal Road just beyond the track. By then a link-up had been made with the British 7th Division, which had taken all but the Red Patch area of the village. Carry on along Diagonal Road to its junction with the D956, where, fittingly, it is signposted **Rue des Australiens**. Stay on the D956 for the church and your car. Before getting into it, consider a drink at **Le Canberra** estaminet across the road.

LOCAL INFORMATION

CEMETERIES

The Australian dead from both battles rest in the same cemeteries as those who fell in the advance to the Hindenburg Line. Falling on 4 May, 2nd Lieutenant Richmond Howell-Price MC, of the 1st Battalion, is in **Vraucourt Copse**

Grave of Captain Percy Cherry VC, MC, Quéant Road Cemetery.

Cemetery at II.B.7. His brother, Owen, commanding officer of the 3rd Battalion, was killed at Flers on 4 November 1916, and another brother, Philip, also from the 1st Battalion, at Broodseinde on 4 October 1917. Richmond was the youngest.

Quéant Road Cemetery, Buissy

Started by British units in the war's last weeks, Quéant Road was enlarged after the armistice. Its 2337 burials include 954 Australians, more than in any other cemetery in the area. Of these, most were Bullecourt casualties and 699 are unidentified. Major Ben Leane, second-in-command of the 48th Battalion, at I.C.1, was killed when the Germans shelled the withdrawal from the start line after the proposed attack on 10 April was called off. His brother, Ray, who led the 48th, dug Ben's original grave and erected the cross. Captain Allan Leane, their cousin, was wounded by a grenade at the end of the 48th's fight in OG2 on 11 April, which he had led. Dying later in a German hospital, he has no known grave. 'Made of all Leanes', the 48th had been known as the Joan of Arc Battalion. The remains of Sergeant John White of the 22nd Battalion, who fell on 3 May, were discovered on the battlefield in 1993 and interred at VIII.B.28a. Captain Percy Cherry VC, MC, whose stellar front-line service ended at Lagnicourt on 26 March 1917, rests at VIII.C.10. To reach the cemetery, take the D38 from Riencourt to Quéant, turn there onto the D38 for Buissy and continue two kilometres to the cross-roads with the D14E2.

The Australian Memorial Park and Bullecourt Digger

Occupying a site that was between OG1 and OG2, the park is on Rue des Australiens, the old Diagonal Road, on the outskirts of Bullecourt. A Bastiaan plaque guards the entrance and a stunning bronze statue, the 'Bullecourt Digger', looks out over the battlefield at the other end. When then Australian Minister for Veterans' Affairs Ben Humphreys opened the park on Anzac Day 1992, he felt that something was needed atop the cairn, which then stood as the memorial. The Office of Australian War Graves subsequently commissioned Melburnian sculptor Peter Corlett to create a work that captured the character of the Australians who fought at Bullecourt.

Corlett, who would later sculpt the Fromelles 'Cobbers', took great pains to replicate the AIF uniform and fighting order. Wanting the digger's face to be the 'fresh face of a young man about to set off on a great adventure', he took the features from an old photograph of his father after discovering that he had fought at Bullecourt. Unveiled on ANZAC Day 1993, the digger stands as a tribute to 'hope, pride and optimism'. Look closely and you can also see determination, resilience and mischievous humour in his unforgettable expression.

The Cross Memorial

Honouring the 2423 Australians killed at Bullecourt who have no known grave, this memorial is situated on the bank

Grave of Major Ben Leane, Quéant Road Cemetery.

above Diagonal Road where OG2 crossed it midway between the Australian Memorial Park and the Six Cross Roads. The inspiration for the memorial, and its location, resulted from a sister's persistent enquiries over many years concerning her brother, who was believed to have fallen near this spot on 12 May 1917. Jean Letaille and other locals built the plinth using cobbles from the roads of

'Hope, pride and optimism'.

Vimy Ridge Canadian National Memorial and park

The results of the Arras offensive were disappointing apart from the capture of the 14-kilometre long Vimy Ridge on the left flank by the Canadian Corps. Perhaps the most important feature held by the Germans in northern France, it was fortified and defended accordingly. The French had lost 135 000 men attacking it before they handed over to the British early in 1916. Unremitting action above and below ground thereafter kept tensions high until the Arras offensive began. After careful planning and thorough rehearsals, the four Canadian divisions advanced side-by-side behind a perfect creeping barrage towards the crest in driving sleet at 5.30 am on 9 April 1917. By mid-afternoon the ridge was effectively theirs. Its capture was a great achievement, recognised by the award of four VCs, but it did not come cheap. The Canadians suffered 10 602 casualties, the Germans twice that.

In 1920 the Canadian government announced a design competition for a standard memorial to mark several significant battle sites. As the winning design, which Toronto sculptor Walter Seymour Allward said came to him in a dream, was too grandiose to duplicate, it became a national memorial instead. In 1922 France gave Canada 107 hectares of Vimy Ridge around Point 145, the highest part of the ridge and where the fighting was grimmest, for the setting. Work began in 1925 and the memorial was unveiled in 1936 by Edward VIII in his only official foreign engagement as king. Dalmatian stone was used for everything apart from the massive concrete base, above which two 27-metre pylons, standing for Canada and France, watch over the figure of a cloaked woman resting her chin in her hands. Mother

the original Bullecourt, while the Arras branch of the Souvenir Française replaced the original wooden cross atop it in 1982. The many private plaques that now adorn the memorial include one installed by Major Black's family from Victoria.

MUSEUMS

Started by Jean Letaille in the late 1980s when he was mayor of Bullecourt, this is one of the best private museums on the old Western Front. Many parts from the tanks knocked at Bullecourt are on show, as well as numerous other relics of the fighting. The focus is very much on the Australian involvement. As the museum is in the grounds of M Letaille's house and does not open regular hours, calling ahead to visit is advisable.

Contact details are: M Jean Letaille, 1 Rue d'Arras, 62128 Bullecourt, France; telephone 33 3 21 48 92 46. Entrance is free but donations are welcome.

Vimy Ridge Canadian National Memorial.

Canada mourning Canada's 66 000 war dead above a sarcophagus that represents them, the figure is one of 20 on the memorial. The names of the 11 285 Canadian missing are etched into the walls.

Standing on the steps of the memorial, it is easy to see why the ridge was gold dust to the Germans. The Douai plain of the Pas de Calais and Nord unfolds as far as the eye can see, with the 'Double Crassier', a huge twin-peaked slag heap, rising like two black pyramids to the left front. They featured in the British attacks at Loos in 1915, and are also a reminder that the Germans utilised France's principal coal-mining region in 1914 for most of the war. The view alone makes a visit to Vimy Ridge a must.

The Visitors Centre, staffed by Canadian student guides, like the one at Beaumont-Hamel, abuts a preserved section of the front lines where the gaping 'Grange' mine crater separates the opposing trenches. Nearby Grange Subway can be toured but only within a group escorted by a guide. It was part of the 9.6 kilometres of tunnels dug to provide covered approaches to the line. Old shell holes pockmark much of the park, large sections of which are off limits because of the dud ordnance that litters them.

Brigadier-General Alexander Ross, then a Canadian battalion commander, said of the capture of Vimy Ridge, 'I thought then … that in those few minutes I witnessed the birth of a nation'. Australians say the same about Gallipoli. Vimy Ridge means as much to Canadians as Gallipoli does to us and for the same reasons. To reach it, follow the D956 through Hendecourt to the A26 autoroute. The Canadian Memorial is signposted and can be seen on the right about eight kilometres after the A26 bypasses Arras.

CHAPTER 8

1917

YPRES

The Belgians call it Ieper. British trench maps used its French name, Ypres. Wanting something easily pronounceable, British soldiers dubbed it 'Wipers'. Whatever name it was given, this Flemish Flanders town was more closely associated with the BEF than anywhere else. The BEF had twice saved it. During First Ypres in October 1914, the original BEF was virtually destroyed while forming a salient around the town. At Second Ypres in April 1915, the Germans used gas for the first time on the Western Front and pushed in the salient to within three kilometres of the town. Symbolising sacrifice and defiance, Ypres meant as much to the British nation as Verdun did to the French by the time the BEF began the third battle of Ypres by attacking from the salient at the end of July 1917. Also known as Passchendaele, this offensive became a byword for the horrors of the Western Front. I and II ANZAC played a leading role in it, spearheading between them the attacks on the Menin Road, at Polygon Wood and Broodseinde, and the first assault on Passchendaele itself.

Destruction and reconstruction

British soldiers had come to Ypres twice before. They besieged it unsuccessfully in 1383 during the Hundred Years War, and stormed it successfully in 1658 while fighting alongside the French against the Spanish. Louis XIV's great military engineer Marshal Sebastien Vauban subsequently oversaw the building of the ramparts and other defences that transformed Ypres into a fortified town. It belonged to the Dutch and Austrians as well as the French before independent Belgium was formed in 1830. A sleepy backwater with a population of 17 500, Ypres in 1914 was a regional gem, whose high-gabled architecture reflected its medieval standing as a great European cloth centre. When the ANZACs first beheld it in 1916, two years of war had rendered it virtually a ruin; the process was complete when they returned in 1917. The town was 'simply one mass of broken walls with piles of bricks and stones everywhere', wrote Private Hartnett, who thought that preserving some of the ruins 'would assist the cause of peace more than the speeches of all the world's most renowned pacifists'. By war's end, one in four of the million British and Empire wartime dead had fallen around Ypres.

Postwar talk by Winston Churchill, among others, of preserving the ruins as a memorial and rebuilding a new Ypres nearby remained talk, for the returning residents immediately started rebuilding the old one. The architecture surrounding the central square, known as the Grote Markt, largely duplicated the original. Tours to Ypres and its salient started almost as soon as the guns stopped firing and were interrupted only by the Second World War, during which the town, fortunately, was barely touched. You will be one of more than 100 000 visitors who come annually nowadays.

WALKING YPRES

Descriptions of Ypres in travel literature usually run something like 'a small, quiet provincial town, where the past is only a step away'. With a population of about 35 000, Ypres is hardly a metropolis, although the hordes of battlefield tourists that base themselves there can make it seem otherwise. The best way, indeed the only practical way, to see the town is on foot. The one-way traffic system and a lack of parking pretty well preclude driving. But the walking is easy and there are plenty of refreshment opportunities on the way.

If arriving from Calais, take the A16/E40 to the outskirts of Dunkirk, and then the A25. On reaching Steenvoorde, follow the D48 to Poperinghe, from where the N38 heads to Ypres. From Paris, head north on the A1/E17 to Lille, then take the A27/E429 (direction Tournai), before swinging onto the A17 and then the A19 to Ypres. Start from the 1.25-hectare **Grote Markt ①**, where you *can* comfortably park. From whichever direction Ypres is approached, the towers and spires of the buildings overlooking the square are visible a long way off. It has been the main thoroughfare, and the commercial and social centre, for most of the town's thousand-year existence. Throughout the war the Grote Markt echoed to the sound of boots crunching over the cobbles as battalion after battalion passed through it. As the Germans pounded it in the hope of catching them, the crash of exploding shells was just as common. The last one struck on 14 October 1918. Today hotels and restaurants line the square, many on the sites of prewar taverns. An outdoor meal or drink at one of them is an enjoyable way of ending a day on the battlefields.

Dominating the Grote Markt, and a reminder of the halcyon days of the cloth industry, is the magnificent **Cloth Hall**. Started in 1200 and taking over a century to build, the original was one of the largest commercial buildings of the medieval period, during which it served as a cloth market and warehouse, and as a centre for numerous trade offices. The first shells to smash into it, in November 1914, began its path to destruction by starting a fire that gutted the upper level. In Australian Official Photographer Frank Hurley's famous photograph of an Australian column marching past in September 1917, the jagged ruins of the Cloth Hall poke skyward like a broken tooth. They were as symbolic of Ypres as the precariously leaning Golden Virgin was of Albert on the Somme. The reconstruction, which took until 1962 to complete, meticulously followed the original medieval architectural plans and utilised those parts of the original that were structurally sound. Today's Cloth Hall houses the Ypres council offices, the regional tourist office and the **In Flanders Field Museum**. When the

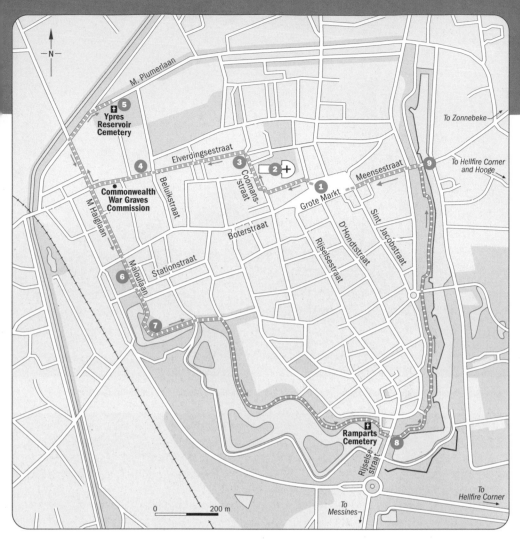

M. Plumerlaan

To Zonnebeke

5 Ypres Reservoir Cemetery

Elverdingsestraat

3

2

To Hellfire Corner and Hooge

4

Meensestraat

9

Commonwealth War Graves Commission

Beluikstraat

Coomans-straat

1

Grote Markt

Sint Jacobstraat

M Haiglaan

Boterstraat

D'Hondtstraat

6

Maloulaan

Stationstraat

Rijselsestraat

7

Ramparts Cemetery

8

Rijselse-straat

0   200 m

To Messines

To Hellfire Corner

early morning sun catches it, there is no grander sight on the old Western Front.

Walk through the archway between the near end of the Cloth Hall and the adjoining restaurant row to **St Martin's Cathedral** ❷. Troops were billeted in its cloisters until 12 August 1915, when prolonged German shelling killed 20 British soldiers sheltering there. St Martin's then shared the Cloth Hall's fate. A pile of

Starting from the famous town square, this walk passes the Menin and Lille Gates (the two main exits into the wartime salient), the Cloth Hall, St Martin's Cathedral and St George's Church, the prison and railway station, and tracks along the remaining stretch of the town ramparts. These were some of the main sites of wartime Ypres, though they show little evidence of this today.

DISTANCE COVERED: 4 km
DURATION: 2 hours

Frank Hurley's shot of an Australian column passing the Cloth Hall on its way to the line on 25 October 1917.

'No grander sight on the old Western Front.' Restored to its former glory, the Cloth Hall on the Grote Markt today, with St Martin's Cathedral behind it.

rubble by the end of the war, it was rebuilt to the original plan, including the 100-metre Gothic spire, which the town had previously been unable to afford, in place of the stubby square-topped one. Inside the cathedral are several war-related memorials, commemorative tablets and stained-glass windows. Outside it are bits of the original that were too damaged to be used in the reconstruction.

Leaving St Martin's by the main door, look left along Coomansstraat to see the imposing memorial to Belgium's dead in both world wars. Now head right for 100 metres to **St George's Memorial Church** ③, on the corner of Elverdingsestraat. In 1924 the BEF's first commander, Field Marshal Sir John French, called for the construction of a British church in Ypres as a memorial, and to serve pilgrims to the battlefields as well as the large British community that lived in the town and tended the many war cemeteries. Its designer, Sir Reginald Blomfield, accordingly sought to re-create a typical English parish church. Funded mostly by public donation, St George's was built between 1928 and 1929 and is filled with memorials, mainly brass plaques on the walls, to the divisions, regiments and battalions that fought in the salient. Families could place plaques to loved ones killed there; each pew commemorates one of the fallen. Plaques honour the Australian and New Zealand dead of both world wars, and the Australians of the 10th Battalion who perished in the unsuccessful raid on Celtic Wood on 9 October 1917. Memorials continue to be added. They make St George's as much a museum as a church, though services are still held regularly. It remains a wonderful place to reflect in quiet solitude.

Head left down Elverdingsestraat, which was the main route into the centre of Ypres from the rear areas. Cross Beluikstraat and walk along the front of **Ypres prison** ④ on the right. Though Rudyard Kipling remarked after visiting Ypres that the prison was 'a fine example of the resistance to

Australians relaxing by the ramparts and the moat on 19 September 1917. They would be going into action in their first battle in the Ypres salient, on Menin Road, the next day.

shell-fire of thick walls', it had been battered into ruin by war's end. An advanced dressing station was set up in the cellars in late 1915. **Ypres Reservoir Cemetery**, which served it, can be reached by continuing past the **Commonwealth War Graves Commission office** at 82 Elverdingsestraat, heading right on M Haiglaan (Maloulaan) for 200 metres, and right again along M Plumerlaan for another 200 metres ⑤.

From the cemetery, return to M Haiglaan, turn left and walk 400 metres to the **railway station square** ⑥. Remaining open until the Germans reached the outskirts of Ypres during their Lys offensive in April 1918, the station was at the apex of a network of branch lines that ran to the plethora of camps and dumps west of the town. It was the offload point for the salient's logistics needs and the evacuation point for its wounded. During the Second World War the Germans removed and scrapped the British tank that stood in the station square.

Continue in the direction you have been walking to the path that heads up onto the remaining section of Vauban's **ramparts**. Impervious to shell fire, they accommodated resting units, dressing stations and headquarters, including those of the Australian divisions during Third Ypres. Telephone lines from the

Australian engineers relaxing in the vaults beneath the ramparts on 1 November 1917.

fetid, damp, rat-infested interior festooned the outside walls, and the surrounding moat was a stinking swamp. The **pillbox** 7 that you will shortly pass on the edge of the path was one of a number hurriedly built by British engineers when it seemed, during the Lys offensive, that Ypres might have to be defended from the ramparts.

Carry on to beautiful **Ramparts Cemetery**, whose grounds run down to the edge of the moat, and stop just past it at the **Lille Gate** 8. The southern exit from Ypres, it straddles Rijselsestraat. As the Menin Gate was more exposed to German observation, and hence shelling, many units entered the salient via the Lille Gate. But they were soon under fire nonetheless for **Shrapnel Corner**, on the site of the roundabout on Rijselsestraat that you can see from the gate, was a frequent German target, particularly at night when most movement occurred.

A well-known trench rag, *The Wipers Times*, was printed in the Lille Gate. On the wall below the span are five cemetery signs from the Commonwealth War Grave's Commission's predecessor, the Imperial War Graves Commission.

Particularly riddled with dugouts, the next section of the ramparts ends at the **Menin Gate** 9. The eastern exit from Ypres, it was originally just a gap in the walls through which Meensestraat, the N8, passed before crossing the moat on a bridge guarded by two stone lions. Muttered by practically every one of the hundreds of thousands of soldiers who passed through it into the salient beyond, 'Tell the last man through to bolt the Menin Gate' became a famous wartime saying. Ferociously shelled, the gate area became a tangle of smashed stonework, smashed vehicles and smashed bodies. The lions were dismembered. Whenever the shelling died down, repair teams dashed out from the ramparts to patch up the road. In a reversal of roles, the British destroyed the bridge in May 1940 to delay the advancing Germans. This time the lions, or their remains at least, were safe for Ypres had given them to Australia as a gesture of friendship in 1936. Repaired in such a way that the original bits can easily be distinguished from the reconstructed ones, they now guard the entrance to the Australian War Memorial.

To return to the Grote Markt from the Menin Gate, simply walk 200 metres along Meensestraat.

The Menin Gate lions welcoming visitors to the Australian War Memorial.

LOCAL INFORMATION

CEMETERIES

Aeroplane Cemetery

Begun in August 1917 on ground captured at the start of the Third Ypres offensive on 31 July, this cemetery took its name from an aeroplane that crashed near the site of the Cross of Sacrifice. Remains from other cemeteries and the surrounding battlefields were re-interred at Aeroplane postwar. Of its 1105 burials, 469 are identified. Many of the 208 Australians and 17 New Zealanders fell in the Polygon Wood and Passchendaele fighting. Three British soldiers, Privates Bert Hartells and John Robinson at II.A.6/7, and Alfred Thompson at II.A.8, were among the five shot at dawn on the Ypres ramparts on 26 July 1915 for desertion. This was the largest British execution of the war. The cemetery is on the right of the N332, the Ypres–Zonnebeke road, just before it crosses the A19 autoroute and just past the French military cemetery.

Langemarck German Cemetery

The only German cemetery in the salient, Langemarck should be visited because of its scale and because of what happened around it. Take the N332 from Ypres and turn left after two kilometres onto the N345 just after **Potijze Burial Ground Cemetery**. At the T-junction one kilometre along, head right onto the N313. Continue through St Juliaan and past the Canadian **Brooding Soldier Memorial** on the right at Vancouver Corner to Poelcapelle. On entering the village at the **mourning stork memorial** to the French ace Georges Guynemer, who came down in this vicinity on 11 September 1917, turn left

for Langemarck. Turn right in the centre of the village and head past the church, following the signs for the cemetery. On arrival, walk to the far wall and face right.

On 22 October 1914, at the start of First Ypres, British troops either side of you annihilated the formations of German university students and high school graduates that attacked down the road towards you. The *Kindermord*, or Massacre of the Innocents, became a catchcry for Hitler's National Socialists in postwar Germany. On 22 April 1915 the cemetery area was at the heart of the German gas attack that began Second Ypres. The French North African troops holding the line to your front folded. At horrific cost, the Canadians around Vancouver Corner blunted the attack. On 9 October 1917, during Third Ypres, Private Frederick Dancox of the 4th Worcesters knocked out one of the three pillboxes, in the cemetery wall to your front, which had almost wiped out his unit. He was awarded the VC.

The Germans began the cemetery in 1915. As a result of the postwar concentration of graves from elsewhere in the salient and Belgian reluctance to provide ground for the interment of enemy dead, Langemarck contains more than 44000 burials, including over 3000 *Kinder*. The flat headstones signify multiple burials; the mass grave near the entrance contains 25000. Many of these unknowns have since been identified and their names, together with regimental insignia and battle honours, are recorded on the bronze panels enclosing the grave. At the rear of the cemetery, Munich Professor Emil Krieger's haunting sculpture of four faceless German soldiers in mourning eerily stands eternal guard over their brothers-in-arms.

Lijssenthoek Military Cemetery

Close to the salient and its lines of communication but beyond the range of most German artillery, Lijssenthoek was an ideal location for casualty clearing stations and field hospitals. By mid-1915 a cluster of them had been established around the village. They were served by this cemetery, which began in a hop field. Only a handful of graves were added after the war, so its 10786 burials reflect Lijssenthoek's wartime scale. It remains the second-largest Commonwealth war cemetery in Belgium after Tyne Cot, near Passchendaele. As those resting in it died here rather than in the front line, 10755, nearly all of them, are known.

Australian burials number 1131, more than anywhere else but Tyne Cot. Major Frederick Tubb of the 7th Battalion, who won the VC at Lone Pine on Gallipoli, is the best known. Mortally wounded by shell fire in the attack at Polygon Wood on 26 September 1917, he rests at XIX.C.5. 2nd Lieutenant William Seabrook of the 17th Battalion at XXIII.B.5. was mortally wounded in the Menin Road attack, in which his two brothers were killed, on 20 September. The cemetery also contains 291 New Zealand burials.

In 1923 as many as a thousand relatives of the dead made a pilgrimage to Lijssenthoek. They could not contain their emotions. Overshadowed by Tyne Cot, the cemetery is hardly visited at all today. You can reach it from Ypres by heading west on the N38 for 10 kilometres to the R33, the Poperinghe ring road. Take the N38 exit after 2.5 kilometres, turn left after 750 metres onto Lenestraat and then right straightaway onto Boescheepseweg. The cemetery is on the right 1.7 kilometres along.

Nine Elms British Cemetery

Started in September 1917 by the 3rd Australian and the 44th Casualty Clearing Stations, Nine Elms contains 150 Australians and 117 New Zealanders among its 1615 burials. Like those at Lijssenthoek, they died of wounds so most are identified. Touring New Zealand All Black rugby teams often visit to honour the legendary captain of the 1905 All Blacks, Dave Gallaher of the Auckland Regiment. Mortally wounded in the attack at Broodseinde on 4 October 1917, he rests at III.D.8. The cemetery is 700 metres along the Helleketelweg, which swings left off the Poperinghe ring road 3.3 kilometres after the ring road meets the N38 from Ypres.

Ramparts Cemetery

Near the Lille Gate on the walking route, this cemetery was started by the French, whose graves were removed postwar, and then used by the British. Its 198 burials span the entire fighting in the Ypres Salient. Six of the 11 Australians were killed by a single shell and are buried in a single row.

The grave of Major Frederick Tubb VC, Lijssenthoek Military Cemetery.

Of the 14 New Zealanders, 10 belonged to the Maori (Pioneer) Battalion, including Lance-Corporal Edward Angel at J.2, who served on Gallipoli.

Ypres Reservoir Cemetery

On M Plumerlaan and visited on the walking tour, this cemetery was one of three that served the dressing station in the nearby prison. The burials from the other two, and from other smaller cemeteries and isolated battlefield graves, were concentrated into it postwar. Renamed Ypres Reservoir, as its original name, Cemetery North of the Prison, might have led mourning relatives to think that their loved ones had died in the slammer, the cemetery contains 2613 burials, 1579 of them known. The 143 Australians include the acting commanding of the 3rd Pioneer Battalion, Major Bill Adams DSO, killed while supervising road construction near Zonnebeke on 15 October 1917, at I.H.43, and Captain Eric Kerr, of the 11th Field Ambulance, at I.C.17. A brilliant doctor, his career was cut short in the Broodseinde attack. Many of those killed in the shelling of St Martin's Cathedral on 12 August 1915 lie in Plot V, Row AA.

You might pause at the graves of two British officers, Major James Knott and Captain Henry Knott, who lie beside each other at V.B.15 and 16 respectively. James fell on the Somme in 1916, almost a year after Henry was killed at Ypres. After the war, their father, Sir James Knott, who funded the tower of St George's church in their memory, asked for James' remains to be brought from the Somme and re-interred alongside Henry's here. Each headstone bears the moving words, 'Devoted in life, in death not divided'.

MEMORIALS

The Menin Gate

After the war, the 'Gap', as British soldiers called the break in the Ypres ramparts at the Menin Gate, was selected as the site of a memorial to commemorate the many thousands of them who fell in the salient beyond 'but to whom the fortune of war denied the known and honoured burial given to their comrades in death'. So reads the inscription on the massive memorial that Sir Reginald Blomfield, designer of St George's Memorial Church and one of the principal architects of British cemeteries and memorials along the Western Front, intended as both a mausoleum and a triumphal arch. Finding shifting sands just below ground level when work started in 1923, Blomfield had to set concrete foundation piles 11 metres deep on which to rest the 10 000-tonne French limestone and marble arch over the N8. It is 41 metres long, 31 metres wide and 26 metres high. Yet there was only room on the Portland stone panels for the names of the 54 896 missing up to 15 August 1917. The 34 888 who fell afterwards, ANZAC troops excepted, are recorded on the screen memorial at Tyne Cot cemetery.

All 6176 Australian missing in the salient are listed on the Menin Gate, mostly on the panels by the stairs of the northern loggia, which has a Bastiaan plaque at the top. Killed on 7 October 1917, Major Alexander Steele DSO, DCM had landed on Gallipoli on 25 April 1915 as part of a machine-gun team with the 9th Battalion. After four days, he was the only one in his section not killed or wounded. Killed

The Menin Gate in the morning sun.

in the Broodseinde attack, Major Philip Howell-Price DSO, MC was one of three decorated officer brothers to fall on the Western Front. Privates Theo and George Seabrook of the 17th Battalion fell in the Menin Road attack. It also claimed their brother, William, who rests at Lijssenthoek. Lieutenant John Lyons MC, MM, MSM of the 17th Battalion had started his war as a sergeant on Gallipoli. It ended before Passchendaele on 9 October 1917 when he was wounded and never seen again. There are no New Zealanders on the Menin Gate. Their missing are recorded on memorials at Messines, Polygon Wood and Tyne Cot, near where they fell.

Field Marshal Lord Plumer, the commander of the Second Army, which had been the salient's long-time custodian, unveiled the Menin Gate on 24 July 1927. Looking at the several thousand relatives, including 700 mothers, of those whose names were on it, he uttered the immortal lines, 'He is not missing. He is here'. Australian artist Will Longstaff painted the well-known *Menin Gate at Midnight* after attending the ceremony. Depicting an army of steel-helmeted ghosts marching through the gate and into a field of blood-red poppies with the salient beyond, it has hung for many years in a shrine-like darkened room at the Australian War Memorial.

During the ceremony, the bugle notes of the 'Last Post' had resounded around the memorial. Sponsored by the local authorities, buglers from the Ypres fire brigade began playing it under the arch every night at 8 pm for two months in 1928 as a gesture of gratitude to the soldiers of the Empire and of sympathy to the relatives of the fallen. In 1929 the ceremony became permanent and, apart from the four years of German occupation in the Second World War, the firemen have carried it on nightly, rain, hail or shine, ever since. Today upwards of a thousand people gather, many from veterans'

organisations with supporting bands. The police stop the traffic through the gate, wreaths are laid and the buglers play the 'Last Post' and the 'Rouse', with the recitation of the 'Ode to the Fallen' and a minute's silence in between. No visitor to Ypres should miss the ceremony. Thanks partly to it, the Menin Gate is probably the most famous of all British war memorials, including the equally imposing Memorial to the Missing of the Somme at Thiepval.

MUSEUMS

In Flanders Fields

Opened in the Cloth Hall in 1998, In Flanders Fields is a far cry from the Ypres Salient Museum that preceded it. Utilising high-technology interactive displays and audiovisual presentations as well as more traditional objects, it explores the social and military dimensions of the war in the salient while seeking to provoke discussion of the twin themes of war and peace. The concluding display on the rebuilding of Ypres reflects 'hope and renewal', in keeping with the museum brochure's declaration that the museum 'wants to be a place where every visitor will pledge to continue to fight for Peace'. Not surprisingly, In Flanders Fields has not been without controversy. Opening hours are 10 am to 6 pm daily between 1 April and 15 November and 10 am to 5 pm Tuesday to Sunday in the remaining months. Entry costs €8 for adults, €1 for those aged between seven and 25. Contact details are: telephone +32 57 23 92 20; flandersfields@ieper.be. See also www.inflandersfields.be.

NEARBY PLACES OF INTEREST

Essex Farm

On the right of the N369 just after it passes under the N38 on the bank of the Ypres/Yser Canal 2.2 kilometres north of Ypres, Essex Farm was the dressing station in which Canadian surgeon Colonel John

McCrae, who had been Professor of Medicine at McGill University prewar, wrote perhaps the most memorable war poem of all time. Revolted by what he had seen during 17 hellish days spent in the dressing station's earthen dugouts during Second Ypres, McCrae was particularly affected by the death on 2 May 1915 of one of his former students, Lt Alexis Helmer. After conducting the funeral service, McRae penned the lines: *In Flanders fields the poppies grow/Between the crosses, row on row/that mark our place*. Published in *Punch* in December 1915, the poem was instantly successful. It also inspired the adoption of the poppy as the symbol of remembrance of the dead. The dugouts that sheltered the dressing station under concrete were constructed in 1916–17. There are no Australians or New Zealanders in the adjacent cemetery but the grave of Private Valentine Strudwick of the Rifle Brigade at I.U.8 gives food for thought. He died on 14 January 1916 aged just 15. McCrae died of pneumonia in 1918.

Hill 60

Now one of the most visited spots in the Ypres salient, Hill 60 was one of the most notorious spots on the entire Western Front during the war. It can be reached by leaving Ypres through the Menin Gate and heading down the third street on the right, Menin Road, for 1.7 kilometres to the roundabout on the site of Hellfire Corner, another of the salient's least-attractive locations. After taking the second exit (direction Zillebeke), look right towards the Zillebeke lakes. Exposed to German gas and high-explosive shelling while crowded almost wheel to wheel in this area, the Australian artillery supporting the Third Ypres offensive suffered its highest casualties of the war, losing 1375 men to the end of August 1917. In Zillebeke, turn left at the T-junction in the village centre, from which Hill 60 is signposted, and continue for another 1.2 kilometres to it. Park on the left before the railway bridge.

Formed by the spoil dug from the adjacent cutting when the railway was built in the 19th century, the hill is only 60 metres above sea level — hence its name. It had been a prewar lover's haunt but the view from it over the then largely treeless flats towards Ypres, whose spires can easily be seen from the car park, gave Hill 60 immense tactical value once war came. The Germans captured it at the end of 1914 and the British immediately began mining operations to blast them off. They

Australian artillery gallop into action at the start of the Third Ypres offensive, in Septimus Power's *Third Ypres: Taking the Guns Through, 31 July 1917*.

Ypres from Hill 60. The spire of Zonnebeke church rises on the right.

succeeded in April 1915, creating the first craters you pass after going through the turnstile at the back of the car park, but were ejected in May.

The British line then ran along the slope 50 metres beyond the road behind you, while the German one, strengthened by pillboxes, paralleled it along the crest behind the car park. As an over-ground attack to retake Hill 60 would now be suicidal, mining continued apace. In August 1915 the British 175th Tunnelling Company started galleries over 30 metres underground for a mine under Hill 60 and another under the **Caterpillar**, across the cutting. The 3rd Canadian Tunnelling Company took over the work in April 1916 and completed it before the 1st Australian Tunnelling Company relieved it in November.

The Australians defended both galleries against German countermining. Once they mastered the technique of clay-kicking, in which a digger lying on his back on an inclined plank used both feet to jab a short spade into the clay face, they advanced four metres daily on

a third mine. Working underground was tense in the extreme, with the risk of entombment constant, and the fighting in the darkness, when one side broke into the other's gallery, ferocious and terrifying. On 24 April 1917, an Australian tunneller defending the Hill 60 gallery heard footsteps that were so loud he thought a German had entered. They came from a German gallery that had gone undetected. Waiting until 17 May, when the German one seemed almost finished, the Australians destroyed it by blowing up their own gallery. Captain Oliver Woodward, who answered the anonymous white feathers, a symbol of cowardice, he received before enlisting by becoming the first Australian tunneller to be decorated, fired the Hill 60 and Caterpillar mines on 7 June 1917. They were the northernmost two of the 19 that went up in the attack on the Messines Ridge, which was the precursor to Third Ypres. The third mine was not completed in time.

Now take the track to your half right and drop into the large crater beside the

The author in the crater of the mine blown under Hill 60 during the Messines attack.

cutting. Originally 80 metres wide and 20 metres deep, it resulted from the explosion of the 21 tonnes of ammonal and 3.6 tonnes of guncotton in the Hill 60 mine. The feature was now back in British hands. In February 1918 Australian engineers reconfigured the German pillbox at the far end of the crest so that it could be used against the Germans. They regained Hill 60 anyway in April 1918. The British got it back in September. Apart from the grass, and the sheep that graze on it, Hill 60 remains as it was at war's end. Many of those who died in its bowels remain there, which makes the feature a cemetery. The Australians among them are remembered on the **1st Australian Tunnelling Company Memorial** alongside the car park, which bears bullet scars from the Second World War. Erected in 1923, it replaced the original, which the tunnellers themselves had put up four years earlier. Information panels in the car park give a good summary of the fighting.

The Caterpillar Crater can be seen by crossing the bridge, turning left and following the fence line to another turnstile. Take the track on the right 20 metres beyond it, which passes the remains of a pillbox before bursting from the trees and into a clearing that the crater mostly fills. The effect is dramatic. Resulting from the explosion of 32 tonnes of ammonal, it is close to its original dimensions, 100 metres across and 27 metres deep. A walk around the rim is blissfully tranquil and drives home the crater's size.

Bethune's post

At the start of March 1918, Lieutenant Frank Bethune's section of the 3rd Australian Machine-Gun Company was near the top end of the line that the 1st Australian Division held immediately south of the Ypres Salient. With a colossal German offensive expected daily, Bethune, a prewar Tasmanian clergyman, had been ordered to hold his position 'at

The bullet-scarred memorial to the Australian tunnellers at Hill 60.

Bethune survived the war. His order lives on still. Australian Wallaby coach Rod McQueen read it out to his team before the final of the 1999 Rugby World Cup. The Wallabies won. To return to Ypres, take Kasteelhoekstraat to the T-junction and turn left onto Werviksestraat for Zillebeke, from which Ypres is signposted.

Poperinghe

'Pop' is 10 kilometres west of Ypres. Far enough away not to be threatened by concentrated shelling, and the closest point that supply trains from the Channel ports could come to in relative safety, it was the main British logistics base supporting the salient. In 1917, 250 000 troops were billeted in and around it, and depots, dumps, hospitals, and hutted and tented training camps covered the surrounding hop fields. The town's restaurants, cafés and estaminets remained open, and it became a thriving metropolis that catered to every need. Like the rest of the BEF, ANZAC soldiers loved it as a haven, the first place where something like normal life was possible on coming out of the line, and the last place before hell on going back into it.

Take the N38 from Ypres and on reaching the R33, Pop's ring road, follow the signs to the **Centrum**, the main square, on which many of the wartime buildings still stand. Head down Gasthuisstraat by the Café de la Paix, and stop on the right at No. 43, the white three-storey house bearing the shingle 'Talbot House Every Man's Club'. Founded in 1915 by two British Army chaplains, Neville Talbot and the Australian-born Phillip 'Tubby' Clayton, in the empty residence of a Poperinghe hop broker, Talbot House — Toc H in the army signallers' phonetic alphabet of the time — became the best-known building in the BEF and perhaps its main social and religious centre. The irreverent Clayton, who ran it and became forever linked with it, welcomed all-comers

all costs'. He scribbled out his own orders. Containing the grim line, 'If the section cannot remain here alive, it will remain here dead, but in any case it will remain here', they became famous.

Bethune's position was near Hill 60. From the car park there, go over the railway bridge to the T-junction and head left on Komenseweg. Park after 1.3km at the bottom of the hill, where Kasteelhoekstraat heads left under another railway bridge. Stand with the bridge at your back. Bethune's section occupied the canal bank to your right front, which was known as **Buff's Bank**. Treeless in 1918, the position offered extensive fields of fire to your left and rear. Bethune wrote his order here on 13 March. The Germans struck eight days later. Ironically they came nowhere near this location, which suffered nothing worse than some sporadic gas shelling.

Gas

Both sides used three types of poison gas in the First World War, and the Germans were the first to employ each of them on a large scale. In January 1915 they drenched the Russians with a **lachrymatory**, or tear, agent but the effect — watering of the eyes and laboured breathing — was extremely short-lived. Deadlier compounds were necessary. Chlorine, introduced at the start of Second Ypres, was the first of the **respiratory** agents, which caused death by asphyxiation. But its green cloud and powerful odour made it easy to detect. Being water soluble, it was also relatively easy to counter, even by covering the mouth and nose with a damp cloth. Phosgene, which was showered on the French at the opening of the Verdun offensive in February 1916, was more potent and harder to detect. But its symptoms often did not present for 24 hours, so its victims could fight on, temporarily at least. Mustard, a blistering agent, or **vesicant**, appeared in July 1917 and was used extensively in Third Ypres. It caused internal and external bleeding, and stripped the mucous membrane from the bronchial tubes. Its victims could linger for five weeks before dying.

> I wish those people who talk about going on with this war whatever it costs could see the soldiers suffering from mustard gas poisoning. Great mustard-coloured blisters, blind eyes, all sticky and stuck together, always fighting for breath, with voices a mere whisper, saying that their throats are closing and they know they will choke.
>
> Brittain, V., *Testament of Youth*, London, 1978, p. 395.
> Brittain was a British nurse

Gas helmets gave protection during gas attacks but made breathing laboured, so fighting in them was not easy. The gas itself was initially released from cylinders brought up to the front line but by 1916 artillery and large-calibre mortars were the main means of projection. By the end of the war, one in four shells fired on the Western Front was a gas shell.

as long as they heeded the enjoinder at the entrance: 'all rank abandon ye who enter'. Availing themselves of the library, cellar cinema, or quiet rooms for letter writing, all fitted out through Clayton's scrounging, officers and soldiers mixed freely in this oasis of peace for a few hours or perhaps overnight. Over 20000 attended services in the Upper Room, the hop store that served as the chapel. Out of the Christian fellowship pervading the house grew the postwar Toc H movement, a charity that is now worldwide.

Named after Talbot's younger brother, Gilbert, who fell in the salient, the house was bought for Toc H in 1929 by Lord Wakefield. Largely unchanged since the war, it is a living museum but also a hostel that offers accommodation on a self-catering basis. You should book ahead. Contact details are: telephone +32 57 33 32 28; info@talbothouse.be. See also www.talbothouse.be. Visiting or staying, make sure you heed the invitation of the old wartime sign to 'come upstairs and risk meeting the chaplain'. Tubby won't be at the top but you will find the Upper Room there preserved as it was.

Return to the square and walk into the courtyard of the town hall, where a number of soldiers were executed following courts martial. The sentences were usually carried out at dawn, and several of the condemned may have spent the night before in the two cells on the right. An execution post that was used on at least one occasion stands behind a plastic screen there.

Nieuport

On 10 July 1917 the Germans launched a surprise attack along the seashore towards the mouth of the Yser River at Nieuport, 40 kilometres from Ypres and the most northerly point of the Western Front. This all-but-forgotten episode was significant for two reasons. Field Marshal Haig had just declared that the Germans would run out of men within six months if the current tempo of fighting continued. This was a strong argument in favour of the Third Ypres offensive, which began at the end of July, and also suggested that far-reaching results might ensue. Proving that the Germans were far from finished, the Nieuport attack therefore came as an inconvenient surprise. Haig discounted it, even though part of the British bridgehead across the Yser, from which a subsidiary attack in support of the Ypres offensive was to jump off, had been overrun. Most of the 50 men from the 2nd Australian Tunnelling Company, who were mining under the German strongpoints in the dunes in preparation for the British attack, and the best part of two British battalions, were captured in what the Germans called 'a beach picnic'. Secondly, the Germans introduced at Nieuport a gas that smelled like 'new mixed mustard'. It would become the most dreaded gas of the war.

Nieuport is hardly a major ANZAC battlefield but it is the only place where you can breathe sea air while visiting the Western Front. Take the N369 from Ypres to Dixmude, continue north on the N35 and then the N355 before turning right on the outskirts of Nieuport onto the N39. At the T-junction on the Yser, head right onto the N34, which tracks between the river on the left and Lombardzyde on the right. Once past the marina, turn left into Helvemaanstraat and right soon after onto Alexisstraat. Follow the Yser through the grassy dunes to its mouth and stop at the lighthouse at the end of Vierboeteweg. Nieuport was a prewar seaside resort town; it has burgeoned as one in the decades since.

Keep the beach on your left. You are now just behind the British line, which ran diagonally to your right, over an old golf course, to Lombardzyde. The German line paralleled it less than 100 metres further on. Preceded by a crushing bombardment, the German attack swamped the British line. Four Australian tunnellers were among the 80 men who got away over the Yser behind you. Australian sapper Tom Burke swam across with one end of a rope. His mate, John Coade, held the rope taut on the near bank, enabling many British non-swimmers to cross, and then crossed himself. Burke and Coade were each awarded the MM. Sapper James O'Connell miraculously got across despite being badly wounded, and burned by a flamethrower. Even more miraculously, he jumped back in and successfully rescued a floundering British soldier. He was awarded the DSM.

CHAPTER 9

1917

MESSINES

When the Messines Ridge was captured on 7 June 1917, British newspapers hailed 'the most sweeping and most brilliant victory won by British arms since the war began'. The 3rd Australian Division, which had joined the New Zealand Division in II ANZAC at the end of 1916, made an auspicious debut in the battle. II ANZAC itself had not seen significant action as a formation before Messines either. It was also the first time that Australians and New Zealanders actually fought alongside each other in a big engagement on the Western Front. As the BEF's first battle after assuming the main burden from the French Army after the collapse of the French offensive on the Chemin des Dames, Messines was of landmark importance for the British too.

The Lark Hill Lancers

Unlike the other Australian divisions, the 3rd Division had gone straight from Australia to England, where it began assembling under Major-General Monash at Lark Hill on Salisbury Plain in July 1916. Whereas much of the training given to the other divisions in Egypt before they went to France was irrelevant, Monash could prepare his from the outset for the type of fighting it would experience. In November the 3rd Division joined the Second Army as part of II ANZAC near the old Armentières nursery sector, where its predecessors had been introduced to warfare on the Western Front several months earlier. General Plumer, the Second Army's commander, was an able general whose determination not to waste lives made him a disciple of 'bite and hold'.

Its sister formations thought the 3rd Division had been enjoying the good life in England while they were fighting hard. Nicknames such as the Neutrals and the Lark Hill Lancers rankled Monash's men when they reached France. Seeking to dispel the animosity, the 3rd began raiding and became the pre-eminent Australian division at it. But Monash knew that the feeling against his formation would not entirely fade until it had fought a major battle.

Flanders

The opportunity came with the Flanders offensive that Field Marshal Haig had advocated since the start of the war. Shortly after becoming the BEF's commander-in-chief in January 1916, he proposed an advance from the Ypres salient to clear the Belgian coast but had to fall in with French plans for a joint Somme offensive. His Ypres scheme was ditched again in 1917 in favour of the Chemin des Dames offensive. Mutinies over heavy casualties and poor conditions after this offensive crumpled sidelined the French Army, which played second fiddle to the BEF thereafter. On

7 May Haig announced that he was shifting the BEF's weight to Ypres. It would shove the Germans off the heights around the town.

The Second Army, which had held the Ypres salient for most of the war, was to take the first step, the capture of the Messines–Wytschaete Ridge. Though just 80 metres at its highest point, the ridge commanded the communications into the salient to the north and Plumer had long considered it the most important objective on his front. He started mining operations in 1915 with the eventual aim of taking the ridge. That was now to be attempted on 7 June 1917.

Plans and preparations

Skirting the western foot of the ridge, above which the German first line ran, the 16-kilometre attack frontage followed a salient that bulged westwards between St Yves in the south and Mount Sorrel, near Ypres, in the north. Plumer's first objective was the German second line, shown on British trench maps as the Black Line. It tracked mainly to the west of the N365, the road that followed the crest, and was up to two kilometres from the British front line. The second objective was the Oosttaverne or Green

Line, a reverse-slope position up to two kilometres back, where some of the German guns might be captured. IX Corps's four-kilometre advance in the centre was longer than those of X Corps and II ANZAC against the northern and southern shoulders of the salient respectively. So the Green Line was to be struck 10 hours after the opening blow, enabling IX Corps to catch up with the others for a simultaneous assault on it.

Begun two years before, the preparations were on a scale unique in the BEF. Twenty-four mines, packed with over 500 tonnes of ammonal, ran under the German front line. As at Arras, the artillery needed was worked out according to the amount of wire to be cut, the length of trench to be destroyed and the number of German batteries to be neutralised. The calculation came to 2226 guns, 756 of them heavy or medium, and 458 heavy mortars. This concentration represented one gun for every 6.5 metres of front, the BEF's highest yet. In the 11 days before the attack, 3.5 million shells reduced Messines and Wytschaete to rubble and the ridge to a brown wasteland. They also stripped the camouflage off the concrete pillboxes that dotted the German lines in

N314

NZ DIVISION

The view from the German line on the ridge. Here, it overlooks part of the line from which the New Zealanders attacked.

checkerboard-fashion. The creeping barrage during the attack would form a steel wall 650 metres deep in order to prevent machine-guns firing at long range. Support also came from 72 Mark IV tanks, far superior to the feeble Mark II's that had let the Australians down at Bullecourt. Almost half went to II ANZAC.

While the New Zealand Division, with the British 25th Division on its left, advanced in the centre of II ANZAC to capture Messines village, the 3rd Australian Division would form the right flank of the entire attack. Its junction with the New Zealanders was at La Petite Douve Farm, which nestled in the Douve Valley

The Germans pummel Messines Ridge on 8 June. The view is as it would have been when the ridge was under British bombardment before the attack. Trees lining Hun's Walk are on the skyline to the right, while the Douve streamlet runs through the centre of the photo.

MONT KEMMEL

ONTARIO FARM

25TH (BRITISH DIVISION)

between the tip of the ridge and Hill 63. From there its line stretched southeastwards for 1.8 kilometres, passing in front of Ploegsteert Wood. Being on the flank of the salient arc meant that the 3rd's right-hand man literally had to stand still while the left-hand man had to go 2.7 kilometres. The 3rd could not advance at all unless the New Zealanders took the ridge on their front because its trenches enfiladed the length of the 3rd's assault across the valley. Once the Black Line was secure, the 4th Australian Division, with the 37th Battalion from the 3rd on its right, would assault the Green Line.

As his untried formation faced a far-from-easy task, Monash's arrangements were meticulous. He told his brigadiers how they should employ even their platoons. Numerous rehearsals followed on terrain like that in the attack sector and against positions laid out according to the latest aerial photos of the German line. This training was important as the attack would be the first in which Australian troops could use effectively the tactical doctrine for platoons derived by the Canadians and recently issued by GHQ. It incorporated in the platoon the Lewis-gunners and bombers who provided the main firepower but who had hitherto been temporarily attached. The New Zealanders left nothing to chance either. For the mopping up of Messines, they went so far as to give each section an objective.

Pillars of fire

Though German gas shelling turned the approach march of the Australian assault battalions through Ploegsteert Wood late on 6 June into a nightmare, they were in position when the mines went up at 3.10 am next morning. For tactical reasons, only 19 of the 24 were fired. Blown seven seconds early, the three on the 3rd Division's front and the one south of it were the first to go up. Another mine went off just to the north of the New Zealanders. The trenches rocked, the bones of the waiting attackers shook. With the earth already spewing pillars of fire, the inferno when the barrage fell was incredible, recalled Captain Robert Grieve of the 37th Battalion. 'The air screamed shells and snapped bullets and above all was the roar of the guns, the crackle of the machine-guns and the hum of aeroplane propellers.' The advance was the easiest carried out by the Australians and New Zealanders to date.

Cowed by the barrage and the explosions, 'The enemy would not stand up to us', said Major Arthur Maudsley of the 38th Battalion. 'They asked us not to kill them.' Machine-gunned from the area of Ultimo Crater, the 33rd Battalion on the right struck the only serious resistance that the Australians encountered. Private John Carroll won the VC for his part in quashing it. Alongside the Australians, the New Zealanders had some brisk fighting in Messines, where Lance-Corporal Samuel Frickleton of the 3rd Rifles knocked out two machine-guns. He, too, won the VC. By 5.15 am the Black Line was being consolidated all along II ANZAC's front.

New Zealand units in training for the attack on Messines. They move in artillery formation, which requires companies to be spread out in order to minimise the effect of German shelling.

The New Zealanders began establishing posts 700 metres beyond on the Black Dotted Line, which would protect the 37th Battalion and the 12th and 13th Brigades from 4th Australian Division when they formed up for the 1.10 pm attack on the Oosttaverne Line.

Pillboxes

Late in the morning the Germans detected the build-up. Their surviving guns concentrated on II ANZAC's end of the ridge, mauling the 37th Battalion and the 12th Brigade as they moved into position for the attack. Then Plumer postponed it until 3.10 pm because some formations were struggling to get forward over the damaged ground. Two more hours of shelling had to be endured. At 1.30 pm it stepped up because the Germans counterattacked. The British bombardment of the Oosttaverne Line forced them back to it, making the line strongly held. The denuded Australians assaulting it had nothing like the earlier cakewalk.

Pillboxes caused most of the trouble. As they were virtually invulnerable, their garrisons could emerge unscathed, set up their machine-guns and pin down the advance. Some pillboxes were loopholed, enabling the guns to fire from within. Under the new platoon structure, the standard drill required Lewis-gunners and rifle grenadiers to fire at the pillbox, covering the riflemen and bombers working around behind it. But the drill broke down if neighbouring pillboxes engaged the outflanking move. The Australians had not met pillboxes on a systematic basis before and the fights around them were so ferocious that the surrender of a garrison once surrounded often went unrespected.

The 37th Battalion was caught by a pillbox that savaged Captain Grieve's company before he knocked it out to win a VC. Attacking alongside the 37th, the 47th Battalion took no prisoners in subduing some pillboxes in the Oosttaverne Line astride Hun's Walk, today's N314. South of the Blauwepoortbeek stream next to the 47th, the 45th Battalion ran into a large concentration of pillboxes and field-guns, and was pinned down. So was the 49th on the far side of the stream. On their left, the 52nd Battalion was hampered from the start because the neighbouring British 33rd Brigade had been held up by

Charles Wheeler's *Battle of Messines* shows the 3rd Division starting its advance after the firing of the mines. Note the straightness of the creeping barrage ahead of it.

A pillbox captured by the Australians.

The barrage on the Oosttaverne Line.

hit them when the Germans counterattacked at 5.30 pm. Though the Germans were repulsed, the 47th Battalion bolted for the Black Line. The New Zealanders there shortened the barrage, thinking that the counterattack had succeeded and was now heading for them. It fell on the 37th and 45th Battalions, forcing them back too. By 9 pm the entire two kilometres of the Oosttaverne Line between the Blauwepoortbeek and the Douve lay open. The 44th and 48th Battalions regained most of the ground on 8 June but pillboxes prevented the full closing of the gap until the Germans retired towards the Warneton Line, 1.5 kilometres rearwards, three days later.

the broken ground. The 52nd spread across the 33rd's objective. British formations took the rest of the Oosttaverne Line. The Australians held half of it, albeit with a 900-metre gap at the Blauwepoortbeek.

At this point the attack turned into a tragicomedy. Afraid of revealing their positions to the Germans, the thinly stretched Australians did not fire flares to show an overflying aircraft where they were. Unsure of their location, the supporting artillery fired a barrage that

Brickbats and bouquets

The contrast between the efficient capture of the ridge and the shambles on the Oosttaverne Line sparked criticism of the 4th Division. Haig defended it, pointing out that it 'was at Bullecourt and lost many officers'. All told, Messines cost

Major-General William Holmes

Commander, 4th Australian Division, January–June 1917

1862–1917

Holmes had been in charge of the Sydney Metropolitan Water and Sewerage Board prewar and presided over the construction of several major dams. He joined the New South Wales militia as a 10-year-old bugler in 1872, and dropped from captain to lieutenant to serve in the South African War. Before being wounded and invalided home, he had made lieutenant-colonel and been awarded the DSO. On the outbreak of war in 1914, he commanded the Australian Naval and Military Expeditionary Force, which captured German New Guinea and other German Pacific territories. On Gallipoli Holmes led the 5th Brigade towards the end of the campaign and the 2nd Division at the evacuation. Resuming command of the 5th Brigade afterwards, he took it to France, where he performed solidly at Pozières on the Somme in 1916 but indifferently in the Somme winter fighting. Commanding the 4th Australian Division from January 1917, Holmes argued strongly against the Bullecourt attack in April, in which his formation was shattered. It had not fully recovered by the time of Messines. He habitually reconnoitred every part of his front line but courted danger by insisting on wearing his red-banded general's cap. Ironically, his mortal wounding occurred well behind the line and had nothing to do with his headdress. He had been appointed CMG before his death.

the 4th Division 2700 men. Only praise attended the 3rd Division's effort. It took 11 of the 48 guns captured and, at a cost of 4100 casualties, proved itself up to the standard of the others. In another positive, Messines started the rebuilding of Australian trust in British generalship, which had evaporated under General Gough. The New Zealand Division itself lost 5000 men, which meant that, altogether, II ANZAC suffered almost 14 000 of the 26 000 British casualties in the battle. Some senior officers became casualties afterwards. On 2 July a chance salvo mortally wounded General Holmes, the 4th Division's commander, while he was taking the New South Wales Premier, William Holman, to the old battlefield. Major-General Ewen Sinclair-MacLagan, who had led the 3rd Brigade since 1914, replaced him. Among the New Zealanders, General Russell narrowly

escaped death when a shell killed Brigadier-General Charles Brown of the 1st New Zealand Infantry Brigade on 8 June. Two days later a sniper parted Russell's hairline. A sniper would soon kill Brigadier-General Francis Johnston of the New Zealand Rifle Brigade.

II ANZAC spent the next six weeks following up the Germans. On 23 June the 11th Brigade from the 3rd Division began its famous '18 days', during which it slowly advanced under constant shell, machine-gun and sniper fire until blocked by posts near a windmill 500 metres in front of the Warneton Line. It successfully cleared them during the Second Army's feint towards Lille on 31 July, which sought to divert attention from the offensive being launched simultaneously at Ypres. The neighbouring New Zealand Division took La Basse-Ville.

DRIVING THE BATTLEFIELD

When retracing the Australian and New Zealand attacks, bear in mind how different they were. The New Zealand Division headed straight up the western slope of the Messines Ridge with each flank going the same distance. The 3rd Division missed the ridge in arcing past the end of it and finishing up in the low ground on the eastern side. As a result, correlating the two assaults can be difficult. The long advance of the 3rd Division's left flank while the right flank marked time also makes it hard to get a handle on the 3rd's assault. Superimpose the 4th Division's confused advance to the Oosttaverne Line onto all of this and frustration looms. The one mitigating factor is the prominence of Messines church, which is a visible reference point from almost everywhere on the battlefield. Frequently relating your location to it will greatly assist you to make sense of the fighting.

MAP NGI 1:20000: 28, 5-6 Heuvelland–Mesen

Leaving Ypres by the Lille Gate, take the second exit from the roundabout onto the N336 (direction Armentières). On reaching the roundabout in Saint Eloi, by which time you will have driven across X Corps's advance, take the second exit onto the N365 (direction Wijtschate/Mesen) and continue through Wytschaete and IX Corps's advance to Messines in II ANZAC's sector. It is nine kilometres from Ypres.

On entering Messines, turn right at the first crossroads onto the N314 (Nieuwkerkestraat) and stop after 450 metres at **Messines Ridge British Cemetery** and the **New Zealand Memorial to the Missing** ❶. They lie on ground that belonged prewar to the Institution Royale, a large convent at the far end of the village. Standing on the site of the Cross of Sacrifice, the convent's windmill, the **Moulin de l'Hospice**, was a German machine-gun post captured by 1st Otago on 7 June. Brigadier-General Brown was killed by a shell while talking to General Russell there next day. The Otagos also took the German forward system. Its support trenches crossed the N314 100 metres further on while the front line went over another 100 metres beyond. When you reach this point, look left to see a German pillbox, then right. The buildings 250 metres away denote the location of **Birthday Farm** on the New Zealanders' boundary with the 25th Division. Flawlessly executing a well-rehearsed plan, the Otagos rushed its machine-guns while covered by snipers.

Noting the superb observation that the Germans had over the British rear areas below as you descend the slope, continue along the N314 for another 700 metres and turn right into Katteputstraat. As parking on the corner can be precarious, drive another 200 metres to **Ontario Farm**. Lying 200 metres ahead of the 25th Division's front line, the original farm buildings, which the Germans had fortified, were atomised by a mine blast that left a soggy patch of earth rather than a crater. Look along Katteputstraat at the tree-covered knoll on the skyline, to which the German line ran from Ontario Farm. It conceals the massive **Spanbroekmolen** crater. Now walk back to the N314, turn left after crossing it and stop just past the **black-roofed house** ❷. Look down the N314 towards the ridge.

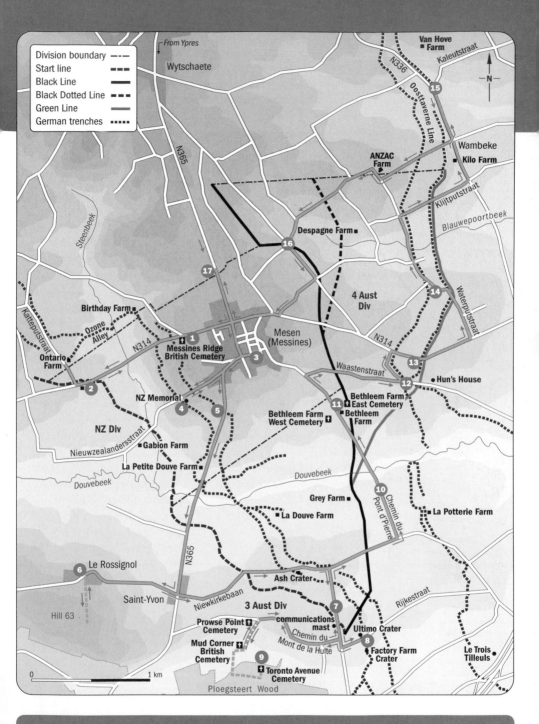

Legend:
- Division boundary
- Start line
- Black Line
- Black Dotted Line
- Green Line
- German trenches

From Ypres

Wytschaete

Van Hove Farm
Kaleutstraat
N336
Oosttaverne Line
15
Wambeke
Kilo Farm
ANZAC Farm
Kilijtputstraat
Blauwepoortbeek
Despagne Farm
16
17
14
4 Aust Div
N314
Waterputstraat
Birthday Farm
Ozone Alley
N314
Mesen (Messines)
13
Ontario Farm
1 Messines Ridge British Cemetery
3
Waastenstraat
12
Hun's House
2
NZ Memorial
4
5
11 Bethleem Farm East Cemetery
Bethleem Farm
NZ Div
Bethleem Farm West Cemetery
Nieuwzealandersstraat
Gabion Farm
La Petite Douve Farm
Douvebeek
Douvebeek
10
Chemin du Pont d'Pierre
Grey Farm
La Potterie Farm
La Douve Farm
Le Rossignol
6
N365
Ash Crater
Rijkestraat
Saint-Yvon
Niewkirkebaan
7
Hill 63
3 Aust Div
communications mast
Ultimo Crater
Prowse Point Cemetery
Chemin du Mont de la Hulte
8 Factory Farm Crater
Le Trois Tilleuls
Mud Corner British Cemetery
9 Toronto Avenue Cemetery
Ploegsteert Wood

0 _____ 1 km

N365
Kattepputstraat
Steenbeek

This drive begins by covering the New Zealand assault on the Black Line and the capture of Messines village from the perspective of the New Zealand front line and from the German positions on the ridge. It then deals with the Australian attack on the Black and Green Lines, in particular the confused fighting on the Blauwepoortbeek, before concluding on the New Zealand Division's left flank. The sites of the mine craters in the Australian sector and the VC actions are also included.

DISTANCE COVERED: 27 km
DURATION: 4.5 hours

You are on the New Zealand Division's front line. Extending this side of Ontario Farm to the N314 200 metres behind you, it followed the road before turning right 100 metres ahead of you and heading through **Gabion Farm** 700 metres off on your right. Naturally worried that **Ozone Alley**, the 700-metre stretch of the German front line paralleling the N314 up the ridge to Birthday Farm, would enfilade their assault, the Otagos dug assembly trenches in no-man's-land to cut their exposure to it to 400 metres. They attacked with the explosions of the Ontario Farm and Spanbroekmolen mine ringing in their ears. Resistance was trifling.

As the barrage fell directly on it, no trouble came from the German front line paralleling the N314. Next to the Otagos in the 2nd Brigade was 1st Canterbury, which stretched to Gabion Farm, and alongside them were the 1st and 3rd Battalions of the Rifle Brigade. Dawn had not yet broken as the two brigades headed up the slope to your front and

easily took the German front and support lines, which ran along it from Birthday Farm and through the New Zealand Memorial to the Missing, in the trees 800 metres to your right front. From there the lines slid down to La Petite Douve Farm, just visible 1.1 kilometres off in the valley beyond Gabion Farm. Once Messines had fallen, the 1st Brigade passed through to the Black Line, 800 metres over the crest. The left of the 4th Australian Division later moved through your location to assault the Oosttaverne Line.

Now return to Messines. At the crossroads, turn right onto the N365, which marked the end of the 2nd Brigade's assault and the start of the 1st's. The 2nd Canterbury and the 4th Rifles subdued the patchy resistance coming from the rubble to which the village had been reduced. Bombing along the streets, they seized five machine-guns before they could come into action, rushed five from the rear and used rifle grenades to knock out two firing across

The 2nd New Zealand Brigade's attack between Ontario and Gabion Farms.

OZONE ALLEY

MESSINES CHURCH

GERMAN LINE

1ST OTAGO

N314

the square, which is on the first street on the left. Private Fred White, the Canterburys' barber, took out another firing from a nearby dressing station and killed its treacherous crew. Near the town hall are a Bastiaan plaque and a New Zealand kowhai tree.

At the next crossroads, turn left off the N365 and park at **St Nicholas Church** ③, outside which is an information panel on Lance-Corporal Frickleton. Hitler did a watercolour of the ruined church, which dated from the 11th century, while probably stationed at nearby Bethleem Farm. He was also reportedly treated for wounds in the crypt, which served as a German aid post. The last resistance in the village came from the maze of concrete cellars under the **Institution Royale**, which occupied the partly open area from the right of the church to the N365. Hauptmann Thomas, the local German commander, and his staff were nabbed in them. Return to the N365 (direction Ploegsteert) and take Nieuwzealandersstraat, the second street on the right. Signposted for the **New Zealand Memorial Park** ④, it was the boundary between the 2nd Brigade and the Rifle Brigade. Park outside the memorial, which was unveiled by the Belgian king, Albert I, on 1 August 1924, and walk to the wall at the lower end. It is on the site of **Uhlan Trench**.

St Nicholas church, Messines, rebuilt.

Look straight ahead. Overlooking the Douve Valley, Uhlan Trench was part of the German front line, which continued, as **Ulna Trench**, parallel to the N365 to **La Petite Douve Farm**, 550 metres to your left. In August 1916 the British blew in the shaft of the mine dug under the farm after German miners began to

suspect its existence. It collapsed but the 35-tonne ammonal charge still remains in place. The boundary between the New Zealand Division and the 3rd Australian Division was on the far side of the farm. The Steenbeek, which runs from your right around the foot of the ridge, joins the more prominent Douve just behind the farm as well. The opposing front lines swung from the farm over the N365 and passed in front of **Ploegsteert Wood** on the left horizon. Following the Steenbeek in the opposite direction, the New Zealanders' front line ran in front of Gabion Farm, 500 metres directly ahead of you, and diagonally across the valley to your right front.

Later reporting that they 'kept very close to barrage, enemy had no time to man his parapet', 1st Rifles advanced up the slope towards your location and took the pillboxes on either side. Normally the Germans sheltering in them would have set machine-guns up on top once the barrage had passed. The 3rd Rifles quickly overran La Petite Douve Farm but had a tough fight at Ulna Trench, where Corporal Henry Jeffery captured 12 prisoners after silencing a machine-gun trained on the Australians. Both battalions took the support line, 100 metres behind you, before 4th Rifles

leapfrogged them and continued to the far side of the N365.

Before leaving, note **Hill 63**, across the valley on the right of the N365, under which the 1st Australian Tunnelling Company chiselled out accommodation for two battalions. Known as the **Catacombs**, it sheltered many of the New Zealanders. Monash carried out his only reconnaissance on the Western Front from an observation post in the ruined Château de la Hutte on the hill's left shoulder. Little trace of the château remains. Further afield, the spires of **Armentières**, which was close to the 'nursery' sector, are at 11 o'clock from your location. Nieuwkerke, whose church breaks the skyline at 1 o'clock, was a billet for the Australians and New Zealanders whenever they were in this area. **Mount Kemmel**, the final objective of the German *George* offensive in April 1918, is at 2 o'clock.

Retracing your route, turn right onto the N365. Lance Corporal Frickleton's VC action occurred in the area of the row of terraced houses, then a ruined expanse, that ends at the flat-roofed commercial building 120 metres along on the right. The support line ran down the left side of the N365 after crossing it just beyond this building. When heavy fire from the ruins

The view from the New Zealand Memorial Park over the 3rd (Rifle) Brigade's attack between Gabion Farm and the N365.

LA PETITE DOUVE FARM

PLOEGSTEERT WOOD

N365

ARMENTIÈRES

3RD (RIFLE) BRIGADE LINE

held up 3rd Rifles on the support line, Frickleton charged up the slope through the barrage, killed the crews of two machine-guns, and then called on nine Germans in a dugout to surrender. Twice wounded, he killed them when they refused.

Continue to the **Island of Ireland Peace Park** ⑤ on the right and stop. Sponsored by the Irish government, it centres on a replica of an Irish round tower and is partly built with stone from an old British barracks at Tipperary. The park commemorates all Irishmen who served on the Western Front, though the nearest place to Messines at which they fought was Wytschaete; captured by the 36th (Ulster) and 16th (Irish) Divisions of IX Corps, it straddles the N365 a few kilometres behind you. Positional confusion aside, the park offers a panoramic view of the ground over which the 3rd Australian Division advanced on the right flank of the Second Army. One other thing: the pillbox on the slope below the park is not German but British. It was built after the battle.

From the park entrance with the tower at your back, look across the N365. The two houses with a large barn on their left, one kilometre directly in front of you and to the left of the power pole on the other side of the road, mark **Bethleem (Bethlehem) Farm**. Tracking just behind it, the **Black Line** went to **Grey Farm**, in the low ground 1.3 kilometres to your right front and in line with the distant chimney stacks, and then cut left of the communications mast, two kilometres away to the left of Ploegsteert Wood. **La Douve Farm**, with the Douve this side of it, is halfway between the park and the mast. Passing the park either side of the N365, the German front and support lines broke left next to La Petite Douve Farm, in the valley over your right shoulder, and ran to the right of La Douve Farm to meet the Black Line beyond the mast. Roughly paralleling them, the Australian lines went through the mast site and along the left of Ploegsteert Wood.

The 3rd Division's advance across your front could be likened to an opening door, whose hinge near the mast formed the divisional right flank, and whose edge, near La Petite Douve Farm, the left flank. After the explosion in front of it of the three mines, all blown by the 3rd Canadian Tunnelling Company, prepared in the Australian sector, the 9th Brigade pivoted on the hinge and swept around to Grey Farm. Alongside, the 10th Brigade to your right had a lot further to go,

HILL 63

GABION FARM

An Australian transport wagon dodges German shelling of the ANZAC batteries' gun lines behind Hill 63 on 5 June. The Germans drenched this area with gas when the 3rd Division was moving through it for the attack two days later.

Brigade advanced down the slope on your left, next to the 10th Brigade, to the Black Line on the left of Bethleem Farm. In the afternoon the 4th Australian Division and the 37th Battalion passed through the 1st New Zealand Brigade to strike the Oosttaverne Line 400 metres beyond Bethleem Farm.

Continue on the N365, passing La Petite Douve Farm on the right, where the road levels out, at the same time as you cross over the German front line at the **Beak**, just before the Douve. A lone German machine-gunner here briefly offered the only opposition met by the 40th Battalion, whose front line on the 3rd Division's left flank straddled the N365 200 metres past the stream. As for the rest of the Germans, 'they made many fruitless attempts to embrace us', said Lieutenant Bill Garrard. To study the New Zealanders' battlefield from Hill 63, turn right at the crossroads at Saint-Yvon hamlet 600 metres further on. Stop just past **Le Rossignol hamlet** ⑥ 850 metres along and look towards Messines. With binoculars you can easily spot the New Zealand Memorial. As the Australian battlefield is mostly hidden by the curve of the slope, take the track from here to the crest of Hill 63 to see it.

The 3rd Australian Division's attack as seen from the Irish Peace Park, illustrating its dependence on the New Zealanders seizing the higher ground from which the photo was taken.

passing this side of La Douve Farm to the Black Line between Grey Farm and Bethleem Farm, where the end of the door rested. The dependence of both brigades on the New Zealanders' capture of the German lines enfilading their attack from the ridge is starkly clear from your location at the park. Having leapfrogged the 2nd New Zealand Brigade and the Rifle Brigade after they did capture them, the 1st New Zealand

GREY FARM

BLACK LINE

The Château de la Hutte was on the slope directly above the N365.

Return to the crossroads and drive straight over onto Niewkirkebaan. The 34th Battalion, followed by the 35th, attacked on the left of the 9th Brigade's line, which crossed the road past the farm buildings 600 metres along. They effortlessly snatched the German front line 200 metres further on, just beyond the five sheds on the left, and support line 250 metres past them near the T-junction. The Germans were dazed, the Australians dazzled, by the explosion of the 40 tonnes of ammonal in the paired **Trench 127 Left** and **Right** mines, of which **Ash crater** from Trench 127 Right can be seen in the field on the right. Trench 127 Left is covered by the sheds.

Turn right at the T-junction and park by the buildings on the far side of the **track junction** 7 at the foot of the knoll on which the communications mast stands. Walk back to the track junction and look along the track with the mast on your right. From Ash Crater, the German front line ran midway between your location and the copse ahead of you, and through Ultimo Crater in the trees on the higher ground 250 metres to your right front. It resulted from the firing of a nine-tonne ammonal charge under **Trench 122 Left**. The support line went through the copse and behind Ultimo. Passing 80 metres behind you to the buildings on your right and then to the right of Ultimo was the 9th Brigade's right flank, the hinge of the door, from which the 33rd Battalion assaulted. It had the 3rd Division's hardest fight on the way to the Black Line. Three men covered by two rifle grenadiers knocked out a troublesome machine-gun in the German support line. A Stokes mortar accounted for another near the crater, which was so exposed that it could not

DOUVE FARM

PLOEGSTEERT WOOD

3RD DIVISION LINE

GERMAN LINE

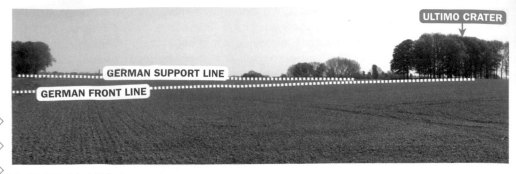

ULTIMO CRATER

GERMAN SUPPORT LINE

GERMAN FRONT LINE

The 9th Brigade's right flank, where Private Carroll won the VC.

be fortified until after nightfall. Private Carroll was awarded his VC for 96 hours' fighting in this area, during which he destroyed a machine-gun after bayoneting four Germans, rescued a captured mate, and extricated two others buried by heavy shelling.

To see **Ultimo Crater** ⑧, which is water-filled like most of the other surviving craters, drive past the mast, turn left onto Rijkestraat, and park after 150 metres by the trees on the left. The crater is on private land and fenced off, so be sure to close the gate after you. Created by the firing of 18 tonnes of ammonal under **Trench 122 Right** just beyond the Australian right flank, **Factory Farm Crater** is across the road in the low ground 200 metres away. The 33rd Battalion's snipers prevented the Germans enfilading the new line from it.

Ultimo Crater.

About 800 metres beyond the crater were the four **'Birdcage'** mines, none of which were fired. One went up after a lightning strike on 17 June 1955; the locations of the other three have been lost.

Returning to the start of Rijkestraat, turn right, and then left just before the mast, onto Chemin du Mont de la Hutte. The plaque affixed to cottage No. 12, 400 metres along on the left, states that Captain Bruce Bairnsfather of the Royal Warwickshires occupied a dugout below the original cottage at the end of 1914. A trained artist, Bairnsfather created the war's most famous cartoon character, the grizzled veteran 'Old Bill', here. Bill proved so popular that his antics were collectively published as *Fragments from France* and *Bullets and Billets*. Carry on past the Khaki Chums' Bairnsfather wooden cross on the right, whose inscription says that both sides briefly left their trenches and fraternised in no-man's-land in this vicinity on Christmas Day in the celebrated Christmas Truce of 1914. On reaching **Prowse Point Cemetery**, park and take the track on the left, following the signs past **Mud Corner British Cemetery** to **Toronto Avenue Cemetery** ⑨.

You are now in Ploegsteert Wood. Just behind the British line for most of the war and packed with resting units, and artillery and depots, it attracted frequent German shelling. Filing through the wood's splintered remains near midnight on 6 June, the Australian battalions heard the 'pht, pht, pht' of gas shells, to which was soon added the crash of high-explosive ones. Though the approach march became a nightmare, they still arrived in good time for the attack because Monash had specified four routes to minimise congestion and delays.

Retracing your route, turn left to pass the mast and continue to the T-junction near Ash crater. Head right on reaching it, then left after 650 metres onto Chemin du Pont d'Pierre. The road on the left 350 metres along ⑩ runs to Grey Farm, from which heavy fire came. Sixteen-year-old Private Herb Sternbeck won the DCM for capturing one of the four machine-guns taken in and around the farm by the 34th and 35th Battalions. When a pillbox to the right of the farm threatened the 39th Battalion's advance, Captain Alex Patterson stood in full view of it to fire his rifle into it, before charging with a few others and capturing another two machine-guns. He won the MC. More or less paralleling the road, the Oosttaverne Line ran through **La Potterie Farm** 300 metres to your right rear. The 36th Battalion took it this side of the Douve, which is in the low ground to your front, on 10–11 June.

Continue on what is now Rue de Lille over the Douve, 500 metres beyond which on the right is the rebuilt **Bethleem Farm** ⑪. Hitler called by in 1940 and presented the farmer's wife with some flowers. He had been billeted in the original farm during the winter of 1914–15. A pillbox on the corner of the minor road on the left, which leads to **Bethleem Farm West Cemetery**, held up the right of the 38th Battalion. When Captain Francis Fairweather and a few others sneaked around behind the pillbox, which protected a co-located headquarters, the occupants of both bolted. Fairweather turned their

The Bairnsfather plaque, Ploegsteert Wood.

machine-gun on them. Giving chase when they scarpered again, he and his men ran into two field-guns to the right of the farm buildings, probably in the vicinity of **Bethleem Farm East**

The Douve near Bethleem Farm.

Cemetery. They captured both. The 38th Battalion and 3rd Auckland linked on the Black Line 180 metres past the farm, where the boundary between the New Zealand and the 3rd Australian Divisions crossed the road.

Just before the crucifix on the left 220 metres further on, turn right onto Waastenstraat and park after 900 metres at the intersection with the minor road that cuts sharply leftwards ⑫. Look back towards Messines. Running through your location from your left, the Oosttaverne Line paralleled the minor road to the N314, atop the spur to your right. One of the pillboxes studding it was at this intersection. It wiped out half of Captain Grieve's company when the 37th Battalion reached the wire after advancing towards you from your left front in the afternoon attack. Grieve's report laconically states that the pillbox 'was put out of action by the aid of Mills bombs and the company were able to get forward onto the objective'. He did not mention that he was the thrower, and that he had rushed up to the loophole and rolled two bombs in before being seriously wounded.

Now head up the minor road and turn right onto the N314, which was called **Hun's Walk** in 1917. Another pillbox of the Oosttaverne Line, which crossed the N314 here, stood on the other side of the junction, with **Oxygen Trench** beyond it. Park after 200 metres on the hardstand-ing at the first building on the right ⑬ and look back along the N314 towards Messines. After capturing the Black Line, which crossed the road 900 metres ahead of you, the 1st New Zealand Brigade established posts on the **Black Dotted Line**. Starting 100 metres this side of the Black Line immediately left of the N314, it crossed the crest and ended up 400 metres in front of the Black Line

MESSINES

DIRECTION OF ATTACK

The location where Captain Grieve won the VC.

to your right front. You are on the **Oosttaverne Support Line**, which the 12th Brigade was to take here in the 4th Australian Division's assault. Word that the attack had been postponed arrived as the 12th reached its jump-off position between the Black and Black Dotted Lines. It had to lie under German shelling for two hours there. Further along the high ground to your right front, the 13th Brigade was relatively sheltered and suffered less. With the 13th alongside, the 12th Brigade duly came down the slope towards you supported by three tanks. The 47th Battalion took no prisoners when it silenced the pillbox on the Oosttaverne Line.

The tanks crushed Oxygen Trench. Pushing through your location, the 47th Battalion dug in 200 metres beyond the bend in the N314 behind you. Face in that direction. With its right flank at **Hun's House**, 200 metres to your right front and the site of a German headquarters, the 47th extended across the road for 350 metres to link up with the 45th Battalion to your left, while the 37th Battalion stretched behind the 47th almost to the Douve to your right rear. When the Germans counterattacked towards you at 5.30 pm, they were beaten off. But the supporting artillery and machine-guns twice mistakenly deluged the Australians. In the confusion, the New Zealanders even thought at one stage that they were about to be attacked. Ravaged by the fire and unable to stop it, the Australians temporarily abandoned the new line.

Continuing on the N314 for 400 metres, turn left at the first house onto the narrow and badly rutted Waterputstraat. Stop 520 metres along at the sharp bend rightwards ⑭ and, keeping the Messines Ridge on your left, look across the Blauwepoortbeek in the low ground ahead. You are between the Oosttaverne and the Oosttaverne Support Lines, which ran from the N314 to your left rear, over the Blauwepoortbeek and through the farm buildings ahead of you on the near bank. Its ruins concealed some of the many pillboxes in both lines as they continued on past the right of **ANZAC Farm**, which is one kilometre distant on the crest of the Wambeke Spur and slightly to the left of the farm buildings.

The 12th and 13th Brigades attacked from your left. At your location, the right of the 45th Battalion took the Oosttaverne Line and linked up with the 47th Battalion near the N314. But the left of the 45th, and the 49th astride the Blauwepoortbeek, were stopped by torrential fire from the pillboxes in the farm buildings, and from field-guns in nearby concrete shelters, whose sole survivor, dubbed 'The Better 'Ole' after the Bairnsfather cartoon, now shelters cattle. Every officer in the 45th here was killed, as were all the 49th's company commanders. The left of the 49th swung up to ANZAC House, which should have been the left flank of the neighbouring 52nd Battalion. But the 52nd had to stretch into the valley of the Wambeke and across the objective of the British

33rd Brigade, which had been delayed. Despite repeated attempts over the next three days, the gap up to ANZAC House was never closed.

Drive past the T-junction to the first crossroads beyond the Blauwepoortbeek and turn right onto Klijtputstraat, which the Oosttaverne front line crosses here. The support line crossed it halfway to the N336. Head left on reaching this road. The northern end of the 4th Division's objective in both lines was just behind the building complex on the left 170 metres along, which is on the site of **Kilo Farm**. Continue for another 600 metres into the Wambeke Valley to the **lone house** 15 on the left. As you cannot park on the N336, pull over in Kaleutstraat on the right, where **Joye Farm** is just ahead of you. After paralleling the N336 — the front line 200 metres on the far side, the support along the near side — both Oosttaverne Lines bent rightwards 500 metres to your left and ran past the left of **Van Hove Farm** on the slope to your left front.

Now turn about and walk back to the N336. In the absence of the 33rd Brigade, which should have advanced along the

valley towards you, the 52nd Battalion swung off the Wambeke Spur on which Kilo Farm sits, and captured the Oosttaverne Lines to the point where they swung up towards Van Hove Farm. As German snipers at the farm picked off those in the area around you, 191-centimetre-tall ANZAC and Somme veteran Captain Arthur Maxwell organised some British troops and three tanks on the far slope to your right front. At his request, they secured the farm. The 33rd Brigade relieved the 52nd Battalion next day.

Head back towards Kilo Farm but turn right at the Wambeke crossroads at the two-storey house. Continue along the Wambeke Spur for 700 metres to the T-junction at ANZAC Farm and turn right onto Waterputstraat. Held by 2nd Auckland on the New Zealanders' left, the Black Dotted Line crossed the road 500 metres after the sharp left turn. At the next T-junction, turn left towards Messines then left again at the next crossroads, where the complex on your left occupies the area of **Fanny's Farm** 16 on the Black Line. The 1st Wellington captured it after advancing down the slope to your front.

The line reached by the 47th Battalion and from which it was shelled out.

OOSTTAVERNE SUPPORT LINE

47TH BATTALION

Van Hove Farm, a German snipers' nest that commanded the area behind the Oosttaverne Line.

Turn right at the next crossroads. After a vicious tussle, the Wellingtons also took **Blauwen Molen**, the fortified artillery headquarters in the mill that stood on the site of the disused brickworks 200 metres along on the left. On reaching Hun's Walk on the outskirts of Messines, head right, and right again onto the N365 at the crossroads. Rebuilt **Swayne's Farm** 17, which was on the New Zealanders' boundary with the 25th Division, looms on the left after 400 metres. Until crushed by a tank, its machine-guns pinned down the Otagos. From here, follow the N365 back to Ypres.

MESSINES

GERMAN COUNTERATTACKS

N314

LOCAL INFORMATION

CEMETERIES

Bethleem Farm East and West Cemeteries

Lying either side of Rue de Lille, midway between the Douve and Messines on the tour route, both cemeteries were established by the 3rd Australian Division after the capture of Bethleem Farm. A medical facility was set up in Bethleem Farm East, located behind the farm buildings. It is the smallest cemetery on the ridge with 44 burials, all but one Australian. They fell mostly between 8 and 10 June, as did many of the 114 Australians among Bethleem Farm West's 166 burials. Despite its name, Bethleem Farm West cemetery is actually in the area of Schitzel Farm, which can be seen behind it. Ungodly Trench, which ran past the eastern wall, was captured by the 38th Battalion very early on.

Messines Ridge British Cemetery and New Zealand Memorial to the Missing

On the N314 on the outskirts of Messines and visited on the tour route, this cemetery was made postwar by the concentration of graves from the battlefield and from smaller cemeteries. It contains 342 Australians and 128 New Zealanders among its 1531 burials. Listing the 840 New Zealanders who fell in the area and have no known grave, the New Zealand Memorial to the Missing occupies the site of one of the buildings of the Moulin de l'Hospice. It is one of seven such New Zealand memorials on the old Western Front.

Mud Corner British Cemetery

Containing 53 New Zealanders and 31 Australians in its 85 burials, Mud Corner is truly an ANZAC cemetery. Started immediately after the Messines attack and named after the muddy track junction nearby, it was close to the old front line. The New Zealand burials include many Gallipoli veterans, some of whom were older soldiers. Private Ed Beach of 2nd Wellingtons, at II.C.6, was 54, and Privates David Cowie and Alex McKenzie of the Aucklanders, at II.A.1 and 9 respectively, were 43 and 47. McKenzie also served in the Boer War. Signposted from the Chemin du Mont de la Hutte, the cemetery is passed on the tour near the entrance to Ploegsteert Wood.

Toronto Avenue Cemetery

In Ploegsteert Wood and also on the tour route, this cemetery was named after one of the tracks up which the 3rd Australian Division struggled during the gas shelling of the wood before the Messines attack. The only exclusively Australian cemetery on the Western Front apart from VC Corner at Fromelles, it contains 78 men from the 9th Brigade who fell during the

The New Zealand Memorial to the Missing, Messines Ridge British Cemetery.

battle. They lie in a mass grave, signified by the conjoined headstones. All but two are known. The 36th Battalion, with 44 burials, erected a wooden cross but it is long gone. Five teenagers lie here. The youngest, Private Cec Wise of the 9th Machine-Gun Company, was killed by a shell aged 18. As the cemetery is tucked out of the way in the wood and few visit, the Menin Gate buglers occasionally come to sound the 'Last Post' over the graves.

MUSEUMS

The small museum in Messines town hall on the marketplace offers interesting displays on the fighting around the village and a wealth of information on the New Zealanders who took it. As the museum is not always open, call the tourist office +32 57 44 50 41 to arrange a visit. The crypt of St Nicholas church is also worth seeing.

NEARBY PLACES OF INTEREST

Bayernwald

Largely empty when captured by the 19th Division, Croonaert Wood, northwest of Wytschaete, is one of the few parts of the German line along the frontage of the Messines attack that remains much as it was at the time. Generally called Bayernwald after the Bavarians who occupied it in the early part of the war, it was well known to Hitler. He won an Iron Cross as a runner in the wood in 1914–15, and served there again in 1916. It was also on the itinerary of his 1940 visit to the battlefields. Local schoolteacher André Becquart restored the German trench system and ran it as a private museum.

After his death in 1986 it closed and fell into disrepair. The site reopened in 2004 after the local council purchased it, cleared it and refurbished the trenches.

Further from Ypres than the preserved British line in Sanctuary Wood, Bayernwald is never crowded, which makes wandering the wattle-lined trenches a pleasure. Apart from a lunch break between midday and 1.15 pm, it is open daily, except for holidays and weekend afternoons between 1 November and 31 March. Gaining access, though, is inconvenient as you have to go to the tourist office in Kemmel (telephone +32 57 45 04 55) and pay €1.50 to get the entry code for the gate. Then leave the N365 at Wytschaete, turn right past the village church and continue for one kilometre to a minor road on the right, which you should follow for 800 metres to the parking area on the left. Before entering the wood, look towards nearby Croonaert Chapel British Cemetery. The remains of the three Hollandscheschurr mine craters are clustered around the farm beyond it.

Toronto Avenue Cemetery.

Spanbroekmolen

An offshoot of Messines Ridge, Spanbroekmolen dominated the surrounding area and the Germans fortified it appropriately. The British appropriately made it the target of their largest mine but damage from German countermining at the start of 1917 necessitated starting a new drive that joined the original one 350 metres along. The 41-tonne ammonal charge was readied only hours before the attack. It was blown 15 seconds late, catching the Ulstermen of the 8th Royal Irish Rifles halfway across no-man's-land. A number were killed by car-sized falling clods. Confronted by a crater 80 metres across and 13 metres deep, the rest met little opposition.

Hearing postwar rumours that the local farmers intended to fill the Messines craters in, Padre 'Tubby' Clayton, Toc H's founder, campaigned for one of them to be left as a memorial. Lord Wakefield, chairman of what was to become Castrol Oil and a prolific benefactor, duly purchased Lone Tree Crater, as Spanbroekmolen was originally known, for the Toc H movement to preserve. Filled with water, it was renamed the 'Pool of Peace'. Upkeep is a problem that has left the rim badly overgrown but a pillbox can still be discerned at the northern edge. The four German officers found dead inside were unmarked. Concussion from the mine explosion had killed them. Lone Tree Cemetery, established in front of the old British line across the road for the first Ulster dead, contains most of the victims of the fallout. The path to its right offers a superb view of the battlefield. To reach Spanbroekmolen, continue another 1.5 kilometres along the road from Ontario Farm on the tour route.

La Basse-Ville/Warneton

After losing the Messines Ridge, the Germans staged a fighting withdrawal to the Warneton Line. II ANZAC kept touch

The 2nd Wellingtons' attack in La Basse-Ville.

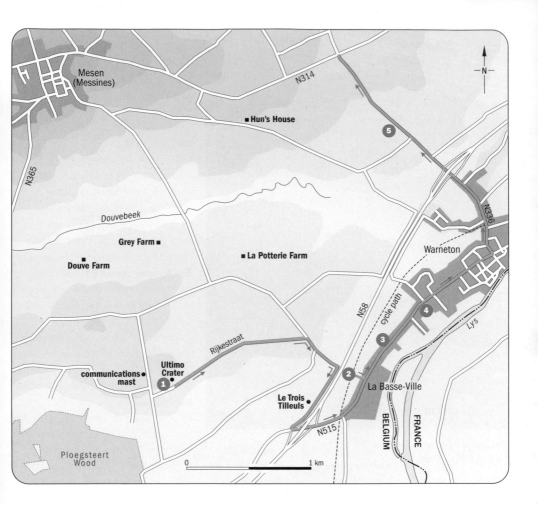

with them. On 13 June the New Zealand
Division, now on the right flank,
advanced towards La Basse-Ville,
Warneton's southern outlier. Its principal
axis was the Rijkestraat, on which you
saw **Ultimo Crater** ❶ on the tour. You
should now follow it all the way to the
N58 autoroute, whose line the New
Zealanders had almost reached next
morning, and turn right, then left onto
the N515. Passing under the autoroute,
the N515 crosses a cycle path, which
follows the track of the old railway in
no-man's-land. Continue past it for
350 metres into La Basse-Ville before
turning left, opposite an industrial estate
that was the site of a sugar refinery in
1917, onto a minor road that leads back
to the **cycle path** ❷.

Park and look along the cycle path
with the N58 autoroute on your left.
Rested for three weeks after sparring with
the Germans until the end of June, the
New Zealanders returned to the line on
the other side of the N58 on 20 July. Five
nights later 2nd Wellingtons attacked
from your left to right, taking La
Basse-Ville, but were driven out in the
morning. They regained it in the feint for
the Ypres offensive on 31 July, during
which Sergeant Charles Rangiwawahia
Sciascia MM, a well-known Horowhenua
footballer selected for the 1913 All Blacks,
was killed in this vicinity. At 1.72 metres,
the monument to him here is the same
height as he was.

Return to the N515 and continue into
La Basse-Ville. When the German

Memorial to Sergeant
Sciascia MM, La Basse-Ville.

Vestey single-handedly held it off long enough for his platoon to withdraw. He received the DCM. Trouble had also come from the **estaminet** that stood near the white house at the bus stop 100 metres further on the left. Lance-Corporal Leslie Andrew ran through the barrage in the 31 July attack to silence it, having already knocked out a machine-gun near the railway. From the estaminet, which marked the northern limit of La Basse-Ville in 1917, Andrew and a companion reconnoitred over the then open ground towards Warneton and captured another machine-gun in the **In den Rooster tavern** 4, which was on the right 280 metres further still, opposite today's **Café au Rooster**. Andrew was awarded the VC.

Continue on the N515 into the centre of Warneton and turn left onto the N336. The farm buildings on the left 600 metres beyond the N58 mark the location of the **windmill** 5 towards which the 11th Brigade advanced from the direction of Messines on your left in the '18 days'. Both the windmill and the line of posts extending to the N314, Hun's Walk, to your right front were captured by the 11th in the 31 July feint.

counterattack on 26 July approached the **Factory area** 3, which was on the left 350 metres along opposite the large windowless building, Private Matthew

CHAPTER 10

1917

MENIN ROAD

With the capture of the Messines Ridge, Field Marshal Haig's offensive from the Ypres salient could proceed. Apart from the artillery, the Australians and New Zealanders were not initially involved, and the offensive had gone badly wrong by the time they joined it. When they did, starting with I ANZAC's attack on Menin Road, they had the central role in major operations for the first time on the Western Front. Menin Road got the offensive back on the rails but conditions, which had been deplorable before, favoured the outcome. That aside, the battle was important for the Australians. It was the first time that two Australian divisions attacked alongside each other. It was also the first time in I ANZAC's experience that an attack was launched only after the most complete preparation and with maximum support, and according to a higher command concept that was operationally feasible and tactically sound. The attacks that followed, in which II ANZAC also participated, were identical to Menin Road. As at Messines, the advance was directed at the high ground, this time the end of the ridge that curved northeast past Ypres through the Gheluvelt Plateau, Broodseinde and Passchendaele.

High ground

Mere speedbumps like Aubers Ridge above Fromelles, these heights gave the same commanding views. The Germans ensconced on them observed everything that went on in Ypres and its salient. Life for the British in both was grim. Not only would it improve if the offensive cleared the heights and broke out of the salient but the strategic consequences if the subsequent advance to clear the Belgian coast succeeded were profound. Hemmed in by the coast and the border with neutral Holland, the Germans could not withdraw, as they had done to the Hindenburg Line. If they crumbled, Belgium would be liberated, thus achieving the objective for which Britain had gone to war. Russian resolve, tottering since huge losses in a string of defeats had led to the storming of the Winter Palace and the Tsar's abdication in March 1917, would be strengthened. The French would be bolstered too. Lastly, the Admiralty wanted Belgian ports captured because it maintained, speciously, that the toll in shipping exacted by U-boats operating from them would otherwise cost Britain the war.

Haig announced that he had 'no intention of entering into a tremendous offensive involving heavy losses', but would advance 'step by step'. After his success at Messines using 'bite and hold', General Plumer was therefore the obvious pick to lead the offensive. But clearing the coast would involve an advance of 40 kilometres, over three times as far as any advance to date. So Haig put General Gough, the 'thruster', in charge instead.

The German view from the 'high ground'. Remember that the view was unimpeded by trees and intact buildings in 1917. The spires of Ypres can be seen centre picture.

The Germans

Able to see from the heights what was coming, the Germans perfected the elastic defence concept that they had been working on since the Somme. It laid down that ground was to be fought over, rather than for. The British would not be faced by a strong front line, through which their more powerful artillery could blast a path. Instead, they would have to advance through a series of defensive zones, becoming weaker the further they went. When sufficiently weakened, they could be thrown back.

In practice this meant packing more pillboxes — ultimately as many as 2000 — into the existing lines, and machine-gun posts into the intervening zones. First came the outpost zone, which was lightly held in order to minimise casualties during the bombardment and included the front line. Extending 1.8 kilometres eastwards from it to the second (Albrecht) line, which ran across the start of the 60-metre-high Gheluvelt Plateau, was the forward zone. More strongly held, it consisted of machine-guns and infantry scattered in shell holes, pillboxes and farm ruins. Similarly organised, the battle zone stretched another 1.3 kilometres east to the third (Wilhelm) line, which crossed the Gheluvelt Plateau near Polygon Wood. Rapid counterattacks would spring from it. If they failed, more formal ones would be launched from the rear zone, which rolled up to six kilometres back to

the Flandern Lines. Skirting Poelcappelle, Flandern 1 passed behind Zonnebeke and Polygon Wood. Flandern 2 branched off Flandern 1 near Passchendaele and paralleled it southwards, while Flandern 3 tracked behind Passchendaele to Menin. Thus organised, the Germans confidently awaited the attack.

Mud

Gough ordered a first-day advance of four kilometres, which exceeded the total first-day advance at Messines, to plant the Fifth Army firmly on the ridge. That entailed taking the Gheluvelt Plateau, which straddled the ridge on the right of the attack, because it enfiladed the rest of the advance across the lower areas to the north. Given the tactical importance of the plateau, Haig suggested capturing it in a separate operation. Gough declined on the ground that this would result in a very pronounced salient. Haig relented.

As it happened, the initial assault did well on the low ground but foundered on the plateau. Then the battlefield became a bog. Having amassed 3106 guns, a greater concentration than at Messines, the artillery had fired three million shells during the 18-day preparatory bombardment. The intricate drainage system of dikes and culverts was destroyed and the country reverted to the vast swampland from which it had been claimed. Drenching rains flooded the ravaged terrain. The infantry soon fell behind the barrages in the morass. At the end of August, when losses had reached almost 70 000, Gough was still barely clinging to the edge of the plateau. He remarked that 'the heart had gone out of the Fifth Army'.

I ANZAC

On 25 August Haig made Plumer responsible for the capture of the high ground. Plumer demanded at least three weeks to prepare his first attack. Comprising 1295 guns firing 3.5 million shells to support an advance of 1.3 kilometres on a central frontage of 3.5 kilometres, the artillery concentration would be the heaviest of the war. Following the five-day bombardment, the Second Army was to assault behind a Messines-style creeping barrage and dig in behind a nine-hour standing barrage. The Fifth Army would keep up on the left, making for an assault by 11 divisions on a 13-kilometre front. After a six-day halt to allow the artillery to be brought forward, Plumer intended to launch a second attack, similar to the first. Four such attacks should result in the capture of the Passchendaele. The initial spearhead would be I ANZAC.

In the four months since Bullecourt, General Birdwood's corps underwent its most relevant training of the war. Brigades practised night assaults on successive objectives, leapfrogging under a creeping barrage and consolidating each objective as quickly as possible, and ran through the latest pillbox fighting techniques in a specially designed exercise area. The 4th Division also rejoined the other three Australian divisions in I ANZAC. Aware that the Australians wanted to fight alongside each other, Birdwood had arranged the transfer so that the divisions in his corps could always be put into battle in pairs, one pair relieving the next. The one Australian and one New Zealand division in II ANZAC would also fight together but

Though taken later in the campaign, this photo shows the dreadful conditions in the Ypres salient that confronted the Fifth Army in August.

be relieved by the two British divisions that made up the rest of Godley's corps.

Plans

As I ANZAC had the main role, Plumer left the tactical planning to the Australian commanders. For maximum punch, Birdwood and General White shrank the frontages for each of their two attacking divisions, the 1st and 2nd, to about 900 metres, spread across the two forward brigades in each. They would assault in three phases, each with fresh troops and each shorter than the preceding one to allow for the progressively greater difficulties as the assault went further. One battalion per forward brigade would advance 720 metres to the first objective, called the Red Line, where a 45-minute halt allowed time for consolidation and another battalion to pass through for the 360-metre advance to the Blue Line. After a two-hour halt for more consolidation, the two remaining battalions were to advance 270 metres to the Green Line. The final assault was therefore twice as strong as the initial one, though going less than half as far.

Fixed for 20 September, the attack crossed Menin Road, today's N8. In 1917 it was a shell-ravaged strip that ran southeast from Ypres and over the Gheluvelt Plateau at Clapham Junction, 3.2 kilometres from the town. The road bisected the Second Army's frontage. Both of the Australian divisions would advance north of it. The 1st Division was to clear Glencorse Wood and its outlier, Nonne Bosschen (Nun's Wood), on the plateau. Like all the woods in the salient, they had been shredded so that just a few splintered trunks pointed skyward. Starting below Westhoek Spur on the 1st Division's left, the 2nd Division was to cross the southern Hanebeek streamlet and take ANZAC Spur, an offshoot of the plateau, before joining the 1st beyond the Wilhelm Line inside the western edge of Polygon Wood. The British X Corps would attack south of Menin Road along the Tower Hamlets Spur on the Australian right. The Fifth Army was to attack across the flats on the Australian left.

Action

September turned out to be as fine as August was wet. Though low-lying areas were still waterlogged, parts of the heights were so dry that shells ricocheted when the bombardment opened on the 15th. The approach march through Ypres and across the wasteland south of it began in the drizzly dusk of 19 September. By 11 pm rain was falling steadily, turning the ground to mud again. Gough wanted to postpone the attack. As better weather had been forecast, Plumer refused. Passing over Menin Road, the two Australian divisions filed into shell holes along the jump-off tapes. At 4.30 am next morning a heavy German bombardment fell on the 3rd Brigade below Glencorse Wood, mauling the 9th and 10th Battalions. 'Annihilation fire' pounded the 2nd Division at 5.37 am after one of its officers, lost and stupidly carrying the divisional operation order, had been captured. The creeping barrage signalled the start of the attack at 5.40 am.

Charles Bean wrote: 'The advancing barrage won the ground; the infantry merely pounced on any points at which resistance survived'. Given their importance, the bulk of the German artillery's effort went into protecting the heights. As the Australian gunners had already seen, it was something to be reckoned with. Now it plastered the advance for 25 minutes. The creeping barrage saved the day by forcing most of the German machine-gunners to stay

Troops from the 1st Division moving along Menin Road past Hooge for the later stages of the attack.

under cover until the Australians were upon them. Even so, the 1st and 2nd Divisions were initiated into the pillbox fighting that the 3rd Division and the New Zealanders had got to know at Messines. Second Lieutenant Frederick Birks of the 6th Battalion was awarded a posthumous VC for his part in silencing two pillboxes in Glencorse Wood.

By 6.09 am the Red Line had everywhere been reached. The Blue Line more or less corresponded with the Wilhelm Line, supposedly the German main line of resistance. But it was being consolidated at 7.45 am, after an even easier advance. Germans firing from pillboxes and shell holes on the far side of the Blue Line were taken out during the break. By 10.30 am the Australians were on the Green Line. Lance-Corporal Reg Inwood of the 10th Battalion won the VC for a series of actions that culminated beyond it.

The standing barrage prevented the deployment of the two German divisions

A pillbox complex captured by the 1st Division. Though the trees have been stripped bare by the artillery, the pillboxes are more or less intact.

designated for counterattack until 6 pm. On seeing them the Australians called on the guns again and the counterattacks barely got started. The battle was over, with the British 41st Division's repulse at Tower Hamlets the only setback. Costing 21 000 men, over a quarter of them Australian, the success was not cheap. German losses were similar.

Australian wounded in Menin Road near Hooge during the attack. Shortly after this photo was taken a shell landed alongside the track, pulping most of those on the stretchers.

DRIVING/WALKING THE BATTLEFIELD

Three things need to be remembered on the Menin Road battlefield. Possibly because the road is arrow-straight, it is easy to get the impression that the stretch relevant to the Australian attack runs due south from Ypres. It doesn't. It runs eastwards, as did the axis of the attack, before bending south-east. Next, the ferocious fighting along this part of it in 1914–15 endowed Menin Road with iconic status. It entered British folklore. Lastly, a road with no history, the A19 autoroute, scythes right through the battlefield. Autoroutes and battlefields don't get on but there are a few positives in this case. The A19 is a useful reference marker to I ANZAC's Red Line and its flyovers offer vantage points that wouldn't otherwise exist. They are also little used by traffic. Don't forget, though, that the A19 wasn't there in 1917!

Though the first part of this tour, from Ypres to Frezenbergstraat, must be driven, you can drive or walk from then on. The tour finishes near the start of the Polygon Wood tour, which traces the next battle of the four along the ridge that involved the ANZACs. This arrangement is continued, allowing all four battles to be driven sequentially and, therefore, the entire ANZAC experience during the Third Ypres campaign to be followed as it unfolded.

MAPS NGI 1:20 000: 28/3-4 Zonnebeke–Moorslede; 28/1-2 Poperinge-Ieper

Leave Ypres through the Menin Gate and take the third street on the right. This is Menin Road, today's N8.

On passing **Menin Road South Military Cemetery** after 800 metres, you will reach a large roundabout 900 metres further on. Just before it on the left is a **demarcation stone**, one of 12 surviving in the salient, that show where the Germans were halted before Ypres during their spring offensive in 1918. The roundabout marks the site of **Hellfire Corner** ❶, the intersection of several roads now but of Menin Road with the Zillebeke–St Jean road in 1917. An easily identifiable choke point on one of the main routes into the salient, it was shelled constantly by the Germans in the hope of catching troops moving up to the line. Pioneers erected hessian and canvas screens in the hope of concealing the movement from their prying eyes. The Germans kept up the shelling anyway and Hellfire Corner became known as 'the most dangerous spot on earth'. It was certainly the most notorious spot in the salient. Approaching Australian transport drivers whipped their horses to speed them through.

Stay on the N8 over the roundabout (direction Gheluvelt/Menen) and Menin Road unfolds dead straight before you

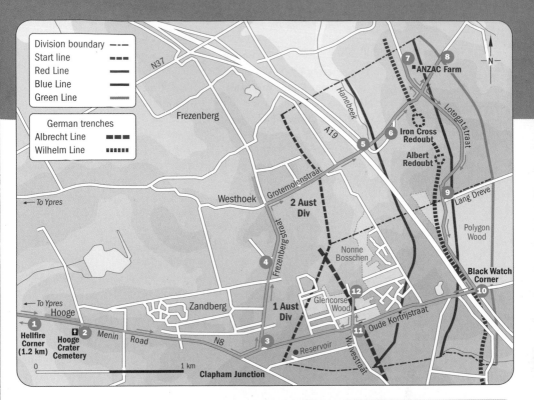

Map labels:

N37
Frezenberg
Hanebeek
A19
7
8
ANZAC Farm
Lotegatstraat
5
6
Iron Cross Redoubt
Albert Redoubt
9
Lang Dreve
Grotemolenstraat
Westhoek
2 Aust Div
To Ypres
Frezenbergstraat
4
Nonne Bosschen
Polygon Wood
Black Watch Corner
10
To Ypres
Hooge
Zandberg
1 Aust Div
Glencorse Wood
12
Oude Kortrijstraat
1
Hellfire Corner (1.2 km)
2
Hooge Crater Cemetery
Menin   Road
N8
3
Reservoir
11
Westrstraat
0   1 km
Clapham Junction

and shortly starts to descend. When the ANZACs arrived in September 1917, the rain and constant shelling had reduced it to a devastated and barely recognisable dirt track that engineers worked nonstop to keep passable for the unending two-way traffic of columns, guns and wagons that moved along it. The detritus of war littered the lunar landscape on either side. British Official War Artist Paul Nash captured the bleak horror in his surreal *The Menin Road* (1919), one of the war's most famous paintings. No road is visible in it. Bottoming out after 1.1 kilometres in an area where wartime

The initial part of the route follows Menin Road, whereupon the drive (or walk) tracks along I ANZAC's start line and over the Hanebeek to the Red Line on the left flank of the attack. After reaching the Blue Line at ANZAC Spur and the Green Line at Garter Point, the route returns to the Blue Line and follows it past Iron Cross and Albert Redoubts to Black Watch Corner at Polygon Wood. The return leg covers the right flank at Glencorse Wood. Also included are the sites of the two VC actions.

DISTANCE COVERED: 9 km
DURATION: 2.5 hours driving; 4 hours walking

tunnelling has caused subsidence problems, the N8 passes Canadalaan on the right, which leads to the preserved trenches at **Sanctuary Wood**, and then starts to climb towards the near end of the Gheluvelt Plateau.

Continue for 650 metres to **Hooge Crater Cemetery** ❷, directly opposite which are **Hooge Crater Museum** and, to its right, in the grounds of the Hotel Kasteel, **Hooge Crater**, some preserved trenches and a few concrete shelters. Ferocious fighting occurred in this area during the first two years of the war. Now a pond, the crater in what used to be the environs of Hooge Château resulted from the explosion of 1.5 tonnes of ammonal under the German line on 19 July 1915. Using flamethrowers for the first time against the BEF, the Germans counter-attacked on 30 July and drove the British 200 metres over Menin Road, beyond the rear wall of the cemetery. There the line stayed until several attacks in August 1917 carried it a kilometre over Menin Road and gained most of the Albrecht Line. Three of the four approach routes used by the 1st and 2nd Australian Divisions for their attack, and a light railway laid by I ANZAC, paralleled Menin Road on your right before crossing between your location and the crest of the plateau. By then the château, and the dwellings of Hooge around it, had disappeared.

The contrast between the grim wartime reminders at Hooge, and the frivolity that emanates from the vast Bellewarde amusement park a little further on, is bizarre. Lending the bizarreness a visual dimension, the lush growth behind the park and to its right covers the site of **Château Wood**, where Australian Official Photographer Frank Hurley snapped five Australian gunners at the end of October 1917 as they walked along a duckboard track through what was then a wilderness of branchless trees rooted in a foul morass. One of the war's most recognisable and widely reproduced images, the photograph came to symbolise the ghastliness of the Western Front, and the Third Ypres offensive in particular.

Past the park, Menin Road bends to the right and Oude Kortrijstraat enters on the left just before a commercial complex. The British line before 20 September curved back from beyond Hooge to cross Menin Road at **Clapham Junction**, on the crest opposite the garage 200 metres further along. Hence the junction marked the limit of the Fifth Army's foothold on the Gheluvelt Plateau. The boundary between the 1st Australian Division and the 23rd Division from X Corps, which attacked on the far side, also ran through it across your front. **Tower Hamlets** lies two kilometres further along Menin Road.

Head left on Oude Kortrijstraat and continue looking along it on reaching **Frezenbergstraat** ❸, the first street on the left, after 120 metres. The only part of the **Albrecht Line** still in German hands passed through the far end of **Glencorse Wood**, on the higher ground to the left of the road, and continued beyond the tree line screening the reservoir on the right of the road 200 metres ahead. The right flank of the 1st Australian Division's start line ran from Clapham Junction on Menin Road to your right and through the reservoir site, before cutting across the left corner of Glencorse Wood.

Now descend Frezenbergstraat, which follows the line of **Westhoek Spur**, for 600 metres to the saddle of the spur, and park near a cluster of sheds and houses by the road on your left ❹. From here, the spur rises to the hamlet of **Westhoek**, on the left of Frezenbergstraat 500 metres along. As far as the eye could see, the area around you before the attack was a shell-torn wasteland, littered by the wreckage of smashed farms and woods. Fine weather had dried out the higher ground, which took on the appearance of a desert, but the low ground was still boggy. Except for the pillboxes strung out along them, the successive German lines were untraceable.

Standing with your back to the houses, look across Frezenbergstraat. You are on

the centreline of I ANZAC's assault. The
boundary between the 1st and 2nd
Divisions ran this side of the sheds
120 metres to your right and through the
left end of **Nonne Bosschen,** the wood
on the far slope 600 metres to your front.
Roughly following the course of the
autoroute, the **Red Line** passed beyond
the far side of Nonne Bosschen, which
today merges with Glencorse, the nearer
wood to your right front. From Glencorse,
the start-line tapes cut diagonally right to
left 300 metres ahead of you. The 11th
Battalion occupied them immediately
right of the boundary, with the rest of the
3rd Brigade arrayed behind in echelon
through your location. At the reservoir
end of the start line, the rest of the 2nd
Brigade was similarly arrayed behind the
6th Battalion. Look in that direction to
appreciate the nature of the attack:
brigades arranged in great depth on
narrow frontages against a nearby

objective. Immediately left of the
boundary, the 25th Battalion, with the
rest of the 7th Brigade behind it,
extended to where the start line passed
in front of Westhoek. Led by the 20th
Battalion, the 5th Brigade took over there.
The frontages in the 2nd Division were
wider because it would not be butting
directly against the Gheluvelt Plateau, as
the 1st Division was, but against ANZAC
Spur running off it.

Waiting for the attack to start, the rear
battalions of the 3rd and 5th Brigades
pressed forward onto the start line to
avoid heavy German shelling of your
location and of the Westhoek area.
Though less affected, the 2nd Brigade
had to do the same before Glencorse
Wood. As the fire kept up when the
advance began, the attack formations
spread right and left across your front
disintegrated as all the waves coalesced
into one dense line ahead of it. Down

Frank Hurley's great shot of
Australian gunners in what
was once Château Wood.

GLENCORSE WOOD

RESERVOIR

START LINE

6TH BATTALION

11TH BATTALION

The left of the 1st Division's start line.

came the creeping barrage at 5.40 am. 'As near to perfect as possible', one Australian officer said. It hung like a thick drape ahead of the line. With cigarettes and pipes lit, the Australians advanced behind the fire, which progressed 90 metres every four minutes.

Continue either on foot or by car along Frezenbergstraat into Westhoek, where the remains of five Australian soldiers killed at the end of September 1917 were uncovered during roadworks in 2007, and head right on Grotemolenstraat down the slope of the spur. Occupied by the 20th and 25th Battalions on the left and right respectively, the centre of the 2nd Division's start line crossed Grotemolenstraat 50 metres before the house on the left, beyond which the road forks at the foot of a flyover on the A19.

Both battalions met feeble resistance. Dazed by the barrage, many Germans simply waved white handkerchiefs or bandages at them. As you proceed up the flyover embankment, look left to see some **concrete artillery shelters** where the 20th Battalion briefly struck trouble. Now stop on the footpath in the centre of the **flyover** ❺ and stand with your back to Westhoek. Following the tree line in the low ground to your immediate left front is the **Hanebeek**.

Innocuous-looking now, it was a flooded expanse 90 metres wide when the 20th Battalion reached it. Some men became bogged as the 20th got to its part of the Red Line, which stretched, on the far side of the stream, just to the right of Grotemolenstraat from a point 500 metres to your left. After an uneventful advance, the 25th Battalion dug in alongside the 20th astride the A19, while the 1st Division took the Red Line between the A19 and Nonne Bosschen over your right shoulder. The Blue and Green Lines ran atop **ANZAC Spur**, the high ground to your front, to **Polygon Wood** on the Gheluvelt Plateau, 700 metres to your right on the other side of the A19. Tracking in front of the Blue Line along the forward slope of the spur and the near edge of the wood was the **Wilhelm Line**, pounded into oblivion

There was the continual swish swish of shells overhead — some high, some low — some indeed too low. With shells bursting around, many indeed were the narrow escapes. Most men were hit at times by flying pieces of high explosive or shrapnel. Unless a man was badly hit, all went eagerly on.

Lieutenant Alex Hollyhoke of the 7th Battalion on following the creeping barrage (Hollyhoke, 'Journal', 3DRL/1465, AWM)

> Here, as in so many pillbox fights, confusion, fatal for the garrison, occurred through weaker spirits being ready to surrender while some brave souls continued to fire. As the first German came out with his hands up, another behind fired between his legs and wounded a sergeant of the 20th. 'Get out of the way, sergeant', shouted a Lewis gunner. 'I'll see to the bastards' and firing three or four bursts into the entrance he killed or wounded most of the crowd inside.
>
> Charles Bean on the 20th Battalion's fight at the artillery shelters
> (Bean, CEW, *The AIF in France. IV. 1917*, Sydney, 1938, p. 766)

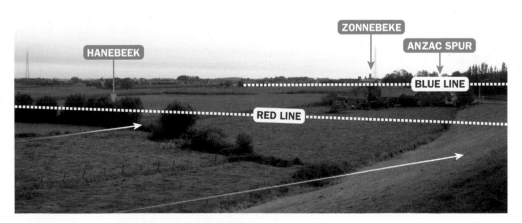

The Hanebeek then and now, showing the 20th Battalion's advance to the Red Line.

apart from the pillbox strongpoints that studded its course. Before leaving, note the large square tower, which is the steeple of Zonnebeke church, to the left of the pylon on ANZAC Spur, and the water tower at Passchendaele on the horizon to its left. Zonnebeke, 2.5 kilometres off, and Passchendaele, 6.5 kilometres off, were the objectives of later attacks.

Continue across the flyover to the gap in the trees on the right of the embankment on the other side and face the gap ⑥. When fire came from two pillboxes near the side road below you while the Red Line 200 metres to your right was being consolidated, men from the 18th and 20th Battalions rushed them, capturing 40 Germans and a machine-gun. These pillboxes mutually supported the **Albert Redoubt**, which was 400 metres to your front across the re-entrant and to the right of the multi-skylit long shed. Sited in the Wilhelm Line to catch in enfilade any assault up the slope on the right of the Grotemolenstraat, it nonetheless fell easily in the 27th Battalion's advance on that side of the road to the Blue Line. Attacking on its left, the 18th Battalion

took **Iron Cross Redoubt** with little difficulty. Another Wilhelm Line strongpoint, it stood just to the right of Grotemolenstraat on the crest, and also gave mutual support to the Albert Redoubt.

Carry on along Grotemolenstraat to the crossroads on the crest of ANZAC Spur, turn left onto Lotegatstraat and stop 40 metres past the overhead power lines ⑦. Look back towards the crossroads. The **Blue Line** ran to the left of the road and included **ANZAC House**, a two-storied artillery observation post that lent its name to the spur. It stood, on the 2nd Division's left flank, on the site of ANZAC Farm, which was to the left of the buildings beside the closest pylon. At the end of an even easier advance than the one to the Red Line, Lieutenant Arthur Hull of the 18th Battalion planted the Australian flag on ANZAC House after the 15-strong garrison had been overpowered. The Germans beyond the Blue Line, though, kept up a harassing fire, catching some men from the 18th as they relaxed.

After ANZAC House's capture, a German messenger dog from Zonnebeke loped in with an order for the German

The Albert and Iron Cross Redoubts, showing how they, and the pillboxes below the embankment, could support each other.

IRON CROSS REDOUBT

POLYGON WOOD

ALBERT REDOUBT

FIELD OF FIRE

PILLBOXES IN BANK

battalion commander to retake the area. The order could not be actioned. A German shell killed the dog next day. Passing through the 18th Battalion, the 17th advanced to the Green Line, here only 50 metres beyond ANZAC House. By briefly stepping back from the local battle, the essence of 'bite and hold' tactics can be grasped from your location. The urban sprawl 800 metres to your left and on the near side of Zonnebeke church is across **Albania Valley** on **Tokio Spur**, the objective of the next 'bite'. The preceding 'bite' started from the low ground in front of the amusement park on your right, which you can see by walking a few metres past the house. As only a modest advance

was involved in each case, the attackers were strong enough at the end to 'hold' the 'bite' against counterattacks. As it was, German attempts to form up in Albania Valley to counterattack during the afternoon were hammered by the artillery.

Return to the crossroads and turn left into Grotemolenstraat. The Green Line crossed it 280 metres along, just past the 70 km speed sign, on the site of the strong **Garter Point pillbox** ❽ above Albania Valley. Some of the fire that disrupted the 18th Battalion's consolidation of the Blue Line behind you came from this pillbox, despite the Red Cross flag flying above it. Successfully rushing the strongpoint, a party from the

The preceding 'bite', taken by the 18th Battalion, as seen from ANZAC Spur on the Blue Line.

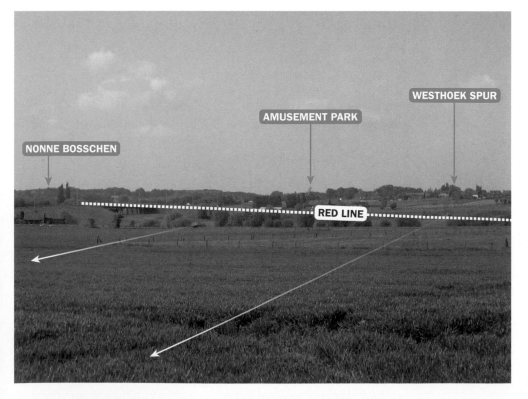

NONNE BOSSCHEN

AMUSEMENT PARK

WESTHOEK SPUR

RED LINE

Garter Point pillbox, with Tokio Spur in the background, after the attack.

18th found two doctors and some wounded inside because it was also being used as a dressing station. The Germans were lucky to survive this instance of 'Red Cross treachery'. The 17th Battalion, whose short advance encountered no opposition, arrived shortly afterwards.

Go back to the crossroads once again and this time head left on Lotegatstraat along the crest of ANZAC Spur. The Green Line ran 150 to 200 metres to the left of the road; the Blue Line crossed the road after 200 metres. Iron Cross Redoubt was 100 metres on the other side of the farmhouse reached by the private road on the right after 230 metres. About 200 metres after Lotegatstraat bends to the right, another private road runs off to a farmhouse on the right. Having taken Albert Redoubt 80 metres beyond the far side of the farmhouse, the 27th Battalion dug in on the Blue Line, which passed the near side facing you, while the 28th Battalion continued the advance to the Green Line on your left. Continue to the **Anzac Rest café** ❾ on the junction with Lang Dreve at the corner of Polygon Wood, where the owner, Johan Vandewalle, displays the many battlefield relics he has found. Known internationally for his exploration of the wartime tunnels around Ypres, Vandewalle led the team that recovered the Westhoek Five. He happily welcomes Australians, as the

name of his café suggests. A Belgian beer is in order there.

Continue on Lotegatstraat along the western edge of Polygon Wood, which the Wilhelm Line also followed, with the A19 on your right. The Blue Line ran just inside the wood, then a wispy stubble of forlorn-looking fir saplings, and was captured here by the 12th Battalion. Attacking from your right, the 12th overran nine machine-guns before their crews, huddled in pillboxes to escape the barrage, had a chance to fire them. The 9th and 10th Battalions carried the 3rd Brigade's advance to the Green Line 300 metres further into the wood. During the two-hour pause beforehand, those appointed as 'newspaper boys' distributed copies of the *Daily Mail* and *Daily Mirror* that Lieutenant-Colonel Maurice Wilder-Neligan had obtained for the 10th Battalion. 'It really is rather comical to think of a whole line of men lying in shell holes, each reading his daily paper, in the middle of an attack of this description', wrote Birdwood.

Proceed to the junction with Oude Kortrijstraat at the south-western corner of Polygon Wood. After 40 men from the Black Watch staged an epic stand here against a powerful German attack on 11 November 1914, the location was immortalised as **Black Watch Corner**. It was given up, along with the rest of Polygon Wood, after the Germans attacked the salient using gas in April 1915. They later installed a formidable pillbox on the corner. Now stand at the nearby **flyover** ❿ with your back to the A19. Crossing the line of the autoroute 150 metres to your left, the Blue Line for the 2nd Brigade ran diagonally into the low ground of the Reutelbeek on the divisional boundary 400 metres over your right shoulder. Entrenching on the Blue Line, the 5th Battalion was heavily engaged by the pillbox, whereupon a party led by Captain Frederick Moore worked either side of your location and surrounded it. The garrison motioned to

ALBANIA VALLEY

ZONNEBEKE

TOKIO SPUR

GREEN LINE

The next 'bite' as seen from the area of Garter Point.

surrender but Moore was shot dead by one of the Germans as he ran towards them. Incensed, his men killed this German and several others. Only the intervention of other officers prevented the slaughter of the rest.

Passing just beyond Black Watch Corner, the Green Line cut across to the line of the A19 250 metres on your right. The 7th Battalion secured this stretch of it, which involved advancing through your location to capture a group of nine pillboxes in the fields to your right front. According to the artillery maps, the barrage should have been 200 metres ahead of them at this stage but part of it fell on the pillbox area as the 7th attacked. One of the 'dropshorts' mortally wounded Major Frederick Tubb, a Lone Pine VC. Now take the flyover and pause at the road on the left on the other side. The Green Line, taken here by the 8th Battalion, ran along the far end of this road, which descends to the

Reutelbeek. When the Germans tried counterattacking there at dusk, the artillery pulverised them for an hour. Some in the 8th laughed, knowing that the Germans could not get through. At the same time they were praying that the Germans would get through so that they could pour their own fire into them.

Continue along Oude Kortrijstraat, which the Blue Line crossed after 120 metres. When a machine-gun in it beyond the tree line on the right of the road fired on the 10th Battalion as it was moving forward, Lance-Corporal Inwood dashed through the barrage to silence it. He killed several Germans and captured nine. The Red Line crossed the road between the t-nonnebos entertainment centre and the housing estate on the right, which ends at Glencorse Wood. Carry on another 200 metres past the corner of the wood to the **crossroads** 11 with Wulvestraat on your left and Sproojesboj Dreef on your right. Emerging from Glencorse just past the crossroads, the Albrecht Line headed leftwards through the fields on the far side of Wulvestraat. Somewhere along its course there was a two-storeyed pillbox where an unfortunate tragedy occurred. The Australians around the pillbox had relaxed, thinking that the battle was over because the Germans on the lower level had surrendered. Unaware they had done so, the Germans on the upper level shot one of the Australians, whereupon his mates bayoneted every prisoner. In no mood to spare one who pleaded for mercy, an Australian whose bayonet was not on his rifle grimly fixed it and killed him.

Second Lieutenant Birks's VC action occurred on your right in Glencorse Wood near the crossroads. When a pillbox in the Albrecht Line there held up the 6th Battalion on its way to the Red Line, Birks and Lance-Corporal William Johnston rushed it. A bomb wounded Johnston but Birks went on through a torrent of bombs and machine-gun fire to the rear entrance. The garrison surrendered. Shortly afterwards, he led an attack that overcame another strongpoint, in which 10 Germans were killed and 16 captured. Next day the Germans shelled the Red Line in the housing estate area and Birks was mortally wounded while digging out those buried by the explosions. A Gallipoli veteran, he had won the MM at Pozières.

Head right on Sproojesboj Dreef to the far end of **Glencorse Wood** 🔢, where the road swings left and runs down the slope to a large **farmhouse**. Look towards it. A machine-gun atop a pillbox sited on the Sproojesboj Dreef between your location and the farmhouse held up the 11th Battalion's advance from your left. Lieutenant Graham Leaver's platoon from the 10th Battalion, which had caught up with the 11th, managed to get behind the pillbox. When a German shot Leaver through the head with a revolver at point blank range, the men, said Charles Bean, 'went mad'. Corporal Harry Hodge received the DCM for rushing the machine-gun.

Return to the crossroads, from which you can head right on Oude Kortrijstraat and, once past Glencorse Wood and the reservoir, turn right onto Frezenbergstraat for your start point. Alternatively, return to Black Watch Corner for the start of the Polygon Wood tour.

The area of the Wulvestraat pillbox incident.

LOCAL INFORMATION

CEMETERIES

Hooge Crater Cemetery

Passed on the right of Menin Road at Hooge on the tour route, this cemetery was begun in October 1917 and contained 76 graves at war's end. The postwar concentration of burials, mostly from the surrounding 1917 battlefields, expanded it to 5892 graves, of which 3850 are unknown. Among the 513 Australians, 178 of them unknown, are Lieutenant Leaver, whose killing in Glencorse Wood provoked a frenzy, at V.J.10. Private Patrick Bugden of the 31st Battalion, who fell in the next 'bite', at Polygon Wood, and was awarded a posthumous VC, rests at VIII.C.5. Some 119 New Zealanders also lie here. Designed by Sir Edwin Lutyens, the cemetery features a stone wall that encircles the Stone of Remembrance in the manner of a mine crater. It is a reminder of the underground warfare that went on at Hooge and, in particular, of the mine blown across the road in July 1915.

Menin Road South Military Cemetery

On Menin Road 800 metres past the Menin Gate, this cemetery was started in January 1916 and always lay within the British line. Field ambulances continually used it to offload wounded who died while being evacuated from the forward areas, which accounts for the small number of unknowns, 120 out of 1658. Most of these were probably postwar burials. Of the 267 Australians, only eight are unidentified. Captain Moore, treacherously killed at Black Watch Corner, rests at I.T.4. There are 52 New Zealand graves.

Hooge Crater Cemetery.

The grave of Private Patrick Bugden VC.

The grave of Captain Frederick Moore, Menin Road South Cemetery.

Maaldestedestraat exit, signposted Zillebeke, on the Hellfire Corner roundabout and It is one kilometre along on the left.

Sanctuary Wood preserved trenches

In October 1914 the wood was in a quiet sector and offered sanctuary — hence its name — to exhausted stragglers trying to rejoin their units. By November the Germans had broken through at Gheluvelt further up Menin Road and the wood was in the firing line. When I ANZAC passed it on the way to the Menin Road attack almost three years later, the wood was said to be worse than anything Dante could have imagined. After the war, the owners decided to leave part of it as it was. Over the years, their descendants have 'maintained' the British trenches and dugouts, as well as the shell holes and splintered trees, and set up a museum displaying a host of battlefield relics and a collection of graphic 3-D images of the war. Now a permanent fixture on any visitor itinerary to the salient, the museum is located on the right of Canadalaan, which you passed on Menin Road on the tour route, 1.5 km along.

You may care to visit the Canadian memorial atop **Hill 62**, 300 metres past the museum. A powerful German assault in this area in June 1916 pushed the Canadians off the hill and threatened to overrun Sanctuary Wood but the outnumbered Canadians grimly held the rear slope above the wood. They subsequently counterattacked and recovered most of the ground lost. Nearby **Sanctuary Wood Cemetery** is one of the largest in the salient with 1989 graves, 88 of them Australian and 18 New Zealand. Lieutenant Gilbert Talbot of the Rifle Brigade, after whom Talbot House in Poperinghe was named, rests at I.G.1.

Perth Cemetery (China Wall), Zillebeke

The 'China Wall' tag derived from a communication trench called the Great Wall of China, which was shielded by a sandbag wall and extended from this location to Menin Road. Originally begun by the French in 1914, the British used the cemetery as a front-line cemetery between June and October 1917. As a postwar concentration cemetery, it expanded from 130 graves to 2791, 1422 of them identified. About half of the 147 Australian burials, 19 of which are unknown, are of gunners, testimony to the losses the Australian field artillery suffered in its gun lines around nearby Zillebeke lake. Of the Menin Road dead, Second Lieutenant Birks VC, MM rests at I.G.45. Also known as Halfway House, the cemetery contains 23 New Zealand burials, and the graves of seven British soldiers executed for desertion. Take the

CHAPTER 11

1917

POLYGON WOOD

Firmly established on the Gheluvelt Plateau after their successful attack two days earlier on Menin Road, in which the south-western end of Polygon Wood had also fallen, the 1st and 2nd Australian Divisions were relieved by the other two divisions in I ANZAC, the 4th and 5th, on 22 September. In General Plumer's second step along the high ground on the southern side of the Ypres salient, they were to capture the rest of Polygon Wood and the Flandern 1 Line beyond it on 26 September, thereby clearing the plateau. X Corps would assault on the right of I ANZAC as before, while V and XVIII Corps from the Fifth Army on I ANZAC's left were to take most of Zonnebeke village and the Windmill Cabaret Spur north of it. Seven divisions altogether would be advancing on a frontage of almost eight kilometres.

Five-sided, appropriately enough, but with an extension on one side, Polygon Wood lent its name to this attack. It was the most prominent terrain feature, it was captured in its entirety, and some of the heaviest fighting took place along its southern edge, where the Australian right flank was genuinely threatened. The wood itself does not extend as far east today as it did in 1917, so it is smaller now than it was then.

Preparations

In the only differences from the Menin Road plan, I ANZAC would attack in two phases instead of three and end up on a wider frontage. After an 800-metre advance, the first phase would finish on the Red Line, which ran for two kilometres along the eastern side of Polygon Wood and, to its north, Albania Valley above the Steenbeek. The second would end 360 metres later on the

2.5-kilometre stretch of the Blue Line that tracked along Tokio Spur almost to Zonnebeke, following Flandern 1 for part of the way. Like ANZAC Spur, on which the Menin Road attack had ended, Tokio was named after a prominent pillbox. Unlike ANZAC Spur, Tokio did not run off the plateau but from where the main ridgeline just beyond it began to swing northwards through Broodseinde towards Passchendaele. As before, each division would assault with two brigades, each brigade attacking the Red Line with one battalion and the Blue Line with two. In its first big attack since the Fromelles disaster over a year before, the 5th Division, which was the more rested, had the harder task of advancing atop the plateau through Polygon Wood. On its left, the 4th would tackle Tokio Spur.

During the six days since the first step, the engineers and pioneers constructed planked 'corduroy' loop roads by night

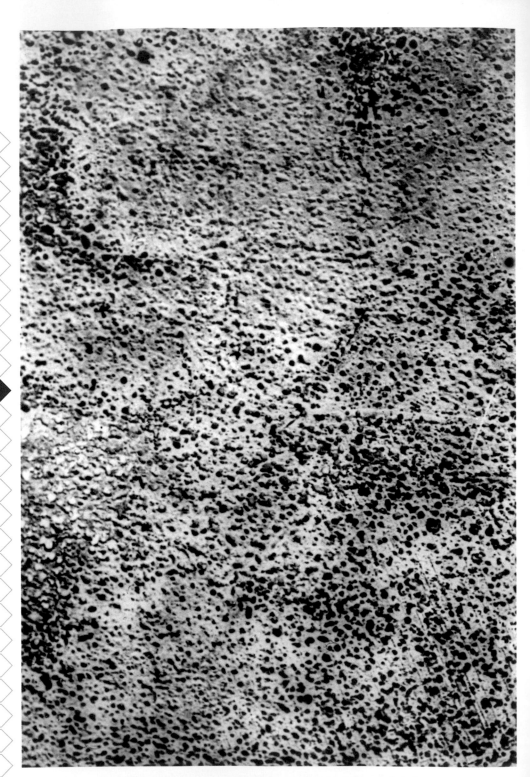

Unrecognisable as anything terrestrial: Polygon Wood bombarded out of existence three weeks before the attack.

across the crater fields in rear that enabled the field artillery to move closer to the line just taken. The result was a replication of the same massive artillery support enjoyed by the earlier attack. Arrayed in five belts, the barrage was almost one kilometre deep.

The 15th Brigade

Aware that an assault was imminent, the Germans sought to disrupt it with a spoiling attack. After a heavy bombardment, the 229th Reserve Infantry Regiment punched up the Reutelbeek re-entrant, which ran alongside Polygon Wood in X Corps's sector, at 5.30 am on 25 September. It was heading for the old Wilhelm Line near the head of the Reutelbeek, which had been lost in the Menin Road attack. British artillery isolated the Germans there by mid-morning. But the 98th Brigade from the British 33rd Division had back-pedalled up to 500 metres to the former German strongpoint at Lone House. On the Blue Line captured in the earlier attack, it was well behind the line of the modern A19 autoroute.

Held by the 58th Battalion, the right flank of the Australian 15th Brigade in Polygon Wood was now exposed. The 58th immediately swung around to face the Germans but it had been battered by their bombardment. Its position was precarious. Brigadier-General Elliott sent the 60th Battalion, under Lieutenant-Colonel Norman Marshall, both to reinforce it and to support a counterattack by the 98th Brigade. The 60th began arriving on the flank of the 58th around noon. Shelled throughout its 1.5-kilometre approach march, it had already lost over 100 men. Set for 2 pm, the 98th Brigade's counterattack barely got going. When Marshall reported that the Germans were still threatening, Elliott ordered the 57th Battalion forward at 7.05 pm. With only the 59th Battalion left, Elliott told Major-General Hobbs at 8 pm that his brigade could not attack next morning. Replacing it with the 8th Brigade, which Hobbs held in reserve, was impossible at this late stage. Hobbs directed Elliott to proceed.

Originally slated for the second phase of the assault, the 59th Battalion would now take the first objective, the Red Line at the far end of Polygon Wood. 'So you know what to do?' Elliott asked Lieutenant Colonel-Charles Mason. He nodded. 'Well, then go and do it.' Elliott had no time to say more for he was organising the nine-kilometre move up of the 29th and 31st Battalions, which the 8th Brigade was giving him for the final advance to the Blue Line. Elliott hurriedly briefed their commanders around midnight. He was assured that the 98th Brigade would restore the right flank. But one of its two battalions got lost and the other waited for it. Elliott's men would have to deal with the flank themselves.

26 September

Low cloud scudded across the sky of what was a fine, mild and surprisingly quiet night. The nerves of those lying out on the start line were stretched taut as they waited for the barrage to open at 5.50 am. It was the same just before any big attack. Then the assault began. With the dust from the barrage and fog hampering control, the 59th, 29th and 31st Battalions advanced as a gaggle. On the exposed right flank, pillboxes that the 98th Brigade should have taken caused problems from the outset. Spilling over into the 98th's sector, part of the 31st Battalion silenced them before being pinned down by the strongpoint at Jerk House. For his part in these actions, ex–NSW north coast hotelier Private Patrick Bugden was awarded a posthumous VC. The rest of the 31st, with the other two

> Half an hour to go. A fog had fallen and we could see Fritz flares only hazily through it. Ten minutes. A man rose here and there to tighten a belt or to stretch his cramped limbs. Three — the fog was more dense, and sections became very restless as they quietly fixed bayonets and prepared to advance. A gun behind boomed louder than the rest, suddenly the whole earth seemed to burst into a seething bubbling roaring centre of eruption and, as at the touch of an enchantress's wand, out of the ground sprang a mass of men in little worm-like columns — each wriggling its way forward to a sparkling shouting seething line of earth, fire and smoke in front of them.
>
> Lieutenant Sinclair Hunt of the 55th Battalion on the tension before the Polygon Wood assault and the relief when it began (Hunt, 'Narrative', 2DRL/0277, AWM)

battalions alongside it, reached the Red Line in Polygon Wood by 6.45 am, only to be hit from Cameron House, a strongpoint on the 98th Brigade's Red Line. As it had still not shown up, the 31st Battalion and part of the 29th on its left stayed put instead of exposing the right flank further by continuing on to the Blue Line. In the event, the 59th Battalion inadvertently reached it while surrounding some pillboxes into which a German counterattack had been driven.

Around midday the 2nd Royal Welch Fusiliers, which had reinforced the 98th Brigade, finally advanced on the right flank. They took Jerk House but pulled back when another German attack threatened at 4 pm to Carlisle Farm, on the edge of the A19 and one kilometre short of the strongpoint in Cameron Covert, a copse on the 98th Brigade's Blue Line. The 15th Brigade's right flank was therefore still open. It was secured after dark when Marshall led a raid by the 60th Battalion on Cameron House,

followed by an advance to Cameron Covert. Advancing along the Reutelbeek during the next afternoon, the Welch braved withering fire to gain the Blue Line alongside the 60th Battalion, which was then holding almost 250 metres of the 98th Brigade's section of it.

The rest of I ANZAC's attack was uneventful. On reaching the Blue Line after advancing through the northern half of Polygon Wood, the 14th Brigade roamed about looking for souvenirs, as their mates in the neighbouring 15th Brigade had done to the amazement of the British soldiers who saw them. The 4th Division had an even easier time. Its only hiccup arose on the way to the Blue Line when parts of the 4th Brigade got too close to the barrage and broke back. Captain Jacka led them on again. Sergeant John Dwyer of the 4th Australian Machine-Gun Company knocked out a German machine-gun that enfiladed the 14th Brigade alongside and brought it back to the 4th's line. Dwyer, who eventually became Deputy Premier

57th Battalion stretcher-bearers 300 metres behind the line in shell-torn Polygon Wood the day after the attack. The butte of the prewar rifle range in the wood rises centre right.

of Tasmania, was awarded the VC. The counterattack that the Germans tried to launch during the afternoon was crushed on the Broodseinde Ridge by artillery and machine-gun fire.

Except on the flanks, the attack had been everywhere successful. On the right the 39th Division failed before Tower Hamlets, as did the 3rd Division from the Fifth Army before the Windmill Cabaret on the left. The two Australian divisions suffered a third of the 15 000 British casualties. Plumer singled out the 15th Brigade's effort in holding the German attack and then taking part of the 98th Brigade's objective. He 'went so far as to thank Elliott for saving the British army from disaster'. During the battle, Elliott learned that his brother George, the 56th Battalion's doctor, had been killed and that he himself was facing likely financial ruin.

DRIVING/WALKING THE BATTLEFIELD

As most of the Australian action occurred along its southern edge on the 15th Brigade's right flank, Polygon Wood is the most important area of the battlefield. Closed to traffic, it must be walked, which takes no more than two hours at a leisurely pace. The rest of the tour can be done on foot but is best driven for two reasons. First, it finishes some distance from its starting point. Second, as the battle began where the Menin Road attack left off, the tour follows part of the Menin Road tour route. So those who have done that tour on foot, as recommended, will be doing so again over some of the same ground and where very little of note happened.

MAP NGI 1:20 000: 28/3-4 Zonnebeke–Moorslede

The approach route is the same as for the Menin Road tour. Leave Ypres through the Menin Gate and take Menin Road, today's N8, which is the third street on the right. Continue on it over the Hellfire Corner roundabout (direction Gheluvelt/Menen). Stop after 1.8 kilometres at **Hooge Crater Cemetery** ❶ on the right. You should read the full description of this locality given in the Menin Road tour. It was where much of the 15th Brigade waited to attack Polygon Wood on 26 September but Brigadier-General Elliott had to deploy the 15th

prematurely after the Germans broke through the 98th Brigade's line the day before. **Zouave Wood**, which covered the slope just beyond the far end of the cemetery, was occupied by the 57th Battalion and, after it was sent forward, by the 59th. The wood was never replanted. Elliott's headquarters was across the road in dugouts at **Hooge Crater**. The main corduroy track from the rear looped around the far side of the crater and was used by the field artillery to deploy guns there and in the environs of the amusement park, further along Menin Road. Packed with troops and guns, the area around you was showered with mustard gas and shelled mercilessly. On 25 September the shelling forced General Hobbs, who was on his way to see Elliott, to turn back 180 metres from Elliott's headquarters. It also killed Elliott's brother while he waited to move forward with the 56th Battalion's headquarters in Château Wood, the modern growth of which is behind the amusement park.

Continue along Menin Road. The 60th Battalion deployed from **Clapham Junction** on the crest of the Gheluvelt Plateau ahead. It was replaced there by the 57th and, when the 57th left, it was replaced in turn by the 59th. Do not proceed to the crest but turn left at the commercial complex 200 metres short of it onto Oude Kortrijstraat. You are now

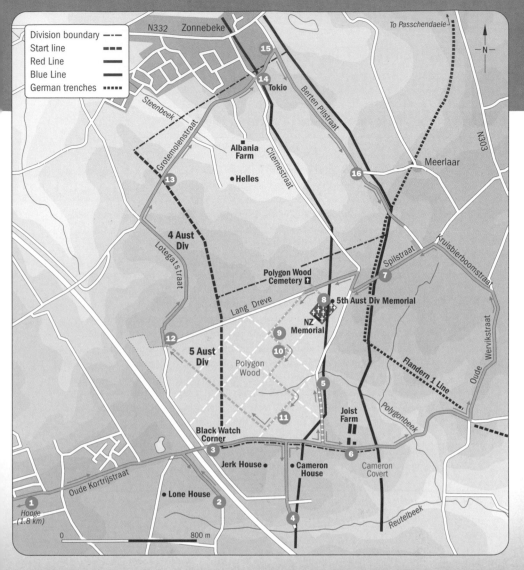

Division boundary ---
Start line - - -
Red Line ——
Blue Line ——
German trenches •••••

To Passchendaele

N332 Zonnebeke

15

14 Tokio

Berten Pilstraat

N303

Steenbeek

Grotemolenstraat

Albania Farm

• Helles

Cijnnestraat

13

16

Meerlaar

4 Aust Div

Lotegatstraat

Polygon Wood Cemetery

Lang Dreve

8 • 5th Aust Div Memorial

Spilstraat

7

Kruisbierboomstraat

Oude Wervikstraat

12

5 Aust Div

9 NZ Memorial

10

Polygon Wood

Flandern 1 Line

5

Joist Farm

11

Polygonbeek

Black Watch Corner

3

6 Cameron Covert

Jerk House •

• Cameron House

1

Hooge (1.8 km)

• Lone House

2

4

Reutelbeek

0   800 m

following the route that the battalions of the 15th Brigade, and the 29th and 31st Battalions from the 8th Brigade, took to Polygon Wood. German shelling had turned **Glencorse Wood**, 700 metres along on the left, into an inferno when

The first part of the drive focuses on the 15th Brigade's actions on the Reutelbeek, on the right flank of the assault. Continuing via the Red and Blue Lines, and Joist Farm in between them, the drive then swings over Flandern 1 and into Polygon Wood. The walk through the wood passes several pillboxes that figured in the attack and sets up the drive around the left flank of the assault, which brushes the outskirts of Zonnebeke before following the Blue Line on Tokio Spur. The sites of the two VC actions are visited.
DISTANCE COVERED: 15 km (Polygon Wood walk: 3 km)
DURATION: 4.5 hours driving/walking; 7 hours walking

Major-General Sir John Joseph Talbot Hobbs

Commander, 5th Australian Division, 1917–18

1864–1938

A highly successful Perth architect and a devout Christian, Hobbs had been a gunner since joining the volunteers in 1883. He commanded the 1st Australian Division's artillery on Gallipoli, after which he was appointed CB, and at Pozières and Mouquet Farm on the Western Front. Given command of the 5th Australian Division at the start of 1917, Hobbs quickly won it over after its less-than-happy experience under General McCay. Never afraid to speak his mind, his insistence to General Birdwood on the need for rest before Second Bullecourt led to all the Australian divisions being withdrawn after that battle. Hobbs was highly regarded by his peers. General Monash thought he occasionally lacked the ruthlessness needed in a general but still praised Hobbs's commonsense and his logical approach to every problem.

Hobbs's finest hour probably came with the recapture of Villers-Bretonneux in April 1918, and he was again prominent in the fall of Péronne in September. Elliott, one of his brigadiers, is better remembered for both. Through his firm but tactful handling of Elliott, Hobbs always got the best out of him. He recognised Elliott's abilities and made allowances that a lesser commander might not. Knighted (KCB) in December 1918 and appointed KCMG in January 1919, Hobbs took over the Australian Corps when Monash became Director-General of Demobilization and Repatriation after the armistice. He died at sea in April 1938 while on his way to France to attend the unveiling of the Australian National Memorial at Villers-Bretonneux. Hobbs had been instrumental in the choice of that location for it, and of Polygon Wood for the 5th Division's memorial.

the 57th and 60th Battalions entered it on 25 September. They suffered severely. When the others passed through, the shelling had died down. The **Albrecht Line**, which crossed the road just past the start of the wood, was the German front line here before the Menin Road attack. Only half-sunken pillboxes broke the featureless moonscape.

Glencorse Wood gives way to the t-nonnebos entertainment centre and a housing estate. Beyond them, a minor road cuts off to the right 100 metres short of the A19. On 25 September the 98th Brigade fell back to a line that ran through the **Lone House** strongpoint, which was on the site of the houses 300 metres along this road. Noting Lone House's location, continue to the flyover

but do NOT cross it. Take the next road on the right, which parallels the A19, instead and stop after 400 metres, where **Carlisle Farm** ❷ stood on the right of the bend. Face the A19. At the end of the Menin Road attack, the Australian line ran diagonally through the farm, across the A19 and into **Polygon Wood** to your left front on the far side, which the 15th Brigade subsequently held. The German spoiling attack, which catapulted the 98th Brigade rearwards to Lone House, came up the low ground of the Reutelbeek to your right front and reached the head of it on this side of the A19 at the bottom of the steep drop to your right. Advancing in the opposite direction on 26 September, the 2nd Royal Welch Fusiliers drove the Germans back over the line of the A19 before having to withdraw to Carlisle Farm. Their advance next day was more successful. The vulnerability of the 15th Brigade's right flank along the edge of Polygon Wood, exposed and thinly held for two days, to the Germans in the Reutelbeek is clearly evident from your location.

Return to the flyover. The tour can be walked from now on, in which case leave your car in the entertainment centre car park. Cross the A19 and proceed to the junction with Lotegatstraat at the tip of Polygon Wood. This is **Black Watch Corner** ❸, where Colonel Marshall set up the 60th Battalion's headquarters. The 29th, 31st and 59th Battalions co-located their headquarters with it. At the start of the war, the wood in front of them had been a Belgian Army training ground. Fir saplings screened off the rifle range, its stop butte and a 'racecourse' that had been used not just by cavalry and horsed artillery but also by Belgium's equestrian team. Before the attack, Lieutenant Sinclair Hunt of the 55th Battalion beheld 'a forest of charred and splintered stumps' standing no more than 1.2 metres high amid thick undergrowth, craters and pillboxes, with the butte at the far end giving the Germans unbroken views.

Stand on the edge of Oude Kortrijstraat, which was the boundary between I ANZAC and X Corps, with the flyover on your right. The new line following the Menin Road attack emerged from Polygon Wood 90 metres on your left and stretched diagonally across your front to Carlisle Farm. After the Germans advanced along the Reutelbeek, the 58th Battalion, which had held the 15th Brigade's part of the front line on the right of the wood, threw back its flank along Oude Kortrijstraat to your location. Scattered in shell holes, the 60th and, later, the 57th extended the flank along the road to your right beyond the A19. All three battalions were badly mauled by German shelling. Counterattacking across the ground to

your right front at 2 pm on 25 September in support of the 98th Brigade, part of the 60th Battalion grabbed a few metres of ground just this side of the A19 but the British could not get past Lone House on the far side.

Now stand with the flyover at your back. Charles Bean described the barrage that preceded the attack next morning as 'the most perfect that ever protected Australian troops'. It 'rolled on like a Gippsland bushfire', raising a thick dust cloud from the powdery surface of the plateau around you, which combined with the fog to reduce visibility so much that compasses had to be used to maintain direction. The 31st Battalion stretched leftwards from your location, with the 29th on its left. Both closed up on the 59th in the wood in front of you so that all three battalions moved off as a solid but ragged line. The 98th Brigade was nowhere to be seen. A group of pillboxes that it should have taken in the field on your right and down the slope towards the Reutelbeek immediately engaged the Australian flank. Too close to the line for the barrage to cover, they may also have halted the 60th Battalion's attack the day before. Captain Reg Hibbs of the 31st Battalion swung his company through your location against these pillboxes, whereupon Private Bugden led attacks through withering fire against several of them. Silencing their machine-guns with bombs, he captured the garrisons at bayonet point. Having crossed almost 200 metres into the 98th Brigade's area, Hibb's advance stalled before **Jerk House**, which was in front of the low buildings in the trees 400 metres to your right front. Hibbs was killed near it.

Continue 300 metres along Oude Kortrijstraat to the junction with the ride in Polygon Wood on the left and look back along the road. Seeing the midday advance by the Royal Welch Fusiliers, which came towards you on your left front through heavy fire, the Germans in Jerk House 160 metres in the field on

JERK HOUSE

PILLBOXES

HIBBS

The area of Jerk House and the pillboxes that Private Bugden knocked out.

your left withdrew. The Red Line emerged from the wood to follow the minor road on the right 150 metres further on. Earlier in the morning the 31st Battalion, with its right flank in the air, elected to remain on the Red Line on the edge of the wood until the British came up. So did part of the 29th on its left. Now actually enter the 98th Brigade's area by turning right onto the minor road. The building among the trees on the left 100 metres along was the site of **Cameron House**, which the Fusiliers' advance did not reach, but which Marshall's raid captured that evening. Carry on to the end of the road, which overlooks the **Reutelbeek** ❹. **Cameron Covert**, now gone, was 450 metres distant on the next spur to your left. When Marshall and his party from the 60th Battalion took it, they had reached the 98th Brigade's Blue Line.

Look straight ahead. **Polderhoek Spur**, named after the château that once graced the area of the industrial buildings 650 metres to your left front, was in German hands. As long as they also held Cameron Covert and the spur down which you have walked, the flank of their counterattack route along the Reutelbeek was protected. The 229th Reserve

advanced from your left in its successful attack on 25 September. But British artillery smashed the 4 pm attack next day well short of your location. Short of ammunition, the Fusiliers to your right rear streamed back just before. The Australians rallied many of them — sometimes at pistol point. Braving artillery and machine-gun fire, the Fusiliers advanced from your right on 27 September to gain the Blue Line alongside the 60th Battalion at Cameron Covert. You can reach the Reutelbeek along the foot track, which passes a German pillbox on the right. As you walk, the spire of **Gheluvelt church** can be seen to your front.

Return to Oude Kortrijstraat and turn right. Stop on reaching the eastern edge of Polygon Wood, which is skirted by a boundary track as it dips down to the low ground of the **Polygonbeek**. Look down the track. Cutting through the wood, the Red Line struck it 200 metres along and followed it over the stream before re-entering the wood. The Blue Line ran behind **Joist Farm** on your right. Now take the track until you can see the **Polygonbeek** ❺, which the Blue Line crossed below the farm. The headquarters of the 1st Battalion of the

CAMERON COVERT

229th Reserve, which was responsible for the right of Polygon Wood, occupied a nest of pillboxes on the near side of the stream there. Around 7.30 am Captain Fischer, the 1st Battalion's commander, personally led a counterattack along the Polygonbeek against the flank of the 14th Brigade on the far side and the 31st and 59th Battalions on the Red Line on your side. When Fischer was wounded in front of the Red Line, his men turned tail. At that moment Captain Stan Neale arrived with some of the 59th who had mistakenly been digging in short of the Red Line. They followed up the Germans, capturing the pillboxes, Fischer, his staff and 60 others. The 15th Brigade was now on part of its Blue Line.

Continue along Oude Kortrijstraat to the **memorial** ⑥ to Sergeant Henry Nicholas VC of 1st Canterbury, opposite Joist Farm. Commemorating the then Private Nicholas's gallantry in the New Zealand Division's attack on the Polderhoek Château on 3 December 1917, its location here is a mystery.

Polderhoek is not just behind the memorial but behind the red-roofed house on the far spur 850 metres away. In 1917, too, Joist Farm was 100 metres further back from the road. The Blue Line crossed the road 100 metres beyond it, and **Flandern 1** ran along the far slope of the Polygonbeek, to which the road descends. Keeping the farm on your right, face Polygon Wood. At the same time as the 60th Battalion took Cameron

The Reutelbeek below Cameron House, along which the German spoiling attack on 25 September came.

The pillbox above the Reutelbeek.

Sergeant Henry James Nicholas VC MM
1891-1918

It was near here, on 3 December, 1917, that Private Henry Nicholas of the 1st Battalion,
Canterbury Regiment, New Zealand, single-handedly destroyed a 16-man machine-gun post
during an advance on the Polderhoek Chateau spur. Later that day he collected ammunition
while under heavy fire. He was awarded the Victoria Cross,
the Commonwealth's highest award for bravery, for these actions.
Sergeant Nicholas was killed on 23 October, 1918, near Le Quesnoy, France, in an action for
which he was awarded the Military Medal.

This plaque was unveiled in 2008 to commemorate the 90th anniversary of the Armistice.

ZONNEBEKE   NEW ZEALAND EMBASSY

The misplaced memorial to Sergeant Nicholas.

Covert, which was on the spur in rear of the memorial, early on 27 September, the 31st Battalion advanced towards you from the wood under heavy machine-gun fire to capture the farm and the rest of the 15th Brigade's Blue Line. Private Bugden again distinguished himself, rescuing Corporal Alf Thompson by shooting one of his German captors and bayoneting the other two, and weathering intense fire on five occasions to bring in wounded. A shell killed him during the sixth.

After another 700 metres on Oude Kortrijstraat, turn left at the Café de Reutel crossroads onto Oude Wervikstraat (direction Zonnebeke) and take the left fork at the Y-junction 800 metres along onto Kruisbierboomstraat. Continue to

the T-junction, turn left onto Spilstraat for Polygon Wood and stop near the trees on the right roughly halfway to the wood 7 . After passing in front of the wood, the Blue Line crossed the road in this location and was captured by the 55th and 56th Battalions from the 14th Brigade. They had recognised Flandern 1, which ran between the Blue Line and the wood, only by the shreds of the entanglement left by the barrage. The pillboxes in it fell easily. Now turn to your right for a panoramic view of the ground over which the 4th Australian Division attacked. Flandern 1, with the Blue Line on its right, continued to the grey buildings under the power lines 300 metres slightly to your right front on the almost indistinguishable **Tokio Spur.**

FLANDERN 1 · REUTEL · POLYGONBEEK · BLUE LINE

From there Flandern 1 broke to the right of the Blue Line and ran to the right of Zonnebeke, whose unmistakeable church spire is visible 1.6 kilometres ahead.

Continue to Polygon Wood, where the road turns abruptly right then left before reaching **Polygon Wood Cemetery** on the right of Lang Dreve 400 metres along the wood's northern side. If driving, park there. Paralleling the wood, the 5th Division's boundary with the 4th passed 50 metres beyond the far end of the cemetery. Now cross the road and take the path to **Buttes New British Cemetery 8**. From the path, face the end of the **Butte**. Crowned by the **5th Australian Division Memorial**, it rises on the site of the original, which shelling had reduced to a rubble heap. Two platoons of the 53rd Battalion scaled it with little opposition and bombed the dugout entrances. Sixty Germans, mainly medical staff, surrendered. The British subsequently used the Butte for brigade and battalion headquarters. The Red Line,

from which the 55th and 56th Battalions attacked, ran diagonally through the cemetery from your right front and passed through the Butte. Lieutenant-Colonel Scott, the 56th's commanding officer, was killed on the left of the Butte while handing the line over to Lieutenant-Colonel Dudley Turnbull of the 20th Manchesters. The same shot nailed Turnbull.

Return to the road, turn left and walk 60 metres along the edge of the wood before entering it at the large ride on the left, where the wood was being replanted at the time of writing. Continue along the ride for 250 metres and take the track on the left, which is not always easy to find. On the left of it, 40 metres along, is a **concrete shelter 9**. Stand with your back to it to see another one 25 metres to your left front. Both were constructed in January 1918 by the New Zealand Division, which held the line here during the 1917–18 winter. Return to the ride, turn left and left again

The Polygonbeek from Joist Farm. The Blue Line was the limit of the advance. Private Bugden was killed here on this side of it.

50 metres further on, which will bring you out onto the wood's wide central ride. It runs just to the right of the south-eastern straight of the old 'racecourse', no trace of which remains, from Buttes New British Cemetery to Black Watch Corner. The advance through the wood came towards you from the Black Watch Corner end.

After turning right onto the central ride, head right again after 30 metres onto a metalled track that ends at a two-roomed **pillbox** ❿. It was most probably captured by the 53rd Battalion in the advance to the Red Line during which, recalled Lieutenant Hunt, whimpering boys emerged from many pillboxes holding out hands full of souvenirs. Their rifles were still racked inside. Named **Scott's Post** in honour of the 56th Battalion's much-loved commander, this pillbox subsequently became a headquarters for British units. It bears the scars of shell hits but most of the damage resulted from postwar efforts to remove the pillbox.

The Butte after the battle (top) and now.

One of the concrete shelters constructed by the New Zealanders.

Continue on the central ride for 120 metres and turn left by the remains of another pillbox onto a smaller ride that enters a large clearing. Just after crossing the head of the Polygonbeek, turn right onto the ride that joins Oude Kortrijstraat opposite Jerk House, where you paused earlier. About 50 metres short of the junction, the remains of two more German **pillboxes** 11 can be seen. The one on the right has lost its roof; the one on the left is more complete. One of them may have been the one that claimed Lieutenant John Turnour of the 59th Battalion after he stood up directly in front of a pillbox in this area to distract the machine-gunners inside while his men got around it. He fell riddled with bullets; they bombed the garrison.

Now turn right just past the pillboxes onto another ride. The dregs of trenches, most probably Australian, and shell holes, rumple the ground either side of it. On the morning after the Menin Road attack on 20 September, Lance-Corporal Inwood and a soldier from the 7th Battalion knocked out a machine-gun that was harassing the new Australian line from somewhere on your right in this vicinity. They killed the crew except for one gunner, whom they made carry the gun back with them. The night before,

Scott's Post.

Inwood had reconnoitred as far forward as the Butte. These actions contributed to the award of Inwood's VC.

You will emerge at the north-western corner of the wood opposite the **Anzac Rest café** 12 on Lang Dreve, where you can inspect the relic collection of the owner, Johan Vandewalle. As the name of his premises suggests, he is a great admirer of the ANZACs. If you are driving, you now have a one-kilometre walk down Lang Dreve to retrieve your car from Polygon Wood Cemetery. The 14th Brigade's start line crossed the road 300 metres along. Its assault got underway more easily than the 15th's on the other side of the wood, from which

The mortal wounding of Lieutenant Turnour as depicted by Australian war artist Fred Leist in *Australian Infantry Attack in Polygon Wood*.

Instantly, a couple of Lewis gunners would open on the defenders, and rifle bombers would drop their volleys of grenades all around them. Under cover of this fire a couple of parties would work round the flanks of the obstruction and in a few minutes further resistance was impossible. It would all happen so quickly that the check to the general advance was imperceptible and touch with the barrage was never lost.

The 14th Brigade's attack (Ellis, AD, *The Story of the Fifth Australian Division*, London, 1920, p. 246)

you have just walked. About 20 machine-guns were firing through the barrage and the line rippled as platoons darted back and forth to knock them out.

Keeping the café on your right, turn right onto Lotegatstraat, which runs along ANZAC Spur. Charles Bean wrote that the 4th Australian Division's advance, which started from the spur, went 'as planned and almost without incident, except for the smothering of pillboxes'. As Lotegatstraat bends right, look towards the crest on your right. The 4th Brigade on the division's right deployed there with the 16th Battalion strung out along the crest ahead of the 15th and 14th Battalions, respectively right and left, echeloned back towards the road. At the second leftwards bend, the 13th Brigade took over, with the 50th Battalion on the crest and the 49th and 51st right and left behind it. Now look left. The Menin Road advance started from the spur on the far side of the autoroute and crossed the valley below you.

On reaching the crossroads, turn right onto Grotemolenstraat. The 13th Brigade's start line crossed it 280 metres along, just past the 70 km speed sign on

the site of the **Garter Point pillbox** ⑬, which was captured during the earlier battle. Ahead of you the Steenbeek runs through **Albania Valley**. The 13th had to slog through its water-filled shell holes and occasional knee-deep mud to Tokio Spur on the far side, and the western end of Zonnebeke beyond it. The 4th Division's left flank ended 220 metres to your left, with the British 3rd Division on the other side.

Continue on Grotemolenstraat. Look right 100 metres after crossing the Steenbeek. Captured by the 50th Battalion, **Albania Farm**, the German strongpoint that gave the valley its name, stood in the vicinity of the farm buildings 300 metres from the road. You are now 'climbing' Tokio Spur. Follow the road from the rightwards bend at the corner of the housing estate for 250 metres to the junction with Citernestraat on the right. This was the site of the **Tokio strongpoint** ⑭. Taken by the 50th Battalion, the Red Line here ran along Citernestraat and on to Polygon Wood. Paralleling it 300 metres ahead, the Blue Line was reached without difficulty by the 51st Battalion, with the 49th on its

The area in front of the Red Line where Captain Jacka rallied the 14th Battalion. ANZAC Spur was the limit of the Menin Road attack on 20 September.

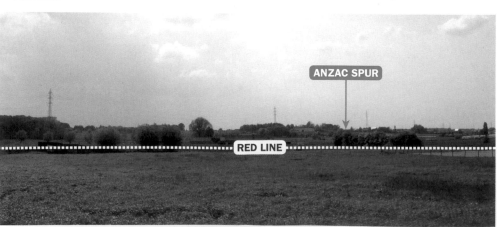

right, after both had passed through the 50th. Carry on along Grotemolenstraat for 200 metres and turn right at the T-junction onto **Berten Pilstraat 15** in Zonnebeke.

The Blue Line ran 100 metres to the left of Berten Pilstraat, on which you should stop at the **fork 16** 850 metres from Zonnebeke. Walk back past the white house among the trees on the left of the road and face left towards ANZAC Spur for an excellent view of the ground over which the 4th Division advanced. After the 16th Battalion took the Red Line in the low ground 350 metres in front of you, the 14th leap-frogged it. Running into the supporting barrage as it advanced towards your location, the 14th turned around but Captain Jacka restored order and hustled it onto the Blue Line on the far side of the road behind you. Now return to the fork. Captain Harold Wanliss, another of the 14th Battalion's outstanding officers, was killed 50 metres short of it while trying to locate a troublesome machine-gun. Some said he was a future Australian prime minister.

At the fork, Berten Pilstraat heads left up a spur on which a communications tower rises among some farm buildings. The machine-gun involved in Sergeant Dwyer's VC action engaged the 14th Brigade on the Blue Line at Polygon Wood, where you stopped earlier, from that location. Its crew did not notice Dwyer rush his own gun to within 30 metres of theirs. Killing them all, he ignored sniper fire and carried the German gun as well as his own back to the 4th Brigade's right flank, which was just beyond **Tabaksbedruf Stubbe**, the large grey building on Plasstraat to your front. He used both guns to help see off two German counterattacks during the afternoon. Raked by other machine-guns as well, and by the artillery, the Germans were shattered as soon as they appeared on the crest. When heavy German shelling of this location destroyed Dwyer's gun next morning, he ran through the bombardment to pick up a reserve gun and braved the shelling a second time to return with it.

From here you can return to the Berten Pilstraat junction in Zonnebeke to start the Broodseinde drive, or head back to Ypres by continuing through the junction on Berten Pilstraat to the N332, turning left and following the signs.

The area of Sergeant Dwyer's VC action.

LOCAL INFORMATION

CEMETERIES

Many of the Australian fallen from the Polygon Wood attack are buried in cemeteries further away, particularly at **Hooge Crater cemetery**. Private Bugden rests there at VIII.C.5.

Buttes New British Cemetery

Off Lang Dreve in Polygon Wood and visited on the tour, this cemetery was built postwar and is one of the most striking in the salient area, not least because of the Butte, and the 5th

The grave of Private Les McMurdo, Buttes New British Cemetery.

Australian Division Memorial on top of it, near the entrance. Of the 2048 graves, 1703 are unknown. Among the 564 Australian burials is Lieutenant-Colonel Scott at II.A.12. Lieutenant-Colonel Turnbull of the Manchesters, who fell alongside him, rests at I.G.9. It is hard not to be moved by the grave of Private Les McMurdo at XXIV.D.7. He fell in the 31st Battalion's assault, aged just 17. Sergeant John Calder and Private George Storey, both of the 51st Battalion, at I.E.20 and 18 respectively, and Private John Hunter of the 49th Battalion at I.E.19, were killed at Westhoek at the end of September 1917. Their remains, and those of the two unidentified burials next to them, were interred here after their discovery in 2007. There are 407 unidentified Australian burials altogether.

The cemetery also contains 167 New Zealand burials. At the far end, opposite the Butte, is the elegant colonnade of the **New Zealand Memorial to the Missing**, on which are recorded the names of the 383 New Zealanders who fell in the New Zealand Division's occupation of this area between November 1917 and February 1918 but have no known grave. Many of them were lost in the unsuccessful December attack on Polderhoek Château.

Polygon Wood Cemetery

Started during the fighting, as the random layout of the graves suggests, this battlefield cemetery is opposite Buttes Cemetery on Lang Dreve and is visited on the tour. It contains 108 burials, of which 60 are New Zealand. Reflecting the cemetery's location, and its name, the surrounding wall is pentagonal. The

350-odd graves from an adjoining German battlefield cemetery in rear were removed, owing to anti-German sentiment in the 1950s, to the German concentration cemetery at Langemarck.

NEARBY PLACES OF INTEREST

Polderhoek Château

In its attacks on Menin Road and, later, at Polygon Wood, I ANZAC had advanced with its right flank on the northern side of the Reutelbeek. The British X Corps had consistently struggled to keep up on the Polderhoek Spur, on which were the

Buttes New British Cemetery and the New Zealand Memorial to the Missing.

1ST CANTERBURY POSTS

SCHERIABEEK

1ST OTAGO

NZ LINE

The New Zealand attack on Polderhoek.

ruins of a château, on the southern side. On 3 December 1917 the 2nd New Zealand Brigade tried to gain ground there. To reach the battlefield, continue on Menin Road through Clapham Junction for 1.7 kilometres before turning left at a cream single-storey house onto Polygonestraat in Veldhoek, an outlier of Gheluvelt. After another 170 metres turn right onto Poezelhoekstraat and park at the right turn above the A19. You are now on the Polderhoek Spur. Look across the autoroute.

Running diagonally from the Scheriabeek, the low ground along the tree line over your right shoulder, the New Zealand Division's front line crossed the road 100 metres behind you before passing over the line of the A19 on your left and the Reutelbeek to your left front. The 2nd Brigade sought to advance 300 metres past the château ruins, which were 100 metres behind the large two-storeyed house to your front on the other side of the A19. 1st Canterbury on your right dropped off posts along the Scheriabeek to protect the flank of 1st Otago, which attacked on your left. Both battalions got as far as the other side of the autoroute before being stopped by torrential fire from pillboxes and posts. Private Henry Nicholas of 1st Canterbury crept around the rear of one post, on a site 50 metres to your right front now obliterated by the A19, and shot the officer in charge before bayoneting 12 of the garrison. Four more wisely surrendered.

Nicholas was awarded the VC. His action was the only highlight of an unsuccessful assault.

CHAPTER 12

1917

BROODSEINDE

'If only every attack could be carried through so cleanly', wrote an 8th Battalion officer after the Menin Road attack. For I ANZAC, the Polygon Wood attack that followed it had gone close. The German spoiling assault on the right flank was the only disruption. But General Plumer's third step along the sickle blade–shaped ridgeline that overlooked the Ypres salient fully lived up to the officer's wish. Carried out on 4 October 1917, by 12 divisions on a 13-kilometre front, it went flawlessly. It was also the most important attack so far for several reasons.

First was the objective, the section of the ridge that curved north from the Gheluvelt Plateau. It was called Broodseinde. As it did in 1917, Broodseinde today consists of little more than the crossroads where the N303, the Passchendaele–Beselare road running along the ridge, meets the N332, the Zonnebeke–Moorslede road, running across it. But unlike the Gheluvelt Plateau at the start of the ridge, which the first two attacks had completely taken, the Broodseinde stretch near the centre of it gave the Germans panoramic views of the entire salient. Its capture would leave the Second Army directly facing Passchendaele, which Field Marshal Haig had hoped to reach at the end of the first week in August.

Second, following on from the Menin Road and Polygon Wood successes, which used the 'bite and hold' tactical formula of limited advances supported by overwhelming firepower, Broodseinde confirmed that, as long as the weather held, the Germans would be hard put to resist blows of this type. Thirdly, the battle was the only occasion in which I and II ANZAC fought together. The Australians and New Zealanders would not fight in a bigger battle until the second half of 1918.

The Germans

'Bite and hold' attacks had not only twice foiled the German tactics of defence in depth coupled with prompt counterattacks. German morale was also affected. Two days after Polygon Wood, an entire German company surrendered to the 30th Battalion near the Butte. So quiet was the front line that the 56th Battalion preferred staying there to being relieved and going back to the heavily shelled rear. The Germans had to counter 'bite and hold', and fast. On 30 September they partially reinstituted the old system of holding the forward positions in strength and counterattacking from them. The change was in place for Plumer's third step.

Plans

II ANZAC had been earmarked as the spearhead because it was thought that I ANZAC would be too tired for another attack. But the 1st and 2nd Divisions from I ANZAC had emerged so fresh from Menin Road that they were able to participate alongside II ANZAC. Sideslipping slightly northward to bring its line of advance directly onto the ridge, General Birdwood's corps retained the central role. II ANZAC would attack on its left. Advancing

Australian pioneers digging out a bogged gun during the Broodseinde attack.

between 1.2 and 1.8 kilometres, both corps would cross the northerly continuation of Flandern 1 from Polygon Wood before reaching the final objective, the Blue Line. Corresponding roughly to the line held in 1914 by the 'Old Contemptibles', as the Kaiser called the BEF then, it ran up to 360 metres beyond the crest of both Broodseinde Ridge and its northerly offshoot, Gravenstafel Spur. The Red Line was nowhere more than 180 metres short of the crest. As usual, the Fifth Army would prolong the attack on the left, while X Corps buttressed the Australian flank on the right.

I ANZAC's preparations were easily made. Its orders largely consisted of those for the previous steps. The 1st and 2nd Divisions, respectively right and left, were each to assault the ridge with two brigades. As before each brigade would employ one battalion for the Red Line and two for the Blue. II ANZAC had to recast its plans at the last minute. Attacking on the northern side of the derelict Ypres–Roulers railway, the 3rd Division was to take Windmill

Cabaret Spur on the northern edge of Zonnebeke, which had defied the British in the Polygon Wood attack, and advance across the marshy valley of the Hanebeek to link up with the 2nd Division on the ridge on its right and the New Zealand Division assaulting the Gravenstafel on its left. The 3rd's advance was the longest but the only pause came on the Red Line well before halfway. So General Monash arranged an additional halt either side of the Red Line to leapfrog fresh battalions through. General Russell ordered extra halts for the New Zealand Division too but without the extra leapfrogs. Spread across wider frontages, its brigades were already employing two battalions in each phase, so the only leapfrog would occur on the Red Line. Spirits soared with the realisation that four ANZAC divisions were attacking shoulder to shoulder.

4 October

Light rain began falling during the move forward. Learning from the earlier attacks, all the assault battalions squeezed up behind the jump-off tape to escape the retaliatory German barrage when the attack began at 6 am. The German guns started half an hour beforehand instead, pummelling I ANZAC. When the British barrage launched the assault, the German one ceased. The leading waves of I ANZAC saw a line of men rise with bayonets fixed 30 metres ahead. I ANZAC and the Germans were attacking simultaneously. The barrage that crunched the Australians had been intended to pave the way for a German attack to regain some of the ground lost between Polygon Wood and Zonnebeke on 26 September, in accordance with the new German policy. But the British barrage had caught the Germans at the moment of their assault. The Australians charged. German dead soon littered the area. The rain ceased.

Before the Australians got much further, some of them felt the stronger forward defence that also resulted from the German tactical changes. The 1st Brigade was briskly engaged by the large pillbox complex at Molenaarelsthoek, called Meerlar today, and the pillboxes confronting the 6th Brigade on the outskirts of Zonnebeke resisted stubbornly. After the Red Line, and with it Flandern 1 in I ANZAC's area, was reached at 6.45 am, the Germans atop the ridge on the N303 near the hamlet of Molenaarelst fired into those trying to dig in along it. The 2nd Brigade had to battle them throughout the hour's pause on the Red Line.

Next to I ANZAC in the 3rd Division, the 37th and 43rd Battalions easily stormed the Windmill Cabaret, a Lewis-gunner, Lance-Corporal Wally Peeler, repeatedly rushing German posts to win the VC. Resistance stiffened near Flandern 1, where the barrage pulled away over the swampy ground, but the injection of fresh battalions at the intermediate halts ensured that momentum was not lost. When heavy machine-gun fire tore at the 10th Brigade, Sergeant Lewis McGee of the 40th Battalion mounted a lone charge to knock out one of the guns. Killed afterwards, he received a posthumous VC.

One by one, the other guns were silenced. By 9 am the 3rd Division was on the Blue Line. The New Zealanders were on its left after tough fighting on parts of the Red Line and all along the Blue Line. After a relatively easy advance, I ANZAC reached the Blue Line about the same time. Seen a long way off from the newly captured high ground, the German counterattacks were scattered by the artillery.

The two ANZAC corps suffered over 8000 casualties but took most of the 4600 German prisoners. 'As they passed us, they were relieved of any valuables that they possessed, souveniring the enemy being a strong characteristic of the Australians', wrote Private Verdi Schwinghammer of the 42nd Battalion. North of II ANZAC, the Fifth Army captured much of Poelcappelle. The rest of the Second Army advanced its line on the right of I ANZAC, though failing to gain the elusive Tower Hamlets.

The 'brick kiln' (foreground) where the left flank of I ANZAC and the Germans, attacking simultaneously, collided in no-man's-land. All that remained of Zonnebeke church can be seen in the background.

The 24th Battalion dug in on Broodseinde ridge the day after the attack. Celtic Wood is on the left horizon.

DRIVING/WALKING THE BATTLEFIELD

As I and II ANZAC attacked alongside each other at Broodseinde, the battlefield covers more than twice the area of the Menin Road and Polygon Wood battles, in which I ANZAC alone participated. Though it can easily be driven, doing it on foot therefore necessitates up to double the walking of those battlefields. But the Broodseinde battlefield naturally divides itself into two areas, the ridge that I ANZAC attacked and the Gravenstafel Spur taken by II ANZAC. Each area makes for an easy walk. Forming the boundary between the two corps, the Ypres–Roulers railway is a prominent landmark in II ANZAC's sector but not in I ANZAC's as it crossed the ridge beyond I ANZAC's Blue Line. Conversely, Flandern 1 lay mostly within I ANZAC's Red Line but ran beyond most of II ANZAC's Blue Line.

MAP NGI 1:20 000: 28/3-4 Zonnebeke–Moorslede

Leave Ypres through the Menin Gate and continue straight ahead on the N332 for Zonnebeke. Cross the A19 autoroute, remain on the N332 after going over the roundabout at the edge of Zonnebeke for 850 metres, and turn right onto Berten Pilstraat before the long brick wall at the sign for the Memorial Museum Passchendaele 1917.

I ANZAC's attack

Park in the **museum car park** ❶ on the left. Each of I ANZAC's two assaulting divisions occupied 850-metre frontages along a start line that ran along the left of Berten Pilstraat. The 2nd Australian Division was on the left of the attack and the boundary between its two brigades ran through your location. Stretching to your left to the **Ypres–Roulers railway**,

300 metres over the far side of the N332, was the 7th Brigade. The 6th Brigade formed up on your right.

At the **fork** ❷ on Berten Pilstraat one kilometre further on, stand with **Zonnebeke** on your left and **Meerlar** hamlet to your right front. Meerlar is on a spur of the Broodseinde Ridge, which is 800 metres behind it. You are on the right of the start line on the barely distinguishable **Tokio Spur**, where the 1st Division attacked. The 1st Brigade extended from the far side of the grey **Tabaksbedruf Stubbe** complex, 400 metres to your right, to your left just beyond the fork, where the 2nd Brigade began. Around you was a wasteland of overlapping shell holes littered with ruined hamlets and farmhouses. German strongpoints were in the ruins, and the pillboxes of the **Flandern 1** line passed to the left of the complex, through Meerlar and over the crest ahead.

Plumer's 'bite and hold' method can easily be grasped from your location on Tokio, which was roughly equidistant between ANZAC Spur behind you and Broodseinde Ridge in front of you. The first 'bite' in the Menin Road attack reached ANZAC Spur, from which the second 'bite' to Tokio in the Polygon Wood attack started. Since then, duckboard tracks had been laid across the ground taken in the second 'bite' so that the infantry could form up on Tokio for the third 'bite' to the ridge.

Approaching from your rear in the rain, the assault battalions slithered over the greasy duckboards. Some were in position at 4 am and had to lie out on the muddy soil or in watery shell holes for two hours chilled to the bone. Crowded along the road in a dense mass

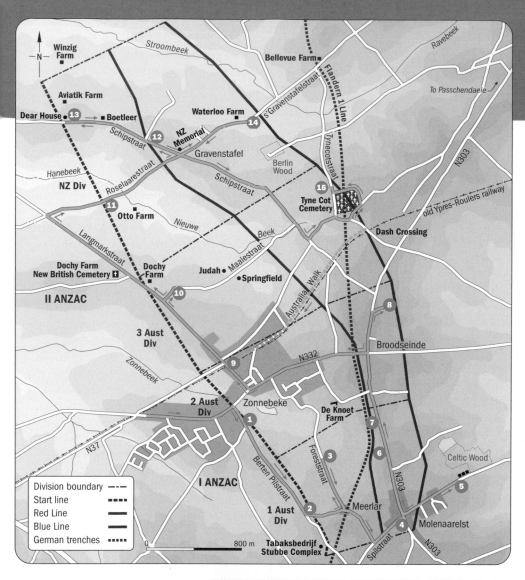

Winzig Farm

Stroombeek

Bellevue Farm

Ravebeek

To Passchendaele

Aviatik Farm

Waterloo Farm

S'Gravenstafelstraat

Flandern 1 Line

Dear House • 13 → • Boetleer

NZ Memorial

Schipstraat

12

Gravenstafel

Berlin Wood

14

Tynecotstraat

N303

Hanebeek

Roselaarestraat

Schipstraat

NZ Div

Tyne Cot Cemetery

15

old Ypres–Roulers railway

11

Otto Farm

Nieuwe

Dash Crossing

Langmarkstraat

Beek

Maalestraat

Dochy Farm New British Cemetery ✠

Dochy Farm

Judah •

• Springfield

10

II ANZAC

3 Aust Div

Zonnebeek

Australia Walk

8

Broodseinde

9

N332

2 Aust Div

Zonnebeke

De Knoet Farm

7

1

N37

3

6

Celtic Wood

Foreststraat

N303

5

Division boundary — —
Start line ▪▪▪▪
Red Line ━━
Blue Line ━━
German trenches ▪▪▪▪

I ANZAC

1 Aust Div

2

Meerlar

Berten Pijlstraat

4

Molenaarelst

Spilstraat

N303

0   800 m

Tabaksbedrijf Stubbe Complex

either side of you, they were dreadfully vulnerable to the German barrage that fell at 5.27 am. Men could do nothing other than huddle in the darkness under waterproof capes. Private Hartnett, in the 2nd Battalion behind you, wrote: 'Five minutes seemed like an hour. Being the only one with a watch in our section, I was kept busy, for every few minutes someone poked his head around the corner to ask the time.' I ANZAC's two divisions had each lost one man in seven when the fire stopped with his watch showing 6 am. The horizon across your rear reddened as the Australian barrage

Starting from Zonnebeke, this drive/walk covers the fight near the start line just after the attack began, then continues via I ANZAC's right flank to the Red Line at Molenaarelst before tracking along the Broodseinde Ridge, parallel to the Blue Line, to the Broodseinde crossroads. It also covers the site of Celtic Wood.
DISTANCE COVERED: 8 km
DURATION: 2 hours driving; 3.5 hours walking

opened. Instead of the usual dust cloud, puffs of smoke and steam rose when the shells struck the wet ground to your front. Hartnett was reassured when a giant Lewis-gun corporal got up from a shell hole. 'He took a cigarette from his pocket, lit it, picked up his gun, and strode off with a cheery "Come on boys", to his mates.'

Both the 3rd Battalion to your front and the 8th Battalion alongside it to your left had advanced 150 metres when the barrage lifted. Three battalions of the German 212th Reserve Infantry Regiment simultaneously emerged from shell holes where the barrage had been. Dazed by the fire, some of the Germans shifted uncertainly along a line that ran along the slope below the near side of Meerlar to Zonnebeke. They were seen 30 metres ahead in the dim light. The Australians hoed into them. German dead soon littered the area to your front and all the way to Zonnebeke. They extended the carpet of Australian dead and wounded, all claimed by the German barrage, along the road.

Continue on Berten Pilstraat, which is the left branch of the fork, to Meerlar. The Molenaarelsthoek pillboxes here, wrote Charles Bean, 'lay so thickly that they resembled a village'. The 3rd Battalion came under heavy fire while outflanking them. Turn left in the centre of Meerlar onto Foreststraat, from which you can easily appreciate how the knoll on which

the hamlet sits enfilades the low ground that an attack must cross to reach Broodseinde Ridge on your right. Stop 500 metres along on the right at **Retaliation Farm** ❸, now a farmhouse that co-exists with a large iron-roofed shed, and look ahead along the road. At **De Knoet Farm**, which was on the right of the road atop the knoll 400 metres to your right front in what is now the outskirts of Zonnebeke, the Germans defied the 22nd Battalion to the end. Working around the flanks of the pillbox there, the 22nd lobbed bombs into it until all the Germans had been killed. The garrison of a neighbouring pillbox was captured after Lance-Corporal Bill Oliver rushed ahead and stood in the open, firing his Lewis-gun from the hip at it to cover the flanking assault. Approaching from your left, the 8th Battalion overcame strong resistance in your location. Every officer in the left company was hit.

Now take the track along the side of the farm to the end of the fence and look straight ahead. The 8th Battalion continued through the stumps of **Romulus Wood**, which extended 200 metres beyond the only remaining part of it, the clump of brush 150 metres

'Bite and hold' from the 2nd Brigade's start line. Its first objective, the Red Line, ran just below the crest of the Broodseinde Ridge. Flandern 1 extended across the lower slope between the ridge and the near trees. A wild melee took place in the area of the trees as soon as the attack started.

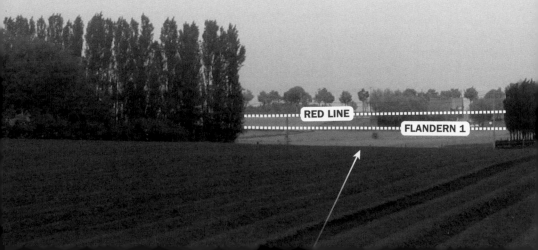

RED LINE

FLANDERN 1

to your left front, and smaller **Remus Wood** to your right front. Descending from Meerlar, Flandern 1 passed behind the two woods and to the right of De Knoet Farm. The **Red Line** was beyond it, running across the slope below the near side of the crest of **Broodseinde Ridge** facing you, then devoid of the trees and buildings past which traffic speeds on the N303 today. As the 8th Battalion crossed Flandern 1 and neared the Red Line, it was belted by a field battery firing over open sights from the crest. The gun line was in the field to the left of the cluster of buildings on the upper slope directly to your front and in the trees on the bump to the left of the field. Moving from shell hole to shell hole to get close, a party from the 8th, and the 7th Battalion trailing it, charged the position, capturing the guns and killing most of the garrison.

This advance had been fired on in turn by a pillbox in the **crater**, which also engaged those digging in on the Red Line. To pinpoint its location, look at the open area to the right of the cluster of buildings. The crater was on the site of the second building on the crest on the right of this area. A party from the 6th and 7th Battalions, spontaneously organised like the one that took the gun line, knocked out the crater pillbox and a post to its right after a sharp 20-minute fight. In this way, important stretches of the crest were seized before the start of the advance to the Blue Line beyond it.

The crater strongpoint.

Returning to Meerlar, turn left onto Berten Pilstraat and left again at the T-junction onto Spilstraat, along which ran the 1st Division's boundary with the British 7th Division. Continue to the crossroads with the N303 in **Molenaarelst** ④ (if driving, park on the right just short of the crossroads). When the 3rd Battalion reached the Red Line, which crossed Spilstraat 150 metres behind you, the 4th Battalion, ignoring the standing barrage that protected the hour's halt for consolidation, careered on through your location towards the Blue Line beyond the N303. Part of the 4th promptly came back over this side of the N303 to avoid the supporting barrage for the Blue Line advance, which came down where you are standing and along the crest at 8.06 am. The rest took their chances in shell holes on the other

BROODSEINDE RIDGE

side of the N303. At 8.10 am the advance began.

Go over the N303 and continue on Spilstraat, which the **Blue Line** crossed 200 metres along. It was easily taken here by the 4th Battalion, and further to your left by the 1st Battalion. Another world unfolded ahead of the screen of posts that both battalions established on the slope just in front of the Blue Line. The country ahead was covered in grass not mud. Copses and hedgerows swayed gently in the wind, cows grazed in the fields as farm carts trundled by and smoke wafted from farm chimneys. No troops of the BEF had beheld such sights in the salient since Second Ypres in May 1915.

Carry on another 400 metres and stop just short of the three houses on the left **5**. Look towards them. The ridge continues across the horizon to your left front to **Passchendaele**, whose church spire is visible. **Celtic Wood**, scene of a catastrophic raid by the 10th Battalion on 9 October, covered the fields behind the houses. Charles Bean remarked that only 14 of the 85 men on the raid returned unwounded and the missing were never heard from again. The war diary of the German regiment in whose sector the wood lay did not mention the action,

leading to suggestions that the missing were buried in an unmarked grave after being captured and shot, possibly in retaliation for the casualties the Germans had suffered in two earlier, successful, Australian raids. Recent research, however, has accounted for all of the raiding party. Of the 59 men who got back to the Australian line, 14 indeed were unwounded. The remains of some of the 29 killed in action were recovered postwar.

Return to the N303 and turn right onto it. Drivers should be very careful on this road as it is very busy and at times seems like a Formula 1 practice track! Passing the Vandenbrouke garage after 400 metres, continue to the second-last house on the left before the field, where the road starts to dip. You are now on the site of the **crater 6**. Thought to have resulted from the explosion of an ammunition dump ages before, it contained two battalion headquarters as well as the strongpoint. When the party from the 6th and 7th Battalions arrived after attacking up the slope that the crater overlooked, Captain Harry Annear walked around the rim, picking off Germans with his revolver until mortally wounded by a bomb. Before the crater fell, some of the garrison withdrew across

The German view from the crater strongpoint. Shell holes on the slope ahead gave some cover to the party from the 6th and 7th Battalions that advanced from the Retaliation Farm area to capture it.

AMUSEMENT PARK

6TH AND 7TH BATTALIONS

FLANDERN 1

Looking towards Passchendaele over the area covered by Celtic Wood at the time of the battle.

the N303 and continued to fight from a trench along the other side. Showered by rifle grenades, they eventually surrendered.

Continue past the house to the **field** ⑦ on the left and look across it. With binoculars, the yellow gantry of a ride at the Bellewarde amusement park on **Menin Road** can be discerned on the horizon to your front. I ANZAC began the first of Plumer's steps from the spur in front of it. Zonnebeke is to your right front and Retaliation Farm is in the low

ground 500 metres directly ahead. Flandern 1 and the Red Line paralleled the road 150 metres below you. The German field battery that took on the 8th Battalion spread across the field into the area of the house set among the trees to your right on the far side. As well as the guns, observation posts, pillboxes and short stretches of trench crowded this area. Outflanking one pillbox, 19-year-old Private Walter Bradby of the 8th saw one of its occupants start towards him. 'I aimed point blank at his

stomach and pressed the trigger. Down he went, on his right knee, and covered his face with his hands.' Bradby shot two more Germans and was upset to find that they looked younger than himself. The 6th and 7th Battalions continued over the N303 here to capture the Blue Line 200 metres down the reverse slope.

Lieutenant Adrian Ball's platoon seized a pillbox on the way to the Blue Line in the 24th Battalion's area 200 metres further along the road. Sending the prisoners off, Ball returned to his men, who were smoking German cigars and getting stuck into Rheinwein, a bottle apiece. Suitably primed, they sent some convivial messages to the Germans after finding two crates of carrier pigeons in the pillbox. Expecting updates on the battle, the Germans read instead: 'Deutschland Über Alles! Ha! Ha!''Hock the Kaiser — I don't think', and a request from Ball himself for certain information of an obscene and personal nature. The remaining pigeons were plucked and stewed.

Proceed along the N303 past the **British 7th Division Memorial** on the left, which commemorates its stand on the ridge in 1914 as well as its role in the 1917 attack, to the Broodseinde crossroads, now a roundabout. Continue over the crossroads on the N303, turn right after 300 metres and stop just past the **last house** 8 . Coming over the crest behind you, the 26th Battalion struck tough opposition from **Daisy Wood** to your right front in the area behind the house at the end of the road. The Blue Line ran through the wood, which no longer exists. German reinforcements were also arriving. Part of the 26th fell back to an old trench on the N303, where the 27th Battalion joined it. They linked with the 44th Battalion from the 3rd Australian Division 250 metres to your left. The only German counterattack against I ANZAC to get through the artillery bombardments approached your

location. Corporal Gaffney of the 26th alone emptied eight magazines from his Lewis-gun into it Rifle-grenadiers wiped out those who remained.

Return to the roundabout and head right on the N332 for Zonnebeke, through which the 25th Battalion chased the Germans who had tried to advance against them at the start of the attack. The 26th Battalion following mopped up those who fought on from the cellars of the ruined village. Passing the church and the **Memorial Museum Passchendaele 1917**, turn left onto Berten Pilstraat for the museum car park. **Zonnebeke lake** in the museum grounds, described as 'a bleak waterhole 200 yards long by 100 wide' then, but a tranquil oasis now, split the assault, the 25th Battalion passing on the far side and the 22nd through your location. Firing from the hip, the 22nd tore into the Germans coming the other way. 'I never had such an enjoyable time', wrote Captain Braithwaite. 'As soon as they saw we were in force, they either up with their hands or rushed off to Berlin.'

II ANZAC's attack

From the museum car park, walk through the museum grounds to the main entrance on the N332 (here Ieperstraat), turn right and then, at the roundabout in front of the church, left onto Langemark-straat. If driving, turn right onto Berten Pilstraat from the car park, right again onto the N332 and left at the roundabout. Once on Langemarkstraat, continue 100 metres past the **Spaar Supermarket** to the bed of the old **Ypres–Roulers railway** 9 on the right, the advance along which is described on panels on the self-guided **Australia Walk**. Look along Langemarkstraat. The railway was the boundary between I and II ANZAC here. Starting 200 metres to your left, the 3rd Australian Division's start line initially ran behind Langemarkstraat. It was also lashed by the German guns at 5.27 am.

Compared with the pounding the 1st and 2nd Divisions took, the 3rd got off lightly. Its supporting barrage, likened to 'a wall of flame' by a 43rd Battalion officer, was also much denser than theirs. Leading the 11th Brigade's advance towards you, the 43rd immediately got into holts with the Germans, some of whom fired from a pillbox in the ruins of the railway station, which occupied the vacant trackside area immediately in front of you. It was quickly quashed. On passing the station site, Langemarkstraat starts over the imperceptible hump of **Windmill Cabaret Spur (Hill 40)**, on which the 43rd took to Germans with the bayonet. Over 350 were reportedly killed. The after-action report laconically remarked: 'Very little further resistance was met as the enemy was only too anxious to surrender'. Continue along Langemarkstraat for 700 metres to the leftwards bend, where Maalestraat runs past the far end of the large farm on the right. Follow Maalestraat to its prominent rightwards bend, on which **Israel House pillbox** ⑩ stood on the right.

Now look straight ahead for a magnificent view of II ANZAC's battlefield. On the far side of the valley of the Hanebeek, then a marsh, the high ground of **Gravenstafel Spur** extends across your front. It was thickly packed with pillboxes, strongpoints and linking trenches. The **Abraham Heights** stretch of the spur is directly ahead, with the obelisk of the **New Zealand Memorial** in Gravenstafel hamlet to its left and **Berlin Wood** in rear. **Tyne Cot Cemetery** appears as a large white patch to your right front just below the crest at Gravenstafel's junction with the Passchendaele section of the main ridge 1.5 kilometres away. Passchendaele's water tower and the spire of its church rise midway between Berlin Wood and the cemetery, and the tree line on the high ground to the right of the cemetery shows the line of the railway. The farmhouse in the copse just below and

Carrying on from where the I ANZAC walk/drive left off, this walk/drive follows II ANZAC's attack from the start line before heading across the Blue and Red Lines in the New Zealand Division's sector and the Gravenstafel Spur between them. It concludes at Tyne Cot Cemetery, from where the 3rd Australian Division's assault is considered in detail. The sites of the two Australian VC actions are also covered.

DISTANCE COVERED: 10 km
DURATION: 2 hours driving; 4.5 hours walking

to the left of the cemetery marks the site of **Hamburg** pillbox. **Bordeaux** strongpoint was in the farm buildings across the Hanebeek and at the foot of the Abraham Heights 700 metres to your front. The concrete shelters at **Judah** were on this side of the Hanebeek in the farm buildings 400 metres to your right front. Just to the right of Judah and on the opposite side of Maarlstraat 600 metres off are the farm buildings whose ruined originals concealed the **Springfield** strongpoint.

Crossing Langemarkstraat on the other side of **Dochy Farm**, 250 metres over your left shoulder, the start line extended to the left of **Dear House**, the lone building on the crest of the Gravenstafel to the right of the farm. The interdivisional boundary stretched on your left from Dochy Farm to the right of Berlin Wood, which meant that the axis of the advance ran diagonally to your right front rather than straight ahead. Leading the 10th Brigade, the 37th Battalion crawled out from its start line

[I] saw many red and green lights go up from the German positions and remarked to the corporal how pretty they looked. He said, 'Now we are for it. The Germans have taken a tumble that we are going to attack them, and now they are sending up their SOS signals to their artillery.' Almost immediately a heavy barrage descended on our positions.

Private Verdi Schwinghammer, who had recently joined the 47th Battalion, betraying his inexperience behind the start line (Schwinghammer, 'Narrative', 2DRL/0234, AWM)

just over Langemarkstraat behind you to within 27 metres of Israel and the **Levi Cottage** pillboxes on the higher ground to your right. Some in the 37th wondered whether the Germans could hear the noise of their chattering teeth and pounding hearts. Like the 43rd on its right, the 37th stormed the Germans 'before they realised what had happened' when the barrage opened at 6 am. A few shots came from your location at Israel before it was engulfed in a cloud of smoke from a phosphorous grenade thrown by those who had outflanked it. Levi Cottages fell even more easily. The assault halted on the intermediate line at Judah.

Attached to the 37th Battalion with a Lewis-gun for anti-aircraft duty, Lance Corporal Peeler may have shot up both Israel and Judah during the five occasions he ran ahead of the line to silence Germans firing from shell holes and posts. In the most dramatic of these actions, Peeler killed a German machine-gunner, tossed a bomb into the dugout into which the rest of the crew had retreated and shot the survivors as they emerged. He killed at least 30 Germans altogether and captured others. Enlisting again in the Second World War, Peeler spent three years as a prisoner of the Japanese only to learn on release that his son had fallen in the Solomons in 1944.

The 38th Battalion leapfrogged the 37th at Judah and continued on to

Springfield and Bordeaux, through which the **Red Line** ran on boggy ground right to left across your front. Taking over there, the 39th Battalion advanced to the next intermediate line halfway up the Gravenstafel, before the 40th Battalion passed through to secure Tyne Cot, behind which the **Blue Line** cut to Hamburg and Berlin Wood. On the right of the 10th Brigade, the 11th had also used all four of its battalions in its assault, which crossed the railway to take the main ridge on the far side of Tyne Cot. In reaching the Blue Line, the two brigades had captured the stretch of Flandern 1 that stretched from Zonnebeke to cross the Gravenstafel behind Hamburg. The New Zealand Division's advance on your left gained the Blue Line at Berlin Wood and over the far side of the Gravenstafel to its left but stopped short of Flandern 1.

Return to Langemarkstraat and head right into the New Zealand 4th Brigade's area. Passing **Dochy Farm New British Cemetery**, continue to the crossroads 750 metres further on and turn right into Roselaarestraat for the New Zealand Memorial. The 3rd Otagos' start line on the left of the 4th Brigade crossed the road by the houses on either side 500 metres along ⑪. Resistance from pillboxes and farm ruins in this vicinity was rapidly overcome. **Otto Farm** pillbox, captured by 3rd Auckland on the Otagos' right, was 350 metres to your

The view from Israel of the ground across which the 3rd Australian Division attacked on the right of II ANZAC towards the Abraham Heights section of the Gravenstafel Spur. Lance-Corporal Peeler operated between Israel and Judah.

BERLIN WOOD

BORDEAUX

PASSCHENDAELE

HAMBURG

RED LINE

right front on this side of the Hanebeek. Carry on another 400 metres to the far side of the Hanebeek, where the Red Line crossed the road in front of the house 100 metres to your left. Both battalions reached it on time. During the halt, 3rd Wellington moved up behind you, with 3rd Canterbury on its right, to take over the advance.

Continue to the crossroads in Gravenstafel, just before which is a concrete shelter on the left. At the crossroads, where the memorial commemorating the New Zealand Division's role in the battle overlooks its sector, head left on Schipstraat along the crest of the spur towards the 1st Brigade's area on the left flank. Stop after 270 metres at the **lone house** 12 on the right. Crossing the road 80 metres further on, at the track on the right, the Red Line cut diagonally over the crest to your right front. When 1st Wellington reached it after advancing up the slope from the Hanebeek on your left, a fusillade rang out from the **Korek Farm** pillboxes that were clustered in the area behind the house. Rushing into the barrage, the

Otto Farm and the New Zealand Division's attack.

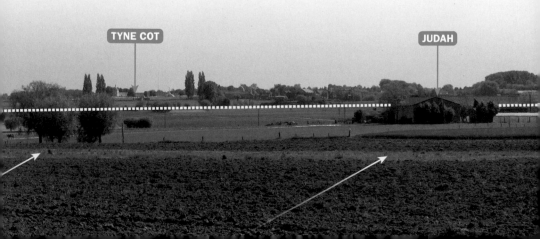

Wellingtons and 3rd Otago hurled bomb after bomb into the entrances. The pillboxes fell silent.

Proceed another 750 metres to the **memorial to the 15th Canadian Battalion (48th Highlanders of Canada)** 13 on the right. If driving, park by the house 50 metres further on, which is on the site of Dear House, and walk back to the memorial. Look towards Dear House. The left of the 1st Brigade's start line crossed the road 200 metres beyond it and ran 350 metres down the slope to your right front. Rising from the start line, 1st Auckland were hit by torrential fire from **Aviatik Farm** strongpoint, which was 100 metres to the right of Dear House. The first line, remarked the New Zealand Official Historian, simply 'withered away'. Using trench mortars, the following waves took Aviatik but were then lashed by the machine-guns at **Winzig Farm** (on the slope 400 metres behind Aviatik and out of sight from your location). The Aucklanders veered towards Winzig. Now turn about. As the Aucklanders had gone off track, 1st Wellington on their right had to shift leftwards astride the Gravenstafel,

occupying most of the 1st Brigade's frontage. It had a torrid time clearing the pillboxes at **Boetleer**, whose houses straddle the road 250 metres ahead of you, only to be hammered again at Korek, whence you have just come.

Return to the Gravenstafel crossroads, turn left onto s'Gravenstafelstraat and continue to the **café** 14 on the right opposite a calvary. Walk to the lower end of the car park, where **Bellevue Spur** rises across the Ravebeek to your front, with **Bellevue Farm** 900 metres away on its crest, and the spire of Passchendaele church to its right. Studded with pillboxes, Flandern 1 crossed the Ravebeek to your right front and went through the farm on the spur. Look back towards Gravenstafel. From your right to left, 2nd Auckland, 3rd Wellington and 3rd Canterbury advanced over the crest and down the slope towards you, meeting strong resistance that was subdued by small groups working from shell hole to shell hole around the flanks. They were also under steady fire from machine-guns on the spur behind you, Passchendaele Ridge on your left and

The 3rd Australian Division's attack as seen from Flandern 1 at Tyne Cot.

11TH BRIGADE

YPRES

10TH BRIGADE

Flandern 1 in between. It subsided when a pre-arranged smoke bombardment blinded the German gunners. As they approached your location, a joint attack by 2nd Auckland and 3rd Wellington captured a German battalion headquarters at **Waterloo Farm**, on the site of the two-storey premises to your right front beyond the calvary. Meanwhile 3rd Canterbury outflanked pillboxes in Berlin Wood, 250 metres to your left, which had stubbornly resisted its advance. Running along the front of Berlin Wood, across your end of the car park and off to your right, the Blue Line was then taken. Revered as the captain of the 1905 All Blacks rugby team, 41 year-old Sergeant David Gallaher of the 2nd Aucklanders fell in this advance. He was one of 13 All Blacks killed during the war.

Go back to the crossroads again, turn left onto Schipstraat and continue along the Abraham Heights before turning left again after 1.3 kilometres onto Vijfwegestraat. At the T-junction head right along Tynecotstraat for 150 metres and then turn left to Tyne Cot Cemetery. Follow the signs to the car park, through which the Blue Line ran to Berlin Wood. Take the downhill path behind past the Visitors' Centre and walk along the front of the cemetery to the corner by **Tynecotstraat** 15. Stand with the cemetery wall at your back. As Flandern 1 ran through your location to Hamburg, on the site of the farm house in the

The New Zealand Memorial, Gravenstafel crossroads.

copse 170 metres to your right front, you now have the German view from it of the ground over which the 3rd Division attacked. Advancing to your left front, the 11th Brigade passed behind the cemetery. With the Ypres skyline as a backdrop, the 10th Brigade moved directly towards you, the 40th Battalion carrying out the final assault against Flandern 1 to gain the Blue Line behind the Visitors' Centre over your right shoulder.

This area was infested with pillboxes, three of which can be seen in the cemetery grounds. Another was just in front of Hamburg, one was in it, and still more lay beyond it, where the New Zealand sector began. At least 10 machine-guns were firing at the 40th from these pillboxes and from shell holes. The 40th was badly pinned down to your left, left

DOCHY FARM

NZ DIVISION

SERGEANT MCGEE

Sergeant McGee's attack on Hamburg.

front and left rear until Captain William Ruddock manoeuvred some men into a fold of dead ground in the New Zealand sector behind Hamburg. They laid down flanking fire that enabled attacks on the pillboxes to go ahead. Sergeant McGee charged 50 metres across the fire-swept ground to your front to the pillbox near Hamburg and, with his revolver, shot the crew of a machine-gun blazing away from its roof. The other pillboxes

were silenced by similar acts of daring. By 9 am the 3rd Division was on the Blue Line.

Return to the car park, from which you can commence the Passchendaele battlefield tour by turning left at the entrance and going to the top of the hill just past the hedge. Otherwise head right and, after 200 metres, left onto Tynecotstraat, which goes over Australia Walk, the bed of the old railway, at **Dash Crossing** 180 metres further on. From the crossing, look along the road. The Blue Line for the 11th Brigade ran diagonally from II ANZAC's boundary with I ANZAC, 500 metres to your right front beyond the houses, through your location to the cemetery. If driving, continue on Tynecotstraat to the N303 and turn right for the Broodseinde crossroads, at which you should turn right again onto the N332 for Zonnebeke and Ypres. If walking, head right on Australian Walk, information panels along which describe the action and, no less interesting, the archaeological work underway at the remains of **Thames** and other pillboxes.

Remains of Thames pillbox on the Ypres–Roulers railway walking track.

LOCAL INFORMATION

CEMETERIES

Dochy Farm New British Cemetery

On Langemarkstraat and passed on the II ANZAC tour route, this cemetery was made after the Armistice and contains 1439 burials, 958 of them unidentified. Most of the 305 Australians and 98 New Zealanders fell during the Broodseinde attack and the Passchendaele battle that followed it. Resting at III.B.27, Lieutenant Roland Glanville of the 8th Battalion was killed by a shell at Broodseinde. He had won the MC in the Menin Road battle for capturing 16 Germans after brandishing his revolver at them. They did not know that the revolver was empty. Private Edward Green at VII.C.16 was killed in the 10th Battalion's raid on Celtic Wood.

Tyne Cot Cemetery

Before the Germans captured this area in 1915, the British dubbed a barn here Tyne Cot(tage). They seemed to be naming local buildings after European rivers — trench maps show others as Seine, Thames and Tiber — which almost certainly renders apocryphal the explanation that the name arose because the five pillboxes subsequently built by the Germans near the ruins of the barn resembled Tyneside cottages. A cemetery sprang up around the largest pillbox, which was used as an advance dressing station after its capture

Tyne Cot Cemetery.

The plaque on the Tyne Cot Cross of Sacrifice.

Grave of Captain Clarence Jeffries VC, Tyne Cot Cemetery.

in the Broodseinde attack. At the Armistice, it contained 343 graves but then underwent an exponential expansion as thousands of remains from the surrounding battlefields and from smaller cemeteries were brought in. Today Tyne Cot's 11 956 burials, 3587 of them identified, make it the largest Commonwealth War Graves Cemetery in the world.

At the suggestion of King George V, who visited Tyne Cot in 1922, the Cross of Sacrifice was built over the largest pillbox. Framed by a bronze laurel wreath, a small part of the original concrete can be seen through an opening in the base. Look closely at the inscription on the plaque there. For many years it stated that the pillbox had been captured by the 2nd Australian Division. The '2nd' has been changed to '3rd' to reflect what really happened! Scattered behind the cross are the original wartime graves. At the back of the cemetery the **Tyne Cot Memorial** records the names of almost 34 000 British soldiers who fell in the salient from 16 August 1917 onwards. They could not be fitted on the Menin Gate, on which British missing before that date, and all Australian Canadian, Indian and South African missing, are listed. In contrast to the triumphal lion above the Menin Gate, mourning angels kneel atop the dome-covered pavilions at each end of the memorial wall, a sombre acknowledgement of the awful fighting towards the close of the Third Ypres offensive.

More Australians rest in Tyne Cot than in any other First World War cemetery — 1368, of whom 791 are unknown. They include Sergeant McGee VC at XX.D.1, and Captain Clarence Jeffries VC, who fell in the later attack at Passchendaele, at XL.E.1. Tyne Cot also contains more New Zealand burials, 520, of whom 32 are unidentified, than any cemetery outside New Zealand. The **New Zealand Memorial** in the Tyne Cot Memorial's central apse also lists the names of the

1176 New Zealand missing from the Broodseinde and Passchendaele battles in accordance with New Zealand's policy of recording its missing close to where they fell.

A roll call of all the fallen in the salient sounds continuously, and hauntingly, from the Visitors' Centre, which contains a small museum and, for Australians, a touch-screen display showing the Australian connection with the cemetery. It is impossible to remain unaffected by Tyne Cot, which is on Tynecotstraat and visited on the tour route.

MUSEUMS

Memorial Museum Passchendaele 1917

Housed in the Zonnebeke château, which was flattened during the war and rebuilt in 1924, the museum covers the fighting throughout the salient but focuses on the battle for Passchendaele. Its centrepiece is a dugout system that includes headquarters, communication and aid posts, and accommodation, all realistically re-created. A large collection of relics is also displayed. Closed in January and February but otherwise open daily between 9 am and 5 pm, the museum is on Ieperstraat (N332) in the centre

Grave of Sergeant Lewis McGee VC, Tyne Cot Cemetery.

of Zonnebeke and charges an entry fee of €5. Contact details are: telephone +32 51 77 04 41; fax +32 51 78 07 50; www.passchendaele.be.

CHAPTER 13

1917

PASSCHENDAELE

The attacks by the ANZAC divisions on Menin Road on 20 September 1917, at Polygon Wood six days later, and at Broodseinde on 4 October, brought the Second Army almost to the village of Passchendaele. Its fall would complete the capture of the ridge around the southern half of the Ypres salient, finally denying the Germans the extensive views that they had enjoyed over the salient since 1915. Each involving a short advance supported by remorseless bombardments and barrages, the three previous steps had 'bitten off' and held small chunks of the ridge. On account of the terrain, the fourth step to Passchendaele would be the most difficult. From the village, the Bellevue Spur curved round from the main ridge to parallel it one kilometre to the west on the far side of the Ravebeek Valley. In defensive terms, the ridge and the spur were mutually supporting. The assault along one would be enfiladed from the other, so both had to be attacked simultaneously. If one assault failed, the other was doomed.

Generals

The German Official History called Broodseinde 'The black day of October 4th'. It forced the Germans to change their tactics again. Holding the front line more densely had not worked, so they reinstituted the lightly held outpost zone, which had rapidly given way in the Menin Road and Polygon Wood attacks. The depth of the zones behind it, from which counterattacks would be launched once the artillery had blasted a path, was greatly increased. Offensive and defensive tactics were now identical. The attackers would occupy a narrow belt of ground that the artillery had pulverised; the defenders would repeat the process in the opposite direction to regain it. But the German artillery could not match the

British. The Germans were desperate. The weather bailed them out.

The return of the rains late on 4 October reduced the battlefield to a quagmire so deep that the British guns needed timber platforms laid on a bed of fascines and road metal. They started sinking after firing a few shells even then, so barrages were feeble and inaccurate, offering no protection to the infantry. On 7 October Generals Gough and Plumer proposed ending the campaign but Field Marshal Haig thought that the strongest defences had been breached. He felt confident that the next attack 'will probably give opportunities for exploitation' and wanted the cavalry readied for it. In the event, he cancelled the exploitation because of the weather but ordered the

The slough to which the battlefield returned after the Broodseinde attack.
An Australian howitzer battery occupied this area.

85TH BATTALION MEMORIAL

9TH BRIGADE 12 OCTOBER

attack to proceed. It would be carried out in two stages, the first reaching the outskirts of Passchendaele and the second taking the village.

Poelcappelle

As Passchendaele lay directly opposite II ANZAC, it had the central role in the first stage on 9 October. Its two British divisions, the 49th and the 66th, had not fought at Broodseinde and would carry out the attack. While the 49th took Bellevue Spur, the untried 66th was to advance on the village. Only 25 guns, a quarter of the normal number, were able to support the attack. The 5th and 6th Brigades from the 2nd Australian Division would secure II ANZAC's right flank on the wrecked Ypres–Roulers railway by advancing to the Keiberg, a southerly offshoot of the ridge between Broodseinde and Passchendaele. Both brigades were in a sorry state. Since Broodseinde they had been helping the engineers build corduroy roads and light railways to assist the forward move of the guns, and also burying telephone cables. Worn out and lacking shelter from the dreadful weather, hundreds of men were evacuated with fatigue and trench feet. Many others 'temporarily deserted'. The average strength of the assault battalions dropped to 157 officers and men.

The battle took its name from the village of Poelcappelle on the northern flank because the Fifth Army and the French advanced 800 metres there. X Corps made some minor gains on the right. But II ANZAC's attack in the centre failed. The barrage had opened at 5.20 am but was barely discernible. On Bellevue Spur the thick, unbroken wire and intact pillboxes of the Flandern 1 line halted the 49th Division, leaving the left of the 66th ferociously enfiladed. It made little headway. With easier going on the crest, the right reached the outskirts of Passchendaele after starting late. The delay had left the 5th Brigade's flank on the railway open. Raked from the 66th's

The Keiberg. On 9 October the 5th Brigade reached the area on the far side of the railway, while the 9th Brigade advanced on the near side three days later. Both brigades were forced to withdraw. The memorial marks the headquarters location of the Canadian 85th Infantry Battalion, which set up there after the Canadian Corps took over the advance from I and II ANZAC.

YPRES–ROULERS RAILWAY

DECLINE COPSE

5TH BRIGADE 9 OCTOBER
12TH BRIGADE 12 OCTOBER

The conditions under which the gunners, in this case New Zealanders, tried to lay down a supporting barrage.

sector across the railway and also meeting tough resistance along the railway, the 5th still completed the 1.1-kilometre advance to the Keiberg but lacked the strength to hold it and had to withdraw. Now isolated, the 66th Division's right pulled back too. Unsubdued machine-guns lashed the exhausted 6th Brigade on the right of the 5th. The few posts it managed to set up had to be abandoned. The two brigades suffered 1253 casualties.

Mud and muddle

Haig remarked: 'It was simply the mud which defeated us ... The men did splendidly to get through it as they did'. The second stage of the attack, which II ANZAC was to carry out as planned on 12 October, would incorporate the objectives of the first. Little thought was given to the fact that the six-day minimum to organise similar attacks in good weather had been whittled down to three in bad. The 3rd Australian Division would assault along Passchendaele Ridge with the New Zealand Division, on its left as usual, attacking Bellevue Spur. Covering the 3rd's right flank would be the 12th Brigade from the 4th Australian Division. To give the infantry a chance in the mud, especially around the flooded Ravebeek, up to 45 metres wide and waist deep, the creeping barrage needed to be much slower and, therefore, required much more ammunition than hitherto. Even if it had been possible to get the shells forward, the bogged guns could only have fired a fraction of them. Yet no attack required artillery support more. The Germans facing II ANZAC had not yet thinned out their front line and they had double the normal number of machine-guns.

Each division was to advance on a 1.5-kilometre frontage with two brigades

The N303 points to the remains of Passchendaele church five days after the attack. Little else of the village is left. The zigzag trench on the right is on the Keiberg.

to the Red Line, which ran 450 metres ahead between Passchendaele Ridge and Bellevue Spur and corresponded to the final objective of the failed 9 October attack. Then came the 720-metre assault to the Blue Line, just short of the village centre. It would be the jump-off line for the final advance to the Green Line 360 metres beyond the village. Each brigade was to use a fresh battalion for each stage and keep its remaining battalion in reserve if Passchendaele's capture proved difficult. But the plan was based on reports that the 66th Division had only withdrawn to its first objective, 550 metres past its start line at Tyne Cot, on 9 October. Next day, it was found to have pulled back all the way to its start line, the position reached by the 3rd Division in the Broodseinde attack.

The 3rd Division would now have to attack from Tyne Cot, which extended its Red Line assault by 550 metres. That meant an overall advance of 2.2 kilometres, 400 metres further than the 3rd's assault at Broodseinde, which was the longest yet. The most important principle of 'bite and hold', a limited 'bite' well within the attacking infantry's capability, had been jettisoned. It was decided to start the 3rd's supporting barrage 270 metres further back but to increase its rate of advance so that it caught the general line of the barrage within 450 metres. But Poelcappelle had shown that the infantry struggling through the mud soon lost the barrage at the existing rate. Given the lack of shells, extending the barrage would also further dilute its density.

In this well-known photograph, Canadian machine-gunners in shell holes manage to smile for the camera. II ANZAC attacked across ground that was in the same glutinous state.

'Things are bloody'

Drenched by high explosive and gas, the approach march fumbled through the rainy darkness. The German shelling continued after the start line was reached. Dawn was breaking when the supporting barrage opened at 5.25 am. It seemed as if a few pebbles were being tossed into the mud. The 40th Battalion 'made no attempt to conform to it', because 'there was really nothing to conform to'. Floundering towards the Flandern 1 pillboxes on Bellevue Spur, behind which the Red Line ran, the 2nd and 3rd New Zealand Brigades faced disaster. Their patrols had reported the night before that the Flandern 1 wire was intact. The New Zealanders were

smashed trying to get through. The Red Line was nowhere reached.

The Bellevue machine-guns were now able to rip into the 10th Brigade from the 3rd Australian Division, which was on the right of the 2nd New Zealand Brigade, as it struggled through the gluey knee-deep, and occasionally waist-deep, mud of the Ravebeek. It had already lost heavily in the German shelling before the attack and had no chance of keeping up with the barrage. About 200 men from the 40th Battalion managed to reach the Red Line. A 20-strong party from the 38th Battalion pushed on beyond the Blue Line and into Passchendaele but turned back on realising that they were alone.

The 9th Brigade had been badly disorganised by the German shelling, and by machine-guns that easily withstood the weak Australian shelling. It reached the Red Line gravely weakened. Captain Clarence Jeffries of the 34th Battalion was posthumously awarded the VC for attacking two pillboxes during the assault. The silencing of the second one enabled mixed parties of the 34th, 35th and 36th Battalions to continue to the Blue Line. Thinly held, it was soon being swept by German machine-guns and snipers, and then by artillery. Holding on meant annihilation, so the remnants withdrew late in the afternoon. The 47th and 48th Battalions from the 12th Brigade, which had reached the Keiberg, also pulled back. With the Germans dribbling down Bellevue Spur behind them, the 10th Brigade's survivors along the Ravebeek pulled out too.

'Things are bloody, very bloody', reported Lieutenant-Colonel Leslie Morshead of the 33rd Battalion. The 3rd Division had lost 3199 men and was almost back where it had started. Comparing the casualties to the ground gained, Messines and Broodseinde both cost it less than one man per metre. Passchendaele cost it over 35 men per metre. On the right of the 3rd Division, the 12th Brigade suffered 1018 casualties. The New Zealand Division lost 2800 men, which made 12 October the costliest day in New Zealand's military history.

Finale

Many of the underlying reasons for the offensive were no longer valid. As the U-boat threat had been contained with the replacement of independent sailing by the convoy system, the need to deprive the U-boats of their bases in Belgian ports had passed. The French had attacked at Verdun and given solid support at Ypres, clear evidence of their recovery. As a combatant, Russia was practically moribund before the Ypres campaign started. The internal chaos following the collapse of Russia's last offensive in July 1917 and the successful German counterstroke rendered it completely so.

Haig now argued that every effort had to be made to defeat the Germans before they could transfer troops from the Eastern Front. That became the justification for continuing the Ypres offensive. He also wanted a winter line that was not under German observation from the Passchendaele end of the ridge, even though the Broodseinde success had given the British observation over much of the German line, as anyone who has done the Broodseinde battlefield tour will appreciate. The Canadian Corps took over the advance. After four attacks between 26 October and 10 November, it did what II ANZAC had been ordered to do in one attack and finally captured Passchendaele Ridge. By then the battle had acquired an infamy that time has not diminished. 'I died in hell. (They called it Passchendaele)', wrote war poet Siegfried Sassoon. In a final irony, the British gave up the ridge to shorten their line during the German spring offensive of 1918. The Germans duly occupied it from April to September.

WALKING THE BATTLEFIELD

It is easy to do two things on the Passchendaele battlefield: clearly follow the action on Bellevue Spur and in the Ravebeek Valley on the left of it, and get disoriented on the ridge on the right of it. The axis of the attacks on 9 and 12 October on the right side paralleled the line of the Ypres–Roulers railway, which ran across the ridge. But natural instinct follows the lie of the land. So you have to remind yourself constantly that the attacks were not intended to proceed along the line of the N303, which runs along the ridge. The 9th Brigade, in particular, tended to give into instinct, which made direction-keeping a frustrating business for it. Remind yourself constantly, too, that today's lush, well-manicured countryside stands in the starkest possible contrast to the appalling conditions under which the attacks took place.

The tour is intended for walkers. A goodly part of it cannot be driven, which means a long walk back to a parked car for drivers. Parking is sometimes difficult as well.

MAP NGI 1:20 000: 28/3-4 Zonnebeke–Moorslede

Leave Ypres through the Menin Gate and continue straight ahead on the N332 for Zonnebeke, 1.1 kilometres past the centre of which turn left onto the N303 at the Broodseinde roundabout. Turn left again 950 metres along onto Tynecotstraat, following the signs for Tyne Cot cemetery. Park in the cemetery car park.

From the car park entrance, head left past the hedges to the top of the hill, which is on the western edge of **Passchendaele Ridge** ❶. Most of the landmarks on the battlefield are visible from this location and much of the action of 9 and 12 October can be grasped from it. Stand with your back to **Tyne Cot Cemetery**. The church at 12 o'clock is in the centre of **Passchendaele**, 1.8 kilometres distant. To your right rear, 1.5 kilometres off at 5 o'clock, is the tower of the church in **Zonnebeke**. The bed of the old **Ypres–Roulers railway** runs across the crest of the ridge to your right front, its course from **Dash Crossing**, 300 metres to your right rear on Tynecotstraat, indicated by the line of trees 250 metres to your right. It went over the N303, Passendalestraat, at **Defy Crossing**, by the building with the high-pitched roof 500 metres to your right front. **Hillside Farm** was further

PASSCHENDAELE

The advance from the 3rd Division's start line at Tyne Cot, here occupied by the 9th Brigade. Opposition came almost immediately from the Hillside Farm area.

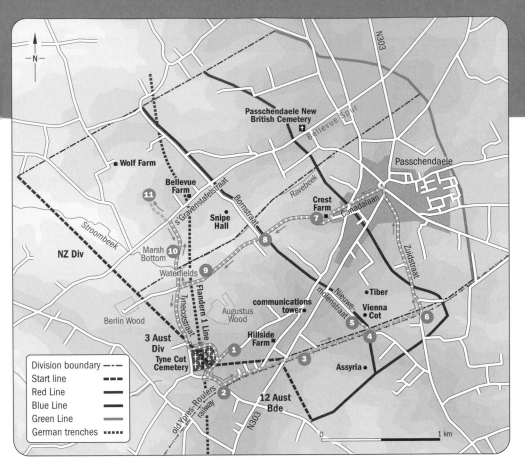

Map legend:
- Division boundary —·—
- Start line — — —
- Red Line ▬▬▬
- Blue Line ▬▬▬
- Green Line ▬▬▬
- German trenches ·····

Labels on map: Passchendaele New British Cemetery, Bellevue Spur, Wolf Farm, Passchendaele, Bellevue Farm, s'Gravenstafelstraat, Bornstraat, Crest Farm, Snipe Hall, Ravebeek, Canadalaan, Stroombeek, NZ Div, Marsh Bottom, Waterfields, Zuidstraat, Tiber, Nieuwe-molenstraat, Vienna Cot, Berlin Wood, Flandern 1 Line, Tynecotstraat, Augustus Wood, communications tower, Hillside Farm, 3 Aust Div, Tyne Cot Cemetery, Assyria, old Ypres-Roulers railway, N303, 12 Aust Bde, 0 — 1 km

left, towards the communications tower on the N303. The low ground 800 metres to your left is the valley of the Ravebeek. Between **Waterfields**, at 9 o'clock beyond the black-roofed barn, and **Marsh Bottom**, behind the seven poplars beyond Waterfields, the stream changes course. **Bellevue Spur** rises on the far side, and the red-roofed house atop the spur, just to the right of the

Starting from Tyne Cot Cemetery, this walk follows the bed of the old Ypres-Roulers railway past the Keiberg in retracing the right flank of the 3rd Division's assault. Cutting back through Passchendaele, it then tracks roughly along the inter-divisional boundary in the Ravebeek Valley before swinging up onto Bellevue Spur to the limit of the New Zealander's advance on II ANZAC's left flank. The Red, Blue and Green Lines and the site of Captain Jeffries's VC action are all included.
DISTANCE COVERED: 8 km
DURATION: 4 hours

HILLSIDE FARM

DEFY CROSSING

black-roofed house, is **Bellevue Farm**. Across the re-entrant 200 metres to your left front was **Augustus Wood**, which no longer exists. **Berlin Wood**, which does, is 650 metres to your left rear on **Gravenstafel Spur**.

Straddling the Ypres–Roulers railway at Dash Crossing, the **British front line** ran diagonally through the cemetery behind you, across the front of Berlin Wood and along the forward slopes of the Gravenstafel. **Flandern 1** tracked to the right of the British line across the low ground to Waterfields and Marsh Bottom before cresting Bellevue Spur at Bellevue Farm. Note how the Germans in Flandern 1 on Bellevue Spur and on the ridge ahead of you could support each other with enfilade fire. The returning rains made the going on these heights difficult. But the valley between them was almost impassable.

At dusk on 8 October, the 49th and 66th Divisions sloshed forward from **Ypres**, on the skyline four kilometres behind you. Five hours had been allowed for the march. As the engineers had concentrated on making roads for the guns, the infantry tracks consisted of little more than guiding tapes. So negotiating the slime-covered crater field for the attack next morning took over 11 hours.

Arriving late, the 197th Brigade from the 66th Division passed from the cemetery diagonally through your location towards the N303 beyond Defy Crossing. Stretching down the slope below you towards the Ravebeek, the 198th Brigade advanced on time at 5.20 am to your left front behind a pathetic barrage. The 49th Division next to it splashed across the Ravebeek but made no impression on Flandern 1 on Bellevue Spur to your left. The Germans there could now lay down enfilade fire in your direction. It ripped into the 198th Brigade, which stalled on the spur 400 metres to your left front.

In order to protect the 66th Division's right flank, the 2nd Australian Division carried out a limited advance on the far side of the railway, which was the boundary between the two formations. The 5th Brigade, next to the railway, reached the final objective, on the Keiberg Spur midway between your location and Passchendaele, but the 197th Brigade had still not caught up on this side of the railway. Facing strong counterattacks with its flank open, the 5th came back to Defy Crossing. When the 197th Brigade, partly sheltered from the enfilade fire from Bellevue, finally arrived opposite the Keiberg, it was in a worse position than the 5th Brigade had

The valley of the Ravebeek, along which the 10th Australian Brigade and the New Zealand Division attacked on 12 October. The New Zealanders were stopped short of Bellevue Farm, which allowed the Germans to enfilade the 10th Brigade. Three days earlier, the attack by the British 98th Brigade and 47th Divisions over this ground had been shot down.

BERLIN WOOD

POELCAPPELLE

FLANDERN 1

been: on its own with both flanks open. It withdrew at dusk.

Now consider this. As the 66th Division was believed to have pulled back to its first objective, a line that ran across your front and through Defy Crossing, the 3rd Australian Division was to have attacked from there on 12 October. When the truth was discovered, the 3rd's start line had to be pulled back to Dash Crossing and the cemetery, from where the 9 October attack began. The 3rd's **Red Line** remained set beyond the house and the barn with the green door ahead of you, halfway to Passchendaele. Only part of the advance on 9 October had got that far and the ground gained could not be held. Yet the 3rd Division on 12 October was to go well beyond Passchendaele, through the same mud and with the same weak barrage.

Attacking on the far side of the valley on 12 October, the New Zealand Division

was cut to pieces in the Flandern 1 wire to the left of Bellevue Farm, just as the 49th Division had been The Red Line ran to the right of the farm. The 3rd Australian Division advanced between the Ravebeek and the railway, with the 12th Brigade on the far side of the railway securing its right flank. On the Ravebeek flank, the 10th Brigade, with the 37th Battalion leading, immediately hit strong resistance at Waterfields and Augustus Wood. The 38th and 40th Battalions joined the 37th to clear it. All three battalions pushed on together under deadly fire from Bellevue to the Red Line. There they halted, apart from the 38th Battalion party that took the Crest Farm strongpoint beyond the distant trees to your front, and reached Passchendaele church. Passing through your location as a disorganised throng and with no hope

The Ypres–Roulers railway cutting east of Broodseinde after the attack on 12 October. The Australian facing the camera on the far right is Private Austin Henderson of the 38th Battalion. Though this well-known photograph is usually credited to Frank Hurley, Hubert Wilkins, another Australian official photographer, was also in the cutting at the time.

The cutting today, now part of the Australia Walk, which follows the bed of the old track to Zonnebeke.

of catching the barrage, the 9th Brigade was held up for an hour by strongpoints at Augustus Wood, Hillside Farm and Defy Crossing. Though the 34th Battalion was supposed to be in the lead, these strongpoints fell to the 35th Battalion. The Red Line was gained under continuing heavy fire, whereupon the 35th went on to Passchendaele's outskirts. Drastic losses precluded going further. The same fire prevented the 12th Brigade from getting much past the Red Line. Too weak to resist counterattacks, the remnants of the 9th fell back to your location; the 12th to Defy Crossing. Now in danger of being outflanked on both sides, the survivors of the 10th Brigade came back too.

Walk down the hill, turn left at Tynecotstraat and stop 180 metres along at **Dash Crossing** ❷. The bed of the old railway, which crossed the road here, has been refurbished as **Australia Walk**. Information panels that start at the

> The New Zealanders were seen coming up on our left in two magnificent waves. They were seen all that day still in two waves, lying dead in the mud in front of the uncut wire … The enemy had great numbers of machine-guns on Bellevue Spur, and he wiped the New Zealanders out with concentrated fire, which played on them like a hose.
>
> The New Zealand advance on 12 October, as witnessed by the 40th Battalion alongside (Green, *The Fortieth*, p. 88)

Zonnebeke end describe the action along it. Stand facing the other end. The 5th Brigade's start line on 9 October ran from your location through the houses on your right; the 197th Brigade's went leftwards to the cemetery. Continue through the cutting to your front, where exhausted Australians were snapped after the 12 October attack. The picture became well-known. Australian Official Photographer Frank Hurley, who probably took it, recalled the scene: 'Under a questionably sheltered bank lay a group of dead men. Sitting by them in little scooped out recesses sat a few living; but so emaciated by fatigue and shell shock that it was hard to differentiate'. Continue over Defy Crossing beyond the cutting to the railway on the far side of the N303. A German post in a pile of cement bags between the railway and road on your left inflicted heavy casualties on the 17th and 20th Battalions from the 5th Brigade as they advanced from your right in the 9 October attack until a party from the 20th got behind it, taking 20 Germans prisoner.

Now walk down the railway and look along it after stopping just past the **industrial complex** ❸ on your right. The bed of the track cuts through the **Keiberg**, the spur running across your front from the Passchendaele Ridge to your left front. On the Keiberg midway between the N303 and the railway is a small cenotaph **memorial** to the 148 Nova Scotia Highlanders of the Canadian 85th Infantry Battalion who fell in the Passchendaele fighting. After reaching this location on 30 October, the 85th set up its headquarters there. The straggly thicket of trees and bushes on both sides of the railway cutting on the

right of the memorial is the remnant of **Decline Copse**. Starting from behind the industrial complex area on 9 October, the 17th and 20th Battalions advanced on your right to a line that ran rightwards along the Keiberg from the copse. The 6th Brigade further right established a line of posts stretching one kilometre back to Broodseinde, over your right shoulder. Unable to hold on the Keiberg, the remains of the 17th and 20th withdrew, as did some of the 6th Brigade posts, to a line that ran from Broodseinde and around the industrial complex area to Defy Crossing.

Advancing on your left on 12 October, the 9th Brigade instinctively followed the axis of the N303 along the ridge instead of crossing diagonally over the ridge and following the line of the railway. A pillbox on the left of the communications tower to your left front halted progress until Captain Jeffries outflanked it with a dozen men, capturing 25 Germans and two machine-guns. The left of the 9th Brigade closed up on the Red Line, which ran just behind the tower, and then

Defy Crossing in November 1917. The track and the N303 have been obliterated.

ASSYRIA

9TH BRIGADE 12 OCTOBER

5TH BRIGADE 9 OCTOBER
12TH BRIGADE 12 OCOTBER

The railway from Defy Crossing today, looking towards the Keiberg, which the 17th and 20th Battalions briefly held between the railway and Assyria on 9 October.

edged towards Passchendaele. The right should have been on the railway but was well short owing to the misdirected advance. As the Germans on the railway flank were therefore untroubled, they prevented the attack there from getting beyond the Red Line, which continued on the far side of Decline Copse. The bulk of the 47th and 48th Battalions, which advanced on your right from the industrial complex area, could not get beyond it either. The survivors from both battalions withdrew to your location during the afternoon.

Proceed through the cutting, which was the scene of grim fighting in both attacks and littered with dead and wounded Australians and Germans after each of them. While others captured the bank on your right on 9 October, Company Sergeant-Major John Raitt led a 17th Battalion party that bombed the dugouts lining the left bank. The surviving Germans bolted down the bed with Raitt on their heels, while Lieutenant Stan Gritten set up a machine-gun on top of the left bank half way along the cutting. Within five minutes, German

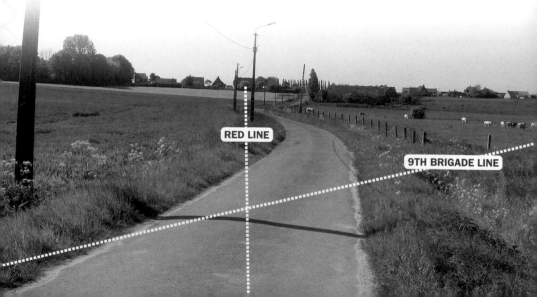

RED LINE

9TH BRIGADE LINE

machine-gunners on the ridge had swept Gritten's post away. Every man was wounded and slid down the bank to the bed. By now Raitt was sheltering in a shell hole just beyond the left bank. Bombing out a nearby machine-gun, he collided with another German. Being too close to bayonet him, he knocked the German down and shot him. Alone, and with other Germans coming at him, Raitt dived back into the cutting and escaped along it the way you have come.

Continuing past Decline Copse, stop at **Nieuwemolenstraat** ❹, which crosses the railway at the end of the cutting, and look back along the track. A large barn, known as **Assyria**, somehow still stood to the left of the house 200 metres to your left front. On 9 October the 17th and 20th Battalions captured the Keiberg between Assyria and Decline Copse, and repelled several counterattacks by Germans who had regrouped to your rear, before being forced back to the industrial complex from where you have come. Now turn about. On 12 October the Red Line ran along Nieuwemolenstraat from the ridge. Taking the same line on the Keiberg to your right rear as the 17th and 20th had done, the 47th Battalion sent the Germans packing from Assyria and reached the Red Line on your right before the 9th Brigade arrived on it

between the ridge and the railway on your left. But the **Vienna Cottages**, a strongpoint 100 metres to your left front, prevented all but a few men of the 48th Battalion carrying the 12th Brigade's advance to the Blue Line 450 metres further on.

Head left for 180 metres along Nieuwemolenstraat ❺. With the railway on your left, face the 85th Battalion memorial on the Keiberg. As the 9th Brigade had reached the Red Line well behind time, parts of the 34th, 35th and 36th Battalions started immediately for the Blue Line behind you, while the rest of the 34th Battalion dug in. The 9th's right flank did not even extend down to your location, leaving a German machine-gun to your left front, between you and the railway, free to enfilade the advance on your right. The gun swung back towards the railway just as Captain Jeffries led a rush from that direction. The rush succeeded but Jeffries was killed. Eventually the 9th Brigade established widely separated posts on a line that ran from the cutting, past the front of Vienna Cottages, and to the left of the stand of tall trees on the ridge to your right rear. When it was compelled to withdraw, the 12th Brigade had to do likewise.

Continuing along the railway, turn left onto the next road, Zuidstraat, at

Looking along the Red Line on Nieuwemolenstraat. The line of the 9th Brigade's posts, which it could not hold anyway, shows how far short of Passchendaele most of the 9th was stopped. Captain Jeffries was killed out of picture on the left.

PASSCHENDAELE

VIENNA COTTAGES

BLUE LINE

Passchendaele church from Crest Farm. The 38th Battalion party passed through the farm strongpoint to reach the church.

The view from Crest Farm down the Ravebeek Valley, along the left of which the 10th Brigade attacked.

Detect Crossing 6 . Bear in mind the line reached by the 9th Brigade as you walk up the slope towards Passchendaele. The brigade's left flank on the N303 was on the Blue Line, which ran diagonally away from the left of Zuidstraat. But the right flank, stuck at your previous location, was well short. As the 10th Brigade on the other side of the ridge had been stopped a long way back, the 9th was effectively strung out along a deep and thinly held salient. Fired on from three sides, including by field-guns over open sights, its position was untenable. Now look across the fields to your right, where the **Green Line** denoting the final objective was among

the line of trees and houses 600 metres off. For its attack to be successful, the 9th and 10th Brigades, already crippled, needed still to go that far!

On reaching the N303, look left. The Blue Line crossed the road at the petrol station 400 metres away. Now turn right for Passchendaele church, which became the furthest point attained by the 3rd Division when the 38th Battalion party reached it. Finding no-one else there, they withdrew and ran into the left of the 9th Brigade. At the end of the battle, only a red smear, which its pulverised bricks had left in the mud, indicated where the church had been. Noting the Bastiaan plaque, take Canadalaan, which leaves the square opposite the church. Stop at the **Canadian Memorial** at **Crest Farm** 7 , which is on the end of the small spur that juts into the Ravebeek Valley between Passchendaele Ridge on your left and Bellevue Spur on your right. A copse of maple trees provides an appropriate setting for the granite memorial stone, which commemorates the capture of Passchendaele by the Canadian Corps. A walk around the memorial and its tranquil gardens shows how the massive pillbox that squatted here could enfilade both the ridge and the spur, as well as fire down the valley.

BELLEVUE SPUR

10TH BRIGADE

The 38th Battalion party was extremely fortunate that its garrison promptly surrendered. But once the party had passed on, the Germans just as promptly reoccupied the pillbox and fired on the scattered groups of the 10th Brigade to their front.

Carry on down the slope behind the memorial. From where the road starts bending leftwards, the boundary between the 3rd Division and the New Zealand Division roughly paralleled it 100 to 150 metres to your right, following the line of the Ravebeek. Pause at **Bornstraat** 8, the first road on the right. As it attacked towards to you, torrential enfilade fire poured into the 10th Brigade from **Snipe Hall**, which was on the far side of the Ravebeek 100 metres to the left of the house halfway up the slope on the left of Bornstraat, and from Bellevue Spur beyond. Reduced to advancing in driblets from shell hole to shell hole, the 10th arrived on the Red Line, which ran to the right of Snipe Hall and up the spur to your left. Only 200 men from the three assaulting battalions got this far. Digging in was futile as the mud poured back into the trench as quickly as they shovelled it out.

The 10th's left flank rested on the road junction and its right flank was on the

crest of Passchendaele Ridge. Before leaving, spare a thought for the wounded here. An Australian doctor, Alec Birnie, remarked that many Germans 'pointed to where the wounded were lying — Hun snipers pointed to where their victims were'. But the stretcher-bearers looking after them were soon exhausted: 'To carry a wounded man from the front line to the R.A.P. was a terrible undertaking. The distance to be covered was less than a thousand yards but it took six men, four, five and even six hours to do the trip'. The 9th Brigade's area on the other side of the Passchendaele Ridge was no different. As the task of clearing the wounded from the slough was so great, anyone on hand had to be pressed into

The conditions under which the stretcher-bearers worked on 12 October.

PASSCHENDAELE
NEW BRITISH CEMETRY

Lieutenant Fisher's report on the 66th Division's line (quoted in Bean, CEW, *The AIF in France. IV. 1917*, Sydney, 1938, pp. 906–7)

The Ravebeek, no obstacle now.

service as emergency bearers. The plight of numerous unwounded was awful too. 'We were bogged up to our armpits and it took anything from an hour upwards to get out', Lieutenant George Carson of the 33rd Battalion recalled. 'Lots were drowned in the mud and water.'

Continue another 300 metres and look left up the re-entrant. The first pillbox that Captain Jeffries attacked was on the near side of the communications tower. In the next re-entrant, 300 metres further on, the bed-and-breakfast farm on the left of the road takes its name from **Waterfields ⑨**, a pillbox in the field opposite, from which a nest of German snipers was cleared out. Look left up this re-entrant. Starting 200 metres from the road, Augustus Wood extended 250 metres towards the crest and across both slopes. The planning for the attack rested on the assumption that the 66th Division's line after the 9 October attack fringed the right side of the wood. On 12 October, fire from pillboxes among its shattered stumps caught the 37th Battalion in the open much further right and mauled it. Sergeant McGee, who had won the VC eight days before at Broodseinde, was among the dead. The 38th and 40th Battalions were drawn into the fight but the Germans only succumbed after Lieutenant William Garrard of the 40th led some men around the wood and attacked it from the rear. Over 100 Germans were killed or captured. At day's end the 10th Brigade had withdrawn to a line that ran from the Ravebeek through Augustus Wood to the crest of the ridge.

Continue to the crossroads and turn right onto Tynecotstraat. Reconnoitring the lower slopes of Gravenstafel Spur to your left on 10 October, Lieutenant Walde Fisher of the 42nd Battalion found them littered with the 66th Division's dead from the previous day's attack, which helped to confirm that its line was on the forward slope of the spur. As you ascend Bellevue Spur after crossing the Ravebeek, Marsh Bottom is on your left and Berlin Wood rises on the Gravenstafel over your left shoulder. The Lamkeek pillboxes were on the site of the long

Looking from Marsh Bottom at the 2nd New Zealand Brigade's advance towards Lamkeek.

farm building on the right of the road in front of you. Bellevue Farm, then another pillbox cluster, is the red-roofed building immediately behind them to the right of the black-roofed one. The Red Line crossed the spur to its right. From your previous location at Waterfields, Flandern 1 crossed the Ravebeek and ran through Lamkeek and the farm. Stop at **Lamkeek** 🔟 and look left across Marsh Bottom.

You are now in the 2nd New Zealand Brigade's area, which stretched between the Ravebeek on your left and the crest of Bellevue on your right. Attacking from the Gravenstafel directly towards you, 2nd Otago slurped through the shell-torn morass of the Ravebeek below you and reached the lip of the spur immediately in front of you, where they struck the uncut entanglements of Flandern 1. Neither the Otagos nor the units behind them could get through. Dead and wounded soon clogged the wire. Only the Lamkeek pillboxes were silenced, and by a true ANZAC assault. Crawling between shell holes, 2nd Lieutenant Allan Cockerell's platoon from 1st Otago managed to get through the wire. By the time they had worked behind one of the pillboxes, capturing 80 Germans, only Cockerell and one other were still in one piece. Meanwhile, Lieutenants Allan Grant and Horace Chamberlain led a

party from the 40th Battalion over the Ravebeek at the road crossing you used. Fighting up Tynecotstraat from your left, they took another two pillboxes but, in rushing a third, all except Chamberlain were killed or wounded. He met up with Cockerell, who was awarded an immediate DSO. The heavy casualties and enfilade fire from Bellevue Farm prevented any further advance, with dire results for the 10th Brigade's attack along the near slope of Passchendaele Ridge to your left rear.

Now walk to the T-junction, turn left onto s'Gravenstafelstraat, and then right onto a track immediately before the house on the right. Continue along the track past the house until you can look down the valley of the Ravebeek, and its continuation, the Stroombeek, on your left. Flandern 1 crossed this spur behind the buildings on your right, giving the German machine-gunners long fields of grazing fire. Emerging from the valley to appear on the slope in front of them, the 2nd Brigade was cut down here as well. 'As the pace slackened and the forward ranks grew thinner, the rear battalions pressed up to fill the gaps in front', remarked the New Zealand Official History. The New Zealanders fell in droves

> He crawled back on his stomach to where Jock was lying, and got hold of his body and dragged him back to the road where we were sheltering. The machine-gun bullets were splashing up the mud all around them. Harold got right through them all. Then, just as he reached us he eased himself up slightly to pull Jock down below the road surface, and a German sniper put a rifle bullet through his throat... His blood gushed out all over me... Whatever was left of the N. Zedders was just a disorganised rabble, so much so that the Germans had become very cheeky. They weren't bothering to take cover, they had come out and were perched on top of their concrete forts picking off any fool who showed his nose.
>
> Private Bill Smith recounts Harold Stewart's reaction to the death of his brother Jock (Macdonald, L, *They Called It Passchendaele*, London, 1978, pp. 206–9)

on the uncut wire that ran 100 metres to the right of the track.

Turn around and look uphill. In the area to your right, Private Bill Smith saw Sergeant Jock Stewart get shot through the heart but Jock's younger brother Harold, who was nearby, did not. 'When he realised it', Smith said, 'we couldn't hold him'. Smith saw Maoris form relays to evacuate the wounded. 'They carried them in their arms like children.'

Continue on the track and stop once past the **trees on the left** 11. Bellevue Farm is to your right rear, with the Red Line behind it paralleling the track. Now look along the track over the valley

ahead. You are on the boundary between the 2nd and 3rd New Zealand Brigades. From its start line, which crossed the Stroombeek to your left front, the 3rd Brigade advanced left to right across your front. It met the same fate as the 2nd Brigade. The 3rd and 4th Rifles moved forward to fill the thinning ranks of the 2nd, and all three battalions finished up on a line that stretched just to the right of **Wolf Farm**, 400 metres away on the lower slope of the far spur directly in line with the track.

From here, return along the track to Tynecotstraat and follow it all the way to Tyne Cot Cemetery and your car. From there, retrace your route to Ypres.

The 'ANZAC' assault on Lamkeek as seen from Marsh Bottom. The failure to get beyond this point exposed the flank of the 10th Brigade on the far side of the Ravebeek.

WATERFIELDS

RAVEBEEK

TYNE COT CEMETERY

FLANDERN 1

40TH BATTALION PARTY

LOCAL INFORMATION

CEMETERIES

Many of the Australian and New Zealand fallen from the Passchendaele attacks lie in Tyne Cot Cemetery. They include the two VCs, Captain Jeffries and Sergeant McGee. Jeffries was missing until remains wrapped in a groundsheet on which his initials had been pencilled were found in a lone grave in 1920. A mining engineer from Wallsend in New South Wales, he was not quite 23 and had just recovered from a bad wound received at Messines when killed.

Passchendaele New British Cemetery

Of the 2101 burials in this cemetery, just 501 are identified, which reflects the nature of the Passchendaele battlefield.

Shellfire smashed many of the small plots and isolated graves that dotted it and the mud swallowed as many again. Still more men were never buried at all but lay where they fell. Most of the 292 Australian and 126 New Zealand burials are from the Broodseinde and Passchendaele battles. Lieutenant Talbert Pitman, the 44th Battalion's signals officer at XIII.C.11, gave up his place in a captured pillbox on 5 October to allow some of his exhausted men to sleep inside. Pitman, who had won the MC at Messines, slept outside and was killed by a shell. The cemetery, which was built postwar, can be reached on the tour route by turning right instead of left onto s'Gravenstafelstraat from Tynecotstraat and continuing for 1.3 kilometres.

CHAPTER 14

1918

FROM LA SIGNY FARM TO PUISIEUX

The grouping of the five Australian divisions into the Australian Corps on 1 November 1917 spelled the end of I and II ANZAC, and signalled the parting of the ways between the Australians and New Zealanders on the Western Front. They would fight alongside each other only one more time there, not in an offensive action as in the past but in a defensive one. Their stay together would be brief. The circumstances that brought it about were part of the most dramatic change in the course of the war since it had begun in 1914.

Hard times

For the British and French on the Western Front, 1917 had ended disappointingly. The British Third Army had scored a major success at Cambrai on 20 November, when an attack led by 381 tanks penetrated eight kilometres. But the 275 000 casualties that Third Ypres cost robbed Field Marshal Haig of the reserves he needed to exploit the breach and the Germans regained most of the ground. Meanwhile 11 British and French divisions had to be sent to shore up the Italians after they disintegrated in the face of an Austrian attack, masterminded and spearheaded by the Germans, at Caporetto in October. At the same time Lenin's Bolsheviks seized control in Russia. They concluded a ceasefire with the Germans in December, enabling the Germans to transfer 35 divisions westwards. Officially First Quartermaster-General but really de facto commander-in-chief, General Erich Ludendorff planned to use this new-found strength in a decisive blow before the American build-up tilted the strategic scales against the Germans. He intended to shatter the BEF. With the northern flank of the Western Front sundered, the French would collapse in turn.

Operation *Michael* dwarfed all previous attacks. It was to be launched on the 80-kilometre front between Croisilles, near Arras, and La Fère on the Oise. Advancing first on Bapaume and Péronne respectively, the Seventeenth Army on the right and the Second Army in the centre would then cross the old Somme battlefield and swing north-west, enveloping Arras and driving the BEF back towards the Channel. As well as protecting the left flank, the Eighteenth Army was to draw in French reserves that might help the British, and sever the connection between the British and the French. Over 6500 guns, 3500 mortars and more than 700 aircraft would support the three armies.

Knowing what was coming, the BEF went over to the defensive for the first time since 1915. This change involved more than a major shift in mindset from the offensive outlook that had dominated in the years since. While the BEF was doing most of the attacking in 1917, the French had held most of the line. Now that the BEF would be defending, Haig had to give in to French insistence that the British hold more of the line. He had to take over an extra 40 kilometres of trenches between Arras and St Quentin, behind which aerial reconnaissance detected the most extensive preparations for the German attack. But the need to retain the Channel ports required Haig to be strongest further north. Part of the German blow would therefore strike the Third Army, whose 14 divisions held 45 kilometres of front either side of Arras. Holding a 60-kilometre front that included the old French line with only 15 divisions, the Fifth Army under General Gough stood in the way of the main thrust.

Michael

At 4.40 am on 21 March 1918, the most spectacular offensive of the war opened. It 'seemed as though the bowels of the earth had erupted', said a British soldier on the receiving end of the bombardment. Storm troops advanced like a tide surging over a rocky shore, penetrating at weak points, ignoring their flanks and bypassing strongpoints, which the following waves took out. The right of the Third Army was pushed back but the Fifth Army crumbled. By 23 March the Germans had opened a breach 64 kilometres wide. The French took over

Lightly equipped for rapid movement, storm troops attack. This photograph was probably taken during a training exercise.

Gough's right flank. His left passed to the Third Army after Haig made the Somme the boundary between it and the Fifth Army. Gough was left only with XIX Corps. Contrasting the dramatic advance in the south with the slower progress in the north, Ludendorff shifted the weight of the attack southwards. The Second Army was to advance astride the Somme towards the vital communications and railway centre of Amiens. But the artillery and logistics could not keep up when it reached the shattered ground of the 1916 Somme battlefield on 25 March. Ordering the drive on Amiens to continue, Ludendorff strengthened the right wing of the Eighteenth Army, which was still advancing rapidly alongside the Second against the French.

Australians

Holding the line around Messines, the Australians could see that the outcome of the war was being decided. They itched to enter the fight. On 25 March, the day that Bapaume fell, the 3rd and 4th Divisions boarded buses and trains

for the move south. Temporarily attached to the British 62nd Division in IV Corps, the 4th Brigade occupied Hébuterne, a village 13 kilometres north of Albert and towards the northern end of the 1916 Somme battlefield, late next day. Reports of German tanks had led to a panicky withdrawal from it and from the line down to the Ancre near Hamel seven kilometres south. The Australians just beat the Germans to the punch. On 27 March the 4th Brigade beheld wave after wave of Germans advancing with wagons and guns strung out behind them. It held the tide and stayed at Hébuterne until 25 April.

New Zealanders

Having spent three tough months in the Ypres salient, the New Zealand Division was in reserve around Hazebrouck when the Germans struck. Also joining IV Corps, with which it spent the rest of the war, it began filling in the gap from the Ancre northwards on 26 March. Spreading five kilometres along the ridge between Englebelmer and Auchonvillers, 1st Rifles

Germans captured by the 4th Brigade assembled outside the brigade headquarters in Hébuterne.

A New Zealander mans a captured German machine-gun in a trench near La Signy Farm.

had several sharp fights while setting up an outpost screen from which the 1st and 2nd Brigades could advance eastwards to a more secure line between Serre and Hamel. With the battalions arriving holus-bolus and no time to organise them into their parent brigades, they were temporarily thrown together in makeshift ones. The 1st and 2nd Brigades became B and A Brigades respectively. Attacking across the D174, which passed through Auchonvillers, and either side of the D919, over ground seamed by old trenches, they met fierce resistance from the sugar factory at the junction of these two roads, from One Tree Hill to the south of the D919, and from La Signy Farm and its screening position, Jeremiah Hedge, to the north. Though A Brigade

reached its objective overlooking Hamel, B Brigade was stopped well short of Serre. But another attack early on 27 March by a third composite brigade further left linked up with the Australians in Hébuterne, thereby plugging the gap between the village and the Ancre.

The New Zealanders joined the Australians in repelling the strong German attacks in the afternoon, although the Germans gained some ground north of the D919. On 28 March a shell mortally wounded the 3rd Brigade's commander, Brigadier-General Harry Fulton. One Tree Hill, La Signy Farm and Jeremiah Hedge were finally taken on 30 March. This success, in which the New Zealanders inflicted 600 casualties on the Germans and captured 110 machine-guns, gave a tremendous fillip to the BEF, which had been on the backfoot since 21 March. It hinted strongly that the worst of *Michael* was over. Of the attacks on 5 April that were among its last gasps, the one against the New Zealanders was the biggest that they ever experienced. Though La Signy Farm was lost, the New Zealanders easily held the rest of their line. Lasting 10 days and costing almost 2500 men, their part in stemming the Germans was the only time that they were involved in a defensive battle on the Western Front.

The humdrum of trench warfare now returned for the New Zealand Division. In July it occupied the 4th Australian Brigade's old trenches, which extended north from Hébuterne towards Rossignol Wood. After the Germans abandoned the wood on 19 July, the New Zealanders steadily made ground beyond it. Sergeant Richard Travis VC of 2nd Otagos, perhaps their greatest front-line soldier, fell on 25 July in one of these 'nibbling' advances. On 13 August the Germans withdrew eastwards to Puisieux. New Zealand patrols harassed the Germans in the village before the New Zealanders captured it in their slice of a set-piece attack on a 15-kilometre frontage by five divisions from the Third Army on 21 August. New Zealand's part in the advance to victory had begun.

The ruins of Hébuterne.

DRIVING THE BATTLEFIELD

Three points about this tour. Driving is necessary for a short distance on the D919, which can be very busy. So be careful. As parking is at a premium on stretches of the tour, you will sometimes have to swing up onto the verges of the roads. So be extra careful. Next, the tour lies within the area of the 1916 Somme offensive. The Germans had surged effortlessly over ground originally captured from them at horrendous cost, which made men reflect. The Australians certainly did. Every man in the old I ANZAC, Charles Bean wrote, asked himself the same question, 'Will he take Pozières?' The Germans did on 26 March. Pozières is just a few kilometres east. I ANZAC had shed more blood there than anywhere else.

MAPS IGN Blue Series, 1:25 000, 24070 Acheux-en-Amienois; 2407E Bapaume

The line established by the New Zealanders on the morning of 26 March as seen from the D174. 1st Auckland lost heavily on this road during the afternoon attack.

From the roundabout between the basilica and the railway station in Albert, take the D50 exit (direction Aveluy). Continue on the D50 through Aveluy to Hamel, turning left there onto the D73 for Auchonvillers.

Shortly after cresting the steep spur above **Hamel**, you will see the **Newfoundland Memorial Park** on the right. The first few of the widely dispersed posts in the screen established by 1st Rifles were 1.3 kilometres to your left, on the distant high ground in front of Englebelmer. Advancing through the screen at 2.15 pm on 26 March, 1st Canterbury in A Brigade made Hamel secure by occupying the crest on your immediate left and the old British trench system that ran through the park. The Canterbury's line continued along the crest on the right of the D73 to the far side of **Auchonvillers**, which everyone called Ocean Villas, 1.5 kilometres further on. At the crossroads in Auchonvillers, turn right onto the D163 and look along it on reaching the junction with the D174 after 400 metres ❶. In its initial encounter in the morning, 1st Rifles drove back German patrols 450 metres to your front. In A Brigade's afternoon attack, 2nd Canterbury passed through your location under fire but pressed on until their left flank lay over the spur 450 metres to your left front.

NEWFOUNDLAND MEMORIAL PARK

KILOMETRE LANE

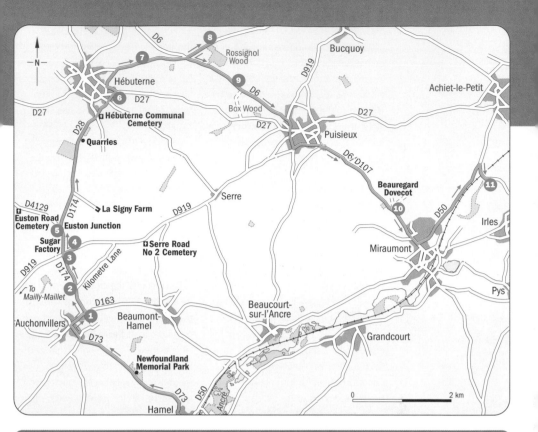

Starting from the area that the New Zealanders held when they arrived on the battlefield, this drive retraces the front line to the D919/174 intersection, around which the heaviest fighting occurred. Passing next through Hébuterne, which the 4th Australian Brigade defended, the route continues via the site of Sergeant Travis's VC exploit at Rossignol Wood to Puisieux before ending on the Ancre heights reached by the New Zealanders near Miraumont.

DISTANCE COVERED: 23 km
DURATION: 3 hours

Heading left on the D174, stop after 500 metres at **Kilometre Lane** ② on the right and look along it. The insignificant knoll to the right of where it crosses the spur to your front is **One Tree Hill**, which the Germans held. Now look along the D174. The **sugar factory** was on the far side of the farm complex 700 metres to your front. Crossing the D174 there, the D919 continues along the crest of the spur ahead of you. Extending beyond your location from Auchonvillers along the slope on your left, 1st Rifles fought their way past Germans on the D174 between Kilometre Lane and the sugar factory, and halted a German advance along the D919 from your right towards the factory. By 11 am 1st Rifles had established their left flank to the left of the factory but the flank lay open. They could do little about the Germans on One Tree Hill, who enfiladed 2nd Canterbury's left flank on the high ground to your right rear.

Continue to the **D174/D919 crossroads** ③ and park. The main buildings of the sugar factory were on the northwest corner. Walk along the D919 past the farm buildings until you have a clear view down the road. The left flank of 1st Rifles rested on the slight rise 500 metres ahead. Given that their right was way beyond Auchonvillers, you should now have a good grasp of the extremely wide frontage the Rifles were holding. Most of the New Zealand battalions entered the battle through **Mailly-Maillet**, 1.2 kilometres beyond the rise. Starting from the village at 5.30 pm on 26 March, B Brigade passed through the Rifles and advanced towards your location with 1st Auckland on the left of the D919 and 2nd Rifles on the right. Machine-guns around the sugar factory were a thorn in the side of both battalions.

Leaving a trail of dead and wounded, the Aucklanders' right sheltered in the D174 while the left continued over it. 2nd Rifles to your right front had an easier time. Concealed by the smoke from a burning ammunition dump until they were almost on the factory, they cleared the Germans in it and on the D174 to your right.

Returning to the crossroads, carry on for another 300 metres on the D919 to the end of the power lines ④ and look down the road. **Serre Road No. 2**, the large cemetery on the right of the D919 in the low ground to your front, is roughly midway between your location and **Serre** hamlet, through which the D919 passes on the high ground beyond. The scene of dreadful fighting in 1916, Serre was B Brigade's objective. The straggly line of trees and bushes to your left front, through which the power lines pass, is the remains of **Jeremiah Hedge**, which started just this side of Serre No. 2 and continued along the crest to your left. Fire from it caused steady loss to 2nd Rifles during their advance. Behind the hedge and directly in line with the power lines is La Signy Farm. One Tree Hill is barely distinguishable at the end of the spur running off to your right, on the far side of Kilometre Lane 500 metres distant.

Knocking out a machine-gun in a trench that ran along the left side of the D919, 2nd Rifles consolidated on a line that started on the road 150 metres ahead of you and cut diagonally across the front of Jeremiah Hedge to the D174 to your left rear. When darkness fell, 1st Auckland's right bayonet charged across the D174 to your right rear. Maddened by their earlier losses, they were merciless

Fritz seemed to have the range to a yard and his shells and bullets from machine-guns and rifles simply deafened one. The screech of bullets was awful and our men began to fall rapidly.

Private Jesse Stayte on the fire as the Aucklanders approached the sugar factory (quoted in Harper, G, *Dark Journey*, Auckland, 2007, p. 228)

JEREMIAH HEDGE

SERRE ROAD NO 2 CEMETERY

2ND RIFLES 26 MARCH

LEFT OF 1ST AUCKLAND 26 MARCH

GERMANS 27 MARCH

D919

and took few prisoners in drawing level with 2nd Rifles and the rest of the Aucklanders. But the Auckland line was still short of One Tree Hill on your right. 2nd Auckland reinforced 1st Auckland that night. The German counterattacks on 27 March stretched left to right across your front and beyond Auchonvillers. Supremely confident, the Germans marched laughing and smoking in column of fours along the D919 towards you in the morning. The New Zealanders let them get within 50 metres before opening fire. Against the Canterburys further right in the afternoon, the Germans barely got within bombing range. Attacking on your left on the afternoon of 30 March, Easter Sunday, 2nd Auckland, with 4th Rifles on their left, caught the Germans napping and took

Jeremiah Hedge and La Signy Farm. Now in full possession of the high ground, the New Zealanders had the same uninterrupted views over the ground to your front as you do.

Return to your car and continue on the D174 to **Euston Junction** ❺, the Y-junction 500 metres along. **Hébuterne** can be seen 2.5 kilometres further on. Look down the D174, which follows the crest of a flat spur towards it. Euston Road, the D4129, runs to your left front past **Euston Road Cemetery**, 600 metres distant, and on towards **Colincamps**, one kilometre past the cemetery and out of sight. From your right rear, Jeremiah Hedge cut diagonally midway between your location and **La Signy Farm**, on the crest to your right front, to meet the D174 700 metres

The remains of Jeremiah Hedge from the D919. The Germans marched up this road seemingly oblivious to the New Zealanders' presence on the morning of 27 March.

> It was like corn before the sicle [sic], machine-guns cracked, every one of the enemy fell like ninepins, horses struggled on the ground, those who did escape flew in a panic and there was congestion all along the road. The dead were heaped on top of one another, the German red-cross were carrying away the corpses for three days afterwards.
>
> Private James McWhirter recalls the moment when the Germans on the D919 were engaged (quoted in Harper, G, *Dark Journey*, p. 240)

One Tree Hill from the D919. The Germans held it stubbornly. Their counterattacks on 27 March crossed this ground.

ahead at the farm's entrance track. Crossing the D174 behind you in B Brigade's 5.30 pm advance on 26 March, the left of 2nd Rifles reached a line that ran 300 metres this side of Jeremiah Hedge, through your location and along Euston Road to the cemetery area. The 4th Australian Brigade reached Hébuterne about the same time. That night the Australians established a line around the right of the village and along the side of it facing you.

At dawn on 27 March, the third composite brigade surged across the fields to your left front. Whipped by fire from La Signy Farm, 2nd Wellington nearer you halted 400 metres short of the D174. In a flawless advance on the left of the Wellingtons, 3rd Rifles took the Germans by surprise, crossed the D174 and linked up with the Australians in Hébuterne. A witness remarked of this bayonet charge that it was 'quite like a moving picture show and quite the old style of things'. The ANZAC line was now unbroken from Hamel to Hébuterne. Four counterattacks came from your right

during the afternoon. The Germans advanced in columns behind leaders carrying small red flags like tour guides in crowded public attractions. Despite the Germans' covering bombardment, the New Zealanders could hear the blasts of the leaders' signal whistles. Only in the last attack, at 7 pm, was any ground lost when the Wellingtons to your left front were driven back 100 metres. Their counterattack failed, leaving the Germans holding a trench along the D174 for 1.2 kilometres from a point 400 metres ahead of you.

After relieving the Wellingtons, 4th Rifles attacked twice on 28 March and gained 100 metres of this trench at the end nearer you. In the larger set-piece attack on 30 March, in which 2nd Auckland rolled through Jeremiah Hedge to your right rear to take La Signy Farm, 4th Rifles reached the hedge to your right but could not dislodge the Germans from the D174 trench further along. Part of 2nd Rifles, which had earlier relieved the 3rd, joined the 4th in a fresh attack at nightfall that took the D174 up to the entrance track to La Signy Farm. A concurrent advance by 2nd Rifles from the far end of the D174 trench towards the track flushed out the Germans in that stretch. The meeting of the 2nd and 4th Rifles on the D174 signalled the recapture of all the ground lost on 27 March.

Now face La Signy Farm. At 5 am on 5 April your location was inundated by part of the heaviest and longest bombardment ever experienced by the New Zealanders. But casualties were light because much of the shooting was short and the wet ground muffled the explosions. When the Germans advanced against the entire New Zealand Line just after 8.30 am, their assault fell heaviest on the stretch, held by the Rifle Brigade, between Hébuterne and the Farm. As the Germans came towards you, those caught in the open on the crest dissolved before withering fire, while New Zealand bombers waiting in the old communication trenches and saps that ran back over the crest blocked those moving along them. Company cooks brought up tea for the front-line men

during the action. The attack failed but another one at 10.30 am took La Signy Farm, the Germans' lone success of the day. The Rifles pulled back to Jeremiah Hedge in front of you to seal off the breach. Their Lewis-gunners and bombers took a fearful toll of the Germans trying to advance further.

Continue along the D174, over which the fighting ebbed and flowed between 27 and 30 March. Note how the ground falls away slightly on either side; note also the track to La Signy Farm heading off on the right. As you approach Hébuterne, keep an eye out for the **Pension de Canine** dog kennels just past the copse on the right. This was the site of the quarries that 3rd Rifles captured on 28 March to improve the observation from the top end of the New Zealand Division's line. The attack was supported from Hébuterne by Australian machine-guns and mortars. Once past the copse, look to your left front. When the 4th Brigade occupied Hébuterne late on 26 March, the 16th Battalion on its right flank stretched leftwards along the side

The fighting along the D174 between Euston Junction and Hébuterne.

FROM LA SIGNY FARM TO PUISIEUX **1918** 297

LA SIGNY FARM

JEREMIAH HEDGE

The view from the D174 along the axis of the New Zealand attack on La Signy Farm on 30 March.

of the village facing you. The 16th poured enfilade fire into the right of the German attack on 5 April, which advanced from your right towards the road. Captain Charles Ahrens told his superiors, 'Don't be alarmed as we can kill 'em as fast as they come'. Stretching around the village to your right front, the 13th and 15th Battalions also riddled the assault. Their enfilade fire broke up the waves of Germans that had attacked over the same ground on the afternoon of 27 March before they even got close to the 16th.

Drive through the crossroads on the outskirts of Hébuterne, passing **Hébuterne Communal Cemetery** on your right. Engaged by at least three machine-guns in the cemetery as they advanced from your left on 26 March, the 13th Battalion established a line along the trees to your left, down the road to your front and around the right of the village. The cemetery was cleared two nights later. Continue through the next crossroads, park immediately after

turning right onto the D27 at the **T-junction ⑥** and look along the road. Relieving an isolated company of the 9th Welch, the 15th Battalion occupied the section of pre–Somme 1916 British support line that ran from the junction across the high ground to your left front. The 14th later extended the Australian line further left. Now walk 100 metres down the D27 to Rue de Cavin. Though cloaked by long grass, the trenches and dugouts of the old Somme battlefield stretched three kilometres ahead of you, seamed here and there by rusting belts of barbed wire. Look to your right to appreciate how well the 15th Battalion behind you and the 13th to your right front could enfilade the Germans attacking left to right in the middle distance through the old diggings on 27 March.

Return to your car, turn left onto Rue de Cavin and head right at the T-junction beyond the cutting onto the **Voie Vieux Moulin**. Turn right at the next junction

GERMANS 27 MARCH

The ground over which the Germans advanced against the 4th Brigade on the outskirts of Hébuterne.

for **Gommecourt British Cemetery No. 2** ⑦ at the bottom of the hill. Some of the hardest fighting of the 1916 Somme campaign occurred in this area. With the cemetery on your left, look along the road, which puts **Rossignol Wood** on the skyline to your front. On 28 March the 62nd Division's right flank was just to the left of the wood. Running along the spur to your front, the 4th Brigade's left flank rested on the Germans' 1916 front line, which crossed the spur in front of the copse to your half right. Australian bombing attacks closed the gap between the two on 29 March.

Now drive over the crossroads with the D6 one kilometre ahead, and continue uphill to the left of Rossignol Wood for another 650 metres to the clear area on the right opposite a **track** ⑧. Face right, so that the near face of the wood is on your right. After paralleling the far side of the wood and then the road along which you have just driven, the New Zealanders' line in July 1918 swung through your location and paralleled the near face of the wood before cutting left to **Biez Wood**, the large wood on your left. On 15 July 2nd Canterbury charged across your front towards Rossignol Wood, while 1st Canterbury did the same from your right. Squeezed from both directions, the

Germans evacuated the wood on 19 July. The New Zealanders occupied it next day and then began 'nibbling' away at the Germans still ahead of them.

Return to the crossroads, turn left on the D6 and stop after 600 metres at the **track** ⑨ on the left, which crosses a small knoll. With your back to Rossignol Wood, look along the D6. Having run up from the low ground over your right shoulder, **Hawk Trench** cut left near the pylon on your right and crossed the D6 180 metres ahead of you. Branching off trenches that tracked on the left of the D6 to the knoll, **Slug Trench** crossed the D6 250 metres behind you to meet Hawk Trench under the power lines. On 24 July 1st and 2nd Otago and 1st Auckland sought to clear all of these trenches. Sergeant Travis knocked out two machine-guns in Slug Trench that held up the right of the attack, killing their crews. Continuing down the trench, he skittled four more Germans as they charged towards him. Arriving at Hawk Trench, Travis grabbed some bombers and captured the 250-metre stretch of it to the D6. Almost single-handedly assuring the success of the attack, he was awarded the VC. A shell killed him next morning.

Continue along the D6 towards **Puisieux**, to which the Germans fell back

62ND DIVISION

ROSSIGNOL WOOD

4TH AUSTRALIAN BRIGADE

The gap between the 62nd Division and the 4th Australian Brigade at Rossignol Wood.

on 13 August with the New Zealanders on their heels. Advancing in IV Corps between the British 37th and 42nd Divisions on the left and right respectively, the 3rd Brigade from the New Zealand Division was to take the village and continue to the Ancre 2.2 kilometres beyond it in the Third Army's attack on 21 August. As you approach the outskirts of Puisieux, look out for **Box Wood**, a copse in the low ground on the right of the D6. The New Zealanders' start line crossed the road at this point. Extending along it onto the high ground beyond the wood was 3rd Rifles, while 4th Rifles stretched 1.1 kilometres to the left of the D6. Launched in dense fog at 5 am behind an excellent creeping barrage, the attack took the Germans by surprise. On entering Puisieux, turn right at the T-junction onto the D919, carry on over the crossroads with the D27 and turn left 400 metres further on at the next crossroads onto the D6/D107. Perhaps

the strongest resistance in a relatively easy assault came from the cemetery area on the right at the far end of the village, where five machine-guns were captured. By 6 am both battalions were digging in on the **Blue Line** either side of the road just past the wood on the left.

From this point, the New Zealanders' frontage narrowed to the apex of a triangle. While the 42nd Division continued to the high ground to your front and the 5th Division passed through 4th Rifles on your left, A Company of 3rd Rifles advanced along the low ground on your immediate left. Continue for another 1.9 kilometres on the D107 to the road that bends sharply back on the left opposite a small wood on the right and park on the track running off the right of this road ❿. Look down the track. A Company was to have waited in the low ground to your front while the 42nd Division took the **Beauregard Dovecot** strongpoint

Sergeant Richard Travis

A legend in the New Zealand Division, probably the best-known New Zealand soldier of the First World War

1884–1918

A horsebreaker and farmhand, Travis was born Dickson Savage at Opotiki in 1884 but severed all family ties and changed his name after a troubled youth. He enlisted in August 1914. The reputation he had gained by the end the Gallipoli campaign for nocturnal scouting and patrolling in no-man's-land burgeoned on the Western Front. Promoted soon after being awarded the DCM for polishing off several snipers that had troubled 2nd Otagos during the New Zealand Division's attack at Flers on 15 September 1916, he took charge of the Otagos' six-man sniper and observation section. Dubbed 'Travis's Gang', it became highly proficient at mapping German defences and grabbing prisoners to gain information. Travis also carried on lone patrols for the same purposes. A small man at 165 centimetres tall and weighing less than 56 kilograms, he was blasé about rank and dress but meticulous in his military work. He received the MM in May 1918. His death in July threw the entire New Zealand Division, which knew him as the 'king of no-man's-land' and the 'prince of scouts', into mourning.

on the crest to your left, opposite the wood. When the fog lifted at 10 am, the Dovecot was still in German hands but A Company, having overshot, was on the side of the spur to your right front overlooking the railway in full view of the Germans in the Ancre Valley. Under heavy machine-gun fire, it pulled back to the low ground ahead of you, where it should have been.

Troops from the 42nd Division reached the Dovecot during the afternoon but were pushed off by a German counterattack from **Miraumont**, on your right, next morning, which was again foggy. Seeing some Germans moving

The scene of Sergeant Travis's VC action.

A section post of the 2nd Canterbury utilises a derelict tank in front of Rossignol Wood in July 1918.

down the slope towards A Company, Lance-Corporal Robert Milne and his Lewis-gun team charged them, killing 12, taking five prisoner, and capturing four machine-guns. The lifting of the fog prevented the Germans going further. They lost the Dovecot but then regained it. During the night 1st Rifles relieved the 3rd. Attacking from your left at 2.30 am on 23 August as part of a further advance by IV Corps, the 42nd swept over the Dovecot, while 1st Rifles on its left advanced across your front over the lower end of the spur almost to the railway. At 11 am 1st Rifles swept over the railway to the left of Miraumont and on to the high ground on the far side of the Ancre.

Continue on the D107 to Miraumont and take the second street on the left, the D50 (Rue d'Achiet), which runs alongside the railway once clear of the village. 1st Rifles advanced from your left, across the track, to the wooded high ground on your right. Follow the D50 as it veers left, away from the railway, and take the first road on the right, which cuts back sharply to cross the track. As the road heads up the slope, look right. The line established by 1st Rifles ran roughly along the line of the wood stretching away to your right ⓫. Now proceed to the T-junction with the D163 on the outskirts of **Irles**, which was captured by the 5th Division on the right of IV Corps's advance on 23 August. 1st Rifles and the 42nd Division had protected the 5th Division's right flank.

To return to Albert, turn right on the D163. On reaching Miraumont, turn left onto the D50 at the crossroads just beyond the railway bridge and continue to Albert. New Zealanders wanting to start the Bapaume battlefield tour should turn left on the D163. Head left again immediately past the two trees on the right of the road 2.1 kilometres along, and drive another 650 metres to the barn on the left at an offset five-ways intersection.

LOCAL INFORMATION

CEMETERIES

Euston Road Cemetery

Started as a front-line cemetery during the disastrous attack on Serre at the beginning of the Somme offensive on 1 July 1916, the cemetery remained in use until the front line moved well to the east when the Germans withdrew to the Hindenburg Line in March 1917. It was put back in service soon after the fighting returned to the area with the German *Michael* offensive in March 1918, and again after the war when graves were brought in from smaller cemeteries and the surrounding battlefields. Of its 1293 burials, 170 of them unknown, 302 are New Zealanders and 26 are Australian. The cemetery can be reached by taking the left fork at Euston Junction on the tour route.

Hébuterne Military Cemetery

Begun by the British in 1915 and used until early 1917, the cemetery was re-opened in 1918. The layout is as it was at the end of the war. It reflects the conditions under which burials were done, which, in turn, accounts for the irregularity of the rows. Of the 757 burials, 712 are known. The 53 New Zealanders, who fell in the area between April and August 1918, include Private Benjamin Morris of the New Zealand (Maori) Pioneer Battalion at I.L.1. To reach the cemetery from the tour route, turn left at the crossroads by Hébuterne Communal Cemetery and left again at the T-junction onto Rue de la Place. Continue to the village green, from where the cemetery is signposted.

Gommecourt British Cemetery No. 2

Visited on the battlefield drive, this cemetery was one of four begun in the Gommecourt area in 1917 when the German withdrawal to the Hindenburg Line allowed the 1916 Somme battlefield to be cleared. The burials from the other three were relocated postwar to Gommecourt No. 2, which now comprises 1357 burials, 682 of them unknown. Some 46 New Zealanders and 26 Australians rest here.

CHAPTER 15

1918

DERNANCOURT AND MORLANCOURT

The major Australian actions during the *Michael* offensive occurred on the Ancre and Somme Rivers south of Albert. Under cultivation, or covered in grass on which sheep and cattle grazed, and almost devoid of shell holes or trenches, the battlefield was pristine. The 3rd and 4th Divisions, less the 4th Brigade, began arriving in this bucolic setting shortly after General Ferdinand Foch was made Allied generalissimo at a landmark meeting between the British and French at Doullens on 26 March 1918. The Allies now had something like a supreme commander. With the Germans striving for Amiens, Foch had insisted at this meeting that there must be no more retreats. 'We must fight in front of Amiens', he thundered. 'We must fight where we are now.'

Amiens had been left wide open almost as Foch spoke. Lieutenant-General Sir Walter Congreve VC, commander of VII Corps, had misinterpreted an earlier order to retire only if 'the tactical situation imperatively demands it' as a direction to fall back regardless. Holding the Third Army's right flank north of the Somme, VII Corps swung behind the Ancre, leaving the seven-kilometre front across Morlancourt Ridge, in the triangle of ground between the two rivers, virtually undefended. The defences were in a poor state anyway. Straddling the triangle between Ribemont-sur Ancre, 7.5 kilometres southwest of Albert, and Sailly-le-Sec on the Somme, the Amiens Defence Line had been dug by the French in 1915 to protect Amiens. As the war had seemingly moved on, local farmers were filling it in before *Michael* broke. Now a scratch force, screened by British cavalry, held it. Dismembered by *Michael*, the Fifth Army under General Gough consisted only of XIX Corps, whose left flank rested on the Somme 9.6 kilometres beyond the Defence Line. Should the Germans jump the Somme in this gap, they could outflank the Fifth Army and hurtle along the southern bank of the river before recrossing to turn the Third Army's right flank. They would then have a clear run to Amiens.

'Thank heavens — the Australians at last!'

The calamity brought the Australians to the Somme. Keen to enter the region in which its sister divisions had been cut up so badly in 1916, the 3rd Division arrived from Doullens amid some of the most memorable scenes in the AIF's experience. 'You're going the wrong way, Digger. Jerry'll souvenir you', retreating British troops shouted. Hordes of French refugees shuffled westwards with whatever belongings they could carry. 'English soldat no bon!', they said, before shouting 'Vive l'Australie!', and embracing 'Nos Australiens!' Hearing the Diggers say 'Fini retreat — beaucoup Australiens ici', which quickly became a great Australian national statement, many returned to their villages.

'Thank heavens — the Australians at last', Congreve gasped when General Monash reached his headquarters at 1 am on 27 March. He directed Monash to occupy the triangle. The 3rd Division began streaming in at 8 am and deployed without interference. Meeting Congreve just after Monash, General Sinclair-MacLagan of the 4th Division was told to secure the high ground on the Ancre. The 12th Brigade relieved the 9th Division, which was strung out along the embankment of the railway that ran alongside the Ancre from German-held Albert through Dernancourt and Ribemont. The 13th Brigade took up a support position behind the D929, the Amiens–Albert road, which followed the crest of the slope that overlooked the Ancre and the railway.

Advancing along the triangle later on 27 March, the Germans tried to cross to the southern bank of the Somme between Sailly-le-Sec and Sailly-Laurette, 1.5 kilometres further east. Monash's men in the Amiens Defence Line watched the cavalry in the screen ahead holding them off. Perhaps the most notable event of the day was Gough's replacement by General Rawlinson, who had led the Fourth Army during the 1916 Somme offensive and was currently the British member of the new inter-allied staff. Gough had become the scapegoat that the British mauling at the hands of *Michael* demanded.

A 3rd Division Lewis-gun crew on the Somme above Sailly-le-Sec at the end of March 1918. The men are looking towards Sailly-Laurette: the spire of its church can be seen on the left of the photo. The Australians and the Germans both got beltings when they attacked across this ground.

Mixed success

On 28 March Congreve told Monash that Foch wanted more ground gained in the triangle to pave the way for an offensive by the Third Army. Monash ordered an afternoon attack towards Morlancourt, three kilometres east. The 10th Brigade laid on a formal assault by the 40th Battalion on the left of the D1, the Bray–Corbie road, which runs along the crest of the ridge. Monash's orders arrived too late for the 11th Brigade on the right of the D1 to replace a plan to grab the ground ahead using patrols with one for an attack alongside the 10th Brigade. When the 40th Battalion advanced unsupported at 5.13 pm, it was soon stopped by intense fire. The 39th Battalion shored up the left flank of the 40th at dusk. Not until late evening did the 41st and 44th Battalions from the 11th Brigade assault. Trying to take Sailly-Laurette, they were ambushed well short. The 3rd Division lost 300 men.

Dernancourt as seen from the air at the end of May 1918. The Australians held the railway embankment against two German attacks, which came from right to left. They smashed the first one but were forced off the embankment in the second.

On the Ancre the story was different. Approaching from Albert and along the river to Dernancourt, the Germans attacked the 47th and 48th Battalions along the railway embankment. Holding a frontage of well over 2.5 kilometres, the two battalions were spread wafer thin in widely separated posts. Though vastly outnumbered, the 47th and 48th, with the 19th Northumberland Fusiliers from the British 35th Division on their right, saw off nine assaults. Sergeant Stanley McDougall of the 47th broke up the first by hosing the Germans with a Lewis-gun as he ran along the embankment. He won the VC. Running out of bombs mid-morning, the 47th pelted the Germans with rocks. Rain set in during the afternoon and the line went quiet. Having gone 72 hours without sleep by then, the 12th Brigade was exhausted.

On 30 March the Germans advanced in daylight against the 3rd Division, just as the 3rd had done against them two days before. The Australians disdained cover in their excitement to shoot at a target they had only ever dreamed of. Three times the Germans came on; three times the 11th Brigade 'swept their lines, wiping them out one after the other', Monash wrote. 'The ground in front of us was literally covered with enemy dead.'

Dernancourt again

On 5 April 1918 the Germans struck the Australians and New Zealanders with the heaviest attacks that they faced on the Western Front. The New Zealanders were hit near Hébuterne, the Australians at Dernancourt. Since the assault on 28 March, the 4th Australian Division had beaten off sporadic probes against its posts along the railway embankment. The pioneers had also dug Pioneer Trench, a strong reserve line on the heights 2.2 kilometres behind it. An old trench 900 metres in front of Pioneer Trench was used as a

support line. But the long, bare slope between these two trenches, and between the support line and the front line on the railway embankment 1.3 kilometres ahead, precluded reinforcement of the front line during daylight. To prevent the Germans capturing the embankment and possibly breaking through on the Ancre to Amiens, General Sinclair-MacLagan on 4 April ordered it held as the divisional 'main line of resistance'. Mist had reduced visibility to 150 metres when the Germans attacked at 9.30 am next morning, intending to reach the D929 and swing southwest for Amiens.

As before, the attack fell mainly on the 47th and 48th Battalions of the 12th Brigade. The bombardment pummelled Pioneer Trench and the support line, and cut communications to the railway embankment. One Stokes mortar battery lobbed 370 bombs, its entire supply, into the Germans massing on the far side of the embankment. But the Australian posts strung out along it went without artillery support because the mist hid their signalling rockets. Sheer weight of

The railway embankment at the end of the war. This was the scene of Sergeant McDougall's VC action.

numbers eventually told. After three attempts, the Germans overran the right of the 47th Battalion at Dernancourt at 10 am. The 52nd Battalion from the 13th Brigade, which had relieved the 35th Division further right, the rest of the 47th and the 48th on its left pulled back, first to the support line and then to Pioneer Trench. Counterattacking from it at 5.15 pm, the 45th and 49th Battalions regained the support line. The 4th Division had lost 1100 men. Newly arrived from Messines, the 2nd Division relieved it.

Following days

With *Michael* now all but dead, the Australians took the fight to the Germans. April marked the start of 'peaceful penetration', whereby patrols used stealth to ambush, cut off posts and take prisoners. Monash also sought to maintain the pressure on the Germans with a series of minor attacks towards the spur above Morlancourt, the objective of the abortive advance on 28 March. It proved elusive once again. The last of the attacks, on 7 May, secured only a foothold. Returning to the line after a brief rest, the 2nd Division relieved the 3rd. It also adopted an aggressive policy. On 19 May the 6th Brigade took Ville-sur-Ancre, on the river below Morlancourt. Sergeant William Ruthven of the 22nd Battalion rallied the faltering right flank of the attack and was awarded the VC. In the next advance, on 10 June, the 7th Brigade firmly established itself on the spur.

Not all of the action had been on the ground. On 21 April Sergeant Cedric Popkin of the 4th Australian Machine-Gun Battalion accounted for the most famous fighter pilot of all time by bringing down Baron Manfred von Richthofen near Vaux-sur-Somme. Known as the Red Baron after the colour of his aircraft, von Richthofen was the war's top-scoring ace.

'Peaceful penetration'

The British press had used this term to describe the spread of prewar German trade through the Empire. The Australians adopted it to describe their pinching out of posts and sections of line. Peaceful penetration was rarely possible in 1916–17, when the German trenches were continuous and well defended. Short of formal attacks, raids were the only means of snatching short stretches of them and they could not be held for long even then. But the fluid conditions on the Somme and Ancre following the German offensive in 1918 were tailor-made for it, especially since the Germans, having expended their best troops, had to use inferior 'trench divisions' to man their line. Local advances through peaceful penetration became for the Australians a competitive private war that gave free rein to individual initiative, patience and field craft. They were not the only practitioners. With Sergeant Travis and his 'gang' at the forefront, the New Zealanders were also peacefully penetrating around Hébuterne. 'We get no sleep at nights', said a German captured by them. 'You have to look out like a watch-dog here. Otherwise Tommy comes over and snatches you out of your trench.'

Baron Manfred von Richthofen, the war's ace of aces with 80 kills.

DRIVING THE BATTLEFIELD

Ranging widely along the Ancre and Somme Valleys and the Morlancourt Ridge in between, this tour covers an area whose appearance has changed little since 1918. You can easily appreciate why the 3rd Division was exhilarated on its arrival. The heights are the real McCoy, not the folds that masquerade as heights on many of the battlefields on which the Australians fought. The views from them are breathtaking. You can also appreciate the one practical difficulty — apart from the Germans — that the Australians faced. Landmarks to use as reference points are lacking, which made it hard to locate advanced posts on ground covered by crops even 30 centimetres high. You should be aware of a modern practical difficulty: the D1 on the crest of the Morlancourt Ridge, which you will cross, re-cross and drive along, is long, straight and busy. BE CAREFUL.

MAP IGN Blue Series, 1:25 000, 24080 Albert

From the roundabout between the basilica and the railway station in Albert, take the D929 exit (direction Amiens) and head left at the Y-junction after 500 metres onto the D52 for Dernancourt. If coming from Amiens, turn sharp right onto the D52 300 metres after crossing the railway bridge on the outskirts of Albert.

Starting near the **railway bridge** on the D929, the Australian front line ran along the **railway embankment** on your right. The initial German attack at **Dernancourt** on 28 March came from your left and crossed the D52. On reaching the village, remain on the D52 but turn left after going through the

underpass in the embankment and then immediately right. Passing **Dernancourt Communal Cemetery and Extension**, continue up the slope to the crossroads just beyond the copse on your right, the site of the **quarry**, and head right. Stop after 250 metres, where a spur runs down into the valley on your right ❶, and face Dernancourt. The **underpass** is in front of you and the Golden Virgin atop the basilica in **Albert** is on your left. The **support line** followed the road on which you are standing.

The 12th and 13th Brigades had to prevent the Germans advancing to your front along the Ancre Valley from Albert and then cutting around to the D929, which leads straight to Amiens, on the crest 900 metres to your rear. From your location, the tricky defensive problem the Australians faced is obvious. The embankment had to be held as any German advance along the other side of it would be shielded otherwise. But the embankment curves around to your left, carrying the railway past the near side of Albert. The front line on it therefore formed a salient. If the Germans broke through on your left, the line to your front would be cut off, and vice versa if they broke through to your front. Reinforcing the embankment if a breakthrough threatened would be suicidal because the reinforcements would have to cross the exposed slope below you. Overgrown and lacking traverses, the support line was inadequate for defensive purposes. The French had earlier constructed it as a training trench. None of this mattered in the attack on 28 March, when the 48th Battalion occupied the embankment to your left front, the 47th on its right

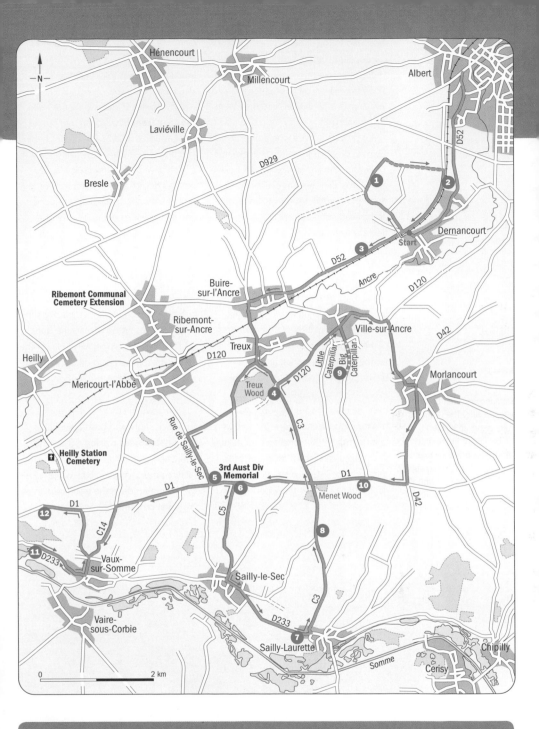

Passing through Dernancourt and covering the two German attacks there both from the heights above the village and from the railway embankment, this drive continues through the areas where the 3rd Division held the triangle between the Ancre and Somme and both the 2nd and 3rd Divisions slowly advanced along the Morlancourt Ridge between the two rivers. It also includes the sites of some notable peaceful penetration exploits, the VC actions and the Richthofen shoot down.

DISTANCE COVERED: 40.6 km

DURATION: 4 hours

extended to the underpass and the 35th Division stretched to your right front. Though two German divisions assaulted along the railway on this frontage, only a few Germans penetrated and they were soon dealt with.

But problems arose when three German divisions assaulted a week later. While the 48th Battalion wiped out wave after wave, the Germans eventually broke through the 47th next to the underpass and spread right and left, dragging a field-gun with them. The 52nd Battalion, holding the railway from the right of the underpass to **Buire-sur-l'Ancre**, 2.2 kilometres to your right, and the rest of the 47th were unaware of the breakthrough until they were fired on and shelled from behind. The remnants of the 47th and the left of 52nd withdrew up the slopes to your left and right respectively, while the 48th narrowly escaped being cut off as it pulled back over the crest to your left rear. Two machine-gun sections, one in the quarry and the other 300 metres to your front, were captured without firing a shot as the Germans swarmed towards the support line, held by the support companies of the 47th Battalion. Without traverses, it was indefensible because the

Germans could fire along it as soon as they reached it. Soon the line through your location was thick with the 47th's dead and wounded.

Fully traversed and two metres deep, **Pioneer Trench** had been dug on the crest astride the D929 900 metres behind you precisely for this eventuality. The trench gave the position some sorely needed depth, and the battalions on the embankment fell back past the support line to it. Having continued after them 300 metres beyond your location, the Germans were now blocked by Pioneer Trench. The 45th Battalion counterattacked from it to your right rear, while the 49th Battalion advanced from it directly behind you. Coming under 'a devilish fire, a tremendous tattoo of machine-guns', said Lieutenant-Colonel Alex Imlay of the 47th Battalion watching on, they drove the Germans back to the support line either side of you.

Now continue another 400 metres, turn sharp right and head downhill to the embankment, turning right at the T-junction there. Stop just before the railway enters a cutting by a white house on the other side of the tracks next to an old **level crossing** ❷. Sergeant McDougall's VC action on 28 March

Dernancourt from the support line. The Germans were repulsed at the embankment in the first attack but broke through in the second. The vulnerability of the embankment and the impossibility of reinforcing it in daylight are clearly evident.

DERNANCOURT

UNDERPASS

GERMANS 5 APRIL

occurred in this location. Look along the embankment towards Albert. Through the dawn mist McDougall heard the flap of bayonet scabbards against the thighs of marching troops. Running along the embankment to warn the next post of his platoon, 100 metres ahead of you, he saw a line of Germans emerging from the murk. Grabbing seven men from the platoon to fill in the gap between your location and the post, he started back but a bomb wounded the Lewis-gunner. Picking up the gun, McDougall wiped out the nearest Germans and ran along the embankment towards you, hosing the Germans he found crouched along it

and those trying to flee towards the Ancre on your right. About 50 Germans had managed to get into the field on your left. McDougall shot them up from the rear before Lieutenant Mitchell of the 48th Battalion charged them, revolver in hand. The Germans surrendered. Further along the embankment, the 48th defied heavy shelling and stood waist high to fire into the masses in front of it.

Carry on along this road. As you approach the underpass, you are passing the area in which the Germans broke through on 5 April. They scaled the embankment to the right of the underpass on 28 March but a charge by a section of

Sergeant McDougall's solo advance along the embankment towards the level-crossing by the house, which is where he was initially positioned. The few Germans who got past him were cleaned up by Lieutenant Mitchell's men.

the 12th Australian Machine-Gun Company and the 19th Northumberland Fusiliers bundled them off.

Picking up the D52 at the underpass, stop after 900 metres ❸ and look along the road towards Buire, 1.4 kilometres ahead. When the Germans fanned out from the underpass on 5 April, they streamed past your right to an abandoned **casualty clearing station** 300 metres to your right front. The 52nd Battalion swung your end of its line along the railway back behind the casualty clearing station to block the advance. When the 49th Battalion counterattacked over the crest to your right, the 52nd, reinforced by part of the 51st, joined it. Together they recaptured the casualty clearing station.

Continue to the crossroads at the far end of Buire, turn left and head over the Ancre to **Treux**. Swing left at the fork just beyond Treux onto the Sailly-Laurette road and drive along the left side of **Treux Wood** to the **crossroads** ❹ in the re-entrant. Park there, keep the Sailly-Laurette road on your left and look

along the Ville road ahead. When the 3rd Division reached the triangle on 27 March, the 10th Brigade occupied the Amiens Defence Line one kilometre to your rear. Passing through the wood behind you, a patrol from the 38th Battalion found some 18th Lancashire Fusiliers holding **Treux Post**, this side of the copse atop the spur on your left. Next morning the Australians and Lancashires beat off a German advance over the spur one kilometre to your right front, whereupon the 38th Battalion itself advanced to occupy the Sailly-Laurette road between your location and the copse.

The spur to your right front, beyond which lay Morlancourt, was to have been reached in two stages in the attack that Monash ordered for the afternoon. Advancing from your right rear, the 39th Battalion occupied the Sailly-Laurette road on your right, which marked the end of the first phase, and linked up with the 40th Battalion on the higher ground further right. As the 40th was unable to progress, the 39th stayed put on the road.

Now head back to the fork, turn left and drive along the right side of Treux Wood. At the corner of the wood, turn right. Running up from the near side of **Méricourt-l'Abbé** on the Ancre to your right front, the **Amiens Defence Line** crossed the road 450 metres along. On 27 March the 38th Battalion held the stretch on the right of the road, the 37th the stretch that extended up to the crest of the **Morlancourt Ridge** on your left.

Turn left at the next crossroads onto Rue de Sailly-le-Sec, which tracks behind the 37th Battalion's line to the D1 and the **3rd Australian Division Memorial** ❺ on the crest. Park at the memorial and

The underpass, alongside which the Germans broke through on 5 April. They hauled a field-gun along the road below.

look across the D1 with the memorial at your back. The 37th's right flank met the D1 80 metres to your left. Directly ahead of you, on the far side of the Somme Valley, is the **Hamel** battlefield, on which the Australian Corps under Monash carried out a small but brilliantly successful attack on 4 July 1918 that became the tactical template for most of the BEF's subsequent major attacks.

Now head left onto the D1 and get into the right-hand lane immediately so that you can turn right after 400 metres onto the C5 for **Sailly-le-Sec**. Park once you have turned ⑥ and, keeping the 3rd Division Memorial to your left rear, face small **Menet Wood** 1.3 kilometres ahead on the right of the D1. The Sailly-Laurette–Treux road, on which you stood at Treux Wood, runs through Menet Wood.

Paralleling the C5 150 metres ahead of you, the Amiens Defence Line ran down to Sailly-le-Sec on the Somme, 1.6 kilometres to your right. On 27 March the 11th Brigade held it, with the 43rd Battalion at the D1 end and the 42nd at the Sailly-le-Sec end. In the attack on 28 March, the 40th Battalion passed through the 37th across the D1 on your left at 5.13 pm but the 41st did not attack alongside it on this side of the D1. Patrols from the 42nd and 43rd had moved forward instead, which meant that the 40th, already without artillery support, advanced alone. Carved up by torrential fire from the German line at Menet Wood, it was forced to ground 500 metres to your left front. The 41st Battalion finally got going on your right at 8 pm and caught up with the 40th. The two battalions advanced together later that night, the 40th reaching the Sailly-Laurette–Treux road on the left of the D1, and the 41st a line that cut diagonally back from Menet Wood across your right front towards Sailly-le-Sec. The Germans still held the wood.

Continue down the C5 to Sailly-le-Sec, bear left at the Y-junction at the

The memorial to the 3rd Australian Division above Sailly-Laurette.

triangular park in the village centre and head left on the D233 to **Sailly-Laurette**. Park opposite the **cemetery** ⑦ on Sailly-Laurette's outskirts, walk to the left corner of the cemetery and look back towards Sailly-le-Sec across the valley. Starting on the Somme in front of Sailly-le-Sec, the 42nd Battalion's line on 27 March ran up the spur to your right front on the far side of the valley. The 41st Battalion's attack late on 28 March started from the line at the top end of the spur. In the final episode of the fiasco that 28 March turned out to be for the 3rd Division, the 44th Battalion advanced towards you at 9.30 pm from the 42nd's posts on the right of the D233. Emerging from the valley, the 44th ran into a wall of fire from the seven German machine-guns in the cemetery area and were forced to shelter behind the bank 60 metres to your front. Advancing towards the Australians through your location and on your right two days later, the Germans got the same treatment.

Head into Sailly-Laurette and turn left 200 metres past the cemetery onto the C3 (the Sailly-Laurette–Treux road). Take the left branch at the Y-junction and stop after 700 metres at **Dive Copse British Cemetery** ⑧. Stand at the back of it with the Somme on your right and Menet Wood on the crest to your left. Attacking on the night of 4 May without a bombardment in order to achieve surprise, the 9th Brigade swung the line,

Dive Copse British Cemetery.

The unsuccessful Australian attack from Sailly-le-Sec and the unsuccessful German one towards it as seen from the cemetery at Sailly-Laurette.

back but got lost. Next morning 45 men from it were captured in the trees just visible over the crest to your right front. They were 700 metres behind the German line.

Crossing the D1 again, continue downhill on the C3 towards Treux. Attacking from this road on the night of 5 May, the 35th Battalion captured the German line paralleling it 600 metres to your right. At the crossroads on the corner of Treux Wood, where you parked earlier, head right for Ville-sur-Ancre. The minor road on the right at the edge of the village was known as the **Little Caterpillar**. Turn right 250 metres further on at the crossroads in the village and park 300 metres along at the start of a deep cutting, as the road from this point on is restricted to local traffic. You are now at the lower end of the **Big Caterpillar**. Noting the faint remains of German dugouts in the sides of the cutting, walk towards the top end **9**. Once through the cutting, look back towards Ville.

In the 6th Brigade's attack at 2 am on 19 May, the 24th Battalion crossed the Ancre and advanced on the far end of Ville, while the 21st and 22nd Battalions started 600 metres to your left. Fighting through the centre of the village, the 21st established a line just to the right of it. The 22nd Battalion nearer you crossed

which had previously bent over the road behind you from the wood, onto the slope ahead of you. Inspecting it shortly afterwards, the 9th's commander, Brigadier-General Charles Rosenthal, and his party captured five Germans 100 metres to your right. Returning alone to his headquarters, Rosenthal was saved from blundering into the German line by the fortuitous firing of a flare. Looking at the featureless landscape, it is easy to see how he became disorientated in the darkness. The 34th Battalion failed to carry the line all the way to the crest to your front on 6 May and tried again on the following night. While the left company near the D1 succeeded, the right one carried on too far after overrunning the German posts. Realising it had overshot, the company turned

SAILLY-LE-SEC

44TH BATTALION 28 MARCH

GERMANS 30 MARCH

Major-General Sir Charles Rosenthal

Commander 9th Brigade, July 1917–May 1918, and 2nd Australian Division from then until war's end

1875–1954

An architect and militia gunner, Berrima-born Rosenthal was also one of Sydney's leading oratorio singers. As commander of the 3rd Field Artillery Brigade, he made his reputation at ANZAC by siting his guns almost in the front line. On the Western Front he was in charge of the 4th Division's artillery before taking over the 9th Brigade when its commander broke down after Messines. Reinvigorated under Rosenthal's leadership, the 9th fought memorably at Villers-Bretonneux on 4 April 1918. At the end of May, he was appointed to command the 2nd Australian Division and led it until war's end.

Rosenthal resembled 'Pompey' Elliott in many respects. Enormous in bulk, he was even more enormous in energy and personality, typically entertaining his fellow wounded on a crowded hospital ship leaving Gallipoli with doses of Handel. He also liked being seen in the front line and was wounded five times. Tactically sound rather than brilliant like Elliott, Rosenthal was not given to the fits of rashness that marred Elliott as a commander. This was a telling factor when the choice of Australians to lead Australian divisions had to be made. Appointed CB in 1915, CMG in 1917, Rosenthal was awarded the DSO and knighted (KCB) in 1918. After the war he returned to architecture and was also elected to the New South Wales parliament.

the Little Caterpillar and dug in on the right of the Big Caterpillar. Approaching the Big Caterpillar, the right company had met stiff resistance from your location, which Sergeant Ruthven quashed. Taking over after his company commander was hit, he bombed a nearby machine-gun that had halted the assault and then ran ahead to the cutting, where he captured eight Germans. While organising the new line to your right front, Ruthven rushed a German post close by and took another 32 prisoners. The 18th Battalion from the

41ST BATTALION

The lower end of the Big Caterpillar in May 1918.

Dugout remains on the Big Caterpillar.

the stillness that the Germans in the post had dozed off. Organising a raid in 10 minutes, he jogged across no-man's-land with 18 men and returned 10 minutes later with 22 prisoners and the machine-gun. The Australians did not fire a shot and suffered no casualties. The Germans were unaware until that evening that the post had gone.

Return to your car, drive to the crossroads in Ville, through which the 21st Battalion had advanced, and head right on the D120. Once clear of the village, take the first road on the right for **Morlancourt**, which is hidden by the surrounding heights until you are almost in it. Turn left 100 metres past the crossroads by the village cemetery onto Rue du Château and then right at the T-junction onto the D42 (Rue d'Albert). On reaching the D1 on the crest of the ridge, turn right and stop after 750 metres at **Beacon Cemetery** ⑩. From the front of the cemetery, look across the D1 towards the Ancre. On 10 June the 7th Brigade attacked from the Australian line, then midway between your location and Menet Wood on your

5th Brigade seized 500 metres of the road to your rear.

If you wish to see the site of one of the great peaceful penetration exploits, carry on another 500 metres to the bend in the road past the end of a smaller cutting and stand with the cutting on your right. To your front, 150 metres away, was a German advance post. Its machine-gun enfiladed the 18th Battalion's line, which ran across your front just beyond the post. On the hot morning of 18 May, Lieutenant Alex Irvine guessed from

VILLE-SUR-ANCRE

ALBERT

SERGEANT RUTHVEN

The scene of Sergeant Ruthven's VC action. The Dernancourt battlefield is on the slope above Ville on the far side of the Ancre.

left. Advancing across your front, the 28th Battalion took the road to your right front, which runs down to the Big Caterpillar, as far as the domed building 700 metres ahead of you. The 18th Battalion had captured it from there to the Big Caterpillar on 19 May. Now look towards the Somme from the back of the cemetery. Assaulting on this side of the D1, the 25th Battalion got to the track to your left. The line that should have been reached in the 3rd Division's attack on 28 March had finally been taken.

Continuing on the D1, take the third road on the left past the 3rd Division Memorial, the C14, to **Vaux-sur-Somme**. Turn right at the crossroads in the centre of Vaux onto the D233 and park on the track on the left just before the wooded area 1.1 kilometres along **11**. Keeping Vaux on your right, look across the D233. Pursuing a rookie pilot, Lieutenant William May, and himself being pursued by a veteran one, Captain Roy Brown, Manfred von Richthofen approached the far side of Vaux as he flew along the Somme on 23 April. Barely clearing the church steeple, he passed directly in front of Sergeant Popkin's machine-gun post to your immediate left. Swerving when Popkin fired at him, Richthofen continued

to gain height over the ridge to your left but was engaged by more machine-guns on the far side of it. When he turned again as if to fly back towards Vaux, Popkin drew a better bead and fired another burst. Mortally wounded, Richthofen came down on the crest above you. For years Brown was credited with the kill, though he broke off the chase before reaching Vaux. Analysis of the trajectory of the bullet responsible proves that it was part of Popkin's second burst.

Return to Vaux, turn left at the crossroads onto the C14 (direction Méricourt) and left again at the crossroads opposite the crucifix on the village outskirts. On reaching the D1, turn left and head past the communications tower on the right to the parking bay at the leftwards bend **12**. As the parking bay information panel explains, the Red Baron came down in the field on the left.

For Amiens, continue on the D1 in the direction in which you were driving. To return to Albert, head back along the D1 in the opposite direction and turn left onto the D42 3.5 kilometres past the 3rd Division Memorial. Carry on through Morlancourt.

LOCAL INFORMATION

CEMETERIES

As the Somme–Ancre triangle was served by the railway running along the Ancre from Albert, casualty clearing stations quickly sprang up around the villages in the triangle through which the railway passed. Those who died before they could be evacuated by ambulance train were buried in the cemeteries established by the casualty clearing stations. After the war, burials from smaller cemeteries and from the nearby

battlefields were concentrated in them. Substantial cemeteries are therefore located around many of the villages that are on, or near, the drive route. The Australians who fell at Dernancourt, and in the triangle between March and June, are scattered throughout them.

Beacon Cemetery

Named after the Brick Beacon, a tall brick chimney that stood in the nearby fields, this cemetery was begun by the British in August 1918 and expanded postwar. Of the 768 burials, 515 are identified. Of the 195 Australians, 137 are known. Among the Australian unknowns are probably men from the 25th Battalion, which suffered 180 casualties in the 7th Brigade's attack here on 10 June. Dying on 22 August aged 48, Lieutenant James McConnell of the 3rd Pioneer Battalion at V.J.1 was one of the oldest Australians to fight. Visited on the drive, Beacon is on the D1, 750 metres from the D42 turn-off to Morlancourt.

Dernancourt Communal Cemetery and Extension

Field ambulances used the communal cemetery in 1915–16, and the extension opened with the arrival of the XV Corps main dressing station in August 1916. The 3rd Australian Casualty Clearing Station was among the units that used both until the Germans took Dernancourt on 26 March 1918. It was recaptured in August. The cemetery now comprises 2164 burials, of which 1986 are known. A number of the 418 Australians, 370 of whom are identified, fell at Dernancourt. They include 14 men from the 49th

Grave of Lieutenant James McConnell, Beacon Cemetery.

Battalion and six from the 48th. Reflecting their 'proud and loving memory' of him, the men of the 26th Battalion arranged for the marble slab that distinguishes the grave of their commanding officer, Lieutenant-Colonel Allan Leane, one of the famous Leane brothers, at A.5 in the communal cemetery. A shell mortally wounded him on 4 January 1917. Passed just beyond the Dernancourt underpass on the drive, the cemetery also contains 51 New Zealanders.

Dive Copse British Cemetery

On the C3 above Sailly-Laurette and visited during the drive, this cemetery served the XIV Corps Main Dressing Station, which set up between the cemetery and the D1 750 metres away. Menet Wood on the junction of the two roads was known as Dive Copse after the dressing station's commander and the copse, in turn, lent its name to the cemetery. Of the 579 burials, all but 20 are identified. Many of the 53 Australians were 18th Battalion casualties from the attack on Ville on 19 May.

Heilly Station

Started in 1916, this cemetery contains 2947 burials, most of them known. The Australians used it between March and May 1918 and 401 of them lie here. They include the senior Australian officer to die in France, Brigadier-General Duncan Glasfurd of the 12th Brigade at V.A.17. Mortally wounded near Flers on 12 November 1916, he succumbed

The ornate resting place of Lieutenant-Colonel Allan Leane, Dernancourt Communal Cemetery and Extension.

shortly after relays of stretcher-bearers struggled through clinging mud for 10 hours to get him to a dressing station. Resting at V.A.14, Lieutenant-Colonel Owen Howell-Price DSO, MC of the 3rd Battalion was shot through the head near Flers a week earlier. He was one of three officer brothers to fall on the Western Front. Lance-Corporal John O'Neill of the 13th Battalion at V.F.29, and Sapper John Greenan of the 6th Field Company, Australian Engineers, at VI.B.14 are remembered in private memorials put up by their families soon after the war. The Imperial War Graves Commission broke with custom by allowing them to remain when it subsequently erected standard headstones for the pair.

Sometimes the rush of burials was so great that the graves contained multiple remains. This is recorded on the relevant headstones. There are also 118 New Zealanders resting in the cemetery, which can be reached by continuing on the D52 through Buire to Heilly, crossing the Ancre there on the original wartime bridge and carrying on for 400 metres past the railway on the other side of the river. The 3rd Australian Division crossed the Ancre at Heilly when it entered the triangle.

Ribemont Communal Cemetery Extension

On the right as the D52 passes the northern end of Ribemont 1.9 kilometres past Buire, the cemetery was begun in May 1918 and expanded postwar. Of its 498 burials, 462 identified, 197 are Australian. Lieutenant John Whittle of the 48th Battalion at III.J.6 was wounded at Dernancourt on 28 March but fought on until killed. Captain Tom Elliot, also of the 48th and next to Whittle at III.J.7, was sniped during the battle while raising his head to see.

NEARBY PLACES OF INTEREST

Querrieu

On the D929 between Albert and Amiens, Querrieu was a billeting centre for Australian formations for much of 1918. Commanding the Fourth Army during the 1916 Somme offensive, General Rawlinson had his headquarters in the château, which, for those coming from Albert, is on the right of the sharp right turn that the D929 makes near the centre of the village. Take the first left towards Bussy-les-Daours 100 metres further on and stop after 400 metres at **Querrieu British Cemetery**, which the 3rd Australian Division started in March 1918. Of its 199 burials, 84 are Australian. They include Sergeant Alex Wilson, DCM, MM and Bar of the 10th Field Ambulance. The war's most decorated Australian medic, he was killed on 20 May near Ville and rests at A.22.

Bertangles

In April 1918 the headquarters of the Australian Corps moved into the majestic 18th-century château in this village, which is just off the N25 10 kilometres north of Amiens. The château became very well known after Monash took command of

The bridge over the Ancre at Heilly then ... and now.

the Corps at the end of May. He planned the Hamel and 8 August attacks in it. In the early morning darkness before both, he paced nervously up and down the gravel driveway, which leads from the ornate wrought-iron gates at the entrance on Rue de Villers-Bocage, the road fringing the eastern side of Bertangles. On 12 August 100 men from each division lined the drive and the grounds either side of it were festooned with several hundred trophies of war, from guns to searchlights, as King George V knighted Monash on the château steps. As the front had moved on, the headquarters began vacating Bertangles next day. Head left from the entrance and right at the T-junction before turning right again onto Rue d'Amiens, which leads to the courtyard at the back of the château. It is unchanged from 1918, when it was crowded with huts and tents and criss-crossed by telephone wires. The château can be visited but times vary. Contact chateau@chateaubertangles.com for details.

Early morning at Querrieu château.

On leaving the château, head right along Rue du Moulin to the **cemetery** on the left just past the village outskirts. The Australians buried Richthofen with full military honours here, a firing party from the Australian Flying Corps unleashing volleys in salute. The depression to the left of the gate indicates where his coffin was laid to rest. After the war, Richthofen's remains were re-interred in Fricourt German Cemetery. Moved to Berlin in 1925, they eventually ended up in the family plot in Wiesbaden.

Australian Corps headquarters, Bertangles château.

CHAPTER 16

1918
VILLERS-BRETONNEUX

On the eastern outskirts of Villers-Bretonneux is one of the 240 demarcation stones that show how far the Germans advanced on the Western Front in 1918. The location of this one suggests that they were stopped short of the town. In fact they took it. Ask the local authorities why the stone is where it is and they'll give a Gallic shrug and say that the Germans held Villers-Bretonneux for less than 24 hours, that the French fought nearby and that, in any case, they paid for the stone. That the Germans held it so briefly was due to a hastily organised counterattack by two Australian brigades at night over unfamiliar ground. Major Neville Lytton, a well-known British artist serving in France, wrote of it: 'The Australians made…one of the most astounding manoeuvres of the war…Even if the Australians achieved nothing else in this war, they would have won the right to be considered among the greatest fighting races of the world.' An Australian battalion had earlier driven the Germans back in a suicidal charge. Today Villers-Bretonneux is probably the best-known Australian battlefield on the Western Front.

To Australians at the start of 1918, though, Villers-Bretonneux was just a name on Somme trench maps. It stood on the edge of the Santerre, a great agricultural plateau on the southern side of the river. The crop-covered fields around the town and the mills within it made the 5200 residents reasonably prosperous. Hill 104, on the northern side of the town, was the highest point of the Santerre. Villers-Bretonneux also barred the way to Amiens, whose urban sprawl could be seen 16 kilometres westwards. An important railway centre, Amiens was vital to the BEF's logistics chain. The ruler-straight D1029 and a trunk railway from the east both ran through the town to the city.

'You needn't go, Ma'

Launched on 21 March 1918, the great German *Michael* offensive was soon blocked everywhere except on the left flank, where it had sliced through the Fifth Army. When the advance there was slowed down by XIX Corps south of the Somme, the Germans swung over to the northern side of the river, from which the British had mistakenly withdrawn. Halted on 28 March after the timely arrival of the 3rd and 4th Australian Divisions, they switched back to the southern side. Meanwhile XIX Corps had joined the British cavalry and some scratch units in the old Amiens Defence Line. Forming the BEF's right flank, it crossed the Somme at Sailly-le-Sec and passed

THAT demarcation stone!

Villers-Bretonneux from the Australian support line. The commercial centre on the edge of town did not exist in 1918, which meant that the town itself was well back — the church was close to the facing edge of it then.

behind Hamel before going over the D1029 trunk road five kilometres beyond Villers-Bretonneux. The only shaky part of this line was its junction with the French

First Army south of the town. Worried about the right flank after the French buckled on 29 March, Field Marshal Haig sent the 9th Australian Brigade to Cachy, a hamlet near the town, for use in counterattacks. The 15th Brigade manned the Somme crossings as an extra precaution.

Realising that *Michael* was on its last legs, General Ludendorff ordered the launching of *Georgette*, an offensive in Flanders. But he was too close to Amiens to resist trying to grab it. Attacks on both sides of the Somme on 30 March failed except at the junction with the French, where the Amiens Defence Line fell and the cavalry and the 33rd Battalion from the 9th Brigade secured Lancer Wood to prevent Villers-Bretonneux being outflanked. Still Ludendorff could not let go of Amiens. The next attack would be five days hence.

During the lull, III Corps, which had been fighting with the French, returned to the Fifth Army and relieved XIX Corps. In the front line when the Germans attacked on 21 March and battered since, all three of its divisions were tired and understrength. Attached to the 18th Division, the Australian 35th Battalion stretched 2.5 kilometres between the D1029 and the railway, the longest part of the Fifth Army's line. As there was nothing between it and the town four kilometres back, a support line was also started 1.5 kilometres ahead of the town. The 33rd Battalion manned it. Still largely intact, Villers-Bretonneux was now virtually in the front line. An Australian told a mother and her children about to join the exodus from it, 'You needn't go, Ma. The Aussies are here. Best stay where you are', and helped her carry her belongings back to her house. On 2 April the Fifth Army was renumbered the Fourth, reviving the title of the army that General Rawlinson, who had replaced

The withdrawal of the 42nd
Brigade on 4 April.

General Gough, led on the Somme
in 1916.

4 April

At 6.30 am on 4 April the Germans
advanced astride the D1029 towards
Villers-Bretonneux. North of the D1029,
the 42nd Brigade from the British 14th
Division abandoned the Amiens Defence
Line at Hamel and backpedalled
4.4 kilometres to Hill 104 and the Somme
crossings. General Elliott told the 58th
Battalion on the river to rally the British. A
line was hastily formed between the river
and the hill, before which the Germans
were halted. The 35th Battalion south of
the D1029 had minced two attacks when
the 7th Buffs on the railway next to them
turned about. Now outflanked on the
right as well as the left, the 35th pulled
back to the support line, where the
Germans were stopped. The 34th and
36th Battalions took up positions either
side of Villers-Bretonneux behind the
support line.

Renewing the attack further south of
the D1029 at 4 pm, the Germans sent the
18th Division reeling. Lancer Wood, the

eastern half of Hangard Wood next to it,
Monument Farm and neighbouring
Monument Wood were all lost. The 7th
Buffs hurtled back into Villers-Bretonneux,
leaving the 35th Battalion hanging again.
It had to pull out as well. The headquarters in the town of Lieutenant-
Colonel Henry Goddard, the 35th's
commander, was now the most
advanced position. Lieutenant-Colonel
John Milne of the 36th Battalion was
there. He agreed to counterattack
immediately.

At 5.15 pm the 36th Battalion shook
out in dead ground below Monument
Farm. 'Goodbye boys, it's neck or nothing',
Milne said. The line jogged forward and
crashed into waves of Germans emerging
from the farm. The assault diverged. The
northern half advanced 1.4 kilometres
along the railway with little difficulty to
outflank the Germans, who started to
withdraw. Whipped by fire, the southern
half faltered before ejecting the Germans
from Monument Farm and Wood and
linking up with the northern half. The
36th Battalion had lost 150 men, a
quarter of its strength. On the other side

of the railway, the 35th also charged. The 33rd joined in, the cavalry rode up and three armoured cars careered along the D1029 to lend a hand. The Germans wilted. By next morning, the 9th Brigade had reoccupied the support line.

Reorganisation

Georgette began on 9 April. On the Somme the 2nd Australian Division had taken over the Fourth Army's right flank between the D1029 and the French. On 7 April a composite battalion from the 5th Brigade tried to recapture Hangard Wood East, held by two German battalions. Poorly planned, the attack failed. Lieutenant Percy Storkey of the 19th Battalion won the VC for leading a charge that saved the left flank from annihilation. On 17 April the Germans drenched Villers-Bretonneux, now in ruins, with gas,

causing over 1000 Australian casualties and disrupting a reorganisation begun on 13 April. Until then, the Somme had been the boundary between the Australians and III Corps. As Haig wanted the Australians made solely responsible for the Somme, their formations still with III Corps returned to the Australian Corps. The 5th Australian Division moved astride the river, keeping the 15th Brigade under Brigadier-General Elliott in reserve at Blangy-Tronville, six kilometres west of Villers-Bretonneux. The 14th Brigade extended from the river to the northern shoulder of Hill 104. On the 14th's right flank, the 8th Division from III Corps held Villers-Bretonneux. Its ranks were filled with partly trained boy-recruits. The Australians worried that they would lose the town, in which case the Australian flank on Hill 104 would be turned. That fear was about to be realised.

Gassed Australians outside a dressing station near Villers-Bretonneux. The eye bandages indicate probable exposure to mustard gas. Though this well-known photograph was taken in May 1918, the scenes after the Villers-Bretonneux gas attack of 17 April would have been similar.

Major-General Sir Thomas Glasgow

Commander 13th Brigade 1916–18, 1st Australian Division 1918.

1876–1955

Taciturn but forceful and rock-steady, Queensland pastoralist Glasgow had won the DSO during the Boer War and been a light horse commander at ANZAC. He impressed sufficiently to be given an infantry command, the 13th Brigade, which he subsequently led with distinction in 1916–17. His performance at Villers-Bretonneux was outstanding. In May 1918 he took over the 1st Australian Division, which had blocked the German advance in the *Georgette* offensive. Appointed CB in 1916 and CMG in 1917, Glasgow was knighted (KCB) in 1918. After the war he entered federal politics and was Minister of Defence between 1927 and 1929. As Australia's first high commissioner to Canada, he took a keen interest in the welfare of Australian airmen training there under the Empire Air Training Scheme in the Second World War.

Villers-Bretonneux lost

Seeking to divert attention from *Georgette*, whose fortunes were flagging, the Germans struck Villers-Bretonneux at 6 am on 24 April 1918. Thirteen tanks supported the assault. Horrified to see them lumbering out of the gloom, the young British soldiers bolted. British gunners stopped one tank as it crawled along the railway west of Villers-Bretonneux and three British tanks fought the first tank-versus-tank duel against three German ones in the fields south of it. The German tanks withdrew after knocking out two of their opponents. By mid-morning the Germans held the town and a pocket around it that included the southern end of Hill 104 and Monument Farm and Wood.

Possibly because they felt that accepting the help offered by Major-General Hobbs, the 5th Division's commander, would be a humiliation, Lieutenant-General Butler of III Corps, who had been involved as Haig's deputy chief of staff in the rotten decision-making before Fromelles, and

Major-General William Heneker of the 8th Division, insisted that the 8th Division could handle things. Its 'handling' came down to a failed counterattack around midday. Meanwhile, Rawlinson had ordered the Australian 13th Brigade, then north of the Somme, southwards at 9.30 am. He also wanted Heneker to contact Hobbs to arrange an afternoon counterattack. Aware from the 8th Division's counterattack that a daylight assault would be massacre, Heneker recommended a night one to Butler. Still waiting for Butler's answer, Heneker was not very forthcoming when he called Hobbs. Not until 3.30 pm did Hobbs find out that the 15th Brigade would be attacking north of the town to meet the 13th attacking south of it in the old British front line.

Brigadier-General Thomas Glasgow of the 13th Brigade had clashed with Heneker a few hours earlier. Glasgow said he would attack north of Cachy. Heneker objected: 'The corps commander says the attack is to be made from Cachy'. As this would put his brigade closer to the Germans at the outset, Glasgow refused.

Heneker relented. Seeking surprise, Glasgow did not want a barrage to precede the attack. Heneker agreed. Glasgow foreshadowed an assault at 10.30 pm. Heneker replied that Butler had said 8 pm. Glasgow snapped. 'If It was God Almighty who gave the order, we couldn't do it in daylight.' They settled on 10 pm. The two Australian brigades faced an assault of over three kilometres.

Villers-Bretonneux regained

No sooner had the 13th Brigade's advance begun than fire ripped into it from Bois d'Aquenne, the wood on its left. Grabbing the survivors of his platoon and some men from the adjacent one, Lieutenant Clifford Sadlier of the 51st Battalion led a charge that routed the Germans. He was awarded the VC. As the rest of the 51st advanced with the 52nd they found remnants of the 8th Division in the Cachy Switch, a trench dug from the town to the hamlet to contain any break through the front line ahead. When the Australians approached the wire protecting the trench, several machine-guns on the far side opened up. Sweeping through them and brushing aside a German counterattack, the two battalions were finally stopped in front of Monument Farm. The British 54th Brigade on their right did not get as far.

Thanks to the fumbling by Butler and Heneker, the 15th Brigade, which had been ready since early morning, ended up counterattacking near midnight, two hours late. Rushing from Blangy, the 59th and 60th Battalions formed up below Hill 104 with the 57th behind them. Villers-Bretonneux was burning but the flames were behind the Germans, who could see nothing. Finally detected after advancing unopposed for 1.4 kilometres, the Australians bayoneted their way through the Germans to the D1029 beyond the town. Early on 25 April the 57th Battalion and the 2nd Royal Berkshires started through the town, while the 2nd Northants charged the southern side of it. Villers-Bretonneux was largely cleared by nightfall and the 13th and 15th Brigades linked up early next morning. A few hours later they watched the French Moroccan Division attack

Lieutenant Sadlier and his tiny band hoe into the Germans in Bois d'Aquenne in Will Longstaff's *Night Attack by the 13th Brigade on Villers-Bretonneux*. Before the town was destroyed, its church had two towers. The ruins of the remaining tower can be seen through the trees on the left.

towards Hangard Wood and get smashed.

Though the old British front line was nowhere reached and the Germans still held Monument Farm and Wood, Villers-Bretonneux had been saved a second time, on ANZAC Day too. Amiens was no longer threatened. The achievement was almost entirely due to the Australian counterattack, which cost the 15th Brigade 455 men and the 13th 1009. Haig now made sure of the BEF's right flank by directing the Australian Corps to swap places with III Corps. The 48th Battalion attacked Monument Wood unsuccessfully on 2 May. It fell to peaceful penetration on 14 July after the Germans were discovered to be holding the line in front of it thinly. *Mephisto*, one of the German tanks that had attacked on 24 April, was found disabled in the wood. It is now on display in the Queensland Museum at Southbank, Brisbane, the sole-surviving A7V *Kampfwagen*. Having won the MM in 1917, Lieutenant Albert Borella was awarded the VC for his part in the

Australians in a support trench after the battle. Behind them, smoke rises from Villers-Bretonneux, which the Germans are shelling. One shell has landed near the trench, wounding the Digger who is making his way back. Putting an umbrella salvaged from the town to good use, another Digger has resumed his siesta on the parapet.

Mephistopheles ('Mephisto'), one of the German tanks used in the attack that took Villers-Bretonneux on 24 April, after its capture in July by the 26th Battalion in Monument Wood.

successful attack by the 25th and 26th Battalions on 16 July on the mound by the railway beyond the wood. The Australian counterattack on 4 April had ended there.

DRIVING THE BATTLEFIELD

A comparison of a trench map of the Villers-Bretonneux battlefield with modern maps shows that the Somme side of the D1029 has changed little. On the other side, the A29 autoroute cuts across the 13th Brigade's advance but the overpass makes an excellent vantage point to follow the course of the advance. The expansion of the industrial and commercial zones on the eastern side of the town, however, has claimed much of the ground over which the 35th and 36th Battalions counterattacked earlier. That's progress.

MAPS IGN Blue Series, 1:25 000, 2308E Corbie; 2309E Moreuil; 24080 Albert; 24090 Harbonnières

The location of the British field-gun that stopped the German tanks getting beyond Bois d'Aquenne, as seen from Adelaide Cemetery.

From Albert, take the D929 towards Amiens and, once through Petit Camon, head left onto the N25 section of the Amiens ring road just beyond the hamlet. Leave the N25 at Longeau on the D1029 exit for St Quentin and Villers-Bretonneux. Amiens-Glisy airfield immediately appears on the left.

The British used this airfield throughout the war. On passing it, look left along the D4029. The headquarters of the 8th Division was in **Glisy** at the far end of the road. Look left again as you cross the D167 after another 1.9 kilometres. The co-located headquarters of the 13th and 15th Brigades was in the château at **Blangy-Tronville**, one kilometre down the road. To see the château, turn left in the village before reaching the Somme and drive 750 metres. The battalions of the 15th Brigade were clustered in reserve around Blangy. As you continue on the D1029, the **Australian National Memorial** on **Hill 104** appears to your left front. The ridge stretching across your front, on which it stands, screens Amiens and provided a natural line of defence against the German advance towards the city. On your right are **Bois de Blangy** and, across a broad clearing from it, **Bois l'Abbé**. Park at the junction with the D523, which separates Bois l'Abbé from **Bois d'Aquenne** ①. German shelling

BOIS D'AQUENNE

BOIS L'ABBÉ

D1029

GUN

RAILWAY

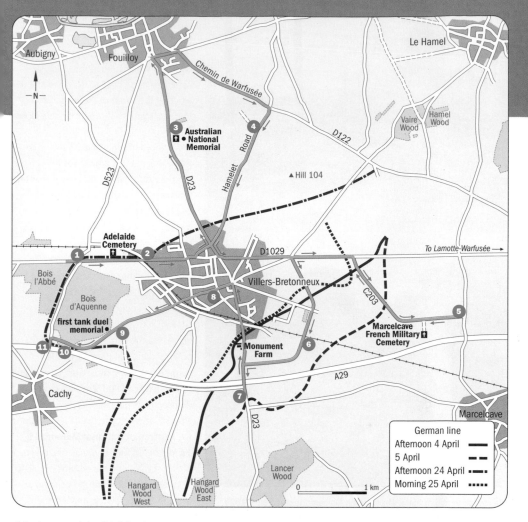

of Cachy caused the 9th Brigade to move into Bois l'Abbé at the end of March. British units sheltered in all three woods from then on.

Now face the railway embankment. Firing from it 250 metres to the right of the bridge over the D523, a British field-gun forced the German tanks and infantry emerging from **Villers-Bretonneux** early on 24 April into Bois d'Aquenne to your right rear. The British held the Germans captured in the battle in a compound under the bridge. Proceed up the slope towards the town, passing **Adelaide Cemetery** on the left after 650 metres. The British line after the German attack extended northwards from the railway behind the cemetery.

The first leg of this drive passes some of the key locations between Amiens and Villers-Bretonneux before entering the town and then retracing the 15th Brigade's advance on the Somme side of it on 24 April. The second leg begins after crossing the D1029 and follows the 13th Brigade's advance on the opposite side of Villers-Bretonneux. Covered at the outset of this leg are the 36th Battalion's counterattack on 4 April, the Hangard Wood assaults and Lieutenant Borella's VC action at Monument Wood.
Distance covered: 26 km
Duration: 3.5 hours

The Germans held the ground to the right of the D1029. Continue to the **gendarmerie** 100 metres past the next railway bridge, park, and look left along the cutting after walking back to the **bridge ❷**. Having passed under the

The stretch of railway along which a tank lumbered towards the D1029, from where the photograph was taken, then ... and now.

arched road bridge to your front, a tank lumbered along the tracks towards you until stopped by a patrol from the 59th Battalion, which fired at the vision slits. Before leaving, check at the gendarmerie whether the tower of the Australian National Memorial is open. If not, pick up the keys.

Once over the next crossroads, look left at the clearing, which was the site of the Delacour Château. Known as the **Red Château**, it was General Gough's headquarters at the start of 1918. Set on fire on 24 April, the château served as a beacon for the 15th Brigade as they advanced between it and Hill 104, indicated by the Australian National Memorial on the skyline. Later housing an aid post and then the Australian Graves Unit, its ruins stood as a mute witness to the battle until they were bulldozed in 2004 to make way for a commercial development as yet unbuilt.

Turn left onto Rue Mme Delacour-Rousseau just past the clearing, left again after 300 metres onto the D23 and stop at the **Australian National Memorial** ❸ 1.6 kilometres further on. As the tower is almost level with the summit of Hill 104 behind it, the all-round panorama easily explains Hill 104's importance. Using the orientation table, **Amiens**

HAMELET ROAD

VILLERS-BRETONNEUX

60TH BATTALION

can be seen spreading across the western horizon. The Santerre runs away to the east. On a clear day, the **Thiepval Memorial to the Missing**, at the centre of the 1916 Somme battlefield, is visible on the northern skyline across the Somme. The 1918 fighting north of the town is easily followed from the tower.

Look south across the re-entrant towards Villers-Bretonneux, ringed on this side by orchards in 1918. Blending into each other along the D1029 to its right are Bois d'Aquennes, l'Abbé and Blangy, all skirted by the railway on the near side of the road. Following the skyline from the left of the town to the river, the church spires of **Marcelcave** and **Lamotte-Warfusée**, then **Vaire Wood**, the spire of **Hamel church**, and **Hamelet** on the bank can all be seen. Attacking from a line that ran across the front of Marcelcave and Lamotte-Warfusée and behind Hamel on 4 April, the Germans reached the near side of Vaire Wood. Coming up from Bois l'Abbé, the 34th Battalion moved around the near side of the town to help the cavalry and the 33rd Battalion to your left front prevent the Germans going further. On 24 April the 14th Brigade stretched between your location and the Somme. After breaking

The ruins of the Red Château, now gone.

into Villers-Bretonneux, the Germans tried to advance from it towards you but the attempt was not coordinated with the artillery and failed. Their line ran along the near edge of the town, over the railway to its right and along the edge of Bois d'Aquenne.

The 15th Brigade counterattacked from the D523, the next road back from the D23 along which you have just driven. Your first stop was at the D523's junction with the D1029 near the prisoner-of-war compound. The 60th Battalion's left flank rested on the D523 to your right and the 59th on its right lined the road as it ran up the re-entrant towards the railway. Behind the 59th was

The advance of the 15th Brigade.

59TH AND 57TH BATTALIONS

> A storm of enemy machine-gun and rifle fire was poured into the oncoming ranks but checked them not at all. A hundred enemy flares lit the terrible scene in vivid light, in which the Germans read too well their fate. Shriek following shriek marked the toll of the deadly bayonets and good round Australian oaths were ripped out in quick succession as the panting men plunged forward to the next victims. The German defences were arranged in a series of strong posts ... If for a moment the slaughter slackened, it was only because new victims were wanted and, in the dark, they were not easy to see. But soon the enemy flares would shoot up again from strong points not yet reached. Those flares were the death-warrant of many a German that night, for, guided by them, the assailants knew exactly where their enemies lay.
>
> The 15th Brigade's charge (Ellis, AD, *The Story of the Fifth Division*, London, 1920, p. 298)

the 57th. Starting near midnight and guided by the light from the burning town, the assault passed the Memorial on its way to the Hamelet road, which bisects the slope between the Memorial and the summit.

Continue on the D523 to **Fouilloy**, the 14th Brigade's headquarters, turn right at the crossroads and right again after 400 metres onto Chemin de Warfusée. On 4 April 58th Battalion posts beyond Hamelet, on the Somme 1.3 kilometres to your left, halted retreating British troops and reformed them into a line that ran up the slope to your left front. Turn right after 1.7 kilometres onto the Hamelet road and stop after 400 metres where a **track** ❹ crosses. Look along the road towards Villers-Bretonneux. Having advanced from your right front, the left of

the 60th Battalion was pivoting through this junction to head towards the D1029 with the 59th alongside when the Germans finally saw them at 12.40 am on 25 April. Charging like a horde of Viking berserkers, the Australians unleashed a banshee yell that the 13th Brigade heard on the far side of the D1019. The area between your location and the town became the scene of one of the most ferocious bayonet assaults of the war.

Yet the assault also featured small-unit tactical skills of a very high order, as the Germans readily admitted. When it was all over at 2 am, the 60th Battalion had established a line that ran down the track to your left. As you continue along the road, you are following the route taken by the 57th Battalion and the 2nd Royal Berkshires into the town. Lewis-gunners

Hamelet road, from where the 15th Brigade charged after its swing towards the D1029 was detected.

sprayed the front of any building from which fire came while bombers grenaded the back. Continue to the junction with the D23, turn left and left again onto the D1029. Passing the wrongly located demarcation stone on the right, go over the roundabout one kilometre along, where the 15th Brigade's right flank rested after the counterattack. Turn right after another 900 metres onto the C203 signposted Cimetière Militaire de Marcelcave. Starting from the D1029 on your left, the Australian support line in the 4 April attack crossed the C203 200 metres along and continued to the railway, which runs across your front. Continue around leftwards, passing the cemetery on your right, and park at the **fork 5** ahead.

Stretching from the D1029 on your left to the far side of the railway beyond the A29 on your right, the 35th Battalion's line on 4 April followed the minor road immediately in front of you. Remember that the 'line' consisted of widely spaced posts in foxholes and fragments of trench. The line from which the Germans attacked ran along the D42 900 metres ahead, starting beyond Lamotte-Warfusée to your left front and passing

A German machine-gun post overrun by the 15th Brigade during its charge.

the near side of Marcelcave to your right front. The 35th shattered two attacks before the Germans laid on a much heavier assault at 7 am. First the 7th Buffs beyond the railway, and then the 8th Rifles across the D1029 hit reverse gear. With the Germans lapping around both flanks, the 35th Battalion left as well. Noting how far the Australian line was in front of the town, return to Villers-Bretonneux the way you have come.

Heading left from the D1029 roundabout, continue over another roundabout and park on the far side

57TH BATTALION/ 2ND ROYAL BERKSHIRES

The opposite end of Hamelet road, from which the clearance of Villers-Bretonneux started.

of the railway bridge by the **gravel works** ⑥. Walk back across the bridge and look to your right along the railway cutting towards the **disused bridge** 500 metres away. You can reach it by walking along the edge of the field. The original bridge there, under which the 35th Battalion had set up an aid post, was at the end of the Australian support line, which ran from the D1029 near the C203 junction. Having pulled back from your previous location beyond Marcelcave French Cemetery in the morning attack on 4 April, the 35th Battalion joined the 33rd in the support line, which the

33rd and British cavalry extended from the D1029 to Hill 104 over your left shoulder. Held before this line, the Germans renewed the attack on the far side of the railway at 4 pm. When the 7th Buffs crumpled again, the right of the 35th Battalion formed a defensive flank by bending its line back along the railway towards you. Thinking that it was withdrawing, the 33rd and the rest of the 35th retired, giving the Germans a free run to Villers-Bretonneux behind you.

In the 36th Battalion's counterattack, the right flank was held up to your right rear. The centre passed through your

The mound, which was regained early on 5 April, and then lost in the attack on 24 April. Lieutenant Borella won his VC on the far side.

The field of fire of the machine-gun that enfiladed the 36th Battalion's right flank in the 4 April counterattack.

location with the left alongside before both were stopped 200 metres from the support line by a machine-gun firing from the bushy mound by the disused bridge. Running along the right of the cutting, this mound was more prominent in 1918. Helped by the cavalry and the armoured cars, the 33rd Battalion advanced astride the D1029 but also stopped short of the support line to conform to the 36th. At 1 am on 5 April, the 34th Battalion overran the mound to regain the support line, which then became the front line. It was lost again when the Germans attacked on 24 April. Assaulting late on 17 July, the 25th Battalion passed to your left and the 26th to your right. When a machine-gun opened from the end of the mound, Lieutenant Borella of the 26th ran ahead and shot the crew. Shell-fire had rendered the track on the right of the disused bridge, where Borella's platoon was supposed to stop, unrecognisable so they continued another 180 metres to **Jaffa Trench**. It was full of Germans. Clearing them with bombs and Lewis-guns, Borella's men took 30 prisoners

and then beat off two counterattacks. The support line had been regained a second time.

Return to your car and stand with the gravel works at your back. **Monument Farm** is on the far side of the D23 to your front and to the right of the hypermarket. Commemorating the defence of Villers-Bretonneux during the Franco-Prussian War in 1870, the monument stood on the near side of the D23 on land donated by the farm owner. **Monument Wood**, the orchard around it, extended from the D23. Starting 100 metres in front of you, its near edge ran 300 metres to your left front. The 36th Battalion counterattacked from behind the farm on 4 April. Hugging the railway, two of the three assault companies advanced passed the farm and the wood, causing the Germans to abandon both. The third company barely progressed past the far corner of the hypermarket. On 24 April German tanks advanced through the gravel works behind you. One, *Mephisto*, ditched in a shell hole halfway to the D23. The 48th Battalion's unsuccessful attack on Monument Wood on 2 May came from the D1029 to your right.

Continue to the hypermarket, park and walk onto the D23 overpass over the A29, on the far side of which is **Crucifix Corner Cemetery** ⑦. A machine-gun in this vicinity had pinned down the 36th Battalion's right company. Now look past the cemetery along the D23. When the Germans attacked on 30 March, the 12th Lancers galloped from your right to secure **Lancer Wood**, on the left of the D23 ahead of you. The 33rd Battalion then charged the Germans in the old British line to its left but were forced to dig in along the left side of the wood. After the attack on 4 April, the German line crossed the D23 250 metres to your front and cut between the two halves of **Hangard Wood**, on the right of the D23 opposite Lancer Wood. In the 5th Brigade's failed attack on 6 April, the Australians advancing from Hangard Wood West, the half further from the road, were flayed by fire from the eastern half. Somehow making it into the near end of that half, Captain Storkey and a few survivors from the 19th Battalion tore into the flank of the Germans engaging the rest of the attack. He and his men used bayonets and rifle butts because pausing to reload was out of the question. Fifty-three Germans were captured in Storkey's VC-winning action.

In planning the attack, Brigadier-General Smith, the 5th Brigade's commander, did not seem to realise that even if it had succeeded, the new line on the D23 would have been dominated from Lancer Wood.

Now stand with the three woods on your left. The Germans captured Hangard Wood West on 24 April. Their line from it passed in front of **Cachy**, three kilometres to your front, and into Bois d'Aquenne beyond the far end of Villers-Bretonneux. Counterattacking that evening, the 13th Brigade advanced towards you from a start line that ran to the left of the wood. After reaching the overpass ahead of you, the advance kept mainly to the right of the A29. When the Germans in the cemetery area saw the 52nd Battalion approach in the flare light, the 7th Bedfords next to it had already been stopped. Under heavy fire and with an open flank, the 52nd halted 500 metres to your front. The 13th Brigade's line ran diagonally from there behind Monument Farm after the 51st, which reached the D23 beyond the farm, pulled back to link up with the 52nd. As the 15th Brigade was way ahead on the far side of the D1029, many Germans in Villers-Bretonneux escaped through the gap between the two brigades on 25 April. A quick look at the open terrain between Hangard Wood and the A29

Hangard and Lancer Woods from Crucifix Corner.

LANCER WOOD

D23

shows why the Moroccan Division's daylight attack towards the D23 on 26 April was annihilated.

Return to Villers-Bretonneux on the D23, which marked the limit of the town in 1918. At the six-way intersection beyond the railway bridge, head left onto Rue Driot. Colonel Goddard's head-quarters was in this street on 4 April. He sent Lieutenant-Colonel Milne of the 36th on his way from it with the parting words, 'Colonel, you must counterattack at once'. Cross Rue de Melbourne to Rue Victoria and visit the **museum** 8 in the primary school on the left. Advancing from your right to clear the town on 25 April, the 57th Battalion and the 2nd Royal Berkshires had taken over 150 prisoners by the time they reached this spot. Continue on Rue Victoria, which becomes Rue de Cachy as it crosses the **railway bridge** that you saw from the D1029 earlier. Noting as you drive the dugout remains that still line the banks as the Cachy Road becomes sunken, stop after 1.1 kilometres on the **track** 9 on the left just behind a line of bushes where the road crosses a deep cut. Climb the bank and walk back along it until you can see Cachy.

Running from the corner of Bois d'Aquenne to your front, the **Cachy Switch** continued over the far slope and passed to the left of Cachy. A

Dugout remains on the Cachy Road.

machine-gun near your location fired along the wire in front of the switch, enfilading the 51st Battalion in the 13th Brigade's counterattack as it tried to get through after passing the British troops sheltering in the switch. Sergeant Charles Stokes knocked the gun out but dawn on 25 April showed the wire covered with the 51st's dead. The lone British counterattack, at midday on 24 April, had been shot down as it started around Bois d'Aquenne on your right towards Villers-Bretonneux.

Now turn about. Part of the 50th Battalion reinforced the 51st after it cleared the wire. On reaching the crest of the spur to your right front, the two battalions routed a German counterattack in a wild melee. Other Germans surrendered. 'No prisoners', went the cry.

HANGARD WOOD EAST

HANGARD WOOD WEST

STORKEY 6 APRIL

12TH LANCERS AND 33RD BATTALION 30 MARCH

In the middle of an attack the Australians did not know what to do with them. The Germans fled towards Villers-Bretonneux Further to your right, the 52nd Battalion's advance was just as vigorous. Swinging leftwards off the spur behind the 51st Battalion to clear the town, 2nd Northants were themselves stopped by torrential machine-gun fire but were then able to rush across to the outskirts mid-morning on 25 April to start the job. The 36th Battalion started its counterattack on 4 April from the re-entrant on the other side of the spur.

Continue on Cachy Road. Heading up the slope from the cut, you will pass on the right a **memorial** to the first tank duel but the tanks actually fought in the fields on your left. The old road went straight on but was consumed by the A29. Bending right to follow Bois

d'Aquenne, the new stretch puts you almost on the scene of Lieutenant Sadlier's VC action on 24 April. Park on the **verge** ❿. Strung out along the edge of the wood from the bend, nine machine-guns fired into the 51st Battalion. Leading the flank platoon, Sadlier recalled: 'We wondered what had struck us. Before we had gone 50 yards, 39 out of the 42 in my platoon were in the mud either dead or wounded. I hit the deck and saw that Charlie Stokes from another platoon was still alive and 2 bombers ... had also escaped the fire. I knew that if we did not clean out the edge of that wood, the 51st Battalion would be sitting ducks.'

Sadlier told Stokes, sergeant of the adjacent platoon, to collect his bombers. Stokes found six. That made nine men in all. They charged. A German shot Sadlier

VILLERS-BRETONNEUX

MONUMENT FARM

The spur from which 2nd Northants attacked Villers-Bretonneux on 25 April and the hollow at the far end from which the 36th Battalion counterattacked through Monument Farm on 4 April.

in the thigh. Sadlier killed him and knocked out two machine-guns. Hobbling at a third with his revolver, he killed its crew too. Another wound paralysed his arm. With only two men left, Stokes took over. He destroyed another three machine-guns. Sadlier received the VC but Stokes, who also silenced the machine-gun wreaking havoc at the Cachy Switch, only got the DCM.

Continue to the junction with the D523, park, and walk to the **overpass** 11 on the A29. From here you have a good view along the axis of the 13th Brigade's assault towards Monument Farm, which is to the right of Villers-Bretonneux by the twin poplars on the skyline. The 13th's start line ran diagonally slightly to your right. General Glasgow positioned it here and not closer to Cachy because he had been informed that the British held the wood, giving him a secure flank for the first part of the assault. The opposite turned out to be the case. Return to your car, turn right on the D523 and then left onto the D1029 for Amiens.

The memorial to the first tank clash.

The 13th Brigade's advance as seen from the D523 overpass on the A29.

LOCAL INFORMATION

CEMETERIES

Adelaide Cemetery

The grave in Adelaide Cemetery from which the remains of the unknown Australian soldier were exhumed.

On the left of the D1029 and passed on the tour route just before Villers-Bretonneux, this cemetery was begun in June 1918 near an advanced dressing station. Plot I is the site of the original

cemetery, which was expanded by graves brought in from smaller cemeteries postwar to 955 burials, 694 of them known. Many of the 519 Australians fell in the town on 25 April or in Monument Wood in May. On 11 November 1993 the remains of an Australian unknown exhumed from III.M.13 were reinterred as the 'Unknown Australian Soldier' in the Hall of Memory at the Australian War Memorial in Canberra.

Bonnay Communal Cemetery Extension

Used between April and August 1918, this cemetery consist of 106 burials, all identified. Many of the 75 Australians fell in the Villers-Bretonneux battles. The Australian Prime Minister, William Morris Hughes, unveiled the Cross of Sacrifice in August 1921. To reach the cemetery, leave Fouilloy on the D1 for Corbie and turn left onto the D23 just past Corbie. Continue through Bonnay and turn left 300 metres beyond it.

Crucifix Corner Cemetery

By the D23 overpass on the A29 and passed on the tour, this cemetery was opened by the Canadians in August 1918 and greatly expanded postwar. Of its 804 burials, 608 known, 296 are Australian. Almost the entire left side of the cemetery is given over to 141 French graves, which face east like the British graves alongside them, symbolising the joint effort of the two armies to stem the German tide in the spring of 1918. A tablet placed by the locals commemorates 'the heroes who died in the defence of Villers-Bretonneux'.

The Australian National Memorial

The laurels the Australians won at Villers-Bretonneux made it their inevitable choice as the location for a national memorial. Its construction was anything but inevitable. In 1927 Melbourne architect William Lucas won the design competition for a memorial that was to be built from Australian materials and cost no more than £100 000. The depression struck before work started and the Scullin Labor government abandoned the project as unaffordable. In 1935 embarrassment that Australia was still without a memorial led to its resurrection but at a cost of £30 000, which meant an entirely new design using local materials. The last of the Dominion memorials to be unveiled, it was dedicated by King George VI on 22 July 1938.

Rising from Hill 104 on the D23 and visited on the tour, Sir Edward Lutyens's creation features a tower 34 metres high flanked by screen walls that enshrine the names of the 10 982 Australians killed in France (except for the 1298 listed at VC Corner Cemetery at Fromelles) who have no known grave. Overlooked by the Memorial, **Villers-Bretonneux Military Cemetery** was established postwar. Of its 2041 burials, 1535 of them known, 779 are Australian and two are New Zealanders. Major Bill Craies, who was mortally wounded while setting up the 52nd Battalion's line on 25 April, lies at X.E.9.

The memorial and cemetery were damaged in June 1940 when a German

Bonnay Communal Cemetery Extension.

The Australian National Memorial.

tank crashed through the lower right-hand corner of the cemetery and engaged a French machine-gun in the tower, which a Bf 109 fighter also strafed for good measure. Spalling on the Cross of Sacrifice and some of the headstones remain as honourable scars of war.

The Franco-Australian museum, Villers-Bretonneux primary school.

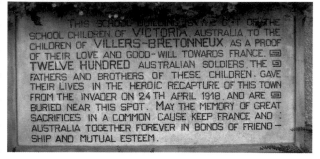

THIS SCHOOL BUILDING IS THE GIFT OF THE
SCHOOL CHILDREN OF VICTORIA, AUSTRALIA TO THE
CHILDREN OF VILLERS-BRETONNEUX AS A PROOF
OF THEIR LOVE AND GOOD-WILL TOWARDS FRANCE.
TWELVE HUNDRED AUSTRALIAN SOLDIERS, THE
FATHERS AND BROTHERS OF THESE CHILDREN, GAVE
THEIR LIVES IN THE HEROIC RECAPTURE OF THIS TOWN
FROM THE INVADER ON 24TH APRIL 1918, AND ARE
BURIED NEAR THIS SPOT. MAY THE MEMORY OF GREAT
SACRIFICES IN A COMMON CAUSE KEEP FRANCE AND
AUSTRALIA TOGETHER FOREVER IN BONDS OF FRIEND-
SHIP AND MUTUAL ESTEEM.

The appreciative plaque.

Amiens Cathedral.

MUSEUMS

The Franco-Australian Museum

On the first floor of the primary school on Rue Victoria and visited on the tour, this museum commemorates the fighting around Villers-Bretonneux in 1918 with an emphasis on the Australian role. A plaque on the front wall states that donations from schoolchildren in Victoria funded the rebuilding of the school after the war. As a result, part of the school is called *Salle Victoria* and a large sign in the playground urges the pupils N'oublions jamais l'Australie – 'Never Forget Australia'. In 1984 Villers-Bretonneux was twinned with the Victorian town of Robinvale. The museum is open 9.30 am to 5.30 pm Monday to Saturday from March to October but closes at 4.30 pm during the winter months. It is also closed in the last week of December and the first week of January. Admission is €4. Contact details are: telephone +33 3 22 96 80 79. See also www.museeaustralien.com.

NEARBY PLACES OF INTEREST

Amiens

The capital of Picardy, Amiens was briefly occupied by the Germans in 1914. Located at the hub of rail and road networks, it became a vital communications centre for the BEF, which held the northern part of the Western Front in 1916. As the city was well behind the line, most of its population remained in place, which meant that it became a bustling recreation centre for soldiers on leave. Australian and New Zealand soldiers got to know Amiens during the Somme offensive in 1916. The Australians flocked to the city in 1918, when they were twice largely responsible for saving it by staving off the Germans at Villers-Bretonneux. Thousands of them visited the 13th-century Gothic cathedral, the largest cathedral in France, which was sandbagged to the roof. Amiens suffered only occasional air attacks until the Germans got close in 1918, whereupon their shelling smashed over 2000 dwellings. The cathedral was also hit but suffered little damage. Plaques in the nave honour all the Dominion forces.

Amiens today has a population of over 150 000. The shopping malls around the station and the cathedral are modern and attractive. For the battlefield tourist, there is plenty of accommodation and many good restaurants but also plenty of traffic.

Corbie

The *Michael* offensive brought the front line close to this picturesque village, which is just across the Somme from Villers-Bretonneux. It was frequently shelled until the Germans were driven back in August and many of its buildings still bear the scars. But the railway that served Corbie ensured that it remained an important logistics centre. The Australian Corps, in whose rear area it was, used Corbie extensively as a rest area. At times as many as 20 000 Australian soldiers were in and around the village, which also housed hospitals, stores dumps and a large military post office.

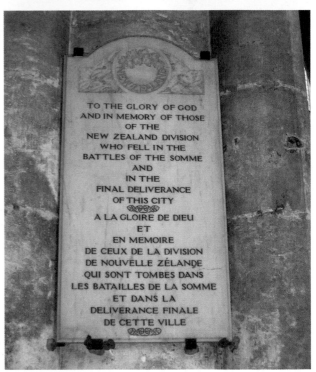

Memorial tablets to the Australians and New Zealanders in Amiens Cathedral.

CHAPTER 17

1918

HAZEBROUCK

The 1st Australian Division spent the four months between April and August 1918 near Hazebrouck in French Flanders, first playing a crucial role in halting the German *Georgette* offensive and then taking the war back to the Germans through minor attacks and peaceful penetration. The other Australian divisions were on the Somme, where their exploits greatly overshadowed what the 1st Division had done. Today names of Somme battles such as Villers-Bretonneux, Dernancourt and Hamel roll off the tongue but those of Flanders fights like Vieux-Berquin, Méteren and Merris only attract quizzical looks. Geography and history didn't help the 1st Division's cause either. The Somme and Ypres were epicentres of the BEF's campaigns for long periods and have always been central to Western Front tour itineraries. But serious fighting at Hazebrouck did not last long and the battlefield is inconveniently located in relation to Ypres and the Somme. It is rarely visited.

Backs to the wall

At the end of 1917, when the Germans were planning their great offensive against the British, they had thought about lunging for Hazebrouck, a railway junction vital for the resupply of the BEF in Flanders. General Ludendorff chose instead to split the British from the French by advancing further south. When the resulting *Michael* offensive stalled within days of its start on 21 March 1918, Ludendorff gave the green light for *Georgette*, the Flanders option. It began on 9 April, a date chosen partly because he wanted to attack before a poorly trained Portuguese division was relieved. Struck by the German Sixth Army, the Portuguese disintegrated. The British First Army, to which they were attached, consisted of divisions cut to pieces during *Michael*. Some resisted stubbornly; others gave way. The Germans were through. Armentières was abandoned. The German Fourth Army

advanced north of it, overrunning the winter line the Australians had built at Messines. Several Australian artillery units and some tunnellers narrowly escaped capture. Pouring across the Lys, the Germans were eight kilometres from Hazebrouck by 11 April. If it fell, the way to the Channel ports would be clear. Field Marshal Haig issued an order that became famous: 'There is no other course open to us but to fight it out! Every position must be held to the last man: there must be no retirement. With our backs to the wall, and believing in the justice of our cause, each one of us must fight on to the end.'

Going north

Haig's words had a special ring for the 1st Australian Division. The last of the Australian divisions to arrive on the Somme from Flanders, it was marching up to the line on 10 April. 'The Huns have broken through up north and they are

Five soldiers from the 1st Brigade prepare for a comfortable night near Hazebrouck. The bedding came from shelled and abandoned farms nearby.

sending us back again', Lieutenant Bill Joynt of the 8th Battalion was told. 'When we reach our destination be prepared to get out of the train and go straight into the fight.' Major-General Charles Harington, the Second Army's chief-of-staff, was waiting on the platform when the first men arrived at Hazebrouck on 12 April. He told them that they were 'the only formed body of troops between here and the Channel Ports'. Without waiting to assemble into their parent brigades, the leading battalions deployed onto an 'army line' that arced across the face of Nieppe Forest, blocking the main approach to Hazebrouck eight kilometres in rear. On 13 April four battalions from the 1st and 2nd Brigades were strung out along a 9.3-kilometre front that two divisions would normally have held.

Standing fast

The Germans advanced next day. One of the 8th Battalion's posts behind Vieux-Berquin was lost but the gap was soon filled. The Australian line was unbroken everywhere else. On Mont de Merris towards the left end of it, Lieutenant Fred Jarvis of the 3rd Battalion played *Die Wacht am Rhein* on a tin whistle in the hope of provoking further attacks. When the next blow came on 17 April, the fire from the Australians and the artillery was so intense that many Germans stayed under cover. The French and the British on the Australian left smashed the attack against them. Abandoning the attempt to reach Hazebrouck, the Germans swung north and took Mount Kemmel, one of the few dominating heights in Flanders, but were unable to exploit the

A reserve platoon from the 9th Battalion waits in a field to escape the shelling of the village in which it was billeted, before the German attack near Hazebrouck on 17 April. Two men were killed during the move out.

success. By the end of April *Georgette* was over.

Advancing

The same fluid conditions that allowed peaceful penetration on the Somme once the German advance ended there now took hold. 'We fight in open fields, among hedges and farm houses', Lieutenant Hubert Chedgey of the 1st Battalion wrote. The cover enabled German posts to be snaffled at will and the Australians soon gained an unchallenged ascendancy over their opponents. At the end of May, the Germans opposite them at Merris expressed relief that their 'bloody tour' was over. On 28 June the 10th Battalion took 450 metres of the 4th Bavarian Division's line at Merris with the loss of 35 men against 300 German casualties.

Corporal Phil Davey was awarded the VC for his part in holding on to the line.

When the 4th Bavarian was relieved, it had lost so many men its commander said that the situation was a disgrace to the division. Its replacement, the 13th Reserve, fared no better. On 11 July the 1st and 4th Battalions cut out over 900 metres of its front line, taking 120 prisoners and 11 machine-guns. During the British capture of Méteren eight days later, the 9th Battalion seized one kilometre of the line south of it. At the start of August, as the 1st Division was about to leave for the Somme, General Plumer, the commander of the Second Army, remarked that 'no division, certainly in my army, perhaps in the whole British Army ... has done more to destroy the morale of the enemy'.

DRIVING THE BATTLEFIELD

Don't worry if you have trouble making sense of this battlefield for the key actions, Vieux-Berquin, Merris and Méteren were widely separated as regards place and time. To minimise the difficulty, the tour is arranged chronologically as far as possible and heads south to north. Remember, though, that peaceful penetration went on continuously. Only the most important instances of it are covered but they do upset the chronology.

MAP IGN Blue Series, 1:25000, 24040 Hazebrouck

Vieux-Berquin church overlooks the village square.

The battlefield is easily reached from Ypres, 20 kilometres away. Leave Ypres on the N375, which becomes the D23 on entering France. Remaining on the D23 through Bailleul, continue another five kilometres through Outtersteene to Vieux-Berquin.

Park in the **square** ❶, where the 7th Battalion established a post on the afternoon of 12 April. Lieutenant Joynt's company from the 8th Battalion arrived just after midnight and took it over. Inspecting the line after dawn, Joynt saw some of his men dancing to a quadrille playing on a gramophone, and suitably clad in the frock coats, top hats, long dresses and Parisian gowns they had found. But dawn also showed that Vieux-Berquin would be hard to defend, so the post was withdrawn behind the village. A plaque on the wall of the **town hall**, which is alongside the **church**, commemorates these events, though not the terpsichorean element.

On leaving the square, turn right onto the D947, right again after 850 metres onto **Rue de Merville**, and right yet again after 1.9 kilometres onto **Rue du Seclin** ❷. Look along it, keeping **Nieppe Forest** on your left. On 13 April the 1st Division's line, held by four battalions, started 700 metres to your left rear, ran along the edge of the forest and extended over **Mont de Merris**, on the skyline to your right front. If you think the battalion frontages were extraordinary, ponder this. The 2nd Brigade's stretch ended at the foot of the Mont and had been held the day before, when it also included additional posts along the face of the forest behind you, as well as Vieux-Berquin, solely by the 7th Battalion. Its length was 6.4 kilometres.

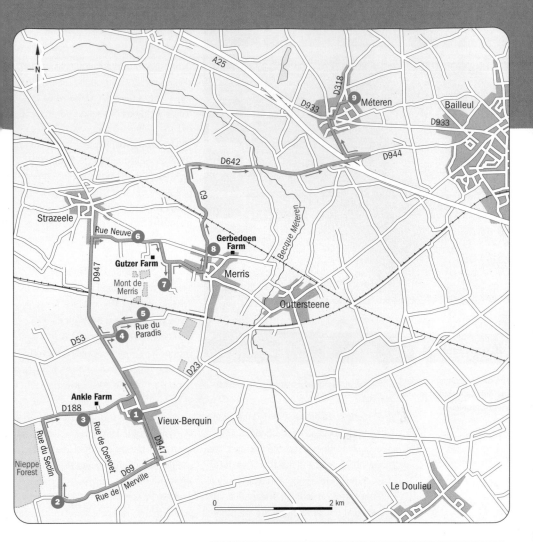

Continue on Rue du Seclin, on which the 7th Battalion's left flank on 13 April rested 800 metres along, giving the 7th a total frontage that day of 1.5 kilometres. After turning right at the T-junction onto the D188 (Rue du Bois), carry on another 750 metres and turn right again between two posts onto Rue de Coevoet, where you should be able to park 50 metres along ❸. Look back along the D188. One of the main arteries to the line, it was well-trodden by the Australian battalions. They gorged on the pigs, rabbits and poultry left behind by the villagers in **La Motte au Bois**, enclosed by the forest at the far end of the road. Its château was a favourite headquarters location. Surrounded by bomb craters,

Starting from the southern end of its line at Vieux-Berquin, this drive follows the 1st Division's major actions chronologically to Méteren in the north, where the New Zealanders had earlier suffered a stinging reverse. Along the way it passes through the sites of some notable peaceful penetration exploits as well as the location of Corporal Davey's VC exploit.

DISTANCE COVERED: **24 km**

DURATION: **3 hours**

the remains of a German V-1 launch complex are on the left of D188 near Nieppe-Bois cemetery, 1.2 kilometres beyond the near end of the wood.

Now face Vieux-Berquin. From Rue du Seclin to your right rear, the 8th Battalion's line ran behind you and across the fields to your left. Just after midnight on 14 April a German battalion marched

The plaque commemorating the Australian stand at Vieux-Berquin.

and a few survivors of his platoon escaped. Blazing away at the Germans pouring out of Vieux-Berquin, Lieutenant Les McGinn's platoon in the post on the other side of the farm took a while to realise what had happened. When they did, they withdrew to a new post 550 metres to your left. The post behind you was shelled out but reoccupied. Crossfire from this post and McGinn's new one covered the gap caused by the loss of Fenton's post. The Germans made no further progress. Nor could they get through the British 5th Division on the 2nd Brigade's right.

On the previous day, the British 29th Division had streamed back via Vieux-Berquin through McGinn's and Fenton's posts, which formed the right flank of Lieutenant Joynt's company. 'Boy, is this your post?' a British colonel had asked McGinn. 'Yes, Sir.' 'You are going to make a fight of it?' 'Yes, Sir.' 'Well, give me a rifle, I am one of your men.' Joining McGinn, the colonel said he was disgusted with his own men. For the first time in the regiment's history, they had abandoned a position they were ordered to hold. Telling McGinn, 'My boy, you can report that the 1st Lancashire Fusiliers held the village to the last', the colonel strode back to Vieux-Berquin at dusk. He settled in with some stragglers he had rounded up. The Australians heard firing throughout the night as the colonel kept his word.

Continue on the D188 and turn left in Vieux-Berquin onto the D947. As you leave the village, you are following the

from your right down Rue de Coevoet towards you. An 8th Battalion post 40 metres behind you opened fire when the leading company reached your location. Panic-stricken, the Germans fled, leaving 21 dead and five machine-guns. Extending across your front all the way to Mont Merris on your left, the main assault started at 6.30 am. During the afternoon, the Germans took the **factory**, the three-storied mill on the left of the D188 200 metres to your front. From the topmost storey, they machine-gunned Lieutenant Horrie Fenton's advanced post at **Ankle Farm**, 300 metres to your left front. Fenton, the only man unwounded,

ANKLE FARM

GERMANS

route taken by two German companies that marched in fours along this road during the afternoon of 14 April, ignoring the fighting to your left. Momentarily stunned, the 3rd Battalion on the higher ground to your front brought every barrel to bear and the Germans scattered into the roadside houses. As a quick glance at the featureless terrain either side of the D947 will confirm, the Australian machine-gunners could engage the Germans advancing from your right at ranges of 700 metres or more. The German attacks were shattered long before they could close with the Australians. It really did not matter that the Australian line was thinly held. This was a perfect example of ground being dominated by fire rather than by numbers of men.

After 1.2 kilometres the D53 appears on your left but you should turn right, between two posts, onto Rue de Christ and park 250 metres along at the sharp bend leftwards ❹. Walk around the bend and past the houses, on what is now Rue du Paradis. Look along it. The road straddles the **Plate Becque** where you are standing, the streamlet's course to your right indicated by the line of bushes, and a railway embankment runs across your front 700 metres away. The high ground beyond the embankment is Mont de Merris, on which the water tower and church spire of **Strazeele** can be seen directly ahead. Held by the 3rd Battalion, the Australian line on 14 April ran across the Mont to the left of the

wood and over the railway embankment before crossing the D947 on your left. The Germans attacked from your right and were belted by the 3rd Battalion. Though heavy, their losses paled against those three days later when the 3rd's machine-guns along the embankment to your left front enfiladed the Germans as they attacked along the slope of the Mont. At least 700 Germans were thought to have been killed on the slope. With the battle stabilised, peaceful penetration began. Some of its best known examples took place around you.

On 22 May 1918 Sergeant John Bruggy, one of the 3rd Battalion's original ANZACs, crept out of the front line on the D947 and stumbled on a trench behind the house on your left. Shooting the six occupants, he took their identity disks and, when his story was doubted, returned with his company sergeant-major so that it could be verified. On 14 June, two days after the 7th Battalion captured the ground to your front as far as the railway, Lieutenant Neil Maddox of the 5th led a patrol from your location to search for a missing corporal. Shortly after crossing the Plate Becque 230 metres on your right the patrol found itself among eight German posts. Quietly emptying six of them by threatening with bomb and revolver, it returned with 12 prisoners.

Continue along Rue du Paradis and stop once past the copse on the left ❺. Face the railway embankment. German posts ran from **Cypress Farm**, in the trees on the right of the road 80 metres

The attack at Vieux-Berquin on 14 April as seen from Rue de Coevoet. Several hours before the attack, the Germans were shot up on the road at the location where the photograph was taken.

FACTORY

VIEUX-BERQUIN

to your right, and across the field to the house enclosed by trees this side of the railway to your right front. The 1st Battalion's outpost line here consisted of Lieutenant Reg Sampson's post at the far end of the copse on your left, Lieutenant Neil Gaskell's before the trees by the railway embankment to your front and Lieutenant Claude Morley's on the other side of the railway. Early on 11 July Gaskell and three men stole through the crops to the house enclosed by trees but found it recently vacated. Heading back across the field towards you, they found three German posts in shell holes. The 14 Germans holding them were captured and made to carry their three machine-guns back to Gaskell's post, after which Gaskell and his men cleared the rest of the German posts to your right front, taking another 18 prisoners. At the same time, Morley and three men from his post worked their way behind the house Gaskell had found empty. They captured eight German posts, 36 prisoners and four machine-guns.

Sampson and four men subsequently moved along the railway embankment to the same house and headed across the field, now devoid of German posts thanks to Gaskell's exploit, towards Cypress Farm. Charging the last 30 metres to seize the farm, they killed several Germans and captured nine along with two machine-guns. Creeping out from its line, which extended diagonally up the slope on the far side of the railway and to the left of Merris to your right front, the 4th Battalion took three posts, 18 prisoners and a machine-gun. In one morning, the 1st Brigade's peaceful penetration had captured over 900 metres of the German line.

Now return to the D947, turn right onto it and right again onto Rue Neuve by the large cream agricultural building one kilometre beyond the railway. The initial Australian line ran through the **junction** **6** with the D69 (Rue de Strazeele) 900 metres along, with the 3rd Battalion on the right of the D69 and the 4th on the left. Peaceful penetration and minor attacks took all the ground between here and Merris, whose church tower is straight ahead. After another 400 metres, turn right onto Rue du Moulin, from which **Gutzer Farm** is 300 metres away on the right. Just past the sharp bend leftwards, head right again onto badly rutted Lynde Straete. Park by the track on the right at the foot of **Mont de Merris** **7** and stand with your back to Merris church.

Advancing on the far side of the railway to your left, part of the German attack on 14 April swung over the tracks

The peaceful penetration exploit of Lieutenants Gaskell, Morley and Sampson on the railway near Merris on 11 July.

GASKELL'S POST

RAILWAY

MORLEY (ON FAR SIDE OF RAILWAY)

GASKELL

at the end of Lynde Straete and onto the slope of Mont de Merris to your front. Manning a Lewis-gun in a forward post at Gutzer Farm, Corporal Perce Turvey remarked that it was 'like firing into a haystack — one could not miss'. Turvey eventually fell back to the 3rd Battalion's thinly spread main line, which ran from the rear of the copse to your front diagonally back to the crest of the Mont 600 metres to your right front. The Germans lost heavily in their unsuccessful attempt to penetrate this line. Launched from the ground to your front and right front, and caught by machine-guns sited further along the embankment, their attack on 17 April was even more costly.

Now turn right and look up the hill along Lynde Straete. By late June peaceful penetration had carried the Australian line on your left to within 150 metres of the road. Attacking on 28 June, the 10th Battalion passed through your location and set up a new line 80 metres to your right. As the left flank entrenched by the hedge, now the line of trees to your right front, point-blank machine-gun fire flayed it. Corporal Davey, who had won the MM near Messines in January 1918, dashed forward and bombed the gun, disabling half the crew. Re-crossing the road to get more bombs, he attacked again and knocked out the gun, which he then used to wipe out a German counterattack. Under fire throughout, Davey was badly wounded himself in his VC-winning action. A month later the Australian line was another 400 metres to your right. Part of the 10th Battalion's

The scene of Corporal Davey's VC exploit and the southern part of the 10th Battalion's attack on Merris on 29 July.

10TH BATTALION

The northern part of the 10th Battalion's attack on Merris on 29 July 1918.

attack that captured Merris on 29 July began there.

Head back up Lynde Straete, turn right onto Rue du Moulin and, after 650 metres, left in Merris onto the C9. Park near the **crucifix** ⑧ on the Rue de Strazeele crossroads 250 metres along and look back towards Merris, which did not extend this far in 1918. At the start of the battle, the Australian line crossed Rue de Strazeele 1.1 kilometres to your right at the junction with Rue Neuve, through which you passed earlier. As a result of peaceful penetration, it had closed up on Merris three months later. On 21 July the

Where's the village? All that was left of Merris at war's end.

11th Battalion continued the process, advancing the line to the left of **Gerbedoen Farm**, 400 metres to your left, through your location and around the right of Merris. In the last Australian attack, on 29 July, a company of the 10th Battalion assaulted through the farm and around the left side of the village while a second company attacked along the far end of the village. Merris was encircled and captured. The 10th lost 35 men out of the 160 involved. The Germans lost 284, 179 of them as prisoners.

Continuing on the C9, pass over the TGV railway, beyond which the Australian line on 13 April ran to your left. The left flank, held by the 4th Battalion, rested on the C9's junction with the D642, where you should turn right. On 16 April the 1st Battalion extended the Australian line over the D642 and across the low ground of the **Becque Méteren** to your left front. The two battalions savaged the Germans when they attacked along the Becque Méteren Valley towards you on 17 April. Look up the slope to your right on crossing the Beque after 1.3 kilometres. Peaceful penetration had taken most of the ground from the C9/D642 junction to this area by the end of July. On 19 July alone, the 9th Battalion bit out one kilometre of the German line beyond the copse on the slope. The Australian line extended from there back towards Merris, still in German hands, over your right shoulder.

Stay on the D642, which is a very busy road. Trying to turn left for Méteren can cause grey hairs, so continue 400 metres past the A25 flyover to the left-turn lane. Head sharp left there onto the D18 (Rue l'Haeghedoorn), right onto the D933 just past the church in Méteren and immediately left onto the D318 (Rue de la Fontaine). Park at the end of the second street on the right, **Rue du Peintre De Coninck** ❾, which was just an open field in 1918. Walk across Hoog Weg at the T-junction and face **Bailleul**. Cluttered with hospitals and headquarters, the town was a major logistics and transportation centre. The Germans took it on 15 April. Next day, two companies of the 2nd New Zealand Entrenching Battalion held the slopes to your front and left front. Attacking from your right and right front across the D933, the Germans took Méteren and began enveloping the New Zealanders. The right company, in your location, was surrounded, losing 100 men as prisoners in the largest single capture of New Zealanders in the war. The left company fought its way back to the crest on your left, where the German advance was stopped.

On 19 April the 1st Australian Division extended its line around the rear of

The D933, cratered, in Méteren, July 1918.

Méteren to link up with the French 133rd Division in the low ground to your left front. Late on 23 April the 3rd Brigade tried to regain Méteren by envelopment in a silent attack; that is, an attack that achieves surprise by dispensing with artillery support. Advancing along the slope across your front, the 10th Battalion was caught in a withering crossfire that came principally from two farm houses, one at the end of the road to your right, the other further down the slope. Concurrently with this advance, the 11th Battalion tried to break into Méteren from your right rear but also failed. The 3rd Brigade held the line around the village until 10 May when it moved back to the far side of the Becque Méteren.

Now return to the D933 and head for Bailleul. The D933 meets the D23, Rue d'Ypres, in the city centre. Continue on the D23 for Ypres.

The location where the right company of the 2nd New Zealand Pioneer Battalion was captured in the German attack on Méteren on 16 April.

BAILLEUL

GERMANS

2ND NEW ZEALAND PIONEER BATTALION

LOCAL INFORMATION

CEMETERIES

Bailleul Communal Cemetery Extension

The 1st Australian Casualty Clearing Station was among the many medical formations based at Bailleul at one time or another. When space in the community cemetery serving them ran out in April 1915, the extension opened. Of the 4404 burials, 398 are Australian. Some graves contain two sets of remains, indicating that neither could be individually identified. This is the case with an Australian and a New Zealander, who lie under a single headstone on which the rising sun and fern leaf are intertwined. There are 252 New Zealanders in the cemetery. To reach it, take the D23, Rue d'Ypres, from the city centre and turn right almost immediately onto Rue des Soeurs. The cemetery is at the back of the civilian cemetery 500 metres along.

Méteren Military Cemetery

Built by the French in 1919, this cemetery is on the left of the D18 200 metres from the village centre. The French and German burials originally in it were later removed, leaving 768 Commonwealth burials, 657 of them identified. Of the 104 Australians, most of whom fell locally in the April 1918 fighting, nine are unknown. Lieutenant Percy Reed of the 12th Battalion at I.E.138 fell at Méteren on 24 April. Charles Bean notes that he had enlisted under the name Eric Heurtley after deserting from the Royal Australian Navy in a quest to see action. Receiving a royal pardon after winning the MC at Bullecourt in May 1917, he resumed using his true name. The cemetery also contains 22 New Zealand burials.

Trois Arbres Cemetery

Started by the 2nd Australian Casualty Clearing Station in July 1916 and used until the Germans captured nearby Steenwerck in April 1918, the cemetery was almost doubled in size by remains brought in postwar from the surrounding battlefields. Of its 1694 burials, 1269 are identified. The 470 Australians include the most senior AIF officer killed on the Western Front, Major-General William Holmes DSO, CMG, VD of the 4th Division at I.X.42, who fell near Messines on 2 July 1917. Killed near Messines three days later, Major Harold Howden of the 48th Battalion had fought at Quinn's Post at ANZAC and won the MC at Pozières and again at Gueudecourt. He rests at I.U.17. There are 213 New Zealanders in the cemetery, which unfortunately receives few visitors as it is out of the way. You can help to change this by leaving Bailleul on the D10 for Steenwerck, taking the D77 (Rue du Pont d'Achelles) in the village, going over the A25 and stopping on the left just before the railway.

The grave of Major-General William Holmes DSO, Trois Arbres Cemetery

CHAPTER 18

1918

HAMEL

Exactly three months after the Germans had taken the Somme village of Hamel in their attack on Villers-Bretonneux on 4 April 1918, the Australian Corps regained it, handing the BEF its first major offensive success since the opening day at Cambrai eight months earlier. The Australian attack went flawlessly, which led Lieutenant-General Monash, the commander of the Australian Corps, to coin an analogy that became famous: 'A perfected modern battle plan is like nothing so much as a score for an orchestral composition, where the various arms and units are the instruments, and the tasks they perform are their respective musical phrases'. Though the name of the village on modern maps is Le Hamel, this book follows the Australian Official Historian's practice of referring to both the village and the battle simply as Hamel.

Conception

Though the BEF had weathered the *Michael* and *Georgette* offensives in March and April 1918, General Ludendorff still sought to crush it. As a preliminary, he unleashed *Blücher* on the Chemin des Dames against the French at the end of May to prevent them helping the British. General Foch asked Field Marshal Haig to tie down German reserves by launching local attacks. Monash initially thought the most useful operation that the Australians could carry out was the recapture of Hamel. It would bring the Australian line on the southern bank of the Somme level with the line on the northern bank, which was a long way ahead. Taking Hamel would also gain more room for the defence of Villers-Bretonneux, whose linchpin was the 4th Australian Division's line on the main spur of Hill 104.

The German divisions opposite were mediocre. Their positions were not. Part of the German front line ran below the brow of the Hill 104 Spur to Vaire Wood and was hidden from the 4th Division.

Pear Trench redoubt in the centre enfiladed attacks towards the Somme to its right or past Kidney Trench redoubt on its left. Vaire Wood, and conjoined Hamel Wood, were fortified. German artillery observers on the Wolfsberg behind Hamel had magnificent views over the 2.5 kilometres separating them from the Australians. Though the line between Vaire Wood and the D1029 on the Santerre plain consisted mainly of rifle pits, the area was devoid of cover and ironing-board flat. Australian and French attempts to take Monument and Hangard Woods, on similar ground south of the D1029, had failed. Monash concluded that the cost of attacking Hamel outweighed the gains.

After seeing the new Mark V tank demonstrated, Monash changed his mind. At 7.2 kilometres per hour it was faster, and had more armour protection and greater endurance than its predecessors. He told General Rawlinson that he would attack Hamel if given some. Monash got 60, which, he calculated, would enable him to cover

Lieutenant-General Sir John Monash

Commander 4th Brigade 1915–16, 3rd Australian Division 1916–18, Australian Corps 1918

1865–1931

A graduate in engineering, arts and law from Melbourne University, a pioneer of reinforced concrete construction in Australia and fluent in German, Monash had a formidable intellect. His career before 1914 in many ways prepared him for high command. Like the big Western Front offensives, the major engineering works he undertook required the organisation, direction and support of labour and the assembly and maintenance of resources. The principles guiding Monash in them were also relevant: foresight, flexibility, cooperation, economy, delegation of authority and an awareness of time. His 30 years of militia service were spent mainly in the garrison artillery and the intelligence corps, both technical arms. Monash became fascinated by the intimate relationship between technology, the development of modern weapons and the changes they wrought on warfare. 'Fighting Machinery', he concluded, had replaced physical force and brute courage. Monash could also visualise the shape of terrain from a map. This power of creative imagination was a priceless asset given the scale of operations on the Western Front.

Commanding the 4th Brigade at ANZAC, Monash experienced the soldiers' war first-hand because the cramped conditions meant that his headquarters was virtually in the front line. At the end of 1916 he took the 3rd Division to France. His meticulous planning showed at Messines in 1917, where every aspect of the division's role was covered in 36 separate instructions. As a result of that battle, and at Broodseinde following, Monash became a disciple of 'bite and hold', the limited attack. 'We can in this way inflict the maximum of losses when and where we like. It restores to the offensive the advantages which are natural to the defensive in an unlimited objective', he said. The Western Front also confirmed what Monash had realised

the five-kilometre attack frontage with 10 battalions. Commanding the 3rd Division at Broodseinde, he had deployed eight battalions on a one-kilometre frontage. The Blue Line, to which tanks and infantry would advance, ran from the Somme, across the Wolfsberg, to the D1029. Monash also opted for a composite infantry force, to be commanded by Major-General Sinclair-MacLagan, so that the losses did not fall entirely on the 4th Division, in whose sector most of the Blue Line lay. The 4th Brigade from it would attack in the centre, with the 11th Brigade from

the 3rd Division assaulting across the Somme flats on the left and the 6th Brigade from the 2nd Division between Vaire Wood and the D1029 on the right.

Monash wanted to give the leading tanks freedom of movement by dispensing with the creeping barrage but he had not reckoned on the legacy of the 4th Division's disastrous experience at Bullecourt in 1917. It had attacked there without a creeping barrage on account of the tanks, and been hung out to dry when they failed miserably. Deferring to the 4th's concerns, Monash retained the barrage and also included smoke in it to before the war: that morale, discipline and an offensive spirit alone could not defeat sophisticated military technology. It had to be countered by technology as well. The hard-pressed infantry, he wrote, would benefit most:

> [Its] true role was not to expend itself upon heroic physical effort … but to advance under the maximum possible protection of the maximum possible array of mechanical resources … guns, machine guns, tanks, mortars and aeroplanes … to be relieved as far as possible of the obligation to fight [its] way forward.

The emphasis on the physical was not at the expense of the moral. Monash insisted on looking to his men's welfare in order to keep them in fighting trim. Erecting optimism into a creed and 'feeding the troops on victory' were other means of creating and maintaining esprit.

Monash possessed in spades the essence of generalship, the capacity to endure great strain and to make quick and clear decisions. By the time he took over the Australian Corps, his ideas on fighting were also highly developed and fully proven. They gave the infantry every conceivable assistance and did not commit them to assaults on distant objectives that they would reach too weak to hold. Monash's technical mastery of all arms and tactics, particularly surprise and deception, was unsurpassed among his contemporaries, and he attached equal weight to logistics. His practical philosophy of 'unity of thought and policy and a unity of tactical methods throughout the corps' enabled the tremendous potential inherent in the grouping of the Australian divisions together to be fully realised. Monash's strengths far outweighed his flaws or the few mistakes he made. For all its own skill, the Australian Corps could not have won its successes without Monash's skill as its commander.

Appointed Director-General of Repatriation and Demobilisation at war's end, Monash planned and oversaw the massive task of returning the AIF to Australia. After his own return at the end of 1919, he accepted the chairmanship of the infant State Electricity Commission of Victoria and planned and supervised the development of the state's power scheme, his greatest engineering project. Appointed CB in 1915, Monash was knighted (KCB) in 1918. His military and civil achievements, centred on the numerous lives his generalship saved, entitle him to be called the greatest Australian.

blind the Germans. He arranged for heavy guns to fire desultorily on the exposed Santerre and for the shell holes to be mapped so that the 6th Brigade knew where to take cover. No. 3 Squadron, Australian Flying Corps, would parachute ammunition to the infantry. No effort was spared to ensure surprise. Guns, ammunition and stores were moved forward at night and camouflaged by dawn, when No. 3 Squadron reported on anything that German pilots might see. Other aircraft patrolled over the German line from dusk to dawn to drown the noise of the tanks'

assembly. Diversions were arranged on the other side of the Somme.

Diggers also met Yanks. Rawlinson had hit on the idea of using troops from the 33rd Division, an Illinois National Guard outfit training in the Fourth Army's rear, to give them some experience. Some 800 Americans joined the Australians for the attack and Monash confirmed American Independence Day as the date on which it would be carried out. When an Australian sarcastically asked an American, 'Are you going to win the war for us?', he replied, 'Well, we hope we'll fight like you'.

Major-General Ewen Sinclair-MacLagan

Commander 3rd Brigade 1915–16, 4th Australian Division 1917–18

1868–1948

A British regular who had won the DSO during the Boer War, Sinclair-MacLagan was sent to Australia in 1901 to assist in the raising and training of the new Australian Army. In 1915 he commanded the 3rd Brigade, which landed first at ANZAC. His pessimistic outlook probably contributed to his controversial decision to halt its advance prematurely, which led to the ANZAC clinging to a tiny bridgehead for the first months of the campaign. MacLagan subsequently led the 3rd Brigade at Pozières and Mouquet Farm in 1916 and, after a stint commanding the AIF depots in England, took over the 4th Division on the death of Major-General Holmes in July 1917. After its battering at Bullecourt in April, it had performed indifferently at Messines in June but did well under MacLagan's leadership at Polygon Wood in September. He led the 4th Division for the rest of the war. Appointed CB in 1917 and CMG in 1919, MacLagan returned to the British Army at war's end. Alluding to his habitual pessimism, Monash summed him up best: 'He never failed in performance and invariably contrived to do what he had urged could not be done'.

Execution

At 3.10 am on 4 July the advance began. As the smoke screens and dust thrown up by the barrage thickened the fog, the Australians had to gauge the barrage line from the flashes of air-bursting shrapnel. The gloom affected the tanks even more. In the rehearsals, they had caught up with the infantry after four minutes, when the barrage made its first lift, but at 3.14 am most were still groping forward, trying to find the battalions to which they were attached.

Advancing with the 4th Brigade, the 15th Battalion was ripped by fire and bombs from Pear Trench. Owing to the lack of observation over the redoubt, the barrage had fallen either side, leaving it untouched behind intact wire. The three tanks allotted had lost their way in the murk, so the 15th clawed its way through the wire and cleared Pear Trench on its own. Private Henry Dalziel became the 1000th recipient of the VC after he charged a machine-gun. It was also awarded to Lance-Corporal Tom Axford in the 16th Battalion for almost single-handedly overcoming Kidney Trench. He had recently won the MM. The 16th then took Vaire and Hamel Wood. Thanks to the tanks, the 6th Brigade's advance on the D1029 flank resembled a peacetime field day.

The 11th Brigade's attack on the Somme flank was almost as easy. Assaulting Hamel with the 43rd Battalion, Corporal Thomas Pope, an American, knocked out a machine-gun to win the

The attack as seen from Pear Trench in George Bell's *Dawn at Hamel, 4 July 1918*. An officer scribbles a message while a runner waits and German prisoners are being brought in. Shells burst on the Wolfsberg above Hamel village in the centre. Hamel Wood is on the right. The smokescreen that covered the advance lingers in the distance.

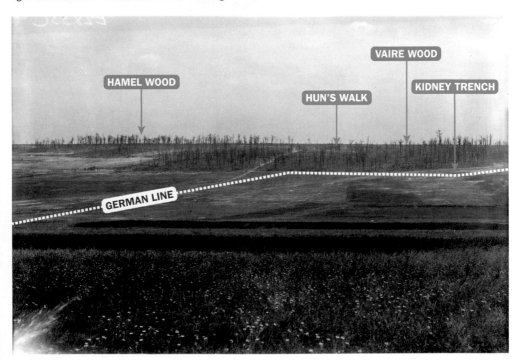

The area over which the 16th Battalion assaulted.

Australian and American dead before Pear Trench.

US Army's first Medal of Honor in France. Dawn had broken when the 44th Battalion started up the Wolfsberg for the Blue Line, its path cleared by the tanks. At 4.43 am, 93 minutes after the attack started, the Blue Line had been reached along its length. Four carrier tanks began delivering the ammunition and defence stores normally carried by 1250 men. The battle cost the Australians 1200 casualties, the Americans 176. German losses amounted to over 2000 men, 177 machine-guns, three field-guns, 32 trench mortars and three anti-tank rifles. Over 1600 prisoners were taken.

A textbook victory

The Supreme War Council asked Australian Prime Minister Hughes to cable its congratulations to Monash. Georges Clemenceau, the French Prime Minister, called at the 4th Division's headquarters at Bussy-les-Daours and enthralled the Hamel veterans gathered around him with an address in English that entered Australian folklore. Haig was delighted. A stream of commanders from other corps and armies in the BEF arrived at Monash's headquarters at Bertangles to study his methods. GHQ included his orders in two instructional pamphlets it published on the battle. They attributed the success to 'the care and skill as regards every detail with which the plan was drawn up', not least the maintenance of secrecy that ensured surprise, and the excellent coordination and cooperation of infantry, tanks, artillery and aircraft that made Hamel an all-arms battle and the model for the far bigger British offensives that followed. It was a textbook victory that cast a long shadow.

When the Australians came to France,
the French people expected a great deal of you...
We knew that you would fight a real fight,
but we did not know that from the very beginning
you would astonish the whole continent...
I shall go back tomorrow and say to my countrymen,
I have seen the Australians. I have looked in their faces.
I know that these men will fight alongside of us
again until the cause for which we are all
fighting is safe for us and for our children...

French Prime Minister Georges Clemenceau
July 1918

Clemenceau's words enshrined on the wall of the monument at the Australian Memorial Park, Hamel.

WALKING THE BATTLEFIELD

The route of this walk is gentle and the battle is easy to follow. With a population of 600, Hamel is leafy, quiet, sleepy even, which is totally in character with this stretch of the Somme. The beauty, tranquillity and splendid views in the valley and on the heights above the river make walking glorious, particularly during the long, lazy summer days. Battlefield touring does not get any better than this.

MAP IGN Blue Series, 1:25 000, 24080 Albert

Australians and Americans share a trench on the Wolfsberg after the attack. The shoulder of Hill 104, from which the assault began, rises on the far side of the valley beyond Hamel.

On leaving Villers-Bretonneux on the D1029, simply turn left onto one of the minor roads signposted for Hamel. From Albert, leave the ring road at the D42 exit and follow the D42 through Morlancourt before crossing the Somme and turning right onto the D71. At Hamel, follow the signs for the Australian Corps Memorial.

The memorial is on the site of the German command post on the **Wolfsberg** ❶. On arrival, take the path leading from the car park to the memorial and stop at the first information panels. Stand facing **Hamel**. As the distance between the car park and the memorial illustrates, the Wolfsberg was not a small position. Part of the old Amiens Defence Line, it was 550 metres across and sown with deep dugouts. Its trenches ran well beyond the access road to your right and reached halfway down to Hamel in front of you. They extended behind you to the scrubby fringe at the end of the car park. Running along the far side of the fringe and across to the right of Accroche Wood on your left was the **Blue Line**. The Wolfsberg makes a superb vantage point from which to consider the Australian advance towards it.

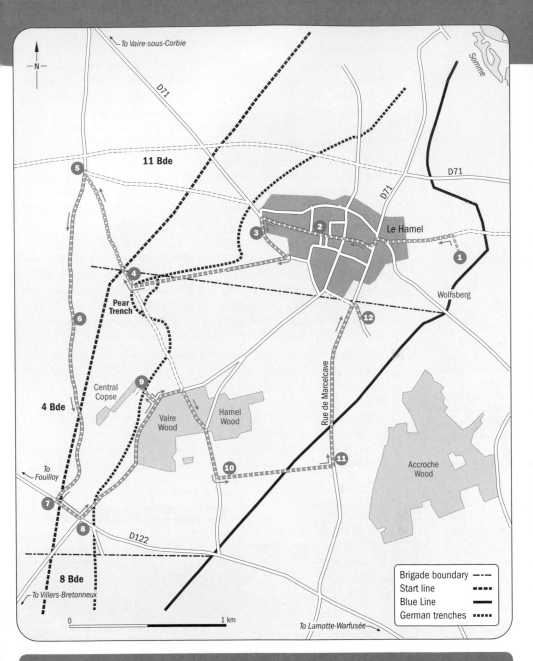

To Vaire-sous-Corbie

N

D71

D71

11 Bde

Somme

Le Hamel

5

3

2

4

1

Wolfsberg

Pear
Trench

12

6

Central
Copse

9

4 Bde

Vaire
Wood

Hamel
Wood

Rue de Marcelcave

Accroche
Wood

To
Fouilloy

10

11

7

8

D122

8 Bde

To Villers-Bretonneux

0   1 km

To Lamotte-Warfusée

Brigade boundary — — —
Start line   ■ ■ ■ ■
Blue Line   ━━━━
German trenches   ▪▪▪▪▪

Starting from the Wolfsberg, which was one of the main objectives of the Australian attack and which offers panoramic views over much of the battlefield, the walk passes through Hamel itself, over the ground on which the 4th and 11th Brigades advanced and along their front line. The route then goes through Vaire Wood before continuing along the left flank of the 6th Brigade's advance and returning to the Wolfsberg. Pear and Kidney Trenches, where the two VCs were won, are also included.

DISTANCE COVERED: 9.5 km
DURATION: 4 hours

The Australian line on the far side of the Somme started midway between **Sailly-le-Sec**, on your right, and **Sailly-Laurette**, over your right shoulder, and went diagonally up the slope behind Sailly-Laurette. On this side it started at **Bouzencourt**, which comprises a few buildings on the bank at the end of the road leading to the river. You turned left onto the D71 stretch of this road. From Bouzencourt, the line tracked over the flats before **Vaire-sous-Corbie**, to your right front, ran up the end of the **Hill 104 Spur** 2.5 kilometres away to your front and then followed the road along the crest, which is crowned by **Mouse Copse**. Notice how far ahead of the line on this side of the Somme the Australian line on the other side was. Capturing the Wolfsberg would bring the two lines level and prevent the Germans on this side enfilading the Australian line on the far side. But the terrific views the Germans had from your location and the vulnerability of infantry advancing over the open ground towards you explain Monash's reluctance to attack until tanks became available.

Also starting from Bouzencourt, the German line skirted around the front of Hamel. After turning sharp right there, it joined the track running along the facing side of the Hill 104 Spur below the crest road and passed around the far side of the conjoined mass of **Vaire** and **Hamel Wood** to your left front. Hamel Wood is at the nearer end of them. **Pear Trench** was almost directly in front of you on the track, while **Kidney Trench** abutted **Central Copse**, the untidy outgrowth at the tip of Vaire Wood. The tower of the **Australian National Memorial** is on the skyline to the right of the wood. As the Memorial is close to Villers-Bretonneux, the town's security would be enhanced by extending the Australian line to the Wolfsberg.

Try putting yourself in the position of the Germans on the Wolfsberg. The Hill 104 Spur extends like a distant wall across your front, behind which the tanks could assemble without your seeing them and, because of the din from the aircraft above you, without you hearing them. Their start line was behind the infantry one and ran along the spur just in front of Mouse Copse but they moved to it in darkness while the aircraft were bombing you as well. The firing data for the Australian and British guns was based on map calculations rather than on ranging shots, so the barrage crashed down on you out of the blue. Your stunned surprise is hardly to be

The German view from the Wolfsberg, showing the German front line and the ground across which the Australian assault came.

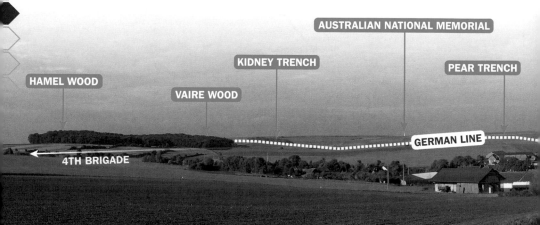

AUSTRALIAN NATIONAL MEMORIAL

KIDNEY TRENCH

PEAR TRENCH

HAMEL WOOD

VAIRE WOOD

GERMAN LINE

4TH BRIGADE

wondered at. Shrouded by fog, smoke and, of course, the darkness, you can see nothing of the advance.

The 4th Brigade advanced to your left front, with the 15th Battalion reaching the Blue Line on your left after taking Pear Trench, and the 16th Battalion clearing Vaire and Hamel Wood after taking Kidney Trench. As no-man's-land was at its widest to your right front, the 11th Brigade attacking there was given almost half the tanks. On the Somme flats, the Germans scattered before the 42nd Battalion and its tanks like ducks fleeing a line of beaters. The 43rd Battalion took Hamel while the 44th passed either side of it and reformed below you for the attack on the Wolfsberg. Dawn had broken and the fire from your location was intense. But the barrage was mainly shrapnel now so the tanks could move underneath it without risk, allowing the 44th to hang back. The tanks lumbered up the slope towards you, trampling German posts or firing grapeshot into them. One tank moved backwards and forwards over a machine-gun position like 'a housewife's flat iron'. With the way open, the 44th Battalion rushed the crest around you, capturing crowded dugouts and a battalion headquarters.

Before leaving, turn about. Following a mustard and phosgene bombardment, a German counterattack reached the scrubby fringe at 10 pm. The Australian response started from the memorial area, with Private James Lynch of the 44th Battalion in the van. A colossus who had been a prewar axeman, Lynch wielded a club and threw bombs until he was shot through the head. The Germans ran. Now head down to Hamel. German machine-guns were scattered along the outskirts ahead of you. Lance-Corporal Francis Shaw of the 43rd Battalion charged one, killing a German officer who rushed at him firing a revolver. When Shaw reached the post, eight Germans lay dead around the gun. A ninth attacked him. Drawing his own revolver while they grappled, Shaw smashed the German's skull and shot him. Three more machine-guns opened up. Shaw led an assault on one that yielded 17 prisoners and a tank flattened the other two.

Turn left at the T-junction onto the D71, then right after 50 metres at the traffic island. Continue on Rue General John Monash, the name given to the D71 as it passes through the village, to the **church 2**, outside which is a Bastiaan plaque. The stone-topped pillars supporting the iron-railing fence on the

wall across the street were among the few parts of prewar Hamel to escape destruction. Since 26 June the Germans had been harassed with 'flavoured smoke', a combination of gas and smoke shelling that drilled them into wearing gas masks whenever smoke shells went off. Smoke only was used in the attack but the Germans donned gas masks nonetheless. The specially designated sections clearing the cellars and dugouts in the village found many Germans, conditioned by the flavoured smoke, sheltering in them still with their gas masks on. 'Everywhere the enemy was unprepared for the assaulting troops', the 43rd Battalion's war diary said. Over 300 prisoners were taken.

Continue to the **four-way intersection** ❸ at the end of the village, before which the 43rd Battalion

was briefly held up. Look straight ahead. When a troublesome post in the German line 100 metres to your front was outflanked by men swinging towards the D71 to your right front, those pinned down by the post charged it, taking 40 prisoners. Now look down the D71. The crew of a machine-gun located where the German line crossed the road 150 metres along got away just before a tank squashed it. Head left on Rue du Tour de Ville and sharp right after 300 metres. This road, which paralleled the German line on your right, becomes a farm track within 400 metres and strikes the rear of Pear Trench 400 metres further on, after which it runs through the centre of the position. Follow the track to the junction with the **sunken road** ❹ and face the slope ahead.

You are now at the business end of Pear Trench. It ran for almost 150 metres just the other side of the sunken road, which was pitted with dugouts, before doubling back on itself in a trench that faced Vaire and Hamel Wood and completed the pear-shaped outline that gave the redoubt its name. Even a brief look shows how Pear Trench could enfilade any advance towards Hamel across the low ground on either side. It was also an excellent reverse-slope position. Accentuated by tall crops, the convex curve of the ground rendered it invisible to the 15th Battalion on its start line 250 metres up the spur but the Germans could make out the 15th against the skyline. When the barrage went astray and the tanks failed to arrive, the 15th faced a frontal assault against concealed defences that were intact.

Covered by Lewis-gunners, who stood and sprayed over the crops, the 15th clawed its way through the wire on the slope ahead of you and rushed the two machine-guns in the trench immediately in front of you that were holding up the advance. When a third gun opened near your location, Private Dalziel leapt into the gun pit and killed two of the gunners.

Rue General John Monash. The fence pillars on the left survived the battle.

Australians on the outskirts of Hamel with one of the three tanks disabled in the attack. A tricolour flies from the ruined house beyond. Captain John Moran of the 43rd Battalion climbed onto the roof to raise it when the assault reached the village.

He spared the third because 'the youngster fought so well'. Dalziel's trigger finger was shot away and he was hit in the head while carrying ammunition up afterwards. His brain was exposed but Dalziel survived. Even as the Germans around you surrendered, those in the depth trenches behind you continued to throw bombs. Infuriated by what they considered to be 'white flag treachery', the Australians moved along the sunken road killing any Germans they found. The stretch in which you are standing was soon littered with over 40 dead.

Now head right on the sunken road, which the Australian start line crossed 150 metres along, on the boundary between the 15th and 43rd Battalions. Carry on another 550 metres to the **crucifix 5** on the junction with the sealed road from Vaire and face Hamel. The German line ran leftwards to the Somme from Hamel; the line from which the

11th Brigade attacked crossed your front midway between your location and Hamel and ran up the Hill 104 Spur to your right. No-man's-land varied from 500 metres ahead of you to as much as 1400 metres on the Somme flank. These distances made surprise and attacking in darkness essential. The open terrain was perfect for tanks. For the onlookers in the 41st Battalion, in reserve behind your location, 'It was a truly wonderful sight watching the tanks creeping over the ground through the grey mists of dawn, and the long line of flashing shell-bursts as the barrage lifted and lengthened, while the colossal din of the whole titanic combat smote upon the ears and set the heart palpitating with awe and tense excitement'.

Take the sealed road up the spur and stop after 900 metres 6. Look towards Hamel. Pear Trench was 450 metres to your left front, hidden by the convex slope from the 15th Battalion's start line, which

German dead in the sunken road behind Pear Trench shortly after the Australian assault passed through.

The sunken road at Pear Trench today.

crossed your front 100 metres ahead. The shape of the ground and the poor light defeated the three tanks supporting the left of the 15th. They started from the area of Mouse Copse behind you but missed Pear Trench. Using binoculars, you can see the sunken road emerging in the fields to your right front and heading up the slope to meet the road from Hamel at Vaire Wood. The German line followed it from Pear Trench but broke across the slope to Kidney Trench at Central Copse, which appears as an untidy extension of the wood. Crowning the Wolfsberg above Hamel, the Australian Corps Memorial signifies the Blue Line, which you can follow towards Accroche Wood. Look rearwards at the tower of the Australian National Memorial on the far side of Hill 104 and the spires of Villers-Bretonneux to its left. Before the Australian attack the town's proximity to the German line behind you left it vulnerable.

Continue along the road. After crossing it 400 metres along, on the boundary between the 15th and 16th Battalions, the start line ran along the right of the road to the **junction** ➐ with the D122. The 13th Battalion took over here. Head left on the D122 and left again onto the **Hamel–Villers-Bretonneux road** ➑ after 150 metres. The barrage obliterated a post in the old quarry on the left of this intersection, giving the 13th a relatively easy advance to the tip of Vaire Wood 650 metres away. Following the right side of the road, the German line crossed over after 200 metres to become **Vaire Trench**, which skirted around the front of Vaire Wood. Walk another 800 metres to the track on the left just before a sharp rightwards bend. **Hun's Walk**, a communication trench, entered Vaire Wood here and ran two kilometres to Accroche Wood. Head along the track, which roughly followed the line of Hun's Walk, for 150 metres to the tip of **Central Copse** ➒.

Stand with the copse on your left and Vaire Wood on your right. You are now on

the end of Kidney Trench, a double line of trenches that stretched 180 metres ahead of you and 90 metres to your right. It enfiladed the line to your front, which met the sunken road 250 metres away and followed it up the far slope to Pear Trench on the crest. Assaulting from your left without its tanks, the 16th Battalion was heavily machine-gunned from Kidney Trench and faltered before its uncut wire. Spotting a gap, Lance-Corporal Axford tore through the wire, hurling bombs that stunned the German machine-gunners. He bayoneted 10 Germans and captured several others. His VC-winning action broke the back of the resistance.

Return to the Hamel road. Head left and, after 150 metres, right onto the sunken road through Vaire Wood. Having cleared Vaire Trench, the 16th Battalion swept through the wood, whose trees had been stripped bare by the shelling. The tanks had caught up and did useful work but the 16th's best asset was the barrage. Firing Lewis-guns from the hip while advancing in an extended line like a bunch of Western gunfighters, the 16th drove the Germans into the shell fire. Traces of shell holes and dugouts can be seen either side of the sunken road, which joins a sealed road near the tree line after 250 metres. Hun's Walk passed through this junction on its way to Accroche Wood. Many Germans withdrew along it.

Continue another 300 metres on the sealed road to the **track** ➓ on the left and look back towards the wood. The area enclosed by the wood to your left front was a **carrier tank dumping point**, while the area around you served as an **ammunition drop zone**. Both were set up for the 13th Battalion, which assaulted from your left between the wood and the D122, 500 metres behind you. Two machine-guns opened from a concealed trench 100 metres to your front, pinning down the 13th. Two tanks trundled to the rescue. Captain George Marper ran in front of one and was shot twice while pointing out the trench. The tank crushed one of the machine-guns, prompting the crew of the second to surrender.

Now take the track. Cutting diagonally from your right, the Blue Line crossed it 300 metres along. In the 6th Brigade's advance on your right, the 21st Battalion was on the far side of the D122 with the 23rd next to it on the D1029. The flat and open terrain towards the D1029 explains why it was the target zone for most of the heavy shelling that created craters for the 21st and 23rd to use as cover. As this ground also favoured tanks more than anywhere else, they were heavily called upon and earned lavish praise from all ranks. The barrage was perfect. On reaching the T-junction turn left for Hamel on **Rue de Marcelcave** **11**. Both the Blue Line and Hun's Walk crossed the road 300 metres past the junction. The Blue Line went on to the Wolfsberg, Hun's Walk to Accroche Wood on your right. As tanks and infantry parties pushed into the wood, many felt afterwards that the Blue Line should have been set on the far side of it. But Monash would not risk a potentially stiff fight for the wood at the end of an already long advance. The nearness of Accroche Wood exemplifies his conception of Hamel as a limited or 'bite and hold' attack.

Walking down the hill towards Hamel, you will pass the protruding corner of Hamel Wood on your left. The Germans in the wood made their last stand there. One captured by the 16th Battalion laughed when told 'Finis le Guerre.' 'Yes my —— oath', he replied, adding that he had learned English as a miner in Western Australia before returning to Germany early in 1914. Several German machine-guns lined the terraced slope that overlooks the Hamel–Villers-Bretonneux road to your left front. Masked by the wood and enfilading the village, they threatened the 43rd Battalion's attack until the 15th Battalion overran them.

Before entering Hamel, stop at the **Chapelle St Roche** **12** on the fork and look back along the road. A trench on the high ground to your left held up the 15th Battalion to your right front until a tank drove along it. Fifty Germans and 27 machine-guns were captured. Ammunition drop zones and dumping points for carrier tanks were established either side of the chapel between Hamel Wood and the Wolfsberg, to which you should now return. But the café in Rue John Monash may be more tempting. Suitably refreshed, you can start the tour of the battlefield over which the Australian Corps advanced on 8 August 1918.

An Australian infantryman's view from the 15th Battalion's front line. The curve of the slope ahead hides Pear Trench.

HAMEL

WOLFSBERG

15TH BATTALION

LOCAL INFORMATION

CEMETERIES

The Australian Hamel fallen rest in many of the cemeteries pertaining to the Villers-Bretonneux and Morlancourt Ridge fighting. Private Lynch, for example, lies at I.F.7 in **Villers-Bretonneux Military Cemetery**. Others sleep in **Méricourt l'Abbé Communal Cemetery Extension**. Details on these and additional relevant cemeteries can be found in the chapters on those battles.

Daours Communal Cemetery Extension

As Daours was on the Amiens–Albert railway line, five casualty clearing stations were set up around it before the 1916 Somme offensive. Though this cemetery served them, most of its 1231 burials, nearly all identified, are from 1918. The bulk of the 459 Australians died between May and September that year. Among the Hamel casualties are Captain Frederick Woods and Company Sergeant-Major Harold Blinman of the 16th Battalion. Both were hit by fire from a machine-gun that Lance-Corporal Axford subsequently knocked out. 2nd Lieutenant Horace Blee, wounded in the same action, also rests in Daours. Woods, Blinman and Blee were all good friends and had been sergeants-major of D Company. Woods is buried at III.D.37 with Blee and Blinman either side. One New Zealander rests in Daours. To visit the cemetery from Hamel, take the D71 via Vaire to Fouilloy and turn left there onto the D1. Continue on the D1 through Aubigny to Daours and turn right at the lights onto the D115. The cemetery is 400 metres along on the left.

MEMORIALS

The Australian Corps Memorial Park

Set among German trenches on the Wolfsberg that were captured by the 44th Battalion, this memorial to the

ACCROCHE WOOD

HAMEL WOOD

SUNKEN ROAD

VAIRE WOOD

16TH BATTALION

The graves of Captain Frederick Woods and Company Sergeant-Major Harold Blinman, Daours Communal Cemetery Extension.

The rebuilt centrepiece of the Australian Corps Memorial Park.

achievements and sacrifice of the Australian Corps on the Western Front in 1918 has had a rocky time since its opening on 4 July 1998. Rain seeped behind many of the granite tiles cladding the massive curved walls that were the memorial's centrepiece and they fell off when the water froze during the winter. As if this were not enough, its remoteness made the memorial an easy target for vandals, who did further damage and repeatedly smashed or defaced the glass information panels. Deteriorating to a point where it drew public criticism for embarrassing rather than honouring the Australian Corps, the memorial had to be rebuilt. The Australian Governor-General rededicated it on 8 November 2008.

The new memorial is a deluxe version of its predecessor. Its three curved walls, still granite-clad, are smaller but bear the Australian 'rising sun' badge worn by every AIF soldier and the extract from Clemenceau's post-battle speech to the Australians that were on the original. New, more resilient information panels have been installed and random security checks instituted. Ceremonies are held at the memorial on 4 July or, if that day falls during the week, on the first weekend after.

CHAPTER 19

1918

THE GERMAN ARMY'S BLACK DAY

As *Michael*, the first of the German offensives of 1918, had been brought to a halt on the Somme, it was appropriate that the Allied counteroffensive should start there. The British Fourth Army, with French support, attacked on 8 August. General Ludendorff famously described the outcome as 'the black day of the German Army'. Consult any list of history's decisive battles and you will more than likely find 8 August, sometimes called the Amiens Offensive, included. The Australian Corps was in the centre of the advance. General Monash initially considered himself 'the prime mover' in the genesis of the offensive. Later, he was less sure of the part he had played. But many of the AIF's senior officers believed that Monash was at the heart of it, particularly his chief of staff, Brigadier-General Thomas Blamey. Patriotic journalism promoted the view, sometimes with the added claim that the AIF thus 'won the war'. The reality was different.

Genesis

On 6 July 1918, two days after the Australian success at Hamel, Sergeant Walter Brown of the 20th Battalion captured a German post in a peaceful penetration exploit that won him the VC. Monument Farm and Wood, in German hands since Second Villers-Bretonneux, fell to peaceful penetration soon after. Determined to capitalise on its ascendancy over the Germans, Monash impressed on General Rawlinson, the Fourth Army's commander, that the Australian Corps could attack on a decisive scale if its front were reduced, the 1st Australian Division were returned from Hazebrouck and the Canadian Corps advanced on the Australian right. On 15 July Rawlinson told Monash that

the Canadians would be available and asked what he needed in tanks and guns. On 21 July Rawlinson, Monash and others thrashed out the plan. So went Monash's version of events.

As a corps commander far removed from the war's strategic direction, Monash did not know that General Foch, the Allied generalissimo, had wanted to attack on the Somme since March to safeguard Amiens. *Georgette* stymied the Anglo-French offensive he proposed in April. He revived it with Field Marshal Haig in May. The Fourth Army would carry out the British role. Haig intimated to Rawlinson that he would receive the Canadian Corps for it. But the Germans were still determined to destroy the BEF. To prevent the French helping the British, they sprang the *Blücher* offensive on the French at the end of May on the Chemin des Dames. The Amiens offensive was put on hold again. By mid-June *Blücher* had fizzled out. Launched in mid-July, its successor, *Friedensturm*, also failed. Rawlinson resurrected the Amiens scheme. Haig approved his proposals on 19 July.

By then the French counterstroke on the Marne had ended German offensive aspirations. On 24 July, Foch announced his intentions for the Allied counter-offensive. The French would again strike on the Marne, the Americans were to eliminate the St Mihiel salient south-east of Verdun, and the British would have the leading role in the Anglo-French advance before Amiens. The Fourth Army would assault on 8 August on an 18-kilometre front between Morlancourt and Démuin with the Australians and Canadians, respectively left and right of the railway, south of the Somme and III Corps north of the river. Supported by 2000 guns and 552 tanks, as well as armoured cars and cavalry, they were to advance up to 11 kilometres in three stages.

Plans

If Monash did not devise the August offensive, he was responsible for his formation's part in it. Spread between the Somme and the railway, the Australian Corps would advance over nine kilometres. Ending after 3.2 kilometres on the Green Line, the first phase included the German gun line, whose capture would put Amiens outside the range of all but the heaviest German guns. Then came the 4.5-kilometre assault to the Red Line, during which the Australian left flank on the Somme at Morcourt would be enfiladed by the Germans on the finger-shaped Chipilly Spur on the far bank. Lacking confidence that III Corps, advancing on that side of the Somme, could take Chipilly, Monash wanted the Australian line extended over the river. Rawlinson refused. The last phase was the

A shot taken nine days after the attack from the Chipilly Spur, looking across the Somme to the Morcourt Valley.

Taken during the attack, this photograph shows troops of the 5th Australian Division clustered around some field-guns and a Mark V Star carrier tank in the re-entrant north of Lamotte-Warfusée, which can be seen on the right. They are waiting for the start of the advance to the Red Line. The tank will be used in the assault on the Blue Line.

1.4-kilometre advance past Harbonnières to the Blue Line, which ran just beyond the outer line of the defences dug by the French in 1915 to protect Amiens.

The eight-kilometre frontage of the Australian assault necessitated two divisions attacking side-by-side. Its depth necessitated leapfrogs, which favoured the divisions attacking first because they could assemble close to their objectives. Those destined for the later phases had to leapfrog them after marching from concentration areas well to the rear. In the deep penetration now proposed, they would have to march a long way. By placing those divisions, the 4th and 5th, closest to the start line, Monash shortened the distance by almost five kilometres. The 2nd and 3rd Divisions would leapfrog them to attack the Green Line and be leapfrogged in turn for the advance to the Red Line by the 4th and 5th, some of whose battalions would go on to the Blue Line. Leapfrogging within

divisions had become commonplace but it was rarely practised between divisions. Monash was now ordering two leapfrogs by two divisions next to each other. He acknowledged the complexity but trusted to the intelligence and competence of troops, commanders and staffs. Calling the plan 'John Monash's masterpiece', Charles Bean wrote it would probably be the classical example for the launching of such operations. Arriving from Flanders just before the attack, the 1st Division was to be in reserve.

At least 24 tanks supported each division. Moving up during the pause on the Green Line, a field artillery brigade, as well as an engineer and a machine-gun company, would assist the advance of each infantry brigade to the Red Line. Thirty-six Mark V Star tanks, stretched Mark V's that could carry up to three infantry machine-gun teams, were laid on for the attack on the Blue Line, so that it could be reached before German reserves occupied the old Amiens Outer Line. Accompanied by some Whippet light tanks, the 1st Cavalry Brigade was to raid the German rear areas along with 16 armoured cars. The extra punch and flexibility given by these groupings meant that the creeping barrage could be dispensed with for the later phases, which would take on the character of open warfare. Conversely, said Monash, the attack on the Green Line in the set-piece first phase reproduced 'the conditions of Hamel'. The methods used to gain surprise at Hamel were again applied.

Advancing

At 4.20 am on 8 August the Fourth Army's 2000 guns spoke and the line moved forward. The fog was so dense that some platoons held hands to stay together. Attacking next to the Canadians, the 7th Brigade struck the only intact wire met that day. As the tanks had not caught up, 2nd Lieutenant Alfred Gaby found a gap and cleared a trench holding up the 28th Battalion. He was awarded the VC. The 5th Brigade alongside moved as a gaggle of intermixed units. Lieutenant John Lane

of the 18th Battalion described the tactics as 'someone telling anyone he met that there were some Germans down in some corner he had passed or where he had seen them; collecting a few men and going round and grabbing the Germans'. Further north, the 9th Brigade rooted them out of Accroche Wood. On the Somme flats the 11th Brigade homed in on the Germans firing blindly into the fog. The German guns were reached as it began to lift. Many had already been smashed by the Fourth Army's counter-battery fire. By 7 am the 2nd and 3rd Divisions were on the Green Line and digging in.

At 8.20 am the advance to the Red Line began, the tanks taking the place of the creeping barrage. No longer blinded by the fog, the German gunners further back fired over open sights. Covered by an extemporised barrage from the accompanying artillery, the Australians and the tanks headed towards them, the tanks forcing the gunners into cover while the infantry attacked. By 11 am the 8th and 15th Brigades had taken the 5th Division's section of the Red Line. They took off for the Blue Line without waiting for the tanks assigned to help.

German prisoners scurry rearwards along the Morcourt Valley just after their capture.

Wounded Australians from the 15th Brigade, and wounded German prisoners shelter beside a Whippet tank near Harbonnières.

At 1.15 pm Monash signalled Rawlinson: 'Australian flag hoisted over Harbonnières at midday'.

In the 4th Division's sector on the Somme flank, the 4th Brigade came across rich logistical pickings and hundreds of unresisting troops in the lower Morcourt Valley. The 12th Brigade captured 500 Germans in the upper part of the valley. Over the Somme, III Corps had failed to take the Chipilly Spur, as Monash expected. Complaining that they had too many targets, the German gunners there laid into the 4th Brigade as it re-formed on the Red Line. Ferocious short-range artillery duels began when the batteries attached to the 4th caught up but the German guns could not be suppressed.

The unbearable conditions inside the Mark V Star tanks precluded full use being made of some, while others were too slow moving forward, so the advance to the Blue Line was largely undertaken without them. Meanwhile,

the 1st Cavalry Brigade and the Whippets had gone beyond the Blue Line. One cavalry column captured a 28-centimetre railway gun used to shell Amiens. The armoured cars ranged over three kilometres out to shoot up the Germans in Vauvillers, Proyart, Framerville and Chuignolles.

For the loss of 2000 men, the Australian Corps had taken 7295 prisoners, 173 guns and enough engineering material to last it for the rest of the war. The Canadians took 6000 prisoners and about the same number of guns as the Australians, while the French took 3500 prisoners. Ludendorff lamented that the decline of German fighting power was 'beyond all doubt'. Next day Rawlinson made Monash responsible for the northern bank of the Somme. Crossing over, a six-man patrol under Quartermaster-Sergeant Jack Hayes of the 1st Battalion found Chipilly abandoned and the German guns gone from the spur.

DRIVING THE BATTLEFIELD

The Australian Corps advance on 8 August covered a vast area. If you have toured any of the 1916–17 battlefields, say Pozières, Bullecourt or even Broodseinde, contrast their size with the size of this one. True, the positions the Germans occupied were ad hoc and a far cry from the established and formidable trench and pillbox systems of the earlier battles. But this was not the only reason for the success on 8 August. Remember that the Australian Corps then was highly experienced at all levels and benefited from technology, such as tanks and artillery ranging techniques, that had resulted from the experience of war since 1914. You are now driving a *modern* battlefield. But avoid being so absorbed that you neglect the views on the Somme flank. They are timeless — and stunning — more than compensating for the fact that the A29 autoroute cuts across part of the battlefield on the opposite flank.

MAPS IGN Blue Series, 1:25000, 24080 Albert; 2408E Bray-sur-Somme; 24090 Harbonnières; 2409E Roye

The tour begins at the Australian Corps Memorial on the Wolfsberg, which is also the start and end point of the Hamel walk Simply follow the directions to the Wolfsberg from either Villers-Bretonneux or Albert given in the Hamel chapter. Using the track along the left side, walk to the far end of the hedged **orchard** ❶ that abuts the memorial's car park and stand with the orchard at your back and the Somme on your left. **Sailly-Laurette** is on the far bank 2.3 kilometres to your left front. Starting from the near bank directly opposite it, the 3rd Division's start line ran through your location and to the right of **Accroche Wood** on your right. The 11th Brigade struck out from here across the **Vallée d'Arbancourt** to your front, while the 9th Brigade passed through Accroche Wood. Both headed for the **Green Line**, which passed across your front and to the far side of **Lamotte-Warfusée**, whose church spire breaks the skyline to the left of Accroche Wood. Having waited behind you, the 4th Brigade then moved

CHIPILLY SPUR

CERISY

11TH BRIGADE

through your location with the 12th Brigade on its right. These two brigades from the 4th Division took over the advance from the Green Line. The 4th Brigade was shot up from the Chipilly Spur, the high ground behind **Cerisy**, whose church steeple can be seen four kilometres ahead on the near bank. Following the 4th Brigade, the 1st Brigade strung out along the Somme there to protect the Australian left flank.

The Wolfsberg was captured by the Australian Corps in the attack on Hamel on 4 July. Unless you have already done so on the Hamel tour, visit the Corps Memorial and the nearby trenches and then head down to **Hamel**. Turn left onto the D71, which soon becomes the C201. The start line crossed it by the track on the right 1.5 kilometres along and the boundary between the 3rd and 2nd Divisions went over after another 500 metres to run along the right side of Accroche Wood on your left. There are blind corners on the D122 just ahead, so be careful when crossing. On reaching the D1029, turn right. The 2nd Division's start line crossed 600 metres along. Now keep a keen eye out for the **layover** ❷ on the right 900 metres further on. Pull into it and stand with your back to the road.

A short German trench ran diagonally across your front and met the road a few metres to your right. Though being sniped from it on 6 July, the Australians beyond the trench were unsure of its exact location. Sergeant Brown took matters into his own hands. When a shot rang out, he charged 60 metres towards a small mound 200 metres to your front, from where he thought the shot had come, throwing a bomb as he ran. Brown, who had won the DCM at Passchendaele in 1917, hit the ground when it fell short. Resuming his attack when all was quiet, he arrived at the mound, which overlooked the apparently empty trench. Jumping into the trench, he clocked a German who emerged from a dugout. When more Germans emerged from another dugout, Brown brandished his remaining bomb and motioned

The start line on the Somme flank from the Australian Corps Memorial Park.

VALLÉE D'ARBANCOURT

9TH BRIGADE

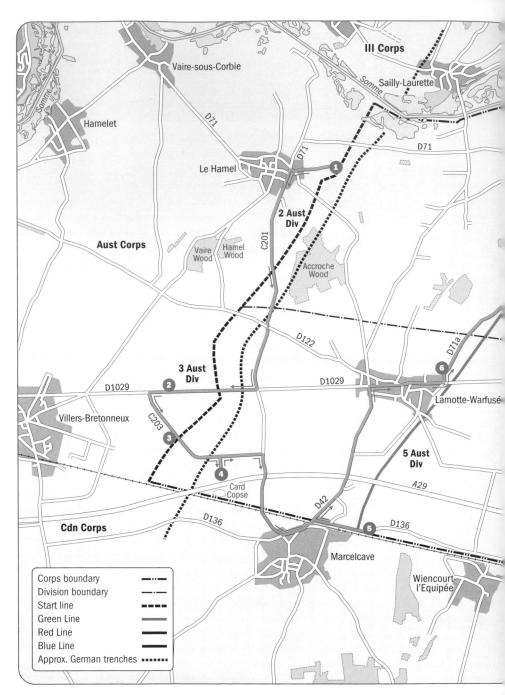

towards the Australian line. He handed
13 prisoners over there. As a 56-year-old
gunner in the 8th Division in the next
war, Brown picked up two grenades, said
'No surrender for me' and walked towards
the Japanese on 14 February 1942, the
eve of the capitulation in Singapore. The
VC recipient was never seen again.

Turn left just past the layover onto the
C203, signposted **Cimetière Militaire
de Marcelcave**. Pull over 800 metres
along ③, where the start line, occupied
by the 7th Brigade, crossed the road at
right angles and ran to the D1029 on
your left and the **railway** on your right.
Formed up behind the 7th was the 15th

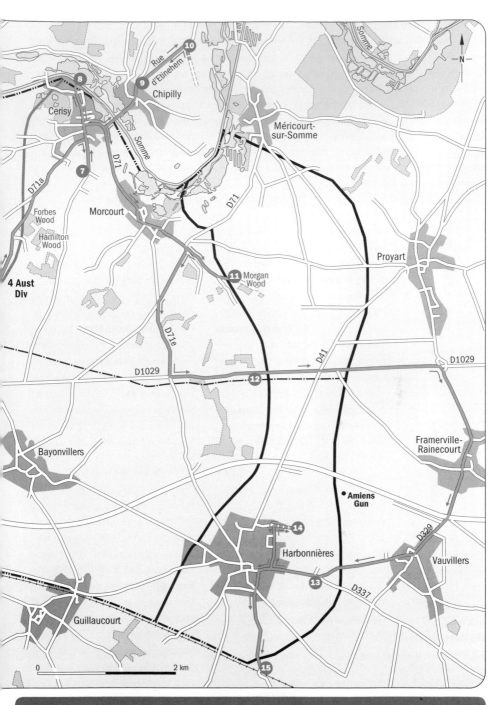

Crisscrossing the 8 August battlefield is necessary if you want to do it justice and this drive does just that. Traversing the start line from the Wolfsberg above Hamel, it heads down the 2nd Division's right flank at Marcelcave, passing the site of Lieutenant Gaby's VC exploit, and back along the Green Line to the 3rd Division's left flank on the Somme and the Chipilly Spur on the far side of the river. Recrossing the Somme, the route continues over the ground on which the 4th and 5th Divisions advanced to the Red and Blue Lines before finishing up on the Blue Line at Harbonnières on the 5th's right flank.

DISTANCE COVERED: 46 km

DURATION: 6.5 hours

> There was a titanic pandemonium...The lighter, more metallic notes of thousands of field guns were blended in one long-drawn chord. The hoarse and frantic rumble of the sixty-pounders, the long naval guns, the great howitzers, was like the rapid burring of a thousand drums. The light pieces were like trombones, for there were no individual sounds except the bark, bark, bark of an eighteen-pounder battery close behind us. And always, thrutter, thrutter, thrutter went the heavies.
>
> White smoke curled over us and hid the flaming skies. There was a thrumming as of gigantic bumble bees, and a low chug-chug-chug, as the ugly noses of the tanks poked through the fog above us. We hastily scattered from the path of one, and found ourselves almost beneath others. They went forward in a line, scarcely thirty yards between them. They were in scores, and their vibrations sounded through the fog from every side, like another layer of sound on the bellow of the guns. Then a rattling of machine-guns told us that the lads in front were at grips with the enemy.
>
> Sergeant Downing's recollection of the barrage (Downing, WH, *To the Last Ridge*, Sydney, 1998, pp. 138–9)

Brigade, in which Sergeant Downing of the 57th Battalion thought that dawn had been flung skyward when the barrage crashed down at 4.20 am.

Follow the C203 around to the left, take the first right and park at the A29 autoroute end of the **French National Cemetery** ❹. The 'lads' Downing referred to when recalling the barrage were in the 28th Battalion, which was stalled before a fully wired trench that extended from your location, through strongly fortified **Card Copse**, on the other side of the A29 but now gone, to the railway. Seeing a break in the wire, Lieutenant Alfred Gaby raced through it and then walked along the parapet between the cemetery and the A29, emptying his revolver into the Germans below. He captured 50, along with four machine-guns. Killed three days later, Gaby never knew he had won the VC. The 26th Battalion took Card Copse in a stiff fight. Turn right on leaving the cemetery and swing over the A29. Look

to your right front on crossing the railway, which was the boundary between the Australians and the Canadians. While providing a flank guard for the 7th Brigade, the 21st Battalion knocked out several machine-guns in this area. The one in **Jean Rouxin Mill**, which stood 250 metres away, put up bitter resistance.

On entering **Marcelcave**, head left at the crossroads onto the D136 (Rue de l'Hirondelle). As the Canadians had not yet taken Marcelcave and visibility was improving, the Germans at this end of the village engaged the 26th Battalion advancing past it on your left. Supported by a tank, the 26th began clearing them, hearing as it did so the Canadians starting to fight through the far end of the village on your right. Turn left on reaching the D42 and, once over the railway, right onto the D136 (direction Wiencourt). Park at the leftwards **bend** ❺ 750 metres along and stand with the railway at your back. Advancing from your left astride it towards the Green Line, which ran from here to the right of Lamotte-Warfusée to your front, the 26th overran a German howitzer battery as it tried to withdraw from your location. But some guns were in depth further to your right. When the 15th Brigade advanced from this stretch of the Green Line in the second phase, a battery in the dip 600 metres to your right knocked out one of the tanks supporting the 57th Battalion before it was silenced. The 15th Brigade continued on past the right

The French National
Cemetery, Marcelcave.

of **Bayonvillers**, 2.7 kilometres to your right front.

Do a U-turn at the next road junction, head back through this location and turn right on the D42 by the railway crossing. Once over the A29, look down the long, shallow re-entrant on your right. The 27th and 28th Battalions between them captured three German batteries in it. Turn right onto the D1029 for Lamotte-Warfusée, conjoined now but separate villages in 1918. While the 17th and 18th Battalions advanced around the outskirts to your right and left respectively, their inner companies bombed the Germans out of the houses. Head left opposite the cemetery at the far end of Lamotte-Warfusée onto the D71a, park at the **fork** ❻ 150 metres along and stand with the D1029 on your left. Accroche Wood is on the skyline to your right front, the Green Line ran 200 metres behind you, paralleling the D71a, and the boundary between the 2nd and 3rd Divisions crossed the D71a 600 metres to your right.

Advancing towards you as part of the 5th Brigade on this side of the boundary, the 18th Battalion found two abandoned batteries in the low ground ahead, while the 33rd and 34th Battalions in the 9th

Brigade on the other side found the gunners in a battery to your right front sitting on the gun trails awaiting capture. Monash's insistence on including the German gun line, which straddled the D71a, within the Green Line had paid off handsomely. At 8 am the sun broke through, revealing a scene on both sides of the D1029 that remained indelibly printed on the minds of the 50 000 Australians who beheld it. 'Everything was on the move forward, guns, tanks, ambulances and everything that was used in an offensive', wrote Lance-Corporal David Wilson of the 24th Battalion. 'No man's land of yesterday was a spot now that one could rest in peace and quiet'. Turn about. Tanks rolled up to

Continuing the advance, an Australian platoon passes Germans killed near Lamotte-Warfusée.

The 5th Brigade's advance to the Green Line, which is behind the location from which the photograph was taken.

the Green Line either side of you to support the 8th Brigade's advance to the Red Line 4.5 kilometres to your front, while field artillery batteries galloped up and rushed into action in the low ground behind you. Forming up on your left and right respectively, the 30th and 31st Battalions headed diagonally over the D1029 at 8.20 am and passed to the left of Bayonvillers, 1.5 kilometres to your right front.

Continue along the D71a. Immediately to the right of **Forbes Wood**, which abuts the right of the road 2.6 kilometres along, is **Hamilton Wood**. After the 41st Battalion took **Gailly Ridge** on your left, the 44th attacked across the re-entrant to the road here, after which 200 Germans were captured in Hamilton Wood. The 13th Battalion then moved through the woods to continue the advance. Cerisy appears as the D71a descends to the Somme. The 42nd Battalion took the area to the left of the village quite easily. On reaching the T-junction on the outskirts, turn right onto sunken Rue de la République and park at the fork 500 metres up the **Cerisy Spur** 7. The Australians experienced their heaviest fighting on 8 August around this location.

Look down the road towards Cerisy. Advancing over the D71a in the second phase, the 14th Battalion cleared several machine-guns sited along the lip of the spur to your left but had to take cover in

How the Chipilly Spur, on the far bank of the Somme, dominates Cerisy. The 4th Division's left flank lay open to the Germans on the spur.

the sunken road when heavily engaged by more machine-guns above the steep tree-lined bank to your right. III Corps had been held up to your left front on the **Morlancourt Ridge** on the far side of the Somme, allowing the German machine-gunners on the ridge opposite Cerisy to enfilade it and prevent the further advance of the 15th Battalion, which had taken several hundred prisoners in the village. Field-guns on the lower slopes of the **Chipilly Spur,** also on the far side of the river but to the right of Cerisy, knocked out several of the tanks supporting both battalions. Fortunately the 13th Battalion advanced untroubled behind you, outflanking the Germans lining the bank to your right and forcing their withdrawal. The 14th and 15th Battalions pressed on to the Red Line.

Now head into Cerisy on Rue de la République and swing right at the fork opposite the village hall onto Rue du Pont, which eventually becomes a lane. Park in the open area at the end of the lane and walk to the bank of the **Somme Canal** 8, beyond which is the river. Though the American 131st Regiment attached to III Corps had made some progress along the crest of the Morlancourt Ridge to your front, the 2/10th Londons from the 58th Division were stuck on the far bank directly opposite you. Owing to the continued

CHIPILLY SPUR

CERISY

threat that the Germans ahead of them posed to the Australian left flank, which was well past your location, the 1st Brigade deployed along the bank here to protect it. At 6 pm next day Quartermaster-Sergeant Hayes and his six-man patrol crossed the canal and the river near the bend in the canal to your left and headed for **Chipilly** village to your right.

Return to Rue de la République, turn left after 250 metres onto the D71 and left again after 300 metres to cross the Somme. Continue through Chipilly, pausing at the **memorial** at the five-way intersection to the 58th (London) Division, which poignantly depicts a soldier farewelling his dying horse and additionally commemorates the Australian, Canadian and French contributions on 8 August. From the five-ways, head up the slope of the Chipilly Spur on Rue d'Etinehem to **Chipilly Communal Cemetery and Extension** 9. From the high ground at the rear of the cemetery, face the entrance. Finding Chipilly deserted, Hayes's patrol advanced to this location, whereupon he led a platoon of Londoners to a chalk pit, among the trees on your right, intending to attack two German posts near it. Though a British smoke barrage forced them back, Hayes utilised the smoke screen to take his patrol across the crest of the spur, which lies over your left shoulder. To see the chalk pit, walk from the cemetery car park 150 metres along the track that runs off the far side of the road. The Germans near the pit had a superb vantage point from which to fire down the valley.

Continue on Rue d'Etinehem for 900 metres and park on the **track** 10 on the right. Look down the track. Passing 500 metres in front of you, Hayes' patrol swung around the slope on your left, where it captured over 60 Germans and two machine-guns. By 10 pm, four hours after the patrol had crossed the Somme, the Chipilly Spur had been cleared. Walk

The 58th (London) Division memorial, Chipilly.

a short distance down the track and the views are memorable. Using binoculars, the Australian Corps Memorial and Accroche Wood, from which the advance began, and the Australian National Memorial at Villers-Bretonneux can all be seen on the horizon to the left of Chipilly. Extend the line of the track across the Somme and you have the approximate course of the Red Line, reached by the 13th, 14th and 15th Battalions. **Morcourt** is on the far bank 2.5 kilometres to your right front and the high ground to its right is the Cerisy Spur, where the 14th Battalion was held up. Starting to the right of **Méricourt-sur-Somme**, one kilometre to your left front, the Blue Line ran along the high ground behind the village to the skyline, where traffic can be seen crawling on the D1029. Consider how easily the Germans here could enfilade the left of the Australian advance and fire into the rear of the Blue Line. Monash's worry over the Chipilly Spur was understandable.

Recross the Somme at Chipilly and turn left on the D71 for Morcourt. Three tanks moving along this road from Cerisy on your right were destroyed by German field-guns on the lower slope of the Chipilly Spur to your left. Remain on the D71 through Morcourt. At the triangular intersection centred on a crucifix 250 metres beyond the village, drive

VILLERS-BRETONNEUX

AUSTRALIAN NATIONAL MEMORIAL

ACCROCHE WOOD

HAMEL

GREEN LINE ········· ← 3RD AUSTRALIAN DIVISION

From Chipilly Spur looking back over the Australian attack on the far bank of the Somme.

straight on, following the minor road that heads up the facing slope of the **Morcourt Valley**. Stop at the **fork** 11 on the crest made by the track on the left and look along the road with Morcourt behind you. The Red Line ran to the left of the road, between your location and **Morgan Wood** 250 metres to your left front. Now walk back towards Morcourt until you can look down into the valley, which extends beyond the D1029 to your left. Descending into it while advancing towards you, the 13th Battalion found stores, hutted officers' messes and canteens replete with cigars and liqueurs, 60 horses and many docile Germans. But on reaching the road up which you drove, the 13th was raked by the field-guns on the Chipilly Spur across the Somme to your right, and by rifle and machine-gun fire from the Germans strung out along this ridge. It suffered over 60 casualties in the rush that secured the Red Line.

Return to the fork and look over the **Proyart Valley**. From the near side of Méricourt, on the bank of the Somme two kilometres to your left front, the **Blue Line** stretched left to right along the crest above the far side of the valley, coinciding with the Amiens Outer Line. Using your route to the fork, four Mark V Star tanks carrying the 16th Battalion's machine-gun teams continued past the facing edge of Morgan Wood before turning left and making for the D71, which you can see running along the bank of the Somme to Méricourt. Turning right on reaching the road, they clattered past the small copse to its right. One tank was knocked out but the other three turned uphill well short of Méricourt for the crest. All were soon hit and disgorged their machine-gunners, who were overcome by fumes, before reaching it. The gunners could provide little support to the 16th Battalion, which advanced from the Red Line on your left. It used

SOMME

MÉRICOURT

D71

16TH BATTALION

TANKS

short rushes to get through heavy fire and capture the Amiens Outer/Blue Line on the crest to your left front. Pounded then from the Chipilly Spur, over your left shoulder, the 16th turned its left flank outwards to face across the river. The tanks proved more useful to the 48th Battalion, which had less trouble taking the Blue Line to your front and to your right front. Méricourt was not secured until 12 August.

Head back towards the triangular intersection but turn left at the fork just before reaching it. Take the road on the right, which crosses the mouth of the Morcourt Valley, and swing left onto the D71e at the crossroads by the grain silo. Turn left again on reaching the D1029. Crossing the upper reaches of the Morcourt Valley on the way, stop after

1.2 kilometres at **Heath Cemetery** 12, opposite a communications tower. Head right on entering the cemetery, walk to the far wall and look back along the D1029 towards the valley. Here too, it was full of German bivouacs, hutments, hospitals and stores. After overcoming some spirited resistance on the far rim, the 30th and 46th Battalions, respectively left and right of the D1029, started across the valley. As the tanks attached to the 46th could not negotiate the steep slopes, they provided fire support from the rim but most of those with the 30th were able to make it, unnerving the Germans ahead. They surrendered en masse. The two battalions then passed either side of you to the Red Line, which crossed the D1029 to your rear, 200 metres beyond the cemetery.

The Morcourt Valley, which the 13th Battalion, advancing from right to left across it, discovered was a land of plenty.

The advance to the Blue Line.

PROYART VALLEY

48TH BATTALION

Continue on the D1029, which the Blue Line crossed 1.4 kilometres along, and turn right onto the D329 after another 1.4 kilometres. Head through **Framerville-Rainecourt** and over the A29 towards **Vauvillers**. The armoured cars wreaked havoc on the Germans in this area. At the war memorial in Vauvillers, head right for **Harbonnières**. Park after 1.2 kilometres by the electricity sub-station and the **crucifix** ⑬ near the junction with the D337, through which the Amiens Outer Line ran, and look along the D337 towards Harbonnières 700 metres off. Lying 350 metres behind you, the Blue Line curved towards the railway, indicated by the tree line 1.5 kilometres to your left, which was the boundary between the Australians and the Canadians. Harbonnières station, a stop on a now non-existent branch line, stood on the site of the large white shed on your right.

Racing ahead of the infantry, a Whippet tank passed to your left and ran amok beyond the Blue Line for an hour before being destroyed. But British cavalry following the tank could not get through the Amiens Outer Line between Harbonnières and the railway on your left. The use of the cavalry and the Whippets in combination had failed. As this example showed, the tanks had a good chance of forging ahead when resistance was met but the cavalry had none. Subsequently advancing between the D1029 and Harbonnières, the 30th and 31st Battalions from the 8th Brigade occupied the Blue Line to your right. Neither battalion had waited for its Mark V Star tanks to arrive. The 15th Brigade cleared Harbonnières with tank support but had trouble going further. Meeting heavy fire from the railway station as it assaulted towards you, the 59th Battalion stalled to your front. The 57th Battalion was held up to your left front. Neither of these battalions had waited for its Mark V Star tanks either. Several attempts to break through to the Blue Line by capturing the station failed badly.

Now head towards Harbonnières. Turn right 150 metres past the cemetery onto Rue du Stade and park at the T-junction at the end of the road. Walk to the end of the line of trees on Rue de Béthisy to your right ⑭, stand with Harbonnières on your left and Vauvillers on your right,

The outskirts of Harbonnières, where the 59th Battalion was pinned down by machine-guns at the railway station, which is just to the right of where the photograph was taken.

and look towards the A29 ahead. As the cavalry approached from your left and front, two trains sped off towards Vauvillers from a siding in the field this side of the A29 and to your right front. Smoke belched several times from a hump on a third train. Just as this train started up, the cavalry engaged it and a British aeroplane bombed the loco, which stopped in a cloud of steam. The 'hump' turned out to be the 28-centimetre railway gun. As the cavalry rode off towards Vauvillers, which it failed to reach though capturing three German field batteries in the attempt, the 31st Battalion took possession of the gun. Its barrel is now displayed at the Australian War Memorial.

Australians surround the 28-centimetre railway gun, soon to be known as the Amiens gun, on 8 August after its capture by the 31st Battalion earlier in the day. The words 'captured' and 'Australia' (partly obscured) have already been painted on the carriage.

Return to the D337, turn right and then take the first left, Rue Jacques Deflandre, at the pharmacy. Continue straight ahead at the five-way intersection, park in the open area on the left just before the railway bridge 15 and face Harbonnières. You are now at the right-hand end of the Blue Line for the Australian attack. Again coinciding with the Amiens Outer Line, it ran to the old railway station to the right of the village. Starting from the railway 1.7 kilometres to your left, the Red Line stretched to the left of the village. The 15th Brigade's advance to it passed the left side of Bayonvillers, 3.5 kilometres to your left

front, with the 59th Battalion on that flank and the 57th beside the railway. In the failed advance to the Blue Line, the 57th was stopped 500 metres to your left. By nightfall, therefore, the Australian Corps had secured all but the extreme ends of the Blue Line, here and before Méricourt on the Somme.

To follow the subsequent advance, return to the old railway station by the D337 junction. Otherwise, take the D337 through Harbonnières and Bayonvillers and turn left onto the D1029, which will get you back to Villers-Bretonneux. For Albert, turn right onto the D42 at Lamotte-Warfusée.

The line reached by the 57th Battalion in its advance from Bayonvillers, as seen from the Blue Line.

BAYONVILLERS

RED LINE

57TH BATTALION

LOCAL INFORMATION

CEMETERIES

Heath Cemetery

On the D1029 and visited on the tour, this cemetery was built postwar and named after the wide, bare heath-like expanse on which it is located. It is one of the most significant cemeteries for Australians on the Western Front. Of its 1860 burials, 1491 known, 984 are Australian. They include some of the AIF's most distinguished fallen. Lieutenant Gaby rests at V.E.14. Another Australian VC recipient, Private Robert Beatham of the 8th Battalion, who fell on 11 August, is at VII.J.13. Lieutenant-Colonel Milne DSO of the 36th Battalion, which charged almost suicidally to save Villers-Bretonneux on 4 April, lies at VIII.J.19. He was pulped by a shell eight days later. Lieutenant-Colonel Ernest Knox-Knight at V.B.15 fell in the 37th Battalion's daring attack near Proyart on 10 August. Two Indigenous soldiers from Victoria, Corporal Harry Thorpe of the 7th Battalion, and his friend, Private William Rawlings of the 29th, rest at IV.J.15 and I.A.19 respectively. Wounded at Pozières and Bullecourt, Thorpe won the MM at Broodseinde and fell on 9 August 1918 near Lihons. Rawlings, who fell on the same day near Vauvillers, had won the MM at Morlancourt in July. Six New Zealanders rest at Heath.

The grave of 2nd Lieutenant Alfred Gaby VC, Heath Cemetery.

The grave of Private Robert Beatham VC, Heath Cemetery.

The grave of Lieutenant-Colonel John Milne DSO, Heath Cemetery.

The grave of Corporal Harry Thorpe MM, Heath Cemetery.

Corporal Harry Thorpe MM.

Aboriginal and Torres Strait service in the AIF

Between 800 and 1000 Indigenous Australians are believed to have served in the AIF. They were treated as equals and paid the same as white soldiers. Joining up wasn't easy though. Many who tried to enlist in 1914 were rejected on racial grounds. By the end of 1917, when recruits were harder to find and the conscription referenda had failed, restrictions were eased. A Military Order stated: 'Half-castes may be enlisted in the Australian Imperial Force provided that the examining Medical Officers are satisfied that one of the parents is of European origin'.

What motivated Indigenous Australians to serve can only be guessed at. Loyalty and patriotism, the belief that they were protecting their land and community, and the incentive of a wage all probably played a part. There may have also been the hope that AIF service would result in some sort of equality after the war. Upon return to civilian life, however, the Indigenous servicemen met the same prejudice and discrimination as before.

CHAPTER 20

1918

SOMME SOUTH

If the attack on 8 August had been a model of coordination and organisation, the follow-up initially was a shemozzle. There were two reasons. Firstly, not all Germans were as panicked as General Ludendorff. Responding with the trademark swiftness that flummoxed their opponents in two world wars, they were deploying six divisions onto the battlefield before the day was out, one more than GHQ expected. Secondly, the Fourth Army, having attacked after a long period on the defensive, now had to carry the transition another step and advance. Static warfare had given way to mobile warfare. The first and last time that this had happened on the Western Front since the first weeks of the war was during the German retirement to the Hindenburg Line in 1917. Just as they did then, senior commanders had to adjust to the changed conditions. Instead of having plenty of time for planning and preparation, they had to do these things while the advance rolled on. Like his colleagues, General Monash found his stride after a patchy start.

Confusion

At the now-Marshal Foch's urging, Field Marshal Haig had directed General Rawlinson before the attack on 8 August to continue advancing after it for another 30 kilometres. Foch thought the Germans were crumbling. The days of 'bite and hold' limited offensives were over; the time was right for an unlimited one. On 6 August Rawlinson announced that the Canadian Corps would carry out the exploitation. Its four divisions fielded at least 12 000 bayonets each, as opposed to 7000 in each Australian division. They had also seen much less recent fighting. On 8 August the Canadians attacked on the right of the Australians. On 9 August the Australians would move their right flank forward in conformity with the Canadians.

In the first stage of the exploitation, the 1st Australian Division was to advance 6.4 kilometres to Lihons. The 8th Brigade from the 5th Division would protect its left flank before being relieved by the 2nd Division. Though Rawlinson promised plenty of supporting artillery and tanks, most of the artillery was still moving forward and only 145 tanks were fit for action in the Fourth Army. The 1st Division got 14, the 2nd and 5th 17 between them. As formations other than the Canadians were involved, Rawlinson should have set the start time for the advance but he left it instead to General Sir Arthur Currie, the Canadian commander. Rawlinson's headquarters blundered too, countermanding the relief of a Canadian division late on 8 August even though it was well underway. The Canadians had to draft fresh orders. The Australians had to wait for them, leaving the 1st Division with no hope of being ready to begin the advance at 10 am on 9 August. In the line next to the Canadians, the 15th Brigade from the 5th Division was simply told to advance in its place until it showed up.

Lihons

The 15th Brigade broke through the Germans just outside Harbonnières, while the 8th Brigade took neighbouring Vauvillers. Finally catching up at 1.45 pm, the 1st Division headed for Lihons, whose location atop a bare, gentle hill gave the Germans terrific fields of fire. They knocked out most of the supporting tanks and halted the assault well short of the village. The 2nd Division should have been alongside because Monash wanted it to attack simultaneously with the 1st in order to prevent the Germans concentrating against either. But in a lapse like Rawlinson's the night before, he left their commanders to coordinate the details when that responsibility was his. Wires got crossed. The 2nd Division's advance did not begin until 4.30 pm and was strongly opposed. Rosières and Framerville were both taken but with great loss. Private Robert Beatham of the 8th Battalion knocked out four machine-guns only to fall in another disjointed attack next day. He was posthumously awarded the VC. Lihons was taken on 11 August.

Proyart

The three days since 8 August, wrote Charles Bean, 'will probably furnish a classic example of how not to follow up a great attack'. They cost the Australians over 3000 men. This figure includes the 3rd and 4th Division's losses on the Somme flank, where Monash ordered an attack that answers any criticism of him as a cautious general. Seeing that the river followed a series of U-shaped bends around protruding spur lines, of which the Chipilly Spur was the first, he decided to take the

next two by cutting them off at the base. At 9.30 pm on 10 August the 13th Brigade was to advance along the D1 north of the Somme and seal off the Etinehem Spur. At the same time the 10th Brigade would swing through Proyart from the D1029 to cordon off the Méricourt Spur south of the river. A few tanks were to accompany each column, mainly in the hope of panicking the Germans. This time Monash instructed the two brigadiers directly, to avoid misunderstandings. Bean called the plan 'ingenious'. The opinions of the infantry and tank officers ran from 'ridiculous' to 'stupid' to 'mad'.

The 13th Brigade easily cleared the Etinehem Spur, but a German aeroplane chanced upon the 10th at the start of its advance and bombed it. Progress was impossible as the Germans were now fully alert. They sent the 10th Brigade packing. Outflanked by the 13th Brigade's advance north of the Somme, and by the capture of Lihons in the south, the Germans evacuated Proyart on 11 August. Vigorous patrolling by the 11th Brigade, during which Sergeant Percy Statton of the 40th Battalion silenced four machine-guns, secured a line beyond the village next day. Statton was awarded the VC.

Chuignes

The Proyart knock and the slog towards Lihons had confirmed that opposition south of the Somme was increasing. Moreover, Lihons was at the edge of the French sector of the 1916 battlefield, a wilderness of old trenches and wire that would slow the advance down, just as it had the Germans in March. General Currie impressed on Haig on 10 August that the Canadian Corps faced the worst of this terrain and could do more useful work if it returned to its old stamping ground around Arras. Haig agreed. Rawlinson and Monash also had reservations. Haig shifted the main offensive north, where the Third Army advanced towards Bapaume on 21 August. The Fourth Army was to carry out supporting attacks

Troops from the 1st Division pass through the 15th Brigade beyond Harbonnières on 9 August.

astride the Somme. With the British III Corps on its left, the 3rd Australian Division moved on Bray next day to protect the Third Army's right flank.

On 23 August the 1st Australian Division advanced three kilometres to secure the Froissy Plateau, south of the river, in a Hamel-type set-piece. The 1st and 3rd Brigades swept through on the left flank to Chuignes, after which the battle was named. Astride the D1029 in the centre, the 2nd Brigade had a harder time Half its tanks were lost at the start to a counter-barrage. The rest rendered great assistance, enabling strongly held St Martin's Wood to be cleared. For leading an attack that captured equally dangerous Plateau Wood South beyond it, Lieutenant Joynt of the 8th Battalion won the VC. On the right flank, the 97th Brigade from the 32nd Division assaulted towards Herleville. Rawlinson had temporarily reinforced the Australian Corps with the British 32nd and the 17th Divisions so that the tired Australian divisions, which had been fighting continuously for five months, could be rotated through brief rest periods. When the 97th's right flank was held up, Lieutenant Lawrence McCarthy of the 16th Battalion almost

single-handedly captured most of the trench it was supposed to attack. He was also awarded the VC.

At a cost of 1000 casualties, the 1st Division took one-quarter of the 8000 prisoners captured by the Third and Fourth Armies. Though disabled by the Germans, a 35-centimetre naval gun, the largest gun that fired on Amiens, also fell into its hands. On 24 August, the 3rd Division took Bray and the Third Army was within three kilometres of Bapaume, which the New Zealand Division had a tough time trying to envelop.

Support troops from the 3rd Brigade move up during the Chuignes attack.

The naval gun captured by the 1st Division on 23 August.

DRIVING THE BATTLEFIELD

Spend even a little time on the Australian 1918 Somme battlefields and you'll realise that the areas closest to the river have been largely untouched by modern development whereas those further south have worn the full force of it. Nowhere is this contrast more apparent than on the post–8 August battlefield. The leafy villages dotting the valleys and spurs that run down to the river bank have an eternal quality about them, which sometimes makes it difficult to pick up the differences between 1918 and now. On the other side of the D1029, though, you are in another world. Not only does the A29 autoroute continue its scything path across the battlefield but wind farms also seem to intrude onto every view. Don't let them put you off because this area saw the hardest fighting in the aftermath of 8 August.

MAPS IGN Blue Series, 1:25000, 2408E Bray-sur-Somme; 2409E Roye; 24090 Harbonnières

From Villers-Bretonneux, take the D1029 for 6.7 kilometres, turn right just past Lamotte-Warfussée onto the D337 and follow it through Marcelcave to Harbonnières. From Albert, take the D42, turn left on reaching the D1029 at Lamotte-Warfusée and then right onto the D337.

Remain on the D337 through Harbonnières and park 500 metres past

The advance along the railway as seen from the strongpoint in Harbonnières station.

the cemetery at the fork by the electricity sub-station and the **crucifix** ❶. Face the village. The final objective on 8 August, known as the Blue Line, ran right to left 300 metres behind you. While the 8th Brigade had reached it to your far right, the 15th Brigade was held up on the edge of Harbonnières by heavy fire from the old **Amiens Outer Defence Line**, particularly from the strongpoint in the village station, which stood on the site of the large white shed on your right and served a now-defunct branch line. From there the Outer Line stretched to the trunk railway indicated by the tree line 1.5 kilometres to your left. The 6th Canadian Brigade had reached it beyond the railway.

When the 1st Australian Division failed to arrive on time for the attack on 9 August, the 15th Brigade helped the Canadians out. Advancing in short rushes, part of the 58th Battalion eventually outflanked the station on both sides, allowing the rest of the 58th, which was pinned down to your front astride the D337, to advance through your location. Using a tank lent by the Canadians, a platoon of the 60th Battalion worked along the railway to your left and enfiladed the Germans at that end of the Outer Line. Stalled to your left front, the rest of the 60th was able to get moving too. Now turn about and face **Vauvillers**, 1.2 kilometres away

← 60TH BATTALION PLATOON AND TANK

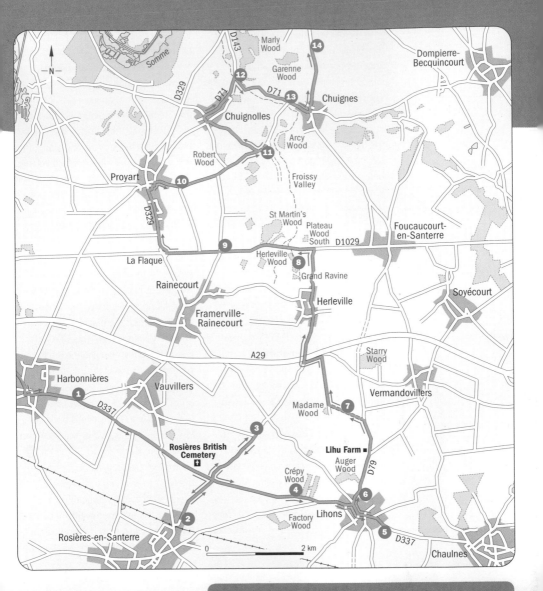

at the end of the minor road. By 1.45 pm the two battalions had reached a line between the village and the railway on your right, completing the first part of what should have been the 1st Division's advance. Having caught up, the 2nd Brigade from the 1st Division took over.

Starting from where the 8 August battlefield drive left off south of the D1029, the route retraces the advance on Lihons before crossing the D1029 to follow the Chuignes attack. It also covers the assault towards Proyart and the VC actions of Lieutenants Joynt and McCarthy and Sergeant Statton.

DISTANCE COVERED: **32 km**

DURATION: **4 hours**

RAILWAY

In the 8th Brigade's attack on your left, a single anti-tank gun in Vauvillers knocked out all six of the 29th Battalion's supporting tanks near the A29 autoroute. The debacle confirmed what had become evident on 8 August once the fog lifted. For all its improved performance, the Mark V tank was still vulnerable while advancing over ground as open as this unless concealed by darkness or fog or screened by smoke. Confronted by fire from field-guns as well as machine-guns, the 29th edged slowly around either side of Vauvillers and took the village. At 4.30 pm the 7th Brigade passed through, with the 5th Brigade alongside it on the far side of the A29. Over six hours late, the 2nd Division's advance was now underway.

Continue along the D337. Once past **Rosières British Cemetery** on your left, turn right at the crossroads onto Rue d'Herleville and park on the outskirts of **Rosières-en-Santerre ❷**. Stand with the outskirts behind you and the D337 to your left. As the Canadians had already taken Rosières beyond the railway on your right, the Germans on your side of the railway withdrew when the 8th Battalion approached from your rear between the railway and the D337. They left a huge dump of timber, construction

tools and barbed wire. But then German field-gun batteries on the long, flat hill to your front, on which squats **Lihons**, swung into action. Soon every one of the 8th's tanks was a flaming wreck, giving the German machine-gunners a free run. By 2.35 pm the 8th Battalion had been brought to a halt more or less along the line of Rue d'Herleville, on which you are standing. On the far side of the D337, the 7th Battalion was fighting its way forward from Vauvillers.

That the advance got past Rue d'Herleville was due very much to Private Beatham. Helped by Lance-Corporal William Nottingham, he rushed four machine-gun posts in the area to your front, killing 10 Germans, and capturing another 10 plus the machine-guns. The pair then laid down covering fire with two of the guns, enabling the 8th to progress. By nightfall the 7th and 8th were astride the D337 just past the copse on the near side of it halfway up the slope to your left front. Head back along Rue d'Herleville, cross over the D337 and continue to the first road on the left ❸. Look down this road. From the copse on the D337 to your left, the line that evening ran across your right front, cutting between **Framerville** and **Rainecourt**, just to its right, on the far side of the A29. This stretch was held by the 2nd Division.

Now turn about and face the hill. Attacking at 8 am on 10 August with the 3rd Brigade on this side of the D337 and the 2nd Brigade on the other, the 1st Division sought to take **Crépy Wood**, on the crest to your right front, and Lihons beyond it. The orders had arrived at midnight on the 9th, too late for any reconnaissance. Supposed to pass to the left of Crépy Wood, the 11th Battalion veered to the right of the quarry ahead of you and was smashed by enfilade fire from Germans lining Rue de Framerville to your left front. It did not get far beyond the quarry. At least the 11th had

Advancing British tanks under fire. German guns took a heavy toll of them on 9 August.

The 3rd Brigade's advance on Crépy Wood. It would be hard to better the fields of fire that the Germans had from the higher ground ahead.

partly shielded the 9th Battalion, which was advancing on your right next to the D337. Trying to secure the 3rd Brigade's flank, the 25th Battalion struggled to reach Rue de Framerville 450 metres on your left. Before leaving, consider how unfavourable the conditions were. Not only did the tardy orders preclude adequate preparation but the barrage fell 800 metres ahead, too far to be of any use, and the mist had lifted, enabling the Germans to see for miles around. There were no tanks left to lend support but then they would have been very vulnerable anyway.

Return to the D337, turn left and park after 1.8 kilometres at **Lihons French National Cemetery 4**, whose 8000 burials include 1638 in four mass graves. Crépy Wood, then a wilderness of dense undergrowth, overgrown trenches and barbed wire, skirts the right side of it. Stand with the cemetery on your left and look down the D337. Coming up the slope to your rear, the 9th Battalion ran into intense fire from posts in the wood and from the crest on the skyline on your left. The 9th cleared the fringes of the wood to your left and on the D337 but could go no further. A company from the 10th Battalion, which was supporting the 9th, formed up along the D337 ahead of you and fought its way right to left past you to the crest end of the wood,

whereupon the 9th advanced and set up posts on the far side of the wood. In the 2nd Brigade's attack on the other side of the D337, the 6th Battalion was raked from **Factory Wood**, 600 metres down the slope to your right, as it passed between the wood and the railway. Jumping into old trenches between the near side of the wood and your location, the neighbouring 5th Battalion turned its Lewis-guns on the wood, after which both battalions rushed it. The Canadian left flank, on the far side of the railway, was ahead of the Australian right at this stage.

Continue on the D337 through Lihons and stop 500 metres past it by the **crucifix 5** in a copse on the right. Face the village. You are looking across no-man's-land at the old French line from 1916, which ran around the near side of Lihons. At 4 am on 11 August 1918, the 8th Battalion advanced in a thick mist towards you between the right of the village and the railway on your left. While the left flank moved through Lihons, a machine-gun sited midway between your location and the railway checked the right. Though already wounded, Private Beatham charged the post but was killed while knocking it out. The 8th Battalion finished up on the German 1916 line just behind you, which brought the Australians level with the Canadians.

Troops from the 6th Battalion rest in an old trench after losing heavily in the attack on Factory Wood, which was carried out simultaneously with the Crépy Wood assault.

The capture of Crépy Wood by the 9th and 10th Battalions, as seen from the direction of the 9th's advance. Lihons is visible in the distance to the right of the wood.

Return to Lihons but continue straight ahead on the D79 instead of following the D337 around to the left. Stop briefly at the **communal cemetery** ⑥ and face left across the D79. Starting from Crépy Wood, on the crest to your front, the 10th Battalion secured your location in the 11 August attack while the 12th Battalion took **Auger Wood** to your right front. Lihons and its hill now belonged to the 1st Australian Division.

Drive another 750 metres along the D79 and swing left past **Lihu Farm** at the Y-junction. Turn left after 700 metres onto a dirt road and stop 400 metres along ⑦. Look down the road. You are standing at the junction of two 1916

trenches, **Courtine Alley**, which ran from your location to the left of **Madame Wood**, 350 metres to your left front, and **Courtine Trench**, which stretched to the left of **Starry Wood**, 900 metres away over your right shoulder. When the 16th Lancashire Fusiliers from the 97th Brigade advanced towards you to capture Courtine Trench on 23 August, its right flank stalled to the right of Madame Wood. Fighting along Courtine Alley to assist, some 16th Battalion bombers found the junction blocked by an earthen 'island' barricade girded with barbed wire. The Australians in Courtine Alley and the Germans in Courtine Trench exchanged bombs for an hour and were in a stand-off when Lieutenant McCarthy arrived. Followed by Sergeant Fred Robbins, McCarthy leapt the block into Courtine Trench and, with his revolver, shot a sentry, silenced a machine-gun blazing away at the Fusiliers and killed an officer trying to rally his men. He then used German bombs against the fleeing Germans. At the end of what Bean called perhaps the most effective individual action in the AIF next to Jacka's counterattack at Pozières, McCarthy had seized 450 metres of Courtine Trench, 15 Germans were dead and 40 had surrendered.

Turn right at Madame Wood, left at the T-junction by the A29 and then right

CRÉPY WOOD

9TH BATTALION

Lieutenant Lawrence Dominic McCarthy

An institution in the 16th Battalion throughout the war

1892–1975

McCarthy was an orphan from Western Australia who could not change his birth name, Florence Joseph, quickly enough. A contractor prewar, he was sent to the 16th Battalion on enlisting in the AIF in October 1914. Nicknamed 'Fats' because of his bulk, McCarthy was at Gallipoli from the start, fought throughout the AIF's 1916 Somme battles and was wounded at Bullecourt in 1917 a day after being commissioned. Popular, kindly and modest, Fats remarked that his VC action, which his own battalion praised as 'a super VC stunt', was 'nothing'. He believed that there was 'a VC in everybody if given a chance'. McCarthy worked as a commercial traveller and building manager after the war. His son and only child was killed in action on Bougainville in 1945.

at the next T-junction for **Herleville**, cleared by the left of the 97th Brigade. On reaching the D1029, head left for 300 metres and park on the track on the right in the cutting. Cross the D1029 and walk back along the edge of the field above the cutting. When you can clearly see **Plateau Wood South** on the crest on the other side of the road, turn about ⑧. Separated by the high, bare **knoll** but merging 500 metres to your right front by **St Martin's Wood**, the

Grand Ravine to your front and the **Rainecourt Valley** behind it form the upper end of the **Froissy Valley**, which stretches to the Somme five kilometres to your right. The Germans held all of these locations. On 23 August the 1st Australian Division sought to gain the high ground on your side of the valley down to the river.

Having come from the 97th Brigade's assault on the right flank of this attack, you are now in the centre, where the

LIHONS FRENCH NATIONAL CEMETERY

LIHONS

10TH BATTALION

D337

down on the far side of the wood. Advancing over the knoll towards you on this side of the D1029, the 6th Battalion struck trouble from the start. It was whipped by fire from **Herleville Wood**, to your left front on the facing slope of the knoll, and from Plateau Wood South. Most of the officers were hit. Moving with his platoon close behind the 6th in support, Lieutenant Joynt of the 8th Battalion rushed over the crest to rally the survivors. They cleared Herleville Wood before being stopped at the edge of the Grand Ravine, where you are standing, by drenching fire from Plateau Wood South. Joynt realised the wood had to be taken.

Running into 15 men from Lieutenant McGinn's platoon, Joynt led them into dead ground in the Grand Ravine, where they captured an aid post and 50 Germans in the hollow to your front. 'Don't treat us as prisoners', two doctors said to Joynt. 'We will stay here and look after your wounded as well as ours if you will let us.' Joynt agreed. He led his party across the D1029 and into a trench. No sooner had they bombed a dugout than 20 Germans appeared behind them. The leader dropped his rifle when Joynt threatened him with a revolver. The rest did likewise. Then the survivors from the dugout emerged with their hands raised. One seemed about to cry. McGinn 'took three or four very slow menacing strides towards the cringing Hun, and bringing his face close to him, said "BOO!" The Hun collapsed on his

Lieutenant William Joynt VC.

2nd Brigade advanced across Rainecourt Valley and through St Martin's Wood. Helped by tanks, one of which silenced 20 machine-guns, the 5th Battalion pushed through the wood, whereupon a soldier celebrated its capture by tickling the ivories on a piano he had found in an abandoned hut. The 5th easily reached the high ground, though heavy fire from Plateau Wood South pinned its right flank

GRAND RAVINE

DUGOUT

knees', Joynt recalled. Offered a choice of 'ratted' (souvenired) watches, Joynt selected one. The situation was 'perfectly absurd'. Plateau Wood South still remained. It was teeming with Germans, precluding a charge, though Joynt's men were itching to make one. Calling an end to the frivolity, he directed them instead along a communication trench he had found that led directly to it. Seeing the Germans start to break, Joynt's men then charged, seizing the wood and another 12 Germans. The 6th Battalion could now secure the high ground behind you.

Continue another 1.5 kilometres on the D1029 and pull over just after turning right at the crossroads onto **Avenue Cross** ⑨. Look along the D1029 and go back in time from 23 August to 10 August when the Australian line ran from Rainecourt, 600 metres to your left, and behind **La Flaque**, in the copse on the D1029 one kilometre to your front, and **Proyart**, 1.5 kilometres to your right front. That night the 10th Brigade, led by the 37th Battalion, was to belt up the D1029 towards you, turn left onto Avenue Cross and then string itself out facing the Froissy Valley between your location and the Somme near Méricourt, four kilometres away. The 37th's commander, Lieutenant-Colonel Ernie Knox-Knight, quipped 'There'll be a train load of VC's waiting for us when we get back, if it's a success, but we won't want them if we get through with our lives'. The column passed through La Flaque at 10 pm and the leading tank was 300 metres from you when the German aircraft skimmed along the road dropping bombs. The Germans on Avenue Cross and in Rainecourt and Proyart let fly a tempest of machine-gun and armour-piercing fire. High-explosive and gas shells also rained down. Though an Australian officer, revolver in hand, tried to prevent the tanks U-turning, progress was out of the question. An anti-tank round killed Knox-Knight and the 37th lost 106 men, a quarter of its strength. The withdrawal was completed just before dawn.

Head right at La Flaque on the D329 to Proyart. Turn right there onto Rue de l'Eglise near the church, right again onto Rue de Péronne and park after 500 metres opposite a **crucifix** ⑩.

The scene of Lieutenant Joynt's VC action.

PLATEAU WOOD SOUTH

JOYNT

LA FLAQUE

PROYART

37TH BATTALION

The fiasco at Proyart, looking back from Avenue Cross.

Stand with Proyart on your left. On 12 August 10th Brigade patrols moved through it unopposed but were shot up by four machine-guns 300 metres to your right front when they tried to go further. Firing from the light railway that ran immediately to your right front, two Lewis-gun teams under Sergeant Statton supported another attempt by the 37th Battalion at 6 pm but it was sent reeling by the same four guns. Statton, who had won the MM at Messines, led four men along the road to your right. Closing on the nearest gun, he charged it and shot two of the gunners. While his mates dealt with the rest of the crew, Statton went on to the next gun but emptied his revolver before he had shot the last of its crew. Statton wrenched the surviving German's bayonet away from him and killed him with it. The crews of the remaining guns fled. Statton's VC– winning action enabled the 37th to advance to the railway. Before leaving, look along the road and leap forward in

time to 23 August. The start line for the 1st Brigade, on the left of the 1st Division's attack that day, crossed the road 200 metres ahead of you and ran to the left of **Robert Wood**, one kilometre away on the left of the road.

Drive another 1.7 kilometres along this road to the sharp left turn and park on one of the tracks **11**. Walk down to the Froissy Valley and face left along it. With 12 tanks in support, the 1st Brigade came over the heights to your rear. You are on the boundary between the 1st Battalion on your left and the 4th on your right. As the advance passed through your location, the naval gun was discovered this side of **Bois du Gros Canon**, the copse on the bank 300 metres to your left front. The Germans had blown the barrel out of the massive carriage on 8 August. Interestingly, the copse takes its name from the gun. The excavation in the side of the valley below the copse, in which the gun was emplaced, looks as it did in 1918. While the right of the

> As we lay there trying to find cover when there was none, the bullets were knocking sparks out of the road beside our heads, whistling between us and missing us by inches... It seemed impossible that any of us could live through it, and I am convinced that it was God Himself that saved me. We struggled on for some distance along the road, but it was impossible to go on. The tanks were the first to turn it up, and when they started to come back we left the road and dug ourselves in.
>
> Private Arthur Sindrey under fire on the D1029 near Proyart on 10 August (letter, 26 September 1918, 3DRL/7514A, AWM)

Bois du Gros Canon, the hollow excavated for the 35-centimetre naval gun.

1st Battalion drew abreast with Bois du Gros Canon, a company of the 3rd Battalion attached to the 1st took the Bois and crossed the valley to occupy **Arcy Wood**, on the slope to your right front. The 4th Battalion captured the crest further to your right. Resistance was minimal as most of the Germans fled. The tanks had little to do.

Take the sharp left turn to **Chuignolles**, head right there on the D71 and stop after one kilometre at the triangular **intersection** ⑫ with the D143. Look back towards Chuignolles. The left of the 1st Battalion took the village and continued down the spur on the right of the D71 to the valley floor either side of your location, which was crowded with hutments, stores depots and railway lines. One track had been the means of installing the naval gun at Bois du Gros Canon, where the 1st Battalion's line to your left met the battalion's right flank. Now stand with Chuignolles at your back. Ahead of you is the **Froissy Plateau**, which ends 1.6 kilometres to your left at the **Froissy Beacon**, a bald headland overlooking the Somme. The slope of the plateau to your front and right front is the **Gibraltar Bluff**, fire from which had greatly troubled the 1st Battalion's advance.

At 2 pm the 3rd Brigade commenced the exploitation beyond the line already gained. As the 12th Battalion moved either side of Chuignolles towards you, the fire from the heights was again intense and it temporarily held up the 12th's left flank. The barrage advanced too quickly for the rest of the 12th Battalion, assisted by the 1st, as it moved past your right and started to climb. But it was now in dead ground to the Germans on the heights. The rim of the plateau was reached above **Marly Wood**, on the slope to your left front, and at Gibraltar. While the 1st Battalion occupied the rim, the 12th fanned out across the plateau. Meanwhile the 11th Battalion had taken the Froissy Beacon to your left.

Turn right on the D71 and stop after 1.3 kilometres at the **track** ⑬ on the right. Look along it into the Froissy Valley, which swings away to your right and down to the Somme. Named after the village 250 metres further along the D71, the **Chuignes Valley** enters on your left. Bois du Gros Canon is 700 metres to your front, with Arcy Wood to its left on the opposite slope. Aiming to take the stretch of Gibraltar behind you, the 3rd Battalion advanced towards you from both woods during the morning. Gibraltar was too steep for the supporting tanks and

The left of the 3rd Brigade's advance onto the Froissy Plateau.

torrential fire came from the slopes to your left, which included grapeshot from an anti-tank gun. The 3rd withdrew but the afternoon attack, when the Germans had to respond along a wider front, brought success. Though still heavy, the fire was not as intense as before and when the 3rd reached your location it was sheltered from the Germans above. They began to break, enabling the 3rd to capture Chuignes and the heights.

Drive into Chuignes, turn left at the crossroads onto Rue de Cappy and park at the dumping area by the **track 14** on the right 750 metres along. You are now squarely on the Froissy Plateau. Stand with Chuignes on your left. **Garenne Wood**, which initially held up the 12th Battalion as it started across the plateau

towards you, is 500 metres to your front. When the 12th began working around both sides of the wood, the Germans abandoned it. Over the next few days, the Australians pushed their line well beyond the high ground behind you and past **Cappy**, the village on the Somme at the end of the road. Manfred von Richthofen's last sortie began there.

To return to Villers-Bretonneux or Amiens, go back to Chuignolles and turn left just beyond it onto the D329. Turn right on reaching the D1029, which takes you to both destinations. For Albert, take the D1 in Cappy, swing right in Bray onto the D329 and stay on this road. Alternatively, continue on the D1 for two kilometres past Bray to start the Somme North battlefield drive.

LOCAL INFORMATION

CEMETERIES

Many of the Australian fallen from the post–8 August advance on the southern side of the Somme rest in **Heath British Cemetery**, including Private Beatham, and in other cemeteries covered in earlier chapters on the 1918 Somme battlefields. **Rosières Communal Cemetery Extension**, reached by continuing into the town from the tour stop and turning right onto the D28, contains the graves of 68 Australians, mostly 1st Division casualties from 9–10 August.

Heath Cemetery.

CHAPTER 21

1918

SOMME NORTH

It will never be known whether General Monash said to General Rawlinson on 9 August, 'I told you so'. Monash had anticipated that the British III Corps, whose sorry record alongside the Australians dated back to Second Villers-Bretonneux, would probably fail again on the northern bank of the Somme in the advance on 8 August. The left flank of the Australian Corps on the southern bank would then be exposed. Monash had therefore sought responsibility for both banks. Rawlinson refused. On 8 August III Corps stalled before the Chipilly Spur, allowing the German guns on it to pummel the Australian left flank. Rawlinson gave Monash control of the northern bank next day, whereupon Quartermaster-Sergeant Hayes and his six-man patrol from the 1st Battalion promptly cleared the spur. Carried out principally by the 3rd Division, the Australian advance on the northern side of the river that followed has been overshadowed by the advance of the bulk of the Australian Corps on the southern side.

Acting as stretcher-bearers, German prisoners bring in 9th Brigade soldiers wounded in Happy Valley on 22 August.

Bray from the northeast. The 10th Brigade's assault struck the village from the right of the photograph.

Australian transport passing a ditched German gun in Happy Valley on 28 August 1918.

Etinehem and Bray

On 10 August the 13th Brigade from the 4th Division moved across the Somme and sealed off the Etinehem Spur, which jutted sharply into the river, by advancing across the base of it that night. Monash, whose idea it was, hoped to increase the shock effect of using tanks in darkness by crashing through on a very narrow front. The attack was completely successful, the Germans abandoning Etinehem in panic and withdrawing to Bray, at the far end of the spur. A simultaneous attempt to cut out the Méricourt Spur on the southern bank failed disastrously when the Germans caught the 10th Brigade near Proyart. German resistance had been increasing on that side of the river, whereas most of the Germans facing the 13th Brigade had just been withdrawn, exhausted, from the battle there.

On 20 August the 3rd Australian Division took over on the northern side of the Somme. III Corps was on its left. On 22 August they carried forward the right flank of the Third Army, which had struck towards Bapaume the day before. The 3rd Division reached Happy Valley above Bray, from which the heavily defended village could be enveloped. A German counterattack drove the 47th Division, next to the 3rd, back to its start line, exposing the 3rd's left flank and forcing a brief postponement of the attack on Bray. It was renewed on 24 August when the 10th Brigade started towards the village in bright moonlight. Advances either side of Bray distracted the Germans from the assault on the village, which was quickly cleared. At a cost of 74 casualties, only three of whom were killed, the 10th took 186 Germans prisoner.

Taking risks

Reviewing the effect on the Germans of operations since 8 August, Field Marshal Haig declared that 'Risks which a month ago would have been criminal to incur ought now to be incurred as a matter of duty'. The Third Army continued the main thrust, with the First Army extending the attack northwards past Arras on 26 August. The Fourth Army was to continue guarding the right of the Third. Rawlinson told Monash on 24 August to 'keep touch' with the enemy: 'no opportunity will be missed of making ground towards Péronne', 14 kilometres east. But Haig denied Rawlinson reinforcements because his was the subsidiary offensive. Backflipping next day, Rawlinson decreed that the Fourth Army would 'mark time and await events elsewhere'. Monash disagreed. Prisoners confirmed that the Germans were withdrawing to the great bend in the Somme at Cléry, 12 kilometres east. Other prisoners said they were pulling back to the Hindenburg Line another 16 kilometres east.

Unwilling to give the Germans a respite when they were on the run, Monash fell back on Rawlinson's earlier directive to 'keep touch'. Through aggressive patrolling, he instructed on 26 August, 'advantage will be taken of any opportunity to seize the enemy's positions and to advance our line'. By 28 August the 3rd Division had reached Cléry after capturing Suzanne, Vaux and Curlu. Lance-Corporal Bernard Gordon was awarded the VC for clearing away the Germans holding up part of the 41st Battalion during the advance. On the southern bank, the 2nd and 5th Australian Divisions and the 32nd British Division were nearing Péronne.

DRIVING THE BATTLEFIELD

Though the fighting for the Australians was harder on the southern side of the Somme than on the northern, there is no doubting which battlefield is the more pleasurable to drive: the northern one, which mostly follows the river, wins handsomely. Do it in the late afternoon, when the sun is at your back, and the memory will always bring a smile. But remember, too, how tired the soldiers of the 3rd Division were. On Monash's promise of 'a good rest later', they carried out the advance without relief. Making the advance an even greater test of endurance, the 3rd, like the other Australian divisions, was also badly understrength.

MAPS IGN Blue Series, 1:25 000, 24080 Albert; 2408E Bray-sur-Somme; 25080 Péronne

The 13th Brigade's advance across the Etinehem Spur.

From Amiens take the D1 through Corbie and continue to the junction with the D42. From Villers-Bretonneux, take the D23 and turn right onto the D1 in Fouillloy. From Albert, follow the D42 through Morlancourt to the D1 and turn left.

On each approach route, continue through the D1/D42 junction, passing **Tailles Wood** on the left and **Gressaire Wood** on the right after 3.8 kilometres. Having formed up along the forward edge of Gressaire Wood, the 49th Battalion next to the D1 and the 50th Battalion alongside it further to your right began the advance across the Etinehem Spur to your front at 9.30 pm on 10 August. You are following in the wake of the two tanks that clattered along the D1, firing as they went and scattering the worn-out Germans ahead of them. Moving to the right of the road behind the tanks, the 49th Battalion faced little opposition as it dropped off posts that faced to your left. At the crossroads 500 metres past the woods, turn right onto the C2, signposted **Cimetière Militaire d'Etinehem**, and head left at the Y-junction 900 metres further on. Continue to the T-junction at the calvary, turn left and, after 200 metres, right. Park on the crest after 250 metres at the **T-junction ❶** with a track.

GRESSAIRE WOOD

50TH BATTALION

BRAY HILL BRITISH CEMETERY

47TH DIVISON

9TH BRIGADE

Stand with the D1 on your right. **Etinehem** is 500 metres to your left front on the bank of the **Somme**, which clearly defines the spur as it curls around behind you to **Bray**. As the 50th Battalion advanced towards you, flares went up from the Y-junction to your right front and the dozen machine-guns strung out on the far side of the C2 near the junction opened. But the 50th, though only 400 strong, looked like an attacking brigade in the ghostly light and the sound of tanks firing came from the D1 to your right. The fusillade ceased as the panic-struck Germans bolted towards Bray. Passing 200 metres to your right, the 50th swung up the crest towards the D1, meeting the right flank of the 49th on the way. The 13th Brigade expected to capture some 300 Germans in Etinehem but when a company from the 51st Battalion entered the village at dawn only one was found.

The 9th Brigade's start line on the C2 for the attack on Bray, which is out of picture to the right, on 22 August.

TAILLES WOOD

49TH BATTALION

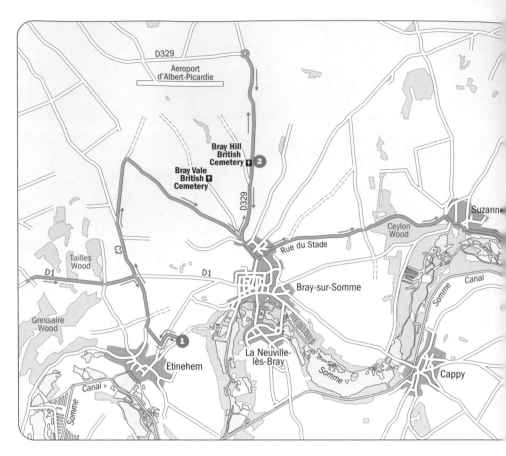

Before leaving, turn about. At 1 am on 12 August the 51st Battalion advanced to your right front to mop up the Germans who remained on the slope and along the river bank. Scouting ahead of the new line below you in the moonlight, Sergeant Bill Lehane was fired on by some men whose identity he had challenged. Lehane chased them to a dugout and called on them to come out. To his astonishment, 60 Germans emerged and surrendered. Now look to your right front across the Somme, where the steeple of **Proyart church** breaks the skyline. Attacking simultaneously with the 13th Brigade, the 10th Brigade was supposed to arc around the left of Proyart and reach the bank of the river. It was smashed even before the turn towards you could begin.

Return to the C2 and cross over the D1. The road ahead was the start line that the 9th Brigade occupied in the 3rd

Division's attack on Bray on 22 August. Head right at the Y-junction and right again after 1.1 kilometres, just before the **Aeroport d'Albert-Picardie**, used by the Airbus consortium as a test strip. This used to be the **Aerodrome d'Albert-Bray**, a local airfield. At the time of writing, the IGN Blue Series maps had not been updated to reflect its expansion and the resulting road changes. You are now in III Corps's sector, held here by the 47th Division. As you descend towards Bray on the badly rutted road, **Bray Vale British Cemetery** appears 500 metres to your left, indicating that you are entering **Happy Valley**. Turn left at the T-junction onto the D329 and stop after 1.3 kilometres at **Bray Hill British Cemetery** ❷ on the left of the road. Look downhill along the D329.

At 4.45 am on 22 August, in a mist thickened by dust and smoke from the creeping barrage, the 9th Brigade started

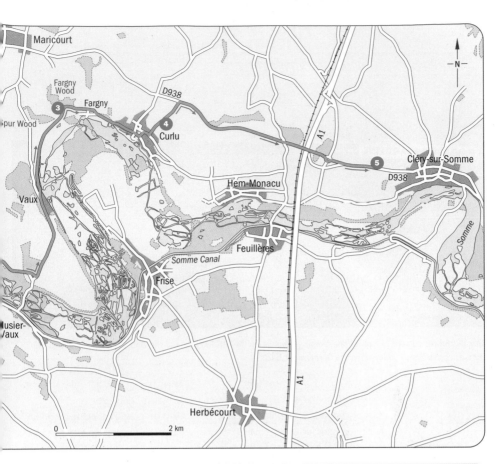

from the C2, along which you have just driven, and crossed Happy Valley to your right front. Its left flank anchored on the **chalk pit**, which straddled the D329 200 metres ahead of you, the 33rd Battalion extended down the D329. The right flank of the 35th Battalion next to it was on the T-junction. With much of the high ground overlooking Bray now secure, the village could be enveloped. But the Germans counterattacked from your left during the afternoon, striking the 47th Division's line, which ran from the chalk pit, through your location and up the hill behind you. Having earlier advanced alongside the 9th Brigade across the head of Happy Valley to your right, the 47th now hit reverse gear and went back across it. As the Germans tore after the 47th, the 33rd Battalion to your front poured fire into their flank, using captured weapons as well as their own. Meanwhile, the 34th Battalion, which had

This drive covers the Etinehem Spur and Bray attacks before following, mostly on the left bank of the Somme, the 3rd Division's advance to Cléry. Along the way, it passes through the site of Lance-Corporal Gordon's VC action.
DISTANCE COVERED: 26 km
DURATION: 2 hours

been in support, hurriedly formed a line of posts that stretched from the chalk pit and over Happy Valley towards the C2. The Germans were halted on the far side of the valley. The 9th Brigade's left flank was intact.

Relieving the 9th next day, the 10th Brigade attacked Bray at 1 am on 24 August. The Germans detected the advance in the moonlight and drenched the valley ahead of you with gas, forcing the 40th Battalion and that part of the 37th carrying out the assault to don masks. Companies from both battalions advanced right to left around the near

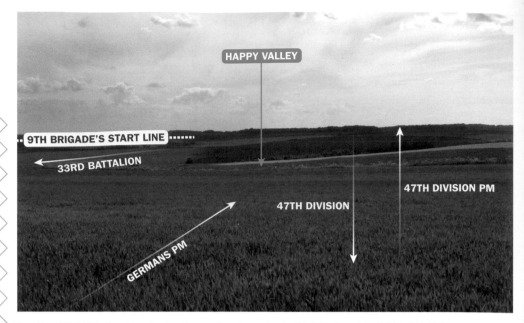

From Bray Hill British Cemetery, showing the morning advance by the 9th Brigade and the British 47th Division and the 47th's retreat across Happy Valley when the Germans hit back.

end of the village while another company from the 40th passed around the Somme end. The Germans already had their hands full when a third company of the 40th entered the right side of Bray at three points. Most of the Germans withdrew to avoid being cut off. At the same time, the 47th Division

A German sniper killed near Bray on 22 August by a shot through the neck. In his pack was found a letter written to his wife the night before, in which he complained how terrible it was to be opposite the Australians and how he hoped he would soon be sent to a sector where there weren't any.

regained the ground behind you that it had lost on 22 August.

As U-turns are a risky proposition on the busy D329, continue along it to the roundabout beyond the airport runway and head back from there towards Bray. The village, which stood on the boundary between the British and the French in 1916, is unique in that it is ringed by French, British and German cemeteries. After entering Bray, turn left onto Rue du Stade where the D329 bends rightward opposite the **Cimetière Nationale de Bray**, outside which is an impressive *poilu* memorial. As they advanced around this side of the village, the companies from the 37th and 40th Battalions were heavily fired on by four machine-guns in the cemetery area. They seized all four of them.

Proceed along Rue du Stade, following the advance of the 10th and 11th Brigades, respectively right and left of the road, at dawn on 25 August. Helped by the creeping barrage and the fog, both brigades easily dealt with the few posts they encountered. As you crest the

Australian pioneers digging in above Bray after the attack on 22 August. The village was still in German hands and snipers firing from it accounted for several of the pioneers.

height, **Ceylon Wood** straddles the road ahead. When the attack reached the crest the fog had cleared and the 11th Brigade, in particular, was hammered by machine-guns and field-guns firing from the wood and the trenches of the 1916 battlefield beyond it. With the 58th Division on the left of the 11th Brigade held up too, the advance stalled. When it resumed after dark, the Germans had withdrawn and Ceylon Wood was cleared. Continue through it. Once the road curves rightwards, the wood no longer straddles it but extends only down to the Somme on the right. By mid-morning on 26 August the 39th Battalion closest to you, and the 44th and 43rd Battalion in that order next to it, had crossed the bare spur on your left and were beyond **Suzanne** to your front.

Turn right at the crossroads on the edge of Suzanne onto the C3, Rue du Calvaire, follow it past the magnificent château on your right and then head right at the Y-junction by the war memorial onto Rue d'en Bas. Continue through the village and along the bank of the Somme marshes to the round-about 1.5 kilometres further on and head left over the spur towards **Vaux**, which the 37th and 39th Battalions, advancing from your left, had cleared by morning on 27 August. Swing right at the Y-junction in the hamlet onto Rue de Fargny, which passes **Spur Wood** on your left after 1.5 kilometres and then descends across a clearing before turning sharp right in front of **Fargny Wood**. Park on the **track** ❸ that heads sharp left at the bend. With your back to Fargny Wood, look along Rue de Fargny.

The 41st Battalion had fought through Spur Wood by daybreak on 27 August. C Company, to which Lance-Corporal Gordon belonged, was consolidating along the high ground to your right front. B Company had pressed on along the river and was strung out between the left

FARGNY WOOD

GORDON

The scene of Lance-Corporal Gordon's VC action. Gordon charged into the wood several times. To get closer to where the action was, park on the track at the rightwards bend.

of the wood and the steep **Chapeau de Gendarme** cliff just beyond **Fargny** hamlet 400 metres to your left. With machine-guns in Fargny Wood behind you pinning B Company down, Gordon, who had won the MM at Hamel, charged across the re-entrant to your right, knocked out one of the guns and took 11 prisoners. His VC action did not end there. Making repeated forays into the wood, he eventually captured 63 Germans and six machine-guns, one of which is now displayed in the Australian War Memorial. The Germans abandoned the wood.

Drive through Fargny, heading right at the Y-junction onto Rue du Four to pass below the cliff from which snipers fired at the leading elements of B Company wedged in by the river. Once in **Curlu** turn left at the far end of the large common onto Rue de la Place, then right at the T-junction and left after 150 metres. On 28 August the 38th Battalion captured the quarries on your right 250 metres along ❹. Turn right at the T-junction opposite the chapel onto the D938. Advancing respectively left and right of the D938 and led by the 13th Light Horse Regiment, the 9th and 10th Brigades pursued the Germans towards **Cléry-sur-Somme**.

Continue over the TGV railway and the A1 autoroute and through the large roundabout. Both brigades had reached the high ground between the roundabout and Cléry during the afternoon. As you approach the village, think of the 38th Battalion pinned down on the outskirts by 10 machine-guns lining the broad slope to your left ❺. It had been on the move for 84 hours and the men were so tired that many of them slept through the German shelling of their positions and, starting at 6.30 pm, the tremendous Australian shelling that softened up the Germans pinning them down. Three companies took the slope shortly after 7 pm. Only 40-strong instead of the usual 200, the fourth company entered the ruined village after dark and found it deserted. The attack on Mont St Quentin and Péronne, which would bring the Australian Corps arguably its greatest success, was about to begin.

The Mont St Quentin/Péronne battlefield drive starts in Cléry. Should you wish to return to Albert, though, simply head back on the D938. For Amiens and Villers-Bretonneux, turn left off the D938 at Maricourt onto the D197, then right onto the D1 2.6 kilometres beyond Suzanne and remain on the D1.

LOCAL INFORMATION

CEMETERIES

Bray Military Cemetery

Started in April 1916 and used extensively by casualty clearing stations until Bray fell to the Germans in March 1918, this cemetery was back in operation within days of the village's recapture by the 40th Battalion in August. Expanded postwar by graves brought in from the surrounding battlefields, it now contains 874 burials, of which 747 are identified. All but two of the 31 Australians are known. The cemetery is 300 metres along on the left of Rue du 11 Novembre, the second road on the left after entering Bray on the D329 on the tour route.

Bray Vale British Cemetery

Containing 279 burials, 107 of them identified, Bray Vale was begun after the 40th Battalion retook Bray. The 17 Australians include Captain Harry Dench of the 38th Battalion at II.C.2, killed trying to rally British troops who had fallen back when the chalk pit area was shelled on 24 August. Many of the burials comprise remains brought in after the war from the nearby 1916 Somme battlefields. Attractively terraced on two levels, the cemetery is passed in Happy Valley on the tour route. Turn sharp left immediately before the D329 near Bray to reach it.

Cote 80 French National Cemetery Etinehem

Passed on the tour route, this cemetery is located on the C2 above Etinehem village. After the 13th Brigade captured the Etinehem Spur on 10 August, 29 Australians were buried in the original French cemetery.

CHAPTER 22

1918

MONT ST QUENTIN AND PÉRONNE

On 30 August 1925 Marshal Ferdinand Foch, the allied generalissimo in 1918, unveiled a memorial to the 2nd Australian Division on Mont St Quentin. The memorial's larger-than-life sculpture depicted an Australian soldier bayoneting an eagle that lay wounded at his feet. As the eagle symbolised the Imperial German Army, the meaning was obvious. In 1940 the occupying Germans removed the sculpture. The 2nd Division's veterans, who had wanted, and paid for, something more dramatic than the obelisk memorials to the other Australian divisions, were now left with just the plinth on which their memorial had stood. In 1971 a new sculpture was unveiled. It showed a slouch-hatted Australian soldier in full battle gear with his head slightly bowed as if reflecting on the cost of the fighting in which he had been involved continuously since March. If less-aggressive looking than the original, it is still unique among the Australian divisional memorials.

This is appropriate for the battle fought here was unique in the AIF's experience of the Western Front. As Charles Bean wrote, 'it was the only important fight in which quick, free manoeuvre played a decisive part'. But it really comprised three interdependent fights, all encapsulated by the name Mont St Quentin. The 2nd Division's capture of the Mont was the most spectacular but it relied on the 3rd Division securing Bouchavesnes Ridge, which ran down towards the Somme hamlet of Cléry, on the left flank. In turn, the 5th Division attacking Péronne on the right flank relied on the fall of Mont St Quentin. The fighting to take all three locations lasted four days and resulted in the award of eight VCs, more than for any other Australian action of the war.

Intentions

After passing Péronne, the Somme abruptly abandons its northerly course at Cléry, 3.5 kilometres further on, to follow a westerly one. The river was canalised but unfordable marshes extended up to 500 metres from the canal. Overlooking Péronne and the river was Mont St Quentin, 100 metres high and defended by a good division, the 2nd Prussian Guard. Cléry lay at the foot of 1916 Knoll, which formed the tip of 1916 Spur, an offshoot of Bouchavesnes Ridge. The Germans on the knoll and spur blocked the approaches to the Mont and commanded the causeway linking Cléry to Omiécourt on the opposite bank of the Somme. Vauban's ramparts rose 20 metres to enclose Péronne, making the town a formidable obstacle.

The memorial to the 2nd Australian Division on Mont St Quentin.

From the line reached by the Australian Corps on 28 August, General Monash knew that the Germans would have to withdraw over the Somme next day. That afternoon he ordered a frontal assault across the river, hoping to swamp them before their retirement was complete. The 2nd Division on the southern bank was to secure the Péronne bridges and swing onto the Mont, while the 5th and the 32nd Divisions seized other crossings on the right of the 2nd. But once the Germans were over the Péronne bridges, they blew them up. As the other crossings were also untenable, Monash utilised the operational flexibility stemming from his insistence three weeks earlier that the Australian Corps must have responsibility for both banks of the Somme. At 5 pm on 29 August he ordered the divisions on the southern bank to sidestep left, which brought the 2nd Division to Omiécourt. Crossing there once the 3rd Division had taken

1916 Spur, it was to attack Mont St Quentin at 5 am next morning. The 5th Division following would move between the 2nd and the river to capture Péronne. Each division was to employ a single brigade initially.

The 10th Brigade from the 3rd Division had captured Cléry late on 29 August. But the Germans still remained on 1916 Knoll, which made the causeway at Omiécourt untenable when the 5th Brigade reached it after an all-night march at 4 am on 30 August. Hopes of launching the attack at 5 am evaporated. Monash postponed it 24 hours, giving the 9th and 10th Brigades more time to secure 1916 Knoll and Spur. Like all the Australian formations they were exhausted and badly undermanned. Their attacks were only partly successful. Using another crossing at Feuillères, two kilometres rearwards, the 5th Brigade reached Cléry during the afternoon, whereupon the 20th Battalion gained a

The 21st Battalion attacks Mont St Quentin village at 1.30 pm on 1 September 1918. It advanced from the trench in the foreground.

The summit of Mont St Quentin shortly after its capture.

strong footing on 1916 Knoll. The start line for next morning's advance on the Mont, two kilometres away, ran across it.

Presumption becomes reality

'So you think you're going to take Mont St Quentin with three battalions! What presumption! However, I don't think I ought to stop you! So, go ahead and try — and I wish you good luck!', Monash's army commander, General Rawlinson, told him. Monash's presumption was greater than Rawlinson imagined for the 5th Brigade was down to 1340 all ranks, an average of 330 men per battalion. Assaulting in the dimness at 5 am on 31 August after a tot of rum, the 17th and 20th Battalions yelled their heads off to convince the Germans that they were much stronger. As the assault streamed across the overgrown ditch of the unfinished Canal du Nord, the Germans disintegrated. 'It all happened like

lightning, and before we had fired a shot we were taken unaware', one of them said. Now able to use the Omiécourt causeway, the 19th Battalion arrived in support. Elsa Trench near the summit of the Mont was passed, but the Germans counterattacked, regaining the crest. Monash ordered the 3rd Division to take Bouchavesnes Ridge in order to secure the open left flank. 'Casualties no longer matter', he told General Gellibrand.

When the 6th Brigade, 1334 strong, moved up to attack the summit at 6 am on a rainy 1 September, Private Robert Mactier was killed while silencing machine-guns that blocked the 23rd Battalion. He was posthumously awarded the VC. Sergeant Albert Lowerson of the 21st Battalion led a charge that overcame the centre of resistance on the critical left flank, where machine-guns under Lieutenant Harry Towner of the 7th Machine-Gun Company provided continuous covering fire. Lowerson and

Towner, who also held the MM, both won VCs. The Mont was taken after two attempts.

Péronne

The 14th Brigade also had great trouble crossing the Somme to attack Péronne, in and around which were parts of three German divisions. Having taken 10 hours to complete an approach that should have taken three, it squeezed between the 6th Brigade and the river at Cléry late on 31 August. Assaulting next morning, the 53rd Battalion was clobbered by a field-gun at Anvil Wood until Private William Currey rushed it. Emerging from the wood into the town cemetery, the 53rd saw Péronne spread out before it but was pinned down. The 54th Battalion on its right met ferocious fire from Johannes Trench. Corporals Arthur Hall and Alex Buckley dealt with the machine-guns and the Germans fled. The 54th reached the moat at Péronne's ramparts, where Buckley was killed near a wooden footbridge that was under fire. Hall found that the moat was passable beside the modern Historial museum a kilometre north, where there was also less resistance, and much of the 54th entered Péronne there. The 54th now controlled the western part of the town. Currey, Hall and Buckley (posthumously) were all awarded the VC.

During the afternoon, the 53rd Battalion lost heavily in a failed attempt to advance beyond the cemetery. Long before then Brigadier-General Elliott had tried to hustle the 15th Brigade over the Somme canal, using the remains of the road bridge, to attack Flamicourt, south of Péronne. When German fire from the far bank forced a halt, he decided that the 15th's best chance was to help the 14th Brigade take the rest of Péronne and attack Flamicourt from it later. Mishaps precluded coordination of the attack before it got underway at 6 am on 2 September, and one of Elliott's

battalions, the 58th, ended up clearing the rest of the town almost by itself. It used the same tactics as the 57th had at Villers-Bretonneux, with Lewis-gunners pouring fire into the houses while riflemen charged them. Meanwhile the 7th Brigade pushed beyond Mont St Quentin and the 3rd Division secured Bouchavesnes Ridge. Privates George Cartwright and Lawrence Weathers, of the 33rd and 43rd Battalions respectively, were awarded VCs for eliminating machine-guns in the 3rd Division's advance.

Reckoning

At a cost of 3000 casualties, the Australians had taken 2600 prisoners and evicted the Germans from one of their key bastions. Monash's deft manoeuvring of his formations during the battle, wrote Bean, furnished 'a complete answer to the comment that [he] was merely a composer of set-pieces'. It established Monash as a superb general. But Monash himself admitted that the outcome was due 'first and chiefly to the wonderful gallantry' of tired soldiers in understrength units who repeatedly attacked strong positions without tanks and, sometimes, without the usual artillery support. He might also have mentioned the brigade and divisional staffs, whose skill and efficiency had enabled his orders to be carried out swiftly. Rawlinson reportedly told him, 'You have altered the whole course of the war'. Field Marshal Haig, too, was amazed. Some contend that the effort was wasted because the Germans planned to withdraw to the Hindenburg Line. But they also wanted to winter in an intermediate line while its defences were thoroughly prepared. On 2 September the Canadian Corps broke through the Drocourt–Quéant Switch Line near Bullecourt. With the Somme line lost to the Australians the same day, they had no choice but to retire to the Hindenburg Line forthwith.

DRIVING THE BATTLEFIELD

Covering the assaults on Péronne and Bouchavesnes Ridge as well as Mont St Quentin, this is a long tour. Péronne is exponentially larger than it was in 1918 and now abuts Mont St Quentin, which it didn't do in 1918. The modern development makes it difficult to follow the fight through the town. Fortunately, this is not the case with the Mont, where you have the option of a short walk that takes you to the sites of Lieutenant Towner's and Sergeant Lowerson's VC actions and some old German trenches. It also gives you a chance to stretch your legs.

MAPS IGN Blue Series, 1:25 000, 2408E Bray-sur-Somme; 25080 Péronne

1916 Knoll and Spur from Omiécourt where the 5th Brigade tried to cross the Somme. The river is in the low ground behind the houses.

From Amiens and Villers-Bretonneux, take the D1 through Corbie and Bray, turn left onto the D197 opposite Cappy and then right onto the D938 just before Maricourt. From Albert simply take the D938.

On reaching **Cléry**, turn right at the first crossroads onto Rue de l'Eglise and then left at the T-junction by the church onto Rue Anne-Marie Vion, which follows the bank of the **Somme**. At the far end of the village, turn right onto Rue d'Omiécourt and cross the river on the arc of its great bend. The Somme flows from your left front towards the causeway and then away to your right beyond it. Park where the power lines cross the road ❶ and look back towards Cléry. Strung out along the bank to your right rear, the 5th Brigade sought to get over the river here in the early hours of 30 August as the causeway was the closest crossing to Mont St Quentin still intact. But the Germans held a strongpoint on the edge of Cléry to your front, and **1916 Knoll** on the far side of the river to your right. They could sweep the causeway from both, precluding any crossing.

1916 SPUR

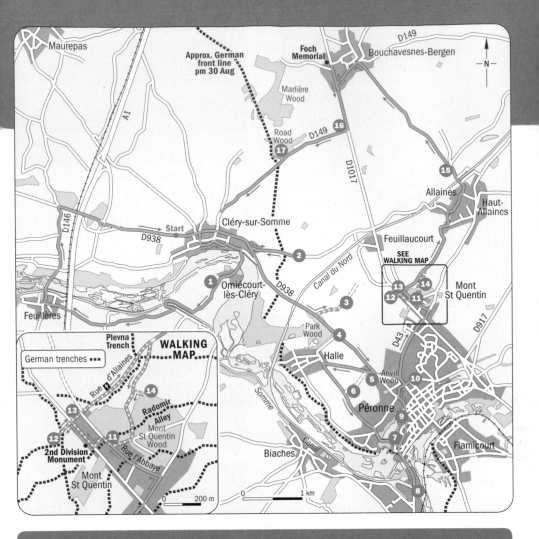

Starting from Cléry, this drive follows the 5th Brigade's attack on Mont St Quentin before retracing the 14th Brigade's advance into Péronne. It covers the capture of the town by the 14th and 15th Brigades and then goes over the Mont itself, which allows the assault to be seen from the German standpoint. The walk here embraces some of the key locations in the 6th Brigade's fight for the crest. Continuing over and along the Bouchavesnes Ridge, the route concludes in the area over which the 3rd Division advanced. The location of every VC action is also included.

DISTANCE COVERED: 35 km (Mont St Quentin walk 1.7 km)
DURATION: 5 hours

1916 KNOLL

Continue along Rue d'Omiécourt, turn sharp right after crossing the Somme canal and carry on to **Feuillères**, passing under the A1 autoroute and the TGV railway on the way. Leaving the 19th Battalion to secure the river bank at Omiécourt, the rest of the 5th Brigade started out at dawn on 30 August on the route you are taking. Having been on the go for the previous two nights and fought the previous day, it hoped for a break out of harm's way near Feuillères. But Monash's planning for the battle was dynamic. The 5th had barely cleaned up when it was ordered to cross the Somme at the village and head along the northern bank to Cléry. Led by the 20th Battalion, it was marching by 10.30 am. You can retrace its route by turning right at the crossroads in Feuillères onto the D146 (Rue de Feuillères) and right again once over the river onto the D938.

On exiting Cléry, head left at the Y-junction by the crucifix onto Rue de Feuillaucourt and continue past the deep gully, where the bitumen gives way to dirt. Park by the fence at the top of the **cutting** ❷, walk to the crest ahead and look along the track. You are now on **1916 Spur**, which runs down from **Bouchavesnes Ridge** on your left and ends at 1916 Knoll above the D938 on your right. At the end of the 1916 Somme campaign, the French and

Germans faced each other along the ridge and spur. Now the 3rd Division, the only one of the Australian formations to advance on this side of the Somme, was drawn up to your left rear facing the Germans, who were back in their old trench system. Its communication trenches and saps stretched across the big re-entrant to your front to **Mont St Quentin**, the broad wooded hill that squats like a sumo wrestler on the far side two kilometres away. Péronne's commercial area extends to the right edge of it.

Late on 30 August the 37th Battalion established posts 600 metres to your left rear above Cléry. But the Germans held 1916 Spur and Knoll when the 20th Battalion arrived in the meantime. It cleared the reverse slopes of both to your right rear at dusk. The Germans had the deep gully behind you particularly well covered. 'Men paused at the corner with bullets smacking into the trench walls and timed their rush and jump', said Lieutenant William Guard. 'A good number of fellows mistimed it.' Eventually the Germans bolted only to be skylined to your right in a deadly crossfire from the reverse slopes. The 20th easily took the rest of 1916 Knoll at the outset of the attack on Mont St Quentin next morning. 'Yelling like a lot of bushrangers', it passed diagonally right to left across your front

MONT ST QUENTIN

D1017

ELSA TRENCH

20TH BATTALION

GOTTLIEB TRENCH

with the 17th Battalion, which had emerged from **Park Wood**, on the river to your right front, alongside.

Return to the D938, turn left onto it and left again into a dumping area 350 metres after crossing the **Canal du Nord**, here barely a ditch in 1918. Walk to the fork at the bushes and then head left for 300 metres to the site of **Brasso redoubt ❸**. Look towards Mont St Quentin, from which the D1017 runs past the far side of **Feuillaucourt** to your left front. The D1017 continues up a steep spur, adjacent to 1916 Spur to your left rear, to Bouchavesnes Ridge. Starting from the D1017, **Elsa Trench** skirted the tree line on the crest of the Mont and ran around towards the edge of Péronne to its right. **Galatz** and **Agram Alleys** extended from Elsa across the skyline to your right front. Starting at Feuillaucourt, **Gottlieb Trench** stretched away to your right front after passing in front of your location. Galatz, Gottlieb and Agram all met on the near side of the D938. **Moineville Alley** went from Gottlieb, 200 metres to your left, directly to the D1017.

As there had been no time to arrange a creeping barrage, the artillery struck selected localities ahead of the assault, including Mont St Quentin. Advancing over 1916 Knoll to your right rear, the 20th Battalion passed to your left to take Feuillaucourt and Gottlieb Trench on your left, while the 17th Battalion got to your location and Gottlieb on your right. Casualties were light as the Germans were taken completely by surprise in the dim early-morning light. The 5th Brigade 'came suddenly', their account states, 'first from the left then in front' racing them from one position to the next. The skillful cooperation of the Australian rifle grenadiers and Lewis-gunners was particularly noticeable. Some 700 Germans were captured. With the resistance broken, the 20th Battalion continued to the D1017, which it lined between the Canal du Nord and the tree line on the Mont. The 17th Battalion continued through the trees to the summit, while the 19th Battalion, having come across the now secure Omiécourt crossing, occupied Galatz and Agram Alleys from the Mont halfway down to the D938.

At 11 am the Germans counter-attacked the summit, driving the 17th Battalion back to Elsa Trench. Meanwhile the 3rd Division tried to protect the left of the attack by securing Bouchavesnes Ridge. The 9th Brigade reached the D1017 on the crest of the ridge to your left. The 10th Brigade below it was unable to progress beyond 1916 Spur to the D1017 on the adjacent spur overlooking Feuillaucourt in order to link up with the 20th Battalion on the canal.

PÉRONNE

GALATZ AND AGRAM ALLEYS

19TH BATTALION

17TH BATTALION

Sheltered by this spur, the Germans moved along the canal during the afternoon and struck the 20th's open left flank on the far side of Feuillaucourt. The left half of the 20th pulled back to Gottlieb as far as your location; the right half stayed on the D1017 on the Mont. The 18th Battalion came forward to occupy Moineville Alley, linking the two halves and giving the 5th Brigade a continuous line. Advancing across your right front next day, the 6th Brigade retook the Mont.

Continue 600 metres on the D938 to the **concrete building** 4 just past the electricity sub-station. Look along the D938. Extending from **Halle** on your right, **Florina Trench** crossed the road 200 metres ahead of you to join Gottlieb 100 metres to the left of the road. The 23rd Battalion had captured Halle and Florina Trench on the right of the D938 after it led the 6th Brigade through Cléry on 31 August. It now had to pass through

Gottlieb and Florina on the left of the D938 to take part in the 6th's Brigade attack on the Mont on 1 September. As the 23rd crossed the D938, a machine-gun opened from Florina close to the road. Lobbing a bomb at it and scrambling over a wire barricade, Private Mactier killed the six Germans in the post and hurled their machine gun out of the trench. Another 20 Germans surrendered as he pushed past them to wipe out another gun. Charging across the open at a third gun, Mactier was killed by a fourth. His VC-winning action allowed the 23rd Battalion to attack on time. The 14th Brigade advanced to your right front to protect the 6th Brigade's right flank.

Proceed along the D938. At the entrance to Péronne, turn right on the roundabout and park on Rue Hector Berlioz at the Y-junction 5. The 14th Brigade advanced towards you astride this road, with the 53rd and 54th Battalions to your right and left

The site of the field-gun that inflicted heavy losses on the 53rd Battalion before Private Currey knocked it out. Anvil Wood extended to the junction in the foreground in 1918.

The area of Johannes Trench, where Corporals Hall and Buckley took on the German machine-guns.

respectively. Now walk back to the D938 and head right for 50 metres to another Y-junction, where Rue de Quinconce branches off to the left. Look back along the D938. The copse at the far end of the **Centre Cultural et Sportiff** on your right is all that remains of **Anvil Wood**, which extended to your location in 1918. The field-gun that pummelled the 53rd Battalion as it advanced towards you fired at point-blank range from where you are standing and caused heavy loss. Charging through intense machine-gun fire, Private Currey killed three Germans and captured another nine as well as the field-gun. The 53rd pressed on through Anvil Wood.

Drive down Rue Hector Berlioz, turn sharp left at the T-junction just before Halle onto Rue de Maismont, and stop after 650 metres at the **track** ⑥ on the left. Look back along Rue de Maismont. Cresting the spur to your front, the 54th Battalion was heavily engaged from densely wired **Johannes Trench**, which ran down the slope to your right front, crossed the track 200 metres to your right and then passed between the church and the pylon to your left. Covered by Lewis-gunners standing to shoot over

them, men pulled up the pickets securing the wire or crawled under it. Once through, Corporals Hall and Buckley both silenced machine-guns but the precise location of the guns is now unknown. The two that Hall dealt with were probably in Johannes Trench to your right. He killed five Germans and captured nine plus both guns. The gun Buckley rushed may well have been in **Toros Alley**, 200 metres to your left rear. He killed its four crew and took 22 prisoners. Shooting from the shoulder, the 54th chased the fleeing Germans to Péronne.

Continue into the town, following Boulevard de Fort Carabit past the end of the lake on your left. Stop in the car park on the left ⑦, walk downhill to the green and stand with your back to the fortifications so that you can look along the lake to your front. It is part of the moat that extended past the castle, which can be seen at the other end, and encircled the town in 1918. Machine-guns were sited on the ramparts along the moat and a field-gun was emplaced by the car park to your right. Intense fire halted the right flank of the 54th Battalion as it approached from your left

Boulevard de Fort Carabit. Corporal Buckley was killed near the far end of the road. The field-gun and the numerous machine-guns firing into this area were located along the ramparts, which were in rear of where the photograph was taken.

on the road on which you are standing, then a wooden footbridge and the only crossing of the moat still intact. Corporal Buckley and Lieutenant Don Macarthur were killed as they reconnoitred. Macarthur was heard to gasp: 'I am happy to die, the war is now won and I have lived to see it and like Nelson I can say thank God I have done my duty'. Once Corporal Hall found that the moat could be crossed beyond the castle, the left of the 54th got over there and swung along the rear of the ramparts towards you. With the footbridge now freed up, the right crossed and the 54th began clearing this end of Péronne.

Turn left out of the car park and right at the second crossroads onto the D1017 (here Rue Saint-Fursy). After passing the

junction of the **Cologne River**, on your left with Flamicourt on the far bank, and the more prominent Somme on your right, cross the Somme Canal on the red-topped bridge and park at the service station on the right. Walk back to the **bridge** ⑧. On 1 September, when the 15th Brigade was on the bank to your rear, General Elliott clambered over the shattered remains of the original bridge, intending to get his battalions across to attack Flamicourt. Fired on when he reached the other side, Elliott started back across but tumbled into the canal. 'Pompey's fallen in the Somme' clogged the 5th Division's telephone lines. Most of the 58th Battalion used the wrecked bridge to enter Péronne, where it linked up with the 14th Brigade. The 59th Battalion tried to cross the intact railway bridge 300 metres to your right and advance directly on Flamicourt but the bridge was swept by a machine-gun firing from the far side of it. The 59th was recalled.

Return to Péronne on the D1017, retracing the route that the 58th Battalion took. It cleared the town to the right of the road on 2 September. Continue to the Y-junction and head left onto the D938, here the narrow Rue du Noir Lion, which will bring you to the castle. It is now the entrance to the **Historial de la Grande Guerre** ⑨. Walk 150 metres past the castle on the D938 to Rue Georges Clemenceau on the right, which ran behind the ramparts, now gone, in 1918. A bridge carried the D938 over the moat, which came around the castle to this location. Though the bridge was demolished, Corporal Hall saw that the moat could be crossed using the planking and other debris. The ramparts appeared deserted. Stumbling over the moat, the 54th Battalion came up the D938 towards you, fired a burst at the Germans on the castle walls, who promptly surrendered, and then continued along the ramparts on the

Where General Elliott took an unintended dip.

Australian Prime Minister William Morris Hughes emerges from the castle, now the facade of the Historial, while being shown through the ruins of Péronne on 14 September.

other side of the castle to the far end of the lake, where you were earlier.

Meanwhile Hall and his five men headed along Rue Georges Clemenceau. Coming across 20 Germans lining the ramparts above them some way along and firing at the 53rd Battalion on the far side, Hall placed his men in houses that offered a good view. 'I gave the order to fire', he said. 'The Germans immediately surrendered.' His tiny band had taken 70 prisoners before machine-gun fire forced them back. Continue on the D938 and head right at the four-way intersection onto Rue Jean Mermoz, which bends to the right before crossing the D43. Anvil Wood was on your left, bounded by these two roads. Continue over the D43 and stop at **Péronne Communal Cemetery Extension** ⑩. Enter the cemetery and face the road. Just as Anvil Wood overlooked the far side of the communal cemetery on your right at the time of the battle, this area was

surrounded by fields, which extended from the wood down to the ramparts to your right front and to the hamlet of St Denis, 800 metres to your left. All of these locations have now been absorbed by Greater Péronne, leaving nothing of the battlefield and little to see from the cemetery. But stopping here is

A Lewis-gun team from the 54th Battalion in Péronne on 2 September.

Dead from the 53rd Battalion in the wire at Anvil Wood. A shell bursts in the background.

The attack on the Mont as seen from Elsa Trench.

worthwhile nonetheless. Some of the hardest fighting occurred in these environs.

After clearing Anvil Wood to your right rear early on 1 September, the 53rd Battalion advanced through the communal cemetery, near which Private Currey captured a machine-gun. But it could barely get beyond the cemetery owing to enfilade machine-gun fire from the ramparts. Heavy fire also came from St Denis. At 5 pm another attempt was made, with the 53rd attacking through your location as well as the communal cemetery, and the 55th assaulting to your left rear next to it. This attack also petered

out with great loss. As a barrage would precede another attack next morning, the survivors out to your right and left front had to be recalled. Lieutenant William Waite's post, furthest out, could not be reached. Crawling forward from the cemetery, Private Currey stood up when he thought he was close to the post and yelled, 'Waitsy, get in!' A welter of fire, including some gas shells, winged towards Currey, whose gas mask was riddled before he could put it on. But he got back. So did Waite's post.

Advancing from your left rear at 6 am on 2 September, the 55th and 56th Battalions were shot up from the ramparts and pinned down to your left. Not until 10 am, when the 58th Battalion had cleared the ramparts, were they able to secure St Denis.

Return to the D43, now Rue du Mont St Quentin, and turn right onto it. After going through a Y-junction, you will again pass the Centre Cultural et Sportiff, much of which occupies the site of Anvil Wood, on the left. During the 53rd Battalion's morning advance from your left on 1 September, Lance-Corporal Cec Weatherby and Private Ron Crank saw an abandoned German field-gun in the tennis court area, which was on the edge of the wood. They turned it on its former owners, lobbing shell after shell at the

PÉRONNE COMMERCIAL AREA

AGRAM ALLEY

GALATZ ALLEY

19TH BATTALION

17TH BATTALIO

Germans engaging the 53rd from Mont St Quentin ahead of you. The pair used the gun again in the early afternoon, despite being shelled themselves, to break up the Germans reinforcing the Mont before the 6th Brigade's attack. Remain on the D43 through three roundabouts, then take the first left, Rue l'Abbaye, and park by the derelict **church** 11 at the Y-junction. Referring to the walking map, head left on Rue Pierre l'Hermit to the D1017, here, appropriately enough, called Rue des Australiennes. Cross over to the **2nd Australian Division Memorial** and note the elaborate bas-reliefs on the plinth, which depict gunners going into action and bombers fighting along a trench. The Germans left these in place when they took the original of the sculpture on the top. A Bastiaan plaque explains the battle.

Head downhill to the track by the last house on the left and walk 100 metres along it to where another track enters on the right 12. For a German view of the attack on the Mont, look along the track down which you have just walked. You are standing in Elsa Trench, which started on the D1017 behind you and swung leftwards through your location to follow the tree line to the commercial area. Feuillaucourt is in the low ground to your right, with Bouchavesnes Ridge, up which

the D1017 runs, to its right and 1916 Spur to its left. Follow the spur leftwards to see the occasional roof and spire of Cléry. The sub-station, where you stopped earlier, is on the left side of the far end of the track. Starting from Elsa Trench 100 metres to your left, Galatz Alley tracked along the slope and ended up near the D938 to the left of the sub-station. Meeting Galatz there, Gottlieb ran back across your front to Feuillaucourt. Agram Alley paralleled Galatz 200 metres in rear.

Advancing towards you from the direction of Cléry early on 31 August, the 17th, 19th and 20th Battalions all crossed Gottlieb. The 17th swept through your location and over the summit of the Mont to your left rear, the 19th to its right took the nearer halves of Galatz and Agram, and the 20th passed to your right to establish a line along the D1017 down to Feuillaucourt. Now turn about. As the facing slope of Bouchavesnes Ridge was still uncaptured, the Germans were able to counterattack towards the D1017 without the risk of being enfiladed. Shrapnel burst three metres above Lieutenant Guard's platoon in the 20th Battalion. Guard's undated account reads: 'A man on my right, firing from a kneeling position, fell forward with a shell splinter piercing his steel helmet. Enfilading and rear fire from our left were playing havoc

A company from the 21st Battalion leaves Elsa Trench as the 6th Brigade renews its attack on the Mont.

Captain James Sullivan MC and Bar, MM of the 21st Battalion leads his company up the D1017 towards the crest of the Mont on 1 September. Sullivan would be killed at Montbrehain on 5 October in the very last Australian attack of the war.

and I ordered the men about me to retire to a line of trenches some 200 yards [180 metres] to the rear.'

Guard was presumably in that part of the 20th that gave up the D1017

between the bend in the road and Feuillaucourt and withdrew to Gottlieb. But the rest of the 20th still held the D1017 down to the bend, while the 18th Battalion occupied Moineville Alley between the bend and Gottlieb. An attack across the summit to your right front drove the 17th Battalion back to Elsa Trench. More counterattacks and heavy shelling were withstood from these locations. You should now be able to understand Monash's insistence on taking Bouchavesnes Ridge. As long as the Germans held it, they could strike his left flank on the Mont with near impunity. The 14th Brigade's advance in Péronne was looking after the right flank.

The 6th Brigade's morning attack on 1 September started behind you from the 5th Brigade's line. Passing to your left, the 24th Battalion crossed the D1017 and recaptured Feuillaucourt. Advancing astride Agram and Galatz Alleys, the 23rd was stopped between Elsa Trench and the D1017 on your right. Now down to 120 men, it sideslipped to the far end of Elsa to give the 21st Battalion the central

The crater charged by Sergeant Lowerson. The author is facing the wood from which the charge came.

position between the track on which you are standing and Agram Alley for the next attempt on the summit at 1.30 pm. As the Germans had begun withdrawing in the meantime, the 21st's advance over the summit to your right front and the 23rd's around the far side of the Mont met only light opposition.

Now cross the D1017 and walk along Rue d'Allaines to the **crucifix** ⓭ by a sunken track on the left. Look down the track. During the morning assault, the Germans stood on the embankment to blaze away at the 24th Battalion, which had crossed the D1017 and was starting its advance across the slope to your front. Lance-Corporal David Wilson, a Lewis-gunner, aimed at 'one whom I thought was an officer and gave him a burst and he burst into flames and fell back. I must have hit bombs he was carrying or his ammunition.' Wilson next fired on what he thought were the German machine-gun positions. 'The fire ceases and we rush on,' he wrote. Then he was hit and went down as if he had been 'kicked by a horse'. But heavy fire from **Plevna Trench**, beyond the

cemetery on your right, halted the assault. The 24th pulled back to this track. Lieutenant Towner, who had been wounded in the head, sited his machine-guns, and a German one he captured near your location, on the right of the embankment 220 metres to your front. They were instrumental in holding this line. The 24th attacked from it during the afternoon.

Continue along Rue d'Allaines. Several machine-guns were captured in the area between the cemetery and Plevna Trench, which crossed the road 250 metres past the cemetery, during the bitterly contested afternoon assault. Pause at Plevna and stand with the cemetery on your left. Parties from the 21st and 24th Battalions fought their way down the trench to the **Tortille** and the trench along it in the low ground to your front. By this stage the 3rd Division had reached a line that began midway between the D1017 and **Allaines**, 1.4 kilometres to your right front, and ran to the crest of Bouchavesnes Ridge above the village. Starting on 2 September from Plevna Trench and the line that ran from it towards the summit of the Mont to your right rear, the 7th Brigade took Allaines and continued 1.5 kilometres over the ground to your right.

Head right on the track 70 metres past Plevna Trench that leads to **Mont St Quentin Wood**. Do not enter the wood but walk 25 metres along the left edge ⑭. Look along the track. After crossing the D1017 in the afternoon attack on 1 September, the 21st Battalion burst from the wood behind you and was hit by a wall of fire and bombs from a strongly manned trench system centred on a large crater 100 metres to your front. If the field is fallow, you can walk to the depression that is the remains of the position. The assault stalled just as Sergeant Lowerson exited the wood to your right. Ordering seven men to attack the flanks, he rushed the crater and bombed the Germans into surrender. Lowerson was hit in the leg and three of his men were killed but they captured 30 Germans and 12 machine-guns.

Return to the track and head though the wood. It is pockmarked by shell holes and riddled by trench remains, the most prominent of which is **Radomir Alley**,

one of the communication trenches along which the Germans counterattacked on 31 August to regain the summit. On reaching Rue du Bois, which crosses the track, head right to the church and your car. Continue along Rue l'Abbaye, turn right at the T-junction onto Rue d'Allaines, along which you have just walked, and head towards Allaines over the ground across which the 27th and 28th Battalions from the 7th Brigade advanced from your left to your right on 2 September. After the road bends sharply right, turn left onto Rue du Pont and then, after crossing the Tortille, right at the T-junction onto Grand Rue. Pass through Allaines and stop at the Y-junction 200 metres after crossing the Canal du Nord ⑮. You are now on the lower slopes of Bouchavesnes Ridge.

Look along the re-entrant to your left, where 150 Germans holed up at the junction of **Scutari**, **Fiume** and **Uslar Trenches** 250 metres away blocked the 43rd Battalion's advance towards you on 2 September. Ignoring heavy fire, Lance-Corporal Weathers bombed the Germans, killing their leader. Going back for more bombs, he returned with three

The area where the 33rd Battalion captured the German field battery on the crest of Bouchavesnes Ridge.

mates who covered him while he stood on the parapet hurling the bombs into the trenches below. The Germans surrendered. Take the left fork. As you head up the slope, you are crossing the ground over which the 41st and 42nd Battalions advanced on 1 September. At the T-junction in **Bouchavesnes-Bergen**, turn left onto the D149. You are now in the British III Corps sector, where the 74th Division was advancing on the left of the 3rd Australian. On reaching the D1017, you should head right to see the memorial to Marshal Foch 350 metres down the hill. Foch considered Bouchavesnes the most significant battle for the French in the 1916 Somme offensive. It marked the limit of their advance. The memorial also commemorates the capture of the village by the French on 12 September 1916 and by the 58th Division on 2 September 1918. Head back along the D1017 after viewing it.

If you do not go to the memorial, turn left onto the D1017 and head uphill. After passing the copse on the left, which hides an old **quarry**, turn right onto the D149 and park 16. You are now on the crest of Bouchavesnes Ridge. Look along the D1017. Péronne is to your front, overlooked by Mont St Quentin to its left. In the 3rd Division's attack on 31 August, the 9th Brigade attacked along the crest from your right. The 33rd Battalion passed through your location, its left reaching the quarry. A battery of six German field-guns to the right of the D1017 in front of you fired over open sights at the right of the 33rd. They were successfully rushed, the battery commander fighting to the end with his revolver. Now only 140 strong, the 33rd lined the D1017 for 500 metres to your front, from where the 10th Brigade extended down 1916 Spur, which joins the ridge 600 metres to your right front.

This advance helped the 5th Brigade's concurrent assault on Mont St Quentin. Had the battery not been taken, it would have turned the slopes of the Mont

facing you into an Australian mass grave. But the steepness of the ridge meant that Feuillaucourt and the Canal du Nord below you were in dead ground, giving the Germans a sheltered counterattack route from your left front. They drove the 20th Battalion off the D1017 there. Resuming the 10th Brigade's attack during the afternoon, the 39th and 40th Battalions advanced from 1916 Spur and reached the D1017 above Feuillaucourt, securing the 24th Battalion's left flank when the 6th Brigade attacked the Mont next day. The 11th Brigade then carried the 3rd Division's advance beyond the D1017.

Continue on the D149 to the far end of **Road Wood**, now Bois Madame, on the right and park by the **memorial** 17 to Gustave Fumery and his 150 comrades in the French 132nd Infantry Regiment, who fell here on 4 October 1916. With your back to the road, look along the edge of the wood. Advancing from your left behind a weak barrage, the 33rd Battalion was halted by a machine-gun firing from the corner of the wood to your front. Standing up, Private Cartwright fired at the post with his rifle and then started walking towards it. Still firing, he killed the gunner and two more Germans who took his place. With the 33rd cheering him on, Cartwright threw a bomb to cover his rush over the last few metres and jumped into the post, capturing the gun and nine prisoners. Clearing the rest of the wood, the 33rd carried on to your previous location. Walk 220 metres to the corner of the wood to see among the trees the remains of the post that was the scene of Cartwright's VC action. Now proceed along the D149, which the 3rd Division's start line for the attack on 31 August crossed 450 metres past the wood.

To return to Villers-Bretonneux, Amiens or Albert, turn right onto the D938 on reaching Cléry and follow the same route, but in reverse, that you took to get here.

LOCAL INFORMATION

Hem Farm Military Cemetery

After taking the D938 from Cléry, turn left onto the D146 once past the A1, then right just before the Somme onto Rue de Monacu. Follow it through Hem-Monacu, turn left at the far end of the village onto Rue de la Ferme and the cemetery is 300 metres along, beside Hem Farm. It was begun in January 1917 by the British, who used it until the Germans overran the area in March 1918 and again after its recapture in September. Many of Hem Farm's 598 burials, 394 of them known, resulted from the postwar relocation of graves from small cemeteries nearby. Most of the 138 Australians fell at Mont St Quentin/Péronne, including Private Mactier at II.J.3 and 18 of his comrades from the 23rd Battalion.

Herbécourt British Cemetery

To reach this cemetery, continue over the Somme on the D146 instead of turning right to Hem-Monacu, pass through Feuillères and head right on the D1 in Herbécourt to the end of the village. Alternatively, just take the D1 from Péronne. Building onto an extension of the communal cemetery previously used by the French and Germans, the British started the cemetery early in 1917. The French and German graves were removed postwar, leaving only the British plot, which the Australians used in 1918.

Of the 59 burials, 51 are Australian. As with Hem Farm, most were killed at Mont St Quentin/Péronne. Resting at C.1, Fromelles survivor Lieutenant Stan Colless MC, DCM of the 55th Battalion fell in the attack on Péronne on 1 September. Captain Fred Cotterell MC of the 55th at D.2 died next day while reconnoitring in Saint Denis. Lieutenant Macarthur rests at C.16. It is a pity that he was not laid to rest alongside Corporal Buckley, as both were killed together. As the cemetery is tiny and out of the way, it is rarely visited. That is an even greater pity.

Péronne Communal Cemetery Extension

On Rue Jean Mermoz/Rue des Platanes and visited on the drive, this cemetery was begun by the British as an extension to the communal cemetery after the Germans withdrew to the Hindenburg Line in 1917. It was used by the Germans after they regained Péronne in 1918 and by the Australians when they wrested the town from the Germans. The postwar concentration of graves from surrounding battlefields and smaller cemeteries expanded it from 177 burials at war's end to 1689, of which 1404 are known. For Australians, the cemetery is very much a testament to the battle. Corporal Buckley lies at II.C.32. Resting at V.P.1, Gallipoli veteran Major Cedric Brodziak DSO fell at Road Wood with the 33rd Battalion while consulting his map. Three-time MM winner Corporal Frederick Thurston, also of the 33rd, was killed on 30 August. He

The Historial de la Grande Guerre.

lies at IV.P.6. Killed on the Péronne side of the Mont on 2 September, Major Augustus Woods DSO of the 26th Battalion is at III.E.2. In all, 517 Australians rest here.

MUSEUMS

Historial de la Grande Guerre

Visited on the drive, this museum is housed in a contemporary building behind Péronne castle, which forms the facade through which it is entered. A Bastiaan plaque is located near the entrance. As its name implies, the museum covers the First World War. Successive halls chart the prewar period, the war years and the war's aftermath. Eye-catching displays of the weapons and equipment used by the combatants are set in the floor rather than behind glass in showcases. The industrial and social impacts of the war are also explained. There is no reluctance to convey the war's horrors — just watch the footage of badly shell-shocked soldiers, one of the 56 films shown as part of the museum's audiovisual and interactive exhibits.

The museum is open 10 am to 6 pm daily but closes from mid-December to mid-January. Admission is €7.50. Contact details are: telephone +33 3 22 83 14 18; www.historial.inovawork.net.

CHAPTER 23

1918

HINDENBURG OUTPOST LINE

'The whole sky was black with the smoke of burning dumps and villages.' This was the scene beheld by Private Harold Shapcott of the 42nd Battalion as the Germans withdrew towards the Hindenburg Line after losing Mont St Quentin and Péronne. When they had retired in 1917 they cratered roads and ripped up railways as part of a systematic scorched-earth policy. Needing roads and railways for his own advance, General Rawlinson, the commander of the Fourth Army, was anxious to prevent a repetition. He ordered a vigorous pursuit. Anxious to keep the Germans on the back foot himself, General Monash needed no telling.

The 3rd and 5th Australian Divisions and the British 32nd Division began the pursuit on 5 September 1918. Each was led by an advance guard that comprised an infantry brigade with its own artillery and a squadron of light horse to scout ahead. But the German rearguards fought in masterful fashion and had to be outflanked one after another. At Field Marshal Haig's insistence, Rawlinson called a halt on 7 September. Haig wanted the divisions rested and communications improved prior to a major offensive with the French and Americans. The halt allowed the 1st and 4th Divisions to relieve the 3rd and 5th Divisions. As the 32nd Division left at this stage, the Australian corps now comprised only the five Australian divisions. The fresh IX Corps moved onto the Australian right flank.

Afternoon tea

The pause did not preclude peaceful penetration, which took the old British reserve line, overrun by the Germans during the March offensive, on 11 September. It cut through Jeancourt and Hésbecourt, 13 kilometres east of Péronne. But Monash foreshadowed that the British front and outpost lines would have to be taken by a set-piece attack as they were more strongly held. Rawlinson concurred. He wanted to strike the Hindenburg Line beyond them before German morale recovered sufficiently to make the cost prohibitive. The British War Cabinet was already worried about the cost, so carrying out the attack would also test the feasibility of assaulting the Hindenburg Line. Haig told Rawlinson to launch it as soon as possible. It was fixed for 18 September. The Third Army would assault on the left of the Fourth. Monash, Rawlinson and the commander of IX Corps, Lieutenant-General Sir William Braithwaite, planned the Fourth Army's attack over a cup of afternoon tea on 13 September.

After the manoeuvre battle at Mont St Quentin, the Australian Corps would now revert to the sort of operation it had carried out on 8 August. The 1st Division, with III Corps on its left, and the 4th Division, with IX Corps on its right, would first advance to the Green Line between Hargicourt and Le Verguier. It corresponded with the old British front line. After another one to 1.5 kilometres, the Red Line, which followed the old British Outpost Line, would be reached. The British wire was on the wrong side of the trenches for the Germans, which would help the attack on both positions. But Monash was hesitant about exploiting to the Hindenburg Outpost Line 1.5 kilometres further on. Designated the Blue Line, it screened the main Hindenburg Line, which stretched over lower ground between Bellenglise and Bellicourt another 1.5 kilometres ahead. Taking the Outpost Line would give excellent observation over the main line but also entailed crossing Ascension Valley, devoid of cover, at the end of an already deep penetration. This part of the attack was not to be pressed if it met strong resistance.

Two of the 10 dummy tanks, made from wood and canvas, used in the attack. Six-man crews inside pushed them along.

By this time, said Monash, 'the methods of the Corps were becoming stereotyped ... we all began to understand each other so well that what I had to say could be taken for granted'. The conference at which he explained the attack to Generals Glasgow and Sinclair-MacLagan lasted only 75 minutes. Each division would assault on a 3.1-kilometre frontage using two brigades, with the battalions leapfrogging at the successive lines. But there were some novel features, chief among them Monash's setting of the start line on a position that he thought could be gained by 18 September using peaceful penetration. It was, on average, 1.5 kilometres from the Green Line. Only eight tanks were available, so dummy tanks were built and placed where the Germans could see them. Also compensating for the tank shortage was the doubling of the machine-gun barrage by adding the guns of the 3rd and 5th Divisions to those of the 1st and 4th, making 200 guns in all.

'Too terrible for words'

Launched from the line Monash predicted would be reached, the attack began at 5.20 am in rainy fog but the Australians were well used to keeping direction in such conditions and the murk hid them from the Germans. The creeping barrage was the heaviest that many Australians had known, while a German officer labelled the machine-gun barrage 'absolutely too terrible for words'. Though the Germans put up a fight for Grand Priel Woods on the left before the 3rd Brigade cleared it, the resistance was generally feeble. The 4th Brigade easily took Le Verguier on the right, which the Germans were expected to defend strongly. Sergeant Gerald Sexton of the 13th Battalion knocked out a field-gun and several machine-guns there, winning the VC. Captain Bill Lynas DSO, MC, the original ANZAC who led the 16th's assault on the village, remarked that 'if the

Germans had had the fighting spirit of a louse', a single battalion of them could have smashed the 4th Brigade.

By 6 am the Green Line, which was defended by more Germans than the Australians who attacked them, had been reached. The advance to the Red Line went just as smoothly, even though the mist had lifted and the Germans could see their targets. While the 11th Battalion took Villeret, the 45th Battalion overran the Tumulus de Vermand, an ancient burial mound, and part of nearby Ascension Spur. Stiff resistance had been anticipated from both. Mass surrenders were the rule instead, ensuring that the exploitation to the Hindenburg Outpost Line would proceed. In parts of the 1st Division's sector, it was very close to the old British Outpost Line and in places the two lines even met. By 10.30 am the 1st had reached it everywhere but on the extreme left next to the British 74th Division.

The 4th Division had to advance over two kilometres across Ascension Valley to get to the Hindenburg Outpost Line. This time the Germans fought. Heavily engaged from the start, the 14th and 46th Battalions leapt between shell holes but were stopped 500 metres from the Outpost Line. Part of the 14th circled back and tried to bomb southwards from the trenches that the 1st Division had captured but was blocked by the Germans in them further along. General Sinclair-MacLagan ordered artillery brought up to lay down a creeping barrage for another attempt at 11 pm. With rain pelting down, the 14th resumed the bombing attack while the 46th assaulted frontally. The Germans eventually bolted and the two battalions met. The 46th's two assault companies, 160 strong, took 550 prisoners. Neither III nor IX Corps was able to reach the Outpost Line, though the 1st Division in IX Corps maintained that it had. Part of a small patrol that proved otherwise, Private James Woods rushed a post and

Private James O'Hehir and other troops from the 45th Battalion snipe at Germans racing back from the old British front line towards the Hindenburg Outpost Line, which runs across the far slope.

held off a counterattack. 'You will I suppose be pleased to hear that I might get some decoration out of it', Woods wrote to his sister. He got the VC.

As they looked down on the Hindenburg Line ahead, the 1st and 4th Divisions did not know that they had fought their last battle. For the loss of 1360 men, they had taken 4300 prisoners and 76 guns, well over a third of all the captures by the Third and Fourth Armies that day. 'All I can say is that you are some bloody soldiers', remarked a German officer to the Australian who had captured him. Other Germans said their men would not now face the Australians. But there was an unpleasant postscript. After III Corps had spent two days trying to close up on the Outpost Line, its commander, General Butler, planned another attack for 21 September and asked Monash to assist by taking over the southern 450 metres of the attack frontage. Monash agreed and the 1st Brigade got the job. When the 1st Battalion received the order just as it was being relieved late on the 20th, 119 men went rearwards in protest at having to make good British failures as well as having to fight themselves. All but one were convicted of desertion, given up to 10 years' imprisonment and pardoned after the Armistice.

DRIVING THE BATTLEFIELD

This battlefield covers a large area that is devoid of reference points, which makes the battle difficult to follow on the ground. A couple of tips may prove useful. The Green, Red and Blue Lines all followed ridges that run north–south. Stand on one of these ridges, therefore, and you will know that one or other of the lines tracked along the ridge to your front or rear. The Hindenburg Outpost or Blue Line for the most part coincided with the modern A26 autoroute, on which you can always see traffic. It will tell you where the attack finished up.

MAPS IGN Blue Series, 1:25 000, 2508E Roisel; 26080 Villers-Outréaux

From the Historial in Péronne head left through the town square on the D1017 and left again after one kilometre at the Y-junction. At the major intersection just beyond the bridge, turn right onto the D6 (Rue de Roisel).

The D6 was the axis of the Australian advance from Péronne and the two brigade groups that comprised the divisional advance guards moved either side of it. Wide intervals separated the trenches they encountered; there was nothing like the lattice-work of trenches that criss-crossed the Mont St Quentin battlefield. Tall grass or self-sown crops

Looking from Hill 140 at the area over which the 1st Division advanced then ...

covered the fields, and the woods, copses and hedges were untouched. Though the villages had been shelled and burned, the landscape overall was pretty much as it is today.

Struck by point-blank field-gun and machine-gun fire from **Roisel**, the 41st Battalion went around the town while the supporting artillery shelled it. The Germans fled, leaving their machine-guns, field-guns and 60 wagons. Continue along the **Cologne River** valley to **Templeux-le-Guérard** and turn right just past the village sign. Head up the spur and park outside **Cayenne Farm,** where the road becomes a track. Now walk 500 metres to the **crest** ❶ and stand with the farm on your left.

You are atop **Hill 140**, which the 4th Battalion attacked at 5.30 am on 11 September, during the peaceful penetration phase. German guns in **Hargicourt**, two kilometres to your left front, plastered the hill after the 4th had taken it and was digging in on the slope to your front. Most of the survivors withdrew but 10 were captured on the road to your left when the Germans successfully counterattacked at 11 am. All told the 4th lost over 100 men. The **Green Line** for the attack a week later ran along the far side of Hargicourt and

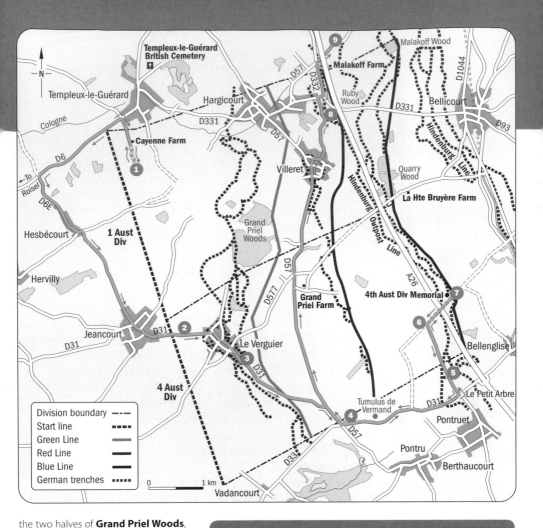

the two halves of **Grand Priel Woods**, 2.2 kilometres to your right front, which had been felled and was just an expanse of stumps and dense undergrowth in 1918. The **Red Line** cut behind **Villeret**, three kilometres to your front. Villeret, Hargicourt and the woods had all been fortified. Tracking across the horizon behind Villeret is the A26, which the **Hindenburg Outpost Line**, and hence the **Blue Line**, generally followed.

On 18 September the 1st Division attacked from a start line that followed the old British reserve line. Paralleling the track on which you are standing, it ran from the D6 to your left rear and passed 300 metres behind you. Advancing through your location, the 1st Brigade, with the 2nd Battalion on the right and the 4th on the left, easily took Hargicourt.

After covering some of the preliminaries to the attack, the drive continues to the vicinity of the start line for the 1st Division's assault. It then follows the 4th Division's advance to each of the objective lines before heading back between the Red and Green Lines to retrace the 1st Division's advance. The site of Sergeant Sexton's VC action is also included.
DISTANCE COVERED: 28 km
DURATION: 3.5 hours

Led by the 11th and 12th Battalions, the 3rd Brigade on your right had a tough fight to capture Grand Priel Woods. With the Green Line now taken the advance pushed on to the Red, where the 9th Battalion was held up at Villeret before the 11th Battalion and a tank cleared it. From there, the 9th's patrols effortlessly reached the Blue Line beyond the A26.

Return to the D6, head left and then left again after 1.8 kilometres onto the

D6E for **Hesbécourt**. Turn left at the T-junction at the far end of the village and then immediately right for **Jeancourt**, where the 10th Battalion rested before the attack on 18 September. Once through the village, where the road becomes the D31, turn left and park at the dumping area on the right 500 metres along ❷. After peacefully penetrating Jeancourt on 10 September and finding it deserted, the 2nd Battalion ambushed a German column marching towards the village on this road later that night.

You are now in the 4th Division's area. Its boundary with the 1st Division was 450 metres to your left. The Green Line ran behind both Grand Preil Woods, on the crest 1.5 kilometres to your left front and in the 1st Division's area, and **Le Verguier**, on the ridge in front of you. The trenches of the old British front line running along the ridge enclosed the village, in which the Germans had set up five strong points, or 'forts'. While the 12th Battalion advanced towards Grand Priel Woods, the 4th Brigade attacked Le Verguier from a start line that crossed the road 250 metres behind you. The 13th and 15th Battalions passed to the right and left of the village respectively, and the 16th, advancing to your right, attacked it. The 16th broke into small groups when fired upon but the Germans mostly took to their dugouts as

it approached, leaving the defences unmanned. At Fort Bell, on the left corner of the village, 70, including a regimental commander, were nabbed. Another 28 and six machine-guns were captured at Fort Lees, which stood among houses at the far end of the tree line to your right front. For the loss of 20 men, the 16th ended up taking 450 prisoners, 60 machine-guns and several field-guns.

Continue on the D31 through Le Verguier and stop at the **crucifix** ❸ on the left at the far end of the village. Look along the D31. Having come around the village to your right rear, the 13th Battalion started to pass across your front when it was held up by two posts in **Hun Trench**, part of the old British front line, which ran to the right of the road. Sergeant Sexton rushed them, firing his Lewis-gun from the hip, and wiped both out. When the advance crossed the D31, it was stopped by fire from a field-gun emplaced on the slope to your left front and from Germans in the copse in the low ground beyond. Charging once more, Sexton killed the gun crew, continued on under heavy fire to clean up the Germans in the copse and then returned to deal with those in the dugouts by the field-gun. Thirty Germans, including a battalion headquarters, surrendered. Sexton, who had won the DCM on 8 August, had originally enlisted under

...and now. The same area today. Hargicourt is out of picture behind the woods on the left skyline.

VILLERET

1ST BRIGADE

his real name, Maurice Buckley, but adopted his mother's maiden name on re-enlisting after returning to Australia for undisclosed reasons in September 1915. He reverted to Buckley after being awarded the VC for his action at Le Verguier.

Proceed on the D31, which the 4th Brigade's boundary with the 12th Brigade crossed 300 metres along. The 48th Battalion advanced on the right of the 13th Battalion here. Crossing the D31 500 metres further on, the Green Line ran to your left along the slope of the valley. Turn right on the valley floor onto the D57 and then left at the crossroads onto, believe it or not, the D31 again. Park after 100 metres in the **layover** 4 on the left and look along the D31. **Ascension Spur**, along which the Red Line stretched, runs away to your left front, with the copse denoting the **Tumulus de Vermand** at its tip on the left of the road. Advancing on your left, parallel to the road and next

to the British 1st Division, the 45th Battalion easily took the Tumulus and captured over 300 Germans, together with a howitzer battery trying to withdraw from the crest of the spur. A second battery further along the spur had already been abandoned.

Carry on over Ascension Spur and **Ascension Valley** and turn left at the crossroads in **Le Petit Arbre** hamlet, 500 metres short of the A26. The road soon becomes badly rutted. Look along it after stopping 600 metres along on the crest of a **spur** 5. You are now on the Hindenburg Outpost Line in the British 1st Division's sector. Attacking from your left over Ascension Spur, at the end of which you can see the Tumulus, and Ascension Valley, the 46th Battalion met intense fire from the Outpost Line, which, in its sector, ran along the crest of the ridge 500 metres to your right front. It made the road embankment to your

front but was pinned down there for the rest of the day. Now turn about. As the British 1st Division was stuck on the Red Line 900 metres to your right front, the 48th Battalion came up to secure the 46th's exposed right flank back towards the Tumulus.

The British 1st Division almost reached the road to your front that night but was forced back into Ascension Valley. Its commander insisted that it was on the road. Private Woods belonged to a three-man patrol sent by the 48th Battalion to check. Creeping from your left rear through your location and then along a tangle of trenches either side of the road it found a German post at the junction of two of the trenches 200 metres to your left front. Rushing the post, Woods captured two Germans. The rest fled, leaving six machine-guns. When the Germans, at least 30 strong, counterattacked along the trenches and over the open soon after, Woods lay on the parapet and bombed them back until the 48th Battalion properly secured the post.

Continue along the road to the T-junction at **Victoria Crossroads** 6 and face the A26. In 1918 the road continued straight on and the 46th Battalion was strung out another 450 metres to your left along it, which puts you roughly at the centre of its line. The front trench of the Hindenburg Outpost Line ran from your left front on the other side of the A26, which, don't forget, didn't exist in 1918, cut through the **bridge** site in front of you and then continued to your right to your previous

location. The 46th's 11 pm attack surprised the Germans who expected a dawn assault next morning. Most of them were sheltering in their dugouts from the rain, leaving their machine-guns unmanned. This was fortuitous because it enabled the 46th to get though the exceedingly dense wire, which the supporting barrage had hardly damaged. Though they were in far greater numbers than their attackers, the Germans, both in this trench and the support trench beyond the A26, surrendered or fled.

The 14th Battalion had been pinned down further along the road. Its left flank was two kilometres from your location. Around midday part of the 14th had looped back into Ascension Valley to your left rear and around into the stretch of the Outpost Line already held by the 10th Battalion. From there it bombed down both trenches towards you until stopped by a post at the elongated copse on the far side of the A26 to your far left. Assaulting again at the same time as the 46th that night, it overcame the post and the two battalions linked. Before leaving, turn about to see the extent of the attack on 18 September. Le Verguier is on the skyline to your right front. The 4th and 12th Brigades advanced either side of it to the Red Line on Ascension Spur and then to the Blue Line beyond the A26 to your rear. To the right of Le Verguier is Grand Preil Woods, on the Green Line for the 3rd Brigade, which then advanced to the Red Line between the water tower in Villeret, on the skyline to your right, and the A26. The 3rd continued over the A26,

TUMULUS

ASCENSION VALLEY

ASCENSION SPUR

12TH BRIGADE

On account of the lead that was flying we all got down flat on the ground. Bullets were kicking up the dirt all around us. I heard a man yell just beside me, and then he lay quiet. What to do was past me; I was just on the point of ordering a bolt, when one of the boys with a Lewis gun crawled up alongside me, and in a second had opened fire along their trench, and to our surprise he silenced the Huns. A little further along another of the lads took his cue from the first one and opened fire, and after each burst these gunners would yell: 'Now's your time to rush them'. They did this several times before anyone moved but at last it sank in and several of the NCO's started to go forward... we all up and ran for dear life towards those Huns, yelling like lunatics... When we were within thirty yards, some of the Huns heaved some bombs, and then they bolted for their lives.

Lieutenant Rule on getting his company from the front trench of the Hindenburg Outpost Line
to the support trench at the start of the 14th Battalion's night time assault
(Rule, E, *Jacka's Mob*, Sydney, 1933, pp. 326–7)

as did the 1st Brigade on its left. Driving the Germans from all this ground was a magnificent achievement for four brigades, each just 1700 strong.

Cross over the A26 to the **4th Australian Division Memorial** 7 on the Blue Line. Walk to the back of the memorial and stand with the A26 on your left. Its front and support trenches generally 100 to 150 metres apart, the Hindenburg Outpost Line ran along the crest towards you, the front trench swinging to your left front over the A26 and the support trench continuing through your location before arcing away to your left rear. Attacking from your left, the 46th Battalion met the 14th Battalion, which assaulted along the trenches towards you, 500 metres to your front after a barrage that Lieutenant Rule thought 'very tame'.

Charles Bean commented that the achievement of the two battalions against five times their own number had 'few parallels on the Western Front'. The 4th Division put their obelisk memorial in this lonely, windswept and rarely visited

location because their war ended here. But the achievement that Bean rightly praised also made the location a fitting one. Now walk to the front of the memorial and look down at **Bellenglise**, 2.3 kilometres ahead of you on the far side of the **St Quentin Canal**. The village was incorporated into the Hindenburg Line. It ran behind the canal here, thereby using the canal as an obstacle. The extensive views from the Outpost Line over the Hindenburg Line explain why Rawlinson and Monash wanted to take the Outpost Line.

Return to Le Petit Arbre, head right on the D31 and right again at the crossroads onto the D57, which runs along the reverse slope of Ascension Spur. The Red Line behind **Grand Priel Farm**, on the right 2.5 kilometres along, was taken by the 13th and 15th Battalions. Grand Priel Woods, along which ran the Green Line, is on the high ground across the valley to your left front and the D57 climbs as you pass by the end of it. Attacking from your left here, the 10th Battalion had to fight through machine-guns on your right to

The 4th Division's advance across Ascension Valley as seen from the bridge over the A26.

LE VERGUIER

GRAND PRIEL WOODS

RED LINE

4TH BRIGADE

The memorial to the 4th Australian Division.

You are now in the centre of the 1st Brigade's area. The 2nd and 4th Battalions took Hargicourt, beyond the small wood on your right, to reach the Green Line, which ran along the far side of the wood. The 1st Battalion, with the 3rd on its left, passed through your location to the Red Line, which paralleled the A26 on your left and ran to the left of Villeret. Patrols from both battalions then took the Blue Line, which stretched on the other side of the A26 through **Quarry Wood**, 1200 metres to your left front. Here the two lines were relatively close. Quarry Wood fell to the 9th Battalion. According to the 1st Battalion's war diary, the mutiny by 119 men on 20 September occurred in the cutting to your front.

get to the Red Line. More guns along the road and in Villeret ahead of you troubled the 9th Battalion alongside the 10th. The 9th cleared the guns on the road while the 11th, which had moved through Grand Priel Woods, carried on with a tank to deal with Villeret. Turn right at the T-junction at the far end of the village, then left after 150 metres at the Y-junction. Park on the track on the right where the road bends sharply left after a cutting **8**, and look back towards Villeret.

Continue to the T-junction, turn right onto Rue de Cologne, then left at the next T-junction onto the D332, across which the 3rd Battalion advanced from left to right to the Blue Line. On reaching the T-junction at the bottom of the re-entrant, head right onto the D57 (Rue de Bony) and park at the layover and dumping area 250 metres past the A26 off-ramp **9**.

A German machine-gunner who fought to the last. The massive pile of spent cartridges in the foreground bears grim testimony to the fire he poured into the Australian advance.

Stand with the A26 on your right. This was the British 74th Division's sector. Its boundary with the 1st Australian Division ran along the slope 400 metres to your front from **Malakoff Farm**, which stood on the left of the A26, to **Malakoff Wood** on the high ground to your left front. The Blue Line ran from **Quennet Copse** to your left rear, to **Quennemont Farm**, near the communication tower on your left, and on through the wood. Attacking via Malakoff Farm, the 3rd Battalion was to take it.

Heavy fire from Quennet Copse and Quennemont Farm doomed the attempt. The 3rd could only capture **Minnow Trench**, which ran from Malakoff Farm and to the right of **Ruby Wood**, the copse on the crest ahead of you, and **Triangle Trench**, which ran from Minnow and crossed the D57 at the bend to your left. Assisting the 74th Division on 21 September, the 1st Battalion reached Ruby Wood, while the 3rd advanced into the re-entrant to your left front before returning to Minnow Trench following another failure by the British formation.

Continue on the D57 for 900 metres to start the Hindenburg Line battlefield drive. Otherwise, head back along the D57 to Hargicourt, pick up the D331 and then turn left at the T-junction in Templeux-le-Guérard onto the D6, which will take you back to Péronne.

Fatigue

The 1st Battalion mutiny reflected the fatigue of the AIF divisions, which had been fighting continuously since March. It had been evident before the Hindenburg Outpost Line attack. 'We were thoroughly worn out and discontented all round', wrote Lance-Corporal Eric Russell of the 58th Battalion, then down to 170 men. Private John Nixon-Smith in the 31st thought it was 'time they gave us a *rest*'.

Monash himself was tired. His chief of staff, Brigadier-General Blamey, observed that he had become very thin and the skin hung loosely on his face. He rode in his car for long periods in silence and his diary suggests that he had nervous tremors. But Monash's attitude was moulded by the decline of the British Army, which, he pointed out to brigade after brigade, was no less overworked than the Australians, and by the obvious demoralisation of the Germans, whom he wanted to hit as hard and as often as he could. But only the ANZACs and Canadians were consistently successful. It was therefore inevitable, said Monash, that the Australians 'should be called upon to yield up the last particle of effort of which they were capable'. Notwithstanding the longing for a rest, many agreed with him. As Corporal Robert Campbell of the 55th Battalion maintained:

All this hard fighting is necessary. There is only one way of finishing this war and that is by force of arms. If they make peace by negotiations … the Hun will make war again in a few years' time … To prevent anything like that ever happening, we must win this war … and the only way to win is on the battlefield.

Charles Bean agreed. Writing in the *Official History*, Bean had no doubt that Monash 'was right to work his troops to the limit of their endurance' in this decisive fighting. 'At such times', he continued, 'victory often goes out to the troops that hold out longest, withstanding strain, toil or exhaustion in perhaps unbelievable degree and for an unbelievable time'.

The scene of the 1st Battalion mutiny viewed through the rain and mist that so often made conditions miserable on the Western Front.

LOCAL INFORMATION

CEMETERIES

Most of the cemeteries in this area were started up by the British after the Germans withdrew from it to the Hindenburg Line in March 1917. They were used to varying degrees until the Germans recaptured the area in March 1918 and then again when the Germans pulled out in September. After the war, they were greatly enlarged by the transfer to them of graves from the surrounding battlefields and from smaller cemeteries nearby.

Jeancourt Communal Cemetery Extension

The Germans built the extension to the communal cemetery to serve the hospitals they set up in Jeancourt and the British took it over. The cemetery now consists of 660 burials, 452 of them identified. Its 114 Australians, 98 of them known, fell in the September advance. There are 168 German burials. Jeancourt is on the drive route. To visit the cemetery, turn left off the D31 just before leaving the village.

Templeaux-le-Guérard British Cemetery.

Templeaux-le-Guérard British Cemetery

Started in April 1917, the cemetery consists of 773 burials, 585 of which are known. The 45 Australians include Captain Francis Fairweather, who had an outstanding career with the 38th Battalion, at II.F.41, and the commanding officer of the 39th Battalion, Lieutenant-Colonel Robert Henderson, at II.F.44. Both were killed in the attack on the Hindenburg Line on 29 September. Follow the D6 through Templeaux-le-Guérard and head right on leaving the village to reach the cemetery.

Tincourt New British Cemetery

Started by the British casualty clearing stations that occupied Tincourt in March 1917, the cemetery contains 1986 burials, of which 1879 are identified. Of the 228 Australians, twice-wounded Gallipoli MM winner, Captain Walter Hallahan, at V.E.6, and 2nd Lieutenant Dudley Elliott, at V.E.16, were killed near Grand Priel Woods. Both were from the 11th Battalion. The cemetery is on the edge of Tincourt-Boucly, seven kilometres past Péronne on the D6. Take the first right,

Rue de la Flaque, on entering the village from the D6 and then turn right again onto Rue du Bas de Tincourt.

The grave of Captain Francis Fairweather MC and Bar.

CHAPTER 24

1918

HINDENBURG LINE

The relatively easy Australian capture of the Hindenburg Outpost Line on 18 September 1918 removed any anxiety Field Marshal Haig may have had about attacking the Hindenburg Line itself. He gave the job of assaulting the main part of it to the Fourth Army. Planned for 29 September, the operation would be the principal British stroke in the series of blows by which Marshal Foch, the Allied generalissimo, intended to conquer territory held by the Germans since the start of the war, as distinct from ground they had captured in their offensives between March and July. Three offensives were to precede it. Having eliminated the St Mihiel salient, the Americans would advance with the French between Rheims and the Meuse, 150 kilometres south of the Australians, on 26 September. Next day, the British were to attack at Cambrai, and on 28 September the British, French and Belgians in Flanders would strike towards Ghent, 100 kilometres north of the Australians. The salients created would be so acute that the Germans between them would have to pull back, resulting in a German retirement along the Western Front as a whole.

The Hindenburg system

The Australian Corps had the main role in the assault on the Hindenburg Line. It mostly ran along the eastern side of the St Quentin Canal, dug during Napoleon's rule to link the Somme and Scheldt Rivers. But on the Australian front, the canal passed through a tunnel that began at Bellicourt and emerged 5.4 kilometres north near Macquincourt. Above the tunnel, the Hindenburg Line jutted up to one kilometre west of the canal's course. Studded with pillboxes and girded by as many as six belts of barbed wire, its twin trenches enclosed the village of Bony. The tunnel itself offered shell-proof accommodation to the Germans, who could counterattack from it through concealed passages and airshafts. Three spurs rose gently to the Knoll, Gillemont and Quennemont Farms,

strongpoints in the Hindenburg Outpost Line 1.4 kilometres further west, that III Corps should have taken on 18 September. The Hindenburg support, or Le Catelet Line, ran through Nauroy and Le Catelet 1.5 kilometres east of the tunnel. A further three kilometres east was the reserve or Beaurevoir Line.

As the 1st and 4th Australian Divisions were resting, General Monash had only three divisions to tackle these formidable positions. General Rawlinson, the Fourth Army's commander, offered him the 27th and 30th Divisions from the American II Corps, then in reserve. With the weakest Australian battalions being disbanded in order to beef up the others, Monash immediately agreed. Comprising two brigades, each of two regiments, each American division was three times stronger than an Australian one. It was

An aerial view of the Hindenburg Line and the St Quentin Canal at the Bellicourt entrance to the tunnel before the attack.

also fresh and, though inexperienced, dead keen.

Plans made

Called on by Rawlinson to shape the plan on which the Fourth Army fought, Monash faced a dilemma. If he attacked on a broad frontage that included the tunnel and the canal on either side of it, the Germans would have to spread their reserves. But the canal was a daunting obstacle and the casualties from a direct assault across it would likely be prohibitive. If the attack was initially confined to the tunnel, which he thought of as a 'bridge' over the canal, the Germans could concentrate their reserves against a much narrower frontage. In the event, Monash decided on this option as the less-risky one.

Supported by a creeping barrage and 60 tanks, the two American divisions would carry out a set-piece assault of four kilometres to the Green Line, which

included the Hindenburg and Le Catelet Lines. Monash knew he was asking a lot of the raw Americans but reckoned that the Germans opposite, shaken from recent battles, would be further rattled by the four-day bombardment, which incorporated the first British use of mustard gas. A specially formed Australian Mission would advise the Americans down to battalion level. Moreover, their part was simpler than the long open-warfare advance without a creeping barrage and just 30 tanks that inevitably fell to the veteran Australian divisions. They would fan out on their way to the Red Line, which embraced the Beaurevoir Line, uncovering the far bank of the canal so that IX Corps could cross it on their right. Rawlinson adjusted this part of the plan. Preferring to hedge his bets rather than staking everything on getting over the tunnel, he let the 46th (South Midland) Division from IX Corps attack directly across the canal at

Riqueval. After capturing Vendhuille, III Corps would cross on the left of the Australians.

Plans unravel

To attack from a line directly opposite the tunnel, the Australian Corps side-slipped left and began taking over part of the III Corps front on 24 September. Monash had gambled that by then III Corps would finally have reached the Hindenburg Outpost Line, from which the attack on the Hindenburg Line was to start. A similar gamble had paid off in the Australian assault on the Outpost Line, for which Monash set a start line that the advance was yet to reach. This time Monash lost out for III Corps, despite repeated attempts, was still 900 metres short of the Outpost Line on what became the left flank of the Australian Corps. The Germans held the Knoll, Gillemont and Quennemont Farms and III Corps was too exhausted to attack again. Monash wanted to pull the start line back but Rawlinson insisted on the 27th Division taking the Outpost Line on 27 September.

The 106th Regiment advanced at 5.30 am but the assault disintegrated as the Americans' inexperience took hold. Some made the Outpost Line but most were scattered in front of it, ending the option of starting the creeping barrage for the coming attack from the 27th's existing line. It would begin from the Outpost Line, which the Americans would simply have to reach in time to advance with the other divisions. The ineffectiveness of III Corps was also recognised. It was now to advance on the Australian left only as far as the canal, where XIII Corps would take over.

'Why we were not all wiped out, goodness knows'

Thinking an attack was imminent, the Germans moved their artillery late on 28 September. It escaped the British counter-battery fire and thumped the

The disbandment troubles

'I welcome any pretext to take the fewest possible [men] into action', Monash said. 'So long as [battalions] have 30 Lewis-guns it doesn't very much matter what else they have.' But mechanical resources could only go so far towards compensating for the increasing numerical weakness of the Australian battalions. Matters came to a head on the eve of the Hindenburg Line battle in a manner Monash probably never expected.

Before the Outpost Line attack, Prime Minister Hughes had announced that 800 original ANZACs were to be sent to Australia immediately for two months' furlough. As 6000 were eligible, many more would follow. Together with the losses on the Outpost Line, Hughes's action was the final factor necessitating the disbandment of more Australian battalions in order to beef up the rest. The War Office had been concerned about the low numbers in the battalions in June, when only 11 of the 57 were at the establishment strength of 900. As numbers dwindled further, it insisted in late August on the reduction of the Australian brigades from four battalions to three as in the British Army. Three had been reduced in April following the defensive battles. Although the four original brigades were exempted, a battalion in each of the other eight was ordered to disband on 23 September.

The 19th, 21st, 25th, 29th, 37th, 42nd, 54th and 60th Battalions were selected. Brigadier-General Elliott's influence in the 15th Brigade persuaded the 60th Battalion to break up but the other battalions refused, though their officers heeded the decision. Taking their lead from the 37th, they 'went on strike', electing their own leaders and asking to go into the Hindenburg Line battle in their old units. Monash deferred action for another fortnight, when the battle would be over. Starved of reinforcements, they would have to disband voluntarily, and they did.

Americans when they advanced in misty conditions at 5.55 am next morning. Unprotected by a creeping barrage, the 27th Division's assault on the left stalled before the Outpost Line, although the Knoll was taken. The result for the Australians was 'Fritz firing wildly through smoke with ... machine-guns in all directions', said Lieutenant Arthur Fullard of the 5th Machine-Gun Battalion. 'Why we were not all wiped out, goodness knows.' In the 3rd Australian Division following closely behind the 27th, Private Schwinghammer saw 'dead Americans piled feet deep'. Coming under heavy fire from Gillemont and Quennemont Farms,

Tanks move up for the attack on 29 September. The apparatus on top would be dropped into a trench, thereby providing the means for the tank to cross.

the 10th and 11th Brigades, despite strict orders not to become enmeshed with the Americans, began launching local assaults to gain breathing space.

Going forward at 9.50 am, General Gellibrand, the 3rd's commander, reported that the Americans were pinned down, holding up his division behind them. Monash preferred to believe aerial reconnaissance and prisoner reports that the Americans had reached the Green Line. Figuring that only a few German posts must be holding up the 3rd Division, he ordered it to advance at 3 pm, without artillery support on account of the Americans ahead, and mop them up. The 10th Brigade took Gillemont Farm but against such heavy fire that nothing more could be attempted in daylight. But the door to the Hindenburg Line was already ajar.

On the 27th's right, the 30th Division had taken over the stretch of the Outpost Line captured by the 1st Australian Division on 18 September. Able to assault from it, the 30th could be supported by a creeping barrage. With the tanks crushing the wire ahead, it got to the tunnel and took Bellicourt. Its advance was also

helped by the 46th Division from IX Corps alongside, which crossed the canal at Riqueval on 'rafts, life-jackets from Channel packets and anything else that would float'. Rawlinson's acceptance of the risk involved in attacking across the canal had paid off. Moving behind the 30th Division, the 5th Australian Division linked up with it short of Nauroy. Led by Major Blair Wark, the 32nd Battalion continued beyond the Green Line towards Joncourt. Wark was awarded the VC.

Le Catelet and Beaurevoir

Next morning, Monash swung the 9th and 14th Brigades, the reserve formations of the 3rd and 5th Divisions, northwards through the 30th Division's line. They were to advance astride the Hindenburg and Le Catelet Lines respectively, and take Bony. 'Slow and methodical hand to hand fighting in a perfect tangle of trenches', wrote Monash on 30 September, during which Private John Ryan of the 55th Battalion won the VC for driving off a determined counterattack. Realising that they were being outflanked, the Germans abandoned Bony and the tunnel on 1 October and withdrew to

the Beaurevoir Line. Totally exhausted, the 3rd and 5th Divisions were relieved by the 2nd.

After weathering a severe gas bombardment during the night, the 5th and 7th Brigades attacked the Beaurevoir Line early on 3 October. They were so widely spread that few platoons knew what their neighbours were doing. The line was captured nonetheless, Lieutenant Joe Maxwell of the 18th Battalion winning the VC for a feat at Estrées, where the attack was briefly held up, that would defy credulity in an action movie. 'You Australians are all bluff', a captured German officer blustered. 'You attack with practically no men and are on top of us before we know where we are.' IX Corps reached the Beaurevoir Line on the 2nd Division's right. The capture of the Hindenburg system cost all three Australian divisions almost 3900 men.

The shell-torn ruins of Gillemont Farm on 1 October. The crater in the left foreground was made by a large shell.

Helped through the wire by the tanks, the infantry mop up in Will Longstaff's *Breaking the Hindenburg Line.*

DRIVING THE BATTLEFIELD

You can spend a day on the Hindenburg Line battlefield, which gives some idea of its size. So keep the German officer's words about the Australians attacking with practically no men in the back of your mind at every stage of the drive. The manpower shortage had reached crisis proportions in the Australian divisions, which meant that they embarked on the battle with next to no men. Its outcome spoke volumes for their spirit, resilience and tactical skill.

Now for the battlefield. The area beyond the Le Catelet Line over which the Australians advanced was devoid of shell holes and covered in grass or old crops. Joncourt and Estrées were intact. The Bellicourt tunnel entrance and the Riqueval bridge are unchanged. With so many things looking as they did in 1918, you do not need much imagination to bring it alive.

MAPS IGN Blue Series, 1:25 000, 2508E Roisel; 26080 Villers-Outréaux

Leave Péronne on the D1017 for Cambrai, veer left at the first Y-junction and turn right onto the D6 (Rue de Roisel) at the major intersection just beyond the bridge. On passing Templeux-le-Guérard, head right on the D331 for Hargicourt and at the crossroads in the village centre turn left onto the D331/D57. Swing right after 500 metres onto the D57 for Bony. Picking up where the Hindenburg Outpost Line drive left off, turn left off the D57 1.1 kilometres past the A26 autoroute onto a track that heads up a spur and park on the **crest** ❶.
Quennemont Farm was in the vicinity of the **communications tower** on the far side of the D57. Keeping the tower on your left, look back along the road. The Hindenburg Outpost Line beyond **Ruby Wood**, on the high ground 1.5 kilometres to your left front near the A26, generally paralleled the autoroute and was captured by the 1st and 4th Australian Divisions on 18 September. III Corps

QUENNET COPSE

HINDENBURG OUTPOST LINE

106TH REGIMENT

D57

attacked it on this side of Ruby Wood, from where its twin trenches ran past **Malakoff Wood**, to your left beyond Quennemont Farm, and through the farm itself. Cutting from there either side of your location, it headed to the right of **Quennet Copse**, 250 metres to your right front, across **Claymore Valley** on your right and through **Gillemont Farm**, which is over your right shoulder on the next spur. Following repeated failures by III Corps, the 106th Regiment assaulted this stretch of the Outpost Line on 27 September.

Look at the tremendous fields of fire the Germans had down the long, bare slopes descending to the line of the A26, from which the 106th set off. Quennet Copse had been turned into an outlying strongpoint that could fire towards the fortified farm on either side. Malakoff Wood was also a strongpoint. Ironically, the Americans advanced in thick fog, the one element

Starting in the section of the Hindenburg Outpost Line ahead of the 27th Division, this drive retraces the 27th's ill-fated attack on that position and the 3rd Australian Division's subsequent advance over the Hindenburg Line to the Le Catelet Line on the left of the Australian Corps. The route then covers the assaults by the 30th Division and the 5th Australian Division on the right flank before following the 2nd Australian Division's advance to the Beaurevoir Line. Also included are the locations of all the VC actions and the site of the British 46th Division's dramatic crossing of the St Quentin Canal at Riqueval.
DISTANCE COVERED: 35 km
DURATION: 4.5 hours

that took the sting out of these well-organised defences.

Tragically, their rawness precluded their taking advantage. The 106th started with 18 officers, whereas an Australian brigade would have had over 40. Soon only one officer was left and the advance, which had lost the creeping barrage at the outset, degenerated into a number of isolated and leaderless groups that failed to recognise the dangers facing them.

Quennet Copse and Quennemont Farm from the bottom of the slope up which the 106th Regiment attacked on 27 September.

QUENNEMONT FARM

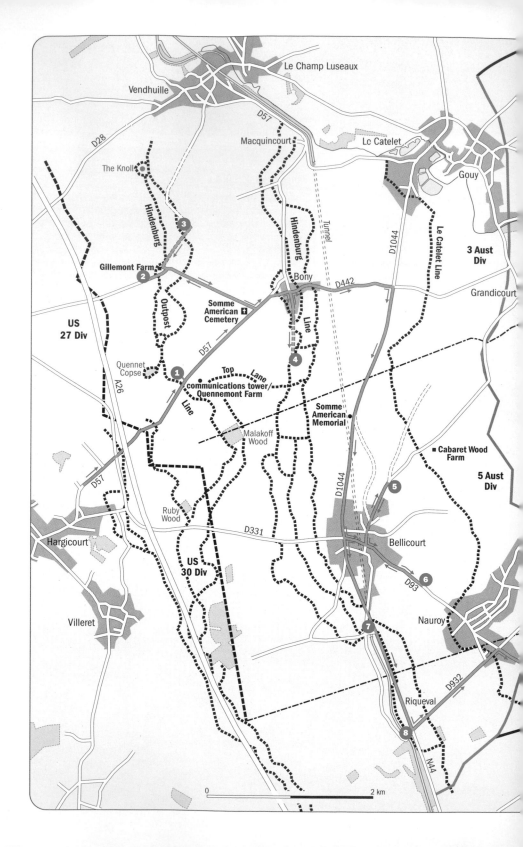

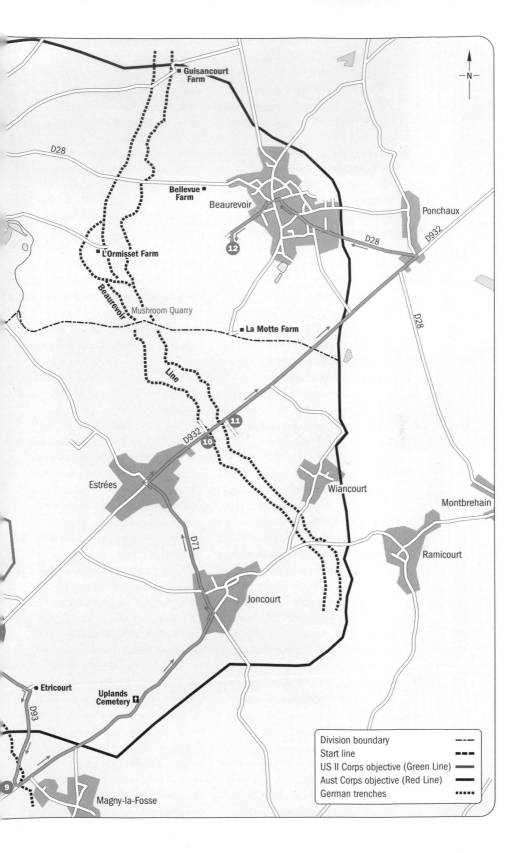

Guisancourt
Farm

D28

Bellevue
Farm

Beaurevoir

Ponchaux

L'Ormisset Farm

D28

D932

Beaurevoir

Mushroom Quarry

La Motte Farm

D28

Line

D932

Estrées

Wiancourt

Montbrehain

D71

Ramicourt

Joncourt

Etricourt

Uplands
Cemetery

D93

Magny-la-Fosse

Division boundary	---
Start line	===
US II Corps objective (Green Line)	—
Aust Corps objective (Red Line)	—
German trenches	.....

Some Americans thought the fog was gas. At day's end, they were pinned down across your front all the way to the A26.

Turn about to see what this reverse meant two days later. The tree line on the horizon two kilometres to your right front tops the three-metre-high mound formed by the spoil from the excavation of the **St Quentin Canal tunnel**, which runs beneath it. Following the near side of the mound and passing through well-defended **Bony**, which is screened by **Somme American Cemetery** in the trees on the left of the D57 to your front, were the two trenches of the **Hindenburg Line**. Not only did the 27th Division have to take them but it also had to carry on to the Le Catelet Line 1.5 kilometres beyond the mound. Assaulting that far would have been hard enough from the Outpost Line, on which you are standing, let alone from a kilometre further back. Furthermore, until the 27th Division got to the Outpost Line, it could not be supported by a creeping barrage for fear of hitting those marooned in no-man's-land after the earlier attack.

Beginning with the mist, the advance of the 107th and 108th Regiments was largely a rerun of the 106th's. Many of the 34 supporting tanks were clobbered by field-guns and anti-tank guns in the 'tank fort' at Gillemont Farm, most of the few officers were hit and the advance broke down. Some small parties moved around Quennemont Farm towards Bony, others passed around the far side of Gillemont Farm but the Hindenburg Line ahead of you was untouched. American dead and wounded carpeted the slopes below the Outpost Line behind you. Trailing the Americans, the 10th and 11th Brigades from the 3rd Australian Division had to bludgeon their way forward. 'The Yanks were heartily cursed', Private Shapcott wrote. Any able-bodied Americans met reinforced the understrength Australian battalions. By mid-morning the 41st Battalion had taken Quennet Copse and

was spread across the spur to your rear. Then the British 17th Armoured Car Battalion and some Whippet tanks sped past your right to raid the German rear areas. The tank fort in Bony crippled three cars in the cemetery and another car and four Whippets during the hasty withdrawal towards you that followed.

Things were rosier on your right, where the boundary between the 27th and 30th Divisions, and hence the 3rd and 5th Australian Divisions, passed through Malakoff Wood. Donning masks on account of gas lingering in the low ground, the 44th and 59th Battalions, on the inner flanks of the 3rd and 5th Divisions respectively, became intermixed to your right rear in the fog. But your location was captured with the aid of a tank, enabling machine-guns to fire in enfilade on Quennemont Farm. It fell to the 59th soon after, its garrison proffering cigars. Meanwhile the 44th Battalion had moved around both sides of the farm and was heading towards the Hindenburg Line, partly along **Top Lane**, a communication trench running across your right front to it from the farm. The 59th followed after taking Malakoff Wood.

Continue on the D57 and turn left on the pot-holed road by the American cemetery for Gillemont Farm. Follow the road around the left of the farm for 200 metres, park and look along it ❷. Skylined as they came over the crest ahead, the 38th and 39th Battalions from the 10th Brigade were whipped by fire from the farm and from **South Gillemont Trench**. The Outpost Line's front trench, it passed to the left of Quennet Copse, 1.1 kilometres to your left, after leaving the farm. Both battalions hunkered down in **Dog Trench**, an old British trench that crossed the road 180 metres along. Lieutenant-Colonel Henderson, commanding the 39th, was killed while reconnoitring it. Captain Fairweather, an institution in the 38th, fell when his company was pinned down in South Gillemont's wire halfway to the

The 10th Brigade's attack on the Outpost Line between Gillemont Farm, from where the photograph was taken, and Quennemont Farm. Note how the strongpoints at the farms and in Quennet Copse between them could support each other.

copse. Most of the supporting tanks were hit when the 38th and 39th reached the farm and South Gillemont during the afternoon. They linked up with the 41st Battalion, which had bombed up South Gillemont towards them from the copse. Running 350 metres to your rear across Claymore Valley as the Outpost Line's support trench here, **Claymore Trench** was found empty at dawn on 30 September. The 41st Battalion took the support trench at Quennemont Farm about the same time.

Returning past the front of Gillemont Farm, drive straight on, following the power lines, to the dumping area at the sharp leftwards bend ❸. Stand with the farm on your left. Stretching from it, the front trench of the Outpost Line, here **Willow Trench**, cut across the **Macquincourt Valley** to your front to the **Knoll**, which is crowned by the copse on the far side. **Lone Tree Trench**, the support line, passed 100 metres to your left and along the line of the road. The 107th Regiment had taken the Knoll and Willow Trench below it, and part of Willow below the farm. Incredible as it may seem, two reserve battalions had also cruised down a sunken road in the valley, unnoticed by the Germans in the fog and smoke, towards the northern end of the canal tunnel in **Macquincourt**

hamlet, 1.5 kilometres to your right and at the foot of the spur on which you are parked. They streamed back to the Knoll when the Germans finally saw them and counterattacked up the valley from your right. The Knoll was held.

Moving along the near slope of the valley, the 40th Battalion arrived just in time to save the farm end of Willow Trench, which was crowded with Americans unsure of what was happening around them. Captain Hubert Wilkins, the Australian official photographer, saw one group in the trench 300 metres to your left front oblivious to the counterattack and cleaning their weapons. Others thought that the bombs being hurled at them from no-man's-land were shells fired by distant guns. A bullet grazed Wilkins' chin as he urged the Americans to the parapet, from where they forced the Germans to ground. During the night the Germans pulled back to the Hindenburg Line, enabling the 40th to occupy Lone Tree Trench next morning.

Return to the D57 at the cemetery, turn left, and then head right at the Y-junction to enter Bony. Turn right at the first crossroads and park at the clearing just past the start of the track on the village outskirts. Walk along the track, which follows the crest of a spur, to the

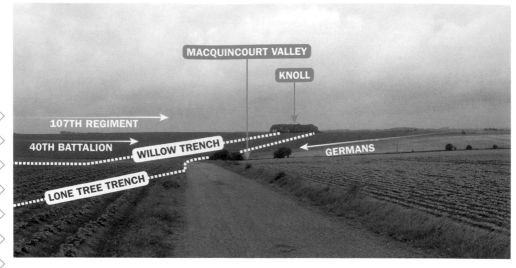

MACQUINCOURT VALLEY

KNOLL

107TH REGIMENT

40TH BATTALION

WILLOW TRENCH

GERMANS

LONE TREE TRENCH

Holding on in the Macquincourt Valley and on the Knoll.

clump of bushes at the rightwards **bend** ④, passing the remains of a German pillbox on the way. It may also have engaged the Whippets. Look along the track. You are on the front trench of the Hindenburg Line, which ran along the crest before crossing the track here and cutting to Bony. The support trench was 250 metres to your left. Extending 100 metres out to your right and paralleling the track 'like a bad nightmare', recalled Private Shapcott, was the wire, 'rows and rows of it, as thick as it could possibly be. It had not been broken to any great extent by either the barrage or the Yanks'. Arcing around your right front from Quennemont Farm, denoted by the communication tower to your right (NOl the one on the A26 that you can see behind the American Cemetery), Top

Lane Trench joined the Hindenburg Line 250 metres ahead of you.

When the 44th and 59th Battalions reached the wire on the far side of Top Lane and on over the skyline to your front, Lieutenant-Colonel Scanlan was directing the 59th through the gaps when his adjutant screamed at him. With a German just about to fire, Scanlan's dive into the barbs saved his life. When the two battalions reached the tunnel mound at the tree line to your left front, they were heavily engaged from the twin-trenched Hindenburg Line stretching back from your location, and from Bony itself. A German counterattack down both trenches was beaten off. The 44th and 50th, as well as the 41st, subsequently formed a line facing Bony that stretched between the two trenches

QUENNEMONT FARM

CLAYMORE VALLEY

> 30 yards from us was a Fritz strong post. A Fritz had stood upon his parapet and taken aim but I fell before he pressed the trigger. There I was acting as a scout for my Battalion. I left a Lewis Gun team to clean up those Huns and directed the companies still on [and] came upon a sight which, in spite of the seriousness of the situation, made me laugh. A big Digger wearing an American raincoat was holding up a dozen prisoners at bayonet point, and making the unhappy devils dance about... I have never seen men so cowed and frightened as these Huns; they were crying for pardon, and dancing Highland flings all about this grinning Digger.

Lieutenant-Colonel Scanlan evades death
(Scanlan, J, 'Account', PR00983, AWM)

and back to the Outpost Line. At 6 am on 30 September, the 43rd and 44th Battalions began bombing along both trenches towards you, clearing the advanced German post at the junction of Top Lane and the Hindenburg Line. They occupied Bony and the line of the tunnel mound next morning after the Germans withdrew during the night.

Having returned to your car, turn right at the crossroads onto the D442, which crosses the tunnel mound, and head right on the D1044. After 1.5 kilometres you will pass the **Somme American Memorial**, which commemorates all American units that served with the BEF, on the right. An orientation table at the rear of the memorial gives the directions to their battlefields. Once in **Bellicourt**, turn left at the mairie onto the D93 (Rue Jean Moulin) and left again at the roundabout onto Rue Victor Trocmé. Drive through the five-way intersection, veering slightly right on Rue des Corneilles, to the next junction, where the road curving to the right by the brick wall follows the bed of an old light railway. Continue straight ahead on Chemin du Bois de Cabaret, passing the water tower, and park at the clearing over the crest **5**, where the road swings right and a track runs down into the valley ahead. With Bellicourt on your left, look across the valley towards the D1044, although you'll get a better view from the bank on the right of the road.

You are standing on an outwork of the single-trench **Le Catelet Line**, which passed behind you after running to the rear of Bellicourt. Crossing the road 550 metres to your right, or two-thirds of the way to **Cabaret Wood Farm** among the trees, it continued diagonally to your right front over the track in the valley and then paralleled the D1044. Having the advantage of starting from the Outpost Line, the 119th Regiment from the 30th Division reached the tunnel mound, topped by the tree line behind the D1044, between the American Memorial, on the D1044 to your right front, and Bellicourt. Part of it entered the village and some men got to the embankment of the light railway, which paralleled the

Looking back from the front trench of the Hindenburg Line at the Outpost Line. On 29 September the advance only got beyond the Outpost Line at Quennemont Farm. The photograph illustrates the protection that it afforded the Hindenburg Line and how exposed any advance from it against the Hindenburg Line would have been. Wire entanglements would have covered the area at least to where the ground starts to fall away.

QUENNET COPSE

HINDENBURG OUTPOST LINE

A typical stretch of the wire entanglements along the Hindenburg Line ahead of the Australian Corps.

D1044 before turning at the memorial to run along the line of bushes to your front into Bellicourt, where you crossed it earlier. Plastered from the farm, which was a tank fort, and by field-guns on the bank around you as the mist cleared, neither they nor the rest of the 119th at the mound could go further.

Behind the Americans came the 8th and 15th Brigades from the 5th Australian Division. While the 8th moved through Bellicourt, the 15th joined the Americans at the mound and attacked with them towards you at 3 pm. Murderous fire from your location, the farm and the Le Catelet Line crippled the accompanying tanks

and stopped most of the 58th Battalion on the spur to your front. Its left made the Le Catelet Line from the valley to your right front to the road on your right. Peeping over the parapet, Lance-Corporal Eric Russell saw 'Huns trickling up, even some carrying MG's', and shot 15 of them. 'Feeling slightly cheered', he settled into the trench, which was 'full of mud, water and dead and wounded men'. Covered by the railway embankment, the 57th Battalion circled around your left front. It reached the Le Catelet Line at its junction with the railway to your left rear behind Bellicourt, where the 29th Battalion from the 8th Brigade had been held up. The

The attack of the 43rd and 44th Battalions on 30 September.

The Somme American Memorial.

57th then bombed along the Le Catelet Line but was stopped behind you.

So 29 September ended well short of the Green Line on your right, where the Germans still held much of the Le Catelet and Hindenburg Lines. After Monash's revamping of the plan, the 43rd and 44th Battalions struck next morning along the Hindenburg Line towards Bony from your previous location. The 58th Battalion seized the uncaptured stretch of the Le Catelet Line between the 57th Battalion and the road to your right, allowing the 53rd and 55th Battalions from the 14th Brigade to advance from a start line that stretched from there to the tunnel mound. Stymied at the mound, the weight of the attack shifted to the Le Catelet Line to your right front and the high ground on this side of the D1044 to the right of the American Memorial was gained. When a counterattack drove the 53rd Battalion down the slope facing you, Private Ryan, despite being wounded, led bombing and bayonet attacks that sent the Germans back over the crest. The Le Catelet Line was now held all the way to Bellicourt. Attacking from it next day, the 5th Division swept past your right, capturing Cabaret Wood Farm.

Return to Bellicourt, head left at the roundabout onto the D93 and, on crossing the valley, park at the **layover** ⑥ on the left of the road. **Nauroy**, on the far side of which the Green Line ran, is directly ahead. Stand with it on your left. The Hindenburg Line ran along the near side of the D1044 to your left front before crossing it to the right of the St Quentin Canal tunnel entrance, among the trees to your right front. At 10.30 am on 29 September, the 32nd Battalion under Major Wark came over the D1044 there with two tanks and advanced across your front. One tank was knocked out on the right side of Nauroy in the improving light. At Wark's direction, two companies and the remaining tank swept through that part of the village, taking 40 prisoners but losing the tank.

The 32nd Battalion at Nauroy.

Now face Nauroy. The Le Catelet Line curved around the front of the village from the high ground to its left. When the 120th Regiment appeared from Bellicourt in the morning mist, the tank fort in the trees at the left end of Nauroy smashed it. Many Americans pulled back to Bellicourt; others held on in small groups either side of you. Having lost three of its four tanks, the 29th Battalion following the Americans bombed along the D93 to your front, along the

The fighting on the Le Catelet Line 29–30 September.

communication trench to your left that linked the tank fort to Bellicourt, and the sunken road beyond the communication trench. Capturing the tank fort and entering the Le Catelet Line, the 29th headed left along it for 900 metres to the railway, where the 57th Battalion linked up with it. Moving through your location at 12.45 pm, the 30th Battalion took Nauroy. The 29th's attempted advance beyond it next day was repulsed.

Return to Bellicourt, turn left onto the D1044 and park after 1.2 kilometres at the **Touage de Riqueval** ⑦ on the right, where the St Quentin Canal emerges from the Bellicourt end of the tunnel. Take the track above the tunnel entrance, pass the German pillbox and face right. Crossing the tunnel mound to your right, the Hindenburg Line trenches ran in front of you before swinging right and stretching over the spur that extends to the left of Bellicourt ahead. Major Wark found 200 leaderless Americans from the 117th Regiment in these trenches and added them to the 32nd Battalion. Tanks helped the 32nd deal with the pillbox. Before leaving, walk down to the tunnel entrance like Private Schwinghammer and many other Australians did. They wanted to check the rumour that the tunnel contained a 'corpse factory' where the Germans boiled down their dead for fat. Instead they found it full of casualties.

Continue along the D1044 for 1.3 kilometres, park by the sign for the **Pont de Riqueval** on the right and walk to the **bridge** ⑧. On 29 September the 137th Brigade from the 46th Division stormed over the canal and its steep banks to your right to take the Hindenburg Line beyond the D1044. A shot of them perched on the banks afterwards and being addressed from the bridge by their commander, Brigadier-General

The St Quentin Canal tunnel entrance at Bellicourt.

Just as it was in 1918: the Riqueval bridge.

Etricourt as seen from the spur above Magny-la-Fosse.

John Campbell VC, became one of the war's standard photographs. Now cross the D1044 to head towards Nauroy on the D932 and turn right onto the D93 on the village outskirts. Swinging sharp right at **Etricourt**, drive 1.1 kilometres across **Springbok Valley** to the **T-junction** 9 on the crest and park. Keeping Nauroy and Etricourt Farm on your left, look along the crest. Passing to the left of the farm, the Le Catelet Line cut from Nauroy directly through your location.

You are now in the 46th Division's sector. After meeting the 4th Leicesters 200 metres to your rear at 11.30 am, the 32nd Battalion was engaged by a field-gun battery in Etricourt. Major Wark personally led an attack that captured it. Continuing along the ridge, the 32nd easily passed through the Le Catelet Line and took **Magny-la-Fosse** to your right front before stopping halfway to **Joncourt**, three kilometres to your front, at 2.30 pm. From there they extended thinly across Springbok Valley to Etricourt, from which the 31st Battalion carried the line to Nauroy. The Germans counterattacked at 5.30 pm but got no closer than 500 metres. On 30 September the 32nd advanced to within 200 metres of Joncourt. In two days it had taken 250 prisoners and captured 20 field-guns, 30 machine-guns and five *minenwerfers* at a cost of 125 casualties.

Passing tiny **Uplands Cemetery** just beyond the line reached by the 32nd Battalion on 29 September, continue to Joncourt, which the 30th and 32nd Battalions took two days later. Turn left at the village, in which Major Wark silenced a machine-gun, onto the D71 for **Estrées**, captured by the 56th Battalion on 1 October. At the crossroads in Estrées, turn right on the D932 and stop at the car park on the right near the crest of the slope ahead 10. Stand facing the village. Running along the crest on your left, the front trench of the **Beaurevoir Line** crossed the D932 at your location and passed through **L'Ormisset Farm**, on the skyline three kilometres away and to the left of **Beaurevoir**. The stretch astride the D932 was the most developed. For 400 metres to your left and 200 metres to your right, it was protected by dense entanglements and sown with pillboxes containing anti-tank guns as well as machine-guns. On the site of the lone house on the crest behind you was the **White Cottage**, in which the Germans had emplaced a field-gun to fire down the D932 into Estrées. The support trench paralleled the front trench on the other side of the crest.

Attacking from the Le Catelet Line on a 5.8-kilometre frontage on 1 October, the 5th Division advanced two kilometres beyond the Green Line, capturing the high ground on the near side of Joncourt, 1.8 kilometres to your left front, through Estrées and beyond L'Ormisset Farm. As the 2nd Division assaulted the Beaurevoir Line at 6.05 am on 3 October with just 2500 men spread across this frontage, it is easy to see why platoons fought in virtual isolation. While the 7th Brigade struck the L'Ormisset Farm end of the line, the 5th Brigade came towards you with the 18th and 19th Battalions respectively left and right of the D932. Their inner companies were pinned down along the wire across your front by fire from machine-guns and anti-tank guns in the pillboxes and the White Cottage, which also kept the supporting tanks at bay.

Ignoring the fire, Lieutenant Maxwell picked his way through the wire 600 metres to your left and silenced the machine-gun holding up his company. Moving along the trench towards you, he knocked out another gun and heard from an English-speaking German he had nabbed that the men in a nearby pillbox wanted to surrender. About to take them prisoner, Maxwell and his small party were instead suddenly surrounded by 20 Germans who seized their rifles. Just then a barrage conveniently landed around the group. Maxwell took the revolver he kept hidden in his gas-mask, shot two Germans and escaped along with his men in the ensuing pandemonium. He added the VC to the MC and DCM he already held.

A tank created a path through the wire 700 metres to your right for the outer flank of the 19th Battalion, which then attacked along the pillbox line towards you while the 20th carried on the advance. But the Whippets supporting the 20th were hit in quick succession by the field-gun in the White Cottage when they emerged from Estrées on the D932 below you. Withdrawn at 9.40 am while the crest was shelled, the pinned-down companies passed around to your right to join the attack from there. The resistance on the crest and in the White Cottage folded; 200 Germans and 18 machine-guns were captured.

Now drive over the crest to the **dumping area ⑪** on the right and look along the D932. The support trench of the Beaurevoir Line crossed the road 50 metres behind you. Ahead of you stretched the Red Line, which ran from the far side of **Wiancourt**, 1.2 kilometres to your right, beyond the ridge to your

ESTRÉES WATER TOWER

18TH BATTALION

BEAUREVOIR LINE

The 18th Battalion's attack on the Beaurevoir Line. Lieutenant Maxwell's action began on the crest on the left.

The remains of Beaurevoir Mill.

The attacks across the Torrens Canal Valley.

front and behind **Beaurevoir** to your left front. On the skyline between the left of Beaurevoir and the **water tower** is the ruin of **Beaurevoir Mill**. The copse to the left of the water tower hides **Bellevue Farm**, while **La Motte Farm** is adorned by the poplars in the valley of the **Torrens Canal**, a storm water channel leading to the Scheldt, below the mill.

Continuing the 5th Brigade's assault, the 17th Battalion took Wiancourt and gained a foothold on the ridge to your right front. The left company, only 20 strong, advanced down the slope on which you are standing and was halted at the bottom. On the left of the D932,

the 20th Battalion swept over the Torrens Canal Valley but was stopped near Bellevue Farm by point-blank fire from machine-guns and field-guns at the mill. The 6th Brigade joined the advance at 6.30 pm. Attacking to your right front, the 23rd Battalion carried the line to the copse on the far slope ahead, while the 22nd moved through your location to extend the line from the copse to La Motte Farm. On its left, the 24th Battalion took the mill with hardly a shot being fired. As Charles Bean noted laconically, 'night was falling, and the enemy generally did not grasp what was happening'.

Proceed on the D932, passing the copse reached by the 22nd Battalion on the right after 1.6 kilometres. On 4 October the 22nd and 23rd Battalions gained the line of the D28 along the ridge on the right one kilometre further on. Continue another 250 metres beyond it and turn left onto the D28 for Beaurevoir. During the advance on the 4th, some men got into **Ponchaux** on your right but were quickly ejected. Turn left at the T-junction in Beaurevoir and, passing the town centre and war memorial on your left, drive straight ahead on Rue de la Tour to **Beaurevoir Mill** 12 just beyond the outskirts. A

BELLEVUE FARM

MILL

20TH BATTALION

24TH BATTALION

The advance on L'Ormisset and Bellevue Farms as seen from Beaurevoir Mill.

great view of the battlefield unfolds from it.

Stand with your back to Beaurevoir. In the 7th Brigade's attack on 3 October, the 26th Battalion took L'Ormisset Farm, in the trees 1.5 kilometres to your front, and, with the 28th on its left, Bellevue Farm to your right. German counterattacks from Beaurevoir, supported by artillery firing over open sights from the near side of the town, regained Bellevue Farm. Estrées, from where the 5th Brigade attacked, is 2.5 kilometres to your left front, beyond the Torrens Canal Valley. Advancing along the right side of the valley, the 20th Battalion was halted 300 metres from the mill. The 24th's attack, which later took the mill, also

came up the Torrens towards you. The Australian line now stretched from the far side of Wiancourt, through your location and to the left of Bellevue Farm. With **Montbrehain**, whose blue water tower can be seen to the left of the grain silo on the skyline four kilometres to your left, and Beaurevoir still held by the Germans, Monash decided not to go further.

To return to Péronne, head back to the D932, follow it to Nauroy and turn right there onto the D93 for Bellicourt. From Bellicourt, take the D331 through Hargicourt to join the D6 in Templeaux-le-Guérard. Then remain on the D6. Alternatively, turn left off the D932 in Estrées and take the D71 to Joncourt for the Montbrehain battlefield.

LOCAL INFORMATION

CEMETERIES

Many of the Australians killed on the Hindenburg Line lie in cemeteries further afield. Colonel Henderson and Captain Fairweather rest in **Templeux-le-Guérard British Cemetery**; others lie in **Tincourt New British Cemetery**. Both cemeteries are covered in the chapter on the Hindenburg Outpost Line.

The grave of Corporal Lawrence Weathers VC, Unicorn Cemetery.

Bellicourt British Cemetery

Started after the capture of the village, this cemetery contains 1204 burials, of which 892 are known. Most of the 307 Australians, all but 46 of them identified, fell in the final battles. Captain Arthur Rogers MC at II.C.9 was killed while leading the two companies of the 32nd Battalion that cleared the lower end of Nauroy during the advance for which Major Wark won the VC. Located on the D331 just outside Bellicourt, the cemetery was greatly expanded by the postwar concentration in it of graves from smaller cemeteries and the surrounding battlefield.

Unicorn Cemetery, Vendhuille

The 78 Australians, 18 of them unknown, in this cemetery fell during September and October 1918. Resting at III.C.5, Corporal Weathers VC of the 43rd Battalion was killed on the Hindenburg Line on 29 September. Lieutenant Henry Davis MC of the 13th Battalion at I.D.9 fell as part of the Australian Mission advising the Americans during the attack. The 50th (Northumbrian) Division, whose symbol was the unicorn, started the cemetery after British and American units captured Vendhuille. Greatly enlarged by postwar concentrations, including from the nearby Cambrai battlefield of 1917, it now contains 1008 burials, 599 of them known. To visit Unicorn, continue through Bony on the D57, pass through Macquincourt to see the northern end of the St Quentin Tunnel and turn left in

The Somme American Cemetery.

Vendhuille onto the D28. The cemetery is three kilometres along, by the A26.

Somme American Cemetery

On the D57 near Bony and passed on the drive, this cemetery is one of the eight First World War American military cemeteries maintained by the American Battle Monuments Commission, the US equivalent of the Commonwealth War Graves Commission. Called the Somme Cemetery because the American 1st, 33rd and 80th Divisions, as well as the 27th and 30th, and some engineer formations fought in the Somme area, it contains 1844 burials, 138 of them unknown. They rest under white crosses rather than headstones. On the interior walls of the chapel-memorial are the names of 333 missing. The literature on the cemetery and the ABMC, which is available from the office, points out that the 107th Regiment's 339 dead and 658 wounded on 29 September was the heaviest loss suffered by an American regiment in a single day during the war.

CHAPTER 25

1918

MONTBREHAIN

In the lead-up to the attack on the Hindenburg Outpost Line, Australian Prime Minister Hughes told General Monash that his job depended on the Australian Corps being relieved by mid-October. By 2 October all the Australian divisions bar the 2nd Division were resting, and it was due for relief on the evening of the 4th, after its successful attack on the Beaurevoir Line. But II American Corps was unable to take over until the following evening. Asked by General Rawlinson to use the extra day to continue the advance, Monash decided to capture Montbrehain, 3.5 kilometres southeast of Beaurevoir, because it crowned a plateau from which the Germans could block further progress. Assaulting on the 2nd Division's right, the British 46th Division had briefly held the village on 3 October.

Montbrehain. This photograph was taken shortly after its capture.

German machine-gunners killed in a makeshift trench during the attack.

As the 5th and 7th Brigades had borne the brunt of the Beaurevoir Line fighting, the 6th Brigade was the 2nd Division's freshest formation. Of its battalions, the 24th had been lightly involved and the 21st not used at all, so they were slated for the Montbrehain attack. Having less than 500 men between them for the 2.1-kilometre advance, the two battalions were joined by the 2nd Pioneer Battalion. As with each division's pioneer battalion, the 2nd's main tasks were trench digging, road repair and light construction, but it had been trained as infantry and could fight in that role if necessary. Though it would now be doing so for the first time, it shared the high spirits of the veteran 21st and 24th. They were to advance on the right and left respectively of the 1.1-kilometre attack frontage and the

pioneers following would wheel outwards to secure the right flank. Eight Australian artillery brigades and 12 tanks would support the attack, which was to begin from nearby Ramicourt at 6.05 am on 5 October.

Was it necessary?

It did not begin well. The tanks were late and part of the barrage struck the 21st Battalion as it advanced on the right of D713. Nonetheless it quickly overran the Germans holding out in two quarries on the edge of the village. By the time the railway station at the far end of Montbrehain was reached, a tank had caught up and the jubilant villagers were plying the Australians with coffee and milk. Meanwhile the pioneers had met torrential fire as they swung towards the railway behind the 21st. Commanding the section from the 6th Machine-Gun Company attached to them, Lieutenant Norm Wilkinson crept through the crops and saw 100 German machine-gunners arrayed along the railway embankment. Wilkinson's two guns swept them away, enabling the pioneers to set up their flanking line.

On the left of the D713, the 24th Battalion was held up at the edge of the village and also hit by the German counter-barrage. Though the timely arrival of a tank helped the 24th on, the prime mover was Lieutenant George Ingram. After leading a charge that dealt with a strongpoint before which the centre of the battalion was pinned down, Ingram rushed several more posts and single-handedly cleared the Germans from a large quarry. He was awarded the VC. The 24th took the northern half of Montbrehain but had to give up the cemetery on the highest part of the village when the Germans counterattacked. Reserves from the 21st Battalion subsequently swept through the cemetery and the orchards around it. The Germans withdrew. Nearly 400 remained as prisoners.

Determination, flexibility, initiative and tactical skill had enabled the 21st and 24th Battalions to wrest Montbrehain from the Germans, who were fresh and held every ace as regards terrain. Not forgetting the 2nd Pioneers, Charles Bean wrote that they fought 'like skilled infantry'. He also remarked that the German guns could pound the narrow salient that resulted, which jutted two kilometres ahead of the British line, from three sides as they had at Mouquet Farm. Perhaps, although in these final days of the war, the Germans lacked the formidable

The surrounds of Montbrehain church, bearing signs of the fight through the village.

capability that they had in 1916. But Bean was right to question the necessity for the attack. Montbrehain could have been taken easily and probably with smaller loss as part of a wider advance instead of in an isolated advance undertaken to fill in time. It cost the Australians 430 casualties, of whom 94 were killed. Some of the dead bore the ANZAC chevron of a Gallipoli veteran on their sleeve. They had fallen at the very last hurdle for the Australian Corps did not return to the line after the Americans relieved the 2nd Division that night.

WALKING THE BATTLEFIELD

It is appropriate that the battlefield on which the AIF fought for the final time on the Western Front can really be done properly only on foot. Walking allows reflection; sitting behind the wheel of a car and concentrating on the road do not. There is plenty of food for thought on this walk. Montbrehain is where the journey that the AIF began in the nursery over two years and almost 200 000 casualties earlier came to an end. In a sense it was anti-climactic, a battle fought by just three battalions rather than an epic involving the entire Australian Corps. But the corps was embodied in the spirit and skill of those battalions. Some of the men in them had started their journey not at the nursery but at ANZAC months before. All of them knew that the war was almost over. Instead of playing it safe, which would have been understandable, they advanced with dash and verve. Think about that.

Few visit Montbrehain. It is too out of the way. Hopefully you will make the effort to come. By doing so, you will be paying tribute to these men. The walk is easy too.

MAPS IGN Blue Series, 1:25 000, 26080 Villers-Outréaux

Leave Péronne on the D1017 for Cambrai, veer left at the first Y-junction and turn right onto the D6 (Rue de Roisel) just beyond the bridge. On passing through Templeux-le-Guérard, head right on the D331 to Bellicourt. Pick up the D93 there for Nauroy and turn left at the far end of the village onto the D932 for Estrées. Head right at Estrées church onto the D71, left on reaching Joncourt and left again at the T-junction onto the D713 (Rue de Ramicourt).

Continue sharp left on the D713 on entering **Ramicourt** and park at the **cemetery** ❶ just outside the hamlet. Look along the D713, which heads over the crest of the spur to your front to **Montbrehain**. Crossing the road by the silo to your left, the **railway** ran through the trees to your right front and contoured around the spur. You are on the start line for the attack. The 21st and 24th Battalions extended along it respectively right and left of the D713, while the 2nd Pioneer Battalion was astride it behind you. Now walk up the spur on the D713, following the axis of the advance into Montbrehain. Some of the guns supporting the 21st Battalion on your right opened fire late. Their shells landed on the 21st, which was already on the move, instead of ahead of it. Casualties were severe. They increased when the German counter-barrage caught the 21st on the railway further to your right. One of the most heart-rending losses of the day occurred on the railway just 50 metres to your right. Lieutenant Bill Hardwick, a 21st Battalion 'original' and a Gallipoli veteran, was killed by a German shell there while briefing the incoming Americans *after* the attack.

Head left at the village war memorial onto the D28 (Rue de l'Abbaye) and left again down the lane after 450 metres. At the leftwards bend 125 metres along the lane ❷, face the silo. Entrenched along the edge of Montbrehain on the D28 behind you, the Germans put up a wall of fire on seeing the 24th Battalion appear through the thin morning mist on the crest ahead of you. It was also thickened by their counter-barrage. Advancing from your right front,

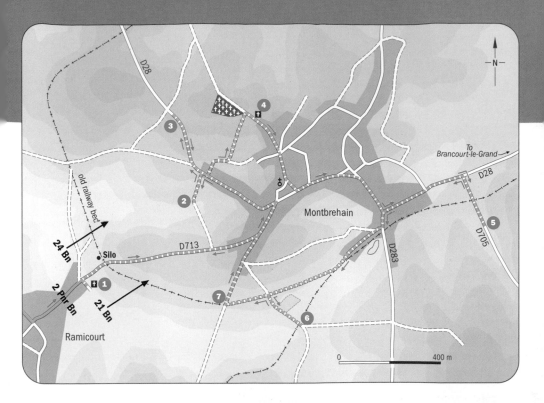

B Company in the centre charged a post on the crest to your right. The charge was shot down, leaving B Company hopelessly stalled until a Lewis-gunner managed to get close enough to the post to pour sustained fire into it. Covered by the fire, charges from each flank, one led by Lieutenant Ingram, took the post, killing 40 Germans and capturing six machine-guns.

Return to the D28 and head left for 300 metres to the rightwards bend, where a large **depression** ❸ abuts the house on the left of the road. Face the silo again. The depression is all that remains of the quarry from which intense fire pinned down B Company after it had reorganised behind the bank crowned by the lone tree 300 metres to your front. A tank in the village to your left was summoned by waving helmets on rifles. Lieutenant Ingram led it towards your location with B Company following. While the tank circled the quarry, he jumped in and shot several of the

Starting from Ramicourt, as the attack did, the walk follows the D713, which was the axis of the attack. The route then follows the 24th Battalion's assault and passes the location of Lieutenant Ingram's VC action before going through Montbrehain and retracing the assaults of the 21st Battalion and the 2nd Pioneers on the opposite side of the village.
DISTANCE COVERED: **9 km**
DURATION: **4 hours**

occupants, prompting 63 more to surrender. Leaving the rest of B Company to mop up the quarry, where 40 machine-guns were captured, Ingram rushed the original house next to it. After shooting a machine-gunner firing from the cellar ventilator, he dashed down the cellar stairs and took another 30 prisoners. Ingram's VC was Australia's last of the war. He already held the MM.

Walking back on the D28, head left onto a track by a low wall 30 metres past the lane. Behind the houses, swing left onto another track that runs up the hill to the civilian cemetery. After crossing the D28, B Company and its tank cleared

The quarry strongpoint on the D28 cleared by Lieutenant Ingram.

The ground over which the Germans counterattacked as seen from Calvaire Cemetery. They advanced well past this location.

the posts in the cemetery and from the surrounding roads and hedges. Turn right on reaching Rue du Cimetière and walk to the far end of **Calvaire Cemetery** ❹, which you will see straightaway on the left. You are now on the highest part of Montbrehain, the scene of severe fighting throughout the day. Enfiladed from the village on your right and in full view of the Germans on the edge of the crest to your left front, D Company of the 24th Battalion on your left could not move beyond the line of the cemetery. Its commander,

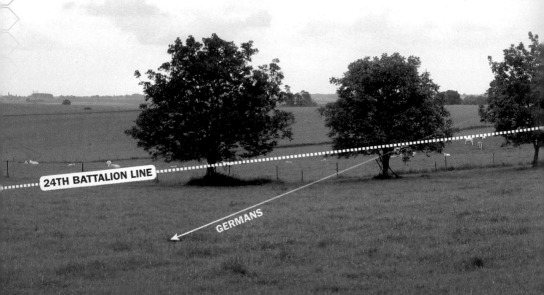

24TH BATTALION LINE

GERMANS

Captain Harry Fletcher, a 24th 'original' and Gallipoli veteran, was killed by a shell while directing a tank. It was knocked out soon after.

To your right front a company from each of the 21st and 24th Battalions and the 2nd Pioneers had advanced through Montbrehain and set up a line of posts that stretched from the far end of the village, through the orchards, to your location and the civilian cemetery to your left rear. Spread across the low ground to your front, the Germans counterattacked towards you at 9 am, driving in these posts and regaining the civilian cemetery. Coming around from your right rear and rushing the Germans before they had time to consolidate, reserve platoons from the 21st Battalion re-established the line.

Continue down Rue du Cimetière, head left at the fork by the church and left again onto the D28 (now Rue Charles de Gaulle). You are following the route of the advance that cleared the village. Moving on your left with A Company of the 24th Battalion under Captain John Mahony MC, Private John Blankenburg's platoon commander banged his head against the muzzle of a German machine-gun while pushing through a hedge. Blankenburg, a Russian, reckoned the gun crew were cowardly and shot

them. He was later killed himself. The 21st Battalion attacked on your right and a company of the 2nd Pioneers mopped up in rear. The residents poured out into the street with refreshments as the Australians passed. By this stage of the walk you're probably wishing that they'd do the same for you. Remain on the D28 through the T-junction 350 metres along, head left on it after another 250 metres and pause at the junction with the D705 500 metres further on. After the attack, the 21st Battalion's line stretched from here to the end of Montbrehain on your left, where Mahony was mortally wounded. He had enlisted with his great pal Fletcher and served on Gallipoli with him.

Now walk 350 metres down the D705 **5** and look along it. German field-guns by **Doon Mill**, which was on the site of L'Arbre Haut Farm to the left of the road on the slope ahead, along the spur extending to your left from it, and in **Doon Copse**, just visible to the left of the mill on the higher ground behind it, hammered the line held by the 21st Battalion and the 2nd Pioneers. It ran to your right along the side of Montbrehain from the D28/D705 junction. The 21st tried to reach the mill but failed. Starting from the mill and the copse, and from **Brancourt-le-Grand** one kilometre along the D28 to your left, the left wing

FAR END OF MONTBREHAIN

DOON COPSE

DOON MILL

GERMANS

Doon Mill from the D705. The mill was a thorn in the side of the 21st Battalion. The Germans also counterattacked from it.

of the 9 am counterattack was halted by the 21st on the slopes to your left and front and in the fields across the D28. At 11 am the Australian artillery blasted the Germans out of Doon Mill, making life easier for the Australian line this side of Montbrehain.

Return to the D28, head left along it, left again at the T-junction onto the D283 and right after 100 metres. You are now on the bed of the old railway. The station, converted into a house, is on your left, opposite the pharmacy, which was formerly a hotel. Much to the delight of the 21st Battalion, the German logistics dump by the station contained a stack of beer barrels as well as the usual stores and ammunition. Continue past the station, where the road ends and the railway continues as a dirt track. Head left after 750 metres onto the cross-track and, passing an old quarry on your left, walk down the slope to where another track

enters on the left. You are now at **Neville's Cross** ⑥. Face to your right. In 1918 another railway line branched off the main line 300 metres to your right rear, passed through your location and headed diagonally to your left front along an embankment before entering a cutting on the far slope to pass by the left of Ramicourt. No trace of the embankment remains.

Advancing towards you on the flank of the attack, the 2nd Pioneers were 400 metres to your front when the German machine-guns along the embankment opened up. The pioneers flattened themselves into the crops that covered the fields then as they do now. Lieutenant Wilkinson saw what had happened from the cutting at the far end of the embankment. He told his two machine-gun crews to set up there. Each fired two 250-round belts into the Germans, killing or wounding 80 of the

Looking from the quarries at the start of the 21st Battalion's advance. The photograph was taken on the misty morning of a fine day, replicating exactly the conditions under which the advance was made.

100 on the embankment. The rest fled, leaving 14 machine-guns. One who was captured said they were sick of the war and would not have fought at all had they known Australians were attacking. Wilkinson went undecorated, even though Charles Bean called his action 'outstanding even in the history of the AIF's machine-gunners'. The pioneers could now establish posts along the embankment and the high ground to your left rear.

Return to the main railway, head left and stop after 200 metres at the **T-junction** 7 between the remains of an old quarry on the right and a newer one on the left. The dregs of a smaller quarry are on the far side of Rue de La Haut on your right. Look across Rue de La Haut towards Ramicourt. Machine-guns in the two old quarries engaged the 21st Battalion as it attacked from Ramicourt towards you. Covered by its Lewis-gunners, the 21st advanced by rushes. As it drew close, the Germans surrendered. Eight machine-guns were captured. At this stage the 2nd Pioneers were moving across the low ground to your left front.

Now head right on Rue de La Haut and swing left at the Y-junction on the outskirts of Montbrehain onto the D713, which will take you back to Ramicourt. Return to Péronne by following in reverse your route to Ramicourt.

LOCAL INFORMATION

The grave of Captain Harry Fletcher, Calvaire Cemetery.

CEMETERIES

As with the Hindenburg Line fallen, many of the dead from the Montbrehain attack lie in cemeteries some distance from the battlefield. Captain Mahony rests at VII.A.20 in **Tincourt New British Cemetery**. Private Joseph Baxter of the 21st Battalion is at Tincourt in X.C.19. An ex-British regular, Baxter had served in Egypt between 1882 and 1885 and won the DCM in the Boer War before enlisting in the AIF aged 54 in 1917.

Calvaire Cemetery

On Rue de Cimetière in Montbrehain and visited during the walk, this cemetery contains 71 burials, of which 55 are known. Of the 48 Australians, 37 fell in the capture of the village. They include Captain Fletcher and Private Blankenburg MM at A.11 and A.10 respectively. Seven of the Australians are unidentified.

High Tree Cemetery

Even more rarely visited than Montbrehain, this cemetery is more or less on the site of Doon Mill and can be reached by continuing on the D705 past the stop on the walk and taking the track on the left that runs by L'Arbre Haut Farm. Of the four Australians among the 48 burials, only two, Privates Charles Bateman and Joseph Taylor, at A.45 and A.1 respectively, are identified. They belonged to the 2nd Pioneers and were killed during the battle. These four graves can be said to mark the furthest point reached by the AIF on the old Western Front. If you do come to Montbrehain, please go to the cemetery. It is not out of your way.

CHAPTER 26

1918

THE NEW ZEALANDERS AT BAPAUME

When the Amiens offensive launched by the Fourth Army astride the Somme on 8 August 1918 ran out of steam, the Third Army took over the main advance. What followed in the last days of August became known as the Battle of Albert. In fact, Albert was taken by III Corps from the Fourth Army, which secured the right flank of the Third. For New Zealanders, though, the last part of August has always been the period of the Battle of Bapaume. The town was the Third Army's main goal. Advancing in the centre of the Third Army was IV Corps. As the New Zealand Division formed the centre of IV Corps, it was at the heart of the Third Army and, therefore, at the heart of the Battle of Bapaume.

The battle was significant for the New Zealanders in several ways. During its course, they received air-dropped supplies and were counterattacked by tanks for the first time. Three of them won VCs, the most for any battle in the nation's history. Involving failed and successful attacks in equal measure, it was their toughest action of 1918 and resulted in 3000 casualties, including 821 dead. Many of these were from the large pool of reinforcements that replaced the losses incurred during the defensive fighting. The veterans started to show the war-weariness that was gripping the Australian divisions. Not for nothing do New Zealanders call the battle 'Bloody Bapaume'.

Preliminaries

As most of the German reserves were facing the Fourth Army in front of Amiens, striking towards Bapaume, 30 kilometres north, promised to catch the Germans off balance. The Third Army might then outflank the Germans opposite the Fourth. Field Marshal Haig wanted Bapaume seized rapidly. Between 21 and 23 August the Fourth Army took Albert and the Third reached the Arras–Albert railway, bringing Bapaume within striking distance. Running from Loupart Wood through Grévillers to Biefvillers-lès-Bapaume, the last ridge to the west of the town had to fall first. Grévillers and the wood were well defended and the 5th Division, on the left of the New Zealand Division, could not capture them on 23 August. The task passed to the New Zealanders, whose role so far had been limited to gaining the line of the Ancre north of Miraumont. On 24 August the 1st New Zealand Brigade was to advance 450 metres past both Grévillers and Loupart Wood, after which the 2nd Brigade would take Bapaume. The 37th Division on the left would capture Biefvillers.

Following up the German withdrawal to the Hindenburg Line early in 1917, the Australians had passed through this area. When the Germans returned in the *Michael* offensive in March 1918, they fortified the ruins of the villages they had devastated during their earlier retirement. From the New Zealanders' point of view, the ground offered good going to tanks as it lay just beyond the 1916 Somme battlefield and was not cut up by shelling. Thirteen heavy tanks and some Whippets supported them. But the uncertainty as to the situation on the evening of 23 August resulted in rushed planning that left no time to organise an artillery barrage. The attack would be a 'silent' one, which initially helped the New Zealanders when they stepped off at 4.15 am next morning. With the darkness and rain blinding the Germans, the absence of a barrage removed their last hope of detecting the assault until it was almost upon them.

The Germans still defended strongly. 1st Wellington took until 12.30 pm to clear Loupart Wood. On their left, 2nd Auckland had enveloped Grévillers by 9 am but could not get beyond it. Engineer Sergeant Sam Forsyth led an assault that took a strongpoint holding up part of the attack. Killed afterwards, he was awarded a posthumous VC. Further left, 2nd Otago and 2nd Canterbury from the 2nd Brigade cleared Biefvillers by mid-morning, thereby securing the 1st Brigade's left flank. The 37th Division, which should have taken the village, had fallen behind. Heading towards the D929, the Albert–Bapaume road, part of 2nd Otago was stopped just beyond Grévillers. The rest continued with 2nd Canterbury towards Bapaume, 1.5 kilometres away on the far side of the D929. Avesnes-lès-Bapaume, then a hamlet west of the town, now an outlying suburb, was taken but could not be held.

New Zealanders advancing towards Bapaume.

'One of the toughest nuts to crack'

Since the start of the Third Army's offensive four days earlier, nine German divisions had reinforced the eight originally opposing it. The Germans ahead of the Third Army thus regained their balance and, as the tough fighting on 24 August showed, were putting up the same stiff resistance that had slowed down the Fourth Army. It was particularly strong in front of Bapaume, which did not bode well for the New Zealanders. In the continuation of the advance on 25 August, in which IV Corps was to reach the line Riencourt–Beugnâtre three kilometres beyond Bapaume, they had to envelop the town, thereby forcing the Germans to abandon it. Costly street fighting through its ruins would then be avoided.

At 5 am on the 25th, 1st Auckland and 2nd Wellington from the 1st Brigade headed for the southern side of Bapaume. Hit by heavy fire, they stalled on the D929. Supported by a creeping barrage and 23 tanks, whereas the 1st Brigade had neither, the 2nd Brigade made for the northern side of Bapaume. 1st Canterbury on the right briefly took Avesnes and reached the D917, the Arras road. 1st Otago on the left was halted on the D917. But both battalions got across the road in capturing Monument Wood and part of Favreuil, 1.5 kilometres north of Bapaume, in a second attack at 6.30 pm. Nonetheless, the town's well-sited and concealed defences had withstood the New Zealanders a second time. As one of them remarked, it was turning out to be 'one of the toughest nuts to crack'.

The First Army joined the offensive on the left of the Third on 26 August but it made no difference to the New Zealand Division, which was to advance a third time against Bapaume. South of the town, the 1st Brigade barely progressed beyond the previous day's line. The only bright spot was the knocking out of three machine-guns by Sergeant Reg Judson of 1st Auckland. He won the VC. North of Bapaume, the Rifle Brigade, which had relieved the 2nd Brigade, reached the D956, the Bapaume–Beugnâtre road, a gain of just 450 metres. Pinpointing the cause of the grinding pace of the advance, a New Zealand artillery observer expressed sentiments that the Australians would have echoed: 'We share great admiration for the way the machine-gunners of the enemy stick to their work. Most died at their post'.

Another attack that evening achieved little but at least the Rifle Brigade was now firmly ensconced east of Bapaume, threatening the Germans with envelopment. A continuous bombardment commenced to give them every

Sergeant Reg Judson VC, DCM, MM

The ruins of Bapaume, overlooked by a camouflaged German observation post.

incentive to withdraw. But on 27 August they belted two attacks by the 63rd Division on Ligny-Thilloy, on the right of the New Zealanders, who stood fast that day and the next. The New Zealanders' patrols still attracted intense German machine-gun fire. An attack on Bapaume was being planned when the fire petered out early on 29 August. Cautiously entering after dawn, New Zealand patrols found the Germans had gone and the town 'nothing but a few acres of bricks', according to Private Stayte of 1st Auckland. It was booby-trapped just as extensively as it had been when the Australians entered in 1917.

Following up

During the day, the Rifle Brigade established a new line 1.4 kilometres beyond Bapaume and Beugnâtre. At last able to move around the southern side of the town, the 1st Brigade took the heavily defended sugar factory on the Cambrai road to the right of the Rifles. Both brigades started the 2.2-kilometre

advance to the ridge behind the villages of Bancourt and Frémicourt at 5 am on 30 August. They reached the crest but could not hold it. A German counterattack with tanks next morning was driven off. Forming the centre of a wider attack on 1 September, the two brigades took all but the Bancourt part of the ridge. Sergeant John Grant was awarded the VC for clearing machine-guns that held up 1st Wellingtons. Relieving the 1st Brigade and the Rifles that night, the 2nd Brigade secured the uncaptured section of the ridge on 2 September.

'Bloody Bapaume' was over. Throughout the battle, the New Zealand Division had fought with one, and sometimes two, open flanks because it consistently outpaced the divisions of IV Corps on either side. Major-General Russell, the divisional commander, seemed out of touch, probably because he was tired and quite ill. Partly for this reason, orders often arrived at the last minute. Like the Australians, the New Zealanders had the skill and experience to know what to do

A fortnight after its capture, Bapaume is a hive of activity. The troops are New Zealanders.

Desolation. New Zealanders head out of Frémicourt on 2 September 1918.

anyway. Their effort at Bapaume deserves more recognition but, ironically, some of the blame for its obscurity rests with them. The New Zealand press misrepresented Bapaume as a pushover that cost few casualties. So no-one gave it a second thought, especially since it coincided with the stunning Australian capture of Mont St Quentin, which stole the limelight from everything else.

DRIVING THE BATTLEFIELD

Remember throughout this drive that after the initial attempt failed, attacking Bapaume directly was the option of last resort. Enveloping the town was the preferred tactic and it worked, though taking longer and involving heavier fighting than anticipated. The drive therefore passes either side of Bapaume, and mainly the northern side, where the envelopment progressed furthest, but does not enter the town itself. Progress has intruded heavily onto the battlefield. A busy ring road encircles most of Bapaume and the town's expansion has absorbed Avesnes. The TGV railway and the A1 autoroute split the eastern side of Bapaume, where the envelopment ended, from the follow-up objectives of Frémicourt and Bancourt. It may be small consolation but the ground appears today pretty much as it did in 1918.

MAPS IGN Blue Series, 1:25 000, 24070 Acheux-en-Amiénois; 2407E Bapaume; 25070 Croisilles

Leave Albert on the D929, continue through Pozières and turn left onto the D74 in Le Sars. Once in Pys, go straight ahead instead of veering left on the D74 and follow the road as it swings right to Irles. Turn right there onto the D163.

GRÉVILLERS

After 2.6 kilometres, turn left immediately past the **two trees** on the right. Park 550 metres along near the barn by the five-way intersection known as **Starfish Crossroads ❶**, in front of which is a memorial to Private Chris Cox VC, a stretcher-bearer in the 7th Bedfordshires. With the barn on your left, look along the road. Moving between **Achiet-le-Petit**, two kilometres to your left front, and **Achiet-le-Grand**, 1.5 kilometres to your front, the 1st Brigade assembled in the area ahead of you in the early hours of 24 August. Now turn about and walk back along the road until you can clearly see **Loupart Wood** to your front and **Grévillers** to your left front. Held by the 5th Division, the British front line ran midway between your location and the wood to Irles, through which you have just driven, on your right. Forming up on your left, 2nd Auckland started for Grévillers, visible on the skyline in the greying dawn, at 4.15 am, precisely on time but alone. 1st Wellington was late. Stretching to your right, it did not set off for Loupart Wood until 5 am. 2nd Wellington moved in support behind the two battalions.

The rushed preparations meant that most men knew only that they had to go

2ND AUCKLAND

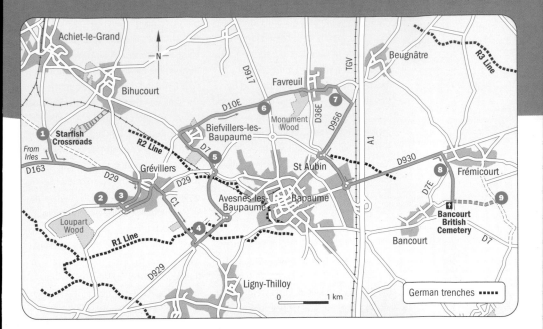

forward. They would be also be attacking without a preliminary barrage for the first time. It was hoped that the 1st Brigade might carry on to **Bapaume**, which can just be seen beyond Grévillers. The most likely outcome, though, was that the 2nd Brigade, which had assembled behind the 1st, would have to pass through it and sweep through the town. In the event, Bapaume held out for another week, showing that the planning was optimistic as well as hasty. Return to the D163 and turn left, whereupon the D163 becomes the D29. Taking the first right on reaching Grévillers, continue 500 metres to the T-junction, head right and then almost immediately left, and pull over after 500 metres ②.

Starting with the Loupart Wood and Grévillers attacks, the route reaches the D929 in the area where the 1st Brigade stalled on the southern side of Bapaume. After following the step-by-step advance of the 2nd Brigade and the Rifle Brigade around the northern side of the town, it carries on to the Frémicourt-Bancourt Ridge. The three VC actions are also covered.
DISTANCE COVERED: **19 km**
DURATION: **3 hours**

With Loupart Wood on your left, look across the road as the Germans did. As the dawn was behind them, they could not see 2nd Auckland approach. The Aucklanders captured two field-guns and several machine-guns in the low

LOUPART WOOD

1ST WELLINGTON

ground to your front. Platoons from the leading company then passed around the far side of Grévillers and the near side to your right, while another company moved through the village. Alerted by this attack, the Germans in Loupart Wood saw 1st Wellingtons' delayed advance to your left front. The wood was infested with machine-guns and the trees were too closely set for the supporting tanks to enter. They could do little during the fight through. No sooner had the Wellingtons knocked out three machine-guns along the front of the wood than they were cut up by another line just inside it. A company from 2nd Wellingtons had to be committed before the wood was cleared. Posts were then set up along the side closest to you and along the end to your left rear.

Head back along the road, stop at the **right-angled bend** ❸ and stand with the copse behind you and the D29 to your right front. When the Aucklanders assaulting this side of Grévillers neared your location, they were pinned down by a machine-gun 30 metres to your left rear in the area of the copse. 'It was impossible to raise a head while the Huns continued to rattle through belt after belt at such a furious pace', Sergeant Ormond

Burton recalled. 'There was nothing to be done but lie still and wait for better times.' Sergeant Forsyth, a Gallipoli veteran, ran through the fire to a tank in the field to your front and guided it towards the gun. The tank was destroyed. Wounded himself, Forsyth led the surviving crew and some Aucklanders in an outflanking move that forced the German gunners to withdraw. Continue 100 metres to the T-junction in the cutting. Forsyth was sniped while organising the defence of the high ground to your right front. Now head left into Grévillers. It fell easily as the Germans were caught napping. Some having breakfast were among the 400 prisoners taken by the New Zealand Division on 24 August.

Drive to the T-junction at the far end of Grévillers and turn right onto the D29 (here Rue de General Frère). When the D29 turns sharp left, go straight ahead on the C1, swinging right at the Y-junction by the cemetery for **Ligny-Thilloy**. At the end of the 24 August attack, 2nd Auckland's line crossed the road on the crest ahead and ran to your right to link up with the Wellingtons at Loupart Wood. The right of 2nd Otago, having come around Grévillers next to the Aucklanders, was pinned down on the crest to your left. On passing the pine

Sergeant Forsyth's advance on the outskirts of Grévillers. The German machine-gun was firing behind the position from which the photograph was taken.

copse on the right, park just short of the D929 on the **track** ④ on the left and look back along the C1. In order to add depth to their positions at Loupart Wood and Grévillers, the Germans also held **R1**, one of the lines they had dug to defend Bapaume during the 1916 Somme offensive. It crossed the D929 on the crest over your right shoulder, passed over the C1 ahead of you and then ran in front of the pine copse before curving leftwards around Loupart Wood. Fire from it over the bare ground to your front and right front had driven back 2nd Otago.

Covered by the morning mist as it advanced towards you from Grévillers on 25 August, the 1st Brigade was able to approach R1 before the German machine-gunners began sweeping the area across your front. 1st Auckland on the right of the C1 took a small stretch of R1 ahead of you, while 2nd Wellington got to the D929 to your left rear. Both battalions were supporting the 63rd Division's advance on **Ligny-Thilloy**, one kilometre behind you. But the 63rd was held up, exposing the Wellingtons' right flank when the mist thinned. The Aucklanders' left could then be seen from Bapaume, 1.5 kilometres along the D929 to your right. Further progress was impossible.

Now face the D929. During the unsuccessful attempt to advance on 26 August, Sergeant Judson's company from 1st Auckland was held up by a section of R1 to your left front that the Germans still held. Managing to crawl into part of the trench, Judson and a few men captured one machine-gun and attacked two more. When the Germans crewing the other two guns withdrew towards the D929, Judson ran along the parapet to cut them off. Getting to the D929 first, he pointed his rifle at the 12 Germans and ordered them to surrender. They fired at him but missed. Judson bombed them and jumped into the trench, bayoneting two of the survivors. His VC capped a stellar month of fighting. Since 25 July he had also won the DCM and MM. The 1st Brigade was only able to get over the D929 and pass around the near side of Bapaume when the Germans left the town on 29 August.

Passing a large bunker on your left, continue to the D929, turn left onto it and left again at the roundabout onto the Bapaume ring road. As you follow the ring road, the developed area on your right is **Avesnes-lès-Bapaume**. At the next roundabout, just over the railway, take the D7 and as it starts curving leftwards, park at the small **loop road** ⑤ on the right. With your back to the roundabout, look along the D7. **Biefvillers-lès-Bapaume** is on the ridge ahead, which continues leftwards to Loupart Wood, while the D917 (the Arras road), runs along the high ground to your right and right front. **Monument Wood** can be seen on the skyline on the far side of the D917.

Sergeant Judson's solo attack on R1.

The railway on your left was the boundary between the New Zealand and the 37th Divisions on 24 August. As the 37th Division was to advance on the right of the track, Biefvillers lay in its sector. But the 37th was held up well beyond the village, leaving the Germans in it free to enfilade 2nd Auckland as they passed on the left of the railway. Tanks silenced some of the machine-gunners, allowing a company from 2nd Wellington to go around the far side of Biefvillers. Helped by 2nd Otago and 2nd Canterbury and their tanks, which arrived in the meantime, it cleared the village by 10 am. Continuing down the slope towards you, the Otagos and Cantabrians were hammered by the German artillery, which knocked out four tanks, and by machine-guns on the D929 to your rear and left rear. 2nd Otago's right stalled on the high ground on the left of Grévillers, to your left. Together with 2nd Canterbury, the remaining Otagos fought through your location to Avesnes behind you, forming a deep salient on which the Germans inevitably concentrated their fire. Lieutenant-Colonel William Pennycook, the Otagos' commanding officer, was killed. Unable to resist a strong counterattack from Bapaume at 1 pm, the survivors withdrew to a line around Biefvillers.

Advancing from the village towards you in the 25 August attack, 1st Canterbury was aided by the mist, which blinded the German machine-gunners, just as it had in the 1st Brigade's concurrent assault on the far side of Grévillers. The Cantabrians recaptured Avesnes but were caught on the D917, on the outskirts of Bapaume to your right rear, when the mist began to lift at 7 am. Having taken 150 prisoners, they could not get beyond the road. Now drive to Biefvillers, turn right onto the D10E and park by the **memorial** 6 at the D917 crossroads. Often mentioned in contemporary accounts of the 1918 action, it commemorates the battle fought at Bapaume in 1870, during the Franco-Prussian War. Look back along the D10E at Biefvillers, from which 1st Otago attacked towards you on the left of 1st Canterbury. The mist cleared when the Otagos reached your location and they were raked from Monument Wood, 600 metres to your left rear, though in 1918 it extended almost to the D917. The supporting tanks were knocked out between the road and the wood. With the tanks gone, and unable to rely on the barrage, which had crept a long way ahead, the Otagos stayed on the D917. They had also captured 150 Germans, as well as 18 machine-guns.

Continue on the D10E past Monument Wood and through **Favreuil** to **Favreuil British Cemetery** 7. Walk to the rear of the cemetery and stand with Favreuil to your right. Running from the village and along the shallow re-entrant below Monument Wood, the D36E extends past your right front to **St Aubin**. The steeple of its church rises ahead of you on the far side of the ring road. At 6.30 pm on 25 August a New Zealand barrage fortuitously crashed down on the Germans forming up on the D36E to counterattack the 2nd Brigade on the D917 beyond Monument Wood. This barrage was the prelude to another attack by the 2nd Brigade, which the Germans, now having lost heavily, were unable to resist. 1st Otago careered through Monument Wood, whereupon 2nd Canterbury leapfrogged them during a thunderstorm and dug in along the D36E between Favreuil and the ring road. Over 400 prisoners were taken, along with 40 machine-guns and a field-gun. The 37th Division took the far end of Favreuil. New Zealand patrols pushing out afterwards towards St Aubin met stiff resistance. So did those making for the D956, which passes 200 metres to your left on its way from **Beugnâtre**, over your left shoulder beyond the TGV railway and A1 autoroute, to Bapaume.

Starting from the D956, the Rifle Brigade was to advance 1.4 kilometres

RING ROAD

GRÉVILLERS

BIEFVILLERS

1ST CANTERBURY

1ST OTAGO

D10E

The 25 August attack from
Biefvillers as seen from the
memorial on the D917.

down the left side of Bapaume on
26 August but it had to spend the early
hours fighting its way across your front
from the D36E just to reach the D956.
Enfiladed from Beugnâtre, which the
5th Division should have captured, at one
end and from St Aubin and Bapaume at
the other, and without tank or artillery
support, most of the Rifles could not
move past the D956 when they attacked
at 6.30 am. It was 'four feet deep and
gave us good cover if we kept down',
wrote Rifleman Les Ross of 2nd Rifles in
the centre. 3rd Rifles on the right reached
the outskirts of St Aubin and got a little
beyond the D956 on the far side of the
hamlet. 4th Rifles to your left halted a
midday counterattack from Beugnâtre
near the A1 but lost heavily itself. A
barrage supported a second attack at
6 pm. 4th Rifles advanced 500 metres
beyond the D956 to your left front and
2nd Rifles took St Aubin. These marginal
gains marked the limit of the New
Zealand advance until the Germans
abandoned Bapaume on 29 August.

Carry on along the D10E to the
T-junction with the D956, turn right and
then left onto the ring road at the
roundabout, from which St Aubin is
directly to your front. Following the signs
to **Cambrai**, head left again onto the
D930 at the roundabout in the industrial
estate. The Rifle Brigade had been trying

to reach this road in its curving advance
from the D956 to your left rear. With the
Germans gone, the 1st Brigade swung
around Bapaume from your right. The
sugar factory strongpoint they took
covered the roundabout area. Continue
over the A1 and turn right just short of
Frémicourt, noting the ridge that
stretches behind the village. Park at the
Y-junction 8 300 metres along and
stand with Frémicourt, which the 15th
Australian Brigade had taken in the
advance to the Hindenburg Line in
March 1917, at your back.

In the 30 August attack, 1st Rifles
attacked towards you astride the D930.
A Company passed to your left with little
difficulty, D Company took a large
strongpoint on the D930 to your right
and then ground its way around the other
side of Frémicourt with the help of a tank.
Passing through your location, C Company
cleared the village while the other two
companies carried on to the crest of the
ridge. Over 400 Germans were captured.
Advancing to your left past the near
side of Bancourt with two tanks, 1st
Wellington reached the ridge but were
unable to remain on it because their right
flank, which 2nd Auckland should have
secured, was lashed by unrelenting
enfilade fire. The Wellingtons pulled back
to the low spur that runs to the left of
the road on which you are standing.

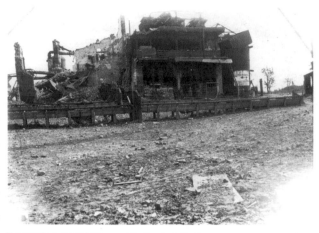
The wrecked sugar factory on the Cambrai Road.

Attacking **Bancourt** to your left front, 2nd Auckland had to wait until the 42nd Division was ready to assault Riencourt, well beyond the far side of the village. It was broad daylight and the Germans were fully alert when the Aucklanders finally got going at 6 am, an hour late. They took Bancourt and clawed their way up the ridge to your left rear against dreadful machine-gun fire. The 42nd Division stalled at Riencourt, leaving the Aucklanders' right flank undefended. Anti-tank guns and mortars now began pounding the Aucklanders. Falling back towards Bancourt, they linked up with the Wellingtons near **Bancourt British Cemetery**, 700 metres along the road to your left.

Turn about. 1st Rifles on the ridge ahead of you were now isolated and unsupported on either flank. Counterattacked at 12.50 pm they withdrew to a trench midway between the crest and Frémicourt. The German counterattack at 4.30 am next morning

The attacks 25–26 August at Favreuil.

stretched across the ridge to your front but the three or four tanks supporting it headed for the village. Pummelled by the New Zealand artillery, they did not try to enter. Going back over the ridge, they were mistaken for British tanks and engaged by German anti-tank guns. Two foundered. The New Zealanders quickly regained the 200 metres of ground they had given up. In the 1 September attack, which started at 4.55 am, 1st Rifles had taken the crest ahead of you by 5.30 am and 1st Wellingtons reached it to your right front. The 2nd Brigade had to attack three times on 2 September before taking the stretch, further right, which looks back towards Bancourt.

You will have to do some walking to see the area of Sergeant Grant's VC action on 1 September. After parking at Bancourt British Cemetery, take the track that runs past the left of the communal cemetery opposite and stop after 900 metres on the **cross-track ❾**. Stand with Frémicourt on your right. Five machine-guns in this locality were firing on 1st Wellingtons as they advanced towards you. They were finally forced to ground 20 metres from the guns. Grant and a mate rushed one of the guns and then Grant single-handedly silenced two more. The resistance fizzled out.

Walk back to the cemetery. To return to Albert, head left on the D930 at Frémicourt and follow the signs after turning right on reaching the Bapaume ring road. To follow the New Zealand Division's advance to the Hindenburg Line and beyond, continue straight ahead on leaving the cemetery and turn left on reaching the D7.

ST AUBIN

3RD RIFLES 26 AUG

2ND RIFLES 26 AUG

LOCAL INFORMATION

CEMETERIES

Bancourt British Cemetery

Begun by the New Zealanders after the battle, this cemetery was greatly expanded by the postwar concentration in it of battlefield graves and graves brought in from smaller cemeteries nearby. Of its 2480 burials, 1018 are known. Many of the 178 New Zealanders fell in the immediate aftermath of Bapaume's capture, such as 2nd Lieutenants Arthur Abel at I.B.23, Gerald Hall at III.B.3, Joseph McCreanor at I.B.9 and James Taylor at I.B.4. All were 2nd Aucklanders killed in the fighting around Bancourt. Most of the 250 Australians died in the advance to the Hindenburg Line early in 1917. The cemetery is located between Frémicourt and Bancourt and visited on the drive.

Favreuil British Cemetery

Also visited on the drive, this cemetery is just outside Favreuil on the D10E. It opened in April 1917 and was used almost continuously until war's end except when the Germans occupied Favreuil between March and August 1918. Becoming a concentration cemetery after the Armistice, it now contains 409 burials, of which all but 10 are identified. The 19 New Zealanders fell in the Bapaume fighting, many in the cemetery environs. Most of the 26 Australians were killed at Bullecourt.

The New Zealand Memorial to the Missing, Grévillers British Cemetery

Grévillers British Cemetery

Started by the 3rd Australian Casualty Clearing Station and two British clearing stations in April 1917, this cemetery was used for concentration purposes postwar. Of its 2122 burials, 1941 are identified. The 153 New Zealanders died in 1918 in the defensive actions around Hamel, Auchonvillers, Hébuterne and Rossignol Wood, and in the capture of Bapaume. They include Lieutenant-Colonel Pennycook of 2nd Otago at VII.AA.3. Most of the 428 Australians fell in 1917 during the advance to the Hindenburg Line and the two Bullecourt battles. At the back of the cemetery, the **New Zealand Memorial to the Missing** commemorates almost 450 New Zealanders killed in the area between March 1918 and the armistice but who have no known grave. Signposted at the D29 exit from the D929 Bapaume ring road, the cemetery is on the right of the D29 650 metres along.

MONUMENT WOOD

D36E

2ND CANTERBURY LINE 25 AUG

CHAPTER 27

1918

THE NEW ZEALAND ADVANCE

While the New Zealanders were attacking at Frémicourt and Bancourt on 2 September, the rest of IV Corps and, indeed, the Third Army as a whole, made good progress. But it was overshadowed by the dramatic news that the Canadian Corps, advancing with the First Army on the left of the Third, had broken the strong Drocourt–Quéant Switch Line. On the right of the Third, the Australian Corps had seized Mont St Quentin, in the Fourth Army's sector, the previous day. Having now lost two of the key bastions on the line that they intended to hold during the winter, the Germans decided on a staged withdrawal of up to 25 kilometres to the Hindenburg Line. On 3 September the New Zealanders discovered that the Germans ahead of them had gone.

Tactics

In the advance that followed, the New Zealand Division moved on a single brigade frontage, which could stretch across three kilometres as the leading brigade usually had three of its four battalions forward. It also had a field artillery brigade attached, resulting in a brigade group. The artillery batteries remained just behind the battalions so that the machine-gun posts on which the Germans based their rearguards could be shelled as soon as they were encountered. Wherever possible, attacks were launched two hours before dawn so that the Germans would have to counterattack in daylight. Having the guns well up enabled the counterattacks to be dealt with instantly. In order to maintain momentum, the brigade

groups leapfrogged through each other. These tactics were much the same as those adopted by the Australian divisions towards the end of August, when Monash allocated each of them a 'corridor' along which it was led by a brigade acting as an advance guard.

Onwards

In the week after 2 September, the 2nd New Zealand Brigade brushed the German rearguards aside during a 13-kilometre advance astride the D7 that ended before Trescault Spur. Extending south from Trescault village past Havrincourt Wood to Gouzeaucourt Wood, it had been captured by the Germans during their *Michael* offensive in March 1918. As the high ground of the spur made a good defensive position

Private James Crichton VC.

and was just five kilometres from the Hindenburg Line, they held in strength the old British trenches, African and Snap, running along it. After relieving the 2nd Brigade, the Rifle Brigade captured Gouzeaucourt Wood while supporting the left of an attack by V Corps south of the spur on 9 September. In the Battle of Havrincourt three days later, the Rifles attacked the spur on the right of VI Corps. They gained the crest but failed to take Snap Trench on the far side, although

Sergeant Harry Laurent of 2nd Rifles led a patrol that surged ahead and nabbed a German company. He was awarded the VC. The Rifle Brigade took 490 prisoners altogether.

On 14 September the New Zealand Division left the line. It returned a fortnight later for the attack on the Hindenburg Line, which was nowhere near as well fortified here as it was above the St Quentin Canal tunnel in front of the Australian Corps further south.

Passing over Welsh Ridge, the New Zealanders were to reach the Cambrai road on Bonavis Ridge two kilometres further on. The Hindenburg Line straddled both ridges. Starting at 3.30 am on 29 September, the 1st and 2nd Brigades swept up Welsh Ridge, which fell easily. After another effortless assault, the 1st Brigade on the left was on the Cambrai road by 8 am. The 2nd Brigade on the right had a hard fight and did not arrive until 1 pm. Both brigades between them took over 1000 prisoners for the loss of 200 men. They now looked down on the St Quentin Canal, and the Scheldt (L'Escaut in French) River alongside it, between Vaucelles and Crèvecoeur. That night the Germans withdrew to the far bank.

Advancing to the canal at 5.45 am on 30 September, 1st Canterbury from the 2nd Brigade found the Vaucelles crossing untenable. 2nd Auckland from the 1st Brigade was also unable to cross on its left. One company of Aucklanders, though, reached the small island between the canal and river at Crèvecoeur, and a platoon from it crossed the river to reach the edge of the village. Both were pinned down. Private James Crichton was awarded the VC for relaying messages under heavy fire between the platoon and the company and for defusing the demolition charges that the Germans had rigged on the bridge over the river. Swinging over the canal further north, 1st Auckland and 2nd Wellington took Crèvecoeur during a bitter action next day. 1st Auckland suffered almost half of the 1st Brigade's 500 casualties.

Along with the rest of IV Corps, the New Zealand Division remained in place until the Germans abandoned the canal line altogether on 5 October after it had been outflanked by the Fourth Army's advance further south. They withdrew to the Beaurevoir–Masnières Line, the northern end of which crossed IV Corps' sector. IV Corps attacked it on 8 October at the start of the Third Army's advance in the Battle of Cambrai. In the New Zealand Division, the 2nd Brigade and the Rifle Brigade breezed through the line and had taken 1400 prisoners, double their own losses, when their advance ended 4.5 kilometres later near Esnes. They were ahead of the British on either flank, which was fortuitous when the Germans, counterattacking using captured British tanks, struck the 2nd Division on the left of the Rifles. Catching the attack in enfilade, the Rifles and some tanks shattered it.

As the advance was now passing through the German back area, there were no organised defensive lines ahead of it and the pace stepped up. Covering 3.5 kilometres virtually unopposed, the New Zealanders reached the Cambrai–Caudry railway on 9 October. With the 37th Division alongside, they pushed on another 15 kilometres without difficulty to cross the Selle River at Briastre early on 11 October. After 1st Wellington cleared the Germans overlooking the river from the D955, the Solesmes road, on the slopes of Belle Vue on 12 October, the New Zealand Division left the line. Since breaking through the Beaurevoir–Masnières Line five days earlier, it had taken over 1400 prisoners and captured 13 field-guns for the loss of 536 men.

DRIVING THE BATTLEFIELD

Whereas a large part of the Australian advance to victory followed the line of the Somme, the New Zealanders faced a series of ridges that ran north–south across their path. This has its benefits as regards vantage points, although occasionally one ridge blocks the view from another. Two autoroutes, the A2 and the A26, cross the battlefield. Cutting right through the axis of the New Zealanders' assault on the Hindenburg Line, the A26 is the more intrusive. Once beyond it, though, you are in the L'Escaut Valley and the scenery is spectacular. Be aware that the drive ends at Esnes, rather than at the Selle 18.5 kilometres further on. The road network makes this last stretch of the advance frustratingly difficult to follow on the one hand and the advance itself was relatively uneventful on the other.

MAPS IGN Blue Series, 1:25000, 25070 Croisilles, 2507E Cambrai, 2607E Le Cateau-Cambrésis

Leave Albert on the D929. Once in Bapaume, turn right at the T-junction onto the D917. Go through the town square and head left after 850 metres onto the D7 (Route de Bancourt).

Continue through or past **Haplincourt**, **Bertincourt** and **Ruyaulcourt**. The New Zealand Division captured these villages in its advance astride the D7 from Bancourt after 2 September. On reaching **Metz-en-Couturé**, turn left onto the D17 and then right after 400 metres at the chapel. Park 700 metres along on the track on the right just before the cutting ❶ and stand with the southern end of **Havrincourt Wood**, in which the British tanks were hidden before the Cambrai attack on 20 November 1917, on your left.

The New Zealanders took this part of the wood, as well as Metz-en-Couturé, on 6 September. Stretching along the far side of the **Grand Valley** to your front is the **Trescault Spur**, across which the old British trenches ran. Emerging from the rear of **Gouzeaucourt Wood**, on the facing slope to your right front, at **Dead Man's Corner**, **African Support** joined **Snap Support** just behind the crest ahead of you. Snap Support continued along the facing slope to your left past Havrincourt Wood. Having withdrawn ahead of the New Zealanders, the Germans now occupied these two

GRAND VALLEY

TRESCAULT SPUR

3RD RIFLES 9 SEP, 1ST RIFLES 12 SEP

The Rifle Brigade's attacks on Trescault Spur.

trenches, which had formed the British support line, as their front line. **Snap** and **African Trenches**, which paralleled them on the far side of the crest and had been the British front line, formed the German support line. As these trenches comprised an outwork of the Hindenburg Line further back, they were strongly held.

At 4.30 am on 9 September, 2nd and 3rd Rifles attacked from the near edge of Gouzeaucourt Wood in order to secure the left flank of the 17th Division's advance on the far side of the D7. The German machine-gunners facing the New Zealanders fired too high in the early-morning darkness. Assaulting to your right astride the D7, the right of 2nd Rifles seized that end of the wood and African Support behind it, which it mistook for its intended objective, African Trench. So the darkness affected both sides alike. Counterattacks came throughout the day but were warded off. The left of the 2nd cleared the wood to your right front in heavy fighting while under fire from the Dead Man's Corner strongpoint. That fire prevented 3rd Rifles from establishing a line running from the strongpoint, across the spur to your front, to the corner of Havrincourt Wood on your left. On 12 September 1st Rifles attacked to your front and 4th Rifles from Havrincourt Wood in heavy rain. Only the left flank of the 4th was able to get past Snap Support.

Return through Metz-en-Couturé to the D7 and head left. After crossing the Grand Valley just past **Metz-en-Couturé Communal Cemetery British Extension** and going through Gouzeaucourt Wood, turn left again at the sunken crossroads, the site of **Queen's Cross Redoubt** in 1918. Park at the dumping area 300 metres along ② and stand with the crossroads on your right. You are now just short of the crest of Trescault Spur. Queen's Cross, the wood behind you and African Support, which passed 150 metres to your front and then skirted the wood on its way to Dead Man's Corner 700 metres to your left, all fell to 2nd Rifles on 9 September. Bombing along African Support, a party under Corporal Franklin Fruin reached Dead Man's but was driven back down the trench to the edge of the wood on your left. The strongpoint was taken next

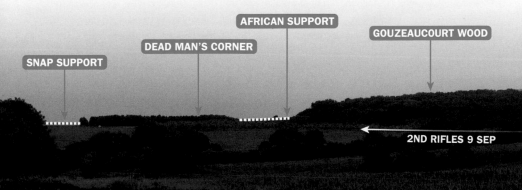

SNAP SUPPORT   DEAD MAN'S CORNER   AFRICAN SUPPORT   GOUZEAUCOURT WOOD

2ND RIFLES 9 SEP

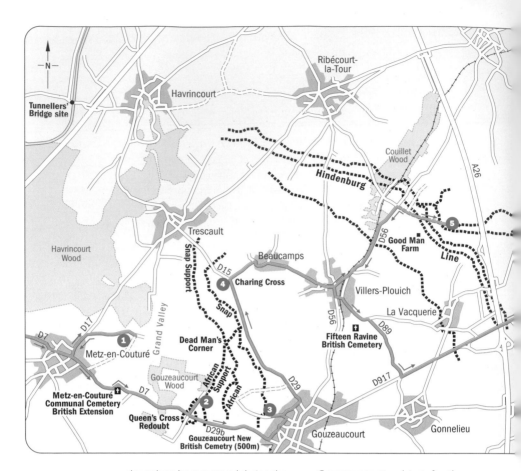

day only to be recaptured during the evening when the Germans bamboozled the New Zealanders by counterattacking while wearing captured British helmets.

Plastered by a hurricane bombardment as well as a creeping barrage, Dead Man's Corner was finally taken soon after the 5.25 am start of the 12 September attack. Despite the failure of the 38th (Welsh) Division's detachment on their right, which infuriated General Russell, 2nd Rifles streamed into African Trench ahead of you. Paralleling African Support, from which the 2nd had assaulted, it ran across the crest 300 metres away. Attacking with flamethrowers early on 14 September, the Germans regained African, driving the New Zealanders back to African Support. Return to the crossroads and continue on what was the D7 but has now somehow become the D29b. Take the first left on the outskirts of

Gouzeaucourt and, just after the three-way junction, head left again onto Rue des Archers. Turn left yet again at the T-junction onto Rue Blanche, head downhill and park by the white shed 400 metres along ❸. Keeping the shed on your left, look along Rue Blanche at the rear of Trescault Spur.

After 2nd Rifles took African Trench, which stretched along the near side of the crest, Sergeant Laurent led a 12-man patrol through shell and machine-gun fire down the slope to your right front. On seeing the extension of Snap Trench, which ran left to right 100 metres ahead of you, Laurent and his men jumped into it, unaware that a German company held this stretch. The Germans were overwhelmed by the ferociousness of the assault. Thirty were killed or wounded and 111, plus two messenger dogs, captured and herded back to the Rifles'

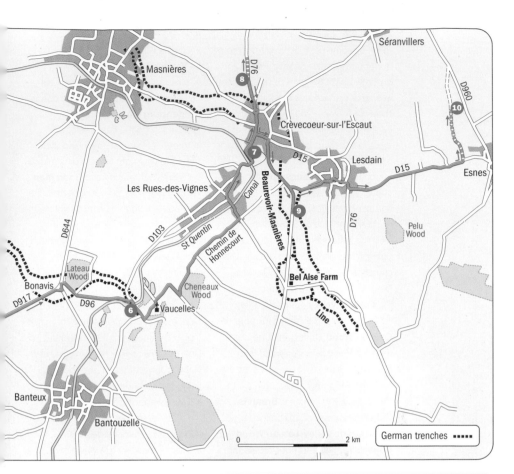

line. Laurent's patrol suffered four casualties. Now turn around, take the first left, Rue de l'Ouest, and head left again at the T-junction onto the D29, here Rue de Trescault. Pull over by the Beaucamps road on the right 2.3 kilometres further on **4** and stand with it at your back.

You are on the site of the **Charing Cross** strongpoint. Passing 400 metres ahead of you, Snap Trench cut diagonally across your left front and ran to the right of the D29. African Trench branched rightwards off it one kilometre along to parallel the near side of the Trescault Spur crest between Gouzeaucourt and its wood. The slope between and in rear of these trenches was a maze of old British communication trenches, saps and dugouts, all of which the Germans exploited. As Snap was also on the reverse slope of the spur, the

The route covers each stage of the New Zealand Division's advance. After passing either side of Trescault Spur and through Gouzeaucourt to follow the attacks on the spur, it continues to Welsh and Bonavis Ridges, between which the 1st and 2nd Brigades passed through the Hindenburg Line. Running next along the L'Escaut canal and river to Crèvecoeur and the location of Private Crichton's VC exploit, it then retraces the breaching of the Beaurevoir-Masnières Line near Bel Aise Farm by the 2nd Brigade and the Rifle Brigade, and their subsequent advance to Esnes. DISTANCE COVERED: **39 km** DURATION: **4.5 hours**

Germans in it saw the 1st and 4th Rifles skylined on the crest when the two battalions advanced towards you on the left of 2nd Rifles on 12 September. They were to take Charing Cross and the line of the D29 to your left. Running into a wall of machine-gun fire, they resorted to the saps and communication trenches but struck advanced German posts in them and were hit by counterattacks along them. The left of 4th Rifles managed to set up some posts 500 metres to your front on the far side of Snap Trench and got to within 100 metres of your location in a second attack that evening. From there the New Zealand line ran diagonally back to Snap Support, to which most in the two battalions had been driven back, on the crest to your left front.

Continue into **Beaucamps**, turn right at the T-junction in front of the château and swing left around the village on Rue Gustave Bulté/Rue de Beaucamps. On reaching **Villers-Plouich**, continue through the village centre, keeping the church on your left, on the D56 (here Rue de l'Argillière). Passing through the **Couillet Valley**, turn right after 1.7 kilometres at the crossroads opposite **Couillet Wood**. Drive over Surrey Road, the track that cuts across your front 200 metres along, and park on the crest of **Welsh Ridge** ⑤ ahead. Stand with Couillet Valley to your rear. **Bonavis Ridge** rises ahead of you on the far side of **Vacquerie Valley**. **Lateau Wood**, and **Bonavis** hamlet to its right, crown the crest of the ridge to your front. Running along the crest to your left front, the D644 from Cambrai meets the D917 in Bonavis hamlet. The D917, in turn, passes over the A26 to the right of the communications tower to your right front and runs along the crest to your right to Gouzeaucourt. In 1918 the D644 and D917 were lumped together in the same breath as the Cambrai–Gouzeaucourt

road. The A26 cuts diagonally across Vacquerie Valley to your front, passing **La Vacquerie** village.

Crossing Bonavis Ridge at the A26/D917 junction, the twin trenches of the **Hindenburg Line**, about 150 metres apart, followed the near side of the autoroute past La Vacquerie and then swung to your right front to pass midway between your location and **Good Man Farm**, 600 metres to your right rear. After curving back from the farm to straddle the road 600 metres behind you, they met cross-trenches that passed through your location from the support line. Running to your left across Vacquerie Valley, its two trenches went over Bonavis Ridge either side of the hamlet. When the New Zealand Division returned from rest to join the attack on the Hindenburg Line, the area to your right, in particular, was a foul wilderness of shell holes and lingering mustard gas, which made any advance across it difficult.

On 28 September the 42nd Division had secured Couillet Valley. With resistance weakening, it was thought that the 42nd might be able to push through the Hindenburg Line and gain Bonavis Ridge that evening. Instead it could not get beyond Good Man Farm. In a waning moon and light mist, the 1st and 2nd New Zealand Brigades formed up along Surrey Road 600 metres behind you at 3.30 am next morning, aiming to reach the Cambrai road. The 42nd had withdrawn behind Surrey Road to avoid

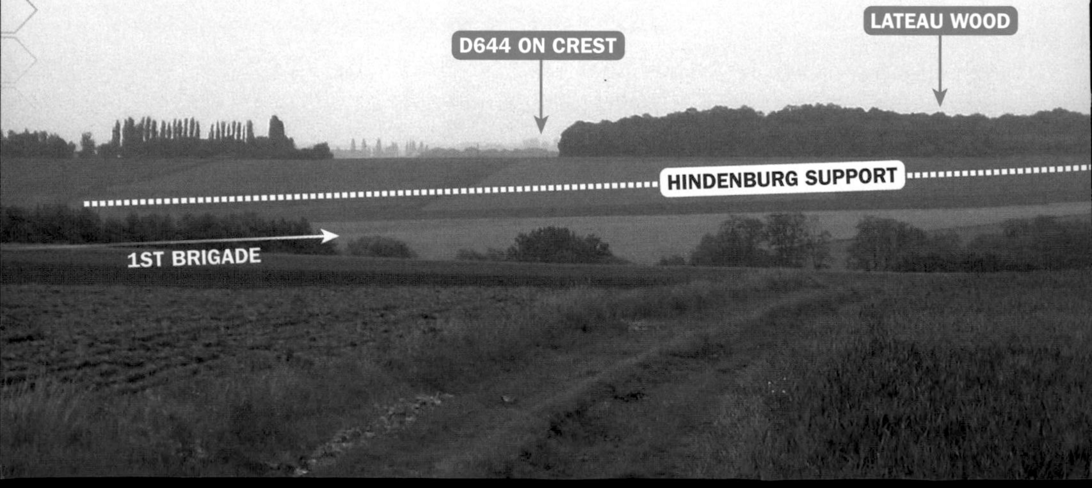

The 1st Brigade's attack towards Bonavis Ridge as seen from Welsh Ridge. The Hindenburg Line is out of picture to the right.

LATEAU WOOD

D644 ON CREST

HINDENBURG SUPPORT

1ST BRIGADE

the creeping barrage that would come down ahead of it. Few tanks were available because as many as possible had been given to the Fourth Army, which was attacking more formidable defences on the right of the Third.

Aided by the barrage, both brigades easily took Welsh Ridge. The 2nd Brigade on your right found Good Man Farm abandoned but then met stiff resistance as it crossed the shell-torn wilderness to the front of and in the Hindenburg Line. The Germans in La Vacquerie fought vigorously and reduced 1st Canterbury's advance through the village to a yard-by-yard affair. Attacking between your location and the Cantabrians, 2nd Otago had to work its way down the maze of trenches and cross-trenches of the Hindenburg Line to your right front, where it was enfiladed by the machine-guns in La Vacquerie. The Otagos ground on but eventually had to halt 350 metres from the Cambrai road and to the left of the A26/D917 junction until reinforcements arrived to shore up the flank facing the village.

To your left, the 1st Brigade's attack took on the nature of a procession. Having got through the Hindenburg Line behind you, the 1st was able to advance to the rear of it, where the going was easier. The darkness and occasional belt of wire proved greater hindrances than the few posts encountered in the support line. Only one post put up a fight and it was knocked out by the artillery.

Crossing Vacquerie Valley, 1st Wellington captured a 13.5-centimetre gun, which is now displayed in the botanic gardens overlooking Wellington Harbour. Reaching the Cambrai road at 8 am, the Wellingtons and 1st Auckland on their left occupied Lateau Wood and Bonavis. The 2nd Brigade reached the Cambrai road between Bonavis and the A26 five hours later. On its right, the 5th Division could not get beyond La Vacquerie. On the 1st Brigade's left, the 62nd Division took **Masnières**, the town to your left beyond the A26. **Marcoing** is just to its left.

Return to Villers-Plouich and turn left off the D56 onto the D89 200 metres past the village centre. After passing **Fifteen Ravine British Cemetery** and then La Vacquerie on your left, turn left again onto the D917. At the large (and confusing) roundabout setup in Bonavis, head left onto the D644 and then immediately right in front of the white two-storey building onto the D96, which Lateau Wood abuts on the left. On gaining Bonavis Ridge, the New Zealanders had reached the extremity of the ground won during the Cambrai battle in 1917 and they occupied the trenches that the British had dug. Below them, at the bottom of the steep slope that you are descending, stretched the **St Quentin Canal**. Beyond it, ahead of them, unfolded green, unspoilt countryside that was alive with activity as the Germans withdrew guns and heavy

VACQUERIE VALLEY

BONAVIS

BONAVIS RIDGE

Now in a more peaceful setting, the 13.5-centimetre gun captured by 1st Wellington in Vacquerie Valley. It is reputedly the only survivor of the 190 guns of this type manufactured by the German Krupp conglomerate.

down by the 20 machine-guns that were estimated to be firing from the area around you. As the bridge was also partly destroyed, no crossing was possible.

Now follow the D96 through the sharp left turn that takes it past the **Cistercian Abbey** in **Vaucelles**. Founded by Saint Bernard in the 12th century, the abbey was partly demolished during the French revolution and much of what remained was destroyed during the First World War. Some of the surviving section has been restored but still bears signs of the damage inflicted then, including in the fighting along the canal that involved the New Zealanders. Once beyond the abbey, swing right and then sharp left at Cheneaux Wood onto Chemin de Honnecourt. At the crossroads 1.9 kilometres along, head left and back over the canal into **Les Rues-des-Vignes**. 1st Wellington tried to cross at this bridge but it, too, was swept by fire. Following the road around to the right, join the D103 at the end of the village, recross the canal at the lock and pull into the canalside parking area 220 metres further on ❼. Face the lock bridge. On your left the D103, as Rue du Moulin, enters **Crèvecoeur-sur-l'Escaut**. Having curved away from the canal beyond the lock bridge, the **L'Escaut** passes under the D103 at the bridge with the yellow railings 200 metres to your left, midway between your location and the church, and rejoins the canal to your rear. You are on the 'island' enclosed by the canal and

The 2nd Brigade's attack on the Hindenburg Line. This photograph was taken from the same location on Welsh Ridge as the one on the previous page but the view is further to the right.

equipment eastwards while at the same time dribbling reinforcements forward to defend the canal line. The ridge was soon being shelled and patrols edging towards the canal were held up by rearguard posts on the slope either side of you.

Continue over the canal and park on the right just past the **bridge** ❻. Walk back to the bridge. Seeking to break through the Beaurevoir–Masnières Line two kilometres to your rear, the New Zealanders needed to cross the canal quickly. Resistance on the far bank waned towards midnight on 29 September as the last of the German rearguards pulled back to your side. Early on 30 September 2nd Otago had reached the far bank to the left of the bridge but was pinned

Wartime damage to the Cistercian Abbey at Vaucelles.

the river. Apart from a few houses on the D103, it was a bare, marshy expanse in 1918.

Advancing on Crèvecoeur on the Wellingtons' left, most of 2nd Auckland got lost and ended up in Rues-des-Vignes, which they cleared before the Wellingtons arrived. Like the Wellingtons, they were unable to cross the canal. The left company of the Aucklanders was on target. Using the lock bridge and a partly destroyed footbridge, which no longer

D917 ON CREST

LA VACQUERIE

2ND BRIGADE

HINDENBURG LINE

2ND BRIGADE

exists, it got over the canal to the island undetected in the rainy darkness. Now walk to the L'Escaut bridge, then a stone bridge, which the current one replaced in 1926, and face the footbridge to its right. The lead platoon of the Aucklanders raced across the island, crossed the river on the footbridge and made for the bridge at your location, which had been prepared for demolition. When they reached the bank to your left front near the end of the bridge, a burst of machine-gun fire from your left rear wiped out several of them. The rest sheltered in a ditch.

Now fully alert, all the Germans along the river opened up, pinning down the rest of the company at the far end of the island. Volunteering to let the company commander know the fate of the platoon here, Private Crichton, despite a severe foot wound, swam the swiftly flowing river and hobbled across the island through the torrential fire. Returning unscathed, he leapt into the river to your front. Screened by the arches of the bridge, Crichton removed the fuses from

the demolitions and braved the river and the fire a third time to report that the bridge was safe. His VC was the last awarded to a New Zealander before the war's end. The company held on but the platoon was overrun that night.

Drive straight ahead on what becomes the D76 (Rue Neuve, in 1918 Crucifix Road) through Crèvecoeur and over the roundabout at the far end of the village. Continue 600 metres up the hill, park at the **cemetery** 8 on the left atop the cutting and look back down the D76. With the canal line between Vaucelles and Crèvecoeur impassable, 1st Auckland and 2nd Wellington looped around and crossed it in the British 3rd Division's sector near Masnières, to your right beyond the crest, on the night of 30 September. Advancing from your right closely behind the barrage at 6 am next day, the Wellingtons took Crèvecoeur within two hours. But the Aucklanders, heading for your location, had a bitter fight to clear the D76, which was strongly garrisoned along this high ground. They took over 200 prisoners here.

The view from the island of the lock bridge where part of the left of 2nd Auckland crossed the St Quentin Canal.

To see how the Aucklanders' attack developed, you will have to walk up the hill along the side of the D76. Taking due care, as the road can be quite busy, continue past the cutting and face right. **Séranvillers** appears over the crest to your left front. The Aucklanders had to reach a road paralleling the D76 roughly halfway between your location and the village. Their advance was bitterly contested and they were very depleted when they got to the road. Too weak to hold on when the Germans counterattacked in strength from Séranvillers at 8.30 am, the Aucklanders fell back to the D76. Their dead and wounded carpeted the slope to your right front. On reaching your location, the pursuing Germans poured a heavy enfilade fire down the road to your right but the banks of the cutting and the bend beyond it afforded the Aucklanders some cover. The Germans were kept at bay. The strongest of the Aucklanders' four companies had just 53 men left.

Return to Crèvecoeur, turn left onto the D15 (Rue de Lesdain) just before the river and right after another 250 metres onto Rue du Pont de Papier. As the canal and the river are on the far side of the pillboxes in the field on the right just past the junction, it is likely that their garrisons engaged 2nd Auckland on the island and Crichton during his VC action. Crossing the **Torrent d'Esnes** stream, continue 1.4 kilometres and park by the **metalled track** ⑨ on the left. Look along it. **Bel Aise Farm**, on the crest to your right, was an outwork of the **Beaurevoir–Masnières Line**. Brushing the left of the farm, its front and support trenches ran either side of your location to finish up on the high ground on your left between Crèvecoeur and, to its right, **Lesdain**. The New Zealanders took that end of the line when they followed up the German retirement from the canal to your rear on 5 October. Forming up between the road and the canal, they had the main role in IV Corps's attack on the rest of the line

The site of Private Crichton's VC action. He approached the original bridge from the left. The view is towards the island, to which he ran back and forth. The St Quentin Canal passes on the near side of the tree line.

three days later. The dense wire ahead of them was intact but the Germans on the other side of it were demoralised. What could have been a difficult and costly assault proved to be a doddle.

Hugging the barrage, which opened at 4.30 am, the 2nd Brigade cut its way through the wire with little interference, moved through your location in the darkness and passed the farm and **Pelu Wood**, directly ahead of you on the far ridge. Using a shovel picked up after his rifle was shot out of his hands, one 2nd Cantabrian promptly bashed in the heads of three Germans. The farm and wood fell to the 37th Division, advancing on your right. 4th Rifles to your left front met some spirited resistance while enveloping Lesdain but still captured over 300 Germans and 30 machine-guns. The rest of the Rifle Brigade on its left moved briskly along the high ground on the far side of the village.

Head back along Rue du Pont de Papier and turn right after 550 metres onto Rue de Vaucelles for Lesdain. Turn right again at the first T-junction, left at the second one and then right almost immediately at the church onto Rue de l'Eglise. Continue through the roundabout onto the D15, which breaks left on leaving the village, for **Esnes**. Park by the chapel on the outskirts of Esnes. As the road up the slope on the left degenerates into a spectacularly rutted dirt track, on which there is no room to turn around, it is best walked. On reaching the crest at the far end of the **cutting 10**, face left.

You are now almost at the end of the New Zealand Division's advance through the Beaurevoir–Masnières Line, which finally halted just over the tree-lined D960 250 metres to your rear. From the far side of Esnes, over your left shoulder, the divisional frontage extended one kilometre to your right. The Rifles attacked along the ridge towards you, troubled mainly by machine-gun fire from Séranvillers, two kilometres to your right front. They passed through your location, 1st Rifles taking several prisoners and machine-guns on the road, to reach the D960 at 8.30 am. 2nd Canterbury moved to your left front, some men helping themselves to a German officers' breakfast after capturing a trench this side of Esnes. 1st Otago on their right cleared the village. Both were on the D960 shortly after 9.30 am. That the two brigades had come 4.5 kilometres in just five hours shows how feebly they were opposed overall. For the most part, the Germans preferred surrender rather than trying to flee, let alone fight.

Before leaving, turn about to view the D960. **Wambaix**, from which the German tank attack struck the 2nd Division to the left of the New Zealanders, is to your left front beyond it. You might care to reflect on the fact that when the British II Corps made its famous stand at Le Cateau against two German corps, over four years earlier, on 26 August 1914, its left flank was in your vicinity. The German IV Corps attacked from Wambaix too.

To return to Bapaume, take the D15 back to Crèvecoeur and head left there onto the D103 for Bonavis, where you turn left again for Gouzeaucourt. Pick up the D29b/D7 for Bapaume in Gouzeaucourt. Should you wish to head to Cambrai, from where the drive that follows the New Zealand Division's final advance starts, continue into Esnes and turn left onto the D960.

PELU WOOD

BEL AISE FARM

2ND BRIGADE

The 2nd Brigade's advance from the Beaurevoir–Masnières Line as seen from the road near Esnes.

LOCAL INFORMATION

Fifteen Ravine British Cemetery

Taking its name from a nearby shallow ravine once bordered by 15 trees, this cemetery was started in March 1917 and used until the Germans overran the area during their *Michael* offensive in March 1918. After the war, graves from smaller cemeteries and from the surrounding battlefields were concentrated in Fifteen Ravine. It now contains 1266 burials, 525 of which are known. Most of the 60 New Zealanders fell during the Hindenburg Line attack on 29 September 1918. Passed on the drive, the cemetery is on the right of the D89 800 metres beyond Villers-Plouich.

Gouzeaucourt New British Cemetery

Started after the Cambrai attack in November 1917, lost to the Germans in March 1918 and reopened when Gouzeaucourt was recaptured the following September, the cemetery was then used for concentration purposes after the Armistice. Of its 1297 burials, 916 are known. The bulk of the 85 New Zealanders are Rifle Brigade fallen from the attack on Trescault Spur. To visit the cemetery during the drive, head right off the D29b at the T-junction on reaching Gouzeaucourt and continue 550 metres. It is just across the D917.

Metz-en-Couturé Communal Cemetery British Extension.

Passed during the drive on the right of the D7 just outside Metz-en-Couturé, this cemetery was started in April 1917 and used until the Germans took the village in March 1918. Of its 486 burials, 431 are identified. The Trescault Spur fighting claimed most of the 43 New Zealanders. An Australian tunneller, Sapper Ernest Brown, lies at II.G.6.

Ruyaulcourt Military Cemetery

Begun in April 1917 and lost, like the other cemeteries in the area, to the Germans in March 1918, Ruyaulcourt cemetery reopened after the New Zealanders recaptured the village in September 1918. Among its 348 burials, all but 10 of which are known, are 20 New Zealanders and two Australians. To visit the cemetery, turn left off the D7 in the centre of Ruyaulcourt. It is 500 metres past the far end of the village.

Histoire et Patrimonie de la Vallée de Vinchy

Located at 12 Rue des Liniers in Crèvecoeur, this small museum contains documents and relics relating to the New Zealand Division and its part in the fighting in the area. There are plans to restore the overgrown pillbox cluster nearby, which probably fell to 2nd Wellington when it swept through the village on 1 October. Opening hours are 3.30 pm to 5.30 pm on the first Saturday of every month, 10 am to midday on the first Sunday, and at other times by appointment. Telephone +33 6 31 14 38 53.

The Tunnellers' Bridge, Havrincourt

Before being driven from the line of the Canal du Nord at the end of September 1918, the Germans destroyed the crossings. In the Third Army's area, the canal was partially constructed and empty but still a major obstacle. The bridge spanning it at Havrincourt, where the canal passed through a cutting 33 metres deep and 60 metres across, was among those demolished. If the flow of supplies and reinforcements to the Third Army was to be kept up, it had to be replaced, and quickly. Some 70 New Zealand tunnellers, who had recently been retrained in bridge construction, played a major part in the task. They built a steel girder bridge weighing 120 tonnes on the west bank, which was then hauled across the canal by winches on two wooden towers on the east bank. From start to finish, the job took just 104 hours.

Though the 'tunnellers' bridge' has gone, the two bridges that span the site now, one for the traffic in each direction, convey a good idea of what it looked like. Stand in the middle of either bridge or look up at them from the canal bank and you'll be impressed by the New Zealanders' achievement. Field Marshal Haig certainly was. He visited the site twice during the construction. To reach it yourself, continue on the D29/D15 from Gouzeaucourt, through Trescault, towards Havrincourt. Turn left onto the D5 just before reaching the village and drive another 1.2 kilometres. As you walk back to the bridge from the parking area on the far side, Havrincourt Wood stretches away to your right front along the far bank.

The site of the tunnellers' bridge over the Canal du Nord then … and now.

CHAPTER 28

1918

THE NEW ZEALANDERS AT LE QUESNOY

Returning to the line for the last time on 20 October 1918, the New Zealand Division joined the general advance from the Selle in its customary position on the left of IV Corps. The Third Army, to which IV Corps belonged, headed for the Sambre Canal, on the far side of the massive Forest of Mormal, between the First and Fourth Armies. Faced by an increasingly brittle defence, the 2nd New Zealand Brigade advanced rapidly in the attack on 23 October. Covering 7.5 kilometres, it finished well ahead of the British 3rd and 37th Divisions on its left and right respectively, and captured over 300 Germans, eight artillery pieces, numerous machine-guns and a tank at virtually no cost to itself. Next day the 2nd Brigade covered three kilometres and captured 260 Germans and almost 50 machine-guns.

The most successful day

The New Zealanders had now closed up on the 12th-century fortress town of Le Quesnoy. Its ramparts had been remodelled by Marshal Vauban, whose work also enclosed Ypres and Péronne, in the 17th century and continually improved up until the 19th century. The seven-sided inner rampart, studded with projecting redoubts from which the walls in between could be enfiladed, rose 20 metres. There were two lines of bastions along parts of the outlying rampart, which was about half as high and ran in zigzag fashion, again to permit enfilade fire. Though the moat between them was largely dry in 1918, both ramparts were covered with trees and underbrush, which hid snipers, machine-guns and even field-guns. The moat below the outer rampart was partly filled. As the crushing preliminary bombardment needed to take these defences by direct assault would cause heavy casualties among Le Quesnoy's 5000 residents, it was decided to encircle the town instead.

After a lull, in which the Rifle Brigade raided towards the railway lines west of Le Quesnoy in order to keep the Germans on edge, the New Zealand Division began the four-step advance at 5.30 am on 4 November. The 300 'oil bombs' that burst into flame after mortars lobbed them onto the ramparts provided the appropriate medieval

The inner ramparts of Le Quesnoy in 1918.

kilometres to Herbignies, leaving the Rifles to mop up the town. The Germans were in a hopeless position but still fired from the ramparts. At 1 pm a prisoner was sent into Le Quesnoy with a message demanding its surrender. Several more followed him before one returned at 3.30 pm with the news that the men were willing but their officers were preventing them.

Tossing caution to the wind, the Rifles' battalions had already decided to race each other into Le Quesnoy. 2nd Rifles on the northern side threatened but 4th Rifles on the western side got in first after hammering a stretch of the outer rampart with intense fire, driving the Germans into the shelters beneath. Things became medieval again when a party under Lieutenant Les Averill, 4th Rifles' Intelligence Officer, got over

atmospherics as the Rifles headed around the southern side of the town and the 1st Brigade moved around the northern side. By mid-morning they had met on the eastern side. With the town encircled, the 1st Brigade advanced another three

A section of the inner ramparts today.

Soldiers from the Rifle Brigade on a sunken road during the attack on Le Quesnoy.

the outer rampart using a scaling ladder. It was too short to climb the inner rampart except at the point where a 30-centimetre-wide bridge led over the moat to a ledge by the wall. When Averill scaled the ladder there, the nearest Germans bolted. The rest of 4th Rifles followed him and resistance collapsed. Losing 180 men between them, 2nd and 4th Rifles captured over 700 Germans, four field-guns and 45 machine-guns in Le Quesnoy. Meanwhile the 1st Brigade had carried on to the edge of the Forest of Mormal.

The New Zealand Division had gained 10 kilometres and taken 2450 prisoners and 60 field-guns altogether, which made 4 November 1918 its most successful day on the Western Front. On 5 November the 2nd Brigade continued another seven kilometres to reach the far side of the Forest of Mormal

on the left of the 5th Division. The New Zealand Division was relieved that night and the war ended six days later. On 20 December the New Zealanders crossed the Rhine into Cologne, entering Germany as part of the allied army of occupation.

Achievement

In the advance during the 11 weeks that began with the Battle of Bapaume and ended with the Armistice, the New Zealand Division had been one of the spearheads of the Third Army, the largest army in the BEF. One or both of its flanks were often exposed throughout the advance because it usually outpaced the divisions either side of it. It captured 8756 Germans, 145 guns, three tanks and 1263 machine-guns. Charles Bean rightly remarked that the New Zealand Division 'shone out wherever it went'.

DRIVING THE BATTLEFIELD

This drive focuses on the action in and around Le Quesnoy. It retraces the 1st Brigade's wheel around the northern side of the town and includes a short walk that covers the storming of the western ramparts by 4th Rifles. The ramparts are unchanged, which makes the tension and drama of the exploit easy to feel even now. It's heart-stopping stuff. The Forest of Mormal leg is optional. It takes you to the line reached by the New Zealanders on their last active day of the war, in effect, the end point of their journey on the Western Front. But their advance was uneventful and there is little to see in the forest.

MAPS IGN Blue Series, 1:25 000, 2606E Valenciennes; 2607E Le Cateau-Cambrésis; 27060T Forêt de Mormal

Leaving Cambrai on the D942, continue through Solesmes to Romeries. Head left onto Rue du Quesnoy at the Y-junction in the village centre, then right after 250 metres at the crossroads onto Rue Paul Bisiau.

Attacking at 3.20 am on 23 October, the 42nd Division took **Romeries** and the far bank of the **Harpies River**, which follows the tree line on the valley bottom to your right. In mist thickened by a smoke screen, the 2nd New Zealand Brigade passed through the 42nd at 8.40 am, splashed over the four-metre-wide 'river' and crossed Rue Paul Bisiau. Turn left at the crossroads on the outskirts of **Vertigneul** hamlet 1.3 kilometres along and head up the slope. You are now roughly following the centre line of the 2nd Brigade's advance. Vertigneul had fallen easily, most of its garrison having been killed by the barrage. To your left, 2nd Canterbury met little resistance but to your right, 1st Otago had to beat down some aggressively handled machine-guns on the crest with concentrated rifle fire.

Head left on reaching the T-junction and then right onto the D942. At the cross-track 1.3 kilometres further on, 1st Canterbury and 2nd Otago took over the

advance. Crossing the **Georges**, another 'river', in the valley to your front, 1st Canterbury on your left maintained the blistering pace that 2nd Canterbury had set. Just as 1st Otago had been, 2nd Otago on your right was confronted by a few stubborn rearguards. Concealed on the river bank and the slopes above it among hedgerows and orchards, which were more numerous then than now, they kept on firing even when directly engaged by the field-guns accompanying the Otagos. Themselves using the hedgerows and orchards as cover, the Otagos skilfully, and rapidly, outflanked the German posts. By 2.30 pm the ridge towards which you are driving, on the far side of the Georges, had fallen. It had been the 2nd Brigade's objective.

Passing through **Pont à Pièrres**, drive over the ridge yourself and continue to **Beaudignies**. As the opposition ahead of it had seemingly evaporated, the 2nd Brigade exploited to this village. Turn left in the village centre onto the D100 (Rue Basse), and pause after 450 metres by the bridge over the tree-lined **Ecallion**, yet another 'river' . By 9 pm 1st Canterbury had secured this bridge and another one on the D942 to your right and set up posts along the high ground ahead of you. Unaware Beaudignies had fallen, some returning Germans blundered into the post 200 metres to your right front, on the far side of Rue des Marlières. It was commanded by Sergeant Henry Nicholas. In a dreadful end to what had been a great day for 1st Canterbury, Nicholas, who had won the VC in the attack at Polderhoek in the Ypres Salient over a year before and recently been awarded the MM, was killed.

After turning right at the T-junction just over the bridge, do so again immediately at the Y-junction onto Rue des Marlières. Passing the area where Nicholas fell, turn left onto the D942. On cresting the slope ahead, swing left between the cream house and the equestrian track, both of which are on

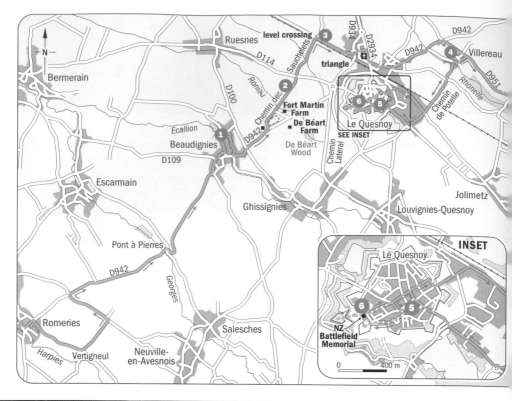

Sergeant Henry Nicholas VC, MM.

the left, onto Chemin des Sauchelets. Continuing past the track, now on your right, and **Fort Martin Farm** on the bank of the Roniau beyond it and also on the right, park on the crest to your front ❷. With your back to the equestrian track, look along Chemin des Sauchelets. Stretching across your front from **Ruesnes** to your left, the D114 (Rue de Ruesnes) enters **Le Quesnoy**, the walled town to your right among the trees. Paralleling the D114 1.2 kilometres further on is the **Valenciennes–Berlaimont railway**, which Chemin des Sauchelets straddles at the **level crossing**. Branching off the main line on the right of the crossing, the defunct **Cambrai–Valenciennes railway** swung along the near side of Le Quesnoy and through the roundabout site, from which it now continues as a road, Chemin Lateral. The area between the two railways to the left of the roundabout was called the **triangle**.

Reaching the crest behind you on 24 October, the 2nd Brigade established posts on the D114 to your left front, beyond which the 3rd Division had taken Ruesnes, and in **De Béart Farm** 700 metres to your right rear, **De Béart Wood** to its left and Fort Martin Farm. Patrols reconnoitred the railways to your front and right, along which the German posts ran, as a precursor to an advance by the Rifle Brigade astride Chemin des Sauchelets late on 25 October. Supposed to end one kilometre over the railway to your front, it was a costly failure. Heavy fighting developed in the triangle, from where the Germans flayed the right of the attack and then fired into its rear.

Now face Le Quesnoy. You are looking at the western end of it. The start line for the attack on 4 November stretched across your front 500 metres ahead, midway between your location and Chemin Lateral. After the rest of the Rifles had cleared the Germans from the Cambrai railway, 3rd Rifles was to move around the right side of the town while the 1st Brigade passed around the left side. The Germans fired from the ramparts even after the link-up had occurred

After following the 2nd Brigade's advance through Pont à Pierres and Beaudignies, the route covers the sharp fighting by the 1st Brigade and the Rifle Brigade around the railways on the western side of Le Quesnoy. On passing through the town itself, it retraces the advance to the far side of the Forest of Mormal.
DISTANCE COVERED: 33.5 km (Le Quesnoy only: 17.5 km);
Le Quesnoy walk: 1.7 km
DURATION: 3.5 hours

beyond the town. In the 'race' to enter it, 1st and 2nd Rifles advanced from the railway towards the ramparts to your right and left front respectively. 4th Rifles won it by getting over them to your front.

Continue over the level crossing, park just beyond it ❸ and look along Chemin des Sauchelets. In the 25–26 October attack, 2nd Rifles advanced 350 metres down this road but were driven back to the crossing by counterattacks that came along the road towards them and from Le Quesnoy on your right. Stretching one kilometre along the railway to your left, the New Zealand line at the end of the attack passed through your location, extended 200 metres to your right and then cut sharply to your rear. Shortly after leaving the crossing at 2 am on 29 October, Sergeant Samuel Hartley's nine-man raiding party from 2nd Rifles chased some Germans whom they heard running down Chemin des Sauchelets ahead of them. Pausing to bomb dugouts in the banks of the road, from which shots had come, they killed three Germans and then resumed the chase. But their quarry had pulled too far ahead. The raiders penetrated 500 metres before a German post halted their progress. All returned safely to the crossing. Hartley was awarded the DCM.

Now head right, beside the railway, on Chemin de Mortry to the roundabout on the D934 and take the second exit. On 4 November the D2934, 200 metres ahead, was the objective of 2nd Rifles, who gained it to your right after a hard fight through the triangle. The 1st Brigade crossed it to your left at the end of the first step of its advance. You should head right on the D2934 and then left at the roundabout opposite **Le Quesnoy Communal Cemetery and Extension** onto Rue du Dr Averill. It is named after Lieutenant Averill, who became a medical practitioner in Christchurch postwar. Turn left again at the T-junction onto Rue du 11 Novembre 1918 and, on reaching the crossroads 250 metres along, head left

once more onto the D942 (here Route de Bavay). Continue over the **Rhonelle 'River'** at **Ramponeau**, which 1st Auckland cleared in the second step of the 1st Brigade's advance, turn right at the roundabout onto the D951 (here Rue Berlandois) and park after 150 metres at the **cemetery** ❹ on the right.

Look across the Rhonelle Valley towards Le Quesnoy. During its advance, the 1st Brigade's left flank progressed from Ramponeau on your right, past the bottom of the cemetery, and then to the left of **Villereau** to your left. In this, the third step of the advance, the 1st and 2nd Wellingtons moved right to left across your front, easily clearing the area between your location and Le Quesnoy, while 1st Auckland protected their right by swinging around to face the town. After a skirmish on the D951, the Wellingtons took Villereau unopposed and swung over the ridge to your left front. When they met 3rd Rifles around 9.30 am, Le Quesnoy was encircled. Now drive to Villereau and turn right at the far end of the village onto Chemin de la Burie, which was the line reached by the Wellingtons in the third step. In the fourth, which started at 10.20 am, they continued to **Herbignies**, three kilometres to your left along the D951.

Follow Chemin de la Burie around to the right, head left to recross the

The Wellingtons' advance past Le Quesnoy, as seen from the cemetery on the D951 above the Rhonelle.

LE QUESNOY

1ST AND 2ND WELLINGTONS

The spot where Lieutenant Averill climbed the inner rampart. The Germans had blocked the arched opening, from which stairs inside the rampart give access to the town.

Rhonelle and go straight ahead onto Chemin de Potelle at the four-way intersection 500 metres further on. After crossing the railway, turn left then immediately right onto **Rue Léon Blum**. On reaching the roundabout, head right (direction Centre Ville), and go through Le Quesnoy's outer ramparts, which overlook Pont Rouge lake on the left, and the town wall. Take the fourth street on the left, Rue Jean Jaurès, then the second left, Rue de Général Bouttieaux, to the **town square** 5 and park. Leave the square through **Porte du Château** and walk along Avenue des Néo-Zéalandais, which leads through the remembrance garden to a path that heads around the now grassed ramparts. Follow the signs to the **New Zealand Battlefield Memorial**, which is set into the wall of the inner rampart. Lieutenant Averill and 4th Rifles scaled the wall from the ledge reached by the narrow bridge, near the sluice gate, on the right of the path 6.

Now go through the tunnel in the wall to your left front and take the path to the first bastion of the outer ramparts. Continue through the tunnel underneath it, from which the path carries on to the outer bastion. Walk to the edge of the outer bastion and look across the outer moat.

2nd Rifles and 4th Rifles were pinned down along the far side of the moat to your right front and front respectively. To your right, one party from the 2nd managed to get onto the outer ramparts and one under 2nd Lieutenant Francis Evans of the 4th actually penetrated beyond them. Both parties were driven back with heavy loss and several other attempts by the 2nd did not even make the wall. With the Germans showing no signs of surrender, 4th Rifles deluged your location, where the wall was already damaged, with fire from trench mortars, rifle grenadiers and all available Lewis-gunners. Now meeting little opposition,

The outer rampart and moat, on the far side of which the 2nd and 4th Rifles were pinned down. Lieutenant Averill's party probably crossed them to the right of where this photograph was taken.

Lieutenant Averill and his men climbed it with a nine-metre-long scaling ladder at 2.30 pm.

Retrace your route to the bridge, which is also the route that Averill took. After reaching the wall above the tunnel in front of the inner rampart, he saw that the inner rampart could only be climbed near the bridge. Met by a shower of bombs from the top of the rampart on heading towards it, his party fell back. No Germans were met when Averill returned at 4 pm with a platoon and another scaling ladder. While a trench mortar and Lewis-guns flayed the inner rampart, Averill and some of the platoon approached the bridge. When you get there, imagine the tension as they crossed in single-file, set up the ladder on the narrow ledge and saw that it reached the top of the wall with 30 centimetres to spare. While two men steadied the

ladder, Averill started the almost vertical climb, expecting a bomb to be dropped on him at any second. None came. Within minutes the 4th Rifles were swarming up the wall after him.

Return to the town square. With the Germans crumpling once 4th Rifles were over the ramparts, 2nd Rifles entered Le Quesnoy. Overjoyed at their liberation, the residents filled the square and the streets, hugging the New Zealanders and plying them with wine, cognac, cakes and cigars. The French President, Raymond Poincaré, reviewed a New Zealand guard of honour in the square when he visited Le Quesnoy six days later. The town has maintained strong links with New Zealand in the same way that Villers-Bretonneux has with Australia. Its primary school is named after Lieutenant Averill, Rue de Général Bouttieaux becomes Rue de Nouvelle-Zélande and ANZAC Day is

INNER RAMPART

WALL

LIEUTENANT AVERILL

commemorated annually. In 1999 Le Quesnoy was twinned with the New Zealand town of Cambridge. The All Blacks visited in 2000.

Should you wish to go on to the **Forest of Mormal**, return to Villereau and turn right onto the D951. Continue through Herbignies, where the 1st Brigade was welcomed just as rapturously on its arrival as the Rifles had been in Le Quesnoy. Beyond the village, the forest stretches across your front. In pouring rain on 5 November, 2nd Otago and 1st Canterbury from the 2nd Brigade passed through the patrols from the Wellingtons that had reached it the previous day. Enter the forest after going over the D932, which runs along the near side, and turn left 2.4 kilometres along at Le Godelot roundabout onto Rte Forestière du Chemin Planté. 2nd Otago was held up at the strongly held **Forester's House** ⑦ at the six-way intersection three kilometres further on but the check did not last long because the Germans pulled out just before the Otagos outflanked them. This was one of the last places in which New Zealanders were killed in the war. Progress to the

D961, the Bavay road, which runs along the far side of the forest four kilometres away, was rapid. You will reach it on the left end of the **New Zealand line** ⑧, which extended 650 metres along the road to your right.

To return to Cambrai, head back through the forest to the D932, turn left for Le Cateau and head right there on the D642.

Lieutenant Averill's approach to the inner rampart. He reached the wall at the tunnel during his reconnaissance.

Why the ramparts could only be scaled from the ledge, seen on the right of the picture. Averill's ladder was not long enough to reach the top from the inner moat.

LOCAL INFORMATION

CEMETERIES

Small groups of New Zealanders rest in some of the village cemeteries in the battlefield area. The 12 who lie in **Beaudignies Communal Cemetery** fell in the last week of October. To visit the cemetery, turn left off the D942 onto the D109 (Rue Capelle) in Beaudignies during the drive. New Zealanders comprise all but one of the 20 burials in **Vertigneul churchyard**. They include Sergeant Nicholas VC, MM at grave 15. The hamlet and its church can be reached by turning right instead of left at the crossroads after leaving Romeries.

Romeries Communal Cemetery Extension

Just outside Romeries on the D942, this cemetery was started in October 1918 and enlarged after the Armistice by the postwar concentration in it of graves from the battlefield and from smaller cemeteries nearby. Of its 832 burials, 703 are identified. The 112 New Zealanders include 2nd Lieutenant Evans of 4th Rifles at X.A.6, who was killed while trying to approach the inner ramparts at Le Quesnoy before Lieutenant Averill reached them.

Le Quesnoy Communal Cemetery and Extension

Begun by the New Zealand Division after the capture of Le Quesnoy, the extension contains 137 burials, of which 126 are identified. All but two of the 50 New Zealanders fell in the 4 November attack. Major Hugh McKinnon MC and bar, who commanded 2nd Wellingtons, was killed by a shell during the evening. Resting at I.B.24, he had started the war as a platoon commander at the ANZAC Landing only to die a week before the war's end. 1st Wellingtons lost their adjutant, Captain Arthur Blennerhassett, early in the battle. He rests at I.B.22. Two Australians, Lieutenant Allan Doig MC of the 17th Battalion at I.A.6 and Private

The grave of Sergeant Henry Nicholas VC, MM, Vertigneul Churchyard.

Walter Hoskins of the 48th Battalion at III.B.2, are among the 63 Commonwealth burials in the adjacent communal cemetery, which served the German field hospital in Le Quesnoy. Doig and Hoskins died of their wounds in the hospital after being captured earlier in 1918. All the German graves were removed after the war. Passed during the drive, the cemetery and its extension are on the D2934 on the outskirts of the town.

Romeries Communal Cemetery Extension.

MEMORIALS

The New Zealand Battlefield Memorial

This memorial is a departure from the obelisk memorials on the Somme and at Messines and Ypres, the other significant New Zealand battlefields on the Western Front. A bas-relief in stone set in the wall of the inner rampart close to where Lieutenant Averill scaled it, the memorial was sculpted by Félix Desruelles, a French sculptor. He based it on a model produced by Alexander Fraser, a Scottish-born New Zealand sculptor. Its main symbolic element is a winged woman, who symbolises freedom, offering a palm, which symbolises victory, to soldiers scaling the ramparts on a ladder. Crosses represent the lives lost. The memorial was unveiled on 15 July 1923 at a ceremony attended by Sir James Allen, the New Zealand High Commissioner in London; Lord Milner, an influential member of the British War Cabinet, who was representing the British government; and Marshal Joffre, France's commander-in chief for the first half of the war.

Le Quesnoy Communal Cemetery Extension. The communal cemetery can be seen beyond the hedge.

The New Zealand Battlefield Memorial.

USEFUL INFORMATION

TOURIST OFFICES

Besides offering advice on accommodation and places to eat and drink, local tourist offices invariably carry a wealth of brochures and maps that provide useful information on the surrounding battlefields and nearby sights. They can also let you know about any events that may be going on at the time of your visit. It is worth dropping by them. Contact details for the main ones are as follows:

Albert

Tourist Office of Poppy Country
9, rue Gambetta
80300 Albert
France
Telephone: +33 3 22 75 16 42
officedetourisme@paysdu
   coquelicot.com
www.paysducoquelicot.com

Amiens

Amiens Métropole Tourist Office
40, Place Notre Dame
BP 11018
80010 Amiens cedex 1
France
Telephone: +33 3 22 71 60 50
ot@amiens-metropole.com
www.amiens-tourisme.com

Arras

Office de Tourisme
Place des héros
62000 – Arras
France
Telephone: +33 3 21 51 26 95
arras.tourisme@ot-arras.fr
www.ot-arras.fr

Péronne

Office de Tourisme
16, Place André Audinot
80203 Péronne Cedex
France
Telephone: +33 3 22 84 42 38
accueil@hautesomme-tourisme.com
www.hautesomme-tourisme.com

Ypres

Ypres Tourist Office
Cloth Hall
Grote Markt 34
B – 8900 Ieper
Belgium
Telephone: +32 57 23 92 20
toerisme@ieper.be
www.toerisme-ieper.be

HANDY WEBSITES

Australian War Memorial (www. awm.gov.au). Contains a wealth of information on Australia's involvement in the First World War and guides to the relevant official and private records within the Memorial's collection. Also offers plenty of advice for researching military service for family history.

Australian Department of Veterans' Affairs (www.dva.gov.au). Among the many interesting sites on its Commemorations: Australia's Wartime Heritage page is *Australians on the Western Front 1914–18* **(www.ww1. westernfront.gov.au)**, which covers battles, cemeteries and memorials.

National Archives of Australia (www.naa.gov.au). Holds the service records of Australian service personnel. All First World War AIF service records and RAN service cards have been digitised and can be viewed, and copies ordered, online.

National Army Museum, Waiorou, New Zealand (www. armymuseum.co.nz). Contains interesting information and occasional articles on New Zealand in the First World War.

Archives New Zealand (www. archives.govt.nz). Holds service records of New Zealanders who served in the First World War.

Commonwealth War Graves Commission (www.cwgc.org). Responsible for Commonwealth War Graves worldwide. Its online database has details of every BEF (and therefore Australian and New Zealand) fatality and the cemetery in which the grave lies.

GLOSSARY

Army A formation comprising a headquarters, two or more corps and assigned 'army troops' such as heavy artillery, cavalry and tanks.

Battalion An infantry unit of 800 to 1000 men, organised into a headquarters and four companies.

Battery An artillery sub-unit of four to six guns or howitzers.

Brigade A formation comprising a headquarters and four infantry battalions.

Brigade: artillery An artillery formation comprising a headquarters and three or four batteries.

Bomb A grenade thrown by hand; also the finned projectile fired by a mortar.

Bombardment The shelling of a target over a set period with the aim of destroying it.

Bunker A concrete structure used to shelter troops, aid posts and headquarters.

Company A 200- to 220-strong infantry sub-unit organised into four platoons.

Corps A formation comprising a headquarters, two or more divisions and assigned 'corps troops' such as heavy artillery, cavalry and tanks.

Creeping barrage A barrage that moves at a set rate to cover the advance of troops following it.

DCM Distinguished Conduct Medal

Dead ground Ground shielded from enemy observation and direct fire.

Division A formation comprising a headquarters, three infantry brigades, three artillery brigades, a field engineer company and logistic units.

DSO Distinguished Service Order

Dugout A shelter dug into the side of a trench or earthen bank for protection from fire.

Enfilade fire Fire from a flank that falls along the length of a line of troops.

Field-gun An artillery piece capable of being easily manoeuvred on the battlefield.

Howitzer An artillery piece capable of delivering shells on a high trajectory so as to hit targets behind fortifications.

Lewis-gun A light machine-gun with a rate of fire of 500 to 600 rounds per minute and an effective range of 800 metres.

Maxim-gun A German heavy machine-gun with a rate of fire of 450 to 500 rounds per minute and an effective range of 2000 metres. Normally served by a crew of four to six, it comprised the gun, a sled and water-cooling can and hose, and weighed 69 kilograms all up.

MC Military Cross

MM Military Medal

Mortar A muzzle loaded weapon delivering a finned bomb that follows a high angle of fire.

Pillbox A bunker from which the occupants can fire, either from inside or from the roof.

Platoon A 40- to 60-strong infantry sub-unit organised into three or four sections.

Re-entrant The low ground between two spurs that project from a ridge.

Section A 10-strong infantry element.

Spur A ridge projecting from a much larger ridge.

VC Victoria Cross. The highest award for valour.

Vickers-gun A British version of the Maxim heavy machine-gun with a rate of fire of 450 to 500 rounds per minute and an effective range of 2000 metres. It weighed 41 kilograms and was also served by crew of four to six.

Zero hour The time fixed for the launching of troops into an attack.

SELECT BIBLIOGRAPHY

Bean, CEW. *Official History of Australia in the War of 1914–18*. Sydney, 1921–42.

—. III. *The AIF in France, 1916*. 1929.

—. IV. *The AIF in France, 1917*. 1933.

—. V. *The AIF in France During the Main German Offensive, 1918*. 1941.

—. VI. *The AIF in France During the Allied Offensive, 1918*. 1942.

Brittain, V. *Testament of Youth*. London, 1978.

Cutlack, FM (ed.). *War Letters of General Monash*. Sydney, 1935.

Dennis, P et al. *The Oxford Companion to Australian Military History*. Melbourne, 2009.

Downing, WH. *To The Last Ridge*. Sydney, 1998.

Edmonds, JEE et al. *Official History of Great Britain in the War of 1914–18*.

—. *France and Belgium, 1916. II. 2nd July 1916 to the End of the Battles of the Somme*. London, 1938.

—. *France and Belgium, 1917. I. The German Retreat to the Hindenburg Line and the Battle of Arras*. London, 1940.

—. *France and Belgium, 1917. II. Messines and Third Ypres*. London, 1948.

—. *France and Belgium, 1918. I. The German March Offensive*. London, 1935.

—. *France and Belgium, 1918. II. March–April: Continuation of the German Offensives*. London, 1937.

—. *France and Belgium, 1918. III. May–July: The German Diversion Offensive and the First Allied Counter-Offensive*. London, 1939.

—. *France and Belgium, 1918. IV. 8th August–26th September: The Franco-British Offensive*. London, 1947.

—. *France and Belgium, 1918. V. 26th September–11th November: The Advance to Victory*. London, 1947.

Ellis, AD. *The Story of the Fifth Australian Division*. London, 1920.

Harper, G. *Dark Journey*. Auckland, 2007.

Holmes, R. *The Western Front*. London, 1999.

Pedersen, PA. *Fromelles*, Barnsley, 2004.

—. *Hamel*. Barnsley, 2003.

—. *Images of Gallipoli*. Melbourne, 1988.

—. *Monash as Military Commander*. Melbourne, 1985.

—. *Villers-Bretonneux*. Barnsley, 2004.

—. *The Anzacs. Gallipoli to the Western Front*. Melbourne, 2007.

Joynt, WD. *Saving the Channel Ports*. Melbourne, 1975.

Knyvett, HR. *'Over There' with the Australians*. London 1918.

Mitchell, GD. *Backs to the Wall*. Sydney, 1937.

Monash, J. *The Australian Victories in France in 1918*. London, 1920.

Pugsley, C. *The Anzac Experience*. Auckland, 2004.

Rule, E. *Jacka's Mob*. Sydney, 1933.

Stewart, H. *The New Zealand Division*. Auckland, 1921.

SOURCES OF ILLUSTRATIONS

Alexander Turnbull Library, Wellington
184 (G-12753-1/2), 301t (F-103803-1/2), 302 (G-13484-1/2), 499 (025461), 500b (013608), 501 (013558), 512 (031675), 532 (031673)

Archives New Zealand, Wellington
526t (WA 10/3/3)

Australian War Memorial, Canberra

Photographs
xv (C01815), xvi (H10400), xvii (P03717.003), xviii (A03376), xix (E02790), xx (A02540), 1 (A03713), 2 (EZ0009), 3 (EZ0007), 4 (H08865), 11 (EZ0057), 13 (H09449), 14t (E04032), 15 (H01890), 16 (E05990), 17 (A03042), 18 (H16396), 19t (A01562), 19b (A01566), 26 (E03963), 30t (E03965), 38b (H12215), 41 (A03754), 42 (E00007), 43t (A02868A), 43b (EZ0100), 44t (J00187), 48t (H08482), 49b (EZ0113), 62 (E05748), 67t (EZ0095), 74 (E04710), 76 (H08347), 92 (E00220), 93 (E00579), 94 (P01465.004), 95 (E00179), 103 (E05701), 106 (E00374), 108 (A03366), 110 (C00440), 124 (P02939.012), 126t (E04581), 136 (A01121), 138b (G01534J), 139 (E00603), 140 (P01489.001), 142 (E00518), 151t (J00369), 168t (E04612), 169 (E04607), 170t (E01400), 183t (H12264), 186t (E01491), 186b (J00272), 187 (133440), 194t (E00650), 209 (E01200), 210 (E00850), 211t (E00901), 211b (E00711), 215 (E01220), 217t (E00889), 220 (E01121), 226 (J00191), 228 (E01912), 238t (J06409), 246 (E01076), 247t (E00914), 247b (E00918), 251t (E01034), 266t (E04591), 269 (J00285), 276t (E03864), 277 (E01162), 289 (E02278), 306 (E04661), 307 (A01058), 308 (E03804), 309 (A04803), 317t (H19207), 318t (E04832), 322t (E00072), 328 (E04851), 329 (A02103), 331t (E04828), 331b (E02877), 334t (E04787), 337t (E02434), 338 (E02685), 350 (E04744), 351 (E02088), 358b (J02577), 359t (E02804), 362 (E02350), 364 (H12187), 365b (02833C), 366 (E02620), 368 (E02844A), 373 (E03843), 374t (E02670), 380 (E02989A), 381 (E03883), 382 (E03014), 383 (E02880), 389t (E02842), 395t (A00006), 397b (P01695.002), 400 (E02847), 401t (E03051), 401b (E04405), 404 (H13436), 406t (E02866), 407t (P01383.016), 408t (A03534), 415 (E02951), 416t (E03116), 416b (E03039), 422b (F03061), 423 (E03067), 429 (E03104), 430 (E03147), 439t (E03302), 439b (E03183), 440t (E03149), 442t (E03139), 442b (E03126), 450 (C04505), 451 (E03260), 452 (E03755P), 458b (E03351), 464 (P00743.026), 466 (H12514), 467t (E03578), 476t (E03481), 487 (E03775), 488t (E03834), 488b (E03605), 528t (A02535), 529 (A02542)

Art
39 (James Quinn, *Major General Sir Harold Walker*; painted in France and London, 1918; oil on canvas, 93.4 x 81 cm; acquired under commission in 1918; ART03349), 138t (Leslie Bowles and Louis McCubbin, *Bullecourt*; created in Melbourne, 1930; diorama [figures: painted composite lead; background: synthetic polymer paint on fibreglass; modelling: plaster over wood and wire with wire, metal and paint], 400 x 730 x 215 cm; acquired under commission in 1930; ART41022), 141 (George Coates, *Major General Sir Neville Smyth*; painted in London, 1920; oil on canvas, 126.7 x 101.4 cm; acquired under commission in 1921; ART00199), 170b (Artist unknown, *Menin Gate lions*; sculpted in Belgium, c. 1200-1300; granite,

150 x 154.5 x 59 cm each; presented by the Burgomaster of Ypres to the Commonwealth of Australia in 1936; ART12510.001-.002), 175 (H. Septimus Power, *First Australian Division Artillery going into the 3rd Battle of Ypres;* painted in London, 1919; oil on canvas, 121.7 x 245 cm; acquired under National War Records Committee commission in 1919; ART03330), 185 (Charles Wheeler, *The Battle of Messines*; painted in Melbourne, 1923; oil on canvas, 137 x 229 cm; acquired under commission in 1923; ART03557), 232 (Fred Leist, *Major General Joseph Talbot Hobbs*; painted in Ypres, Belgium, 1917; oil on canvas board, 60.3 x 50.4 cm; acquired under the official war art scheme in 1917; ART02926), 239b (Fred Leist, *Australian infantry attack in Polygon Wood*; painted in London, 1919; oil on canvas, 122.5 x 245 cm; acquired under National War Records commission in 1919; ART02927), 330 (Will Longstaff, *Night attack by 13th Brigade on Villers-Bretonneux*; painted in London, 1919; oil on canvas, 131 x 208 cm; acquired under the official war art scheme in 1920; ART03028), 365t (George Bell, *Dawn at Hamel, 4 July 1918*; painted in Melbourne , 1921; oil on canvas, 127.7 x 244 cm; acquired under commission in 1921; ART03590), 467b (Will Longstaff, *Breaking the Hindenburg Line*; painted in London, 1918; oil on canvas, 127 x 234 cm; acquired under the official war art scheme in 1920; ART03023)

Imperial War Museum, London
5 (Q53), 270 (CO2246), 281t (Q5935), 288 (Q47997)

Kippenberger Military Archive, National Army Museum, Waiouru
268 (199-929), 290 (1993-1031 H484), 291 (1993-1031 H578), 498 (199-1031 H972), 500t (1993-1031 H986), 508t (1993-1031 H975)

Private Collections
14b, 20-1, 22, 24, 25t, 25b, 27, 28t, 28-9, 30b, 31, 32, 33t, 33b, 34, 35t, 35b, 315, 318b, 326t, 326b, 327, 332, 334m, 334-5, 335t, 336, 337b, 339, 340-1, 341t, 342, 343t, 343b, 344, 345t, 345b, 346t, 346m, 367, 370-1, 372, 376-7, 378t, 378b, 388 (Peter Pedersen); 70, 162, 163, 428, 458t (Robyn Van Dyk); 71, 447 (Karl James); 87, 322b, 323b (Gerard Pratt); 520t (Robbie Munro)

All other images are copyright to the Australian War Memorial

INDEX